SOURCE BOOK IN ANTHROPOLOGY

by

A. L. KROEBER

and

T. T. WATERMAN

REVISED EDITION, ILLUSTRATED

HARCOURT, BRACE AND COMPANY

NEW YORK

CONTENTS

HISTORY OF ANTHROPOLOGY

EVOLUTION

HEREDITY AND RACE

Contents

PREFACE

THE PASSAGES in this volume have been selected for their utility in stimulating discussion. They are included not because they present ultimate scientific truth, but because they embody facts and interpretations which are useful for the exercise of thought on some of the larger problems of anthropology.

The book was undertaken and first published in several smaller editions of *Selected Readings* as an auxiliary to an ordinary working library in anthropology. In that stage it embodied chiefly articles which are out of print or accessible in journals of which even a great library often possesses only a single file. In 1920, the volume was enlarged to about the present size and issued under the present title as a University of California Syllabus. In this form the book was intended as a basis for study in courses of instruction in general anthropology, with collateral and special reading provided according to available library facilities. A reprint in 1924 began to circulate increasingly in a number of institutions where anthropology, sociology, and related branches of social science were taught. The present edition has been prepared with a view to such wider use.

To this end, a thorough revision has been made. Only twenty of the fifty-four original selections have been retained unchanged. Sixteen have been altered, mostly by further cutting, but in one or two cases by additions to bring their information up to date. Eighteen articles have been entirely omitted, and replaced by nineteen new ones.

There are some famous and many useful passages in anthropological literature which might well have been included. In some of these cases, copyright privileges conflicted; in others, the fact of being written in a foreign language. In still other instances, articles have been omitted because they were essentially interpretative or controversial, assuming the facts as known, instead of presenting them. Passages have been included with whose conclusions the editors do not agree: Galton's on race worth, for instance. In all such instances, however, the author has presented evidence for his case. It is for the reader to analyze his interpretation and accept or reject it. Thus, contrary inferences can be and have been drawn, as to the native or foreign origin of American Indian culture, from the articles on the one hand of Nordenskiöld, Spinden,

and Waterman, and on the other, of Tylor and Rivers. Our aim has
been to present material not as it favors one or the other view but as it
lends itself to understanding of problem and method of attack.

That the passages dealing with America about balance in number
those from the other continents combined, is not the outcome of the
editors' choice, nor, they hope, of any provinciality. English ethnographers mostly publish in copyright books; their American colleagues
more often publish in monographs in the series issued by scientific institutions. Beyond that, it is easier to assemble ten selections, usable in a
work like this one, dealing with Oceania, than five dealing with Africa.
We do not know why.

Nothing has been included here which is available in W. I. Thomas'
Source Book for Social Origins. The two works differ much more than
their titles suggest. Thomas' range is wholly within the social field, his
emphasis often on society, the implied interest psychological. A third
of our volume is concerned with biological, the remainder with cultural
anthropology.

The editors have not tried to make this volume cover systematically
all the principal facts of anthropology, though they have tried to give
some representation to nearly every major subject in anthropological
science. They have included no passages purely definitional, concerned
with theory alone, or wholly conceptual. Every selection admitted, they
trust, has an explicit or implicit bearing on some significant principle
or idea. But it always approaches this principle or idea through the
medium of concrete fact.

A. L. Kroeber
T. T. Waterman

September 3, 1930

AN ALTERNATIVE CLASSIFICATION OF SELECTIONS

ENVIRONMENT: 18, Douglass; 20, Barrows; 21, Fourie; 23, Spinden; 50, Nordenskiöld; 53, Rivers.

ARCHÆOLOGY: 6, Hrdlička; 12, von Luschan; 17, Avebury; 18, Douglass; 19, Holmes; 23, Spinden; 25, Nelson; 39, Budge; 43, Aztec; 52, Waterman.

INVENTION, INDEPENDENT ORIGIN: 2, Lucretius; 19, Holmes; 23, Spinden; 24, Galton; 26, Mason; 39, Budge; 49, Kroeber; 50, Nordenskiöld; 52, Waterman; 54, Laufer.

DIFFUSION: 23, Spinden; 38, Tylor; 50, Nordenskiöld; 51, Wissler; 52, Waterman; 54, Laufer.

POLITICAL INSTITUTIONS: 27, Brown; 28, Thurnwald; 29, Hoernlé; 32, Sapir; 35, Barton; 55, Mead.

PSYCHOLOGY, INDIVIDUAL AND RACIAL: 8, Galton; 16, Woodworth; 24, Galton; 49, Kroeber.

PSYCHOLOGY, SOCIAL: 28, Thurnwald; 30, Lowie; 32, Sapir; 34, Danks; 35, Barton; 36, Grinnell; 40, Codrington; 41, Callaway; 42, Thalbitzer; 50, Nordenskiöld; 51, Wissler; 53, Rivers; 55, Mead.

METHOD: 1, Herodotus; 2, Lucretius; 18, Douglass; 38, 48, Tylor; 50, Nordenskiöld; 51, Wissler; 53, Rivers.

STATISTICAL METHOD: 7, Hooton; 8, Galton; 11, 14, Boas; 12, von Luschan; 48, Tylor.

SOURCE BOOK
IN
ANTHROPOLOGY

History of Anthropology

1. SOME GREEK ANTHROPOLOGICAL EXPLANATIONS

BY HERODOTUS [1]

THE EGYPTIANS [2]

CONCERNING Egypt itself I shall extend my remarks to a great length, because there is no country that possesses so many wonders, nor that has such a number of works which defy description. Not only is the climate different from that of the rest of the world, and the rivers unlike any other rivers, but the people also, in most of their manners and customs, exactly reverse the common practice of mankind. The women attend the markets and trade, while the men sit at home at the loom; and here, while the rest of the world works the woof up the warp, the Egyptians work it down; the women likewise carry burdens upon their shoulders, while the men carry them upon their heads. They eat their food out of doors in the streets, but retire for private purposes to their houses, giving as a reason that what is unseemly, but necessary, ought to be done in secret, but what has nothing unseemly about it, should be done openly. A woman cannot serve the priestly office, either for god or goddess, but men are priests to both; sons need not support their parents unless they choose; but daughters must, whether they choose or no.

In other countries the priests have long hair, in Egypt their heads are shaven; elsewhere it is customary, in mourning, for near relations to cut their hair close; the Egyptians, who wear no hair at any other time, when they lose a relative, let their beards and the hair of their heads grow long. All other men pass their lives separate from animals, the Egyptians have animals always living with them; others make barley and wheat their food; it is a disgrace to do so in Egypt, where the grain they live on is spelt, which some call *zea*. Dough they knead with their feet; but they mix mud, and even take up dirt, with their hands. They

---

[1] Herodotus, the "father of history," but equally that of anthropology, wrote in the fifth century B.C. The extracts here given are from the translation by George Rawlinson.

[2] Book II, Sec. 35-37.

3

are the only people in the world—they at least, and such as have learnt
the practice from them—who use circumcision. Their men wear two
garments apiece, their women but one. They put on the rings and fasten
the ropes to sails inside; others put them outside. When they write or
calculate, instead of going, like the Greeks, from left to right, they
move their hand from right to left; and they insist, notwithstanding,
that it is they who go to the right, and the Greeks who go to the left.
They have two quite different kinds of writing, one of which is called
sacred, the other common.

They are religious to excess, far beyond any other race of men, and
use the following ceremonies: They drink out of brazen cups, which
they scour every day; there is no exception to this practice. They wear
linen garments, which they are specially careful to have always fresh
washed. They practice circumcision for the sake of cleanliness, considering it better to be cleanly than comely. The priests shave their whole
body every other day, that no lice or other impure thing may adhere
to them when they are engaged in the service of the gods. Their dress
is entirely of linen, and their shoes of the papyrus plant; it is not lawful
for them to wear either dress or shoes of any other material. They bathe
twice every day in cold water, and twice each night; besides which they
observe, so to speak, thousands of ceremonies. They enjoy, however, not
a few advantages. They consume none of their own property, and are
at no expense for anything; but every day bread is baked for them of
the sacred corn, and a plentiful supply of beef and of goose's flesh is
assigned to each, and also a portion of wine made from the grape.
Fish they are not allowed to eat; and beans—which none of the Egyptians ever sow, or eat, if they come up of their own accord, either raw
or boiled—the priests will not even endure to look on, since they consider it an unclean kind of pulse. Instead of a single priest, each god
has the attendance of a college, at the head of which is a chief priest;
when one of these dies, his son is appointed in his room.

THE ANTIQUITY OF EGYPT
AND THE ORIGINAL LANGUAGE OF MANKIND [3]

Now the Egyptians, before the reign of their king Psammetichus, believed themselves to be the most ancient of mankind. Since Psammetichus, however, made an attempt to discover who were actually the
primitive race, they have been of opinion that while they surpass all
other nations, the Phrygians surpass them in antiquity. This king, finding it impossible to make out by dint of inquiry what men were the most

[3] Book II, Sec. 2-4.

ancient, contrived the following method of discovery: He took two children of the common sort, and gave them over to a herdsman to bring up at his folds, strictly charging him to let no one utter a word in their presence, but to keep them in a sequestered cottage, and from time to time introduce goats to their apartment, see that they got their fill of milk, and in all other respects look after them. His object herein was to know, after the indistinct babblings of infancy were over, what word they would first articulate. It happened as he had anticipated. The herdsman obeyed his orders for two years, and at the end of that time, on his one day opening the door of their room and going in, the children both ran up to him with outstretched arms, and distinctly said "Becos." When this first happened the herdsman took no notice; but afterwards when he observed, on coming often to see after them, that the word was constantly in their mouths, he informed his lord, and by his command brought the children into his presence. Psammetichus then himself heard them say the word, upon which he proceeded to make inquiry what people there was who called anything "becos," and hereupon he learnt that "becos" was the Phrygian name for bread. In consideration of this circumstance the Egyptians yielded their claims, and admitted the greater antiquity of the Phrygians.

That these were the real facts I learnt at Memphis from the priests of Vulcan. The Greeks, among other foolish tales, relate that Psammetichus had the children brought up by women whose tongues he had previously cut out; but the priests said their bringing up was such as I have stated above. I got much other information also from the conversation with these priests while I was at Memphis, and I even went to Heliopolis and to Thebes, expressly to try whether the priests of those places would agree in their accounts with the priests at Memphis. The Heliopolitans have the reputation of being the best skilled in history of all Egyptians. What they told me concerning their religion it is not my intention to repeat, except the names of their deities, which I believe all men know equally. If I relate anything else concerning these matters, it will only be when compelled to do so by the course of my narrative.

Now with regard to mere human matters, the accounts which they gave, and in which all agreed, were the following: The Egyptians, they said, were the first to discover the solar year, and to portion out its course into twelve parts. They obtained this knowledge from the stars. (To my mind they contrive their year much more cleverly than the Greeks, for these last every other year intercalate a whole month, but the Egyptians, dividing the year into twelve months of thirty days each, add every year a space of five days besides, whereby the circuit of the seasons is made to return with uniformity.) The Egyptians, they went on to affirm, first brought into use the names of the twelve gods, which the Greeks adopted from them; and first erected altars, images, and temples to the gods; and also first engraved upon stone the figures of animals. In most of these cases they proved to me that what they said was true. And they told me that the first man who ruled over Egypt was Mên, and that in his time all Egypt, except the Thebaic canton, was a marsh, none of the land below Lake Moeris then showing itself above the surface of the water. This is a distance of seven days' sail from the sea up the river.

THE ORIGIN OF A RELIGIOUS ORACLE [4]

The following tale is commonly told in Egypt concerning the oracle of Dodôna in Greece, and that of Ammon in Libya. My informants on the point were the priests of Jupiter at Thebes. They said "that two of the sacred women were once carried off from Thebes by the Phœnicians, and that the story went that one of them was sold into Libya, and the other into Greece, and these women were the first founders of the oracles in the two countries." On my inquiring how they came to know so exactly what became of the women, they answered "that diligent search had been made after them at the time, but that it had not been found possible to discover where they were; afterwards, however, they received the information which they had given me."

This was what I heard from the priests at Thebes; at Dodôna, however, the women who deliver the oracles relate the matter as follows: "Two black doves flew away from Egyptian Thebes, and while one directed its flight to Libya, the other came to them. She alighted on an oak, and sitting there began to speak with a human voice, and told them that on the spot where she was, there should henceforth be an oracle of Jove. They understood the announcement to be from heaven, so they set to work at once and erected the shrine. The dove which flew to Libya bade the Libyans to establish there the oracle of Ammon." This likewise is an oracle of Jupiter. The persons from whom I received these particulars were three priestesses of the Dodonæans, the oldest Promeneia, the next Timareté, and the youngest Nicandra— what they said was confirmed by the other Dodonæans who dwell around the temple.

My own opinion of these matters is as follows: I think that, if it be true that the Phœnicians carried off the holy women, and sold them for slaves, the one into Libya and the other into Greece, or Pelasgia

[4] Book II, Sec. 54-58.

(as it was then called), this last must have been sold to the Thesprotians. Afterwards, while undergoing servitude in those parts, she built under a real oak a temple to Jupiter at Thebes—to that particular god. Then, having acquired a knowledge of the Greek tongue, she set up an oracle. She also mentioned that her sister had been sold for a slave into Libya by the same persons as herself.

The Dodonæans called the women doves because they were foreigners, and seemed to them to make a noise like birds. After a while the dove spoke with a human voice, because the woman, whose foreign talk had previously sounded to them like the chattering of a bird, acquired the power of speaking what they could understand. For how can it be conceived possible that a dove should really speak with the voice of a man? Lastly, by calling the dove black the Dodonæans indicated that the woman was an Egyptian. And certainly the character of the oracles at Thebes and Dodôna is very similar. Besides this form of divination, the Greeks learnt also divination by means of victims from the Egyptians.

The Egyptians were also the first to introduce solemn assemblies, processions, and litanies to the gods; of all which the Greeks were taught the use by them. It seems to me a sufficient proof of this, that in Egypt these practices have been established from remote antiquity, while in Greece they are only recently known.

A RACIAL PECULIARITY AND ITS CAUSE [5]

On the field where this battle was fought I saw a very wonderful thing which the natives pointed out to me. The bones of the slain lie scattered upon the field in two lots, those of the Persians in one place by themselves, as the bodies lay at the first—those of the Egyptians in another place apart from them. If, then, you strike the Persian skulls, even with a pebble, they are so weak that you break a hole in them; but the Egyptian skulls are so strong, that you may smite them with a stone and you will scarcely break them in. They gave me the following reason for this difference, which seemed to me likely enough: The Egyptians (they said) from early childhood have the head shaved, and so by the action of the sun the skull becomes thick and hard. The same cause prevents baldness in Egypt, where you see fewer bald men than in any other lands. Such, then, is the reason why the skulls of the Egyptians are so strong. The Persians, on the other hand, have feeble skulls, because they keep themselves shaded from the first, wearing turbans upon their heads. What I have here mentioned I saw with my

[5] Book III, Sec. 12.

own eyes, and I observed also the like at Paprêmis, in the case of the Persians who were killed with Achæmenes, the son of Darius, by Inarus the Libyan.

BABYLONIAN CUSTOMS [6]

But that which surprises me most in the land, after the city itself, I will now proceed to mention. The boats which come down the river to Babylon are circular, and made of skins. The frames, which are of willow, are cut in the country of the Armenians above Assyria, and on these, which serve for hulls, a covering of skins is stretched outside, and thus the boats are made, without either stem or stern, quite round like a shield. They are then entirely filled with straw, and their cargo is put on board, after which they are suffered to float down the stream. Their chief freight is wine, stored in casks made of the wood of the palm tree. They are managed by two men who stand upright in them, each plying an oar, one pulling and the other pushing. The boats are of various sizes, some larger, some smaller; the biggest reach as high as five thousand talents' burden. Each vessel has a live ass on board; those of larger size have more than one. When they reach Babylon, the cargo is landed and offered for sale; after which the men break up their boats, sell the straw and the frames, and loading their asses with the skins, set off on their way back to Armenia. The current is too strong to allow a boat to return upstream, for which reason they make their boats of skins rather than wood. On their return to Armenia they build fresh boats for the next voyage.

The dress of the Babylonians is a linen tunic reaching to the feet, and above it another tunic made in wool, besides which they have a short white cloak thrown round them, and shoes of a peculiar fashion, not unlike those worn by the Bœotians. They have long hair, wear turbans on their heads, and anoint their whole body with perfumes. Every one carries a seal, and a walking-stick, carved at the top into the form of an apple, a rose, a lily, an eagle, or something similar; for it is not their habit to use a stick without an ornament.

Of their customs, whereof I shall now proceed to give an account, the following (which I understand belongs to them in common with the Illyrian tribe of the Eneti) is the wisest in my judgment: Once a year in each village the maidens of age to marry were collected all together in one place, while the men stood round them in a circle. Then a herald called up the damsels one by one, and offered them for sale. He began with the most beautiful. When she was sold for no small sum of money, he offered for sale the one who came next to

[6] Book I, Sec. 194-196.

her in beauty. All of them were sold to be wives. The richest of the Babylonians who wished to wed bid against each other for the loveliest maidens, while the humbler wife-seekers, who were indifferent about beauty, took the more homely damsels with marriage-portions. For the custom was that when the herald had gone through the whole number of the beautiful damsels, he should then call up the ugliest—a cripple, if there chanced to be one—and offer her to the men, asking who would agree to take her with the smallest marriage-portion. And the man who offered to take the smallest sum had her assigned to him. The marriage-portions were furnished by the money paid for the beautiful damsels, and thus the fairer maidens portioned out the uglier. No one was allowed to give his daughter in marriage to the man of his choice, nor might any one carry away the damsel whom he had purchased without finding bail really and truly to make her his wife; if, however, it turned out that they did not agree, the money might be paid back. All who liked might come even from distant villages and bid for the women. This was the best of all their customs, but it has now fallen into disuse. They have lately hit upon a very different plan to save their maidens from violence, and prevent their being torn from them and carried to distant cities, which is to bring up their daughters to be courtesans. This is now done by all the poorer of the common people, who since the conquest have been maltreated by their lords, and have had ruin brought upon their families.

2. ROMAN SPECULATIONS ON THE ORIGIN OF MAN AND CIVILIZATION

BY LUCRETIUS [7]

THE ORIGIN OF MAN

IN THE beginning the earth gave forth all kinds of herbage and verdant sheen about the hills and over all the plains; the flowery meadows glittered with the bright green hue, and next in order to the different trees was given a strong and emulous desire of growing up into the air with full unbridled powers. As feathers and hairs and bristles are first born on the limbs of four-footed beasts and the body of the strong of wing, thus the new earth then first put forth grass and bushes, and next

[7] Lucretius lived from 98 to 55 B.C. The passages here printed are selected from lines 783-1360 of the fifth book of the philosophical poem "De Rerum Natura," as translated by H. A. J. Munro and published by Deighton, Bell and Co. in 1873. By permission.

gave birth to the races of mortal creatures springing up many in number in many ways after divers fashions. For no living creatures can have dropped from heaven nor can those belonging to the land have come out of the salt pools. It follows that with good reason the earth has gotten the name of mother, since all things have been produced out of the earth. And many living creatures even now spring out of the earth taking form by rains and the heat of the sun. It is therefore the less strange if at that time they sprang up more in number and larger in size, having come to maturity in the freshness of earth and ether. First of all the race of fowls and the various birds would leave their eggs, hatched in the springtime, just as now in summer the cicades leave spontaneously their gossamer coats in quest of a living and life. Then you must know did the earth first give forth races of mortal men. For much heat and moisture would then abound in the fields; and therefore wherever a suitable spot offered, wombs would grow attached to the earth by roots; and when the warmth of the infants, flying the wet and craving the air, had opened these in the fullness of time, nature would turn to that spot the pores of the earth and constrain it to yield from its opened veins a liquid most like a milk, even as nowadays every woman when she has borne, is filled with sweet milk, because all that current of nutriment streams toward the breasts. To the children the earth would furnish food, the heat raiment, the grass a bed rich in abundance of soft down. Then the fresh youth of the world would give forth neither severe colds nor excessive heats nor gales of great violence; for all things grow and acquire strength in a like proportion.

Wherefore again and again I say the earth with good title has gotten and keeps the name of mother, since she of herself gave birth to mankind and at a time nearly fixed shed forth every beast that ranges wildly over the great mountains, and at the same time the fowls of the air with all their varied shapes. But because she must have some limit set to her bearing, she ceased like a woman worn out by length of days. For time changes the nature of the whole world and all things must pass on from one condition to another, and nothing continues like to itself: all things quit their bounds, all things nature changes and compels to alter. One thing crumbles away and is worn and enfeebled with age, then another comes into honor and issues out of its state of contempt. In this way then time changes the nature of the whole world and the earth passes out of one condition into another; what once it could, it can bear no more, in order to be able to bear what before it did not bear.

And many monsters too the earth at that time essayed to produce, things coming up with strange face and limbs, the man-woman, a thing between the two and neither the one sex nor the other, widely differing from both; some things deprived of feet, others again destitute of hands, others too proving dumb without mouth, or blind without eyes, and things bound fast by adhesion of their limbs over all the body, so that they could not do anything nor go anywhere nor avoid the evil nor take what their needs required. Every other monster and portent of this kind she would produce, but all in vain, since nature set a ban on their increase and they could not reach the coveted flower of age nor find food nor be united in marriage. For we see that many conditions must meet together in things in order that they may beget and continue their kinds; first a supply of food, then a way by which the birth-producing seeds throughout the frame may stream from the relaxed limbs; also in order that the woman may be united with the male, the possession of organs whereby they may each interchange mutual joys.

And many races of living things must then have died out and been unable to beget and continue their breed. For in the case of all things which you see breathing the breath of life, either craft or courage or else speed has from the beginning of its existence protected and pre-served each particular race. And there are many things which, recom-mended to us by their useful services, continue to exist consigned to our protection. In the first place the fierce breed of lions and the sav-age races their courage has protected, foxes their craft and stags their proneness to flight. But light-sleeping dogs with faithful heart in breast and every kind which is born of the seed of beasts of burden and at the same time the woolly flocks and the horned herds are all consigned, Memmius, to the protection of man. For they have ever fled with eagerness from wild beasts and have ensured peace and plenty of food obtained without their own labor, as we give it in requital of their useful services. But those to whom nature has granted none of these qualities, so that they could neither live by their own means nor perform for us any useful service in return for which we should suffer their kind to feed and be safe under our protection, those, you are to know, would lie exposed as a prey and booty of others, hampered all in their own death-bringing shackles, until nature brought that kind to utter destruction.

THE FIRST BEGINNINGS OF CIVILIZATION

But the race of man then in the fields was much hardier, as beseemed it to be, since the hard earth had produced it; and built on a ground-work of larger and more solid bones within, knit with powerful sinews throughout the frame of flesh; not lightly to be disabled by heat or cold or strange kinds of food or any malady of body. And during the revolution of many lusters of the sun through heaven they led a life after the roving fashion of wild beasts. No one then was a sturdy guider of the bent plow or knew how to labor the fields with iron or plant in the ground young saplings or lop with pruning-hooks old boughs from the high trees. What the sun and rains had given, what the earth had produced spontaneously, was guerdon sufficient to content their hearts. Among acorn-bearing oaks they would refresh their bodies for the most part; and the arbute berries which you now see in the winter time ripen with a bright scarlet hue, the earth would then bear in greatest plenty and of a larger size; and many coarse kinds of food besides the teeming freshness of the world then bare, more than enough for poor wretched men. But rivers and springs invited to slake thirst, even as now a rush of water down from the great hills summons with clear plash far and wide the thirsty races of wild beasts. Then too as they ranged about they would occupy the well-known woodland haunts of the nymphs, out of which they knew that smooth-gliding streams of water with a copious gush bathed the dripping rocks, trickling down over the green moss; and in parts welled and bubbled out over the level plain. And as yet they knew not how to apply fire to their purposes or to make use of skins and clothe their body in the spoils of wild beasts, but they would dwell in woods and mountain-caves and forests and shelter in the brushwood their squalid limbs when driven to shun the buffeting of the winds and the rains. And they were unable to look to the general weal and knew not how to make a common use of any customs or laws. Whatever prize fortune threw in his way, each man would bear off, trained at his own discretion to think of himself and live for himself alone. And Venus would join the bodies of lovers in the woods; for each woman was gained over either by mutual desire or the headstrong violence and vehement lust of the man or a bribe of some acorns and arbute berries or choice pears. And trusting to the marvelous powers of their hands and feet they would pursue the forest-haunting races of wild beasts with showers of stones and clubs of ponderous weight; and many they would conquer, a few they would avoid in hiding-places; and like to bristly swine just as they were they would throw their savage limbs all naked on the ground, when overtaken by night, covering themselves up with leaves and boughs.

FIRST SPEECH

Next after they had got themselves huts and skins and fire, and the woman united with the man passed with him into one (domicile and the duties of wedlock were) learnt (by the two), and they saw an off-spring born from them, then first mankind began to soften. For fire made their chilled bodies less able now to bear the frost beneath the canopy of heaven, and Venus impaired their strength and children with their caresses soon broke down the haughty temper of parents. Then too neighbors began to join in a league of friendship mutually desiring neither to do nor suffer harm; and asked for indulgence to children and womankind, when with cries and gestures they declared in stammering speech that meet it is for all to have mercy on the weak. And though harmony could not be established without exception, yet a very large portion observed their agreements with good faith, or else the race of man would then have been wholly cut off, nor could breeding have continued their generations to this day.

But nature impelled them to utter the various sounds of the tongue and use struck out the names of things, much in the same way as the inability to speak is seen in its turn to drive children to the use of gestures, when it forces them to point with the finger at the things which are before them. For every one feels how far he can make use of his peculiar powers. Ere the horns of a calf are formed and project from his forehead, he butts with it when angry and pushes out in his rage. Then whelps of panthers and cubs of lions fight with claws and feet and teeth at a time when teeth and claws are hardly yet formed. Again we see every kind of fowl trust to wings and seek from pinions a fluttering succor. Therefore to suppose that some one man at that time apportioned names to things and that men from him learnt their first words, is sheer folly. For why should this particular man be able to denote all things by words and to utter the various sounds of the tongue, and yet at the same time others be supposed not to have been able to do so? Again if others as well as he had not made use of words among themselves, whence was implanted in this man the previous conception of its use and whence was given to him the original faculty, to know and perceive in mind what he wanted to do? Again one man could not constrain and subdue and force many to choose to learn the names of things. It is no easy thing in any way to teach and convince the deaf of what is needful to be done; for they never would suffer nor in any way endure sounds of voice hitherto unheard to continue to be dinned ruthlessly into their ears. Lastly what is there so passing strange in this circumstance, that the race of men whose voice and tongue were in full force, should denote things by different words as different feelings prompted? Since dumb brutes, yes, and the races of wild beasts are accustomed to give forth distinct and varied sounds, when they have fear of pain and when joys are rife.

THE USE OF FIRE

And lest haply on this head you ask in silent thought this question, it was lightning that brought fire down on earth for mortals in the beginning; thence the whole heat of flames is spread abroad. Thus we see many things shine dyed in heavenly flames, when the stroke from heaven has stored them with its heat. Aye, and without this when a branching tree sways to and fro and tosses about under the buffeting of the winds, pressing the boughs of another tree, fire is forced out by the power of the violent friction, and sometimes the burning heat of flame flashes out, the boughs and stems rubbing against each other. Now either of these accidents may have given fire to men. Next the sun taught them to cook food and soften it with the heat of flame, since they would see many things grow mellow, when subdued by the strokes of the rays and by heat throughout the land.

THE ORIGIN OF RELIGION

And now what cause has spread over great nations the worship of the divinities of the gods and filled towns with altars and led to the performance of stated sacred rites, rites now in fashion on solemn occasions and in solemn places, from which even now is implanted in mortals a shuddering awe which raises new temples of the gods over the whole earth and prompts men to crowd them on festive days, all this it is not so difficult to explain in words. Even then in sooth the races of mortal men would see in waking mind glorious forms, would see them in sleep of yet more marvelous size of body. To these then they would attribute sense, because they seemed to move their limbs and to utter lofty words suitable to their glorious aspect and surpassing powers. And they would give them life everlasting, because their face would ever appear before them and their form abide; yes, and yet without all this, because they would not believe that beings possessed of such powers could lightly be overcome by any force. And they would believe them to be preëminent in bliss, because none of them was ever troubled with the fear of death, and because at the same time in sleep they would see them perform many miracles, yet feel on their part no fatigue from the effort. Again they would see the system of heaven and the different seasons of the years come round in regular succession, and could not find out by what causes this was done; and therefore they would seek a refuge in handing over all things to the gods and supposing all things to be guided by their nod. And they placed in heaven the abodes and realms of the gods, because night and moon are seen to roll through heaven, noon

day and night and night's austere constellations and night-wandering
meteors of the sky and flying bodies of flame, clouds, sun, rains, snow,
winds, lightnings, hail, and rapid rumblings and loud threatful thunder-
claps.

THE DISCOVERY OF METALS AND EVOLUTION OF MILITARY ART

To proceed, copper and gold and iron were discovered and at the
same time weighty silver and the substance of lead, when fire with its
heat had burnt up vast forests on the great hills, either by a discharge of
heaven's lightning, or else because men waging with one another a
forest-war had carried fire among the enemy in order to strike terror,
or because drawn on by the goodness of the soil they would wish to
clear rich fields and bring the country into pasture, or else to destroy
wild beasts and enrich themselves with the booty; for hunting with the
pitfall and with fire came into use before the practice of enclosing
the land with toils and stirring it with dogs. Whatever the fact is,
from whatever cause the heat of flame had swallowed up the forests
with a frightful crackling from their very roots and had thoroughly
baked the earth with fire, there would run from the boiling veins and
collect into the hollows of the ground a stream of silver and gold, as
well as of copper and lead. And when they saw these afterwards cool
into lumps and glitter on the earth with a brilliant gleam, they would
lift them up attracted by the bright and polished luster, and they
would see them to be molded in a shape the same as the outline of the
cavities in which each lay. Then it would strike them that these might
be melted by heat and cast in any form or shape soever, and might by
hammering out be brought to tapering points of any degree of sharpness
and fineness, so as to furnish them with tools and enable them to cut
the forests and hew timber and plane smooth the planks, and also to
drill and pierce and bore. And they would set about these works just
as much with silver and gold at first as with the overpowering strength
of stout copper, but in vain, since their force would fail and give way
and not be able like copper to stand the severe strain. At that time
copper was in higher esteem and gold would lie neglected on account
of its uselessness, with its dull blunted edge; now copper lies neglected,
gold has mounted up to the highest place of honor. Thus time as it
goes round changes the seasons of things. That which was in esteem
falls at length into utter disrepute; and then another thing mounts up
and issues out of its degraded state and every day is more and more
coveted and blossoms forth high in honor when discovered and is in
marvelous repute with men.

And now, Memmius, it is easy for you to find out by yourself in what way the nature of iron was discovered. Arms of old were hands, nails and teeth, and stones and boughs broken off from the forests, and flame and fire, as soon as they had become known. Afterwards the force of iron and copper was discovered; and the use of copper was known before that of iron, as its nature is easier to work and it is found in greater quantity. With copper they would labor the soil of the earth, with copper stir up the billows of war and deal about wide-gaping wounds and seize cattle and lands; for everything defenseless and unarmed would readily yield to them with arms in hand. Then by slow steps the sword of iron gained ground and the make of the copper sickle became a byword; and with iron they began to plow through the earth's soil, and the struggles of wavering war were rendered equal. And the custom of mounting in arms on the back of a horse and guiding him with reins and showing prowess with the right hand is older than that of tempting the risks of war in a two-horsed chariot; and yoking a pair of horses is older than yoking four or mounting in arms scythed chariots. Next the Pœni taught the Lucan kine with towered body, hideous of aspect, with snake-like hand, to endure the wounds of war and to disorder the mighty ranks of Mars. Thus sad discord begat one thing after another, to affright nations of men under arms, and every day made some addition to the terrors of war.

ORIGIN OF THE TEXTILE ARTS

A garment tied on the body was in use before a dress of woven stuff. Woven stuff comes after iron, because iron is needed for weaving a web; and in no other way can such finely polished things be made, as heddles and spindles, shuttles and ringing yarnbeams. And nature impelled men to work up the wool before womankind; for the male sex in general far excels the other in skill and is much more ingenious; until the rugged countrymen so upbraided them with it, that they were glad to give it over into the hands of the women and take their share in supporting hard toil, and in such hard work hardened body and hands.

Evolution

3. THE STRUGGLE FOR EXISTENCE AND NATURAL SELECTION [1]

BY CHARLES DARWIN

BEFORE entering on the subject of this chapter I must make a few preliminary remarks to show how the struggle for existence bears on natural selection. It has been seen in the last chapter that among organic beings in a state of nature there is some individual variability: indeed I am not aware that this has ever been disputed. It is immaterial for us whether a multitude of doubtful forms be called species or subspecies or varieties; what rank, for instance, the two or three hundred doubtful forms of British plants are entitled to hold, if the existence of any well-marked varieties be admitted. But the mere existence of individual variability and of some few well-marked varieties, though necessary as the foundation for the work, helps us but little in understanding how species arise in nature. How have all those exquisite adaptations of one part of the organization to another part, and to the conditions of life and of one organic being to another being, been perfected? We see these beautiful co-adaptations most plainly in the woodpecker and the mistletoe; and only a little less plainly in the humblest parasite which clings to the hairs of a quadruped or feathers of a bird; in the structure of the beetle which dives through the water; in the plumed seed which is wafted by the gentlest breeze; in short, we see beautiful adaptations everywhere and in every part of the organic world.

Again, it may be asked, how is it that varieties, which I have called incipient species, become ultimately converted into good and distinct species, which in most cases obviously differ from each other far more than do the varieties of the same species? How do those groups of species, which constitute what are called distinct genera and which

---

[1] Chapter 3, "Struggle for Existence," and summary of Chapter 4, "Natural Selection: or the Survival of the Fittest," of *The Origin of Species*, by Charles Darwin, first published in 1859. From the A. L. Burt edition, 1890 (reprinted from the sixth London edition).

differ from each other more than do the species of the same genus,
arise? All these results, as we shall more fully see in the next chapter,
follow from the struggle for life. Owing to this struggle, variations,
however slight and from whatever cause proceeding, if they be in any
degree profitable to the individuals of a species, in their infinitely complex relations to other organic beings and to their physical conditions
of life, will tend to the preservation of such individuals, and will generally be inherited by the offspring. The offspring, also, will thus have
a better chance of surviving, for, of the many individuals of any
species which are periodically born, but a small number can survive. I
have called this principle, by which each slight variation, if useful, is
preserved, by the term natural selection, in order to mark its relation
to man's power of selection. But the expression often used by Mr. Herbert Spencer, of the Survival of the Fittest, is more accurate, and is
sometimes equally convenient. We have seen that man by selection
can certainly produce great results, and can adapt organic beings to
his own uses, through the accumulation of slight but useful variations,
given to him by the hand of Nature. But Natural Selection, we shall
hereafter see, is a power incessantly ready for action and is as immeas-
urably superior to man's feeble efforts as the works of Nature are to
those of Art.

We will now discuss in a little more detail the struggle for existence. In my future work this subject will be treated, as it well
deserves, at greater length. The elder De Candolle and Lyell have
largely and philosophically shown that all organic beings are exposed to
severe competition. In regard to plants, no one has treated this subject
with more spirit and ability than W. Herbert, Dean of Manchester,
evidently the result of his great horticultural knowledge. Nothing is
easier than to admit in words the truth of the universal struggle for
life, or more difficult—at least I found it so—than constantly to bear
this conclusion in mind. Yet unless it be thoroughly engrained in the
mind, the whole economy of nature, with every fact on distribution,
rarity, abundance, extinction, and variation, will be dimly seen or quite
misunderstood. We behold the face of nature bright with gladness, we
often see superabundance of food; we do not see or we forget that the
birds which are idly singing round us mostly live on insects or seeds,
and are thus constantly destroying life; or we forget how largely these
songsters, or their eggs, or their nestlings, are destroyed by birds and
beasts of prey; we do not always bear in mind, that, though food may
be now superabundant, it is not so at all seasons of each recurring year.

THE TERM, STRUGGLE FOR EXISTENCE, USED IN A LARGE SENSE

I should premise that I use this term in a large and metaphorical sense, including dependence of one being on another, and including (which is more important) not only the life of the individual, but success in leaving progeny. Two canine animals, in a time of dearth, may be truly said to struggle with each other which shall get food and live. But a plant on the edge of a desert is said to struggle for life against the drought, though more properly it should be said to be dependent on the moisture. A plant which annually produces a thousand seeds, of which only one on an average comes to maturity, may be more truly said to struggle with the plants of the same and other kinds which already clothe the ground. The mistletoe is dependent on the apple and a few other trees, but can only in a far-fetched sense be said to struggle with these trees, for, if too many of these parasites grow on the same tree, it languishes and dies. But several seedling mistletoes, growing close together on the same branch, may more truly be said to struggle with each other. As the mistletoe is disseminated by birds, its existence depends on them; and it may metaphorically be said to struggle with other fruit-bearing plants, in tempting the birds to devour and thus disseminate its seeds. In these several senses, which pass into each other, I use for convenience sake the general term of Struggle for Existence.

GEOMETRICAL RATIO OF INCREASE

A struggle for existence inevitably follows from the high rate at which all organic beings tend to increase. Every being, which during its natural lifetime produces several eggs or seeds, must suffer destruction during some period of its life, and during some season or occasional year, otherwise, on the principle of geometrical increase, its numbers would quickly become so inordinately great that no country could support the product. Hence, as more individuals are produced than can possibly survive, there must in every case be a struggle for existence, either one individual with another of the same species, or with the individuals of distinct species, or with the physical conditions of life. It is the doctrine of Malthus applied with manifold force to the whole animal and vegetable kingdoms; for in this case there can be no artificial increase of food, and no prudential restraint from marriage. Although some species may be now increasing, more or less rapidly, in numbers, all cannot do so, for the world would not hold them.

There is no exception to the rule that every organic being naturally increases at so high a rate, that, if not destroyed, the earth would soon be covered by the progeny of a single pair. Even slow-breeding man has doubled in twenty-five years, and at this rate, in less than a thousand years, there would literally not be standing-room for his progeny. Linnæus has calculated that if an annual plant produced only two seeds—and there is no plant so unproductive as this—and their seedlings next year produced two, and so on, then in twenty years there would be a million plants. The elephant is reckoned the slowest breeder of all known animals, and I have taken some pains to estimate its probable minimum rate of natural increase; it will be safest to assume that it begins breeding when thirty years old, and goes on breeding till ninety years old, bringing forth six young in the interval, and surviving till one hundred years old; if this be so, after a period of from 740 to 750 years there would be nearly nineteen million elephants alive descended from the first pair.

But we have better evidence on this subject than mere theoretical calculations, namely, the numerous recorded cases of the astonishingly rapid increase of various animals in a state of nature, when circumstances have been favorable to them during two or three following seasons. Still more striking is the evidence from our domestic animals of many kinds which have run wild in several parts of the world; if the statements of the rate of increase of slow-breeding cattle and horses in South America, and latterly in Australia, had not been well authenticated, they would have been incredible. So it is with plants; cases could be given of introduced plants which have become common throughout whole islands in a period of less than ten years. Several of the plants, such as the cardoon and a tall thistle, which are now the commonest over the wide plains of La Plata, clothing square leagues of surface almost to the exclusion of every other plant, have been introduced from Europe; and there are plants which now range in India, as I hear from Dr. Falconer, from Cape Comorin to the Himalaya, which have been imported from America since its discovery. In such cases, and endless others could be given, no one supposes that the fertility of the animals or plants has been suddenly and temporarily increased in any sensible degree. The obvious explanation is that the conditions of life have been highly favorable, and that there has consequently been less destruction of the old and young and that nearly all the young have been enabled to breed. Their geometrical ratio of increase, the result of which never fails to be surprising, simply explains their extraordinarily rapid increase and wide diffusion in their new homes.

In a state of nature almost every full-grown plant annually produces seed, and among animals there are very few which do not annually pair. Hence we may confidently assert that all plants and animals are tending to increase at a geometrical ratio—that all would rapidly stock every station in which they could anyhow exist—and that this geometrical tendency to increase must be checked by destruction at some period of life. Our familiarity with the larger domestic animals tends, I think, to mislead us; we see no great destruction falling on them, but we do not keep in mind that thousands are annually slaughtered for food, and that in a state of nature an equal number would have somehow to be disposed of.

The only difference between organisms which annually produce eggs or seeds by the thousand, and those which produce extremely few, is, that the slow breeders would require a few more years to people, under favorable conditions, a whole district, let it be ever so large. The condor lays a couple of eggs and the ostrich a score, and yet in the same country the condor may be the more numerous of the two. The Fulmar petrel lays but one egg, yet it is believed to be the most numerous bird in the world. One fly deposits hundreds of eggs, and another, like the hippobosca, a single one. But this difference does not determine how many individuals of the two species can be supported in a district. A large number of eggs is of some importance to those species which depend on a fluctuating amount of food, for it allows them rapidly to increase in number. But the real importance of a large number of eggs or seeds is to make up for much destruction at some period of life; and this period in the great majority of cases is an early one. If an animal can in any way protect its own eggs or young, a small number may be produced, and yet the average stock be fully kept up; but if many eggs or young are destroyed, many must be produced, or the species will become extinct. It would suffice to keep up the full number of a tree, which lived on an average for a thousand years, if a single seed were produced once in a thousand years, supposing that this seed were never destroyed and could be insured to germinate in a fitting place; so that, in all cases, the average number of any animal or plant depends only indirectly on the number of its eggs or seeds.

In looking at Nature, it is most necessary to keep the foregoing considerations always in mind—never to forget that every single organic being may be said to be striving to the utmost to increase in numbers; that each lives by a struggle at some period of its life; that heavy destruction inevitably falls either on the young or old during each generation or at recurrent intervals. Lighten any check, mitigate the destruction ever so little, and the number of the species will almost instantaneously increase to any amount.

NATURE OF THE CHECKS TO INCREASE

The causes which check the natural tendency of each species to increase are most obscure. Look at the most vigorous species; by as much as it swarms in numbers, by so much will it tend to increase still further. We know not exactly what the checks are, even in a single instance. Nor will this surprise any one who reflects how ignorant we are on this head, even in regard to mankind, although so incomparably better known than any other animal. This subject of the checks to increase has been ably treated by several authors, and I hope in a future work to discuss it at considerable length, more especially in regard to the feral animals of South America. Here I will make only a few remarks, just to recall to the reader's mind some of the chief points. Eggs or very young animals seem generally to suffer most, but this is not invariably the case. With plants there is a vast destruction of seeds, but from some observations which I have made it appears that the seedlings suffer most from germinating in ground already thickly stocked with other plants. Seedlings, also, are destroyed in vast numbers by various enemies; for instance, on a piece of ground three feet long and two wide, dug and cleared, and where there could be no choking from other plants, I marked all the seedlings of our native weeds as they came up, and out of 357 no less than 295 were destroyed, chiefly by slugs and insects. If turf which has long been mown, and the case would be the same with turf closely browsed by quadrupeds, be let to grow, the more vigorous plants gradually kill the less vigorous, though fully grown plants; thus out of twenty species grown on a little plot of mown turf (three feet by four) nine species perished, from the other species being allowed to grow up freely.

The amount of food for each species, of course, gives the extreme limit to which each can increase; but very frequently it is not the obtaining food, but the serving as prey to other animals, which determines the average number of a species. Thus, there seems to be little doubt that the stock of partridges, grouse, and hares on any large estate depends chiefly on the destruction of vermin. If not one head of game were shot during the next twenty years in England, and, at the same time, if no vermin were destroyed, there would, in all probability, be less game than at present, although hundreds of thousands of game animals are now annually shot. On the other hand, in some cases, as with the elephant, none are destroyed by beasts of prey; for even the tiger in India most rarely dares to attack a young elephant protected by its dam.

Climate plays an important part in determining the average numbers of a species, and periodical seasons of extreme cold or drought seem to be the most effective of all checks. I estimated (chiefly from the greatly reduced numbers of nests in the spring) that the winter of 1854-5 destroyed four-fifths of the birds in my own grounds; and this is a tremendous destruction, when we remember that ten per cent. is an extraordinarily severe mortality from epidemics with man. The action of climate seems at first sight to be quite independent of the struggle for existence; but in so far as climate chiefly acts in reducing food, it brings on the most severe struggle between the individuals, whether of the same or of distinct species, which subsist on the same kind of food. Even when climate, for instance, extreme cold, acts directly, it will be the least vigorous individuals, or those which have got least food through the advancing winter, which will suffer the most. When we travel from south to north, or from a damp region to a dry, we invariably see some species gradually getting rare and rarer, and finally disappearing; and the change of climate being conspicuous, we are tempted to attribute the whole effect to its direct action. But this is a false view; we forget that each species, even where it most abounds, is constantly suffering enormous destruction at some period of its life, from enemies or from competitors for the same place and food; and if these enemies or competitors be in the least degree favored by any slight change of climate, they will increase in numbers; and as each area is already fully stocked with inhabitants, the other species must decrease. When we travel southward and see a species decreasing in numbers, we may feel sure that the cause lies quite as much in other species being favored, as in this one being hurt. So it is when we travel northward, but in a somewhat lesser degree, for the number of species of all kinds, and therefore of competitors, decreases northward, or in ascending a mountain, we far oftener meet with stunted forms, due to the *directly* injurious action of climate, than we do in proceeding southward or in descending a mountain. When we reach the Arctic regions, or snow-capped summits, or absolute deserts, the struggle for life is almost exclusively with the elements.

That climate acts in main part indirectly by favoring other species, we clearly see in the prodigious number of plants which in our gardens can perfectly well endure our climate, but which never become naturalized, for they cannot compete with our native plants nor resist destruction by our native animals.

When a species, owing to highly favorable circumstances, increases inordinately in numbers in a small tract, epidemics—at least, this seems generally to occur with our game animals—often ensue; and here we have a limiting check independent of the struggle for life. But even some of these so-called epidemics appear to be due to parasitic worms, which have from some cause, possibly in part through facility of diffusion among the crowded animals, been disproportionally favored: and here comes in a sort of struggle between the parasite and its prey.

On the other hand, in many cases, a large stock of individuals of the same species, relatively to the numbers of its enemies, is absolutely necessary for its preservation. Thus we can easily raise plenty of corn and rape-seed, etc., in our fields, because the seeds are in great excess compared with the number of birds which feed on them; nor can the birds, though having a superabundance of food at this one season, increase in number proportionally to the supply of seed, as their numbers are checked during the winter; but any one who has tried knows how troublesome it is to get seed from a few wheat or other such plants in a garden; I have in this case lost every single seed. This view of the necessity of a large stock of the same species for its preservation, explains, I believe, some singular facts in nature such as that of very rare plants being sometimes extremely abundant, in the few spots where they do exist; and that of some social plants being social, that is abounding in individuals, even on the extreme verge of their range. For in such cases, we may believe, that a plant could exist only where the conditions of its life were so favorable that many could exist together, and thus save the species from utter destruction. I should add that the good effects of intercrossing, and the ill effects of close interbreeding, no doubt come into play in many of these cases; but I will not here enlarge on this subject.

COMPLEX RELATIONS OF ALL ANIMALS AND PLANTS TO EACH OTHER IN THE STRUGGLE FOR EXISTENCE

Many cases are on record showing how complex and unexpected are the checks and relations between organic beings, which have to struggle together in the same country. I will give only a single instance, which, though a simple one, interested me. In Staffordshire, on the estate of a relation, where I had ample means of investigation, there was a large and extremely barren heath, which had never been touched by the hand of man; but several hundred acres of exactly the same nature had been inclosed twenty-five years previously and planted with Scotch fir. The change in the native vegetation of the planted part of the heath was most remarkable, more than is generally seen in passing from one quite different soil to another: not only the proportional numbers of the heath-plants were wholly changed, but twelve species of plants (not counting grasses and carices) flourished in the plantations, which could not be found on the heath. The effect on the insects must have been still greater, for six insectivorous birds were very common in the plantations, which were not to be seen on the heath; and the heath was frequented by two or three distinct insectivorous birds. Here we see how potent has been the effect of the introduction of a single tree, nothing whatever else having been done, with the exception of the land having been inclosed, so that cattle could not enter. But how important an element inclosure is, I plainly saw near Farnham, in Surrey. Here there are extensive heaths, with a few clumps of old Scotch firs on the distant hilltops: within the last ten years large spaces have been inclosed, and self-sown firs are now springing up in multitudes, so close together that all cannot live. When I ascertained that these young trees had not been sown or planted I was so much surprised at their numbers that I went to several points of view, whence I could examine hundreds of acres of the uninclosed heath, and literally I could not see a single Scotch fir, except the old planted clumps. But on looking closely between the stems of the heath, I found a multitude of seedlings and little trees which had been perpetually browsed down by the cattle. In one square yard, at a point some hundred yards distant from one of the old clumps, I counted thirty-two little trees; and one of them, with twenty-six rings of growth, had, during many years tried to raise its head above the stems of the heath, and had failed. No wonder that, as soon as the land was inclosed, it became thickly clothed with vigorously growing young firs. Yet the heath was so extremely barren and so extensive that no one would ever have imagined that cattle would have so closely and effectually searched it for food.

Here we see that cattle absolutely determine the existence of the Scotch fir; but in several parts of the world insects determine the existence of cattle. Perhaps Paraguay offers the most curious instance of this; for here neither cattle nor horses nor dogs have ever run wild, though they swarm southward and northward in a feral state; and Azara and Rengger have shown that this is caused by the greater number in Paraguay of a certain fly, which lays its eggs in the navels of these animals when first born. The increase of these flies, numerous as they are, must be habitually checked by some means, probably by other parasitic insects. Hence, if certain insectivorous birds were to decrease in Paraguay, the parasitic insects would probably increase; and this would lessen the number of the navel-frequenting flies—then cattle and horses would become feral, and this would certainly greatly alter (as indeed I have observed in parts of South America) the vegetation: this again would largely affect the insects; and this, as we have just seen in Staffordshire, the insectivorous birds, and so onward in ever-increasing circles of complexity. Not that under nature the relations will ever be as simple as this. Battle within battle must be continually recurring with varying success; and yet in the long-run the forces are so nicely balanced that the face of nature remains for long periods of time uniform, though assuredly the merest trifle would give the victory to one organic being over another. Nevertheless, so profound is our ignorance, and so high our presumption, that we marvel when we hear of the extinction of an organic being; and as we do not see the cause, we invoke cataclysms to desolate the world, or invent laws on the duration of the forms of life!

I am tempted to give one more instance showing how plants and animals, remote in the scale of nature, are bound together by a web of complex relations. I shall hereafter have occasion to show that the exotic Lobelia fulgens is never visited in my garden by insects, and consequently, from its peculiar structure, never sets a seed. Nearly all our orchidaceous plants absolutely require the visits of insects to remove their pollen-masses and thus to fertilize them. I find from experiments that humble-bees are almost indispensable to the fertilization of the heartsease (Viola tricolor), for other bees do not visit this flower. I have also found that the visits of bees are necessary for the fertilization of some kinds of clover; for instance twenty heads of Dutch clover (Trifolium repens) yielded 2,290 seeds, but twenty other heads, protected from bees, produced not one. Again, one hundred heads of red clover (T. pratense) produced 2,700 seeds, but the same number of protected heads produced not a single seed. Humble-bees alone visit red clover, as other bees cannot reach the nectar. It has been suggested that moths may fertilize the clovers; but I doubt whether they could do so in the case of the red clover, from their weight not being sufficient to depress the wing petals. Hence we may infer as highly probable that, if the whole genus of humble-bees became extinct or very rare in England, the heartsease and red clover would become very rare, or wholly disappear. The number of humble-bees in any district depends in a great measure upon the number of field-mice, which destroy their combs and nests; and Colonel Newman, who has long attended to the habits of humble-bees, believes that "more than two-thirds of them are thus destroyed all over England." Now the number of mice is largely dependent, as every one knows, on the number of cats; and Colonel Newman says, "Near villages and small towns I have found the nests of humble-bees more numerous than elsewhere, which I attribute to the number of cats that destroy the mice." Hence it is quite credible that the presence of a feline animal in large numbers in a district might determine, through the intervention first of mice and then of bees, the frequency of certain flowers in that district!

In the case of every species, many different checks, acting at different periods of life, and during different seasons or years, probably come into play; some one check or some few being generally the most potent; but all will concur in determining the average number, or even the existence of the species. In some cases it can be shown that widely different checks act on the same species in different districts. When we look at the plants and bushes clothing an entangled bank, we are tempted to attribute their proportional numbers and kinds to what we call chance. But how false a view is this! Every one has heard that when an American forest is cut down, a very different vegetation springs up; but it has been observed that ancient Indian ruins in the Southern United States, which must formerly have been cleared of trees, now display the same beautiful diversity and proportion of kinds as in the surrounding virgin forests. What a struggle must have gone on during long centuries between the several kinds of trees, each annually scattering its seeds by the thousand; what war between insect and insect—between insects, snails and other animals with birds and beasts of prey—all striving to increase, all feeding on each other, or on the trees, their seeds and seedlings, or on the other plants which first clothed the ground and thus checked the growth of the trees. Throw up a handful of feathers and all fall to the ground according to definite laws; but how simple is the problem where each shall fall compared to that of the action and reaction of the innumerable plants and animals which have determined, in the course of centuries, the proportional numbers and kinds of trees now growing on the old Indian ruins!

The dependency of one organic being on another, as of a parasite on its prey, lies generally between beings remote in the scale of nature. This is likewise sometimes the case with those which may be strictly said to struggle with each other for existence, as in the case of locusts and grass-feeding quadrupeds. But the struggle will almost invariably be most severe between the individuals of the same species, for they frequent the same districts, require the same food, and are exposed to the same dangers. In the case of varieties of the same species, the struggle will generally be almost equally severe, and we sometimes see the contest soon decided: for instance, if several varieties of wheat be sown together and the mixed seed be resown, some of the varieties which best suit the soil or climate, or are naturally the most fertile, will beat the others and so yield more seed, and will consequently in a few years supplant the other varieties. To keep up a mixed stock of even such extremely close varieties as the variously colored sweet peas, they must be each year harvested separately, and the seed then mixed in due proportion, otherwise the weaker kinds will steadily decrease in number and disappear. So again with the varieties of sheep; it has been asserted that certain mountain varieties will starve out other mountain varieties, so that they cannot be kept together. The same result has followed from keeping together different varieties of the medicinal leech. It may even be doubted whether the varieties of any of our domestic plants or animals have so exactly the same strength, habits, and constitution, that the original proportions of a mixed stock (crossing being prevented) could be kept up for half a dozen generations, if they were allowed to struggle together, in the same manner as beings in a state of nature, and if the seed or young were not annually preserved in due proportion.

STRUGGLE FOR LIFE MOST SEVERE BETWEEN INDIVIDUALS AND VARIETIES OF THE SAME SPECIES

As the species of the same genus usually have, though by no means invariably, much similarity in habits and constitution, and always in structure, the struggle will generally be more severe between them, if they come into competition with each other, than between the species of distinct genera. We see this in the recent extension over parts of the United States of one species of swallow having caused the decrease of another species. The recent increase of the missel-thrush in parts of Scotland has caused the decrease of the song-thrush. How frequently we hear of one species of rat taking the place of another species under the most different climates! In Russia the small Asiatic cockroach has everywhere driven before it its great congener. In Australia the imported hive-bee is rapidly exterminating the small, stingless native bee. One species of charlock has been known to supplant another species; and so in other cases. We can dimly see why the competition should be most severe between allied forms, which fill nearly the same place in the economy of nature; but probably in no one case could we precisely say why one species has been victorious over another in the great battle of life.

A corollary of the highest importance may be deduced from the foregoing remarks, namely, that the structure of every organic being is related, in the most essential yet often hidden manner, to that of all the other organic beings, with which it comes into competition for food or residence, or from which it has to escape, or on which it preys. This is obvious in the structure of the teeth and talons of the tiger; and in that of the legs and claws of the parasite which clings to the hair on the tiger's body. But in the beautifully plumed seed of the dandelion, and in the flattened and fringed legs of the water-beetle, the relation seems at first confined to the elements of air and water. Yet the advantage of the plumed seeds no doubt stands in the closest relation to the land being already thickly clothed with other plants, so that the seeds may be widely distributed and fall on unoccupied ground. In the water-beetle, the structure of its legs, so well adapted for diving, allows it to compete with other aquatic insects, to hunt for its own prey, and to escape serving as prey to other animals.

The store of nutriment laid up within the seeds of many plants seems at first sight to have no sort of relation to other plants. But from the strong growth of young plants produced from such seeds, as peas and beans, when sown in the midst of long grass, it may be suspected that the chief use of the nutriment in the seed is to favor the growth of the seedlings, while struggling with other plants growing vigorously all around.

Look at a plant in the midst of its range! Why does it not double or quadruple its numbers? We know that it can perfectly well withstand a little more heat or cold, dampness or dryness, for elsewhere it ranges into slightly hotter or colder, damper or drier districts. In this case we can clearly see that if we wish in imagination to give the plant the power of increasing in numbers, we should have to give it some advantage over its competitors, or over the animals which prey on it. On the confines of its geographical range, a change of constitution with respect to climate would clearly be an advantage to our plant; but we have reason to believe that only a few plants or animals range so far, that they are destroyed exclusively by the rigor of the climate. Not until we reach the extreme confines of life, in the Arctic regions or on the borders of an utter desert, will competition cease. The land may be extremely cold or dry, yet there will be competition between some few species, or between the individuals of the same species, for the warmest or dampest spots.

Hence we can see that when a plant or animal is placed in a new country, among new competitors, the conditions of its life will generally be changed in an essential manner, although the climate may be exactly the same as in its former home. If its average numbers are to increase in its new home, we should have to modify it in a different way to what we should have had to do in its native country; for we should have to give it some advantage over a different set of competitors or enemies.

It is good thus to try in imagination to give any one species an advantage over another. Probably in no single instance should we know what to do. This ought to convince us of our ignorance on the mutual relations of all organic beings; a conviction as necessary, as it is difficult to acquire. All that we can do is to keep steadily in mind that each organic being is striving to increase in a geometrical ratio; that each, at some period of its life, during some season of the year, during each generation, or at intervals, has to struggle for life and to suffer great destruction. When we reflect on this struggle we may console ourselves with the full belief that the war of nature is not incessant, that no fear is felt, that death is generally prompt, and that the vigorous, the healthy, and the happy survive and multiply.

NATURAL SELECTION: SUMMARY

If under changing conditions of life organic beings present individual differences in almost every part of their structure, and this cannot be disputed; if there be, owing to their geometrical rate of increase, a severe struggle for life at some age, season or year, and this certainly cannot be disputed; then, considering the infinite complexity of the relations of all organic beings to each other and to their conditions of life, causing an infinite diversity in structure, constitution and habits, to be advantageous to them, it would be a most extraordinary fact if no variations had ever occurred useful to each being's own welfare, in the same manner as so many variations have occurred useful to man. But if variations useful to any organic being ever do occur, assuredly individuals thus characterized will have the best chance of being preserved in the struggle for life; and from the strong principle of inheritance, these will tend to produce offspring similarly characterized. This principle of preservation, or the survival of the fittest, I have called natural selection. It leads to the improvement of each creature in relation to its organic and inorganic conditions of life; and consequently, in most cases, to what must be regarded as an advance in organization. Nevertheless, low and simple forms will long endure if well fitted for their simple conditions of life.

Natural selection, on the principle of qualities being inherited at corresponding ages, can modify the egg, seed or young as easily as the adult. Among many animals sexual selection will have given its aid to ordinary selection by assuring to the most vigorous and best adapted males the greatest number of offspring. Sexual selection will also give characters useful to the males alone in their struggles or rivalry with other males; and these characters will be transmitted to one sex or to both sexes, according to the form of inheritance which prevails.

Whether natural selection has really thus acted in adapting the various forms of life to their several conditions and stations, must be judged by the general tenor and balance of evidence given in the following chapters. But we have already seen how it entails extinction; and how largely extinction has acted in the world's history, geology plainly declares. Natural selection, also, leads to divergence of character; for the more organic beings diverge in structure, habits and constitution, by so much the more can a large number be supported on the area, of which we see proof by looking to the inhabitants of any small spot, and to the productions naturalized in foreign lands. Therefore, during the modification of the descendants of any one species, and during the incessant struggle of all species to increase in numbers, the more diversified the descendants become, the better will be their chance of success in the battle for life. Thus the small differences distinguishing varieties of the same species, steadily tend to increase, till they equal the greater differences between species of the same genus, or even of distinct genera.

We have seen that it is the common, the widely diffused and widely ranging species, belonging to the larger genera within each class, which vary most; and these tend to transmit to their modified offspring that superiority which now makes them dominant in their own countries. Natural selection, as has just been remarked, leads to divergence of character and to much extinction of the less improved and intermediate forms of life. On these principles, the nature of the affinities, and the generally well defined distinctions between the innumerable organic beings in each class throughout the world, may be explained. It is a truly wonderful fact—the wonder of which we are apt to overlook from familiarity—that all animals and all plants throughout all time and space should be related to each other in groups, subordinate to groups, in the manner which we everywhere behold—namely, varieties of the same species most closely related, species of the same genus less closely and unequally related, forming sections and sub-genera, species of distinct genera much less closely related, and genera related in different degrees, forming sub-families, families, orders, sub-classes and classes. The several subordinate groups in any class cannot be ranked in a single file, but seem clustered round points, and these round other points, and so on in almost endless cycles. If species had been independently created, no explanation would have been possible of this kind of classification; but it is explained through inheritance and the complex action of natural selection, entailing extinction and divergence of character. . . .

The affinities of all the beings of the same class have sometimes been represented by a great tree. I believe this simile largely speaks the truth. The green and budding twigs may represent existing species; and those produced during former years may represent the long succession of extinct species. At each period of growth all the growing twigs have tried to branch out on all sides, and to overtop and kill the surrounding twigs and branches, in the same manner as species and groups of species have at all times overmastered other species in the great battle for life. The limbs divided into great branches, and these into lesser and lesser branches, were themselves once, when the tree was young, budding twigs; and this connection of the former and present buds by ramifying branches may well represent the classification of all extinct and living species in groups subordinate to groups. Of the many twigs which flourished when the tree was a mere bush, only two or three, now grown into great branches, yet survive and bear the other branches; so with the species which lived during long-past geological periods, very few have left living and modified descendants. From the first growth of the tree, many a limb and branch has decayed and dropped off; and these fallen branches of various sizes may represent those whole orders, families and genera which have now no living representatives, and which are known to us only in a fossil state. As we here and there see a thin, straggling branch springing from a fork low down in a tree, and which by some chance has been favored and is still alive on its summit, so we occasionally see an animal like the Ornithorhynchus or Lepidosiren, which in some small degree connects by its affinities two large branches of life, and which has apparently been saved from fatal competition by having inhabited a protected station. As buds give rise by growth to fresh buds, and these, if vigorous, branch out and overtop on all sides many a feebler branch, so by generation I believe it has been with the great Tree of Life, which fills with its dead and broken branches the crust of the earth, and covers the surface with its ever-branching and beautiful ramifications.

4. ON THE RELATIONS OF MAN TO THE LOWER ANIMALS [2]

BY THOMAS H. HUXLEY

A CAREFUL study of the resemblances and differences presented by animals has . . . led naturalists to arrange them into groups, or

[2] From Thomas H. Huxley, *Man's Place in Nature and Other Anthropological Essays*, second essay: "On the Relations of Man to the Lower Animals." Originally published 1863, in *Evidence as to Man's Place in Nature*.

assemblages, all the members of each group presenting a certain amount of definable resemblance, and the number of points of similarity being smaller as the group is larger and *vice versâ*. Thus, all creatures which agree only in presenting the few distinctive marks of animality form the 'Kingdom' ANIMALIA. The numerous animals which agree only in possessing the special characters of Vertebrates form one 'Sub-kingdom' of this Kingdom. Then the Sub-kingdom VERTEBRATA is subdivided into the five 'Classes,' Fishes, Amphibians, Reptiles, Birds, and Mammals, and these into smaller groups called 'Orders'; these into 'Families' and 'Genera'; while the last are finally broken up into the smallest assemblages, which are distinguished by the possession of constant, notsexual, characters. These ultimate groups are Species.

Every year tends to bring about a greater uniformity of opinion throughout the zoölogical world as to the limits and characters of these groups, great and small. At present, for example, no one has the least doubt regarding the characters of the classes Mammalia, Aves, or Reptilia; nor does the question arise whether any thoroughly wellknown animal should be placed in one class or the other. Again, there is a very general agreement respecting the characters and limits of the orders of Mammals, and as to the animals which are structurally necessitated to take a place in one or another order.

No one doubts, for example, that the Sloth and the Anteater, the Kangaroo and the Opossum, the Tiger and the Badger, the Tapir and the Rhinoceros, are respectively members of the same orders. These successive pairs of animals may, and some do, differ from one another immensely, in such matters as the proportions and structure of their limbs; the number of their dorsal and lumbar vertebræ; the adaptation of their frames to climbing, leaping, or running; the number and form of their teeth; and the characters of their skulls and of the contained brain. But, with all these differences, they are so closely connected in all the more important and fundamental characters of their organization, and so distinctly separated by these same characters from other animals, that zoölogists find it necessary to group them together as members of one order. And if any new animal were discovered, and were found to present no greater difference from the Kangaroo or from the Opossum, for example, than these animals do from one another, the zoölogist would not only be logically compelled to rank it in the same order with these, but he would not think of doing otherwise.

Bearing this obvious course of zoölogical reasoning in mind, let us endeavor for a moment to disconnect our thinking selves from the mask of humanity; let us imagine ourselves scientific Saturnians, if you will, fairly acquainted with such animals as now inhabit the Earth, and em-

ployed in discussing the relations they bear to a new and singular "erect
and featherless biped," which some enterprising traveler, overcoming
the difficulties of space and gravitation, has brought from that distant
planet for our inspection, well preserved, may be, in a cask of rum.
We should all, at once, agree upon placing him among the mammalian
vertebrates; and his lower jaw, his molars, and his brain, would leave
no room for doubting the systematic position of the new genus among
those mammals, whose young are nourished during gestation by means
of a placenta, or what is called the "placental mammals."

Further, the most superficial study would at once convince us that,
among the orders of placental mammals, neither the Whales nor the
hoofed creatures, nor the Sloths and Ant-eaters, nor the carnivorous
Cats, Dogs, and Bears, still less the Rodent Rats and Rabbits, or the
Insectivorous Moles and Hedgehogs, or the Bats, could claim our
'Homo,' as one of themselves.

There would remain then, but one order for comparison, that of the
Apes (using the word in its broadest sense), and the question for discussion would narrow itself to this—is Man so different from any of
these Apes that he must form an order by himself? Or does he differ
less from them than they differ from one another, and hence must take
his place in the same order with them?

Being happily free from all real, or imaginary, personal interest in
the results of the inquiry thus set afoot, we should proceed to weigh the
arguments on one side and on the other, with as much judicial calm-
ness as if the question related to a new Opossum. We should endeavor
to ascertain, without seeking either to magnify or diminish them, all
the characters by which our new Mammal differed from the Apes; and
if we found that these were of less structural value than those which
distinguish certain members of the Ape order from others universally
admitted to be of the same order, we should undoubtedly place the
newly discovered tellurian genus with them.

I now proceed to detail the facts which seem to me to leave no choice
but to adopt the last-mentioned course.

It is quite certain that the Ape which most nearly approaches man, in
the totality of its organization, is either the Chimpanzee or the Gorilla;
and as it makes no practical difference, for the purposes of my present
argument, which is selected for comparison, on the one hand, with
Man, and on the other hand, with the rest of the Primates, I shall select
the latter (so far as its organization is known)—as a brute now so
celebrated in prose and verse, that all must have heard of him, and
have formed some conception of his appearance. I shall take up as
many of the most important points of difference between man and this

remarkable creature, as the space at my disposal will allow me to discuss, and the necessities of the argument demand; and I shall inquire into the value and magnitude of these differences, when placed side by side with those which separate the Gorilla from other animals of the same order.

In the general proportions of the body and limbs there is a remarkable difference between the Gorilla and Man, which at once strikes the eye. The Gorilla's brain-case is smaller, its trunk larger, its lower limbs shorter, its upper limbs longer in proportion than those of Man.

I find that the vertebral column of a full-grown Gorilla, in the Museum of the Royal College of Surgeons, measures 27 inches along its anterior curvature, from the upper edge of the atlas, or first vertebra of the neck, to the lower extremity of the sacrum; that the arm, without the hand, is 31½ inches long; that the leg, without the foot, is 26½ inches long; that the hand is 9¾ inches long; the foot 11¼ inches long.

In other words, taking the length of the spinal column as 100, the arm equals 115, the leg 96, the hands 36, and the foot 41.

In the skeleton of a male Bosjesman [Bushman], in the same collection, the proportions, by the same measurement, to the spinal column, taken as 100, are—the arm 78, the leg 110, the hand 26, and the foot 32. In a woman of the same race the arm is 83, and the leg 120, the hand and foot remaining the same. In a European skeleton I find the arm to be 80, the leg 117, the hand 26, the foot 35.

Thus the leg is not so different as it looks at first sight, in its proportion to the spine in the Gorilla and in the Man—being very slightly shorter than the spine in the former, and between 1-10 and 1-5 longer than the spine in the latter. The foot is longer and the hand much longer in the Gorilla; but the great difference is caused by the arms, which are very much longer than the spine in the Gorilla, very much shorter than the spine in the Man.

The question now arises how are the other Apes related to the Gorilla in these respects—taking the length of the spine, measured in the same way, at 100. In an adult Chimpanzee, the arm is only 96, the leg 90, the hand 43, the foot 39—so that the hand and the leg depart more from the human proportion and the arm less, while the foot is about the same as in the Gorilla.

In the Orang, the arms are very much longer than in the Gorilla (122), while the legs are shorter (88); the foot is longer than the hand (52 and 48), and both are much longer in proportion to the spine.

In the other man-like Apes again, the Gibbons, these proportions are still further altered; the length of the arms being to that of the

spinal column as 19 to 11; while the legs are also a third longer than
the spinal column, so as to be longer than in Man, instead of shorter.
The hand is half as long as the spinal column, and the foot, shorter
than the hand, is about 5-11ths of the length of the spinal column.

Thus *Hylobates* is as much longer in the arms than the Gorilla, as
the Gorilla is longer in the arms than Man; while, on the other hand,
it is as much longer in the legs than the Man, as the Man is longer
in the legs than the Gorilla, so that it contains within itself the ex-
tremest deviations from the average length of both pairs of limbs. . . .

These examples might be greatly multiplied, but they suffice to show
that, in whatever proportion of its limbs the Gorilla differs from Man,
the other Apes depart still more widely from the Gorilla and that,
consequently, such differences of proportion can have no ordinal value.

We may next consider the differences presented by the trunk, consisting of the vertebral column, or backbone, and the ribs and pelvis,
or bony hip-basin, which are connected with it, in Man and in the
Gorilla respectively.

In Man, in consequence partly of the disposition of the articular
surfaces of the vertebræ, and largely of the elastic tension of some of
the fibrous bands, or ligaments, which connect these vertebræ together,
the spinal column, as a whole, has an elegant S-like curvature, being
convex forwards in the neck, concave in the back, convex in the loins,
or lumbar region, and concave again in the sacral region; an arrangement which gives much elasticity to the whole backbone, and diminishes
the jar communicated to the spine, and through it to the head, by locomotion in the erect position. . . .

The vertebral column of the Gorilla, as a whole, differs from that
of Man in the less marked character of its curves, especially in the
slighter convexity of the lumbar region. Nevertheless, the curves are
present, and are quite obvious in young skeletons of the Gorilla and
Chimpanzee which have been prepared without removal of the ligaments. In young Orangs similarly preserved, on the other hand, the
spinal column is either straight, or even concave forwards, throughout
the lumbar region.

Whether we take these characters then, or such minor ones as those
which are derivable from the proportional length of the spines of the
cervical vertebræ, and the like, there is no doubt whatsoever as to the
marked difference between Man and the Gorilla; but there is as little,
that equally marked differences, of the very same order, obtain between
the Gorilla and the lower apes. . . .

Thus, whatever system of organs be studied, the comparison of their
modifications in the ape series leads to one and the same result—that

the structural differences which separate Man from the Gorilla and the Chimpanzee are not so great as those which separate the Gorilla from the lower apes.

But in enunciating this important truth I must guard myself against a form of misunderstanding, which is very prevalent. I find, in fact, that those who endeavor to teach what nature so clearly shows us in this matter, are liable to have their opinions misrepresented and their phraseology garbled, until they seem to say that the structural differences between man and even the highest apes are small and insignificant. Let me take this opportunity then of distinctly asserting, on the contrary, that they are great and significant; that every bone of a Gorilla bears marks by which it might be distinguished from the corresponding bone of a Man; and that, in the present creation, at any rate, no intermediate link bridges over the gap between *Homo* and *Troglodytes*.

It would be no less wrong than absurd to deny the existence of this chasm; but it is at least equally wrong and absurd to exaggerate its magnitude and, resting on the admitted fact of its existence, to refuse to inquire whether it is wide or narrow. Remember, if you will, that there is no existing link between Man and the Gorilla, but do not forget that there is a no less sharp line of demarcation, a no less complete absence of any transitional form, between the Gorilla and the Orang, or the Orang and the Gibbon. I say, not less sharp, though it is somewhat narrower. The structural differences between Man and the Man-like apes certainly justify our regarding him as constituting a family apart from them; though, inasmuch as he differs less from them than they do from other families of the same order, there can be no justification for placing him in a distinct order. . . .

5. EVOLUTION OF THE PRIMATES AND MAN [3]

BY WILLIAM K. GREGORY

THE assumption of the erect attitude in the Hominidæ has involved many . . . readjustments and reversals in the proportional lengths of the limb segments—readjustments, of which the true significance has

[3] From pages 333-342 of "Studies on the Evolution of the Primates" in *Bulletin of the American Museum of Natural History*, Volume 35, Number 19, 1916; and from "How Near is the Relationship of Man to the Chimpanzee-Gorilla Stock?" in *The Quarterly Review of Biology*, Volume 2, Number 4, pages 549-560, 1927. The last section quoted is from the second article. By permission.

been largely missed by those who put their trust in ratios and indices. It is often held that the relatively long arms and short legs of the chimpanzee and gorilla as compared with those of man are aberrant specializations which remove these apes from the direct ancestry to man. But long arms and short legs are used in brachiating, and short legs are especially advantageous in squatting, the favorite posture of the gorilla. Now both brachiating and squatting form I believe a necessary introduction to the upright posture of man. The habit of brachiating, or swinging from branch to branch with the arms, trained the arms in the all important power of supination and improved the brain, eyes, and all the balancing mechanism. The habit of sitting upright conditioned the loss of the tail and the further development of all those characters of the backbone, thorax, and pelvis which give to the anthropoid skeleton a distinctly subhuman look. Moreover the habit of sitting upright tended greatly to encourage the use of the hands.

But long arms and short legs are also very useful in progression upon the ground and especially in the forest, as one can readily see from Mr. Raymond L. Ditmar's excellent motion pictures made in the New York Zoölogical Park. This peculiar method of taking great strides with the forearms, in a semi-erect posture, again forms a necessary prelude to fully erect bipedal progression. It must have been abandoned only when the primitive ape-men took to carrying weapons or food in their hands, and when through the use of jagged flints the arms became terrible fighting weapons.

With all respect to the contrary views of very eminent authorities, such as M. Boule and Professor Klaatsch, it seems perfectly evident that the long legs and short arms of man form a secondary specialization for erect bipedal progression upon the ground and that all resemblances in the proportions of the fore and hind limb between man, the cynomorphous monkeys, and certain lemuroids are entirely secondary. Both the long femur and the long tibia of man greatly lengthen the stride and increase the speed, factors of vital importance in a hunting and fighting animal, but of less importance to the clumsy frugivorous anthropoids. The short arms in man are also more powerful and of greater advantage in fighting with weapons. On the other hand the opposite proportions, namely long legs and short arms, in the tree-living anthropoids would be inconsistent with the fully upright posture in sitting and with the habit of brachiation, and such arboreal animals as happen to have long legs and shorter arms, as in the *Galago*, although accidentally approaching man in this respect, have these proportions because they are specialized for leaping, in a manner utterly different from the erect bipedal progression of man. Moreover long hind limbs, while permissible in a small arboreal animal like the gibbon, would be quite inconsistent with the upright pose, in the trees, of a heavy animal like a full-grown chimpanzee or gorilla, since they would make it more difficult to maintain the balance. . . .

In brief I can discover no valid objection to the view that the Upper Miocene forerunners of the Hominidæ had short stout femora and

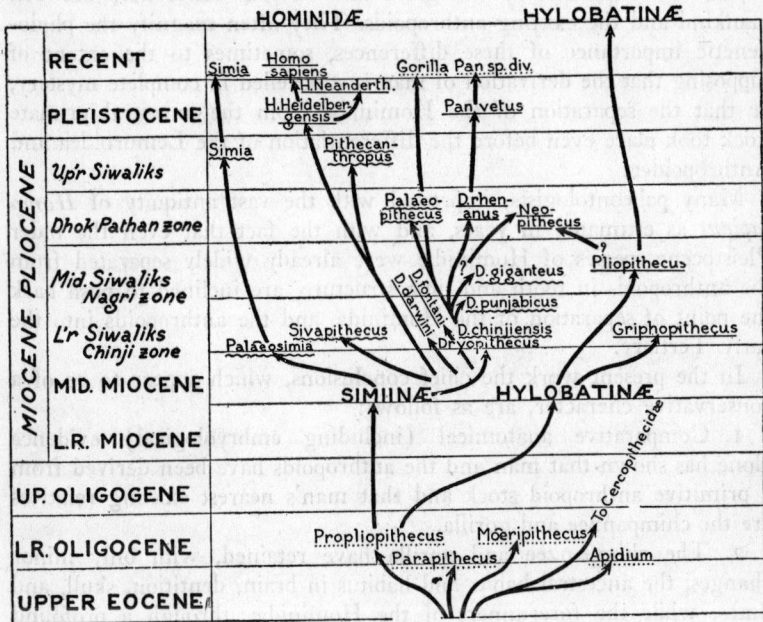

Geological Succession and Relationship of the Ancestors of Man and the Anthropoid Apes

long arms much like those of baby gorillas. As terrestrial bipedal progression was adopted the femora and tibiæ lengthened out while the forearm was reduced in length but gained in thickness. . . .

In short I hold that as the ancestral Hominidæ gave up arboreal frugivorous and semi-quadrupedal habits and assumed the life of hunters upon the ground, the hind limb, especially the femur, became longer, the hallux was lengthened, rotated about its own axis, and brought into alignment with the other digits, the forearm shortened, and the pollex became larger. . . .

THE ORIGIN OF MAN

Most anthropologists have specialized almost exclusively in their own field and have not acquired a practical knowledge of the evolution of the mammals, so far as it is known in many orders and families of mammals throughout the Tertiary and Quaternary Periods. Such specialists are impressed by the great and obvious differences between mankind and the existing anthropoids. They often magnify the phylogenetic importance of these differences, sometimes to the extent of supposing that the derivation of man is still veiled in complete mystery, or that the separation of the Hominidæ from the ancestral primate stock took place even before the differentiation of the Lemuroidea and Anthropoidea.

Many palæontologists, impressed with the vast antiquity of *Homo sapiens* as estimated in years, and with the fact that even the older Pleistocene species of Hominidæ were already widely separated from the anthropoids in tooth and limb structure, are inclined to push back the point of separation of the Hominidæ and the anthropoids into the early Tertiary.

In the present work the chief conclusions, which appear to be of a conservative character, are as follows:

1. Comparative anatomical (including embryological) evidence alone has shown that man and the anthropoids have been derived from a primitive anthropoid stock and that man's nearest existing relatives are the chimpanzee and gorilla.

2. The chimpanzee and gorilla have retained, with only minor changes, the ancestral habits and habitus in brain, dentition, skull, and limbs, while the forerunners of the Hominidæ, through a profound change in function, lost the primitive anthropoid habitus, gave up arboreal frugivorous adaptations, and early became terrestrial, bipedal, and predatory, using crude flints to cut up and smash the varied food.

3. The ancestral chimpanzee-gorilla-man stock appears to be represented by the Upper Miocene genera *Sivapithecus* and *Dryopithecus*, the former more closely allied to, or directly ancestral to, the Hominidæ, the latter to the chimpanzee and gorilla.

4. Many of the differences that separate man from anthropoids of the *Sivapithecus* type are retrogressive changes, following the profound change in food habits above noted. Here belong the retraction of the face and dental arch, the reduction in size of the canines, the reduction of the jaw muscles, the loss of the prehensile character of the hallux. Many other differences are secondary adjustments in relative propor-

tions, connected with the change from semi-arboreal, semi-erect, and semi-quadrupedal progression to fully terrestrial bipedal progression. The earliest anthropoids, being of small size, doubtless had slender limbs; later semi-terrestrial, semi-erect forms were probably not unlike a very young gorilla, with fairly short legs and not excessively elongate arms. The long legs and short arms of man are due, I believe, to a secondary readjustment of proportions. The very short legs and very long arms of old male gorillas may well be a specialization.

5. At present I know no good evidence for believing that the separation of the Hominidæ from the Simiidæ took place any earlier than the Miocene, and probably the Upper Miocene. The change in structure during this vast interval (two or more million years) is much greater in the Hominidæ than in the conservative anthropoids, but it is not unlikely that during a profound change of life habits evolution sometimes proceeds more rapidly than in the more familiar cases where uninterrupted progressive adaptations proceed in a single direction.

6. *Homo heidelbergensis* appears to be directly ancestral to all the later Hominidæ.

THE ORDER OF RELATIONSHIP

I submit the evidence recorded in my previous papers together with the considerations advanced in the present paper, in support of the following conclusions:

1. Considering the evidence afforded by comparative studies on the brains of primates, the anthropoid apes as a whole are undoubtedly man's nearest known relatives, the order of structural relationship being: (1) modernized man; (2) primitive man; (3) gorilla; (4) chimpanzee; (5) orang; (6) gibbon; (7) Old World monkey; (8) New World monkey; (9) *Tarsius;* (10) lemur; (11) pentailed treeshrew (Elliot Smith, Tilney, Le Gros Clark). Modern students are also convinced that the general order of evolution was the reverse of this, namely, from primitive tree-shrew to lemuroid, to stem tarsioid, to pro-anthropoid, to man.

2. Considering the evidence afforded by the comparative study of the teeth of all known recent and fossil primates, the order of structural evolution is as follows: (1) generalized tree-shrew (*cf.* Paleocene, *Indrodon*); (2) primitive lemuroid (*cf. Pelycodus ralstoni,* Lower Eocene); (3) primitive tarsioid (*Parapithecus,* Lower Oligocene); (4) proto-anthropoid (*Propliopithecus,* Lower Oligocene); (5) primitive anthropoid (e.g. *Dryopithecus rhenanus*); (6) primitive man (e.g. *Eoanthropus*); (7) modernized man (*Homo sapiens europæus*). Among existing primates the general order of resemblance to man

in the dentition is: (1) chimpanzee; (2) orang; (3) gorilla; (4) gibbon; (5) *Tarsius*.

3. Dr. Gerrit S. Miller and Professor Wood Jones seem to have over-emphasized the fact that the known remains of fossil anthropoids consist mostly of broken jaws and teeth. Apparently they think that because the specimens are broken and imperfect, any conclusions based on them must be equally defective. But these specimens, imperfect as they are, supply highly important and significant landmarks in the evolution of the primates, and when considered in the light of the great body of evidence from anatomy, embryology, physiology, they are sufficient to establish a high degree of probability that the separation of man from the anthropoid stock did not occur before the middle of the Tertiary period.

4. Turning to another aspect of the question, how near is the relationship of man to the chimpanzee-gorilla stock, we have to ask: About how many generations may have existed since the final separation of man from the anthropoid stock, that is, since interbreeding between the two ceased? Assuming that this occurred in the Middle Miocene, that would give a period of about ten million years to the Upper Pliocene *Eoanthropus*. The anthropoids approach sexual maturity at ten years of age, while certain races of man can breed at twelve years. Assuming twelve years, or about eight generations to a century as the average rate, that would give 800,000 generations as the transitional period between *Dryopithecus* and the Piltdown man.

Dr. Gerrit S. Miller once said that if the divergent great toe of a chimpanzee were to be pressed around so as to be parallel with the other toes, it would cause the animal intense pain and that he would therefore not walk in such a way as to produce such pressure. Hence a chimpanzee-like foot could never be changed into a human foot. But even an acute pain, divided among 800,000 generations, might be supportable. In other words, much might be done toward bridging the remaining gap between some member of the *Dryopithecus* group and man during 800,000 generations, especially in view of the relatively high structural variability of all the known races of man and of anthropoid apes. . . .

6. THE MOST ANCIENT SKELETAL REMAINS OF MAN [4]
BY A. HRDLIČKA

THE early history of the human race, though merged in the darkness of ages, is step by step being traced and reconstructed; and apparently the time is drawing near when science will be able to announce, in the main at least, the definite solution of the profound and involved problem of man's origin, when, in other words, it will be in a position to show, however imperfectly, when, where, and how man ascended from the lower orders.

Actual research into the antiquity of mankind began considerably less than a century ago, and the more intensive investigations in this field cover hardly a generation. Such investigations have been fraught with many difficulties and are growing in complexity. They demand patient watchfulness, diligent and long-extended exploration, and considerable expense. The most careful attention must in every case be given to geological and paleontological evidence. And, after all, the net results of a prolonged quest may be no more than a few stone chips and implements, or perhaps a tooth, or a few badly crushed bones, belonging to human antiquity. But, as there are many hands at work, invaluable materials are accumulating. Besides this every now and then the search is more richly rewarded, or some important specimen is discovered accidentally; and every new, well-authenticated addition to the remains of early man or his predecessors, more particularly if it is a part of the skeleton, means a fresh, highly valuable document which throws supplementary light on the natural history of the human being. . . .

PITHECANTHROPUS ERECTUS

In 1891-92 Dr. E. Dubois, then a surgeon in the Dutch army, while engaged in paleontological excavations along the left bank of the Bengavan River, near Trinil, in the central part of the Island of Java, discovered several skeletal parts of a primate evidently higher in scale and nearer to man than any before known.

The remains were thoroughly petrified and comprised, in all, the vault of a skull, two molar teeth, and a femur.

[4] From an article of the same title in the Smithsonian Report for 1913, pages 491-552, 1914; and from "The Skeletal Remains of Early Man," constituting Smithsonian Miscellaneous Collections, Volume 83, 1930. The latter is the fuller source, but on account of greater compactness of the descriptions, the earlier article has been used except for Eoanthropus and Rhodesian man. A few of the illustrations have been simplified.

The bones were not found simultaneously nor in the same place. They lay some distances apart, though at the same horizon and embedded in the same stratum of volcanic matrix. This stratum was rich in fossil remains of various organic forms and, in the locality where the excavations were carried on, was about 1 meter below the dry-season water level, or 12 to 15 meters below the plain in which the river had cut its bed.

In September, 1891, the excavations in the volcanic matrix yielded unexpectedly, among other fossils, a remarkable tooth, a molar, which was determined as having belonged to a large unknown primate. A month later the unique and most interesting skullcap was discovered, only 1 meter distant from the place where lay the tooth. It now became certain that traces had come to light of a hitherto unknown primate of large size, standing in many respects nearer to man than any of the actual anthropoid apes. It was seemingly an intermediate form between the apes and man, and was characterized by the name of *"pithecanthropus."*

Then came the rainy season and work had to be suspended. Exploration was recommenced, however, as early as possible in 1892, and in August of that year the femur was found about 15 meters (50 feet) from the locality where the other specimens had been embedded. Finally, in October of the same year, the second molar was secured, at a distance of not more than 3 meters (13 feet) from the original position of the skullcap, and in the direction of the resting place of the femur.

The accompanying illustration (Fig. 1) shows the locality of the discovery and the approximate positions of the specimens.

All four specimens were considerably mineralized, being of chocolate-brown color, very heavy, and "harder than marble." Numerous bones of mammals found in the same bed belonged to species now extinct or, so far as known, not now living in Java, and showed fossilization similar to that of the bones of the Pithecanthropus. The contours of the teeth and the femur were sharp, indicating that it has not been washed or rolled about to any great extent; but the skullcap showed the effects of erosion, probably caused by acidulous water seeping through the deposits.

All indications and a detailed study of the specimens led Dubois to the conclusions that: (1) The four skeletal pieces in question were contemporaneous; (2) they were of the age of the stratum in which found; (3) they belonged to one skeleton; and (4) they represent a transitional form of beings between the anthropoid apes and man, belonging to the direct line in the genealogy of the latter. . . .

While Dubois and other scientific men regard the Pithecanthropus remains as all belonging to the same skeleton, as dating chronologically from the latest part of the Tertiary or the earliest phase of the Quaternary period, and as representing a true intermediary form between the anthropoid apes and man, others have expressed doubts as to whether the four bones belong to the same form; or they consider the age of

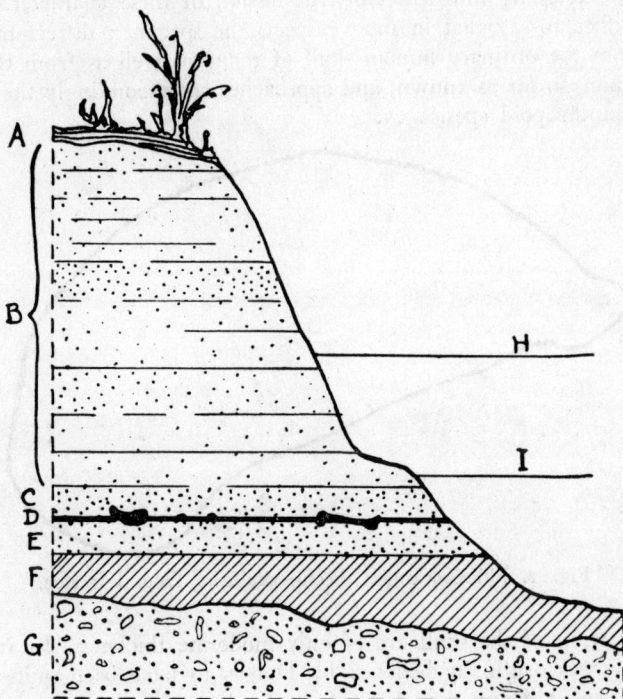

Fig. 1. Section of the strata where the Pithecanthropus bones were discovered. B, soft sandstone; D, level at which the skeletal remains were found; F, argillaceous layer; G, marine breccia; H, wet-season level of the river; I, dry-season level of the river.

the remains, though no doubt early Quaternary, to be less than that estimated by Dubois. . . .

The skullcap (Fig. 2) measures in greatest length 18.5 cm., in greatest (parietal) breadth 13 cm., and at the minimum of the frontal constriction 8.7 cm. It is dolichocephalic, its outline as seen from above is oblongly ovoid, narrowing considerably forward, and it is very low. It presents excessively prominent though not massive supra-orbital arch and a very sloping front. The frontal bone, in addition, shows externally and along its middle a well-defined ridge, running from a short dis-

tance above the glabella toward bregma, and a marked low protuberance just forward of the bregma. The sagittal region is relatively flat
and smooth and the occiput presents a dull transverse crest, connecting
as in apes, though in much less pronounced manner, with the supra-
mastoid crest on each side.

Without going into a detailed discussion of these characteristics, it
will suffice to say that in most respects the specimen differs more or
less from the ordinary human skull of today as well as from those of
early man, so far as known, and approaches correspondingly the crania
of the anthropoid apes. . . .

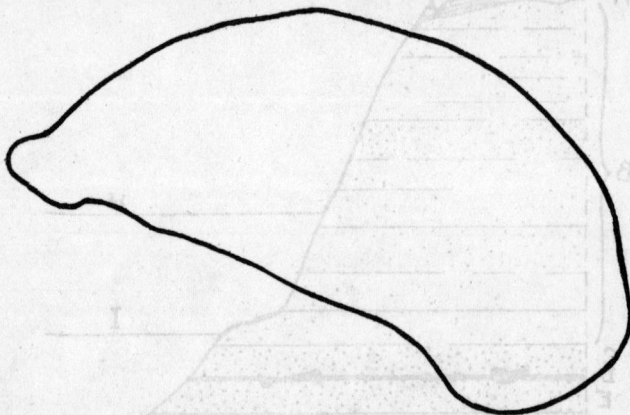

Fig. 2. Pithecanthropus erectus skullcap, from left side.

The walls of the skull are of only moderate thickness. Its internal
capacity was originally believed by Dubois to have been quite large,
namely about 1,000 c.c., but eventually he reduced this estimate to
900 c.c. or a little over. The capacity of an average cranium of a white
American would amount in the male to about 1,500, in the female to
about 1,350 c.c., while in the largest living anthropoid apes it only
rarely attains or exceeds 600 c.c.

The impression which a comprehensive study of the whole skullcap
carries to the observer is, that it represents a hitherto unknown primate
form, which, whatever it may eventually be identified with and whether
or not man's direct ancestor, stands morphologically between man and
the known anthropoid apes, fills an important space in the hitherto
existing large void between the two, and constitutes a precious document for the natural history of man.

On the whole, it seems evident that the two teeth represent a higher primate form; in all probability they come from one individual, and their morphological characteristics are such that they may well have belonged to the same species or even the same individual as the before-described skullcap. Their size, as seen from a comparison with the teeth of larger existing anthropoid apes, is not incompatible with the size of the skullcap, and that even if the latter belonged to a female individual.

The Trinil femur, according to Dubois, Manouvrier, and others, bears a close resemblance to the human thigh bone, both in size and shape; nevertheless it presents also some important differences. Its length, 45.5 cm., equals that of a human femur from a man 1.70 meters (5 feet, 7 inches) in stature, and of proportionate strength. . . .

The femur plainly belonged to a strong being maintaining erect or near-erect posture and marching mostly or entirely biped, as man. . . .

THE EOANTHROPUS DAWSONI

The remains attributed to the Eoanthropus consist of two lots, the first comprising nine fragments of a skull (joined now into four pieces), a pair of nasal bones, a portion of a lower jaw, and a canine; the second, two fragments of another skull and presumably a loose molar.

The initial remains of the first group were unearthed from the ancient river gravels of the Ouse river, at Piltdown, near Fletching, in the weald of Sussex, between 1909 (approximately) and 1913, by laborers, but discovered, with additional finds, by Charles Dawson, A. Smith Woodward and P. Teilhard. The second lot is believed to have been found, in 1915, among the surface rakings of a field two miles from the site of the earlier discovery, by Dawson; it was not reported until 1917 by Woodward, on the basis of oral information given by Dawson.

The earlier remains "were first found by workmen when digging the gravel for use on roads, and among them was the human skull which they broke up and threw away. One fragment was fortunately preserved and given to Mr. Dawson, who recognized its importance and at once began a search for the remainder of the specimen. Enough pieces were recovered to show the essential peculiarities of the skull. Part of the lower jaw and the lower canine tooth were eventually found in the adjacent undisturbed gravel, and some implements of human workmanship and fragmentary remains of animals were also met with."

With the earlier remains were found worn fossils evidently washed out of Pliocene formations (mastodon, stegodon, rhinoceros); fossils of probably early Pleistocene age (hippopotamus, beaver, elk); and primitive stone implements, with one large crude tool of a bone of an elephant.

The discoverers and the English anthropologists in general associate the first group of finds as those of one individual, the loose molar and possibly the parts of the second skull to another, and all the specimens as belonging to one early form of man, the Eoanthropus.

From the same gravels came also waterworn "eoliths," that may have been washed out from an even older formation; and rare flints with "obvious signs of human workmanship" and representing a very old type of paleolithic implements.

Taking all the circumstances of the find into consideration, Dr. Woodward decided that "it appeared probable that the skull and mandible cannot safely be described as being of earlier date than the first half of the Pleistocene Epoch. The individual probably lived during a warm cycle in that age." In 1922, in his "Guide to the Fossil Remains of Man," Dr. Woodward says: "So far as can be judged from present evidence, it is therefore reasonable to suppose that Piltdown man dates back to the beginning of the Pleistocene period." The latter is about the generally accepted opinion today. . . .

From the nine fragments of the cranium, together with the portion of the lower jaw and the loose canine, a number of the most prominent students of the remains have attempted with infinite pains a reconstruction of the whole skull. . . .

Probably the most striking character of the bones of the skull (exclusive of the lower jaw), is their massiveness. The bones measure 8 to 12 mm. in thickness to 20 mm. at the internal occipital protuberance. This is just about twice the thickness of an average modern white skull. . . .

The sum of the indications, it is generally recognized, are that the skull is that of a female. . . .

The capacity of the skull has been estimated by the different authors who attempted its reconstruction, as follows:

	Approximately c.c.
Smith Woodward's original estimate	1,070
Barlow's brain cast, first Smith Woodward reconstruction	1,200
Second Smith Woodward reconstruction	1,300
Elliot Smith	1,200
Keith	1,400

If the skull was that of a female, as is most probable, its mean approximate diameter $(L \times B \times H \div 3)$, after reduction for the extra thickness of the specimen, would indicate an internal capacity of about 1,300 c.c. . . .

The various determinations show that:

1. The skull, taken as female, was in size above rather than below the present average of female crania;

2. The skull cavity and hence the size of the brain were about the average of the ordinary white females of today;

3. The vault of the skull was not low as in all the other known early forms of man.

In addition it is certain that the forehead of this skull was well arched and filled out; the parietal, temporal, and occipital regions were fashioned practically as they are in modern skulls; the supraorbital ridges were very moderate and did not form a connected arch; there were no occipital or other crests; the glenoid fossa and the mastoids were well developed.

In general this skull, though it may show some secondary inferiorities, if it were not for the exceedingly primitive lower jaw and canine tooth found near it, would inevitably have to be classed among those of modern man. . . .

The lower jaw, as stated, was found personally by Dawson, apparently close to the spot where the skull was discovered, in "a somewhat deeper depression of the undisturbed gravel. . . ."

It is this jaw, together with the subsequently found canine, that has become the great "bone of contention" in the case. The reason is that, as tersely stated by Dr. Woodward, "while the Piltdown skull is thus completely human, the half of the lower jaw, so far as preserved, is almost precisely that of an ape." And in another place Dr. Woodward expresses the uncertainty thus created: "It may next be questioned whether this ape-like mandible belongs to the skull. We can only state that its molar teeth are typically human, its muscle-markings are such as might be expected, and it was found in the gravel near to the skull. The probabilities are therefore in favour of its natural association. If so, it is reasonable to suppose that the skull will prove to be that of a very primitive type, not that of a highly civilized man."

No such jaw, or even an approach to it, has ever before or since been found with such a skull. . . .

In 1917 Dr. Woodward announced the discovery of parts of the second skull, together with a loose molar, both evidently connecting with the first find, the skull bones with the skull, the tooth with the jaw. . . .

It appears to the author that it is no longer possible to regard the jaw as that of a chimpanzee or any other anthropoid ape; but that it is the jaw of either a human precursor or very early man. Dr. Smith Woodward's designation of this form as "Eoanthropus"—a being from the dawn of the human period—seems very appropriate.

An individual, or even genetic, specific, association of the Piltdown jaw with the massive remains of the two Piltdown skulls is, it may be repeated once more, exceedingly difficult of acceptance.

HOMO HEIDELBERGENSIS

One of the oldest thoroughly authenticated skeletal relics so far discovered and attributable to a primitive human being, is the priceless specimen known as the Mauer jaw. This precious document of man's evolution is deposited in the Paleontological Institute of Heidelberg. For its preservation and thorough description we are indebted to Dr. Otto Schoetensack, professor of Anthropology at Heidelberg University, who for years had been watching the finds in the sand pits near Mauer which eventually yielded the specimen. . . .

The deposits in which the specimen was discovered are located near the village of Mauer, which lies in the picturesque Elsenz Valley, six miles southeast from Heidelberg. . . .

The portion of these deposits owned by H. Rösch, located about 500 paces north of the Mauer village, have now been worked, in open manner, for upward of thirty years, in which time great quantities of building sand have been removed. During this work, particularly in the lower strata, the workingmen often unearthed fossil shells and fossil bones of various Quaternary animals. Many of these specimens found their way, mostly as gifts of Herr Rösch, to the Heidelberg University, and the diggings were repeatedly visited by scientific men, among whom was Prof. Schoetensack. Both the owner and the workmen were enjoined to watch for better preserved specimens, and particularly for anything relating to the presence of man.

On the date of the find, two of the laborers were working in undisturbed material at the base of the exposure, over eighty feet in depth from the surface, when one of them suddenly brought out on his shovel part of a massive lower jaw which the implement had struck and cut in two. As the men knew it was worth while to carefully preserve all fossils, the specimen was handled with some care. The missing half was dug out, but the crowns of four of the teeth broken by the shovel were not recovered. The men were struck at once with the remarkable resemblance of the bone to a human lower jaw; but it looked to them too thick and large to be that of a man. They called Herr Rösch and he also was bewildered; but he recognized immediately that the specimen might be of considerable interest to Prof. Schoetensack and so he took charge of it. Returning to the village he telegraphed to the professor, who came the next day, and "once he got hold of the specimen, he would no more let it out of his possession." He took it to Heidelberg, cleaned it, repaired it, and in 1908 published its description in an exemplary way. Since then the valuable specimen has been preserved in the Paleontological Institute of the Heidelberg University, where, thanks to the liberality of those in charge, it is available for examination to men of science.

Shortly following the discovery of the jaw a most careful examination and study were made of the Mauer deposits. They were found to range from recent accumulations on the surface to Tertiary deposits in the lowest layers. The jaw lay a little less than three feet above the floor of the excavation and seventy-nine feet from the surface. The same level, as well as some of the higher layers, yielded fossil bones of the *Elephas antiquus, Rhinoceros etruscus, Felis leo fossilis,* and various other extinct species. The age of the human jaw has been determined

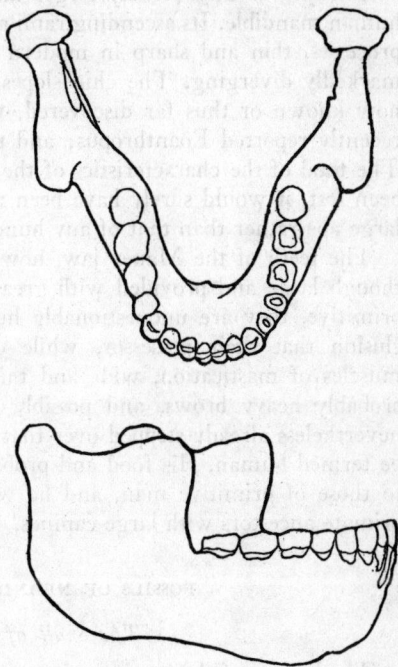

Fig. 3. The Heidelberg jaw.
(After Schoetensack.)

by these and subsequent exploration to be earlier Quaternary, though there seems to be some uncertainty as yet as to the exact subdivision of the period to which it should be attributed.

The original specimen, when seen, impresses one at once and potently as one of the greatest anthropological treasures. It is a huge lower jaw, which looks simultaneously both human and ape (Fig. 3).

It presents no abnormality or any diseased condition that could have altered it in shape, so that it may well be regarded as a perfect representative of its type. The bone is dull yellowish-white to reddish in color, with numerous small and large blackish spots. The crowns of the teeth are dirty creamy white, with blackish discolorations on the somewhat worn-off chewing surfaces of the canines and incisors, and a few similar spots over the molars; while all the parts of the teeth beneath the enamel are dull red, as if especially colored. It is much mineralized and feels more like so much limestone than bone. It weighs nearly seven ounces.

The jaw is considerably larger and stouter than any other known human mandible. Its ascending rami are exceedingly broad. Its coronoid processes, thin and sharp in modern man, are thick, dull, broad, and markedly diverging. The chin slopes backward as in no human being now known or thus far discovered, with the possible exception of the recently reported Eoanthropus; and there are other primitive features. The total of the characteristics of the bone are such that, had the teeth been lost, it would surely have been regarded as the mandible of some large ape rather than that of any human being.

The teeth of the Mauer jaw, however, are perfectly preserved, and though large and provided with great roots and in various other ways primitive, they are unquestionably human teeth. They force the conclusion that their possessor, while of heavy, protruding face, huge muscles of mastication, wide and thick zygomatic arches, thick skull, probably heavy brows, and possibly not yet quite erect posture, had nevertheless already stepped over that line above which the being could be termed human. His food and probably his mode of life were related to those of primitive man, and he was already far removed from his primate ancestors with large canines. . . .

FOSSILS OF NEANDERTHAL MAN

The Skull of Gibraltar

The history of the specimen is, regrettably, somewhat defective. The first mention of it occurs in Falconer's Paleontological Memoirs. . . .

Taking all the available data into consideration, it appears that the skull was discovered, accidentally, as early as 1848, therefore eight years before the Neanderthal cranium made its appearance, in the "Forbes Quarry, situated on the north front of the Rock of Gibraltar." . . .

The skull was presented to the Gibraltar Scientific Society by its that time secretary, Lieut. Flint, but for many years received no scientific attention. In 1862 it came to England, with the collections from the Gibraltar caves, and was studied to some extent by Busk and Falconer. The latter, perceiving how much it differed from recent human skulls, proposed to refer it to a distinct variety of man, the *Homo colpicus*, after Calfé, the old name of Gibraltar. In 1868 finally Busk presented the cranium to the Museum of the Royal College of Surgeons of England, where it is still preserved.

The first descriptive account of the specimen was published, as mentioned above, by Broca, but the adhering stony matrix prevented at that time any attempts at accurate measurements. Subsequently it received attention from Huxley, Quatrefages, and Hamy, and later from Macnamara, Klaatsch, Schwalbe, Sollas, Sera, and Keith, as well as the writer. It is a very remarkable specimen which, even though the geo-

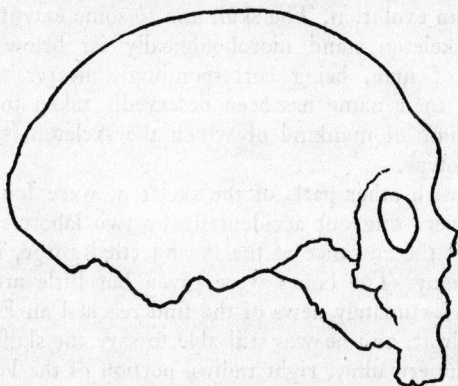

Fig. 4. The Gibraltar Skull.

logical and paleontological evidence relating to its antiquity is imperfect, does not allow for one moment any doubt as to its representing an early form of the human being; and its characteristics are such that it is now universally regarded as a representative, possibly a very early one, of the *Homo neanderthalensis*.

The cranium (Fig. 4) is dirty yellowish to whitish in color. It is considerably mineralized. The stony matrix has been so far removed that all important determinations and measurements which the defective state of the bone itself permits, can now be made. A fortunate circumstance is that the frontal and facial parts are relatively well preserved; the vault on the other hand is largely defective, but even here sufficient portions remain to permit of a number of valuable determinations, and a fairly correct reconstruction. . . .

The vault, viewed from above, is ovoid in shape and decidedly low. The forehead is low and sloping. The cranial bones are thick, exceeding any in this line that can be found in normal modern European.

The external dimensions of the skull are fairly large, but the brain was small. The cranial capacity is estimated by Keith as having been under 1,100 c.c.—that in an adult white woman of the present time averaging about 1,325 c.c.

The Neanderthal Skull and Bones

The most famous of the skeletal remains representing early man are unquestionably the imperfect but highly characteristic specimens known as the Neanderthal skull and bones. This important find more than any other has aroused scientific men to intense realization of the earlier phases of human evolution. The skull and to some extent also the other parts of the skeleton stand morphologically far below those of any existing type of man, being correspondingly nearer to the ancient primates; and their name has been deservedly taken to designate the entire early phase of mankind of which the skeleton is, as now well known, a prototype.

The skull, with other parts of the skeleton, were found in August, 1856. They were dug out accidentally by two laborers from a small cave, located at the entrance of the Neanderthal gorge, in Westphalia, western Germany. The bones were given but little attention by the workmen, but fortunately news of the find reached an Elberfeld physician, Dr. Fuhlrott, and he was still able to save the skullcap (Fig. 5), the femora, humeri, ulnæ, right radius, portion of the left pelvic bone, portion of the right scapula, piece of the right clavicle, and five pieces of ribs. . . .

The principal details of Dr. Fuhlrott's report were as follows:

A small cave or grotto, high enough to admit a man and about 15 feet deep from the entrance, which is 7 or 8 feet wide, exists in the southern wall of the gorge of the Neanderthal, as it is termed, at a distance of about 100 feet from the Düssel and about 60 feet above the bottom of the valley (Fig. 6). In its earlier and uninjured condition this cavern opened upon a narrow plateau lying in front of it and from which the rocky wall descended almost perpendicularly to the river. It could be reached, though with difficulty, from above. The uneven floor was covered to a thickness of 4 or 5 feet with a deposit of mud, sparingly intermixed with rounded fragments of chert. In the removing of this deposit the bones were discovered. The skull was first noticed, placed nearest to the entrance of the cavern; and further in were the other bones lying in the same horizontal plane. Of this I was assured in the most positive terms by two laborers who were employed to clear out the grotto, and who were questioned by me on the spot. At first no idea was entertained of the bones being human; and it was not till several weeks after their discovery that they were recognized as such by me and placed in security.

But, as the importance of the discovery was not at the time perceived, the laborers were very careless in the collecting and secured chiefly only the larger bones; and to this circumstance it may be attributed that fragments merely of the probably perfect skeleton came into my possession. . . .

Following the early notices concerning the Neanderthal cranium, and before other specimens of similar nature, such as the Spy, Gibraltar and others became known, an extensive controversy arose as to the real significance of the find. Virchow, and after him others, were at first inclined to look upon the skull as pathological; to Barnard Davis its sutures appeared to show premature synostosis; while Blake and his followers regarded the specimen as probably proceeding from an idiot. But there were also those, such as Schaaffhausen, Broca, and others,

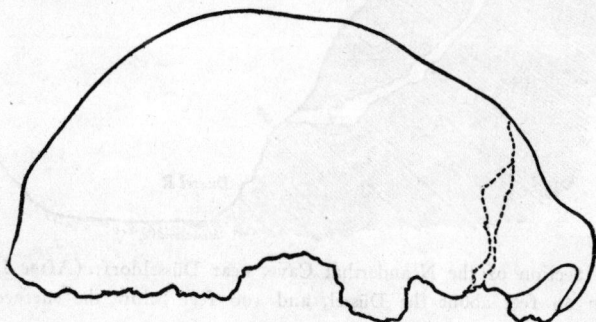

Fig. 5. The Neanderthal skull.

who from the beginning saw in the cranium (the other bones received at first but little attention) not any pathological or accidental monstrosity, but a peculiar, thereto unknown type of ancient humanity. Then gradually new examples of this same early type appeared in different parts of Europe, under circumstances which steadily strengthened the claim of the whole class to geological antiquity; and when eventually a thorough comparative study of the Neanderthal remains was carried out by modern methods and in view of new knowledge, the cranium and bones were definitely recognized as representing, in a normal and most characteristic way, a most interesting earlier phase or variety of mankind, our mid-quaternary predecessor or close relative *Homo neanderthalensis*. The credit for deserving work in this field is due especially to Prof. G. Schwalbe, of Strassburg, whose numerous publications on the early forms of human remains in Europe are well known to every anthropologist. . . .

The skull is gray in color, with large mud-brownish patches on the outside, and whitish gray to whitish brown on the inside. It is decidedly heavy and mineralized. It is plainly non-pathological. . . .

The facial and basal parts are lacking. The vault shows very good dimensions in length and breadth, but is strikingly low, and the bones are considerably thicker than in the white man of today, so that the brain cavity was only moderate.

Besides its lowness the vault is characterized by a very decided protrusion of the whole supra-orbital region. The supra-orbital forestructure or arch formed through this protrusion is heavier than in any other known example of the *Homo neanderthalensis*. . . .

Fig. 6. Section of the Neanderthal Cave, near Düsseldorf. (After Lyell.)

a. Cavern 60 feet about the Düssel, and 100 feet below the surface of the country at *c.*

b. Loam covering the floor of the cave, near the bottom of which the human skeleton was found.

The forehead is very low and also slopes markedly backward, nevertheless it presents a moderately well-defined convexity. . . . The thickness of the frontal bone at the eminences is 8.5 mm.; of the left parietal, along and 1 cm. above the squamous suture, 6 to 8 mm.; these measurements are about one-third greater than those of the skull of an average modern European. . . .

The internal capacity of the skull has been estimated by Schaaffhausen at 1,033 c.c., by Huxley at 1,230 c.c., and by Schwalbe at 1,234 c.c.

The brain which filled the skull was lower and narrower and slightly more pointed than the human brain of today, approaching in these features more the anthropoid form. The right frontal lobe was slightly larger and longer than the left, and the whole right hemisphere was slightly longer than that of the opposite side. In the present man it is generally the left hemisphere which is the longer, but this exception in the Neanderthal man is not necessarily of any special significance.

The long and other bones of the skeleton, so far as preserved, show many features of anthropological inferiority, demonstrating plainly that not merely the skull, but the whole body of the Neanderthal man occupied a lower evolutionary stage than that of any normal human being of the historic times. However, many of the details on these points are technical and must be reserved for another publication. The bones in general indicate a powerful musculature. They belong doubtless to a male individual. The stature of the man was about like the average of the present man in central Europe, or but slightly lower (the femora indicate, according to Manouvrier's scale, approximately 165 cm.). . . .

A careful examination and comparison of the Neanderthal skull and bones can leave only one impression on the anatomist or anthropologist of today, which is that while individually and jointly the various parts represent a human being already far advanced above any anthropoid, they are still in many respects decidedly more primitive in form—that is, on a lower scale of evolution—than the skull and bones of any man of today.

The remains are unquestionably the most precious representatives of the important phase of early humanity which we now include under the name of *Homo neanderthalensis.*

The Spy Skeletons

In June of 1886 Messrs. Marcel de Puydt, member of the Archeological Institute of Liege, and Maximin Lohest, at that time assistant of geology of the University of Liege, discovered in the terrace fronting a certain cave at Spy, in the Province of Namur, Belgium, the remains of two human skeletons associated with the débris of extinct Quaternary animals. The discovery was immediately brought to the attention of Prof. J. Fraipont, of the Liege University, and on the 16th of August, 1886, he announced the important find to the Congrès archéologique of Namur. . . .

The human bones lay in the lowest parts of the deposits, one 6, the other 8 meters in front of the entrance to the cave. They represented two individuals. One of these lay on its side, the hand touching the lower jaw; in the case of the other the original position could not be determined.

The terrace containing the Spy skeletons was situated 47.5 feet above the shallow bed of the stream running at the foot of the mountain, and the bones lay at the depth of 13 feet from the surface. The accumulations which formed the terrace included calcareous débris, various archeological traces of man's presence, and numerous remains of fossil animals. They could be separated into several strata, none of which showed any perceptible disturbance.

The layer in which the human skeletons were inclosed yielded also bones of the following fossil Quaternary mammals: *Rhinoceros tichorhinus* (abundant); *Equus caballus* (very abundant); *Cervus elaphus* (rare); *Cervus tarandus* (very rare); *Bos primigenius* (fairly abundant); *Elephas primigenius* (common); *Ursus spelæus* (rare); *Meles Taxus* (rare); *Hyæna spelæa* (abundant).

This layer further contained a sliver of an animal bone which showed a crude adaptation for use, and worked stones of inferior workmanship, referable to the Mousterian period. The layer immediately above, undoubtedly of lesser age, gave besides the bones of similar fossil animals also those of a few living species, several thousand worked flints, some of which still of the Mousterian type, many worked bones including arrow points, and also fragments of pottery.

Considering the animal and archeological remains associated with the human skeletons, together with the absence of disturbance in the superimposed more recent layers, Lohest believed himself justified to refer the Spy remains to the Mousterian period; and the deductions of Fraipont, based on the study of the skeletal remains themselves, were that they belonged to the Neanderthal man. Since then the Spy remains have received careful consideration by every student of early man and the above classification was found to need no radical revision. . . .

The bones of skeleton No. 1 are in general weaker than those of No. 2, but whether this is due to sexual difference of the two individuals, or is merely accidental, is difficult to determine. No. 2 was of a decidedly powerful musculature. The stature of the Spy man, so far as it can be determined from these remaining bones, was slightly less than that of the Neanderthal man and somewhat below the medium of white man of central Europe of the present day. . . .

The two skulls are plainly normal specimens, free from disease or deformation, and belonged to adults, approaching in No. 1 middle age, while No. 2 was younger. . . .

No. 1 is almost a replica of the Neanderthal cranium. There is a similarly prominent, though not quite as heavy, supra-orbital arch; the forehead is even a trace lower and a trace more sloping than in the Neanderthal skull, and the general shape of the vault is much the same. The vault is also very low, but the sagittal region shows a slightly more perceptible elevation than that in the Neanderthal specimen.

Skull No. 2 on the other hand, while possessing similar prominent supra-orbital arch as No. 1, has a considerably higher and more convex forehead, the whole vault is higher as well as more spacious, and the form approaches in many respects that in modern man. The brain cavity in No. 1 is anteriorly low and relatively narrower, as well as somewhat more pointed, than in recent human crania; in No. 2 these features are also more like those in the present man. On the whole it may be said that No. 2, while in some respects still very primitive, rep-

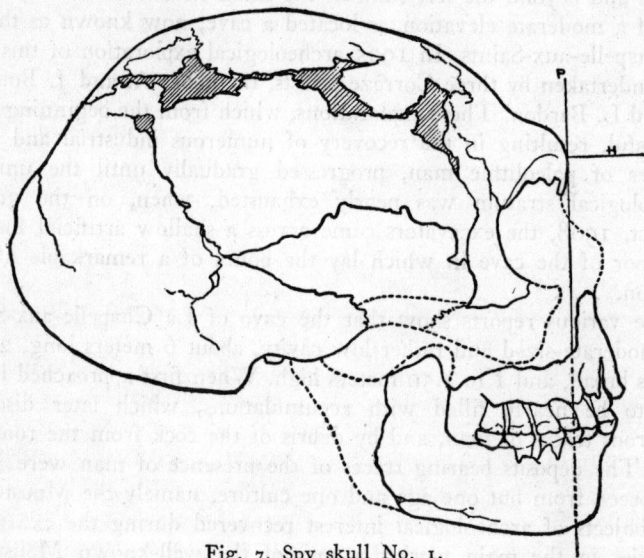

Fig. 7. Spy skull No. 1.

resents morphologically a decided step from the Neanderthaloid to the present-day type of the human cranium.

The lower jaw of No. 1, while yet of a primitive form, possesses nevertheless already a trace of the chin prominence, and in size and anatomical characteristics is closer to the present-day form than any of the other known lower jaws dating from the Mousterian period; and the same is true of the teeth which, though considerably worn, were evidently much like human teeth of today. . . .

The remaining bones of the Spy skeletons show various anatomical peculiarities and secondary primitive features, but these call for a technical description and comparisons. A rather unexpected condition, found since in other skeletons of *Homo neanderthalensis*, is the relative shortness of the forearms, as well as the legs. . . .

The Fossil Man of La Chapelle-aux-Saints

One of the most interesting, best authenticated, and thanks to Prof. Marcellin Boule, now best known skeletons of Early Man, is that of "the fossil man of La Chapelle-aux-Saints."

La Chapelle-aux-Saints is a small village in the Department of Corrèze, near the small railroad station of Vayrac and south of the town of Brive, in southern France. A little over 200 yards from the village and beyond the left bank of the small stream Sourdoire, in the side of a moderate elevation, is located a cave, now known as that of La Chapelle-aux-Saints. In 1905 archeological exploration of this cave was undertaken by three Corrèze priests, the abbés A. and J. Bouyssonie and L. Bardon. These explorations, which from the beginning were successful, resulting in the recovery of numerous industrial and other vestiges of paleolithic man, progressed gradually until the uniform archeological stratum was nearly exhausted, when, on the 3rd of August, 1908, the excavators came across a shallow artificial fossa in the floor of the cave in which lay the bones of a remarkable human skeleton. . . .

The various reports show that the cave of La Chapelle-aux-Saints is a moderate-sized and rather low cavity, about 6 meters long, 2 to 4 meters broad, and 1 to 1.50 meters high. When first approached it was seen to be nearly filled with accumulations, which later disclosed numerous traces of man, and by débris of the rock from the roof and sides. The deposits bearing traces of the presence of man were found to proceed from but one age and one culture, namely the Mousterian. The objects of archeological interest recovered during the excavation comprise in the main worked stones of the well-known Mousterian types, and remains of bones of fossil animals, such as the reindeer, bison, *Rhinoceros tichorhinus*, etc. . . .

Under the accumulations the floor of the cavern was found to be whitish, hard, marly calcareous; and in this hard base, at the distance of a little over four meters from the entrance of the cave, was located the nearly rectangular, moderate-sized cavity which lodged the fossil human skeleton. The depression was clearly made by the primitive inhabitants or visitors of the cave for the body and the whole represents very plainly a regular burial, the most ancient intentional burial thus far discovered.

The body lay on its back, with the head to the westward, the latter being surrounded by stones. The left arm was extended, the right probably bent so that the hand was applied to or lay near the head. The lower limbs were partly flexed. Above the head were found three or four large flat fragments of long bones of animals, and somewhat higher there lay, still in their natural relation, some foot bones of a large Bovid, suggesting that the whole foot of the animal may have been placed in that position. About the body were many flakes of quartz and flint, some fragments of ocher, broken animal bones, etc., much as in the rest of the archeological stratum above the skeleton. . . .

The La Chapelle skull (Fig. 8), notwithstanding its many peculiarities, is plainly a normal specimen, not affected (except in the dental arches) by any disease or by any premature closure of sutures.

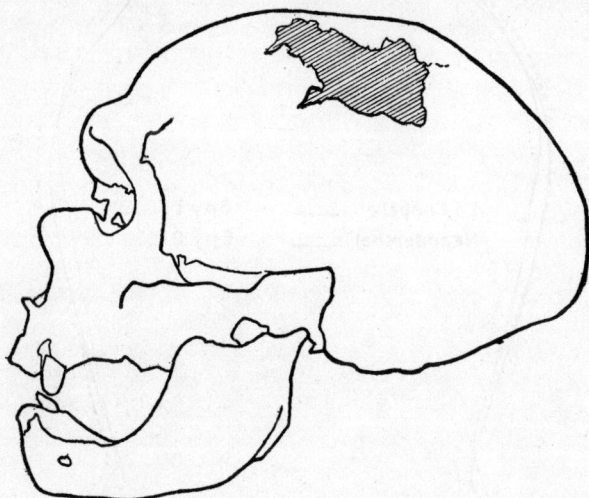

Fig. 8. La Chapelle-aux-Saints skull.

The skull is distinctly masculine, and proceeds from an adult of somewhat advanced age.

Its vault is remarkably like that of the Neanderthal cranium, though somewhat larger. There is the same huge, prominent, complete supra-orbital arch. The nasal process is equally broad and sloping considerably downward and backward. Due to the pronounced supra-orbital arch the upper half of the orbits, as in the Neanderthal skull, has a somewhat forward and downward inclination, wholly unlike that of any man of today. The forehead, while low, is somewhat better formed than in the Neanderthal and Spy No. 1 crania and less sloping. . . .

The bones of the vault, again, as in the Neanderthal and other crania of this type, are thicker than in the skulls of modern man; nevertheless the capacity of the skull was quite large. Prof. Boule estimates it at from 1,600 to 1,620 c.c. This indicates not necessarily a superior brain, but rather one subserving to largely developed organs and powerful musculature. . . .

The lower jaw is large, stout, chinless—though not sloping backward at the symphysis, and otherwise primitive. It was doubtless high,

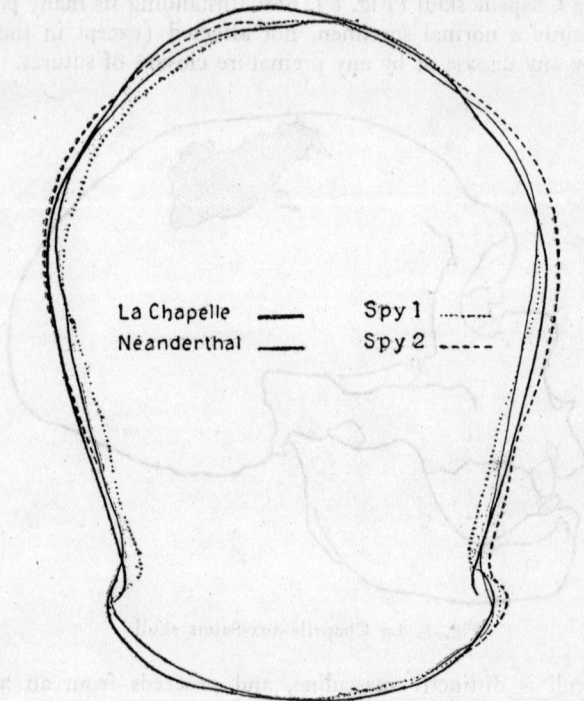

Fig. 9. Outline of four skulls of Neanderthal man, seen from above.

but the reduction of the alveolar process through pyorrhœa and absorption does not permit a definite appreciation of this character. . . .

The long and other bones of the skeleton are, on the whole, less remarkable than those of the Neanderthal or Spy remains, but the peculiarities and primitive features which they possess are of much the same order. The stature of the Chapelle-aux-Saints man is estimated by Prof. Boule to have been about 1.611 meters (5 ft. 3 in.), which is close to that of the Neanderthal man and the man of Spy. The bones are robust; the extremities of the long bones are large. The radii and ulnæ and especially the tibiæ and fibulæ, are again, as in other skeletons of the Neanderthal type, relatively short. There is also the pronounced curvature to the radius; and there are other peculiarities about the specimens an enumeration of which in this place is not feasible. Certain of these peculiarities indicate, according to Prof. Boule, that the individual from whom the Chapelle-aux-Saints skeletal remains proceed had, in common with others of the Neanderthal type, not as yet reached a fully erect posture.

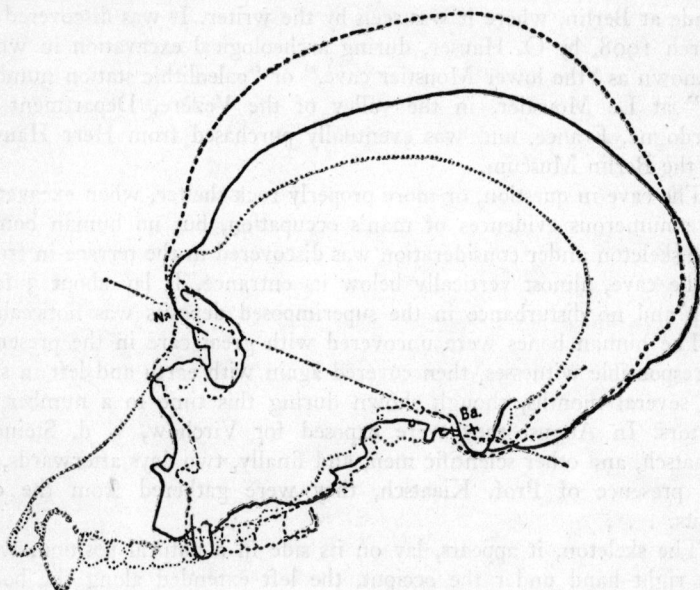

Fig. 10. Profiles of the cranium of a chimpanzee, the cranium of La Chapelle-aux-Saints, and that of a modern Frenchman superposed, and with a common basi-nasal line equal in length for each. (After Boule.)

The study of the brain of this individual, so far as possible from a cast of the cranial cavity, also shows various features of importance. Among the more strictly human characteristics are its large size, normally always a very favorable feature, though not necessarily an index of high intelligence; a predominance in size of the left over the right hemisphere; and certain other anatomical features. The more simian characteristics included especially the general form of the organ, the evident simplicity and coarseness of the convolutions, and the relatively poor development of the frontal parts, which is more pointed forward than obtains in man of today. "The brain, on the whole," to quote Prof. Boule, "is already human by the abundance of the cerebral substance;

but this substance is still lacking the advanced organization which characterizes the brain of present man." . . .

The Moustier Man

Still another highly interesting and scientifically valuable skeleton of early man, recently discovered, is that of the so-called *"Homo mousteriensis* Hauseri." The skeleton is preserved in the Museum für Völkerkunde at Berlin, where it was seen by the writer. It was discovered in March 1908, by O. Hauser, during archeological excavation in what is known as "the lower Moustier cave," or "paleolithic station number 44," at Le Moustier, in the valley of the Vezère, Department of Dordogne, France, and was eventually purchased from Herr Hauser for the Berlin Museum.

The cave in question, or more properly rock shelter, when excavated gave numerous evidences of man's occupation, but no human bones. The skeleton under consideration was discovered in the terrace in front of the cave, almost vertically below its entrance. It lay about 3 feet deep and no disturbance in the superimposed deposits was noticeable.

The human bones were uncovered with great care in the presence of responsible witnesses, then covered again with earth and left in situ for several months, though shown during this time to a number of visitors. In August they were exposed for Virchow, v. d. Steinen, Klaatsch, and other scientific men, and finally, two days afterwards, in the presence of Prof. Klaatsch, they were gathered from the deposits. . . .

The skeleton, it appears, lay on its side in a natural position, with the right hand under the occiput, the left extended along the body. About the body and among the bones were found seventy-four worked flints, ten of which were of a well-defined form. On the skull rested a charred bone of a *Bos primigenius*, and in the neighborhood of the thorax lay a tooth of the same animal. Besides this, 45 other fragments of animal bones were gathered in a close vicinity to the human remains.

The examination of the human bones was begun on the spot by Prof. Klaatsch, who eventually reached the following conclusions:

The skeleton belongs to an adolescent of perhaps 16 years of age and probably of the male sex. The height of the boy, as estimated from the long bones, was probably 1.45 to 1.50 meters (4 feet 9 inches to 4 feet 11 inches).

The skull, notwithstanding the youth of the subject, shows a number of characteristics which are peculiar to the Neanderthal group. While of a good size, with only moderately thick bones of the vault and the latter of a fair height, it shows nevertheless a rather low and sloping forehead; a well-marked complete supra-orbital arch or torus, which later in life would doubtless have become much more prominent; relatively large dental arches, with large and in a number of particulars primitive teeth; a massive lower jaw with complete absence of the chin eminence; and other interesting features. . . . .

Klaatsch reached the deduction that the skeleton belongs undoubtedly to the *Homo neanderthalensis* variety of the early European.

THE RHODESIAN MAN

On June 17, 1921, a very remarkable human skull was discovered in the Broken Hill Mine, Northern Rhodesia. It was the skull of a man whose features were in many ways so primitive that nothing quite like it has been seen before; and coming from a part of the world which hitherto has given nothing similar and in which nothing of that nature was ever suspected, it aroused much scientific attention.

Fortunately the specimen was saved with but a minor damage, and later in the same year was brought by the manager of the mine to the British Museum of Natural History where, safely preserved, it constitutes one of the scientific treasures of that Institution.

The detailed circumstances of the find were, however, not as fully and definitely established from the start as would have been desirable. The specimen was found and taken out by a miner, there was no scientific man on the spot, and the wonder is that so much was saved and done. The whole occurrence is to the lasting credit of all concerned. . . .

The "broken" kopje consisted of hard dolomitic limestone impregnated with lead, zinc salts and vanadium. It was originally full of crevices and holes, and, as shown in the course of mining, also at least two large caves leading deep into the interior. The cave of special interest became known as the bone cave. This cave in the course of time had become filled with sand, soil, bones of animals and detritus of various kinds, which in turn were impregnated by seepage carrying in solution mineral salts and lime. The salts formed incrustations on the walls, here and there new ore deposits and in general consolidated most of the contents, bones included, into a "paying ore." . . .

The skull was found at some distance beneath a layer of this ore, which was, according to Mr. Zwigelaar's [5] recollection, about 10 feet thick. It was not itself embedded in the ore but in a detrital material not mineralized to any extent, and containing a quantity of "bat" bones.

[5] The actual discoverer.—Eds.

The skull was an isolated object. It lay upright. There was no lower jaw, nor any other bone in apposition. Beneath it was something which looked like a large flattened skin bundle, thoroughly mineralized. This may or may not have been merely a natural laminar formation of the lead ore. Barring a few fragments it was smelted.

Somewhere in the vicinity of the lower portion of this "bundle" was found a remarkably straight but otherwise not peculiar, full-sized human male tibia, and lower at some distance were portions of a mineralized lion's skull. . . .

The main part of the bone cavern was for a long time a habitat or a feasting-place of the ordinary Africans, bushmen or negro. The larger bones were none of them brought in by animals, but were the remains of the repasts of the black men. A very large majority were broken for the marrow. Similarly broken human bones suggest cannibalism. There were apparently no human burials in the cave. How the strange Rhodesian skull got in is unexplainable.

The skull was found alone in the lowest and most remote part of the cave, some distance beneath considerable accumulations of soft pure lead ore. There was no lower jaw. There was no skeleton. One human bone, the tibia, and parts of a lion's skull, it is well established, lay from a few to about ten feet from and at a lower level than the skull. . . .

The skull itself is positively not the skull of any now known African type of man or their normal variants. Neither is it any known pathological monstrosity, such as gigantism or leontiasis. It is a most remarkable specimen of which the age, provenience, history, and nature are still anthropological puzzles.

Morphologically the skull is frequently associated now with the Neanderthal type of Europe. This may be fundamentally correct, but only to that extent. In its detailed characteristics the specimen in some respects is inferior, in others superior to anything known as yet of the Neanderthal man. . . .

Professor Elliot Smith shows the volume of the brain of the Rhodesian skull to have been but 1,280 c.c., which is markedly smaller than in any of the Neanderthalers with the probable exception of the Gibraltar female.

The very successful cast shows the brain to have been in general very definitely human, related to that of the Neanderthalers, and superior to both that of the Pithecanthropus and Eoanthropus (? skull too defective). . . .

The skull is monstrous; its frontal and most of the facial parts exceed in primitiveness every other known specimen of early man. The skullcap, on the other hand, from behind the frontal ridges is of a decidedly higher grade, equaling in many respects and in some even exceeding those of the more typical Neanderthal crania.

The subject was plainly a very powerful male, probably over forty years of age. The skull is in no way pathological, though showing some diseased conditions; and it cannot be diagnosed as a reversion. It represents a distinct crude variety of man, which strangely combines many ancient, even pre-Neanderthal conditions with others that are relatively modern. It could represent, conceivably, a very brutish individual development of the upper Neanderthal or the post-Neanderthal period. . . .

The study of the specimen leaves an impression of anamorphism. It is a combination of pre-Neanderthaloid, Neanderthaloid, and recent characters. It is not a Neanderthaler; it represents a different race, a different variety. The specimen does not fit with its surroundings. It does not fit at all with the fine, long, essentially modern-negro-like tibia. It does not fit with any of the other human remains saved from the cave, skeletal or cultural. It does not fit with anything, the negro in particular, found thus far in Africa. . . .

Measurements, in centimeters: [6] Skull vault, length 20.6, breadth 14.5-14.6, height (at bregma) 13.0, cranial index 71.8. Face, height 9.3, breadth 14.8, index 63.0. Facial angle 63°. Nose, height 5.8, breadth 3.1, index 53.4. Palate, length 7.0, breadth 8.0, index 87.5.

7. THE ASYMMETRICAL CHARACTER OF HUMAN EVOLUTION [7]

BY E. A. HOOTON

. . . THE object of this paper is to attempt a demonstration of the essentially asymmetrical character of human evolution. It will be shown that all fossil types of man heretofore discovered manifest certain morphological inequalities in the development of various cranial parts, identical in kind, and differing in degree only, from those displayed by the Piltdown specimen. Further it will be demonstrated that similar disharmonic, contradictory, or asymmetrical features are by no means uncommon in modern human races, but are in fact characteristically present. For present purposes the demonstration of such asymmetries

[6] Extracted from a longer table.
[7] From an article of the same name in *American Journal of Physical Anthropology*, volume 8, pages 125-141, 1925.

TABLE II

Character	Gorilla ♂	Gorilla ♀	Orang ♂	Orang ♀	Chimpanzee	Pithecanthropus	Piltdown	Heidelberg	Neanderthal	Broken Hill	Combe Capelle	Talgai	Australian	Eskimo	Negro	Guanche	Alpine	Mongol	Mediterranean	Nordic
Frontal Region																				
1. Brow ridges	1	2	5	5	2	2	5	?	2	1	4	4	4	6	5	5	5	6	6	5
2. Elevation	2	2	4	4	2	3	5	?	3	2	5	4	4	5	5	5	6	5	5	5
3. Slope	1	2	4	4	2	3	5	?	3	2	5	4	4	5	5	5	6	5	5	5
4. Postorbital constriction	1	2	1	2	2	2	5	?	3	3	4	4	4	5	5	5	5	5	5	5
5. Breadth	1	2	2	2	2	3	5	?	3	3	5	4	4	5	4	5	6	5	5	5
Sagittal Region																				
6. Breadth	2	2	2	2	2	4	5	?	5	4	4	4	4	4	4	5	6	6	5	5
7. Crest, elevation	1	2	1	3	3	4	4	?	5	3	4	4	4	4	5	5	6	5	6	6
Temporal Region																				
8. Zygomata	1	2	2	3	3	?	?	?	5	3	4	4	4	3	5	5	5	5	5	5
9. Fossæ	1	2	2	2	2	?	4	?	5	3	4	4	4	4	4	4	5	4	5	5
10. Supramastoid crest or ridge	1	2	2	2	2	2	4	?	5	4	4	4	4	4	5	5	6	5	6	6
11. Fullness	2	2	2	2	2	2	4	?	5	4	4	4	4	4	4	5	6	5	6	5
Occipital Region																				
12. Shape	1	2	2	2	2	2	4	?	3	3	5	4	4	4	4	5	6	6	5	5
13. Crest or torus	1	1	1	2	2	?	4	?	4	4	4	4	4	5	5	5	5	4	5	6
14. Slope of Foramen	1	1	1	2	2	2	2	?	2	4	5	4	4	4	4	4	5	4	5	5
Skull base																				
15. Mastoids, size	2	2	2	1	2	?	4	?	3	3	5	4	4	3	4	5	6	5	5	6
16. Glenoid fossa	2	2	1	1	1	?	5	?	3	3	5	?	3	5	5	6	6	3	6	6
17. Postglenoid spine	2	2	2	2	2	2	4	?	4	3	3	?	4	5	4	4	5	6	4	5
18. Petrous parts	2	2	1	1	1	?	?	?	?	2	5	?	2	5	4	5	6	5	6	6

	G	G	O	O	C	P	P	H	N	B	C	T	A	E	N	G	A	M	M	N
Facial Region																				
19. Malars, size	5	2	1	2	5	?	?	?	5	4	4	4	2	4	4	4	4	4	5	5
20. Orbits, proportions, shape	2	2	2	2	3	?	?	?	3	3	5	4	3	6	5	6	5	5	4	4
21. Inclination	2	2	2	2	2	?	?	?	4	5	6	6	4	4	3	3	4	4	4	5
22. Suborbital fossæ	2	2	2	2	2	?	?	?	2	2	4	6	4	5	5	5	5	4	6	6
23. Nasal bones, form	1	1	1	2	2	5	?	?	5	5	5	4	5	4	5	4	4	4	2	2
24. Angle or arch	3	3	2	2	2	4	?	?	4	3	2	4	3	4	6	4	5	4	5	6
25. Nasal profile	3	3	2	1	2	4	?	?	4	4	4	4	4	4	4	5	5	4	6	6
26. Nasal bones, size	3	2	2	2	2	4	?	?	5	4	5	5	2	2	6	5	4	5	2	2
27. Lower borders of nasal aperture	2	2	2	1	1	2	?	?	4	3	2	2	4	4	4	6	4	5	6	6
28. Nasal spine	2	1	2	1	2	?	?	?	4	4	5	2	4	4	4	4	5	3	6	6
29. Nasion depression	2	2	2	2	2	?	?	?	4	3	6	6	3	5	5	5	6	3	5	5
Prognathism																				
30. Facial	1	2	2	1	2	?	?	3	3	3	4	3	4	5	5	5	5	5	5	5
31. Alveolar	2	2	1	1	2	?	?	3	4	5	4	3	4	5	5	6	5	5	5	6
Palate																				
32. Proportions	2	2	1	1	2	3	3	3	4	5	4	3	3	4	4	6	6	5	6	6
33. Shape	1	1	1	1	1	4	4	4	5	6	5	3	4	5	5	6	6	5	5	5
Mandible																				
34. Size	1	2	1	2	2	2	2	2	3	?	4	4	4	4	5	6	5	5	5	5
35. Chin	2	2	2	2	2	2	2	3	5	3	4	5	4	4	5	6	6	5	6	6
36. Genial tubercles	2	2	2	2	2	2	3	4	4	6	6	4	5	6	6	6	6	6	6	6
37. Mylo-hyoid ridge	2	2	2	3	3	2	3	3	4	3	5	5	5	5	5	5	4	5	5	5
38. Breadth of ascending ramus	1	1	2	1	2	2	3	3	3	3	4	4	4	4	4	4	5	4	5	5
Teeth																				
39. Canines, projection, diastema	2	1	2	2	2	4	4	4	4	4	2	4	4	5	5	4	4	4	4	4
40. Molars, proportions of crowns	1	2	2	2	2	4	2	4	4	4	4	4	4	5	5	5	5	6	6	6
41. Relative size of m1 and m2	2	2	2	2	2	4	2	3	2	3	4	4	4	4	4	4	4	4	4	4

is confined to morphological cranial features, because measurements and indices provide in themselves no satisfactory criteria of evolutionary development, and are, in any event, impracticable, because of the imperfect and fragmentary state of most fossil remains. With respect to asymmetries of skeletal parts other than the crania, a few remarks only will have to suffice.

The method of this investigation is as follows: The most important cranial morphological features have been graded under six heads, according to presence or absence, degree of development, and form. Thus we have six morphological grades: (1) Excessively anthropoid, (2) Typically anthropoid, (3) Supra-anthropoid, (4) Sub-human, (5) Typically human, (6) Ultra-human. In some instances a character does not present six observable grades of development and in such cases the arrangement of the successively higher gradations is not necessarily consecutive.

A numerical value ranging from 1 to 6 is given to each character in every specimen studied in accordance with the number of the morphological grade to which it is assigned. The anthropoid apes, the more important types of fossil man, and certain modern races have been assigned rank with respect to each of 41 cranial characters, or as many of such characters as are available for examination. The mean ranking of each race or individual specimen is then calculated from the sum total. The asymmetries of cranial morphological features are appraised by contrasting the mean rating of each specimen with respect to (a) brain-case, (b) face and jaws, (c) total cranial rating, and by calculating the standard deviations for each specimen or race in terms of morphological grades.

Table II shows the individual ratings of the several types and races for each of the cranial characters considered.

Table III permits us to contrast the rating of brain-case and face in each type and to judge of its variability by means of the standard deviation. The gorillas, male and female, show higher ratings for face than for brain-case because of certain humanoid nasal features and because of the frontal deficiency and supraorbital torus. On account of precisely opposite tendencies in these same regions the orang-utans show higher ratings for the brain-case than for the face. The standard deviation for orang-utans is high, because of the man-like frontal region which is the markedly asymmetric feature of these apes.

Pithecanthropus erectus is rated on the brain-case only, for obvious reasons. Similarly the Heidelberg specimen is rated only on the face. The brain-case rating for Pithecanthropus is 2.64 and the facial rating for Heidelberg is 2.70. The standard deviations 0.77 and 0.83

respectively are also nearly the same. The Broken Hill skull has a low sub-human rating for the brain-case (3.05), and a considerably higher rating for the face (3.86). The standard deviation (1.00) is very high on account of the association of a gorilloid frontal region and supra-orbital torus with an essentially human palate-form, teeth, etc.

TABLE III. MEAN RATINGS OF CRANIA [8]

	Brain Case	Face	Total	Standard Deviation
Gorilla, male	1.33	1.65	1.51	0.59
Orang-utan, male	1.77	1.52	1.68	0.90
Gorilla, female	1.89	2.00	1.95	0.66
Orang-utan, female	2.27	1.74	1.98	0.81
Chimpanzee, male	2.00	2.13	2.07	0.64
Pithecanthropus	2.64	...	2.64	0.77
Heidelberg	...	2.70	2.70	0.83
Broken Hill	3.05	3.86	3.46	1.00
Piltdown	4.31	2.30	3.63	1.17
Neanderthal	3.47	3.74	3.63	0.89
Talgai	4.00	3.65	3.81	0.88
Eskimo	4.16	3.91	4.00	0.96
Australian	3.83	4.30	4.10	0.65
Combe Capelle	4.39	4.13	4.24	0.88
Negro	4.50	4.22	4.34	0.65
Mongol	4.94	4.43	4.71	0.67
Guanche	4.89	4.78	4.83	0.69
Mediterranean	5.22	5.00	5.10	0.93
Nordic	5.33	5.09	5.20	0.96
Alpine	5.61	4.96	5.24	0.69

The maximum variability is encountered in the Piltdown specimen with a standard deviation of 1.17 grades. This is in consequence of the inferior human rating of the brain-case (4.31) and the anthropoid rating of the mandible and teeth (2.30). The disharmony of this association is clearly evident and is 17 per cent in excess of that of any other type. The total mean rating of the Piltdown skull is 3.63, which is, curiously enough, exactly equal to the total mean rating for Neanderthal man, a type which shows a much more symmetrical distribution of characters and a far lower standard deviation (0.89).

The Eskimo shows a remarkable blend of anthropoid and human features in consequence of his extraordinary masticatory development. The nasal skeleton and aperture is often excessively simian and a total absence of suborbital fossæ is not uncommon. The mean rating of the

[8] Broken Hill, Rhodesian man; Talgai, ancient Australian; Combe Capelle, a Cro-Magnon form; Guanche, Canary Islander.—*Eds.*

Eskimo is 4.00, just a little lower than that of the Australian. In this case only I feel that our 41 morphological cranial features fail to provide a satisfactory mean rating for the type. If one were to take into consideration the cranial capacity of the Eskimo, which is very large, the essential disharmony of the type would be greatly increased, but the mean rating would surpass considerably those of the Australian and of the Negro.

The Negro and the Australian both grade as inferior human types and in each case the variability is the same (0.65). The Negro shows a markedly higher average grade (4.34 as against 4.10). In these two types the standard deviation is at its minimum for man, according to our measure. The position of the Combe-Capelle fossil between the Negro and the Australian is of considerable interest. The variability of this Aurignacian specimen is, however, considerably higher (0.88).

The Mongol and the Guanche are hardly more variable than the Negro, but each surpass the latter both in ratings for brain-case and for face. The remarkably high variabilities of the Mediterranean and Nordic types are due to the anthropoid proportions of the nasal bones more than to any other features. The mean ratings of both types are, however, very high.

The Alpine type shows a slightly higher mean rating than the Nordic, because of more advanced features of the brain-case. Its standard deviation is very low (0.69).

The ranking of the several specimens and types with respect to standard deviations in terms of morphological grades is as follows: Piltdown 1.17, Broken Hill 1.00, Nordic and Eskimo 0.96, Mediterranean 0.93, Orang-utan male 0.90, Neanderthal 0.89, Talgai and Combe-Capelle 0.88, Orang-utan female 0.81, Pithecanthropus erectus 0.77, Alpine and Guanche 0.69, Mongol 0.67, Gorilla female 0.66, Negro and Australian 0.65, Chimpanzee male 0.64, Gorilla male 0.59. If these standard deviations are in any sense valid as criteria of variability, it becomes clear that the morphological stability of a type is no measure of its evolutionary position. . . .

It seems to me that the evidence of asymmetrical evolution in both fossil and modern types of man and in the anthropoid apes, can be interpreted satisfactorily in but one way. We must abandon monogenism. I do not mean by this that we must revert to the idea of independent creation of several distinct types of man, but only that our proto-human ancestors must have shown tendencies toward variation along separate lines of development before the essentially human status was attained. For my own purposes, and perhaps arbitrarily, I consider man to have become man at the time when his giant Primate ancestor definitely took to the ground and assumed an upright posture and biped form of progression. The processes of bodily adaptation whereby the essentially human posture and gait were ultimately acquired must have varied considerably among individual anthropoids and may not always have resulted in identical end products. The gorilla certainly represents an unsatisfactory compromise between arboreal and terrestrial adaptation, an imperfect development toward the erect posture and the biped form of progression. I can see no reason why the gorilla has not attained a perfectly human status in these respects except the inherent incapacity of the gorilloid stock to proceed beyond a certain point, an incapacity probably conditioned by ineradicable tendencies toward variation and specialization in other directions.

We know that not every Primate that has adopted a terrestrial habitat has become man. The ancestors of the baboon assumed a pronograde posture and have converged upon the quadrupeds. Why did they not stand upon their hind legs and become man? I cannot conceive of any environmental factor which could have determined this unfortunate choice. If the gorilla and the baboon have taken to the ground and have adapted themselves in diverse ways with respect to posture and mode of progression, is there any reason for supposing that these and a single ancestor of man have been the only large Primates to descend to the ground and that there have been only these three types of Primate terrestrial adaptation? Nature does not put all of her eggs in one basket and one must conclude that there have been several differentiations of anthropoids in a humanoid direction, resulting not only in varied postures and diverse methods of attaining the erect posture, but also in varied and asymmetrical development of other bodily parts not directly concerned with posture and gait. One such humanoid development may have attained an almost completely erect posture without any consequent reduction of the jaws or any vast increase in the size of the brain. Pithecanthropus erectus may well represent an anthropoid differentiation in which essentially human position and progression were realized, but in which the impulse of the organism toward hypertrophy of the brain and masticatory reduction were lacking. Natural selection would account for the extinction of this and other relatively unsuccessful experiments. On the other hand a type in which the brain grew to essentially human proportions, but in which the face and jaws remained essentially anthropoid might survive for a longer period of time before succumbing in the struggle for existence, or might even undergo a subsequent modification of the jaws, thus realizing the human status in this respect also. When one studies growth in individual children month by month he notes an alternation and asymmetry in the growth of various parts of the body. One month, for instance, stature increases disproportionately, and weight remains almost stationary. One month the head broadens; another month it lengthens. Growth energy seems to be directed toward different parts of the body in succession or alternation. Nor is there any reason for believing that these growth sequences are invariably the same for all individuals or that the ultimate development of the several organs is identical.

Similarly one may conceive that the process of human evolution must have varied considerably in the individuals and groups which ultimately attained an erect or nearly erect posture, and such asymmetry would presumably be most pronounced in those parts of the body in which adaptation to the new posture was least necessary. The modification of the foot from a mainly prehensile to a primarily supporting organ was a fundamental requisite for the radical change in its function. This modification has been realized almost completely in every modern race and every fossil type available for study. On the other hand, most of the bodily characters which we regard as criteria of race are not fundamentally concerned in the modifications necessitated by the assumption of the erect posture. It seems to me that many, and even most of them, must be classified as non-adaptive variations. I am not acquainted with any peculiar use of the jaws or teeth in Negroes or Australians which can be considered the functional basis of their prognathism. It appears to be an ancestral feature which has been retained simply through the inertia of heredity. Nor is it apparent that a moderate alveolar projection is a less favorable variation than a condition of hyper-orthognathism. I cannot see how the possession of a brachycephalic head-form, on the one hand, or a dolichocephalic, on the other, can be of any advantage or disadvantage in the struggle for existence. It is not demonstrable that curly hair as contrasted with straight hair, or short hair as contrasted with long hair, are anything else than indifferent variations. And even if one admits that a certain accumulation of pigmentation in the lower strata of the epidermis may be useful in cutting off the actinic rays of the sun, it can hardly be argued that an amount of melanin sufficient to impart a yellow-brown color to the skin is less efficient for that purpose than the excessive pigmentation which renders the skin black. Anthropologists have made ingenious efforts to show that the elevation of the nasal bridge and the narrowing of the nasal aperture in certain races is an adaptation for the breathing of cold air, roughly analogous to our American habit of placing radiators behind a window and opening the sashes slightly so that fresh air may enter the room after being warmed by passing over and through the radiating surface. I am much more inclined to regard the long and narrow nose as a retention of the anthropoid condition, nor is it apparent that the elevation of the nasal bridge can be ascribed to any such adaptation, in the absence of such elevation among the Eskimo. The nasal cartilages, which by their size and shape impart to the tip of the nose characteristic forms which are racially distinct seem to vary independently and in a non-adaptative manner. Equally non-adaptative are thickness or thinness of lips, relatively long or relatively short fore-arms, shovel-shaped or plane-backed incisors, the presence or absence of epicanthic folds, sacral pigmented spots, pharyngeal fossæ, and other features often or occasionally recognized as racially variable. It seems very probable that the extremes of racial variability in these features are mainly explicable by the indifferent or unimportant character of such variations, which consequently are determined by the inherent tendencies of the several human stocks, independent of adaptations due to environment. Nature evidently likes to proceed to extremes in non-essentials. And, indeed, certain of the changes in bodily form which have been ascribed with some probability to environmental causes, appear to be of a totally non-adaptive character, e.g. change in the head-form of children born in America of immigrant parentage.

All this tedious discussion grows from my conviction that most racial differences and most evolutionary asymmetries are to be ascribed to the fact that several distinct stocks whose common ancestry must be sought in a proto-human or very inferior human stage of development have developed along lines roughly parallel, but with many unimportant divergences. Not all of these stocks attained to precisely the same status of evolutionary development as measured by the degree of their departure from characteristically anthropoid forms. Some of these became extinct without having realized essentially human levels of development; others have survived at varying stages of morphological evolution, the asymmetry of their development being manifested far more in the mosaic of primitive and highly evolved characters within the same type than by the average development of the sum total of their bodily characters.

Let me not be understood to think that in the Tertiary epoch the tropical forests rained anthropoids, many of which evolved into men, resulting in the dozen or more present human groups which we crudely classify as races. Most of these extant races of man are due to mixtures of the ingredients of two or three primary types. Such miscegenation may well have occurred whenever propinquity permitted, even in proto-human times. Although the present anthropoid apes are not positively known to have produced interspecific hybrids, the existence of hybrids between the gorilla and the chimpanzee has been reported several times and is not wholly incredible. Moreover there seems to be no good reason for doubting that the ancestors of man have displayed throughout the process of becoming human, superior adaptability, greater initiative, and less conservatism in their mating habits as well as in other directions, when compared with the existing anthropoid apes or the progenitors of the latter. An occasional hybridization, followed by a process of inbreeding, would satisfactorily account for the varying characteristics of modern races, if the existence of two or three fundamental humanoid stocks is admitted. . . .

Heredity and Race

8. HEREDITARY GENIUS [1]

BY FRANCIS GALTON

I PROPOSE to show in this book that a man's natural abilities are derived by inheritance, under exactly the same limitations as are the form and physical features of the whole organic world. Consequently, as it is easy, notwithstanding those limitations, to obtain by careful selection a permanent breed of dogs or horses gifted with peculiar powers of running, or of doing anything else, so it would be quite practicable to produce a highly-gifted race of men by judicious marriages during several consecutive generations. I shall show that social agencies of an ordinary character, whose influences are little suspected, are at this moment working towards the degradation of human nature, and that others are working towards its improvement. I conclude that each generation has enormous power over the natural gifts of those that follow, and maintain that it is a duty we owe to humanity to investigate the range of that power, and to exercise it in a way that, without being unwise towards ourselves, shall be most advantageous to future inhabitants of the earth. . . .

The general plan of my argument is to show that high reputation is a pretty accurate test of high ability; next to discuss the relationships of a large body of fairly eminent men—namely, the Judges of England from 1660 to 1868, the Statesmen of the time of George III, and the Premiers during the last one hundred years—and to obtain from these a general survey of the laws of heredity in respect to genius. Then I shall examine, in order, the kindred of the most illustrious Commanders, men of Literature and of Science, Poets, Painters, and Musicians, of whom history speaks. I shall also discuss the kindred of a certain selection of Divines and of modern Scholars. Then will follow a short chapter, by way of comparison, on the hereditary transmission of physical gifts, as deduced from the relationships of certain classes of

[1] From Francis Galton, *Hereditary Genius: An Inquiry into Its Laws and Consequences*, 1883. (Pages 1-36, 55-64, 316-324, 336-342 have been drawn upon.) Originally published in 1869.

Oarsmen and Wrestlers. Lastly, I shall collate my results, and draw conclusions. . . .

CLASSIFICATION OF MEN ACCORDING TO THEIR REPUTATION

The arguments by which I endeavor to prove that genius is hereditary, consist in showing how large is the number of instances in which men who are more or less illustrious have eminent kinsfolk. . . .

I look upon social and professional life as a continuous examination. All are candidates for the good opinions of others, and for success in their several professions, and they achieve success in proportion as the general estimate is large of their aggregate merits. In ordinary scholastic examinations marks are allotted in stated proportions to various specified subjects—so many for Latin, so many for Greek, so many for English history, and the rest. The world, in the same way, but almost unconsciously, allots marks to men. It gives them for originality of conception, for enterprise, for activity and energy, for administrative skill, for various acquirements, for power of literary expression, for oratory, and much besides of general value, as well as for more specially professional merits. It does not allot these marks according to a proportion that can easily be stated in words, but there is a rough common-sense that governs its practice with a fair approximation to constancy. Those who have gained most of these tacit marks are ranked, by the common judgment of the leaders of opinion, as the foremost men of their day.

The metaphor of an examination may be stretched much further. As there are alternative groups in any one of which a candidate may obtain honors, so it is with reputations—they may be made in law, literature, science, art, and in a host of other pursuits. Again: as the mere attainment of a general fair level will obtain no honors in an examination, no more will it do so in the struggle for eminence. A man must show conspicuous power in at least one subject in order to achieve a high reputation.

Let us see how the world classifies people, after examining each of them, in her patient, persistent manner, during the years of their manhood. How many men of "eminence" are there, and what proportion do they bear to the whole community?

I will begin by analyzing a very painstaking biographical handbook, lately published by Routledge and Co., called "Men of the Time." Its intention, which is very fairly and honestly carried out, is to include none but those whom the world honors for their ability. The catalogue of names is 2,500, and a full half of it consists of American and Continental celebrities. . . .

On looking over the book, I am surprised to find how large a proportion of the "Men of the Time" are past middle age. It appears that in the cases of high (but by no means in that of the highest) merit, a man must outlive the age of fifty to be sure of being widely appreciated. It takes time for an able man, born in the humbler ranks of life, to emerge from them and to take his natural position. It would not, therefore, be just to compare the numbers of Englishmen in the book with that of the whole adult male population of the British isles; but it is necessary to confine our examination to those of the celebrities who are past fifty years of age, and to compare their number with that of the whole male population who are also above fifty years. I estimate, from examining a large part of the book, that there are about 850 of these men, and that 500 of them are decidedly well known to persons familiar with literary and scientific society. Now, there are about two millions of adult males in the British isles above fifty years of age; consequently, the total number of the "Men of the Time" are as 425 to a million, and the more select part of them as 250 to a million. . . .

Another estimate of the proportion of eminent men to the whole population was made on a different basis, and gave much the same result. I took the obituary of the year 1868, published in the *Times* on January 1st, 1869, and found in it about fifty names of men of the more select class. This was in one sense a broader, and in another a more rigorous selection than that which I have just described. It was broader, because I included the names of many whose abilities were high, but who died too young to have earned the wide reputation they deserved; and it was more rigorous, because I excluded old men who had earned distinction in years gone by, but had not shown themselves capable in later times to come again to the front. On the first ground, it was necessary to lower the limit of the age of the population with whom they should be compared. Forty-five years of age seemed to me a fair limit, including, as it was supposed to do, a year or two of broken health preceding decease. Now, 210,000 males die annually in the British isles above the age of forty-five; therefore, the ratio of the more select portion of the "Men of the Time" on these data is as 50 to 210,000, or as 238 to a million.

Thirdly, I consulted obituaries of many years back, when the population of these islands was much smaller, and they appeared to me to lead to similar conclusions, viz., that 250 to a million is an ample estimate. . . .

These considerations define the sense in which I propose to employ the word "eminent." When I speak of an eminent man, I mean one who has achieved a position that is attained by only 250 persons in each million of men, or by one person in each 4,000. Four thousand is a very large number—difficult for persons to realize who are not accustomed to deal with great assemblages. On the most brilliant of starlight nights there are never so many as 4,000 stars visible to the naked eye at the same time; yet we feel it to be an extraordinary distinction to a star to be accounted as the brightest in the sky. This, be it remembered, is my narrowest area of selection. I propose to introduce no name whatever into my lists of kinsmen (unless it be marked off from the rest by brackets) that is less distinguished. . . .

CLASSIFICATION OF MEN ACCORDING TO THEIR NATURAL GIFTS

I have no patience with the hypothesis occasionally expressed, and often implied, especially in tales written to teach children to be good, that babies are born pretty much alike, and that the sole agencies in creating differences between boy and boy, and man and man, are steady application and moral effort. It is in the most unqualified manner that I object to pretensions of natural equality. The experiences of the nursery, the school, the University, and of professional careers, are a chain of proofs to the contrary. I acknowledge freely the great power of education and social influences in developing the active powers of the mind, just as I acknowledge the effect of use in developing the muscles of a blacksmith's arm, and no further. Let the blacksmith labor as he will, he will find that there are certain feats beyond his power that are well within the strength of a man of herculean make, even although the latter may have led a sedentary life. Some years ago, the Highlanders held a grand gathering in Holland Park, where they challenged all England to compete with them in their games of strength. The challenge was accepted, and the well-trained men of the hills were beaten in the footrace by a youth who was stated to be a pure Cockney, the clerk of a London banker.

Everybody who has trained himself to physical exercises discovers the extent of his muscular powers to a nicety. When he begins to walk, to row, to use the dumb bells, or to run, he finds to his great delight that his thews strengthen, and his endurance of fatigue increases day after day. So long as he is a novice, he perhaps flatters himself there is hardly an assignable limit to the education of his muscles; but the daily gain is soon discovered to diminish, and at last it vanishes altogether. His maximum performance becomes a rigidly determinate quantity. He learns to an inch, how high or how far he can jump, when he has attained the highest state of training. He learns to half a pound, the force he can exert on the dynamometer, by compressing it. He can strike a blow against the machine used to measure impact, and drive its index to a certain graduation, but no further. So it is in running, in rowing, in walking, and in every other form of physical exertion. There is a definite limit to the muscular powers of every man, which he cannot by any education or exertion overpass.

This is precisely analogous to the experience that every student has had of the working of his mental powers. The eager boy, when he first goes to school and confronts intellectual difficulties, is astonished at his progress. He glories in his newly-developed mental grip and growing capacity for application, and, it may be, fondly believes it to be within his reach to become one of the heroes who have left their mark upon the history of the world. The years go by; he competes in the examinations of school and college, over and over again with his fellows, and soon finds his place among them. He knows he can beat such and such of his competitors; that there are some with whom he runs on equal terms, and others whose intellectual feats he cannot even approach. Probably his vanity still continues to tempt him, by whispering in a new strain. It tells him that classics, mathematics, and other subjects taught in universities, are mere scholastic specialties, and no test of the more valuable intellectual powers. It reminds him of numerous instances of persons who had been unsuccessful in the competitions of youth, but who had shown powers in after-life that made them the foremost men of their age. Accordingly, with newly furbished hopes, and with all the ambition of twenty-two years of age, he leaves his University and enters a larger field of competition. The same kind of experience awaits him here that he has already gone through. Opportunities occur—they occur to every man—and he finds himself incapable of grasping them. He tries, and is tried in many things. In a few years more, unless he is incurably blinded by self-conceit, he learns precisely of what performances he is capable, and what other enterprises lie beyond his compass. When he reaches mature life, he is confident only within certain limits, and knows, or ought to know, himself just as he is probably judged of by the world, with all his unmistakable weakness and all his undeniable strength. He is no longer tormented into hopeless efforts by the fallacious promptings of overweening vanity, but he limits his undertakings to matters below the level of his reach, and finds true moral repose in an honest conviction that he is engaged in as much good work as his nature has rendered him capable of performing. . . .

To conclude, the range of mental power between—I will not say the highest Caucasian and the lowest savage—but between the greatest and least of English intellects, is enormous. There is a continuity of natural ability reaching from one knows not what height, and descending to one can hardly say what depth. I propose in this chapter to range men according to their natural abilities, putting them into classes separated by equal degrees of merit, and to show the relative number of individuals included in the several classes. Perhaps some persons might be inclined to make an offhand guess that the number of men included in the several classes would be pretty equal. If he thinks so, I can assure him he is most egregiously mistaken.

The method I shall employ for discovering all this, is an application of the very curious theoretical law of "deviation from an average." First, I will explain the law, and then I will show that the production of natural intellectual gifts comes justly within its scope.

The law is an exceedingly general one. M. Quetelet, the Astronomer-Royal of Belgium, and the greatest authority on vital and social statistics, has largely used it in his inquiries. He has also constructed numerical tables, by which the necessary calculations can be easily made, whenever it is desired to have recourse to the law. . . .

So much has been published in recent years about statistical deductions, that I am sure the reader will be prepared to assent freely to the following hypothetical case: Suppose a large island inhabited by a single race who intermarried freely, and who had lived for many generations under constant conditions; then the average *height* of the male adults of that population would undoubtedly be the same year after year. Also—still arguing from the experience of modern statistics, which are found to give constant results in far less carefully-guarded examples—we should undoubtedly find, year after year, the same proportion maintained between the number of men of different heights. I mean, if the average stature was found to be sixty-six inches, and if it was also found in any one year that 100 per million exceeded seventy-eight inches, the same proportion of 100 per million would be closely maintained in all other years. An equal constancy of proportion would be maintained between any other limits of height we pleased to specify, as between seventy-one and seventy-two inches; between seventy-two and seventy-three inches; and so on. Statistical experiences are so invariably confirmatory of what I have stated would probably be the case, as to make it unnecessary to describe analogous instances. Now, at this point, the law of deviation from an average steps in. It shows that the number per million whose heights range between seventy-one and seventy-two inches (or between any other limits we please to name) can be *predicted* from the previous datum of the average, and of any one other fact, such as that of 100 per million exceeding seventy-eight inches.

The diagram will make this more intelligible. Suppose a million of the men to stand in turns, with their backs against a vertical board of sufficient height, and their heights to be dotted off upon it. The board would then present the appearance shown in the diagram. The line of average height is that which divides the dots into two equal parts, and stands, in the case we have assumed, at the height of sixty-six inches. The dots will be found to be ranged so symmetrically on either side of the line of average, that the lower half of the diagram will be almost a precise reflection of the upper. Next, let a hundred dots be counted from above downwards, and let a line be drawn below them. According to the conditions, this line will stand at the height of seventy-eight inches. Using the data afforded by these two lines, it is possible, by the help of the law of deviation from an average, to reproduce, with extraordinary closeness, the entire system of dots on the board.

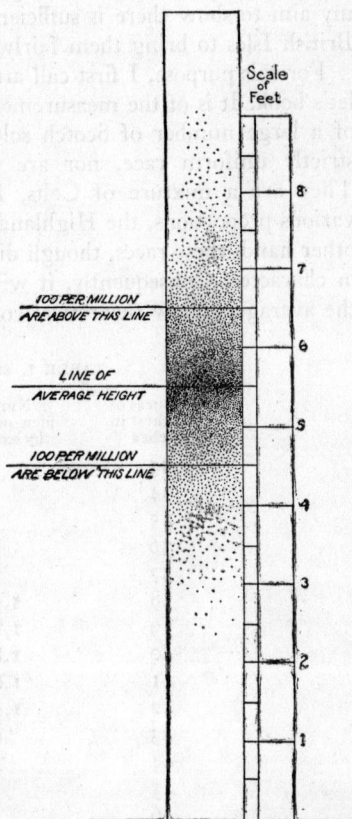

M. Quetelet gives tables in which the uppermost line, instead of cutting off 100 in a million, cuts off only one in a million. He divides the intervals between that line and the line of average, into eighty equal divisions, and gives the number of dots that fall within each of those divisions. It is easy, by the help of his tables, to calculate what would occur under any other system of classification we pleased to adopt.

This law of deviation from an average is perfectly general in its application. Thus, if the marks had been made by bullets fired at a horizontal line stretched in front of the target, they would have been distributed according to the same law. Wherever there is a large number of similar events, each due to the resultant influences of the same variable conditions, two effects will follow. First, the average value of those events will be constant; and, secondly, the deviations of the several events from the average, will be governed by this law (which is, in principle, the same as that which governs runs of luck at a gaming-table). . . .

I selected the hypothetical case of a race of men living on an island and freely intermarrying, to insure the conditions under which they were all supposed to live, being uniform in character. It will now be my aim to show there is sufficient uniformity in the inhabitants of the British Isles to bring them fairly within the grasp of this law.

For this purpose, I first call attention to an example given in Quetelet's book. It is of the measurements of the circumferences of the chests of a large number of Scotch soldiers. The Scotch are by no means a strictly uniform race, nor are they exposed to identical conditions. They are a mixture of Celts, Danes, Anglo-Saxons, and others, in various proportions, the Highlanders being almost purely Celts. On the other hand, these races, though diverse in origin, are not very dissimilar in character. Consequently, it will be found that their deviations from the average, follow theoretical computations with remarkable accuracy.

TABLE I. SCOTCH SOLDIERS

Measures of the chest in inches	Number of men per 10,000, by experience	Number of men per 10,000, by calculation
33	5	7
34	31	29
35	141	110
36	322	323
37	732	732
38	1,305	1,333
39	1,867	1,838
40	1,882	1,987
41	1,628	1,675
42	1,148	1,096
43	645	560
44	160	221
45	87	69
46	38	16
47	7	3
48	2	1

The instance is as follows. M. Quetelet obtained his facts from the thirteenth volume of the *Edinburgh Medical Journal*, where the measurements are given in respect to 5,738 soldiers, the results being grouped in order of magnitude, proceeding by differences of one inch. Professor Quetelet compares these results with those that his tables give, and here is the result. The marvelous accordance between fact and theory must strike the most unpracticed eye. I should say that, for the sake of convenience, both the measurements and calculations have been reduced to per ten thousandths.

I argue from the results obtained from Frenchmen and from Scotchmen, that, if we had measurements of the adult males in the British Isles, we should find those measurements to range in close accordance with the law of deviation from an average, although our population is as much mingled as I described that of Scotland to have been, and although Ireland is mainly peopled with Celts. Now, if this be the case with stature, then it will be true as regards every other physical feature—as circumference of head, size of brain, weight of grey matter, number of brain fibers, etc.; and thence, by a step on which no physiologist will hesitate, as regards mental capacity.

This is what I am driving at—the analogy clearly shows there must be a fairly constant average mental capacity in the inhabitants of the British Isles, and that the deviations from that average—upwards towards genius, and downwards towards stupidity—must follow the law that governs deviations from all true averages. . . .

The number of grades into which we may divide ability is purely a matter of option. We may consult our convenience by sorting Englishmen into a few large classes, or into many small ones. I will select a system of classification that shall be easily comparable with the numbers of eminent men, as determined in the previous chapter. We have seen that 250 men per million become eminent; accordingly, I have so contrived the classes in the following table that the two highest, F and G, together with X (which includes all cases beyond G, and which are unclassed), shall amount to about that number—namely, to 248 per million.

It will, I trust, be clearly understood that the numbers of men in the several classes in my table depend on no uncertain hypothesis. They are determined by the assured law of deviations from an average. It is an absolute fact that if we pick out of each million the one man who is naturally the ablest, and also the one man who is the most stupid, and divide the remaining 999,998 men into fourteen classes, the average ability in each being separated from that of its neighbors by *equal grades*, then the numbers in each of those classes will, on the average of many millions, be as is stated in the table. The table may be applied to special, just as truly as to general ability. It would be true for every examination that brought out natural gifts, whether held in painting, in music, or in statesmanship. The proportions between the different classes would be made up of different individuals, according as the examination differed in its purport.

TABLE II. CLASSIFICATION OF MEN ACCORDING TO THEIR NATURAL GIFTS

Grades of natural ability, separated by equal intervals		Proportionate, viz. one in	In each million of the same age	Numbers of men comprised in the several grades of natural ability, whether in respect to their general powers, or to special aptitudes					
Below Average	Above Average			In total male population of the United Kingdom, viz. 15 millions, of the undermentioned ages:					
				20–30	30–40	40–50	50–60	60–70	70–80
a	A	4	256,791	651,000	495,000	391,000	268,000	171,000	77,000
b	B	6	162,279	409,000	312,000	246,000	168,000	107,000	48,000
c	C	16	63,563	161,000	123,000	97,000	66,000	42,000	19,000
d	D	64	15,696	39,800	30,300	23,900	16,400	10,400	4,700
e	E	413	2,423	6,100	4,700	3,700	2,520	1,600	729
f	F	4,300	233	590	450	355	243	155	70
g	G	79,000	14	35	27.	21	15	9	4
x all grades below g	X all grades above G	1,000,000	1	3	2	2	2	2	
On either side of average		500,000	1,000,000	1,268,000	964,000	761,000	521,000	332,000	149,000
Total, both sides				2,536,000	1,928,000	1,522,000	1,042,000	664,000	298,000

It will be seen that more than half of each million is contained in the two mediocre classes a and A; the four mediocre classes a, b, A, B, contain more than four-fifths, and the six mediocre classes more than nineteen-twentieths of the entire population. Thus, the rarity of commanding ability, and the vast abundance of mediocrity, is no accident, but follows of necessity, from the very nature of these things. . . .

The class C possesses abilities a trifle higher than those commonly possessed by the foreman of an ordinary jury. D includes the mass of men who obtain the ordinary prizes of life. E is a stage higher. Then we reach F, the lowest of those yet superior classes of intellect, with which this volume is chiefly concerned. . . .

THE JUDGES OF ENGLAND BETWEEN 1660 AND 1865

The Judges of England, since the restoration of the monarchy in 1660, form a group peculiarly well adapted to afford a general outline of the extent and limitations of heredity in respect to genius. A judgeship is a guarantee of its possessor being gifted with exceptional ability; the Judges are sufficiently numerous and prolific to form an adequate basis for statistical inductions, and they are the subjects of several excellent biographical treatises. It is therefore well to begin our inquiries with a discussion of their relationships. We shall quickly arrive at definite results, which subsequent chapters, treating of more illustrious men, and in other careers, will check and amplify.

It is necessary that I should first say something in support of my assertion, that the office of a judge is really a sufficient guarantee that its possessor is exceptionally gifted. In other countries it may be different to what it is with us, but we all know that in England, the Bench is never spoken of without reverence for the intellectual power of its occupiers. A seat on the Bench is a great prize, to be won by the best men. . . .

If not always the foremost, the Judges are therefore among the foremost, of a vast body of legal men. . . .

There are 286 judges within the limits of my inquiry; 109 of them have one or more eminent relations, and three others have relations whom I have noticed, but they are marked off with brackets, and are therefore not to be included in the following statistical deductions. . . .

First, it will be observed, that the Judges are so largely interrelated, that 109 of them are grouped into only 85 families. There are seventeen doublets, among the judges, two triplets, and one quadruplet. In addition to these, might be counted six other sets, consisting of those whose ancestors sat on the Bench previously to the accession of Charles

TABLE III

Name of the degree	Degrees of Kinship	Corresponding letter		A.	B.	C.	D.	E.
1 Degree—								
Father	22 F.	....	....	22	26	100	26.0	9.1
Brother	30 B.	....	....	30	35	150	23.3	8.2
Son	31 S.	....	....	31	36	100	36.0	12.6
2 Degrees—								
Grandfather	7 G.	6 g.	....	13	15	200	7.5	2.6
Uncle	9 U.	6 u.	....	15	18	400	4.5	1.6
Nephew	14 N.	2 n.	....	16	19	400	4.75	1.7
Grandson	11 P.	5 P.	....	16	19	200	9.5	3.7
3 Degrees—								
Great-grandfather	1 GF.	1 gF.	0 gF.	2	2	400	0.5	0.2
Great-uncle	1 GB.	2 gB.	0 gB.	3	4	800	0.5	0.2
First-cousin	5 US.	2 uS.	1 uS.	9	11	800	1.4	0.5
Great-nephew	7 NS.	1 nS.	0 nS.	15	17	800	2.1	0.7
Great-grandson	2 PS.	2 pS.	0 pS.	5	6	400	1.5	0.5
All more remote	....	....	....	12	14	?	0.0	0.0

A. Number of eminent men in each degree of kinship to the most eminent man of the family (85 families).
B. The preceding column raised in proportion to 100 families.
C. Number of individuals in each degree of kinship to 100 men.
D. Percentage of eminent men in each degree of kinship to the most eminent member of distinguished families; it was obtained by dividing B by C and multiplying by 100.
E. Percentages of the previous column reduced in the proportion of (286—24, or) 262 to 85, in order to apply to families generally.

II., namely, Bedingfield, Forster, Hyde, Finch, Windham, and Lyttleton. Another fact to be observed, is the nearness of the relationships in my list. The single letters are far the most common. Also, though a man has twice as many grandfathers as fathers, and probably more than twice as many grandsons as sons, yet the Judges are found more frequently to have eminent fathers than grandfathers, and eminent sons than grandsons. In the third degree of relationship, the eminent kinsmen are yet more rare, although the number of individuals in those degrees is increased in a duplicate proportion. When a judge has no more than one eminent relation, that relation is nearly always to be found in the first or second degree. . . . I annex a table (Table III) . . . which exhibits these facts with great clearness. Column A contains the facts just as they were observed, and column D shows the percentage of individuals, in each degree of kinship to every 100 judges, who have become eminent.

What I profess to prove is this: that if two children are taken, of whom one has a parent exceptionally gifted in a high degree—say as one in 4,000, or as one in a million—and the other has not, the former child has an enormously greater chance of turning out to be gifted in a high degree, than the other. Also, I argue that, as a new race can be obtained in animals and plants, and can be raised to so great a degree of purity that it will maintain itself, with moderate care in preventing the more faulty members of the flock from breeding, so a race of gifted men might be obtained, under exactly similar conditions. . . .

COMPARISON OF RESULTS

Let us now bring our scattered results side to side, for the purpose of comparison, and judge of the extent to which they corroborate one another,—how far they confirm the provisional calculations made in the chapter on Judges from more scanty data, and where and why they contrast.

The number of cases of hereditary genius analyzed in the several chapters of my book, amounts to a large total. I have dealt with no less than 300 families containing between them nearly 1,000 eminent men, of whom 415 are illustrious, or, at all events, of such note as to deserve being printed in black type at the head of a paragraph. If there be such a thing as a decided law of distribution of genius in families, it is sure to become manifest when we deal statistically with so large a body of examples.

In comparing the results obtained from the different groups of eminent men, it will be our most convenient course to compare the

TABLE IV

	Separate Groups								All Groups together	Illustrious and Eminent Men of all Classes		
	Judges B	Statesmen B	Commanders B	Literary B	Scientific B	Poets B	Artists B	Divines B		B	C	D
Number of families, each containing more than one eminent man	85	39	27	33	43	20	28	25	300			
Total number of eminent men in all the families	262	130	89	119	148	57	97	75	977			
Father	26	33	47	48	26	20	32	28		31	100	31
Brother	35	39	50	42	47	40	50	36		41	150	27
Son	36	49	31	51	60	45	89	40		48	100	48
Grandfather	15	28	16	24	14	5	7	20		17	200	8
Uncle	18	18	8	24	16	5	14	40		18	400	5
Nephew	19	18	35	24	23	50	18	4		22	400	5
Grandson	19	10	12	9	14	5	18	16		14	200	7
Great-grandfather	2	8	8	3	0	0	0	4		3	400	1
Great-uncle	4	5	8	6	5	5	7	4		5	800	1
First cousin	11	21	20	18	16	0	1	8		13	800	2
Great-nephew	17	5	8	6	16	10	0	0		10	800	1
Great-grandson	6	0	0	3	7	0	0	0		3	400	1
All more remote	14	37	44	15	23	5	18	16		31	?	..

columns B of the several tables. Column B gives the number of kinsmen in various degrees, on the supposition that the number of families
in the group to which it refers is 100. All the entries under B have
therefore the same common measure, they are all *percentages*, and
admit of direct intercomparison. I hope I have made myself quite clear:
lest there should remain any misapprehension, it is better to give an
example. Thus, the families of Divines are only 25 in number, and in
those 25 families there are 7 eminent fathers, 9 brothers, and 10 sons;
now in order to raise these numbers to percentages, 7, 9, and 10 must
be multiplied by the number of times that 25 goes into 100, namely
by 4. They will then become 28, 36, and 40. . . .

The general uniformity in the distribution of ability among the
kinsmen in the different groups, is strikingly manifest. The eminent
sons are almost invariably more numerous than the eminent fathers.
On proceeding further down the table, we come to a sudden dropping
off of the numbers at the second grade of kinship, namely, at the grandfathers, uncles, nephews, and grandsons: this diminution is conspicuous
in the entries in column D, the meaning of which has already been
described. On reaching the third grade of kinship, another abrupt
dropping off in numbers is again met with, but the first cousins are
found to occupy a decidedly better position than other relations within
the third grade. . . .

I reckon the chances of kinsmen of illustrious men rising, or having
risen, to be 15½ to 100 in the case of fathers, 13½ to 100 in the case
of brothers, 24 to 100 in the case of sons. Or, putting these and the remaining proportions into a more convenient form, we obtain the following results. In first grade: the chance of the father is 1 to 6; of each
brother, 1 to 7; of each son, 1 to 4. In second grade: of each grandfather, 1 to 25; of each uncle, 1 to 40; of each nephew, 1 to 40; of
each grandson, 1 to 29. In the third grade, the chance of each member
is about 1 to 200, excepting in the case of first cousins, where it is
1 to 100. . . .

THE COMPARATIVE WORTH OF DIFFERENT RACES

I have now completed what I have to say concerning the kinships
of individuals, and proceed, in this chapter, to attempt a wider treatment of my subject, through a consideration of nations and races. . . .

Let us, then, compare the negro race with the Anglo-Saxon, with
respect to those qualities alone which are capable of producing judges,
statesmen, commanders, men of literature and science, poets, artists,
and divines. If the negro race in America had been affected by no

social disabilities, a comparison of their achievements with those of the whites in their several branches of intellectual effort, having regard to the total number of their respective populations, would give the necessary information. As matters stand, we must be content with much rougher data.

First, the negro race has occasionally, but very rarely, produced such men as Toussaint l'Ouverture, who are of our class F; that is to say, its X, or its total classes above G, appear to correspond with our F, showing a difference of not less than two grades between the black and white races, and it may be more.

Secondly, the negro race is by no means wholly deficient in men capable of becoming good factors, thriving merchants, and otherwise considerably raised above the average of whites—that is to say, it can not infrequently supply men corresponding to our class C, or even D. It will be recollected that C implies a selection of 1 in 16, or somewhat more than the natural abilities possessed by average foremen of common juries, and that D is as 1 in 64—a degree of ability that is sure to make a man successful in life. In short, classes E and F of the negro may roughly be considered as the equivalent of our C and D— a result which again points to the conclusion, that the average intellectual standard of the negro race is some two grades below our own.

Thirdly, we may compare, but with much caution, the relative position of negroes in their native country with that of the travelers who visit them. The latter, no doubt, bring with them the knowledge current in civilized lands, but that is an advantage of less importance than we are apt to suppose. A native chief has as good an education in the art of ruling men, as can be desired; he is continually exercised in personal government, and usually maintains his place by the ascendancy of his character, shown every day over his subjects and rivals. A traveler in wild countries also fills, to a certain degree, the position of a commander, and has to confront native chiefs at every inhabited place. The result is familiar enough—the white traveler almost invariably holds his own in their presence. It is seldom that we hear of a white traveler meeting with a black chief whom he feels to be the better man. I have often discussed this subject with competent persons, and can only recall a few cases of the inferiority of the white man,— certainly not more than might be ascribed to an average actual difference of three grades, of which one may be due to the relative demerits of native education, and the remaining two to a difference in natural gifts. . . .

The ablest race of whom history bears record is unquestionably the

ancient Greek, partly because their master-pieces in the principal de-
partments of intellectual activity are still unsurpassed, and in many
respects unequaled, and partly because the population that gave birth to
the creators of those master-pieces was very small. Of the various Greek
sub-races, that of Attica was the ablest, and she was no doubt largely
indebted to the following cause, for her superiority. Athens opened her
arms to immigrants, but not indiscriminately, for her social life was
such that none but very able men could take any pleasure in it; on the
other hand, she offered attractions such as men of the highest ability
and culture could find in no other city. Thus, by a system of partly
unconscious selection, she built up a magnificent breed of human
animals, which, in the space of one century—viz., between 530 and
430 B.C.—produced the following illustrious persons, fourteen in
number:

Statesmen and Commanders.—Themistocles (mother an alien),
Miltiades, Aristeides, Cimon (son of Miltiades), Pericles (son of
Xanthippus, the victor at Mycale).

Literary and Scientific Men.—Thucydides, Socrates, Xenophon,
Plato.

Poets.—Æschylus, Sophocles, Euripides, Aristophanes.

Sculptor.—Phidias.

We are able to make a closely-approximate estimate of the population that produced these men, because the number of the inhabitants
of Attica has been a matter of frequent inquiry, and critics appear at
length to be quite agreed in the general results. It seems that the little
district of Attica contained, during its most flourishing period (Smith's
Class. Geog. Dict.), less than 90,000 native free-born persons, 40,000
resident aliens, and a laboring and artisan population of 400,000 slaves.
The first item is the only one that concerns us here, namely, the 90,000
free-born persons. Again, the common estimate that population renews
itself three times in a century is very close to the truth, and may be
accepted in the present case. Consequently, we have to deal with a
total population of 270,000 free-born persons, or 135,000 males, born
in the century I have named. Of these, about one-half, or 67,500,
would survive the age of 26, and one-third, or 45,000, would survive
that of 50. As 14 Athenians became illustrious, the selection is only 1
to 4,822 in respect to the former limitation, and as 1 to 3,214 in respect
to the latter. Referring to the table [on page 86], it will be seen that
this degree of selection corresponds very fairly to the classes F (1 in
4,300) and above, of the Athenian race. Again, as G is one-sixteenth
or one-seventeenth as numerous as F, it would be reasonable to expect
to find one of class G among the fourteen; we might, however, by

accident, meet with two, three, or even four of that class—say Pericles, Socrates, Plato, and Phidias.

Now let us attempt to compare the Athenian standard of ability with that of our own race and time. We have no men to put by the side of Socrates and Phidias, because the millions of all Europe, breeding as they have done for the subsequent 2,000 years, have never produced their equals. They are, therefore, two or three grades above our G— they might rank as I or J. But, supposing we do not count them at all, saying that some freak of nature acting at that time, may have produced them, what must we say about the rest? Pericles and Plato would rank, I suppose, the one among the greatest of philosophical statesmen, and the other as at least the equal of Lord Bacon. They would, therefore, stand somewhere among our unclassed X, one or two grades above G—let us call them between H and I. All the remainder—the F of the Athenian race—would rank above our G, and equal to or close upon our H. It follows from all this, that the average ability of the Athenian race is, on the lowest possible estimate, very nearly two grades higher than our own—that is, about as much as our race is above that of the African negro.

9. THE DEVELOPMENT OF RACE MEASUREMENTS AND CLASSIFICATION [2]

BY GUSTAV RETZIUS

THE first scientist who found place in the natural system for human beings was . . . Linnæus, the Swedish naturalist. He was also the first to subdivide human beings into distinct zoölogical categories. Men, he says, form one species, but among them are to be found several varieties. He differentiated four, one in each of the continents then known, characterizing them principally by the colors of their skins: Americanus rufus, Europæus albus, Asiaticus luridus, Afer niger. He also gave a category which he named, monstrosus, embracing certain varieties of an abnormal type with which he was not [personally] acquainted. The people living in Polynesia were wholly unknown to him. As for the white man, Europæus, the description he gives of him shows that he was only familiar with that section of Europeans living

[2] From Gustav Retzius, "A Review of, and Views on, the Development of some Anthropological Questions" (Huxley lecture for 1909), *Journal of the [Royal] Anthropological Institute [of Great Britain and Ireland]*, Volume 39, pages 279-295, 1909.

in the northern parts of the continent. Linnæus himself had not extended his foreign travels beyond Northern Germany, Holland, Northern France, and England. Thus, when he defines his Europæus as: "Albus, Sanguineus, Torosus, Pilis Flavescentibus, Prolixis, Oculis Cæruleis," the characterization, especially in the last item, does not, generally speaking, suit the population of the whole of Europe, but rather only that of its northern districts, i.e. the peoples usually classed as belonging to the Teutonic family; the Scandinavians, and the inhabitants of Holland, England, and the northern parts of Germany and France. Linnæus himself, however, undoubtedly included the peoples of Europe in general under his Europæus, differentiating them as a whole from the varieties of Homo sapiens to be met with in Asia, Africa, and America. . . . His "homines Alpini," it must be observed, are classified in the imagined group "Homo Monstrosus," along with "Monorchides, Macrocephali, Plagiocephali," i.e. forms of a more or less abnormal character, his knowledge of which was probably derived from the works of other writers or from hearsay evidence. . . . Moreover, I have personally investigated all the different editions of Linnæus' Systema Naturæ as well as the hitherto unprinted notes taken by his pupils during his lectures and have come to the definite conclusion that he only assumed that there is one variety of Homo sapiens in Europe, viz.: Europæus, but that he described that variety in accordance with the observations he had made personally in intercourse with those around him in his native country and in other parts of Northern Europe, and that he placed this variety side by side with those of the other continents: Africa's black variety, Asia's yellow variety, and America's red variety. . . .

Blumenbach, the German anatomist, was the first to enter upon the investigation of the human race in a serious manner from the standpoint of a natural scientist, and to study its different varieties comprehensively and exhaustively. His subdivision, like that of Linnæus, was in accordance with the continents and with the color of the skin and hair. He, however, noted for the first time variations in the *shape of the skull and the face*. Blumenbach added one more to the four principal varieties into which Linnæus divided Homo sapiens, this fifth variety, which was unknown to Linnæus, being located in the islands of the Pacific. Blumenbach's names for his five varieties were, we may remember: the Caucasian, the Mongolian, the Ethiopian, the American, and the Malayan. The Caucasian embraced all the peoples of Europe except the Finns and the Lapps, but also included the peoples of Western Asia as far as the River Ob, the Caspian Sea, and the Ganges, and also the inhabitants of Northern Africa. This variety was characterized as possessed of *white skins, red cheeks, brown or nut-brown hair, rounded skulls, oval face, slightly arched and rather slender noses, small mouths, perpendicular front teeth, and as not having big lips.*

The only peoples in Europe Blumenbach did not classify in this group, viz.: the Finns and Lapps, he placed among the Mongolians.

Blumenbach published his characterization of the five varieties of the human race in his well-known work, *De generis humani varietate nativa* (ed. 1, 1775; ed. 3, 1795). It is very clear from several remarks he makes, that he was concerned with the *shape of the skull* as well as with the color of the hair and the skin. . . . Blumenbach took into consideration . . . especially its length and breadth, its sincipital aspect (which he calls its *norma verticalis*) and . . . he distinguished between "the square shape" characteristic of the Mongols, and the "pressed-in-from-the-sides form," as found in Negroes. . . . In his anatomical museum at Göttingen he had a fairly large collection—for that time—of human skulls, containing representatives of even very distant regions of the earth. . . . One can perceive that Blumenbach concentrated his attention, in his craniological researches, primarily upon the physiognomical elements in the appearance of the cranium and especially of the forehead and the other parts of the face, i.e., upon the typical features of the physiognomy. A confirmation of this may be found in the circumstance that, so far as is known, he never, or practically never, carried out measurements of the crania, either in his investigations or when he was describing the differences of shape in the crania he had collected. The most remarkable evidence, however, of Blumenbach's not having grasped and appreciated the real value of the *norma verticalis* of the crania, and especially the importance of the ratio existing between the length and the breadth of the skull, lies in the fact that he included in one or other of his five varieties peoples whose sincipital aspects, and especially also the indices of length and breadth, are exceedingly different one from another. To take for an example: he placed in his Mongolian variety Lapps and Eskimos, races of men that are very divergent as far as the shape of the cranium, especially their length and breadth relation, is concerned. In the Caucasian group, too, he collected a number of peoples whose crania show very marked differences one from another. It is very remarkable, moreover, that he selected the name Caucasian as suitable for the peoples of Europe, with the Caucasus and its round-headed population as the central point. . . . It is quite clear that Blumenbach has the merit, as above stated, of being the first to make a serious and extensive study of the form of the crania of the different races of mankind, but he appears to have been fettered by his absolute belief in the uniformity of his five varieties, and he neglected to observe that within them there are assembled races, whose crania-forms are so typically different, that these races cannot be brought together in the system. It seems singular to us that, although he was a thorough naturalist, he should have classed together such widely separated races as Lapps and Eskimos, to confine ourselves to that one striking example already adduced. It would seem that his attention had become closely fixed upon the physiognomical character of the facial features of the crania, as indeed is plainly apparent from a study of the *Decades,* his principal work on the crania. If, in pursuing his investigations, he had made use of his *normæ,* and especially his *norma verticalis,* he might have advanced science more than he really did. Blumenbach has the merit of having introduced into the science of anthropology the study of the form of the skulls—he is the real founder of Craniology.

In the year of Blumenbach's decease, 1840, Anders Retzius, the Swedish anatomist, laid before the Academy of Sciences in Stockholm the first draft of his theory regarding the shape of the crania, and in 1842 he lectured on "The Form of the Skulls of the Northern Peoples of Europe" to an assembly of Scandinavian natural scientists in Stockholm. That lecture was subsequently translated and published in Holland, France, and Germany. It aroused no little attention in the scientific world, for it brought forward new suggestions and new points of view.

Up to then it had been usual to regard each of the varieties, into which the human race had been subdivided by Linnæus and Blumenbach, as essentially uniform. Anders Retzius, however, now showed, as a result of his unprejudiced and accurate investigation of the forms of crania upon which Blumenbach principally founded his theory, that not even the Caucasian variety, established as a unit by Blumenbach, was uniform throughout; that it indeed, on the contrary, included races of men possessed of very different forms of the skull. He not only proved that the Lapps, Finns, and Eskimos, whom Blumenbach brought together and placed in the Mongolian variety, have crania so widely differing from each other, that they cannot possibly belong to one and the same variety, but also that the proper inhabitants of Scandinavia, i.e., the Swedes, Danes, and Norwegians, differ materially in the shape of the cranium from the inhabitants of Russia, and from the other peoples related to them, i.e., the Slavs.

The skull of the Scandinavian is narrow and more extended backwards, and when looked at from above is more or less oval in outline; that of the Slavs on the other hand is broader, shorter, and when seen from above is more or less round in outline or squarer. The peoples with the longer shape of the cranium Anders Retzius called *Gentes Dolichocephalæ*, those with the shorter *Gentes Brachycephalæ*. In arriving at his conclusions he made use of *measurements* of the crania in various directions. For the ratio between the measurements of maximum length and maximum breadth of cranium he adopted 1000:x. In Swedes the ratio of length to breadth was found to be 1000:773, in Slavs 1000:888, etc. Anders Retzius had thus given the initiative to the index-measurement system which has since played so important a part in anthropology.

In the following years, until his death in 1860, there appeared a succession of treatises and reports, in which he placed on record the results of his continued investigations, and in them he made it abundantly evident that the relation between the length and the breadth of the cranium forms one of the most important criteria for race distinctions that those engaged in making a comparative study of the races of mankind can employ. He tried to group the peoples both in and beyond Europe by the aid of this relation, but it was not by any means his idea thereby to establish any sort of "system of the races of mankind," as is mistakenly supposed by some. In his works Anders Retzius spoke of the classification as merely an attempt to arrange the forms of crania. He was able to show that dolichocephaly and brachycephaly are to be found all the world over, except in Africa, but he was not able, any more than those who have taken up the question subsequently have proved able, to explain the real purport of the phenomenon or how it has arisen. This difficulty of arriving at the explanation of the ultimate cause of a phenomenon is, as we know, characteristic in fact of all the phenomena we meet with in Nature. Research enables us to reveal their existence, to describe and register them, but it is rare indeed that we are enabled to discover their origin and cause. That is the case, too, with the majority of the other race-characters. We are aware that the Negro's skin is black, the Indian's red, the Mongolian's yellow, and the European's more or less white. But has any one ever been able to demonstrate why the coloring is so varied in the skins of these different races? The same difficulty arises when an explanation is required of the differences in the color and character of the hair, the color of the iris, the stature or length of the body, etc. It is therefore essential for us to rest content with having established the fact, that dolichocephaly and brachycephaly are to be found disseminated throughout Europe, Asia, Polynesia, and America, not, however, merely promiscuously without rule, but existing as a criterion of race for the different peoples inhabiting those regions of the globe.

Anders Retzius did not lay down any definite figures by way of limit to mark off dolichocephaly from brachycephaly. He had come across intermediary forms between the two varieties, and he seems to have thought it best to adopt a central point as characteristic for each. Thus, he states that the length of the head of the dolichocephali exceeds the breadth by about one-fourth of the length, i.e. the length stands to the breadth in the ratio of 100:75, whereas the ratio for the brachycephali is 100:80-87, i.e. the length exceeds the breadth by one-fifth to one-eighth.

From the account given by Anders Retzius we may see in general that he did not regard dolichocephaly and brachycephaly as merely a matter of measurement and nothing more, but looked upon them rather as a typological character, a ratio indicative of form, possessing a very close relationship to other criteria of form, which he also described in several of his works.

That he paid attention in his researches, not only to the shape of the skull itself but also to the parts of the face, is evident from two circumstances, first, that in his classification he registers the greater or less degree with which the jaws project, their orthognathic and prognathic properties; and, second, that he gives the dimensions of the face (height of face, jugular breadth) both in his series of measurements and in his descriptions of the characters of the face.

It is not my intention, however, here to enter upon a further discussion of this phase in the history of anthropology. I have only desired to bring forward some of its salient points, seeing that they are of fundamental importance for us in seeking to arrive at a clear idea of the history of the race question even as regards Europe alone. In accordance with the theory of Linnæus and Blumenbach it was generally supposed, as has been stated above, that the white, European, variety of the human race—Blumenbach's Caucasian variety—consisted of a uniform group of people more or less homogeneous among themselves. The idea put forth by Anders Retzius first directed attention to the existence of considerable divergences of race even within the white variety, i.e., among the peoples of Europe itself. The Swedish anatomist and anthropologist demonstrated that the skull of a Swede and that of any other representative of the same stem, the so-called Teutonic stem, differ very widely not only from those of the Lapp and the Finn but also from that of the Russian, and broadly speaking, from that of a Slav. Anders Retzius laid strong stress, consequently, upon the fact that languages do not afford any certain guide for determining criteria of race. As early as 1847 he expressed himself as follows in one of the publications that issued from his pen: "The whole of mankind belongs to one species; the varied types are varieties of several different grades, which, in many localities, have become hybridized one with another. In most countries more than one type of nationality is to be found naturalized; thus in many countries migrations of people have taken place, small sections of the tribes previously dwelling there still remaining distributed—though sparsely—among the more numerous newcomers. In several countries the people who thus remained adopted the language of the tribe that won its way in amongst them; that is said to have been the case in North Germany, where the population, originally Slavs, adopted German as their language in course of time, and by degrees, through acquiring familiarity with German ways and customs, became thoroughly amalgamated with the German nation. Similar conditions have produced the same results in many other regions both in the New and Old Worlds. . . ."

There remains, however, one more criterion of race to be mentioned, stature or length of body. This has, indeed, for a long time past been a point to which anthropologists have been attentive, and in the tabulated measurements of the recruits for the army they have been provided with material ready to hand for purposes of investigation. It was not, however, until towards the close of last century, when several special inquiries on a large scale were carried out in different European countries, that this character came by its rights and received due attention and notice.

Thanks to the systematic investigations made by fully competent persons regarding the most important anthropological characters of large army contingents, the distribution and numerical amount of these several characters have at last been made known for some of the nations of Europe, especially by Dr. Otto Ammon in Baden in 1886-1899 and by Dr. Rid. Livi in 1896-1905. . . .

There are five principal characters that were made the subject of inquiry:

1. The length and breadth of the head, and consequently the length and breadth index;
2. The form of the face;
3. The stature or length of the body;
4. The color of the hair of the head;
5. The color of the iris. . . .

In conjunction with a number of more or less exhaustive investigations into certain of these characters for . . . the countries of Europe, such a general knowledge of the race-characteristics of the European nations has been obtained, that it has been considered possible to draw some general conclusions. Professor Ripley of Harvard University, and Dr. Deniker, of Paris, have been specially occupied with summarizing the general results of investigations in this department. The former gives three separate races called by him: "The Teutonic Race," "The Alpine Race," and "The Mediterranean Race." . . . Dr. Deniker, on the other hand, went further in his subdivision of races; besides the three named he added some others, but has on different occasions arrived at different results. In his last publication, however, in the Huxley Memorial Lecture of 1904, Dr. Deniker fixed the number of European races at six. . . . Until a thorough investigation has made matters clearer, it seems to me to be wisest only to admit of the existence of such races as have really been proved, and to leave the classification of the remainder to the future.

The following may, however, be admitted as surely existing:

1. The Northern European Dolichocephalic, Blue-eyed, Tall Race (Anders Retzius' Dolichocephalic Germanic type), which latterly has been designated by several writers (Wilson and others) *Homo Europæus* (the term Linnæus used), and which is now often termed the Northern Race (La Race Nordique, Nordische Rasse).

2. The Middle-European Brachycephalic, Dark-haired, Dark-eyed, Short-statured Race, probably closely related to the similar population in the eastern portions of Europe (Anders Retzius' Slavonic and Rhætian people). This race has been designated recently *Homo Alpinus* (Linnæus' term); there may be some justification for this term in the fact of a large section of the race being resident in the Alpine regions of Southern and Central Europe. But it should not be forgotten that this race during the lapse of centuries has extended its habitat to a considerable part of France and even to a large portion of Central and Northern Germany. Linnæus certainly did not mean this race by his term *"Homo Alpinus,"* a fact already stated above.

3. The South-European Dolichocephalic, Dark-haired, Dark-eyed, Short-statured Race, called *Homo Mediterraneus* (Sergi, Ripley, Wilser, and others), which may possibly embrace variations of distinct character in the various Mediterranean countries.

To name only the first of these three races, Europæus, as appears often to be the fashion nowadays, seems to be very strange, since the other two great races, too, have inhabited Europe from times immemorial, and it is by no means possible of proof that they originated in other Continents and migrated into Europe subsequently. I consider, moreover, that it is an entirely incorrect use of the nomenclature established once for all for zoölogy, to call these races "Homo Europæus," "Homo Alpinus," "Homo Mediterraneus," as is so often done in modern anthropological literature. This leads to a confusion of our ideas about *species*. They can, of course, only be regarded as variations of one and the same species, *Homo sapiens,* and in reality only as sub-variations of a variety, viz. the so-called white race of men. It is unfortunate that the notions, *species, variety,* and *race,* have not been more definitely fixed in value as regards the races of mankind. The majority of anthropologists are probably of the same opinion as Linnæus, that the living races of mankind at the present time are all to be referred to one species, *Homo sapiens* Lin., and that their variant representatives are to be regarded as varieties of the species, even though very weighty reasons might be alleged for regarding some of these variations as *species themselves.* This question has now lost much of its significance since the triumphs of the theory of descent, but it is of importance for systemology, and for the formation of terms. As regards the population of our own continent and the problems concerning them, it is of no great significance whether the white man, the European, is put down as a particular *species* or as a variety. But it is of real importance that its *subsections* should not be put down as separate *species.* For my own part, I am at present most inclined to agree with Linnæus and Blumenbach in regarding the great racial groups of the human species as varieties, though it must be admitted that the Australian, the Negro, and the American differ very widely from the European. There are to be found, however, remarkable transitional (intermediary) forms to bridge the gulf between the peoples of Asia and Europe, and there also exist similar transitional forms uniting the people of Asia with those of America and a portion of Polynesia. But if the term *variety* is to be preserved for the various large race-groups, we require a suitable term for the sub-sections under *Varietas.* . . . It seems to me, therefore, to be indicated that these sub-sections of the varieties should be designated as *sub-varieties* or *sub-races* (race branches).

10. ESSENTIALS OF ANTHROPOMETRY [3]

BY LOUIS R. SULLIVAN

THERE is practically no limit to the number of measurements and observations which may be taken on the living human body. A majority of these measurements and observations are of interest and importance,

[3] From *Essentials of Anthropometry: A Handbook for Explorers and Museum Collectors.* Issued by the American Museum of Natural History, New York, 1923. By permission.

but it is a physical impossibility to employ all of them on any considerable number of individuals. Experience has shown that it is necessary and wise to limit the number of measurements and observations and to increase the size of the series studied, and in order that observers may proceed in a uniform manner several international and intranational congresses have agreed upon and published lists of preferred measures with details as to how they should be taken. The purpose of these lists or agreements is to insure comparability of the data the world over. Yet, these agreements were made for physical anthropologists primarily and schedule long detailed series of measurements for all parts of the body. This is all well enough for professional specialists, but, as a matter of fact, trained physical anthropologists have contributed only a small part of our anthropometric data. So we must depend upon ethnologists, archeologists, physicians, army and naval officers, and travelers, for anthropometric data on little known and inaccessible peoples with whom they come in contact. Many valuable data have been contributed in this way, but most of these men have carried this work as a side line. Consequently, the number of measures were reduced according to the taste and convenience of each observer. Some measured stature only, some stature and two head diameters; in fact, about ninety per cent. of the studies end here. A few more observers have taken face height or width, the nasal diameters, or one or two other measurements. There are times when it is only necessary to make one measurement, but this is when a particular and concrete problem is in mind. Moreover, if one has a definite and specific problem it is legitimate to select only such measures as bear on or help solve that problem. Yet, unfortunately, most of these observers had no specific problem in mind, but gathered their data as general contributions to our knowledge of the races of mankind. While it is true that a knowledge of the stature and cephalic index of all peoples is a very desirable thing, this in itself does not go far towards advancing our knowledge of race relationships. In fact, the popularity of the cephalic index has probably done much to retard our knowledge of race relationships because so many have relied upon this measure alone. It does not follow that this measure is useless or worthless, far from it, for it is one of the most valuable descriptive measures. Yet it is *one* of many and by itself of little value except in special studies of the cephalic index. Again, what is true of the cephalic index is true of any other one measure or observation, since the larger and finer relationships of the various types of mankind are problems which require a definite number of measures and observations for their solution and upon which all the data of physical anthropology must be brought to bear. For example, most of us desire such schemes of relationship as those devised by Deniker, Sergi, Giuffrida-Ruggeri, and others. We wish to know also just how many and what physical types inhabit such areas as Polynesia, Micronesia, Melanesia, and Malaysia, as well as the relationship of the various physical types to each other and to other known types of mankind. Fortunately a minimum number of measures and observations will give these larger relationships. Thus, for Polynesia, Micronesia, Malaysia, and Melanesia, it appears that with seven measurements, the resulting four indices, and nine descriptive observations, we can untangle the relationships of the many physical types involved. While we speak specifically of these four areas, it is probable that the same seven measures, four indices, and nine observations would give us a key to the relationships of racial groups in any part of the world.

The absolute measurements recommended are: stature, head length, head breadth, face breadth, anatomical face height, nasal height, and nasal width. From these measures we derive the cephalic length-breadth index, the transverse cephalo-facial index, the anatomical face index, and the nasal index. These measures and indices should be supplemented by descriptive observations on the color of the skin, color of the hair, form of the hair, eye color, the epicanthic or Mongoloid eyefold, thickness of the lips, form of the upper front (incisor) teeth, the amount of beard development, and the development of body hair.

The main reason for this choice of measures, indices, and observations, is that the races differ most markedly in these characters and that certain of them in combination are characteristic of the different races. Another reason is the simplicity of the technique involved.

The purpose of this outline is not merely to urge uniformity of technique, but also uniformity in the number and kind of measures and observations taken, to the end that we may attain the maximum result with a minimum expenditure of time, effort, and money. Further, we wish to encourage the coöperation of archeologists, ethnologists, and others who find themselves suitably situated to make such studies, and while the physical anthropologist needs no such guide, it is hoped that he too will coöperate in these minimum specifications. Naturally, there is no objection to increasing the number of measures and observations indefinitely, but all should agree on a desirable minimum to be taken by all. . . .

THE MEASURING POINTS, OR LANDMARKS

The measuring points described below are illustrated in Figs. 4 and 5.

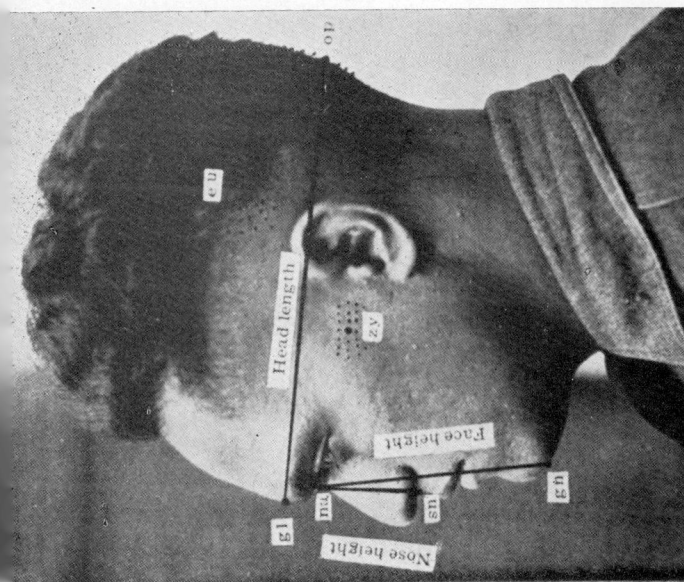

Fig. 4. Landmarks and Length and Height Measurement. gl = glabella; op = opisthocranium; na = nasion; sn = subnasale; gn = gnathion; eu = euryon; zy = zygion. Note that the euryon, zygion, and opisthocranium are not definite anatomical points like the nasion and subnasale, but are located wholly by measuring.

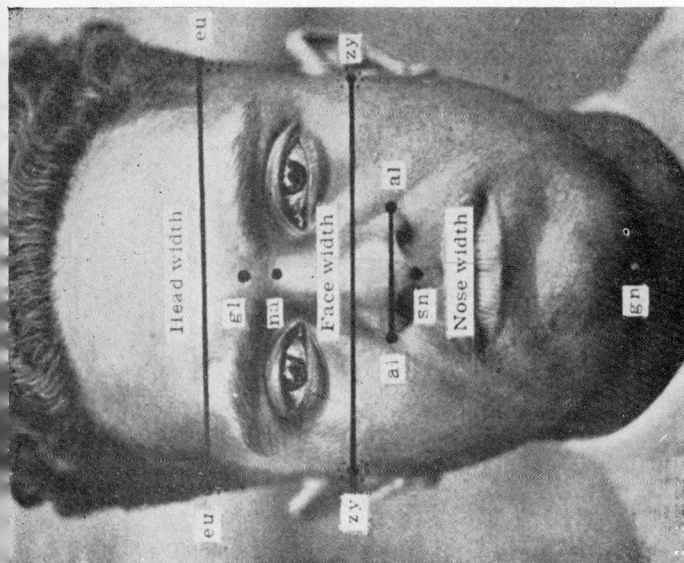

Fig. 5. Measuring Points and Measurements of Width. gl = glabella; na = nasion; sn = subnasale; gn = gnathion; eu = euryon; zy = zygion; al = alare. Note that the euryon, zygion, and alare are not definite anatomical points like the nasion and subnasale, but are located wholly by measuring. Note also that all the above measurements of width are maximum measurements.

Vertex: The highest point on the top of the head in the median sagittal line (not illustrated).

Glabella (gl): The most anteriorly projecting point on the frontal bone (forehead) in the median sagittal line. Usually it is about on a line with the tops of the eyebrows or very slightly below.

Opisthocranium (op): That point in the median sagittal line of the occiput (back of the head) which is most distant from the glabella. It is found by measuring.

Euryon (eu): The most laterally projecting point on the sides of the head above the supra mastoid and zygomatic crests. It is the point at which greatest width of head is measured. It is very variable in location and determined solely by measuring until the maximum width is found. Obviously, the euryon is found on both sides of the head.

Nasion (na): The nasion is the point in the median sagittal line where the nasal bones join the frontal bone. It is one of the most important and at the same time most difficult points to locate on the living. It is best found by running the left thumb up the bridge of the nose with moderate pressure until a distinct angulation is felt where it joins the frontal bone. It is easy to find in people with a high nasal bridge since the angle is moderately abrupt; in races with a very low nasal bridge it cannot be felt, but must be located from our knowledge of anatomy. If possible see this point on a skull before attempting any measuring. It is usually on a line with the lowest hairs of the eyebrows where they sweep down upon the nose or very slightly below. It is always above the inner corners of the eyes. It is usually at least a centimeter below the glabella. Once found it is well to mark this point.

Gnathion (gn): The gnathion is the lowest point in the middle of the bony chin. Of course, it is impossible to measure to the bony chin. But enough pressure should be used to insure that one is really measuring as closely as possible (with the comfort of the subject in mind) to the bony chin.

Subnasale (sn): That point where the septum of the nose joins the upper lip.

Zygion (zy): The zygion is the most laterally projecting point on the zygomatic arches. It is found only by measuring. It is the point on either zygomatic arch where the maximum width of the face occurs.

Alare (al): The alare is the most laterally projecting point on the wings of the nose or nostrils.

THE ESSENTIAL MEASUREMENTS

The most marked measurable differences in the races of man are in stature, head form, face form, and nose form. It is only when we have the measurements necessary to define these peculiarities that we can untangle their relationships. This necessitates taking seven measurements.

1. *Stature,* with shoes removed, to the nearest *centimeter.* The subject should stand with heels together in the attitude of attention, looking straight to the front. The most frequent reaction encountered is for the subject to throw the head too far back on the neck. When the subject is markedly round-shouldered or deformed in such a way as to affect the normal stature, be sure to indicate this by recording stature and then drawing a line through the number so that it will not be included in the average. When it is necessary to choose between omitting the measure or taking it with the shoes on (in other words when the subject refuses to remove shoes), take the measure with shoes on and measure the height of the heel with the sliding calipers. Deduct this at once before recording stature.

2. *Head length* (glabella to opisthocranium). It is to be taken to the nearest *millimeter* with the spreading calipers. This is the maximum length of the head from the glabella to the most distant point on the occiput in the median sagittal plane. Stand on the left side of the subject, who should be seated. Grasp one branch of the compass with the thumb and finger of the left hand and the other branch with the right hand. Have the hinge pointed towards your own chest and the scale up so you can read it at all times. Rest the middle finger of the left hand on the nasal bridge in such a manner that you can hold the tip of the left branch of the caliper stationary or fixed against the glabella. With the right hand move the right branch of the caliper up and down in the median sagittal line of the occiput until you obtain the maximum measurement. Remove the calipers and then repeat. Repeat until you succeed in obtaining uniform results. Do not use painful pressure, but be sure to penetrate the hair. Usually the weight of the hands furnishes enough pressure without any conscious effort. Do not get too far down on the neck. Be sure the right branch of the caliper does not deviate from the midline of the head.

3. *Head breadth* (euryon to euryon). This is the maximum width of the head in a transverse direction wherever it occurs. It is usually slightly above and behind the tips of the ear. Stand directly in front of the subject. Grasp one branch of the caliper in each hand as before. Be sure that the subject's head is in a vertical position and that the

points of the calipers are in a true horizontal plane. Place the points of
the caliper on what appears to be the maximum width of the head. Read
the scale and explore with the calipers all the neighboring area until
the maximum width has been found. Do not get too low down. In
general it is safer to keep above the tips of the ears. In any event do
not go below the plane where the ear joins the head.

4. *Face breadth* (zygion to zygion). This is the maximum width
of the face and is to be measured with the spreading calipers, as were
the length and breadth of head. Hold the calipers as in measuring width
of head. With the tips of the index fingers find the most convex or outstanding point on the zygomatic arches and apply the points of the
calipers. Read the scale. Remove the calipers and repeat the process
until you are sure that you have obtained the maximum face width.
Only moderate pressure is to be used. Appearances are deceiving and
most beginners measure too far forward. The maximum width is usually
back within two or three centimeters of the ear. This varies in different
racial types, so explore thoroughly with the calipers before recording
the measurement.

5. *Face height*, anatomical (nasion to gnathion). This is the distance from the nasion to the gnathion or lower border of the chin. It
is best taken with the sliding compass. Gauge approximately the height
of the face and open the scale a little more than the height of the face.
The subject should now be made to stand. With the left thumb find the
nasion. The nasion is the point where the nasal bridge joins the forehead or frontal bone. In skeletal material it is a suture. Place the left
thumb on the nasal bridge and with considerable pressure follow up
until it reaches the point where the nasal bridge joins the forehead.
There is usually an angle here which can be felt. When located, either
mark with a wax pencil or with the thumbnail held in place. See that
the subject has the mouth closed and the teeth in occlusion. He will not
unless you make a special effort to see that he does. Then measure from
the nasion to the *lowest* point on the chin (gnathion). Again use only
moderate pressure, but be sure to feel the bone of the chin.

6. *Nasal height* (nasion to subnasale). To be measured with sliding
calipers, from the nasion, as described above, to the point where the
nasal septum joins the upper lip. Be sure to touch the septum, but avoid
pressure which distorts the nose.

7. *Nasal width* (alare to alare). This is the maximum width of the
nose or nostrils. Measure from the most outstanding point on one nos-
tril to that of the other. See that the subject is not laughing or otherwise distorting the nasal width. Avoid pressure. Do not compress the
nose, but be sure to touch the wings with the compasses. . . .

DERIVED INDICES

From these seven measures, four important indices, or proportions, are derived.

1. The *cephalic length-breadth* index is derived by dividing the width of the head by the length of the head. In other words, it expresses the width of the head in terms of percentage of the length of the head. If a head is 150 millimeters wide and 200 millimeters long the cephalic length-breadth index is 75.0 or the width of the head is 75 per cent. of the length of the head.

2. The *transverse cephalo-facial* index is derived by dividing the width of the face by the width of the head.

3. The *anatomical face* index is obtained by dividing the anatomical height of the face by the width of the face.

4. The *nasal* index is derived by dividing the width of the nose by the height of the nose. . . .

DESCRIPTIVE OBSERVATIONS

In addition to the above measurable characters the races of man differ widely from each other in characters which are not readily measurable. Examples of such traits are skin color, hair form, eye color, etc. While it is impossible to measure these and similar characteristics accurately, an effort is made to describe them as uniformly as possible. To this end certain descriptive words have come to have a fairly uniform and widely accepted meaning in anthropology. Low waves, deep waves, and curly, have definite meaning in anthropology, when applied to hair, which they lack in popular usage. These conceptions are described and illustrated below. The observer will have less difficulty in this part of the work if he appreciates at the start that these classes (such as low waves, deep waves, etc.) are merely arbitrary stages in a widely variable distribution. Just as stature varies from 130 to 200 centimeters so does hair vary from straight through all gradations to the closely coiled spiral hair of some Negroes. In the case of stature we have an accurate measuring rod for measuring it accurately. 150 centimeters means the same the world over. In the case of hair form, hair color, eye color, skin color, and the other characters mentioned below, we have no accurate measuring rod. So we must set up arbitrary standards of color and form and describe the characteristics as nearly as possible in terms of these standards or conceptions.

The following observations are recommended:

A. Skin color. Skin color is best described by use of some of the standards devised for the purpose. Von Luschan's is the best, but if not obtainable, use any available standard. If possible, before publication, standardize with Broca's or Von Luschan's scale or else publish the scale used. Skin color is to be taken on an unexposed and an exposed portion of the skin. The under side of the upper arm, which is not usually exposed, is a good place to record skin color unexposed to light and wind. If this part has been exposed, the chest will serve. The cheek is usually studied for the effects of light and wind in pigment. Both are important. Record by number. Hold the scale against the part of the skin being studied and find the closest match. An absolute match will not be found in many cases, but one sufficiently close to indicate the degree of pigmentation will suffice.

B. Hair color. The choice of descriptive terms gives black, dark brown, reddish brown, light brown, blond, golden, red. Red hair should be further qualified as light, brick or auburn. When one is studying Caucasians of lighter tints it is very desirable to make up standards of real hair, giving samples of the most outstanding shades of the range. Whenever possible, a small sample of the hair should be collected. These can be used as a check upon the field observations.

C. Hair form. Hair form is one of the most important characters. . . . Straight hair is easy to recognize, but in this day and age even in the most out-of-the-way places one must look for artificial waves. The natural hair form is of course to be recorded. Following straight hair three degrees of waviness are recognized. While they are described in terms of depth only as low, medium, or deep waves, the degree is really determined by the depth in relation to the width of the wave. The width of a wave is the distance from the apex of one wave to the apex of another wave. The depth is the distance from a line tangent to these two points to the greatest dip between the two waves. When the depth is from 1/12 to 1/10 of the width the hair is described as low waved. When the depth fluctuates above or below 1/6 of the width, it is described as a medium or moderate wave. When the depth fluctuates above and below one-half of the width it is described as deeply waved. The next class, curly, is most often abused. Medium and deep waves are often described as curly. Real curly hair is rare. When long, curls are easily recognized of course. We are all familiar with the artificial curls of childhood. In races characterized by curly hair the same long spiral curls from two to three centimeters in diameter are found. But when the hair is cut it is more difficult to recognize curly hair. Tousled, or unkempt, wavy hair is often described as curly. But curly hair does not form waves. It is always tousled in appearance when short. Each hair, even when cut quite short, forms a more or less complete circle or a large spiral. Before a hair can be called curly it should form at least three-fourths or more of a circle. On the other hand it is not to be mistaken for the matted woolly hair of Negroes. It is easily distinguished from this by the diameter of the curl or spiral

Fig. 9. A Standard to aid in describing the Form of the Hair. It is a modification of Martin's (*Lehrbuch der Anthropologie*). a = straight; b = low waves; c = medium wave; d = deep wave; e and f = curly; g = frizzly; h and i = woolly; j = coiled or spiral tufts.

which fluctuates around 2 centimeters near the head and dwindles gradually as the spiral continues. Curly hair does not form such a close, low mat, as does the woolly hair of Negroes. Frizzly hair is hair with a very short deep wave, but it does not form a curl or a spiral. It is distinguished by the small dimensions of the wave. A low wave is frequently about 5 centimeters wide and about .5 centimeter deep; a medium wave is about 3.5 or 4 centimeters wide and 6 or 7 millimeters deep; a deep wave is about 2.5 centimeters wide and about 12 millimeters deep, but frizzly hair has a wave only about 5 millimeters wide, and about the same depth or slightly less. It looks very much like Negro hair which has been treated with "anti-kink." Woolly hair is the familiar Negro hair consisting of more or less closely coiled spirals linked together forming a matted mass. In Bushmen and some other Negroid types one frequently sees very closely coiled hair grouped together in *tufts* which are more or less isolated from each other. The scalp is clearly visible between the tufts. Now, while mention is made of these classes, it is to be clearly understood that these forms do not exist as distinct types. The measures given are only approximate and arbitrary standards of judgment. In the field one will encounter a complete gradation from the stiff straight hair of the Mongol to the tufted or spiral hair of the Bushmen. These artificial standards are given as an aid to description. Match the hair as nearly as possible with the standards given. If it is impossible to say whether it is low waved or medium waved, etc., mark it intermediate between the two or in some way indicate your doubt. It should be possible, however, to allocate a large proportion of the individuals encountered to one class or another. Study these standards until they are firmly fixed in the mind. Keep them constantly with you in the field since one easily loses his perspective in a new racial environment.

D. Eye color. Eyes range in color from the unpigmented albino to the very dark brown eyes of the heavily pigmented Negro races. These very dark brown eyes are often described as black. Describe the eye color as nearly as possible with the following terms: black, dark brown, medium brown, light brown, gray, green, blue-brown, gray-brown, dark blue, light blue. Gray is used not for a very light blue, but for a very light-brown eye. Such gray eyes are frequently described as blue in Jews and Slavs. Green eyes are also a very light brown. Blue-brown and gray-brown are mixed eyes in which the brown pigment is scattered throughout the iris in patches, rings, or rays. The background of the iris is either blue or gray in such instances. Eye color varies from time to time in different states of health, temper, and age. In the aged of very heavily pigmented races the eyes are frequently a light or medium brown due to a thickening of the covering. If working on Caucasians, it is best to make up a standard series of glass eyes to aid in description.

E. The Epicanthic or Mongoloid fold. This is a very important character, but unless the structure of this fold is thoroughly understood it is impossible to note its presence or absence accurately. In Fig.

10 the details of a European and of a Japanese eye are given. The canthus is the corner of the eye opening. There is an inner canthus and an outer canthus. Occasionally in Whites, sometimes in Negroes, and very often in the Mongoloid peoples a fold of skin covers the inner canthus; hence, it is called an epicanthic fold and because of its frequency in the Mongols it is sometimes spoken of as a Mongoloid fold. Further, it should be clearly understood that this fold is not the upper lid overlapping the lower, but a fold of skin arising three or four millimeters above the free edge which bears the eyelashes. In extreme cases this fold may sag down over the upper lid and conceal it completely. Often when it is attached far down on the nasal bridge it also tends to draw up the skin below in such a way that the lower lid is partly concealed. A careful study of Fig. 10 will make clear just what the difference is between eyes having this fold and eyes which do not have it. . . .

This fold often makes eyes appear oblique or slant. But all obliquely placed or slant eyes do not have this fold. Each eye must be studied in detail. It frequently happens that the fold appears on one eye and not on the other. A very high percentage of Mongols do not have this fold even though their eye-slits may be narrow and obliquely placed. It is found in Negroes and Whites to some extent. Look for it in all races.

F. Thickness of lips. Describe as thin, medium, thick, and very thick. . . .

G. Shovel-shaped incisor teeth. The upper incisor (front) teeth of some Mongoloid and other peoples have a depression or fossa on the inner surface which is surrounded by a rim or ridge of enamel. This looks not unlike a coal shovel and has been described as shovel-shaped by Hrdlicka. In the field it is best described in terms of rim development. . . . It is possible to observe this character by having the patient open the mouth and hold the head back. A dental mirror . . . helps in observing this character without contorting the subject.

H. Amount of beard. The development of the beard is an important character in males. It is usually described as absent, scant, medium, or marked. By absent is meant that nothing is found but the soft downy hair common to women and children, scant is used when the well-developed hairs are decidedly scattering in distribution, and could easily be counted. Heavy is applied to well-developed dense beards such as occur in some of the darker Caucasians and other peoples. Medium is applied to the intermediate density. In recording do not be deceived by length, which depends on shaving or trimming. Consider only the density of distribution. The density varies in different parts of the cheek

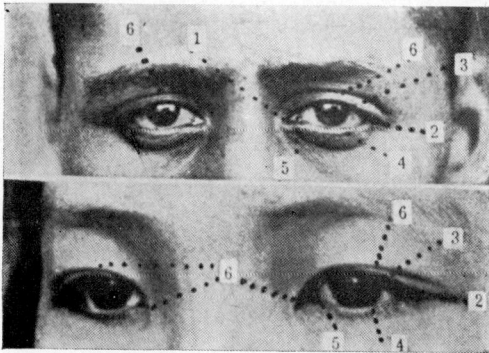

Fig. 10. A Caucasoid Eye compared with a Japanese Eye to show the Structure of the Epicanthic or Mongoloid Eyefold. 1 = inner canthus; 2 = outer canthus; 3 = free upper lid with lashes; 4 = free lower lid with lashes; 5 = caruncula lacrimalis; 6 = the fold in the skin which in the Japanese type below sweeps down and covers the inner canthus (1) and the caruncula lachrymalis (5). This fold (6) is the characteristic to be described. Note especially that the free upper lid (3) plays no part in forming the epicanthic fold but is often itself covered by the fold (6).

and chin so its degree of development should be recorded separately for the upper cheek (from the hair to a point opposite the angle of the lower jaw), the lower cheek (from the above to a point below the corner of the mouth), and the chin. Describe as absent, scant, medium, heavy. . . .

I. Body hair. Describe as above: absent, scant, medium, heavy. Observe the chest, forearm, and leg separately. It is best to restrict this to male subjects also.

11. THE TYPE OF THE HALF-BREED INDIAN [4]

BY FRANZ BOAS

THERE are few countries in which the effects of intermixture of races and of change of environment upon the physical characteristics of man can be studied as advantageously as in America, where a process of slow amalgamation between three distinct races is taking place. Migration and intermarriage have been a fruitful source of intermixture in the Old World, and have had the effect of effacing strong contrasts in adjoining countries. While the contrasts between European, Negro, and Mongol are striking, their territories are connected by broad stretches of land which are occupied by intermediate types. For this reason there are only few places in the Old World in which the component elements of a mixed race can be traced to their sources by historical methods. In America, on the other hand, we have a native race which, although far from being uniform in itself, offers a marked contrast to all other races. Its affiliations are closest toward the races of Eastern Asia, remotest to the European and Negro races. Extensive intermixture with these foreign races has commenced in recent times. Furthermore, the European and African have been transferred to new surroundings on this continent, and have produced a numerous hybrid race, the history of which can also be traced with considerable accuracy. We find, therefore, two races in new surroundings and three hybrid races which offer a promising subject for investigation: the Indian-white, the Indian-negro, and the negro-white. The following study is devoted to a comparison of the Indian race with the Indian-white hybrid race.

It is generally supposed that hybrid races show a decrease in fertility and are therefore not likely to survive. This view is not borne out by statistics of the number of children of Indian women and of half-blood

[4] From Franz Boas, "The Half-Blood Indian: An Anthropometric Study," *Popular Science Monthly*, pages 761-770, October, 1894.

women. The average number of children of five hundred and seventy-seven Indian women and of one hundred and forty-one half-blood women more than forty years old is 5.9 children for the former and 7.9 children for the latter. It is instructive to compare the number of children for each woman in the two groups. While about 10 per cent. of the Indian women have no children, only 3.5 per cent. of the half-bloods are childless. The proportionate number of half-bloods who have one, two, three, four, or five children is smaller than the corresponding number of Indian women, while many more half-blood women than full-blood women have had from six to thirteen children. This distribution is shown clearly in Fig. 1, which represents how many among each

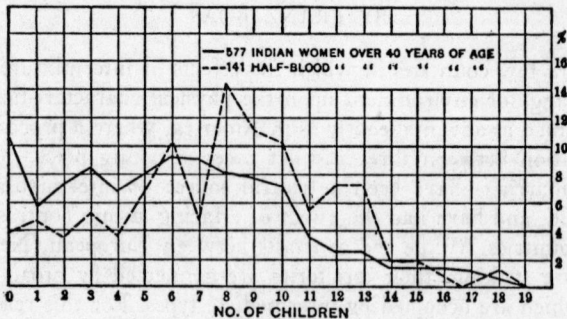

Fig. 1. Number of Children of Indian Women and of Half-blood Women.

one hundred women have a certain number of children. The facts disclosed by this tabulation show that the mixed race is more fertile than the pure stock. This can not be explained by a difference of social environment, as both groups live practically under the same conditions. It also appears that the small increase of the Indian population is almost entirely due to a high infant mortality, as under better hygienic surroundings an average of nearly six children would result in a rapid increase. It is true, however, that a decrease of infant mortality might result in a decreased birth rate.

Among the Indians of the Pacific coast the infant mortality is also very great, but we find at the same time a still larger proportion of women who bear no children.

It is of some interest to note the average number of children of women of different ages as indicating the growth of families. Among the Indians there is an average interval of four years and a half—as shown in the following table—which, however, must not be confounded with an average interval between births:

Indian women 20 years of age have on the average 1 child.
Indian women 25 years of age have on the average 2 children.
Indian women 28 years of age have on the average 3 children.
Indian women 33 years of age have on the average 4 children.
Indian women 38 years of age have on the average 5 children.

Among the half-bloods the interval is shorter, but the number of available observations is insufficient for carrying out the comparison in detail.

The statures of Indians and half-bloods show differences which are also in favor of the half-bloods. The latter are almost invariably taller than the former, the difference being more pronounced among men than among women. The white parents of the mixed race are mostly of French extraction, and their statures are on an average shorter than those of the Indians. We find, therefore, the rather unexpected result that the offspring exceed both parental forms in size. This curious phenomenon shows that size is not inherited in such a manner that the size of the descendant is intermediate between those of the parents, but that size is inherited according to more intricate laws.

From investigations carried on among whites we know that stature increases under more favorable surroundings. As there is no appreciable difference between the social or geographical surroundings of the Indians and of the half-bloods, it seems to follow that the intermixture has a favorable effect upon the race.

The difference in favor of the half-blood is a most persistent phenomenon, as may be seen by a glance at the following table:

DIFFERENCES OF AVERAGE STATURES OF INDIANS AND HALF-BLOODS

Tribes	Men, centimeters	Women, centimeters
Eastern Ojibwa	— 0.1	0.0
Omaha	0.0	— 0.7
Blackfeet	0.1	...
Micmac	0.6	— 0.2
Sioux	1.0	0.9
Delaware	1.6	0.4
Ottawa	1.7	0.4
Cree	2.0	2.8
Eastern Cherokee	3.2	...
Western Ojibwa	3.2	0.7
Chickasaw	4.5	...
Choctaw	7.0	...
Tribes of medium stature (165 to 169 centimeters)	3.3	2.5
Shortest tribes (less than 165 centimeters)	8.3	14.8

The last two entries in this table embrace mainly the Indians of the Southwest and of the Pacific coast.

The facts which appear so clearly in the preceding table may be brought out in a different manner by grouping all the Indian tribes

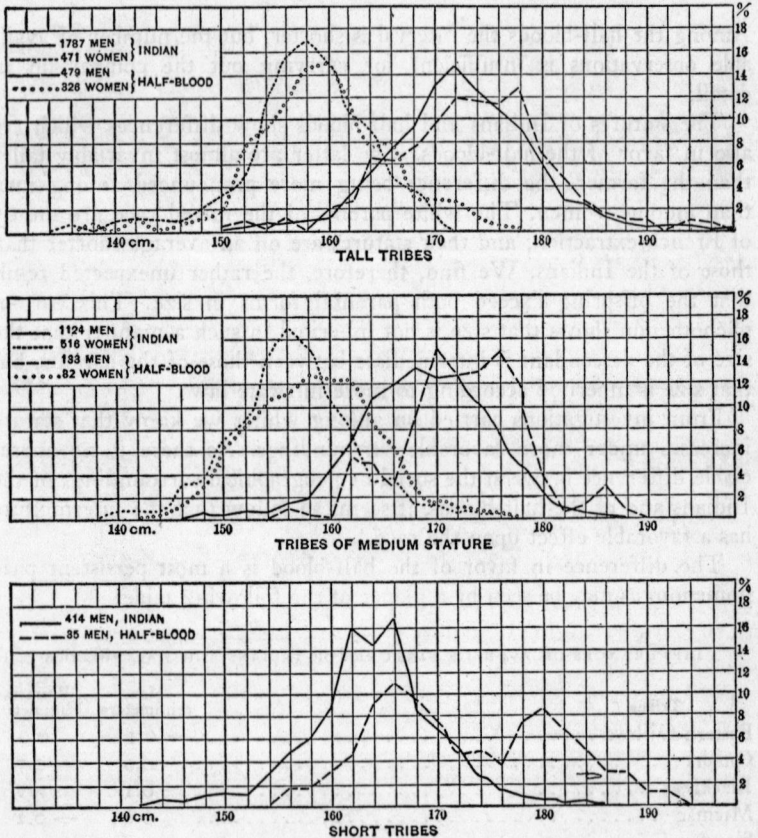

Fig. 2. Statures of Indians and of Half-bloods.

according to their statures in three classes: those measuring more than 169 centimeters, or tall tribes; those measuring from 165 to 169 centimeters, or tribes of medium stature; and those measuring less than 165 centimeters, or short tribes. The frequencies of various statures in each of these classes have been plotted in Fig. 2. The horizontal line represents the individual statures from the lowest to the highest. The vertical distance of the curves from any point of the horizontal line shows how many among each one hundred individuals have the stature represented by that particular point. Thus it will be seen that 14.4 per cent. of the full-blood men of the tallest class have a stature of 172 centimeters, while only 12.3 per cent. of the half-blood of the same class have the most frequent stature, belonging to them—namely, 178 centimeters. Among the Indian women of the full-blood tribes 16.8 per cent. have a stature of 158 centimeters, while only 14.4 per cent. of the half-bloods have their most frequent stature—namely, 160 centimeters.

This tabulation brings out the peculiarity that the statures of the half-bloods are throughout higher than those of the full-bloods; and that, at the same time, the most frequent statures are more frequent among the pure race than in the mixed race. This is expressed by the

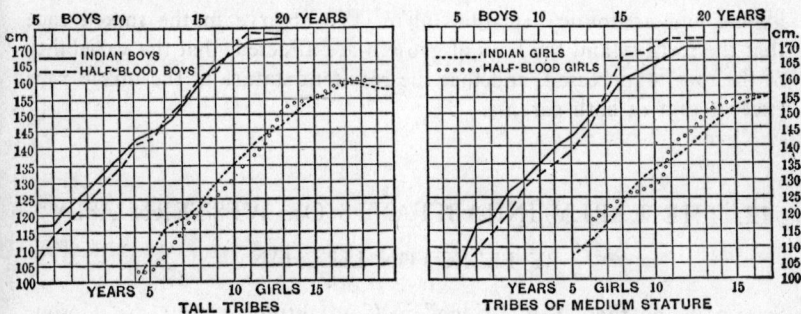

Fig. 3. Growth of Indian and Half-blood Children.

fact that the curves illustrating the distribution of statures among the half-bloods are flatter than those illustrating the same feature among full-bloods. This peculiarity may be noticed in all the curves of Fig. 2, with the exception of that of the men of the second group.

The statures near the average of each group are most frequent, and as these values do not occur as often among the half-bloods as among the full-bloods, the values which are remote from the average are at the same time relatively more frequent. Thus it becomes apparent that the mixed race is less homogeneous than the Indian race.

Another important phenomenon is revealed by a comparison of the growth of Indians and half-bloods (Fig. 3). When the average statures of children of both races are compared, it appears that during the early years of childhood the Indian is taller than the half-blood, and that this relation is reversed later on. This is found in both the groups for tall tribes and for tribes of medium stature. It is to be regretted that this comparison cannot be carried on for whites also. The social surroundings of the white child are, however, so entirely different from those of the Indian and of the half-blood children that no satisfactory conclusions can be drawn from a comparison. It is difficult to see why the laws of growth of the Indian and half-blood should differ in this manner; why the Indian child at the age of three years should be taller than the half-blood child, and then develop more slowly than the latter. This peculiarity is most striking in the growth of the tribes of medium stature, as in this case the difference in the statures of adults is so considerable. Unfortunately we do not know if the same difference prevails at the time of birth; but even if this were the case the difference in the rate of growth would remain mysterious. The various phenomena described here merely emphasize the fact that the effect of intermixture is a most complicated one, and that it acts upon physiological and anatomical qualities alike. We observe in the mixed race that the fertility and the laws of growth are affected, that the variability of the race is increased, and that the resultant stature of the mixed race exceeds that of both parents.

12. THE EARLY INHABITANTS OF WESTERN ASIA [5]

BY FELIX VON LUSCHAN

STANDING on the "New Bridge" in Constantinople, near the Mosque of the Sultan Validé, I have more than once tried to count the languages and dialects spoken by the crowds pressing and pushing between Galata and Stamboul. Turkish and Greek are naturally the most frequently spoken, but one also easily distinguishes much Armenian, Arabic, Kurdish, and Persian. We hear the harsh voices of some Circassian soldiers, and learn from an Abkhasian friend that he does not understand their language and that "it might be" Lesghian. He also tells us that many of his Circassian friends serving in the same regiment are obliged to speak Turkish when they want to understand one another.

We then meet Albanians, Bulgarians, Roumanians, and are addressed in Serbo-Croatian by an old priest from Bosnia. You are sure to hear in less than five minutes five other modern European languages, English, French, German, Italian, and Russian, and then

[5] From Felix von Luschan, "The Early Inhabitants of Western Asia," the Huxley Memorial Lecture for 1911, published in *Journal of the [Royal] Anthropological Institute [of Great Britain and Ireland]*, Volume 41, 1911, republished in *Smithsonian Report for 1914*, pages 553-577, 1915.

your ear is delighted by the melodious Spanish of some Spaniole Jews from Salonika, who still retain the idiom spoken in Spain when they were expelled from there more than 400 years ago, and have thus actually preserved the language spoken by Cervantes. And we hear other Jews on their pilgrimage from Russia and Poland to Jerusalem, speaking their curious Yiddish, a sort of German that no German could understand without making it a special study. Once on this bridge, I had to play the interpreter between a Hungarian Gypsy and some Aptals or other Gypsies from Anatolia, and an instant later I saw a Dinka eunuch sitting on the motor car of an imperial princess and making his selam to a group of equally dark and equally tall Bari or Shilluk. . . .

Another day, on the same bridge, I met some East Indians, speaking, as they told me, Hindi, Hindustani, and Gujerati, and trying in vain to come to an understanding with a large troup of African hajjis returning from Mecca, some of whom were Hausa, others from Zanzibar and the Swahîli coast, others from Wadai and Baghirmi. One may also meet on this bridge Mohammedans from China and from Indonesia, and, to complete this Babylonian confusion of languages, some day or other even a Papuan from Doreh or some other place in Dutch New Guinea may appear there on his hajj to Mecca.

Not less numerous than the languages are the types one meets in Constantinople or in any other of the larger towns in western Asia, and even within a linguistic group there is generally a most striking diversity of somatic qualities. There are Turks with fair and Turks with dark skin; Greeks with short and Greeks with long heads; Arabs with broad and low noses; and other Arabs with narrow and high noses; Kurds with blue and Kurds with black eyes; and the more one studies the ethnography of the Ottoman Empire the more one sees that "Turks" in reality means nothing else than Mohammedan subjects of the Padishah, that "Greeks" means people belonging to the Orthodox church, and that "Arabs" are people speaking Arabic—the somatic difference between a Bedouin from Arabia or Mesopotamia and an "Arab" farmer from near Beyrout is striking, and they have nothing in common except their language.

Also the study of the modern religions in western Asia is of no help to us in this labyrinth of types. There are Greeks who look like Mohammedans, and many Ansarîyeh or other ("Moslem") sectaries are not to be distinguished from Armenians. Religion, too, is here much more closely connected with late historical events than with races or nations, and is only too often of a merely accidental character.

Even the old historians do not help us. Their anthropological interests were generally trifling, and important statements like the note that the Armenians *"πολλὰ φρυγίζουσιν τῇ φωνῇ,"* [6] or that a tribe from the Solymian Mountains spoke Phœnician, are extremely rare in the old writers, who give us names like Lycians, Carians, Cilicians, Paphlagonians, Cappadocians, Lydians, and so on, but, generally, do not give us the slightest details as to their place in an anthropological system.

So we can well understand how, 50 years ago, G. Rosen, then perhaps the best authority on the nations of Asia Minor and Syria, could say that the anthropology of Western Asia would "always remain a mystery."

Since then minute anthropometric researches and vast excavations have both thrown light on most of the problems connected with this "mystery," so that it may now be considered as practically solved.

My own way of proceeding was to eliminate one by one every national or racial element that could be traced as having come from outside, and then to study the remainder. It was my good fortune to begin archæological and anthropometric field work in Lycia as early as 1881, and since that time I have never ceased to collect all available data connected with the natural history of man in western Asia. So it is the work of thirty years of which I shall now try to give a short account, and this will be done best by beginning with the ostensible foreign elements and then describing the remaining tribes and groups.

A. DARK AFRICANS

These are naturally by far the easiest to eliminate, and they have only in a very insignificant way contributed to the building up of the white communities in Asia Minor and in Syria, although they have been imported there from the earliest historical times down to our own days. Even now there are few houses of wealthy Mohammedans without dark servants, male or female, and without half-caste children of the most various tints. Nowhere, perhaps, with the exception only of Brazil, could miscegenation be better studied than in the large towns of the Levant. Domestic slavery is still flourishing there, and "black ivory" generally comes, as in the old times, from the Upper Nile, but also from Bornu. In the Turkish-speaking south of Asia Minor a dark African is generally called "Arab," in Syria, "Maghrebi" or "Habeshi." As far as I know, social inferiority is never connected with color; half-castes frequently intermarry with whites, but still there is no real negro permeation of the other natives, probably because that section of the offspring which reverts to negro qualities does not stand the climate.

[6] Speak much like the Phrygians.

B. CIRCASSIANS

About a million of the Mohammedan inhabitants of the Caucasus immigrated into Asia Minor and Syria after the fall of Shamyl. The lot of these muhajir (refugees) was generally a melancholy one; the Ottoman Government did its best to give them land, but land without a master is rare also in Turkey, and in many places the result was a fight of all against all or a state of regular brigandage, often resulting in the final extinction of the Circassians. Where the land given to them was really masterless, it lay in unhealthy swamps and marshes, where malaria raged and carried them off at a terrible rate year by year. I know a place near Islahiyeh where more than 1,000 Circassian families were settled about 1880; now only seven of them remain, and these in a wretched state of fever and disease. Only a very few of these Circassian colonies are really thriving, and probably most of these glorious sons of snowy mountains will in a few generations have paid with their lives for their fidelity to Islam.

Till now the Circassian blood has not seriously influenced that of their Turkish neighbors and probably never will. The colonists very seldom give their daughters to Turks or Arabs, and the "soft Circassian beauties" play a larger part in fiction than in actuality.

F. FRANKS AND LEVANTINES [7]

Frenghi (Franconians or Franks) is the common name for the European Christians (and also for syphilis) all over the nearer Orient, and the descendants of European, generally French and Italian, and therefore Roman Catholic, families are called Levantines. They take only a minimum share in the building up of the oriental populations. In Marmaritza near Halikarnassos, where a British squadron had a winter station for many years, a very great proportion of the children are said to be flaxen-haired, and at Kynyk, the ancient Xanthos in Lycia, I met in 1881 a Mohammedan, quite fair, with light blue eyes, of rare intelligence, and with nearly a fanatical interest in geographical and archæological problems. He was born in 1841, a year after the second expedition of Sir Charles Fellows, at Xanthos. Near Sendjirli I know an Armenian woman who is very fair; her own people pretend that she is the daughter of an American. But all these are rare exceptions,

[7] The accounts of the following nationalities have been omitted in the present extract: C, Albanians; D, Bulgarians; E, Bosnians; I, Turkomans; J, Yuruks; K, Kurds; L, Tahtadji; M, Bektash; N, Ansariyeh; O, Kyzylbash; P, Druses; Q, Maronites; R, Persians; S, Arabs.

of no general importance, and I feel sure that the modern admixture of European blood is in no way responsible for the great number of light-colored people also in the interior of Asia Minor and Syria.

That in Oriental towns with very hot summers the death rate of light-colored children in Frankish and Levantine families is essentially larger than that of dark-colored has been often asserted, and would naturally be of universal anthropological interest if proved by serious statistics. Personally I do not know of one single light-colored Levantine family in places infected with heavy malaria.

G. JEWS

As the oriental Jews practically never mix with the other orientals, and so do not contribute in any way to the physical qualities of their oriental neighbors, they would be of no interest for this paper if we could not trace them back to very early times. But their racial position can only be investigated in connection with the old and oldest anthropology of Syria and Palestine. So for the moment we must here confine ourselves to the statement that there are several very distinct groups of oriental Jews.

By far the most numerous are now the Sephardim, speaking an early Spanish dialect, and descended chiefly from Jews expelled from Spain by the narrow-minded fanaticism of the fifteenth century. They have contributed not a little to the intellectual and economic development of the Ottoman Empire.

Of far less importance are the Ashkenazim, speaking "Yiddish," and descended from Jews emigrated from eastern Europe. The difference between these two groups was originally merely geographical and accidental, but now they are holding themselves rigidly apart, and I know of a small Ashkenazic community in southwestern Asia Minor that abstains from meat rather than eat of an animal killed by a Sephardic butcher. I could not learn if there were also differences in creed, but practically these two groups are like different sects, and in most places there is less intercourse between them than there is between Protestants and Catholics in the most backward villages of Central Europe. This is perhaps of some importance in connection with the fact that both Ashkenazim and Sephardim are equally distinguished by a complete absence of uniform racial characteristics, just as it is with our Jewish friends in Europe.

The "enlightened public" of course knows better. Some Jews themselves state that they are "pure Semites, chosen and selected," and even in modern scientific papers one may still read of the complete "uniformity" of the Jewish type. But this uniformity only exists in the books and not in reality. There are Jews with light and with dark eyes, Jews with straight and with curly hair, Jews with high and narrow, and Jews with short and broad noses; their cephalic index oscillates between 65 and 98—as far as this index ever oscillates in the genus homo. Indeed, since my paper on the anthropological position of the Jews there is, as far as I know, no serious anthropologist who still maintains the cranial uniformity of the Jews. It is also conceded that the great majority of the Jews is decidedly brachycephalic, whilst the typical Semites are essentially dolichocephalic. But even giving up the cranial uniformity, one still speaks of the marvelous tenacity, frequency, and distinctiveness of the Jewish type of face. Now this "Jewishness" is much more easily felt than defined, and Joseph Jacobs (1885) was the first to try an exact definition. It is a certain and typical development of the nostrils (Jacobs's "nostrility") that is the best characteristic of what we generally call "Jewish."

Weissenberg, wanting to prove a specific Jewishness of type, relates how he showed some hundred photographs of Russians and Russian Jews without distinguishing or peculiar dress, etc., to two friends, a Russian and a Jew; the first was correct in 50 per cent., the second in 70 per cent. of his statements. I do not think this experiment very convincing; Weissenberg should have shown his friends photos of Greeks, Armenians, and Persians. The number of correct identifications would then have been certainly very much smaller, and it would have become evident that what Weissenberg takes to be "Jewishness" is nothing more than oriental, pure and simple. I shall refer to this statement toward the end of this paper, and meanwhile only want to advert to Fig. 2, showing in the thick line the cephalic indices of 1,222 Jews; 52 per cent. of these were Sephardim, whom I measured at Smyrna, at Constantinople, at Makri, and in Rhodes; the rest were Ashkenazim measured by myself when I was one of the medical assistants in the Allgemeine Krankenhaus at Vienna, Austria.

Besides these two large groups there are other Jews in Turkey and in Egypt, who have been there since the early times of the Diaspora and longer. But they are few in number and I had no opportunity to measure any of them.

H. GYPSIES

A small but highly interesting group is formed by the Gypsies and their kin. About 30,000 of them are said to infect Turkey with their disorder and inclination for theft and larceny. On the other side, they are cheerful company, men and women, not seldom with a certain beauty. They make baskets and sieves; the men are mostly blacksmiths and shrewd horsedealers. They are never settled in houses, but wander with their goat-hair tents, in winter time on the plains, in summer high up in the mountains. I once met a small "village" of about ten Gypsy tents as high up as 8,000 feet. Unhappily, nothing is known about their early migrations and history; they speak Turkish in Asia Minor, Arabic in Syria, and keep secret their own language with so much care that my various and repeated efforts to get at least a few phrases turned out a complete failure.

In northern Syria I met a kind of Gypsies calling themselves "Aptal"; they lay a certain stress upon their *not* being Gypsies, but I could find no real difference either in their somatic qualities or in their ethnographic or social standing. Some of them often wander about like dervishes in groups of four or five, and with a large red or green banner; others are jugglers and conjurers and play tricks with serpents.

Gypsies never, or hardly ever, mix with other tribes in Syria or Asia Minor. They naturally pretend to be Mohammedans and have Islamic names, but they are always treated with a certain contempt or disesteem. Mohammedans hardly ever curse; but one of their rare abusive phrases is *tchingene* = gypsy.

T. TURKS

It is customary in most European languages to call the Mohammedan subjects of the Padishah "Turks." But the word should never be used in this sense without inverted commas; it is more than ambiguous and easily leads to serious misunderstandings.

A Turkoman tribe, the Othmanli, commenced from 1289 to conquer a great part of what is now the Ottoman Empire. A good many of the former inhabitants were then forced to speak Turkish and to turn Mohammedans. It is easy to understand that the descendants of the conquerors and of the conquered renegades intermarried freely, and, as the number of the conquering troops was naturally very much smaller than that of the original population, the great bulk of the ten or fifteen, or perhaps more, millions of so-called "Turks" has now the physical qualities, not of the conquering Othmanli, but of the old pre-Othmanic inhabitants.

So the anthropology of Turkey is, like that of Hungary, a typical example showing how language, religion, nationality, and race are quite distinct conceptions, and it is interesting to see how they are again and again confounded by the general public and by the press.

In my paper on the Tahtadji I gave the indices of 187 "Turks" (Turkish-speaking Mohammedans) from Lycia, and was able to show that in the mountain villages, and in some swampy marshes not easy of access, people were generally short headed, and in the towns and on the coast long headed. Since then I have measured 569 more "Turks" from southern Asia Minor and northern Syria, so that I can now publish the cephalic indices of 756 adult men; they run from 69 to 96; if we count the indices 77 to 81 as mesaticephalic, 172 of these 756 men would be dolichocephalic, 151 mesaticephalic, and 433 brachycephalic, with a very pronounced maximum of 77 and 83 men respectively at indices 85 and 86.

These numbers speak for themselves, but it is perhaps useful to study first the corresponding figures for the two large remaining groups, the Greeks and the Armenians, and then to compare the results.

U. GREEKS

What has been said of the "Turks" is valid too in absolutely the same way for the "Greeks" of Anatolia and Syria. Some of them are certainly the direct descendants of old Ionians, Dorians, or Æolians, but the greater part are descended from other groups which spoke Greek and had accepted the orthodox religion.

I must here pass over the interesting problem of the Dorian and Ionian wandering and must restrict myself to some measurements taken on a series of 179 adult men calling themselves Greek and belonging to the orthodox church. I published this series in 1890, in my paper on the Tahtadji, and reprint here a graphic table (Fig. 1) showing the frequency of the cephalic indices. It is very striking to see how the curve shows a maximum of 22 men with an index of 75, and a second maximum of 18 men with an index of 88.

Seventy-nine out of the 179 men are dolicho-, 84 are brachy-, and only 16 are mesaticephalic. If we reckon the arithmetic mean for the whole series, we get an average index of about 80, closely conforming to Weisbach's 95 skulls of Asiatic and European Greeks with an average index of 81.2, and with the series of Klon Stephanos, who found 80.8 for the Greeks in Europe and 80.7 for the Asiatic Greeks.

It is easily understood how dangerous and mystifying such an average index may be, if the material is composed of individuals from at least two different groups, as it manifestly is.

I am in possession of 93 skulls from a modern Greek cemetery in Adalia; they show about the same distribution of indices.

Long before the rediscovery of Mendel and his laws I tried to study the heredity of the cephalic index in the Greek families of Adalia. Here, in the old capital of Pamphylia, there is a large Greek colony, and as I had by good chance been able to give medical help to some of the influential members, I was permitted to measure parents, children and other relations in 67 families. The results were striking. I published a short abstract of them in 1889, in the Reisen in Lykien, and in 1890 in my paper on the Tahtadji.

There was a family A; the father had an index of 87, the mother of 73; of the two sons, the elder had an index of 70, the younger 87.

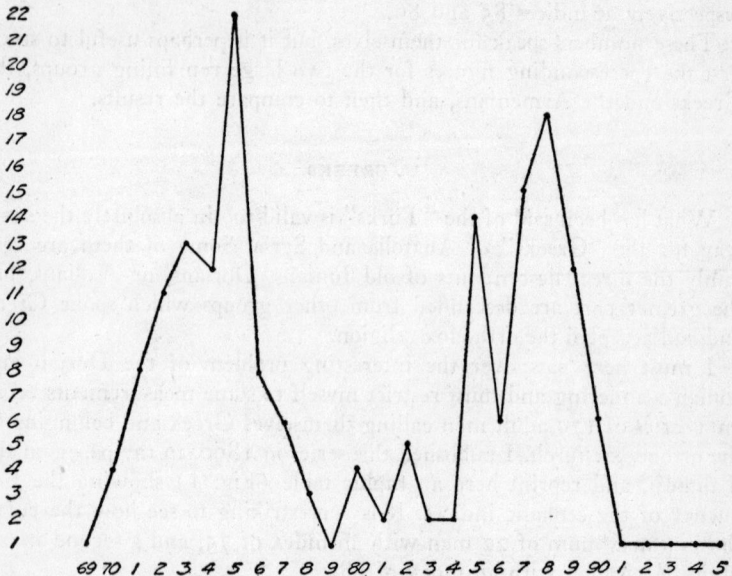

Fig. 1. Frequency of cephalic indices in a series of 179 adult male Greeks.

In another family, B, the brother of the dead father had an index of 70, the mother 86, a son 82, a daughter 75. In a third family, C, both parents were brachycephalic, with indices of 85 and 86. Of their five children, only the youngest daughter was short headed, with an index of 86, and four elder brothers had long heads with 72, 73, 75, and 73, respectively; 74 was the index of a brother of the mother.

If I now study these 67 families in the light of Mendelian researches, it seems as if neither brachy- nor dolichocephaly were dominant or recessive; they seem to be transmitted now with equal frequency, and this has probably been the case for more than 2,000 years. At least, that is the age of the Greek colony of Adalia and for sixty or seventy generations short and long headed "Greeks" have been freely inter-

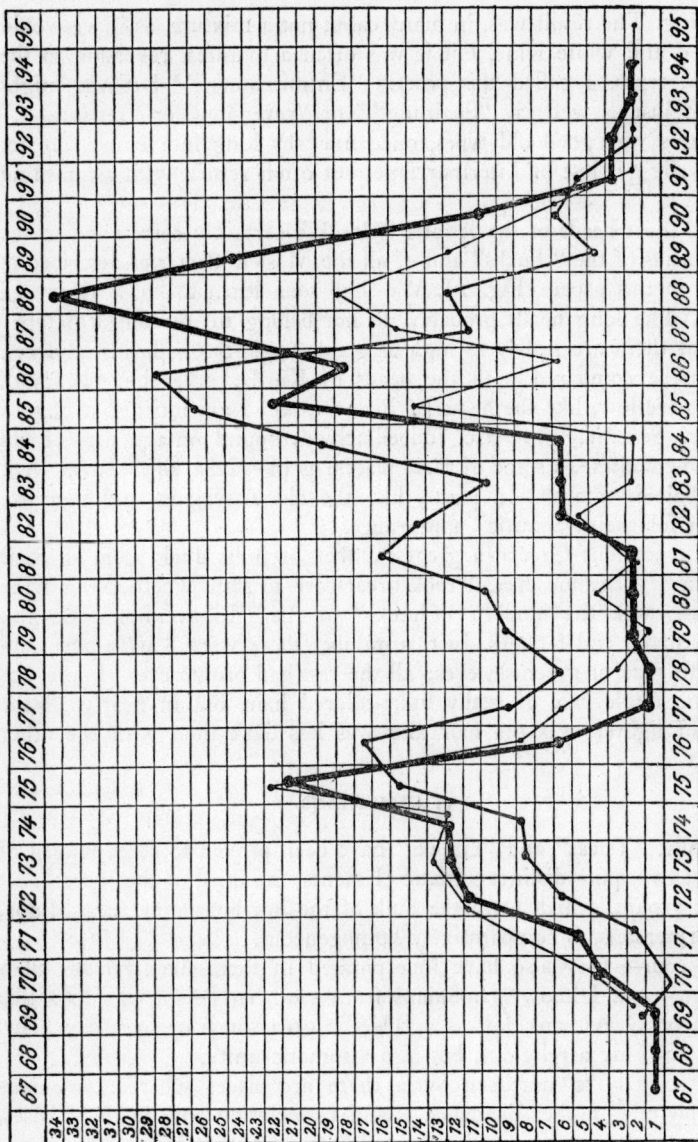

Fig. 2. Frequency of cephalic indices: 179 Greeks (light line); 756 Turks, reduced to one-third (medium line); 1,222 Jews, reduced to one-fifth (heavy line).

marrying. The result was, in many cases, not a mixture, as if we would mix red and white wine, but it was often a manifest reversion to the original types. I called this process "Entmischung," [8] but one might perhaps just as well say "Spaltung" [9] or "reversion" or "restitution."

In this way good old types, once fixed by long inbreeding, do not necessarily get lost by intermarriage, but often return with astonishing energy.

The short heads of the Asiatic "Greeks" certainly correspond to the short heads of the "Turks" and of all the Moslem Sectaries described at length in this paper (Fig. 2). We shall soon learn to know their real origin. The long heads probably do not belong to one uniform type; some of them are nearly as high as good Anglo-Saxon heads, and can perhaps be compared with the heads of Kurds; other long heads of Greeks are low, like the heads of Bedawy, and I am inclined to regard them as Semitic. They are, indeed, chiefly found on the sites of old Semitic colonies. In some of these places, as in Adalia, the women wear their hair in many thin plaits, like the old Assyrians, and they are famous for their "Semitic" appearance.

As in ancient Greece a great number of individuals seem to have been fair, with blue eyes, I took great care to state whether this were the case with the modern "Greeks" in Asia. I have notes for 580 adults, males and females. In this number there were 8 with blue, and 29 with gray or greenish, eyes; all the rest had brown eyes. There was not one single case of really light-colored hair, but in nearly all the cases of lighter eyes the hair also was less dark than with the other Greeks. . . .

V. ARMENIANS

Whilst "Turks" and "Greeks" have been proved to be composed of at least two quite distinct somatic elements, the third of the three great ethnic groups, which form the bulk of the inhabitants of Asia Minor, the Armenians, is comparatively homogeneous.

Of course they also have incorporated in themselves various alien elements, and I know Armenians from southern Persia who look like Biloch or Dravidians, but as a rule the great mass of the Armenians forms not only a religious, but also a somatic unity.

Particularly in northern Syria there are places where Armenians resemble one another like eggs. Religious seclusion and, in many cases, life in remote mountain villages, have both contributed to prevent intermarriage with strangers, and thus we may assume from the beginning that they represent an old type.

[8] "Unmixing."   [9] "Splitting."

More frequently than any other group in western Asia they show the "planoccipital" form of the profile curve, great brachycephaly with extreme height of the skull and a particularly narrow and high nose. . . .

SUMMARY

If we now sum up the results of our researches and try to review them in regard to the origin of the different ethnic groups of western Asia, we need not linger over the Negroes, the Circassians, the Albanians, the Bulgarians, the Bosnians, the Franks, and the Levantines. Their origin lies outside the scope of this paper. The same is true of the Gypsies and their kin, but it must be stated that perhaps one of the nomadic tribes in Asia Minor, the Yuruks, is in some way or other related with them.

Of far greater importance are the Kurds. From the great frequency of fair individuals among them, it is evident that their home must be in the north, and it is probable from their Aryan language that they are in some way connected with the Mitanni, who had Aryan divinities about 1280 B.C.

I am well aware that at present there is no real proof or decisive evidence for this statement, but, by way of a working hypothesis, I might be allowed to suggest that the Kurds, the Amorites of the Bible, the Mitanni of the Boghaz-köi tablets and the Tamehu of the old Egyptian texts are, if not identical, at least somehow related to one another. About 1500 B.C., or earlier, there seems to have begun a migration of northern men to Asia Minor, Syria, Persia, Egypt, and India. Indeed, we can now connect even Farther India with the Mitanni of Central Asia Minor. On the tablets of Boghaz-köi the king of Mitanni not only calls himself and his people "harri," but he speaks of his noblemen as "mari," and Hugo Winckler and F. C. Andreas remind us of the word "marya" for "young man" or "hero" in the Vedic texts. So we find the same Aryan nobles in Mitanni about 1280 B.C., and very much later also in India.

If really, as it seems, the old texts state that the Amorites and the Tamehu were fair, we should thus get a historic explanation of the great number of xanthochroic people we find down to our time everywhere in Asia Minor and in Syria, and among the modern Jews.

Resuming now the thread of this paper, we have a great number of different "Moslem" Sectaries spread over a vast part of western Asia under different names, as Tahtadji, Allevi, Ali-Ullahîya, Ansarîyeh, Fellah, Kyzylbash, Yezidi, and Bektash, speaking the different languages of their orthodox neighbors, Turkish, Arabic, and Kurdish, but still absolutely homogeneous as to their somatic characteristics. And to this self-same group belong also the Druses and the Maronites. They also have the enormously high and short "planoccipital" heads and the narrow and high noses we find with the Sectaries.

Now this same hypsicephalic [10] element with the high aquiline noses, which forms the entire stock of all these Sectaries, we find again in Persia, and in a high percentage among the Turks and the Greeks, and in a still higher among the Armenians—everywhere under circumstances that would make it appear to be old and aboriginal, whilst the dolichocephals seem to represent later immigrations.

This theory, based entirely on anthropometric research, is confirmed by historic considerations and by the results of modern excavations. We now know that about 1280 B.C., when Khattusil made his peace with Rameses II, there existed a large empire, not much smaller than Germany, reaching from the Ægean Sea to Mesopotamia and from Kadesh on the Orontes to the Black Sea. We do not know at present if this Hittite Empire ever had a really homogeneous population, but we have a good many Hittite reliefs, and all these, without one single exception, show us the high and short heads or the characteristic noses of our modern brachycephalic groups.

When I first upheld in 1892, in my paper on the anthropological position of the Jews, the homogeneous character of these groups, I called them "Armenoids." But there can be no doubt that they are all descended from tribes belonging to the great Hittite Empire. So it is the type of the Hittites that has been preserved in all these groups for more than 3,000 years, and this is certainly a Jewish type, and corresponds with the old Jewish ideal of beauty as we read in the Song of Songs, vii, 4: "Thine eyes are as the pools in Heshbon, by the gate of Bath-rabbim, thy nose is like the tower of Lebanon, which looketh toward Damascus."

But this Jewish type is not Semitic and is rarely found among the only real Semites, the Bedawy. The Hittite inscriptions have not yet been read, but our orientalists are unanimous in assuming that there is not the slightest doubt that the Hittite language was not Semitic. These non-Semitic aborigines had their own language, their own writing, and their own religion. Semitic influence is completely absent in the earlier times and is perceptible only later on at different times in the different territories—first in Babylonia, then in Palestine, where Abraham is the eponymous hero of a Semitic invasion, and still later in Northern Syria. . . .

[10] High-headed.

Greek, Levissi.

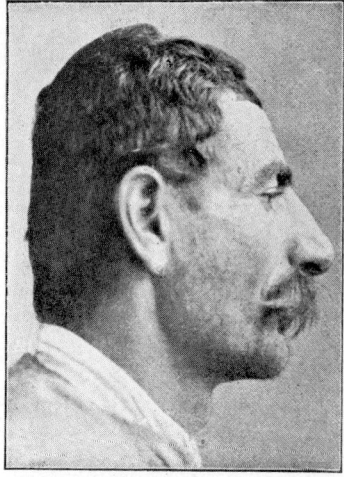

Armenian, Kessab, Djebel Akrah.

Hittite Divinity, Sendjirli, Syria.

For the present population of northern Syria, as well as of all western Asia, our anthropometric tables show evidence that this old type is still extant in a high percentage among the actual inhabitants.

Only as to the primordial home of the Hittites, or however else we may term all these hypsi- and brachycephalic people with the high and narrow nose, is there some difficulty. The "Alpine race" of central Europe is certainly somehow related to or connected with them and a priori it is not easy to determine if the Hittites came from central Europe or if the "Alpine race" came from western Asia. I do not know if the first possibility has many champions left now. If so, they might certainly lay stress on the fact that the modern Armenians and the modern Persians, both typical "Hittites," are now speaking Aryan languages, but we know how often ethnic groups change their language entirely without losing their somatic type, and we can in this special case well imagine that early precursors of the xanthochroic Kurds and their relations may have brought their Aryan language to the Old Armenians and Persians without being able to impress their somatic type upon them.

We should not forget, too, that Europe is only a small peninsular annexe to Asia, and that there are infinitely more typical "Hittites" in western Asia than there are in Europe. It seems surer, therefore, to locate the cradle of the Hittites in Asia, where we find extreme brachycephals as far to the east as Burma and Siam and the Malay Archipelago.

We could then also understand how the essential somatic difference between the Hittites and the other brachycephalic Asiatics—their high and narrow nose—originated as a merely accidental mutation and was then locally fixed, either by a certain tendency of taste and fashion or by long, perhaps millennial, inbreeding. The "Hittite nose" has finally become a *dominant* characteristic in the Mendelian sense, and we see it, not only in the actual geographical province of the Alpine race, but often enough also here in England. Certainly, similar noses may originate everywhere, quite independently of the Hittites, by mere mutation, but it seems safer to explain by atavism and by Asiatic or Alpine origin noses like those of the late Cardinal Newman, Ralph Waldo Emerson, or Charles Kingsley.

So, to sum up, we see how all western Asia was originally inhabited by a homogeneous, melanochroic race, with extreme hypsi-brachycephaly and with a "Hittite" nose. About 4000 B.C. began a Semitic invasion from the southeast, probably from Arabia, by people looking like modern Bedawy. Two thousand years later commenced a second invasion, this time from the northwest, by xanthochroöus and long-headed tribes

like the modern Kurds, half savage, and in some way or other, perhaps, connected with the historic Harri, Amorites, Tamehu, and
Galatians.

The modern "Turks," Greeks, and Jews are, all three, equally
composed of these three elements, the Hittite, the Semitic, and the
xanthochroöus Nordic. Not so the Armenians and the Persians. They,
and still more the Druses, Maronites, and the smaller sectarian groups
of Syria and Asia Minor, represent the old Hittite element, and are
little, or not at all, influenced by the somatic characters of alien invaders.

Combinations of philology with anthropology have in former times,
especially through Friedrich Müller and his school, often led to serious
mistakes. One spoke of Aryan races instead of people with Aryan languages, and one went so far as to speak of Aryan skulls and of Aryan
eyes, so that Max Müller formally protested against the intrusion of
linguistics into ethnology, stating that one might just as well speak of a
brachycephalic grammar as of an Aryan skull.

Still there is a solidarity between the historical sciences and natural
history, and in proof of this solidarity I have ventured—in the spirit
and in honor of Thomas Henry Huxley—to give argument and
evidence.

13. RACE, LANGUAGE AND NATIONALITY
IN EUROPE [11]

BY HUMPHREY J. JOHNSON

OF THE various physical characteristics which mark off the different
branches of mankind from each other the color of the skin is that
which most easily attracts the eye of an observer; hence it was most
natural that the early attempts to classify the races of man should have
been made upon this basis. In the eighteenth century Linnæus assigned
to "Homo Europæus albus" the position of being one of his four
primary divisions of the human species. The name was not strictly
accurate, however, as under it there had to be tabulated the populations of North Africa and Southwestern Asia, which were little if any
darker than the peoples of Southern Europe. In the early nineteenth
century Blumenbach gave to the white-skinned peoples of Europe,
Asia and Africa the name Caucasian, after a skull from Georgia which
he greatly admired. This name has lasted long, and is still in use, but

[11] *The Sociological Review*, Volume 11, pages 37-46, 1919.

since it has to include such peoples as the dark Arabs and the fair Swedes, some further division of the white race was recognized to be a necessity. This step was taken by Huxley, who in 1870 divided into two stocks "fair whites" (xanthochroi) and "dark whites" (melanochroi). The two stocks overlapped in Central Europe, and Celtic-speaking peoples were found belonging to both. Of these two Huxley supposed that the xanthochroi of Northern Europe were the original stock and that the melanochroi of the Mediterranean area were produced by intermixture between the former and a brown race. At this time, however, the problem of devising a satisfactory method of classifying the population of Europe was complicated by that confusion between philological and anthropological terms which has wrought such dire havoc with ethnological nomenclature. Comparative philology had made it clear that with few exceptions all the languages of Europe could be traced back to a single ancestral stock, offshoots of which had also found their way into Persia and India. This family of languages received the names "Aryan," "Indo-European" or "Indo-Germanic," and it began to be readily assumed that there must have existed an Aryan race, a doctrine which still lingers in modern geography books. No one, however, could say whether the early Aryans were dark whites or fair whites. Max Müller ventured to launch the opinion that their original "habitat" had been "somewhere" in Asia, though he later abandoned the hypothesis that an Aryan race had existed. With the exception of Greek and Albanian, the Aryan languages of Europe fall into four groups—Romance, Celtic, Teutonic and Letto-Slavic.

It has of course always been known that the Romance languages owe their present distribution not to the circumstance that they were carried to the lands in which they now prevail by a single race, but to the fact that these lands were once under the influence of a common civilization. Hence, although we meet the expression "Latin race" in newspapers and reviews, we do not encounter it in manuals of ethnology. The origin, growth and distribution of the Celtic, Teutonic and Slavic branches of the Aryan family are, however, shrouded in much obscurity, and this fact has enabled writers to employ these terms now in a linguistic and now in an ethnological sense. The tall fair-haired barbarians who swarmed down from the Alps upon the Italian plains were called by the classical writers Celts, though in the first century before the Christian era, at the time of Cæsar's conquest of Gaul, a distinction between the Celts and the Teutons began to be made. The Slavs do not, however, figure prominently in European history till Byzantine times. The precedent set by the classical writers was followed, and it was customary to regard the Celts as a fair-haired race, till about 1850, when Broca, who was then conducting his anthropo-metrical researches into the composition of the French nation, showed that the Bretons—the only Celtic speaking people on the continent of Europe—had dark hair, from which discovery it followed that a dis-tinction must be made between the use of the word Celtic as a lin-guistic and an anthropological term.

The recognition of this fact has simplified the work of subsequent investigators, and in the two most comprehensive attempts to classify the European peoples which have been made in recent years, those of Ripley and Deniker, "Celtic" does not appear as a racial term. These two investigators, fully alive to the errors into which their predecessors have fallen through failing to distinguish clearly between language and race, have attempted to systematize the European peoples solely by the use of physical criteria. Their results are at first sight strikingly dis-similar, although they have been reached by the use of almost identical material. Professor Ripley recognizes three European races (1) a tall, fair-haired dolichocephalic race, which predominates in the countries bordering upon the Baltic and the North Sea, which he names the Teutonic race; (2) a brachycephalic race of medium height, brown hair and eyes, stretching from Brittany through the highlands of Cen-tral Europe, the plateau of Central France, the Auvergne and Vosges through South Germany, Switzerland, the Austrian Empire and the Balkan states, across the sea of Marmora, through Asia Minor and Armenia to Persia and Afghanistan. This race he names the Alpine; and (3) a short, dark-haired, dark-eyed dolichocephalic race, which is found in the lands lying round both basins of the Mediterranean and which is found in its greatest purity in such isolated areas as the island of Sardinia. The existence of this physical type in the Iberian penin-sula, Italy, Greece and North Africa has been recognized by the Italian craniologist Professor Sergi, who has named it the Mediter-ranean race, a name retained by Ripley. The scheme of classification adopted by Deniker, the late Librarian of the Musée d'Histoire Nat-urelle at Paris, is somewhat more elaborate than Professor Ripley's. This authority postulates the existence of no less than six primary and four secondary races in Europe. It is possible to some extent to equate the two schemes. Thus Deniker has a Nordic and "sub-Nordic" race corresponding to Ripley's Teutonic, a Cévenole or Occidental and a Dinaric or Adriatic corresponding respectively to the Western and Eastern ends of Ripley's Alpine, and two more which correspond to the Mediterranean race.

Can the more elaborate scheme be said to possess any advantages over the simpler one? By the recognition of an Adriatic or Dinaric race the taller portion of the brachycephalic race prevalent throughout Central Europe which occupies Bosnia, Herzegovina, Montenegro and Albania is differentiated from the shorter portion in West and Central Europe. It is impossible, however, to suppose that Deniker's six races and four sub-races ever existed as independent types, rather it appears that they represent local combinations of physical traits. With Ripley's three races, however, the case is somewhat different. It seems that they can put forward some sort of claim to have had an objective existence.

This does not mean that if we take a given area in Northern, Central or Southern Europe we shall find that in any particular area a majority of the inhabitants possess all the characters of the ideal racial type. All we can say is that some of the various characters which go towards making up the racial type are possessed by the majority of the population. For instance, in a given area in Northern Europe 60 per cent. of the population may be tall and 60 per cent. may be blonde, but not more than 20 per cent. need be tall blonde. The pure racial type has dissolved like a lump of sugar in a cup of tea. Ripley accounts for the present population of Europe as follows. In very early times there existed two races of man—a long-headed African race and a broad-headed Asiatic one. In Quaternary times the various migrations of African long-heads invaded Europe by the three routes then open to them; that is, across the land bridges which then connected Spain with Morocco, Tunis with Sicily, and Cyrenaica with Greece.

The palæolithic races of Europe were all long-headed, broad-headed skulls becoming common only in the Azilian or Mesolithic period. We must suppose that the long-headed population of Europe ultimately developed, probably under climatic influences, into two types, one tall and fair in the North, and another short and dark in the South. The population of the Mediterranean basin seems to have remained substantially unchanged since Neolithic times and the present distribution of the Mediterranean race to have been then already achieved. No remains of Pleistocene man have as yet been forthcoming from Ireland, Scotland or Scandinavia, but the basin of the Baltic has been surrounded since Neolithic times by a tall, long-headed population. The round-headed race of Central Europe which has become wedged in between the two long-headed races is regarded by most authorities as an intrusive Asiatic element, though the alternative theory that a mountainous environment induces brachycephaly has been maintained by Professor Ridgeway. On the former theory the existence of the short-headed race of Central Europe is to be accounted for by successive waves of migration from Asia into Europe from Neolithic times onwards. It has its counterpart in the broad-headed element found in the highlands of Asia Minor, Persia and Afghanistan. The Mediterranean type is also represented in Southwestern Asia.

Professor Ripley's hypothesis of the origin of the European peoples appears to fit the facts as well as any other which has been advanced up to the present, and his three types certainly have some claim to the possession of an independent existence. The names which he assigns to them are, however, not entirely above criticism. He calls his northern race the Teutonic. The defect of name is that in popular etymology it includes all peoples who speak Teutonic languages, the English, Scotch, Irish, Flemings, Dutch, the Germans, Danes, Norwegians and Swedes. Now these peoples embrace a very large population which does not correspond physically to his Teutonic type. For instance, the Alpine type predominates in South Germany, German-Austria and German-Switzerland, and Teutonic-speaking people of Mediterranean type are found in England and Ireland, while the physical type which Ripley calls Teutonic is found in the Hebrides, in what were the Baltic provinces of the defunct Russian empire, and in Finland, in which countries Celtic, Slavonic and Finno-Ugrian languages prevail. If we consider these facts it becomes clear that the use of the term word Teutonic, both as a linguistic and as an anthropological term, may beget as much confusion as the similar misuse of the terms "Aryan" and "Keltic."

When therefore we come to choose in which sense we shall use the word Teutonic there can be little doubt that the linguistic one will be the wisest, since it has been hallowed by long use. We must then find an alternative name for the blonde dolichocephalic race of Northern Europe. Deniker calls it the Northern or Nordic race, and this term, being a geographical one, involves no question-begging assumptions with regard to languages, etc. The name Boreal has also been suggested, but it is somewhat ugly and perhaps has too much of an Arctic sound about it. Ripley gives a geographical name to the broad-headed race of Central Europe by calling it the "Alpine." Some writers have called it Celtic or Celto-Slavonic, but both these terms are misleading since its members speak a Celtic language in Brittany, Romance languages in Central France, Northern Italy and Roumania, a Teutonic language in South Germany, Switzerland and Austria, a Finno-Ugrian one in Hungary, and Slavonic ones in Eastern Europe. The term Alpine has this in its justification that the Alps are the most striking physical feature of the part of Europe which the race inhabits; one cannot but feel, however, that it is a somewhat narrow one to apply to a physical type which stretches from Brittany to Afghanistan. The term Celtic has been suggested owing to the belief that this race brought Celtic languages into Western Europe and Celto-Slavonic as embracing its most

westerly and most easterly limits in Europe, but both are unsatisfactory, as Celtic and Slavonic languages are spoken by peoples who
do not belong to it. To rectify the narrowness of the name "Alpine"
the term "Alpine-Armenoid" has been devised, "Armenoid" referring
of course to the brachycephalic substratum of the population of Anatolia, a population which may with some probability be identified with
the ancient Hittites. Its chief defect is of course its clumsiness. The
term Eurasian would have been a good one to express the geographical distribution of this race, but unfortunately it is needed for another purpose. On the whole it seems best to use the term "Alpine-
Armenoid" when we wish to speak of both its European and Asiatic
halves, and "Alpine" when we are confining ourselves to the European
one. As to the third of the three great European races the term "Mediterranean" in every way suits it. It indicates its geographical position,
and begs no question with regard to language. If then ethnologists
would agree to denominate the three main physical types in Europe the
Nordic, Alpine or Alpine-Armenoid and the Mediterranean, and to
use the term "Celtic," "Teutonic" and "Slavonic" solely as linguistic
terms as is now being done with the term "Aryan," an immense amount
of confusion would be saved. By persisting in their use as racial terms
we are only inviting confusion, as all must admit when we reflect that
Celtic languages are spoken by peoples of Nordic type in Scotland,
Mediterranean type in Ireland, and Alpine type in Brittany; Teutonic
languages by peoples of Nordic type in Britain, Holland, Scandinavia
and North Germany, and by members of the Alpine race in South
Germany, Switzerland and Austria, while Slavonic tongues are spoken
by Nordic peoples upon the shores of the Baltic and by Alpine ones in
the Balkans, and, lastly, we find the Romance languages spread among
the three races. These are spoken among peoples of Nordic type in
Northern France and Belgium, among peoples of Alpine type in Central France and Northern Italy and among peoples of Mediterranean
type in Southern France, Spain, Portugal and Italy. When we have
got the distinction between race and language clearly fixed we may
turn to consider the question among which of the races in Europe did
the various linguistic families originate. We know of course that the
source from which all the Romance languages have sprung was the
speech of a people of mixed Alpine and Mediterranean race in Central
Italy. Again there can be little doubt that Celtic tongues were introduced into Western Europe by a migration or migrations of the Alpine
race, but whether the speakers of the original Slavic dialects were
members of the Alpine or of the Nordic race does not seem to be clear.
Teutonic speech seems to have been communicated to peoples of

Alpine stock by southerly and westerly migrations of the tall, blonde dolichocephals of Northern Europe. These problems are, however, all subordinate to the main one in the relations of race and language in Europe, viz. to which of the three European races must we ascribe the original introduction of Indo-European languages into our continent?

Max Müller, after he had abandoned his belief in an Aryan race, said that it would be just as sensible to speak of one as to speak of a brachycephalic grammar or a dolichocephalic dictionary. Nevertheless, although we cannot speak of an Aryan race, it is obvious that the tribe which spoke the original Aryan dialect must have existed somewhere. That they were a pastoral people is admitted, and so far as geographical considerations go their "habitat" might have been anywhere between the Carpathians and the Pamir. The fact, however, that comparative philologists regard the Baltic group which comprises the Lithuanian, Lettish and now extinct old Prussian languages as the most archaic branch of the Indo-European family has led to the belief that the locality of this people may have been somewhere in the neighborhood in which tongues have been spoken. If this inference is correct it seems that the original Aryan-speaking people belonged most likely to the tall, blonde North European race, which since the close of Neolithic times has dwelt round the basin of the Baltic. These Nordic peoples would have passed on Indo-European languages to the Alpine race who would diffuse them throughout Central Europe and into Southeastern Europe; offshoots of the Alpine race migrated both in historic and prehistoric times into the Iberian peninsula, into Italy and Greece, and very likely brought Indo-European languages with them. If, however, on the other hand, it were shown that the Indo-European languages originated among a people of Alpine stock then the history of their diffusion must have been somewhat different, and their introduction into Northern Europe have been due to a northern migration of a part of the Alpine race. That such a movement must have at one time taken place we know from the fact that a considerable proportion of brachycephaly is found in Denmark and Southern Norway. The third alternative that Aryan languages were first spoken by peoples of Mediterranean stock seems to be the least probable.

The only non-Aryan language in Western Europe is Basque, spoken by a people dwelling on both sides of the Pyrenees. There seems little doubt that it is the last remnant of a great family of agglutinative languages which prevailed widely throughout Europe and probably also on the Southern shores of the Mediterranean in Neolithic times.

Having considered the question of how far languages and race are coterminous in Europe, we may turn to the question of their relation to what we call nationality. The outbreak of the late war found Europe divided into twenty-one different States; of these ten, viz., the German Empire, the kingdoms of Italy, Belgium, Norway, Greece, Roumania, Bulgaria, Serbia and Montenegro, and the Principality of Albania— had existed as independent political entities for less than a century, and of the remaining continental States only Spain and Portugal retained the frontiers with which the Congress of Vienna left them a century ago. In no single case was language absolutely coterminous with nationality, that is to say was one language spoken by all the inhabitants of a single political organism and by no one else. Norway and Sweden appear to furnish the nearest approach to this ideal, as with the exception of the Lappish element in the North of the Scandinavian Peninsula which is of alien race as well as of alien speech the languages which take their names from these States are more or less coterminous with the States themselves. This is also practically true of Holland, but in other cases the ideal (if it be an ideal) is rarely even approximately reached. Thus we see that while the French nation is ethnologically made up of the three Great European types we find that in the political organism which we call France there exist strata of speech which enable us to reconstruct something of the linguistic as well as of the anthropological history of the continent. In the southwest corner of the country we still find a vestige of some pre-Aryan linguistic family brought in probably by the Mediterranean race which ultimately broke down in this part of Europe before the invasion of Celtic-speaking tribes belonging to the Alpine race; their language in its turn gave way except in Brittany before Latin, another language of the Indo-European family which in a modified form spread over practically the whole country.

We are, however, reminded of the fact that peoples of Teutonic speech overran the country in the 5th century on the withdrawal of the Roman legions by the circumstance that Flemish, a Teutonic tongue, lingers, especially in place names in Northeastern France. But the bulk of the Teutonic as well as of the Celtic tribes changed their own languages for a Romance one; in the former case the conquerors adopting the speech of the subject people, in the latter the conquered accepting the language of the conquerors.

On the other hand the French language is spread beyond the political boundaries of the country into the territories of all its Eastern neighbors in Belgium, Luxemburg, Germany, Switzerland and into the Val d'Aosta in Northwestern Italy. The relation of the late German Empire to language and race is less complicated, but still presents some features of interest. Only two instead of the three great European races are represented, the Nordic and the Alpine, while traces of the pre-Aryan and Celtic tongues which must once have been spoken over a large part of the country have vanished. Within its limits were to be found, however, another Teutonic language, viz., Danish in Schleswig, and representatives of two other branches of the Indo-European on the Western and Eastern marches of the Empire respectively, viz., French in the part of Lorraine annexed in 1871 and Polish in the Eastern provinces.

When we turn to Eastern Europe the problem of the relation of nationality to language and race becomes far more complicated. Three instances, however, especially arrest our attention—Hungary, Roumania, and Bulgaria. The Hungarian language belongs to the Finno-Ugrian stock, and was, of course, brought in by one of the numerous tribes of Mongoloid origin who wandered into Eastern and Central Europe during the Dark Ages. This language is now, however, spoken by a people who approximate to the Alpine type of Central Europe and have lost their Asiatic features. On the other hand, the Bulgarians, another Finnic people, have settled in the Eastern half of the Balkan Peninsula, and have exchanged their original language for a Slavonic one; while the Roumanians physically resembling their neighbors of Slavonic speech have exchanged a Slavonic tongue for a Romance one.

We see thus that in the history of Europe the races appeared first, the languages second and the nationalities last. The three great European races have been established roughly in their present position since the Bronze Age, perhaps even since the Neolithic. The great linguistic divisions, Romance, Celtic, Teutonic, Slavonic, and Finno-Ugrian, occupy approximately the same geographical areas which they occupied a thousand years ago, but nationality is a phenomenon which scarcely existed before the Renaissance. Political accidents have determined why certain linguistic areas have attained to the dignity of independent States while others have been divided between two or more States and others again are in the position of submerged nationalities. This may be best illustrated by the political history of the Iberian Peninsula. The physical characters of the inhabitants of this part of Europe are remarkably uniform, the population being dolichocephalic and brunet. There is not a single brachycephalic province in Spain. Throughout the Peninsula four languages are spoken, the pre-Aryan Basque in three Northern provinces, Guipozcoa, Viscaya, and Alava, and three Romance tongues, Catalan in the Eastern portion of the Peninsula, Castilian throughout the center from north to south, and Portuguese in the west extending across the Northern frontier of Portugal into the Spanish province of

Galicia. If race in the physical sense was to decide political boundaries then the whole Peninsula ought to be under a single Government; if language then (setting aside the Basques) we should have three States, viz., Portugal, Castile, and Catalonia. As a matter of fact, we have two—Portugal and another embracing Castilians and Catalans which we call Spain. When we look into the cause of this we find that it is due to a marriage contracted in the 15th century between a Queen of Castile and a King of Aragon; if, on the other hand, as Freeman has pointed out, Isabella of Castile had married the King of Portugal instead of the King of Aragon, we should still have had one race and four languages in the Peninsula, but different nations from those which we find today. Since the inhabitants of Portugal and Castile would have formed a nation which we should still probably call Spain, while Aragon and Catalonia would have either formed a separate nation or would have become absorbed into France.

A nation, it seems, may be formed in two ways; either a political accident has forced a group of people to live under a common government or else a common language, and more especially a literature, has produced a common social consciousness which makes those who speak the tongue and read the literature desire to form an independent political organism. The relation of nationality to language and race ought to be carefully considered at a time when so many are clamoring for the drawing of political frontiers along what are miscalled ethnological boundaries.

14. CHANGES IN BODILY FORM OF DESCENDANTS OF IMMIGRANTS [12]

BY FRANZ BOAS

THE Immigration Commission's anthropological investigation had for its object an inquiry into the assimilation of the immigrants with the American people as far as the form of the body is concerned.

On account of the magnitude of such an undertaking, it was deemed advisable to select certain important problems with a view to clearing up a few fundamental points, rather than to attack the whole problem with the prospect of not being able to give a definite answer to any of the questions involved.

[12] From *Abstract of the Report on Changes in Bodily Form of Descendants of Immigrants*. The Immigration Commission, Washington, Government Printing Office, 1911.

An attempt was made to solve the following questions:

1. Is there a change in the type of development of the immigrant and his descendants, due to his transfer from his home surroundings to the congested parts of New York?

2. Is there a change in the type of the adult descendant of the immigrant born in this country as compared to the adult immigrant arriving on the shores of our continent?

The investigation was confined strictly to an inquiry into the physical development of members of certain races in the congested districts of New York City, only immigrants and their direct descendants being included in the study. The important problem of the selection which takes place during the period of immigration, and which is indicated by the change of type of immigrants after the panics of 1893 and 1907; the effect of rural environment and that of the climatic conditions of different parts of our country; the questions relating to the mixture of European races and of the mixture of immigrants with Americans of various types—these have not been studied.

The investigation has shown much more than was anticipated, and the results are briefly summarized in the following pages.

GENERAL RESULTS OF THE INVESTIGATION

In most of the European types that have been investigated the head form, which has always been considered one of the most stable and permanent characteristics of human races, undergoes far-reaching changes due to the transfer of the people from European to American soil. For instance, the east European Hebrew, who has a very round head, becomes more long-headed; the south Italian, who in Italy has an exceedingly long head, becomes more short-headed. . . .

The head form may conveniently be expressed by a number indicating the transversal diameter (or width of the head) in per cents of the diameter measured from forehead to the back of the head (or the length of the head). When the head is elongated (that is, narrow when seen from the front, and long when seen in profile), this number will be low; when it is rounded (that is, wide when seen from the front, and short when seen in profile), this number will be high. The width of the head expressed in per cents of the length of the head is about 78 per cent. among Sicilians born in Sicily and about 83 per cent. among Hebrews born in eastern Europe. Among Sicilians born in America this number rises to more than 80 per cent., while among east European Hebrews born in America it sinks to 81 per cent.

This fact is one of the most suggestive discovered in the investigation, because it shows that not even those characteristics of a race which have proved to be most permanent in their old home remain the same under the new surroundings; and we are compelled to conclude that when these features of the body change, the whole bodily and mental make-up of the immigrants may change.

These results are so definite that, while heretofore we had the right to assume that human types are stable, all the evidence is now in favor of a great plasticity of human types, and permanence of types in new surroundings appears rather as the exception than as the rule.

The disagreement of the changes in distinct types may be illustrated by Table 1 and figure 1 following, which show the head form of Sicilians and east European Hebrews of American birth in comparison with that of Sicilians and east European Hebrews of European birth.

The diagram shows very clearly that the two races are quite distinct in Europe and that their descendants born in America differ from their parents in opposite directions.

TABLE I. CEPHALIC INDEX, OR WIDTH OF HEAD EXPRESSED IN PER CENT. OF LENGTH OF HEAD, OF FOREIGN-BORN AND AMERICAN-BORN HEBREWS AND SICILIANS

MALES.

Age (years)	5.	6.	7.	8.	9.	10.	11.	12.
Hebrews {Foreign-born	85.0	84.1	84.0	84.3	84.9	84.6	84.5	84.6
American-born	83.0	84.1	83.1	83.0	82.3	82.5	82.3	82.3
Sicilians {American-born	79.6	80.8	80.8	80.4	80.2	80.2	81.3	81.6
Foreign-born	80.8	79.6	79.9	78.6	78.9	80.2	79.8	78.3

Age (years)	13.	14.	15.	16.	17.	18.	19.	20 and over.
Hebrews {Foreign-born	84.0	84.1	84.1	83.7	83.0	83.0	82.9	83.0
American-born	82.3	82.0	81.7	81.5	80.9	79.6	82.0	81.4
Sicilians {American-born	80.7	79.0	81.0	79.2	76.0	80.0	....	81.5
Foreign-born	79.4	78.9	78.6	76.9	76.5	77.2	78.2	77.7

FEMALES.

Age (years)	4.	5.	6.	7.	8.	9.	10.	11.
Hebrews {Foreign-born	87.0	85.7	85.1	85.4	84.8	84.3	84.4	85.2
American-born	85.5	83.1	82.8	83.6	82.6	82.6	83.1	82.7
Sicilians {American-born	80.6	80.6	82.0	81.7	80.5	81.1	80.3	80.6
Foreign-born	77.0	79.6	80.2	80.0	78.9	79.6	79.8	79.2

Age (years)	12.	13.	14.	15.	16.	17.	18 and over.
Hebrews {Foreign-born	84.4	85.1	83.6	83.8	83.6	84.1	83.6
American-born	82.3	81.7	81.7	82.7	82.5	80.0	82.3
Sicilians {American-born	80.3	81.1	80.6	80.0	84.2	78.7	80.3
Foreign-born	78.3	77.8	78.9	79.0	78.4	78.2	77.8

In order to understand the causes which bring about these alterations of type, it is necessary to know how long a time must have elapsed since the immigration of the parents to bring about a noticeable change of type of the offspring. This investigation has been carried out mainly for the cephalic index, which during the period of growth of the individual undergoes only slight modifications. It appears in those cases that contain many individuals whose parents have been residents of America for a long time that the influence of American environment upon the descendants of immigrants increases with the time that the immigrants have lived in this country before the birth of their children.

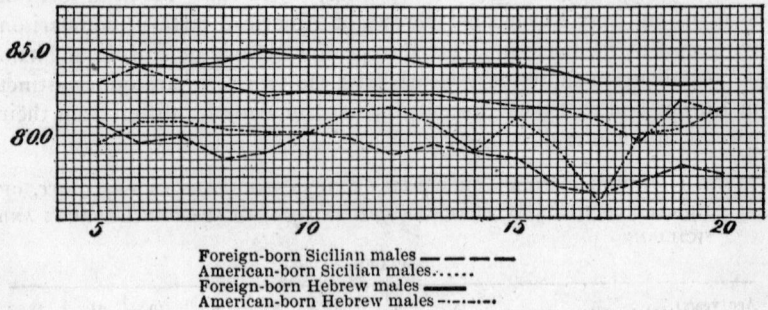

Foreign-born Sicilian males — — — —
American-born Sicilian males......
Foreign-born Hebrew males ▬▬▬
American-born Hebrew males —··—··—·

Fig. 1. Comparison of head form of American-born and foreign-born Hebrew and Sicilian males.
Scale, 1 square = 0.5 unit.

The measurements of males of 5 years of age and older are indicated in this diagram. The head form, expressed by the ratio between width and length of head and its change with increasing age, is indicated by the four lines. The diagram shows that foreign-born Sicilian males have the lowest value for this ratio and the foreign-born Hebrews the highest, while the American-born Hebrews and the American-born Sicilians stand between these two extremes, and are more alike than foreign-born individuals of the same races.

We have proved this statement by comparing the features of individuals of a certain race born abroad, born in America within ten years after the arrival of the mother, and born ten years or more after the arrival of the mother. It appears that the longer the parents have been here, the greater is the divergence of the descendants from the European type. . . .

MEASUREMENTS OF DISTINCT TYPES

The features that have been studied are stature, weight, length of head, width of head, width of face, and color of hair. While it seems doubtful that changes in pigmentation occur, all the other features show notable differences. These are not in the same direction in all cases. Stature, weight, length of head, and width of head show increases in some cases, decreases in others; the width of the face decreases among all the types that have been studied, except the Scotch.

The types that have been subjected to examination are the Bohemians, Slovaks, and Hungarians, Poles, Hebrews, Sicilians, Neapolitans, and Scotch. These have been selected because they represent a number of the most distinct European types, and because they constitute a large percentage of our immigrants. The changes that have been observed may be summarized as follows:

The Bohemians, Slovaks, and Hungarians, and Poles, representing the type of central Europe, exhibit uniform changes. Among the American-born descendants of these types the stature increases and both length and width of head decrease, the latter a little more markedly than the former, so that there is also a decrease of the cephalic index. The width of the face decreases very materially.

The Hebrews show changes peculiar to themselves. Stature and weight increase; the length of the head shows a marked increase, and the width of the head decreases, so that the cephalic index decreases materially; the width of the face also decreases.

Sicilians and Neapolitans, representing the Mediterranean type of Europe, form another group which shows distinctive changes. These are less pronounced among the Neapolitans than among the Sicilians, who are also purer representatives of the Mediterranean type, notwithstanding the many mixtures of races that have occurred in Sicily and the adjoining parts of Italy. The stature of the Sicilians born in America is less than that of the foreign-born. This loss is not so marked among the Neapolitans. In both groups the length of the head decreases, the width of the head increases, and the width of the face decreases. . . .

RELATIONS BETWEEN TIME OF IMMIGRATION AND CHANGE OF TYPE

The differences in type between the American-born descendant of the immigrant and the European-born immigrant develop in early childhood and persist throughout life. This is indicated by the constant occurrence of the typical differences in the measurements of children of all ages. . . . The influence of American environment makes itself felt with increasing intensity, according to the time elapsed between the arrival of the mother and the birth of the child. In Table 8 [omitted here] and figure 11 we have compared the measurements of the foreign-born child, of the child born within ten years after the arrival of the mother, and of the child born ten years or more after the arrival of the mother, with the general average of children of that particular race. The table shows clearly the strong and increasing effect of American environment. . . .

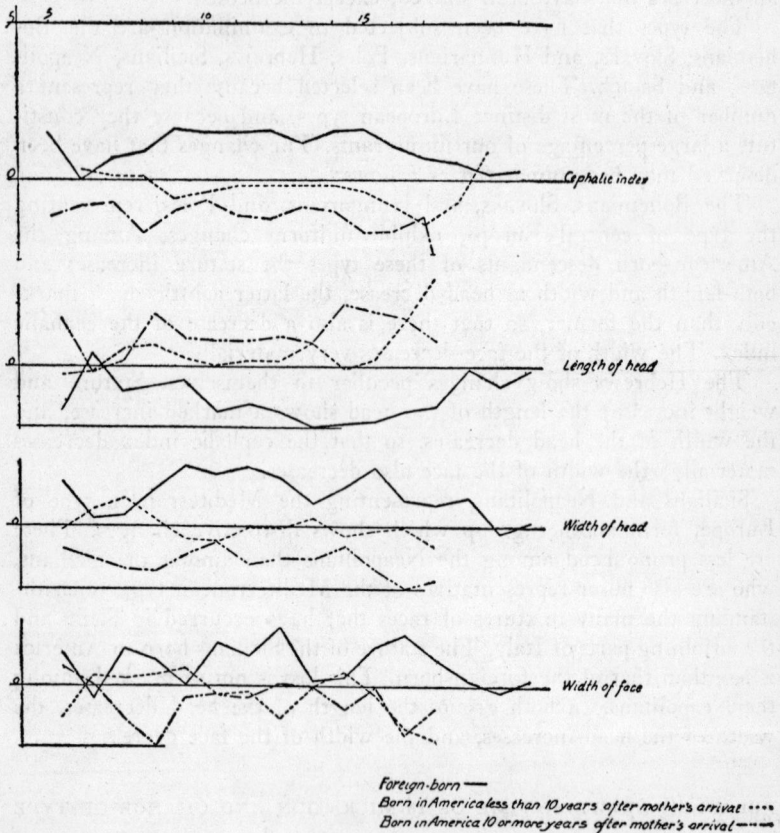

Foreign-born ———
Born in America less than 10 years after mother's arrival ····
Born in America 10 or more years after mother's arrival ——·——

Fig. 11. Comparison of head measurements of foreign-born and American-born Hebrew children.

A more detailed study of these phenomena illustrates still more clearly the increased modification of the descendants of immigrants born a long time after the arrival of their parents in America. Among the Hebrews the cephalic index of the foreign-born is practically the same, no matter how old the individual at the time of immigration. This might be expected when the immigrants are adult or nearly mature; but it is of interest to note that even children who come here one year or a few years old develop the cephalic index characteristic of foreign-born. This index ranges around 83. When we compare the value of this index with that of the index of the American-born, according to the time elapsed since their immigration, we find a sudden change. The value drops to about 82 for those born immediately after the immigration of their parents, and drops to 79 in the second generation, i.e., among the children of American-born children of immigrants. In other words, the effect of American environment makes itself felt immediately, and increases slowly with the increase of the time elapsed between the immigration of the parents, and the birth of the child.

The conditions among the Sicilians and Neapolitans are quite similar to those observed among the Hebrews. The cephalic index of the foreign-born remains throughout on almost the same level. Those born in America immediately after the arrival of their parents show an increase of the cephalic index. In this case the transition, although rapid, is not quite so sudden as among the Hebrews, probably because among the Italians born within a year before or soon after immigration, there is some doubt as to the place of birth. These uncertainties are due to the habit of the Italians to migrate back and forth between Italy and America before finally settling here, and to the indefiniteness of their answers in regard to the place of birth of the child, which sometimes had to be inferred from the age of the child and the year of immigration of the mother. As long as this uncertainty exists, which is hardly present at all in the data relating to the Hebrews, it does not seem necessary to assume any other cause for the more gradual change of the cephalic index about the time of immigration. . . .

Among the east European Hebrews the American environment, even in the congested parts of the city, has brought about a general more favorable development of the race, which is expressed in the increased height of body (stature) and weight of the children. The Italian children, on the other hand, show no such favorable influence of American environment, but rather a small loss in vigor as compared to the average condition of the immigrant children. It therefore appears that the south Italian race suffers under the influence of American city life, while the east European Hebrew develops under these conditions better than he does in his native country. It seems that the change in stature and weight increases with the time elapsed between the arrival of the mother and the birth of the child. This is indicated by the increased differences between children born more than ten years after

the arrival of the mother, as compared to those born less than ten years
after the arrival of the mother. . . .

PROBABLE CAUSES OF CHANGE IN TYPE

The explanation of these remarkable phenomena is not easy. Whatever their causes may be, the change in form cannot be doubted. It
might, however, be claimed that the causes are no deep, physiological
changes, but due to the changes of certain external factors. It is obvious
that a change in the composition of the immigrants of a certain region
that have arrived in America at different times might bring it about
that the people who came here at different periods had distinct physical
characteristics, and that those are now reflected in the descendants of
the older generations when compared with those of the more recent
immigrants. An investigation of this question has shown that the differences between the Bohemians, Hebrews, Sicilians, and Neapolitans,
immigrating at different periods between 1860 and 1909, are so
slight that they cannot account for the change of type of the descendants
of immigrants. This result has been obtained first by a direct comparison of types immigrating at different periods. Furthermore, I have
compared the cephalic index of all immigrants of a certain year and
that of their descendants. I have tabulated in the same manner the
width of face of Bohemians. It appears from these tabulations . . .
that the differences which are exhibited by the whole series exist also
between the immigrants who arrived here in a certain year and their
descendants. The purely statistical explanation of the phenomenon
may therefore be dismissed.

In order to overcome all possible objections based on the assumption
of a different composition of the immigrant series and of the American-
born series, I have also compared the measurements of parents and their
own foreign-born and American-born children. The results of this
tabulation are contained in Table 14. The figures contained in this
table were obtained in the following manner: For each year the
difference between father and his American-born son, father and his
American-born daughter, mother and her American-born son, and
mother and her American-born daughter, were determined; and these
were compared with the series giving the same differences for the
parents and their foreign-born children. After these differences had
been obtained for each year and for the four possible combinations of
sexes, the difference obtained for parents and their American-born
children was compared with the difference between parents and their
foreign-born children, the latter being subtracted from the former.

Since the parents of both groups, foreign-born and American-born, are of the same type, when the American-born child has a larger measurement than the foreign-born child the difference of the values compared will be negative, and when the measurement of the American-born is less than that of the foreign-born the difference will be positive. The values in Table 14 were obtained by averaging the results for all ages and for all combinations of sexes. It will be seen that the results of the observations agree with the results obtained by the generalized comparison of the foreign-born and American-born. . . . Among the Bohemians, for instance, we find the stature increased, all the other measurements decreased; among the Sicilians we find stature, length of head, and width of face decreased, while width of head and cephalic index increase. This shows clearly that an actual difference between the two groups must have developed.

TABLE 14. EXCESS OF DIFFERENCE BETWEEN PARENTS AND THEIR AMERICAN-BORN CHILDREN OVER DIFFERENCE BETWEEN PARENTS AND THEIR FOREIGN-BORN CHILDREN: BOHEMIANS, HEBREWS, SICILIANS, AND NEAPOLITANS

Measurements	Bohemians	Hebrews	Sicilians	Neapolitans
Stature (mm.)	— 5.60	— 13.10	+ 2.60	— 11.90
Length of head (mm.).....	+ 0.74	— 1.65	+ 2.91	+ 1.56
Width of head (mm.)	+ 1.31	+ 1.52	— 1.05	— 0.48
Cephalic index	+ 0.69	+ 1.50	— 1.78	— 0.97
Width of face (mm.)	+ 1.04	+ 2.10	+ 1.33	+ 1.55

More difficult to investigate is the hypothesis that the mechanical treatment of infants may have a decided influence upon the form of the head, and that the changes in cradling and bedding which are made by immigrants almost immediately after their arrival in America account for the changes of head form. If this were true, the continued changes among the Hebrews might indicate merely that the American method of cradling is used the more frequently the longer the family has resided in this country. A number of investigators have claimed that the position of the child on the back tends to produce short-headedness, and that the position on the side tends to produce long-headedness. There is good evidence that a flattening of the occiput occurs when a very hard pillow is used and the child lies permanently on its back. This is the case, for instance, among many Indian tribes; and similar results might obtain if a swathed child were to lie permanently on its back. The prevalence of rachitis in New York would favor distortion due to pressure. While I cannot disprove the existence of such influences, I think weighty considerations are against their acceptance. If we assume that among the Hebrews the children born abroad have a lesser length of head than those born here, because they are swathed and lie more permanently on their backs than the American-born children who can move about freely, we must conclude that there is a certain compensatory decrease in the other diameters of the head of the American-born. Since this compensation is distributed in all directions, its amount in any one direction will be very small. The decrease in the width of head that has been observed is so large that it cannot be considered simply as an effect of compensation; but we have to make the additional hypothesis that the American-born children lie so much on their sides that a narrowing of the head is brought about by mechanical pressure. The same considerations hold good in all the other types. If, therefore, in one case the greater freedom of position of the child increases the length of its head, it is difficult to see why, among the Bohemians, the same causes should decrease both horizontal diameters of the head, and why, among the Sicilians, the length should decrease and the width increase. . . .

The development of the width of the face seems to my mind to show most clearly that it is not the mechanical treatment of the infant that brings about the changes in question. The cephalic index suffers a very slight decrease from the fourth year to adult life. It is therefore evident that children who arrive in America very young cannot be much affected by American environment in regard to their cephalic index. On the other hand, if we consider a measurement that increases appreciably during the period of growth, we may expect that in children born abroad but removed to America when young, the total growth may be modified by American environment. The best material for this study is presented by the Bohemians, among whom there are relatively many full-grown American-born individuals. The width of face of Bohemians, when arranged according to their age at the time of immigration, shows that there is a loss among those who came here as young children—the greater the younger they were. Continuing this comparison with the American-born, born one, two, etc., years after the arrival of their mothers, the width of face is seen to decrease still further. It appears therefore that the American environment causes a retardation of the growth of the width of face at a period when mechanical influences are no longer possible. . . .

I have not carried through the analogous investigation for stature, because in this case the increase might simply be ascribed to the better nutrition of most of the north and central European immigrants after their immigration into this country.

There is another hypothesis which might account for the observed changes of type. If it were assumed that among the descendants of immigrants born in America there are an appreciable number who are in reality children of American fathers, not of their reputed fathers, a general assimilation with the American type would occur. Socially this condition is not at all plausible, but on account of the importance of the phenomenon that we are discussing it should be considered. I do not think that any of the observations that have been made are in favor of this theory. The changes that occur in the Bohemians who arrive here as young children, the different directions of the changes in distinct types, particularly the shortening of the head of the Bohemians and of Italians, do not favor the assumption. Furthermore, if the modification were due to race mixture the similarity between fathers and American-born children should be less than the similarity between fathers and foreign-born children. There is no indication that this is the case, for the index of correlation which expresses the degree of similarity is about the same in either group. . . .

That the index of correlation is a sensitive index of similarity and, we may say, of purity of sexual relations, is shown by the correlation for color of hair between Hebrew mothers and daughters, which is exceptionally low (0.13 for 616 cases), because many mothers wear wigs, and perhaps some daughters dye their hair.

This hypothesis is also shown to be untenable by the comparisons of fathers and mothers with their own foreign-born and American-born children. These comparisons show that the differences are the same in the case of fathers and children and of mothers and children, so that obviously the same conditions must control the relations between fathers and their children and mothers and their children. In other words, the fathers must be considered as the true fathers of their children.

It seems to my mind that the changes that have been observed in the transition of Europeans to the environment of New York must be considered as analogous to those that the European rural population undergoes when it moves from the country to the city. Ammon, who was the first to observe these changes in Baden, ascribes them to the effects of natural selection, which weeds out among the south Germans that move to the city the more short-headed type, while the long-headed type survives. Livi, who made similar observations in Italy, believed that the changes are simply due to the wider range of territory from which urban populations are drawn. The more varied descent, from which the urban population is derived, brings it about that in a region inhabited by short-headed people the urban population will be more long-headed, while in a region inhabited by long-headed people it will be more short-headed, than the rural population.

I believe that this factor is of considerable importance in the development of differences between urban and rural population; but our American observations show that there is also a direct influence at work. Ammon's observations are in accord with those on our American city-born central Europeans; Livi's with those on our American city-born Sicilians and Neapolitans. Parallel observations made in rural districts and in various climates in America, and others made in Europe, may solve the problem whether the changes that we have observed here are only those due to the change from rural life to urban life. From this point of view the slight changes among the Scotch are also most easily intelligible, because among them there is no marked transition from one mode of life to another, most of those measured having been city dwellers and skilled tradesmen in Scotland, and continuing the same life and occupation here.

On the whole, it seems more likely that the phenomena observed in the cities of Europe and among the descendants of immigrants in America are analogous, but not the same; that both are expressions of the general plasticity of human types when living under different conditions. The variability of the Hebrew type in different parts of Europe, which has been so clearly demonstrated by Maurice Fishberg, is also in favor of this theory. Doctor Fishberg has shown that the Hebrew type in various parts of eastern Europe varies somewhat, and generally in accordance with the type of the surrounding population. He was inclined to interpret this phenomenon as due to intermixture, but it may well be an expression of the effect of environment upon the same type.

It may be possible that the wider range of intermarriages which occur in America may have an effect upon human types. The actual intermarriages in small villages in Europe are preponderantly of such character that the same strain will persist for a long period with very slight disturbance by intermixture from outside, the majority of intermarriages in small communities being generally in that community. When immigrants leave their home and settle in large cities this permanence of strain is entirely broken; and it seems at least possible that the changes which have been noticed in urban types, both in Europe and in America, may in part be due to this cause. Our present views of heredity would make it plausible that a disturbance of the established type would occur in such a case, even if the two intermarrying types are not markedly distinct. It has not been possible up to this time to investigate the material thoroughly from this point of view; but I believe the theory deserves to be followed up. Modifications in the distribution of sexes have been observed in an analogous case in the Argentine Republic, where it has been shown that in intermarriages between Spaniards and Italians the proportion of the sexes changes materially. The information contained in our material will permit us to investigate the question here suggested.

Earnest advocates of the theory of selection might claim that all these changes are due to the effects of changes in death rate among foreign-born and American-born; that either abroad or here individuals of certain types are more liable to die, and that thus these changes are gradually brought about. On the whole, it seems to my mind, the burden of proof would lie entirely on those who claim such a correlation between head index, width of face, etc., and death rate— a correlation which I think is highly improbable, and which could be proposed only to sustain the theory of selection, not on account of any available facts. I grant the desirability of settling the question by actual observations, but until these are available we may point out that the very suddenness of the changes after immigration, and the absence of changes due to selection by mortality among the adult foreign-born, would require such a complicated adjustment of cause and effect in regard to the correlation of mortality and bodily form that the theory would become untenable on account of its complexity.

It would be saying too much to claim that all the distinct European types become the same in America, without mixture, solely by the action of the new environment. First of all, we have investigated only the effect of one environment, and we have every reason to believe that a number of distinct types are developing in America. But we will set aside this point and discuss only our New York observations. Although the long-headed Sicilian becomes more round-headed in New York and the round-headed Bohemian and Hebrew more long-headed, the approach to a uniform general type cannot be established, because we do not know yet how long the changes continue and whether they would all lead to the same result. I confess I do not consider such a result likely, because the proof of the plasticity of types does not imply that the plasticity is unlimited. The history of the British types in America, of the Dutch in the East Indies, and of the Spaniards in South America favors the assumption of a strictly limited plasticity. Certainly our discussion should be based on this more conservative basis until an unexpectedly wide range of variability of types can be proved. It is one of the most important problems that arise out of our investigation to determine how far the instability or plasticity of types may extend.

Whatever the extent of these bodily changes may be, if we grant the correctness of our inferences in regard to the plasticity of human types, we are necessarily led to grant also a great plasticity of the mental make-up of human types. We have observed that features of the body which have almost obtained their final form at the time of birth show modifications of great importance in our new surroundings. We have seen that others which increase during the whole period of growth, and are therefore subject to the continued effect of the new environment, are modified even among individuals who arrive here during their childhood. From these facts we must conclude that the fundamental traits of the mind, which are closely correlated with the physical condition of the body and whose development continues over many years after physical growth has ceased, are the more subject to far-reaching changes. It is true that this is a conclusion by inference; but if we have succeeded in proving changes in the form of the body, the burden of proof will rest on those who, notwithstanding those changes, continue to claim the absolute permanence of other forms and functions of the body.

15. HUMAN BLOOD GROUPS [13]

BY LAURENCE H. SNYDER

THIS paper is a presentation of some racial considerations evolving from the heredity and distribution of the blood groups among human beings.

In previous papers . . . the general question of the blood groups has been taken up. It was pointed out that they occur rarely, if at all, in the lower animals. Recently evidence has been brought forward that they may occur in the anthropoid apes. In the human race the blood groups occur as fixed bio-chemical conditions, subject to the laws of heredity. As such they provide a method of studying racial origins and relationships.

Blood groups were first discovered by Landsteiner (1900) and Shattock (1900) working independently. They found that there were definite substances in the serum of some bloods that would agglutinate, or clump, the cells of certain other bloods. On the basis of the agglutinating reactions, blood can be classified into four groups. Two classifications, the Moss and Jansky, are in current use. The Jansky clas-

[13] From "Human Blood Groups: Their Inheritance and Racial Significance," in *American Journal of Physical Anthropology*, Volume 9, pages 233-263, 1926.

sification is recognized as having priority rights, and is used here. The scheme of this classification is given in Table 1.[14]

The specific substances in the serum, causing the clumping of the cells, are known as agglutinins. The equally specific receptors in the red cells are designated agglutinogens. Agglutinogen A is the one found

TABLE I. SCHEME OF THE JANSKY CLASSIFICATION OF BLOOD GROUPS

Group	Effect of Serum	Capacity of Cells
I	Agglutinates cells of II, III, IV	Not agglutinated by any serum
II	Agglutinates cells of III and IV	Agglutinated by serum of I and III
III	Agglutinates cells of II and IV	Agglutinated by serum of I and II
IV	Does not agglutinate any cells	Agglutinated by serum of I, II, III

in group II. Agglutinogen B is the one found in group III. Group IV contains both, while group I contains neither.

The four blood groups, thought at first to be present only in diseased persons, were soon found to be of general occurrence. Within each race there occur fairly definite and characteristic proportions of the four groups. As few unit characters are yet known in man, the blood groups form a welcome addition to the list, since they can be accurately studied on a bio-chemical basis, and, depending as they apparently do, on two dominant mutations at the same genetic locus, they afford a means of investigating racial origins and relationships by correlating the frequencies of the hereditary factors concerned. . . .

Although most of the early investigators of the blood groups reported the frequency of the groups in the peoples among which their observations were made, the first work undertaken for the express purpose of studying the group frequency in various parts of the world was that of Hirszfeld and Hirszfeld (1919). These authors took advantage of the concentration of nationalities in the Macedonian battlefront during the war, and studied five hundred members of each of sixteen different peoples. They reported the frequency of occurrence of each of the four groups in each of the nationalities. They found that the sixteen peoples could be roughly divided into three types, as follows. One type contained a high percentage of agglutinogen A, and a correspondingly low percentage of B. This type comprised nearly all the European countries, and was therefore named the European type. Another type contained a high frequency of B and a correspondingly low percentage of A. The Mongolian and Ethiopians fell into this

[14] The Moss classification is the same but uses opposite designations for the groups: IV, III, II, I respectively corresponding to the I, II, III, IV here used. Another terminology now frequently employed is O, A, B, AB for the same four classes. *Eds.*

category, and it was accordingly named the Asio-African type. The third type, which the authors called the Intermediate type, contained approximately equal proportions of A and B, and comprised Russians, Turks, Arabs and Jews. . . .

I use in this paper the terms "nationalities" or "peoples," where other authors have used the term "races." This distinction must be carefully drawn from the anthropological standpoint. The study of the American Indians reported in this paper is the nearest approach to a true "racial" study of blood groups. . . .

It has been amply established that the agglutinogens are present at birth, but that the agglutinins may be delayed in their appearance for several months (von Dungern and Hirszfeld 1910, Hirszfeld and Hirszfeld 1919, Jones 1921, Robertson, Brown and Simpson 1921, Unger 1921, de Biasi 1923, Kirihara 1924). Tebbutt and McConnel (1922), noting this, suggest that the agglutinogens probably preceded likewise in evolution.

This assumption, however, is not warranted by the fact that primitive or isolated peoples show a very high percent of group I. As will appear later, group I reaches more than 90% among full-blooded American Indians. The peoples which show more than 50% of group I are the American Indians, the Filipinos, the Melanesians of New Guinea, the South African natives, the Australian aborigines, and the Icelanders: all island folk or otherwise isolated. . . .[15]

TABLE XI. PERCENTAGES OF THE FOUR BLOOD GROUPS AMONG
VARIOUS PEOPLES

Race	No.	I [O]	II [A]	III [B]	IV [AB]
EUROPEAN TYPE					
English	500	46.4	43.4	7.2	3.0
Americans	....	47.0	34.0	10.0	9.0
Americans	1,600	43.0	40.0	7.0	10.0
Americans	1,536	46.9	40.8	8.5	3.6
Americans	5,000	41.0	38.0	18.0	3.0
Americans	286	44.0	42.0	12.0	2.0
Americans	1,000	45.0	42.0	10.0	3.0
(insane)	100	45.0	42.0	9.0	4.0
(epileptics)	100	48.0	41.0	9.0	2.0
(feeble-minded)	175	44.0	42.2	9.7	4.0

[15] A somewhat technical section on the inheritance of the blood groups is omitted. Table XI is simplified by omission of columns giving the supposed hereditary factors and the names and dates of authors whose findings have been used. The hereditary factors are computed thus: $p = 1 - \sqrt{I + III}$; $q = 1 - \sqrt{I + II}$; $r = \sqrt{I}$; (or, $1 - \sqrt{O + B}$, $1 - \sqrt{O + A}$, $\sqrt{O}$).—Eds.

Race	No.	I [O]	II [A]	III [B]	IV [AB]
EUROPEAN TYPE					
French	500	43.2	42.6	11.2	3.0
Italians	500	47.2	38.0	11.0	3.8
Italians	139	35.9	51.0	8.6	4.1
Italians	1,391	35.9	51.1	8.6	4.2
Maltans	150	46.0	44.0	6.0	4.0
Germans (Heidelberg)	500	40.0	43.0	12.0	5.0
(in Hungary)	476	40.8	43.5	12.6	3.1
(in Hungary)	543	42.6	43.1	8.8	5.5
(in Berlin)	750	37.8	39.4	16.4	6.4
(Schleswig-Holstein)	1,679	42.7	42.7	11.7	2.9
(Leipzig)	1,000	34.5	41.5	16.5	7.5
(Kiel)	500	39.8	42.8	14.0	3.4
German Jews	230	42.1	41.1	11.9	4.9
Austrians	....	42.0	40.0	10.0	8.0
Dutch	200	42.0	44.0	9.0	5.0
Norwegians	436	35.6	49.8	10.3	4.3
Swedes	533	36.9	46.9	9.7	6.4
Swedes	500	33.5	51.0	10.0	5.5
Danes	150	47.3	36.7	12.0	4.0
Danes	512	43.0	42.0	12.0	3.0
Icelanders	800	55.6	32.1	9.6	2.6
Serbians	500	38.0	41.8	15.6	4.6
Greeks	500	38.2	41.6	16.2	4.0
INTERMEDIATE TYPE					
Arabs	500	43.6	32.4	19.0	5.0
Turks	500	36.8	38.0	18.6	6.6
Russians	1,000	40.7	31.2	21.8	6.3
Slovaks	461	44.7	31.3	15.8	8.2
Spanish Jews	500	38.8	33.0	23.2	7.0
Roumanians	1,521	33.7	43.3	15.6	6.4
Roumanians	....	32.1	34.5	16.1	17.3
(mountains)	2,372	36.5	40.9	14.5	7.9
(valleys)	1,278	33.5	41.2	19.0	6.3
Bulgarians	500	39.0	40.6	14.2	6.2
(in Roumania)	372	31.5	45.4	14.8	8.3
Polish Jews	818	33.1	41.5	17.4	8.0
Armenians	213	22.5	51.6	13.1	12.6
HUNAN TYPE					
South Chinese (Hunan)	1,296	31.8	38.8	19.4	9.8
(Setshuan)	....	44.8	28.9	23.7	2.6
(Tschekiang)	....	37.0	29.8	22.5	10.7
(Kuangtung)	....	40.4	31.4	23.8	4.8

Race	No.	I [O]	II [A]	III [B]	IV [AB]
HUNAN TYPE					
North Japanese (Sendai) ...	151	32.5	37.0	19.2	11.3
(Sendai)	642	29.4	39.3	21.5	9.8
(Sendai)	468	29.1	39.7	21.6	9.6
Middle Japanese (Nagano) ..	353	24.4	40.5	16.0	20.0
(Tokyo)	501	31.5	38.5	22.4	8.0
(Tokyo)	317	30.5	37.5	21.5	10.4
(Kyoto)	509	28.7	41.7	20.2	9.4
South Japanese (Fukuoka) ..	87	23.0	46.0	20.0	11.0
South Japanese (Fukuoka) ..	363	26.8	40.9	18.4	13.9
Japanese (in Korea)	502	29.4	42.2	20.6	7.8
South Koreans (Zennan)	171	19.9	41.5	25.7	12.9
Hungarians	....	26.3	38.1	18.8	16.8
Hungarians	1,500	31.0	38.0	18.8	12.2
Hungarians	1,172	22.3	31.6	27.4	18.7
Hungarians	688	27.8	40.8	20.2	11.2
Poles	11,488	32.5	37.6	20.9	9.0
Ukranians	400	18.0	39.2	22.5	20.3
Roumanian Jews	211	26.1	38.8	19.8	15.3
INDOMANCHURIAN TYPE					
North Chinese (Pekin)	1,000	30.7	25.1	34.2	10.0
(Shantung)	....	21.1	31.6	36.8	10.5
(Nganhai)	....	47.9	21.7	21.7	8.7
(Kiangsu)	....	39.0	29.7	26.4	4.9
Chinese	100	28.0	36.0	25.0	11.0
(in United States)	111	29.0	32.0	29.9	10.0
North Koreans (Heihoku) ..	354	30.5	27.4	34.5	7.6
Middle Koreans (Keiki)	311	27.3	32.8	32.8	7.1
(Chuhoku)	112	17.9	36.6	33.7	12.5
(Seoul)	179	24.5	35.7	25.1	14.5
(Phyengyang)	184	31.5	29.9	27.7	10.8
Manchus	199	26.6	26.6	38.2	8.5
Indians (natives of India)...	1,000	31.3	19.0	41.2	8.5
Gypsies	385	34.2	21.1	38.9	5.8
Ainus	205	19.0	32.7	34.5	13.7
AFRICO-MALAYSIAN TYPE					
Senegalese	500	43.2	22.6	29.2	5.0
South Africans	250	52.0	27.2	19.2	1.6
Madegascans	400	45.5	26.2	23.7	4.5
American negroes	270	49.0	26.9	18.4	5.5
American negroes	500	47.0	28.0	20.0	5.0
Melanesians (New Guinea)..	753	53.7	26.8	16.3	3.2
Annamese	500	42.0	22.4	28.4	7.2

Race	No.	I [O]	II [A]	III [B]	IV [AB]
AFRICO-MALAYSIAN TYPE					
Javanese	1,346	39.9	25.7	29.0	5.4
Sumatrans	546	43.7	23.0	29.0	4.3
Sumatran Chinese	592	40.2	25.0	27.6	7.2
PACIFIC-AMERICAN TYPE					
North American Indians	862	77.7	20.2	2.1	0.0
North American Indians	1,104	79.1	16.4	3.4	0.9
(full-blooded)	453	91.3	7.7	1.0	0.0
Filipinos	204	64.7	14.7	19.6	1.0
AUSTRALIAN TYPE					
Australian aborigines	204	57.0	38.5	3.0	1.5

TABLE XII [16]

p ＼ q	0 – 5	6 – 10	11 – 15	16 – 20	21 – 25	26 – 30	31 – 35
0 – 5	AMERICAN INDIANS	AMERICAN INDIANS			AUSTRALIANS		
6 – 10		FILIPINOS		ICELANDERS	DANES	AMERICANS ENGLISH FRENCH ITALIANS MALTANS GERMANS GERMAN JEWS AUSTRIANS DUTCH SERBS GREEKS	NORWEGIANS SWEDES
11 – 15			SO. AFRICANS	AMER. NEGROES MADEGASCANS MELANESIANS	ARABS TURKS RUSSIANS SPANISH JEWS CZECHS	ROUMANIANS BULGARIANS POLISH JEWS	ARMENIANS
16 – 20			SENEGALESE SUMATRANS	ANNAMESE JAVANESE SUMATRAN CHINESE	SO CHINESE	SO. CHINESE NO. JAPANESE HUNGARIANS POLES	MID. JAPANESE SO. JAPANESE ROUMANIAN JEWS
21 – 25				NO KOREANS	MID. KOREANS		SO. KOREANS UKRANIANS
26 – 30			NATIVES OF INDIA GYPSIES	NO. CHINESE MANCHUS		AINUS	

[16] This diagram, while based upon the correlation of the hereditary factors "p" and "q," conveniently classifies the various peoples into the seven types recognized in Table XI and discussed below. It will be seen that the ratio of the numerical values indicated by position in column and row corresponds approximately to the ratio of the figures given for each people in the columns headed II and III in Table XI.—*Eds.*

. . . To show the effects of crossing on the proportions of the groups, the author chose the American Indians. . . . The percent of group I in all of the Cherokees studied was 74.4. In those known to be mixed, it dropped to 59.3, much closer to that of the whites, while in those said to be pure it was 93.6. This is a definite indication that full-blooded American Indians are all of group I, and the occurrence of the other groups is due to white admixture. Even those said to be pure may have some trace of white blood, as the records seldom go back more than three or four generations. . . .

From these analyses, a graded series can be made, starting with pure Indians, and ending up with whites. This gives an excellent indication of the effect of crossing on the proportions of the groups. This is shown in table XIV.

TABLE XIV. GRADED SERIES SHOWING THE EFFECT OF CROSSING ON THE PROPORTIONS OF THE GROUPS

Race	Number Studied	Percent in Group			
		I	II	III	IV
Indians said to be pure	453	91.3	7.7	1.0	0.0
All Indians (mixed and pure)..	1,134	79.1	16.4	3.4	0.9
Indians known to be mixed	409	64.8	25.6	7.1	2.4
Americans (white)	1,000	45.0	42.0	10.0	3.0

There can be no doubt that racial crossing can profoundly modify the proportions of the groups. . . .

Let us then examine in more detail the peoples which have been studied, and the classification offered here. We shall take each type separately.

The European Type. This type includes all west-European peoples. It has the lowest percent of B found in any peoples with the exception of the American Indians and the Australian aborigines.[17] The percent of A is correspondingly high, being surpassed only among some of the peoples of the Hunan type. From northwest to southeast in Europe the percent of A decreases. It continues to decrease as we proceed farther east, reaching its lowest ebb in India. Exceptions to this rule are the Armenians, Japanese, Koreans, and Australian aborigines, all of whom show a high frequency of A. These will be considered under their own types. . . .

It seems probable that factor A originated in west Europe, and was carried eastward by successive migrations, while factor B was introduced into Europe by westward migrations of Mongolian peoples.

[17] A and B are the agglutinogens found in groups II and III respectively.—*Eds.*

The Intermediate Type. The peoples of the Intermediate type represent a departure from the European type in that the percent of B has increased, and the percent of A has somewhat decreased. The peoples of this type lie geographically intermediate between Europe, with its high frequency of A, and Asia, with its high frequency of B, and show corresponding intermediate blood group proportions. . . .

The Hunan Type. This type derived its name from the fact that South Chinese of the province of Hunan are included in it. However, the researches of Liang (1924) on South Chinese of Setshuan, Tschekiang, and Kuangtung, indicate that these people belong rather in the Indomanchurian type. The Hunan type is a difficult one to define. It has an exceptionally high frequency of A, with a low frequency of B. The presence in it of Hungarians, Poles and Ukranians, suggests a possible Mongolian ancestry for these peoples. The inclusion of Japanese and South Koreans indicates that southern Korea and adjacent southern Japan provide an additional center for the spread of agglutinogen A. . . .

The Indomanchurian Type. This type includes north Koreans, Manchus, Chinese, Ainus, Gypsies and natives of India. It has a high frequency of B, and a rather low frequency of A. The Ainus do not exactly fit in here, but are included for want of a better place. They could as well have been included in the Hunan type. Both agglutinogens are highly developed in the Ainus, and they remain a puzzle from the standpoint of their blood groups, just as they have long been an anthropological puzzle.

The gypsies (Zigeuner) studied by Verzar and Weszeczky are said by these authors to be originally from India. Their blood group proportions agree with those of natives of India, even after these many centuries. The lowest frequency of A, and the highest of B, is found in India.

The high frequency of B in Asia, growing less and less to the west, offers strong evidence that mutation B took place somewhere in Asia, possibly in India, after the American Indian branch had become isolated.

The Africo-Malaysian Type. This type includes all the Africans yet studied, as well as the Malay peoples. The Malays (Javanese, Annamese, Sumatrans) show a slightly higher frequency of B than the Africans and one is tempted to attribute this to their Mongolian affinities. However, the Senegalese of west Africa have just as high a frequency of B as the Malay races. There is no doubt that both agglutinogens are well developed among both the blacks of the continent and those of the Pacific Islands. Much remains to be done in intensive work among the peoples of Africa.

The Pacific-American Type. My studies of American Indians confirm the fact that they have a large proportion of group I, and indicate that full-blooded American Indians are entirely group I. The assumption is obvious that the American Indians branched off or were isolated from the old-world peoples before either mutation took place. In North America they are now reduced to insignificant numbers, and it is hard to be sure of racial purity. In Latin America it is practically impossible to find any pure race, as twelve generations have now passed

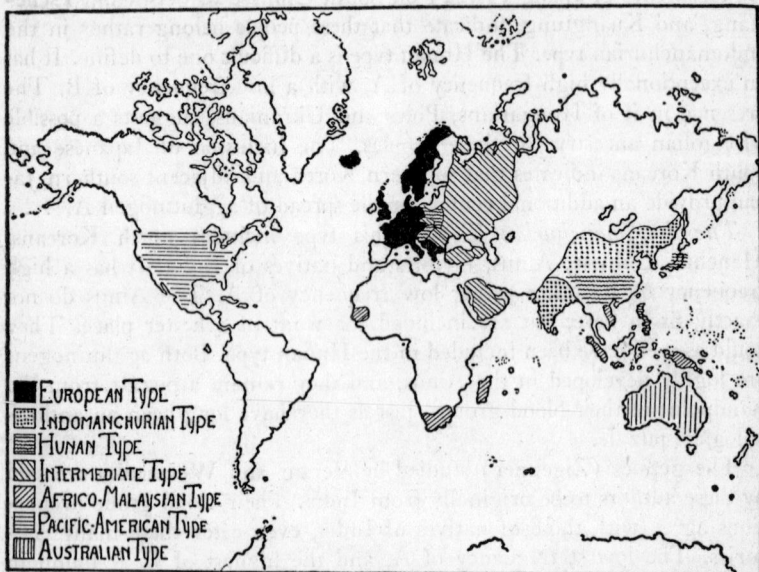

Fig. 1. Distribution of the seven types throughout the world.

since the first Europeans arrived. These first arrivals nearly all married native women, and every degree of mixed blood is now found, with corresponding changes of blood group proportions. The Indians from Mexico give the nearest approach to the group distribution of the whites.

The interior of South America may afford some pure races of American aborigines, and they should by all means be studied. It is to be hoped also that blood group studies will soon be made of Eskimos and Patagonians.

The small amounts of A and B present in American Indians are in the relative proportions in which they are found in whites. Similarly, the small amounts of A and B found in Filipinos are in the relative proportions found in the surrounding Ethiopian and Maylayan peoples, indicating that full-blooded Filipinos would likewise all be group I. In other words, both of these races were isolated from the other peoples of the Eurasic continent before either mutation took place.

The Australian Type. The Australian aborigines show a rather large proportion of group I, indicating their early separation from the Eurasic continent. . . . One hesitates to include them in the European type, however, because of their very low frequency of B. Ottenberg included them in the Pacific American type, but their high frequency of A seems to preclude this. Possibly the Australians became separated after the appearance of A but before the appearance of B. On the other hand, the frequencies are such as to suggest an invasion by a race of the European type, possibly a race whose blood group proportions are as yet unstudied. A knowledge of the proportions of the groups in Dravidians would be of interest in this connection. In Pliocene times Australia was accessible on the north and west to primitive migrations from both India and Maylasia. It is to be regretted that it is too late to learn the group proportions of the Tasmanians. A further study of Australians, particularly those known to be full-bloods, is needed.

Figure 1 shows the distribution of the seven types throughout the world. . . .

16. RACIAL DIFFERENCES IN MENTAL TRAITS [18]

BY R. S. WOODWORTH

ONE of the most agreeable and satisfying experiences afforded by intellectual pursuits comes from the discovery of a clean-cut distinction between things which are superficially much alike. The esthetic value of such distinctions may even outweigh their intellectual value and lead to sharp lines and antitheses where the only difference that exists is one of degree. A favorite opportunity for this form of intellectual exercise and indulgence is afforded by the observation of groups of men. The *type* of man composing each group—that is what we should like to find; and we hear much of the "typical" scientist, the typical business man, the typical Englishman or Frenchman, the typical southerner, the typical Bostonian. The type of any group stands as a sort of ideal within the group, and, more or less caricatured, as the butt of the wit of other groups. There is one peculiar fact about these types: you may have to

[18] From address of the vice-president and chairman of Section H—Anthropology and Psychology—of the American Association for the Advancement of Science, Boston, 1909. *Science*, pages 171-186, Feb. 4, 1910.

search long for an individual who can be taken as a fair example. And when you have at last found the typical individual, you may be led to ask by what right he stands as the type of the group, if he is a rarity amidst it.

If we would scientifically determine the facts regarding a group of men, we should, no doubt, proceed to examine all the individuals in the group, or at least a fair and honest representation of them. The first fact that meets us when we proceed in this way is that the individuals differ from each other, so that no one can really be selected as representing the whole number. We do find, indeed, when we measure the stature or any other bodily fact, or when we test any native mental capacity, that the members of a natural group are disposed about an average, many of them lying near the average, and few lying far above or far below it; and we thus have the average as a scientific fact regarding the group. But the average does not generally coincide with the type, as previously conceived, nor do the averages of different groups differ so much as the so-called types differ. Moreover, the average is itself very inadequate, since it does not indicate the amount of variation that exists within the group—and this is one of the most important facts to be borne in mind in understanding any collection of individuals. It is especially important in comparing different groups of men, since the range of variation within either group is usually much greater than the difference between the averages of the groups. The groups overlap to such an extent that the majority of the individuals composing either group might perfectly well belong to the other.

No doubt statements like this will be readily accepted as far as concerns the different nations belonging to the same race. One could not seriously doubt that the nations of Europe, though they might differ slightly on the average, would so much overlap one another that, except for language and superficial mannerisms, the great majority of the members of one nation might be exchanged with a majority from another nation without altering the characteristics of either. But when we extend our view to all the peoples of the earth, the case would at first appear quite changed. Certainly whites and negroes do not overlap, to any extent, in color of skin, nor negroes and Chinamen in kinkiness of hair, nor Indians and Pygmies in stature. Such specialization of traits is, however, the exception. Whites and negroes, though differing markedly in complexion and hair, overlap very extensively in almost every other trait, as, for example, in stature. Even in brain weight, which would seem a trait of great importance in relation to intelligence and civilization, the overlapping is much more impressive than the difference; since while the brain of negroes averages perhaps two ounces lighter than the brain of Europeans, the range of variation within either race amounts to twenty-five ounces.

Our inveterate love for types and sharp distinctions is apt to stay with us even after we have become scientific, and vitiate our use of statistics to such an extent that the average becomes a stumbling-block rather than an aid to knowledge. We desire, for example, to compare the brain weights of whites and of negroes. We weigh the brains of a sufficient number of each race—or let us at least assume the number to be sufficient. When our measurements are all obtained and spread before us, they convey to the unaided eye no clear idea of a racial difference, so much do they overlap. If they should become jumbled together, we should never be able to separate the negroes from the whites by aid of brain weight. But now we cast up the average of each group, and find them to differ; and though the difference is small, we straightway seize on it as the important result, and announce that the negro has a smaller brain than the white. We go a step further, and class the white as a large-brained race, the negro as a small-brained. Such transforming of differences of degree into differences of kind, and making antitheses between overlapping groups, partakes not a little of the ludicrous. . . .

All in all, the discovery of true inherent differences between races and peoples is an intricate task, and if we now turn to the psychologist to conduct an examination of different groups, and to inform us regarding their mental differences, we must not allow him to present a hasty conclusion. His tests must be varied and thorough before we can accept his results as a serious contribution to this difficult subject. The psychologist may as well admit at once that he has little to offer; for, though the "psychology of peoples" has become a familiar phrase, and though books have been written on the subject, actual experimental work has so far been very limited in quantity. . . .

First, as to the senses. The point of special interest here is as to whether the statements of many travelers, ascribing to the "savage" extraordinary powers of vision, hearing and smell, can be substantiated by exact tests. The common opinion, based on such reports, is, or has been, that savages are gifted with sensory powers quite beyond anything of which the European is capable; though Spencer explains that this is a cause of inferiority rather than the reverse, because the savage is thus led to rely wholly on his keen senses, and to devote his whole attention to sense impressions, to the neglect and atrophy of his intellectual powers. Ranke, however, on testing natives of Brazil, a race notable for its feats of vision, found that their ability to discern the position of a letter or similar character at a distance, though good, was not remarkable, but fell within the range of European powers. The steppe-dwelling Kalmuks, also renowned for distant vision, being able to detect the dust of a herd of cattle at a greater distance with the naked eye than a European could with a telescope, have also been examined; and their acuity was indeed found to be very high, averaging considerably above that of Europeans; yet only one or two out of the forty individuals tested exceeded the European record, while the great majority fell within the range of good European eyes. Much the same result has been obtained from Arabs, Egyptians and quite a variety of peoples. Among the most reliable results are those of Rivers on a wholly unselected Papuan population. He found no very exceptional individual among 115 tested, yet the average was somewhat better than that of Europeans. I had myself, through the kindness of Dr. McGee, the opportunity of testing individuals from quite a variety of races at the St. Louis Fair in 1904, and my results agree closely with those already cited, though I did not find any cases of very exceptional powers among about 300 individuals. There were a number who exceeded the best of the 200 whites whom I also tested under the same conditions, but none who exceeded or equaled the record of a few individuals who have been found in the German army. Indians and Filipinos ranked highest, averaging about 10 per cent. better than whites, when all individuals of really defective vision were excluded. The amount of overlapping is indicated by stating that 65-75 per cent. of Indians and Filipinos exceeded the average for whites. It did not seem possible, however, to assert anything like a correspondence between eyesight and the degree of primitiveness or backwardness of a people; since, for instance, the Negritos of the Philippine Islands, though much more primitive than the Malayan Filipinos in their mode of life, and, indeed, the most primitive group so far tested, were inferior to the Filipinos, and, in fact, as far as could be judged from the small number examined, no whit superior to whites. Nor does it seem possible, from results hitherto reported, to believe in a close correspondence between keen sight and dark skin, though it is true that pigment is important in several ways to the eye, and that therefore, as Rivers has suggested, the amount of pigmentation might be a factor in vision. But it does not seem to be specially the darkest races that show the keenest vision. We may perhaps conclude that eyesight is a function which varies somewhat in efficiency with difference of race, though with much overlapping. No doubt, however, the results as they stand need some qualification. On the one hand, inclusion of individuals with myopia and similar defects would lower the average of Europeans considerably more than that of most other races; so that the actual condition of eyesight differs more than the results show. On the other hand, it would not be fair to include near-sighted individuals, if what we wish to discover is native differences between peoples; for the different prevalence of myopia is certainly due to the differing uses to which the eye is put. And this matter of use may have considerable influence on the individuals not classed as near-sighted, and so admitted to the comparison. Rivers has made an observation in connection with the test for eyesight, which I am able to confirm, and which is perhaps of much importance. He found that when the letter or character used in his test, the position of which had to be recognized at the greatest possible distance, was removed from him beyond the distance at which he felt that he could judge it, he could still guess it right nearly every time, though without confidence. By such guessing, one's record in this test can be bettered considerably; and careful study enables one to see the slight and blurred indications of position which form the basis of the guessing. Now it may well be that the occupations of civilized life breed a habit of depending on clear vision, whereas the life of those who must frequently recognize objects at a great distance breeds reliance on slight indications, and so creates a favorable attitude for the test of eyesight. When this possibility is taken in connection with the deterioration of many European eyes from abuse, and in connection with the observed overlapping of all groups tested, the conclusion is not improbable that, after all, the races are essentially equal in keenness of vision. Even if small differences do exist, it is fairly certain that the wonderful feats of distant vision ascribed to savages are due to practice in interpreting slight indications of familiar objects. Both Rivers and Ranke, on testing some of the very individuals whose feats of keen sight seemed almost miraculous, found that, as tested, they had excellent but not extraordinary vision. A little acquaintance with sailors on shipboard is enough to dispel the illusion that such feats are beyond the powers of the white man.

The hearing of savages enjoys a reputation, among travelers, similar to that of their sight; but there can be little doubt that the case is the same. In fact, the tests which have so far been made tend to show that the hearing of whites is superior. Such was the result of Myers on the Papuans, and of Bruner in his extensive series of measurements made at the St. Louis Fair. Only 15 per cent. of 137 Filipinos tested did as well as the average of whites; other groups made a somewhat better showing, but all seemed inferior on the average to whites. In spite of the experimental results, there is perhaps reason to doubt that the hearing of whites is essentially and natively much superior to that of other races. Civilized life protects the ear from some forms of injury to which it is exposed in more primitive conditions; and, then, the question of cleanliness must be considered in regard to the meatus. Besides, the ear is known to be highly susceptible of training in the perception of particular sorts of sound—as overtones and difference tones—and it is likely enough that the watch ticks and similar clicks used in the tests are not equally within the repertory of all peoples.

Much the same can be said regarding keenness of smell. On account of the high olfactory powers of dogs and some other lower animals, it has often seemed natural and proper that this sense should be highly developed among savages; and feats of primitive folk have been reported quite analogous to those already referred to under sight and hearing. No doubt here again, special interests and training are responsible, since what few tests have been made tend to show no higher acuity of smell among negroes and Papuans than among Europeans.

The sense of touch has been little examined. McDougall found among the Papuans a number with extremely fine powers of discrimination by the skin. The difference between two points and one could be told by these individuals even when the two points were brought very close together; on the average, the Papuans tested excelled Europeans considerably in this test. On the other hand, Indians and Filipinos, and a few Africans and Ainu, tested in the same manner, seem not to differ perceptibly from whites.

The pain sense is a matter of some interest, because of the fortitude or stolidity displayed by some races towards physical suffering. It may be, and has been conjectured, that the sense for pain is blunt in these races, as it is known to be in some individuals who have allowed themselves to be burned without flinching, and performed other feats of fortitude. The pain sense is tested by applying gradually increasing pressure to some portion of the skin, requiring the person tested to indicate when he first begins to feel pain. Now, as a matter of fact, the results of McDougall on the Papuans, and those of Dr. Bruner and myself on Indians, Filipinos, Africans and Ainu, are in close agreement on this point. Greater pressure on the skin is needed to produce pain in each of these races than in whites. This is the average result, but in this test the distribution of the cases is specially important. Though most whites feel pain at or about a certain small pressure, there is quite a respectable minority who give no sign till much higher pressures are reached, their results corresponding very closely to those of the majority of Indians. And similarly, a minority of Indians feel pain at much lower pressures than the bulk of their fellows, falling into the ranks of the white man. In each group, the distribution is bimodal, or aggregated about two points instead of one; but whites are principally aggregated about the lower center, and Indians and other races about the higher center. Introspection comes to our aid in explaining this anomaly, for it shows that there is some difficulty in telling just when the pressure becomes painful. If one is satisfied with slight discomfort, a moderate pressure will be enough; but if a sharp twinge is demanded, the pressure must be considerably increased. Most whites, under the conditions of the test, are satisfied with slight discomfort, while my impression in watching the Indians was that they were waiting to be really hurt. The racial difference would accordingly be one in the conception of pain, or in understanding the test, rather than in the pain sense.

On the whole, the keenness of the senses seems to be about on a par in the various races of mankind. Differences exist among the members of any race, and it is not improbable that differences exist between the averages of certain groups, especially when these are small, isolated and much inbred. Rivers has in fact found such small groups differing considerably from whites in the color sense. One such group showed no cases of our common color blindness or red-green blindness, while another group showed an unusually large percentage of color-blind individuals. In the larger groups, the percentage of the color-blind is, very likely, about constant, though the existing records tend to show a somewhat lower proportion among Mongolians than among whites. Very large numbers of individuals need, however, to be tested in order to determine such a proportion closely; even among Europeans, the proportion can not yet be regarded as finally established. One thing is definitely shown by the tests that have been made for color blindness in various races: no race, however primitive, has been discovered in which red-green blindness was the universal or general condition; and this is a fact of some interest in connection with the physiology of color vision, for it seems probable that red-green blindness, since it is not by any means a diseased condition, represents a reversion to a more primitive state of the color sense. If this is so, no race of men remains in the primitive stages of the evolution of the color sense; the development of a color sense substantially to the condition in which we have it, was probably a prehuman achievement.

In the actual history of the discussion of the color sense in various races, quite a different view of the evolution has been prominent. It was Gladstone who first, as an enthusiastic student of Homer, was struck by the poverty of color names in ancient literature, and who suggested that the Greeks of the Homeric age had a very imperfectly developed eye for color. He was especially impressed by the application of the same color name to blue and to gray and dark objects. Geiger,

adhering to the same sort of philological evidence, broadened its scope
by pointing out the absence of a name for blue in other ancient literatures. It is indeed curious that the sky, which is mentioned hundreds
of times in the Vedas and the Old Testament, is never referred to
as blue. The oldest literatures show a similar absence of names for
green. Geiger found that names for black, white, and red were the
oldest, and that names for yellow, green, and blue have appeared in
that order. He concluded that the history of language afforded an insight into the evolution of the color sense, and that, accordingly, the
first color to be sensed was red, the others following in the same order
in which they occur in the spectrum. Magnus found that many languages at the present day were in the same condition as that shown in
the ancient Greek, Hebrew, and Sanscrit. Very many, perhaps the
majority, have no specific name for blue, and a large proportion have
none also for green. A smaller number are without a name for yellow,
while nearly all have a name for red. It seemed that the backward
races of today had just reached the stage, in the matter of color sensation, which was attained by other races some thousands of years ago.
The underlying assumptions of this argument are interesting—the
notion that the list of sensations experienced by a people must find expression in its vocabulary; and the conception of certain peoples now
living as really primitive. Fortunately, Magnus submitted this theory
to the test of facts, by supplying travelers and traders with sets of colors,
by which various peoples were tested, first, as to their ability to name
the colors in their own languages, and second, as to their power to
recognize and distinguish the colors. The results of this inquiry were
that names were often lacking for blue and green, but that every
people was able to perceive the whole gamut of colors known to the
European. This was a severe blow alike to the philological line of argument and to the ready assumption that early stages of evolution were to
be found represented in the backward peoples of today. Accepting the
facts as they stood, Magnus still felt that there must be some physiological or sensory reason for the curious lack of certain color names in many
languages; and he therefore suggested that blue and green might be
less vividly presented by the senses of many tribes, and that, being
duller to their eyes than to Europeans, these colors did not win their
way into the language. The theory was, however, practically defunct
for many years till Rivers recently took it up, as the result of tests on
several dark-skinned peoples. His test called for the detection of very
faint tints of the various colors, and the result was that, as compared
with two score educated English whom he also tested, these peoples
were somewhat deficient in the detection of faint tints of blue—and

also of yellow—but not of red. One group, indeed, was superior to the English in red. The results made it seem probable to Rivers that blue was indeed a somewhat less vivid color to dark-skinned races than to Europeans, and he suggested that pigmentation, rather than primitiveness, might be the important factor in producing this difference. A blue-absorbing pigment is always present in the retina, and the amount of it might very well be greater in generally pigmented races. The suggestion is worth putting to a further test; but, meanwhile, the difference obtained by Rivers in sensitiveness to blue needs to be received with some caution, since the Europeans on whose color sense he relies for comparison were rather few in number, educated and remarkably variable among themselves. We were able, at St. Louis, to try on representatives of a number of races a difficult color matching test, so different indeed from that of Rivers that our results cannot be used as a direct check on his; with the result that all other races were inferior to whites in their general success in color matching, but that no special deficiency appeared in the blues. We also could find no correlation between ill success in this test and the degree of pigmentation. On the whole, the color sense is probably very much the same all over the world.

That linguistic evidence is a very treacherous guide to the sensory powers of a people is well seen in the case of smell. Certainly many odors are vivid enough, yet we have no specific odor names. Only a psychologist would require a complete vocabulary of sensations; practical needs lead the development of language in quite other directions.

When we turn from the senses to other functions, the information which the psychologist has to offer becomes even more scanty.

Some interest attaches to tests of the speed of simple mental and motor performances, since, though the mental process is very simple, some indication may be afforded of the speed of brain action. The reaction time test has been measured on representatives of a few races, with the general result that the time consumed is about the same in widely different groups. The familiar "tapping test," which measures the rate at which the brain can at will discharge a series of impulses to the same muscle, was tried at St. Louis on a wide variety of folk, without disclosing marked differences between groups. The differences were somewhat greater when the movement, besides being rapid, had to be accurate in aim. The Eskimos excelled all others in this latter test, while the poorest record was made by the Patagonians and the Cocopa Indians—which groups were, however, represented by only a few individuals. The Filipinos, who were very fully represented, seemed undeniably superior to whites in this test, though, of course, with plenty of overlapping.

The degree of right-handedness has been asserted to vary in different races, and the favoring of one hand has been interpreted as conducive to specialization and so to civilization. We were, however, unable to detect any marked difference in the degree of right-handedness in different races, as tested by the comparative strength, quickness or accuracy of the two hands. The Negritos, the lowest race examined, had the same degree of right-handedness as Filipinos, or Indians, or whites.

We are probably justified in inferring from the results cited that the sensory and motor processes, and the elementary brain activities, though differing in degree from one individual to another, are about the same from one race to another.

Equitable tests of the distinctly intellectual processes are hard to devise, since much depends on the familiarity of the material used. Few tests of this nature have as yet been attempted on different races.

There are a number of illusions and constant errors of judgment which are well-known in the psychological laboratory, and which seem to depend, not on peculiarities of the sense organs, but on quirks and twists in the process of judgment. A few of these have been made the matter of comparative tests, with the result that peoples of widely different cultures are subject to the same errors, and in about the same degree. There is an illusion which occurs when an object, which looks heavier than it is, is lifted by the hand; it then feels, not only lighter than it looks, but even lighter than it really is. The contrast between the look and the feel of the thing plays havoc with the judgment. Women are, on the average, more subject to this illusion than men. The amount of this illusion has been measured in several peoples, and found to be, with one or two exceptions, about the same in all. Certain visual illusions, in which the apparent length or direction of a line is greatly altered by the neighborhood of other lines, have similarly been found present in all races tested, and to about the same degree. As far as they go, these results tend to show that simple sorts of judgment, being subject to the same disturbances, proceed in the same manner among various peoples; so that the similarity of the races in mental processes extends at least one step beyond sensation.

The mere fact that members of the inferior races are suitable subjects for psychological tests and experiments is of some value in appraising their mentality. Rivers and his collaborators approached the natives of Torres Straits with some misgivings, fearing that they would not possess the necessary powers of sustained concentration.

Elaborate introspections, indeed, they did not secure from these people, but, in any experiment that called for straightforward observation, they found them admirable subjects for the psychologist. Locating the blind spot, and other observations with indirect vision, which are usually accounted a strain on the attention, were successfully performed. If tests are put in such form as to appeal to the interests of the primitive man, he can be relied on for sustained attention. Statements sometimes met with to the effect that such and such a tribe is deficient in powers of attention, because, when the visitor began to quiz them on matters of linguistics, etc., they complained of headache and ran away, sound a bit naïve. Much the same observations could be reported by college professors, regarding the natives gathered in their class rooms.

A good test for intelligence would be much appreciated by the comparative psychologist, since, in spite of equal standing in such rudimentary matters as the senses and bodily movement, attention and the simpler sorts of judgment, it might still be that greater differences in mental efficiency existed between different groups of men. Probably no single test could do justice to so complex a trait as intelligence. Two important features of intelligent action are quickness in seizing the key to a novel situation, and firmness in limiting activity to the right direction, and suppressing acts which are obviously useless for the purpose in hand. A simple test which calls for these qualities is the so-called "form test." There are a number of blocks of different shapes, and a board with holes to match the blocks. The blocks and board are placed before a person, and he is told to put the blocks in the holes in the shortest possible time. The key to the situation is here the matching of blocks and holes by their shape; and the part of intelligence is to hold firmly to this obvious necessity, wasting no time in trying to force a round block into a square hole. The demand on intelligence certainly seems slight enough; and the test would probably not differentiate between a Newton and you or me; but it does suffice to catch the feeble-minded, the young child, or the chimpanzee, as any of these is likely to fail altogether, or at least to waste much time in random moves and vain efforts. This test was tried on representatives of several races, and considerable differences appeared. As between whites, Indians, Eskimos, Ainus, Filipinos, and Singhalese, the average differences were small, and much overlapping occurred. As between these groups, however, and the Igorot and Negrito from the Philippines and a few reputed Pygmies from the Congo, the average differences were great, and the overlapping was small. Another rather similar test for intelligence, which was tried on some of these groups, gave them the same relative rank. The results of the test agreed closely with the general impression left on the minds of the experimenters by considerable association with the people tested. And, finally, the relative size of the cranium, as indicated, roughly, by the product of its three external dimensions, agreed closely in these groups with their appearance of intelligence, and with their standing in the form test. If the results could be taken at their face value, they would indicate differences of intelligence between races, giving such groups as the Pygmy and Negrito a low station as compared with most of mankind. The fairness of the test is not, however, beyond question; it may have been of a more unfamiliar sort to these wild hunting folk than to more settled groups. This crumb is, at any rate, about all the testing psychologist has yet to offer on the question of racial differences in intelligence.

Prehistory

17. THE DIVISIONS OF PREHISTORIC TIME [1]

BY LORD AVEBURY

OUR knowledge of geology is, of course, very incomplete; on some questions we shall no doubt see reason to change our opinion, but on the whole, the conclusions to which it points are as definite as those of zoölogy, chemistry, or any of the kindred sciences. Nor does there appear to be any reason why those methods of examination which have proved so successful in geology, should not also be used to throw light on the history of man in prehistoric times. Archæology forms, in fact, the link between geology and history. It is true that in the case of other animals we can, from their bones and teeth, form a definite idea of their habits and mode of life, while in the present state of our knowledge the skeleton of a savage could not always be distinguished from that of a philosopher. But on the other hand, while other animals leave only teeth and bones behind them, the men of past ages are to be studied principally by their works; houses for the living, tombs for the dead, fortifications for defense, temples for worship, implements for use, and ornaments for decoration.

From the careful study of the remains which have come down to us, it would appear that Prehistoric Archæology may be divided into four great epochs.

I. That of the Drift; when man shared the possession of Europe with the Mammoth, the Cave bear, the Woolly-haired rhinoceros, and other extinct animals. This we may call the "Palæolithic" period.

II. The later or polished Stone Age; a period characterized by beautiful weapons and instruments made of flint and other kinds of stone; in which, however, we find no trace of the knowledge of any metal, excepting gold, which seems to have been sometimes used for ornaments. This we may call the "Neolithic" period.

[1] From pages 1-5 of Sir John Lubbock [later Lord Avebury], *Pre-historic Times, as illustrated by Ancient Remains, and the Manners and Customs of Modern Savages*, 1865. It was in this passage that the terms Palæolithic and Neolithic were first used.

III. The Bronze Age, in which bronze was used for arms and cutting instruments of all kinds.

IV. The Iron Age, in which that metal had superseded bronze for arms, axes, knives, etc.; bronze, however, still being in common use for ornaments, and frequently also for the *handles* of swords and other arms, though never for the blades.

Stone weapons, however, of many kinds were still in use during the Age of Bronze, and even during that of Iron, so that the mere presence of a few stone implements is not in itself sufficient evidence that any given "find" belongs to the Stone Age. In order to prevent misapprehension, it may also be well to state, at once, that, for the present, I only apply this classification to Europe, though, in all probability, it might be extended also to the neighboring regions of Asia and Africa. As regards other civilized countries, China and Japan for instance, we, as yet, know nothing of their prehistoric archæology. It is evident, also, that some nations, such as the Fuegians, Andamaners, etc., are even now, or were very lately, in an Age of Stone.

It is probable that gold was the metal which first attracted the attention of man; it is found in many rivers, and by its bright color would certainly attract even the rudest savages, who are known to be very fond of personal decoration. Silver does not appear to have been discovered until long after gold, and was apparently preceded by both copper and tin, as it is rarely, if ever, found in tumuli of the Bronze Age; but, however this may be, copper seems to have been the metal which first became of real importance to man: no doubt owing to the fact that its ores are abundant in many countries, and can be smelted without difficulty; and that, while iron is hardly ever found except in the form of ore, copper often occurs in a native condition, and can be beaten at once into shape. Thus, for instance, the North American Indians obtained pure copper from the mines near Lake Superior and elsewhere, and hammered it at once into axes, bracelets, and other objects.

Tin also early attracted notice, probably on account of the great heaviness of its ores. When metals were very scarce, it would naturally sometimes happen that, in order to make up the necessary quantity, some tin would be added to copper, or *vice versa*. It would then be found that the properties of the alloy were quite different from those of either metal, and a very few experiments would determine the most advantageous proportion, which for axes and other cutting instruments is about nine parts of copper to one of tin. No implements or weapons of tin have yet been found, and those of copper are extremely rare, whence it has been inferred that the art of making bronze was known elsewhere, before the use of either was introduced into Europe. Many of the so-called "copper" axes, etc., contain a small proportion of tin; and the few exceptions indicate probably a mere temporary want, rather than a total ignorance, of this metal.

The ores of iron, though more abundant, are much less striking in appearance than those of copper. Moreover, though they are perhaps more easily reduced, the metal, when obtained, is much less tractable than bronze. This valuable alloy can very easily be cast, and, in fact, all the weapons and implements made of it in olden times were cast in molds of sand or stone. The art of casting iron, on the other hand, was unknown until a comparatively late period. . . .

Hesiod, who is supposed to have written about 900 B.C., and who is the earliest European author whose works have come down to us, appears to have lived during the transition between the Bronze and Iron Ages. He distinctly states that iron was discovered after copper and tin. Speaking of those who were ancient, even in his day, he says that they used bronze, and not iron. . . . His poems, as well as those of Homer, show that nearly three thousand years ago, the value was known and appreciated. . . . We may, therefore, consider that the Trojan war took place during the period of transition from the Bronze to the Iron Age.

In the Pentateuch, excluding Deuteronomy, bronze, or as it is unfortunately translated, brass, is mentioned thirty-eight times, and iron only four times.

18. TREE GROWTH AND CHRONOLOGY OF PUEBLO PREHISTORY [2]

BY A. E. DOUGLASS

THE method which we have used in extending the historical calendar of the Southwest is the outcome of a long attempt to read the diaries of trees. Every year the trees in our forests show the swing of Time's pendulum and put down a mark. They are chronographs, recording clocks, by which the succeeding seasons are set down through definite imprints. Every year each pine adds a layer of new wood over its entire living surface of trunk and branches.

If every year were exactly the same, growth rings would tell the

[2] From "The Secret of the Southwest Solved by Talkative Tree Rings," in *National Geographic Magazine*, December, 1929, pages 736-770. By courtesy of the National Geographic Society.

age of the tree and little more. Only in rare cases would they record exceptional events of any interest to us. But a tree is not a mechanical *robot*; it is a living thing, and its food supply and adventures through life all enter into its diary. A flash of lightning, a forest fire, insect pests, or a falling neighbor may make strong impressions on its life and go into its diary.

But in the arid regions of our Southwest, where trees are few and other vegetation scarce, the most important thing to man and trees is rainfall. So, in the rings of the talkative pines we find lean years and fat years recorded. The same succession of drought and plenty appears throughout the forest. This fact has helped vastly in our dating work, for certain sequences of years become easily recognized from tree to tree, county to county, even from State to State.

No living, diary-keeping tree in the semi-arid region inhabited by the Pueblo Indians goes back more than a few hundred years; and the giant sequoias of California register in a different way those seasonal fluctuations that control the pines of northern Arizona. So when we reached the earliest date which the oldest living weather-recording Arizona tree could tell us about, it became necessary to search for beams that had been cut and used by man before the now living trees took up the story. Here and there we found beams the latter years of which were contemporaneous with the early life of trees still living.

By arranging these beams in their proper sequence, so that the inner diary entries of each one dovetailed into and matched the outer entries of its predecessor, we knew that we had an unbroken succession of beams and trees.

In this way, step by step, we pushed historical dates back further and further until we found a beam whose earliest ring was formed A.D. 1260, less than half a century after the Children's Crusade.

The development of this tree-ring study presents an example of how a scientific research starting with a definite idea may lead into unforeseen channels. Originally my work was a study of sun spots. It is known that there is a periodicity in their occurrence; they are most numerous at intervals of eleven years. As an aid in that astronomical investigation, I studied trees, for solar changes affect our weather, and weather in turn affects the trees in Arizona's dry climate, as elsewhere.

Our study of sun spots and their influence upon weather and the consequent effect upon vegetation as recorded by tree rings progressed most successfully. The first confirmation of our general interpretation of a relationship between tree rings and sun-spot periods came in a most dramatic way.

Evidence of the eleven-year sun-spot cycle had been easily found in

Arizona pine trees. The regularly recurring periods had been recorded for 500 years by tree rings, *except for the interval from 1650 to 1725*. During that seventy-five years the tree rings gave no evidence of periodical changes in the weather such as were to be expected.

Several years after we had encountered this puzzling fact the late Dr. E. Walter Maunder, an eminent English astronomer, unaware of my findings, wrote to me that he had discovered that *there were no*

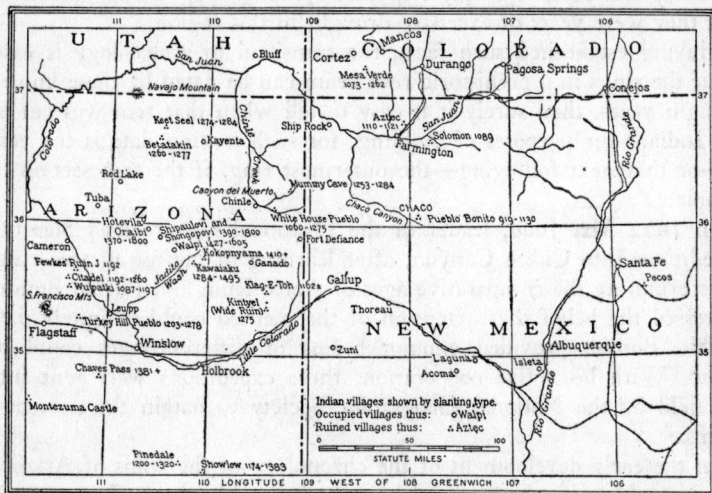

Tree Rings Have Given Definite Dates to These Indian Ruins

In many instances one group name is applied to several ruins. For example, in the Chaco group, various portions of Pueblo Bonito were under construction at different times—919, 1017, 1033-92, 1102, and 1130; Pueblo del Arroyo was being built in 1052-1103. In the Mesa Verde group, Cliff Palace is dated 1073; Oak Tree House, 1112; Spring House, 1115; Balcony House, 1190-1206; Square Tower House, 1204, and Spruce Tree House, 1216 and 1262. Mr. Earl H. Morris, in collaboration with the author, supplied beams from which the dates 1110-21 for Aztec Ruin and 1133-1135 for cliff dwellings in Grand Gulch, Utah, were ascertained. In the Chinle district Mr. Morris aided in fixing the years 936-57 for Sliding Ruin, 1253-84 for Mummy Cave, and 1060-96, 1219, and 1275 for White House Pueblo.

sun spots between 1645 and 1715, and that if my tree rings did not indicate some effect of this absence of sun spots, my work was being conducted on an erroneous hypothesis.

The coincidence between the failure of Arizona trees to register any sun-spot effect upon the weather during those years, and establishment of the fact, by entirely independent study, that the customary sun-spot cycle did not occur during approximately the same period of years, helped confirm the relationship between the growth of trees and solar changes.

The remarkable dependence of rings in the Arizona pines on rainfall, and especially on winter precipitation, showed that trees are Nature's rain-gauges, and in them we now have the history of drought and plenty in this plateau country for 1,200 years. We can point to certain years, such as 1632, 1379, 1067, and 840, and say definitely that they were years of excessive drought in this region.

Having established such facts, the transition to archæology is easy, for if the rings in a prehistoric roof beam can be dated by these known drought years, then surely it is easy to tell when that tree was cut by the Indians for purposes of building, for such cutting date is the year of—or that next following—the outermost ring, if the tree section be complete.

In 1922 Mr. Judd, leader of the [National Geographic] Society's expeditions into Chaco Canyon, after learning of my use of tree rings in ascertaining the comparative ages of Aztec Ruin and Pueblo Bonito, expressed the belief that extension of the method could definitely date Pueblo Bonito, provided enough beams of different ages could be found. With his active coöperation, three expeditions were sent into the field by the National Geographic Society to obtain the necessary beams.

In the early development of the chronology of the ruins of Arizona and New Mexico, the material brought in by Mr. J. A. Jeancon and Mr. O. G. Ricketson, Jr., of The Society's first expedition in search of beams, was invaluable. The expedition started from Flagstaff in June, 1923, and first visited the Hopi villages, where I accompanied them as supercargo for ten days. It was my first experience in picking up old, dried-up pieces of wood, which had formed portions of Indian houses, and trying to assign exact dates to them.

The experience developed only slowly toward satisfactory results, for while the age of some of the pieces was promptly recognized by comparison with Flagstaff trees, others leaped over the centuries and the time when they flourished was still a mystery.

Jeancon and Ricketson proceeded to examine certain old ruins on the mesa to the north of the Hopi villages—Fire House to the east; Wide Ruin, south of the latter; and the ruins of Chaco Canyon, Mesa Verde, and the Rio Grande Valley. As a result, 100 excellent timber specimens came to me for examination.

This material was examined as fast as time allowed. In July, 1927, it was evident that a new chronology had been discovered. Wupatki and Citadel ruins, near Flagstaff; Mummy Cave, in Canyon del Muerto; and Mesa Verde, in southwestern Colorado, had first been developed, each by itself, into local chronologies covering one hundred years or more. Subsequently it was found that all three joined into one continuous sequence 180 years in length.

Archæologists agreed, from study of the cultural remains, that these ruins were generally later than Pueblo Bonito. Therefore we had a second chronology partly filling the uncharted interval of time between the prehistoric timbers of Chaco Canyon and modern trees near Flagstaff and leaving two gaps shorter than before, but of unknown length. On a trip to Betatakin and Keet Seel, out in the northern Navajo country, in 1927, excellent timber specimens, which showed that they belonged to the latter part of this second chronology, were obtained.

Thus the newly developed chronology showed that Citadel, Fewkes' Ruin J, Wupatki, Mesa Verde and Mummy Cave, Betatakin, Keet Seel, and other pre-Spanish pueblos belonged to the same general period. Between all of these and Pueblo Bonito, however, there was a gap which Mr. Judd believed to be short, but which bothered us a great deal. Finally, we checked over the records given us by a juniper and a pine and compared them with the latest rings from Pueblo Bonito, and, lo, what was a distressing gap yesterday today was filled in and two chronological periods were united into one.

Thus . . . I was able to write Mr. Judd that the gap between the Pueblo Bonito period and that of Citadel and associated ruins had been bridged, that we had more than 580 years in a continuous prehistoric sequence.[3]

I now made an effort to discover very old trees in the hope that thereby we could link this united and extended prehistoric sequence with our modern chronology, and offered a reward for any pine 600 years old. We already had a section from a 640-year-old tree, but it had a serious injury near the center, which we did not understand then, but which we now know was caused by the great drought of 1276 to 1299. The next 100 years of that tree's life were very complacent and gave no configurations of rings that could readily be recognized.

An attempt was made to match our prehistoric pine sequence with

[3] This "prehistoric sequence" means that there had been determined a block of 580 consecutive years somewhere in the past within which tree rings could be identified; but the place of this block in historic time was as yet unknown. The remainder of the account is the story of how this "floating block" of 580 years was tied to the "historic chronology" obtained from living trees and occupied pueblos.—*Eds.*

that of the long-lived sequoias of California. This failed to give any certainty in dating, for there was no point at which the correspondence between the two stood out in a striking manner. I was compelled to renew the search for beams.

As successive generations of Hopi Indians had dwelt among the mesas 100 miles north of where the Santa Fe Railroad crosses the Little Colorado River, near Winslow, we believed that here was a promising field for search. Oraibi, for instance, has long been regarded as the only one of the present Hopi villages that has been continuously occupied since a period antedating the advent of the Spaniards, in 1540. We knew that many of its logs were cut by stone axes. Some of these, we reasoned, must be very old. . . .

We went at once to the abandoned Kwan Kiva, at the southeast edge of town, and bored all the logs in sight, only to find that many were of cottonwood or juniper, which were almost useless for our purpose. Eventually we realized that the much-desired older logs were generally of pine and Douglas fir, whose rings are the best of all. After dating numerous sections, we discovered that the use of these trees ceased about A.D. 1770. Evidently by that time all the available trees within portable distance had been cut down. Thus we learned something of the injurious effects of human occupation on forests.

Ends cut with a stone ax then became the distinguishing character. Small chips taken off showed whether the rings had the strong marking of pine or fir, the weak lines of cottonwood, or the narrow, erratic lines of juniper. Length also helped in the selection. Pre-Spanish beams used in the dwellings are rarely more than eight feet long. Spanish beams are easily twice that and are nearly always found in the kivas, or ceremonial chambers.

We call them "Spanish" because these timbers were salvaged by the Hopi when they destroyed the missions, in 1680; they have been in use ever since, and tradition has it they were originally carried by Indians on foot, mostly from the San Francisco Mountains. There are probably a few long pre-Spanish beams still in use. . . .

Naturally I wanted the oldest log. The oldest we found was in that section of Oraibi abandoned in 1906. We entered on the second floor of a three-story house, over a terrace consisting of older rooms filled with rubbish. We went through several chambers and entered into a part of the structure still in good condition. Mr. Hargrave lifted a flat stone on the floor, revealing a hole into the room below. . . .

In the center was an upright post, not more than six inches in greatest diameter, supporting the center of the ceiling. It was partly flattened, and as it was holding up the floor of the room above, no cross-section could be taken, but its longer diameter was bored by Mr. Hargrave. The rings of this beam gave a superb series from 1260 to 1344. Allowing for wearing, it was probably cut as early as A.D. 1370 and had been in use continuously for well over 500 years. . . .

After making large collections from old Oraibi and from Shongopovi and seeing a few specimens from the other villages, it seemed to me fairly evident that we would gain nothing by further search in the Hopi villages. The earliest cutting date discovered was close to the year 1400. One or two logs could be interpreted as having been cut a little before that, but after all our effort no additional piece was found whose inner rings began earlier than 1300. The inference seemed obvious; the pueblos abandoned following the revolt of 1680, when the Hopi erected their present villages, were built about 1400; in the case of Oraibi, alone, the original site has been occupied ever since.

Thus the early work of 1928 indicated that available Hopi beams were not sufficiently old to link definitely our two tree-ring chronologies. The question was, Where should we next look for some older locality whose building period preceded that of Oraibi—in short, the locality from which the Hopi Indians had last migrated?

To answer this question a survey was made of that area known archeologically to have been inhabited by the Hopis in pre-Spanish times. Fragments of pottery were collected at each important ruin; from the shards a sequence of development was obvious. Black-on-white and a form of red ware began in very old times. Then the red changed into a polychrome-on-red. Later the beautiful yellow Hopi pottery began to appear. The development continued with improving fineness of decoration until interrupted by the Spanish influence. Then pottery-making fell into a decline which lasted until about 1897, when Nampeyo saw her opportunity to inspire a revival of the art.

The relationship between the latter years of the prehistoric and the earlier years of the historic chronologies to this sequence of pottery types was easy to determine. Pueblo Bonito, in New Mexico; Keet Seel, near the northern border of Arizona; and Turkey Hill Pueblo, near Flagstaff, had given final building dates covering the late prehistoric chronology. Their pottery, therefore, would necessarily belong to the prehistoric period. It had not developed beyond a polychrome-on-red. But Kawaiku, which has given numerous historic building dates from 1357 to 1495, showed not only polychrome-on-red but, in addition, Hopi yellow ware in great abundance, with both primitive and late designs.

Evidently the point where the two sequences could be joined was close to the latest use of polychrome-on-red and the earliest development of Hopi yellow.

Not until the preliminary work of 1929 did we recognize that a transition orange color, which could be depended on as pottery of the linking area, came between the red and the yellow. This was an important guide in the selection of ruins for our subsequent search. . . .

Absolute certainty was finally obtained in a piece of charcoal as big as one's fist, found in an old kiva at Kawaiku. The rings looked favorable; we carefully bound the fragment and soaked it in paraffin solution. Subsequent examination showed that the rings could be followed from center to outside, and they gave an absolutely perfect sequence from 1400 to 1468, as reliable as if they had been dated at the time and sworn to before a notary. This established conclusively the correctness of all the other dates which had been obtained of approximately that same period.

Then other specimens came to light, carrying our ring sequence back to 1300 and forward to 1495, and showing that new dwellings were erected in this village shortly before the first Spaniards, Pedro de Tobar and Fray Juan de Padilla, reached Awatobi in 1540.

A group of wood fragments in another place showed a series of cutting dates from 1357 to near 1400. At the same time, a bit of pine built into the wall as a door lintel gave a very dependable late prehistoric date for the original walls.

Thus we had ample evidence that Kawaiku was occupied both in the latter years of our prehistoric sequence and the earlier years of our historic chronology. Hence this ruin, or one of its neighbors, gave promise of being a desirable site in which to search for those particular rings that might unite the two series. No doubt the desired wood was here, but the ruin covered some nine acres and it would be difficult to say where that wood could be found. . . .

What then was the next step? We had identified a locality in the Jadito Valley which was apparently inhabited during portions of our two time periods and presumably through the years that linked them together. Other Jadito ruins, especially Kokopnyama, seemed favorable and equally likely to contain material covering this period. But each of these ruins was nearly ten acres in extent and we were without any means of knowing just where to dig.

Probably beams at a depth of ten feet or more were in good condition, but a search for them would mean deep, long-continued excavation. Nearer the surface, timber of the age which we desired would be badly decomposed unless previously burned by fire. Hence evidence of rooms destroyed by fire was the essential clew in future work. Several of the ruins south of Holbrook gave indications of being near the right age and were in the midst of the pine forest. Their colder climate and the abundance of freely burning wood made charcoal far more likely to be found there in quantity.

These considerations provided a background on which to plan the third expedition. In the early spring of 1929 a reconnoissance was made of the pre-Spanish Hopi region where orange-colored pottery or its imitations were found. After excluding wonderfully interesting sites along the Little Colorado River, four ruins—Kokopnyama, in the Jadito Valley; Kintyel or Wide Ruin, to the southeast; Showlow and Pinedale, 100 miles south, in the great pine forest of the Mogollon Rim— were selected for examination. . . .

Mr. Judd and I left Flagstaff early Saturday morning, June 22, for Showlow. When we arrived there, shortly before noon, we found that another log had just been discovered at the extreme north end of the ruin. It had been found only a foot below the present level of the ground, in an area, however, from which earth had been removed in recent years. . . .

Among the valuable material we found at Showlow first place must go to this log taken out just after Mr. Judd and I arrived. It was found in a horizontal position and resembled an ordinary round beam which had been burnt off at the end in the form of a cone, as is common with burnt logs.

As a precautionary measure for holding it together, we bound it carefully with cotton twine; but, even so, the specimen fell to pieces, and not until then did we discover that our supposedly solid log was merely a conical shell of charcoal and near-charcoal from which most of the wood untouched by fire had decayed.

But, for all that, it was clearly a fragment of exceptional value. We gave it the field number HH39 after which I commandeered an old tool house and spent most of the afternoon working on it there.

Its outer parts were at once recognized as belonging to the 14th century, rings being traceable nearly to A.D. 1380. The record it gave us after 1300 was absolutely satisfactory, with no question whatsoever remaining as to the dating.

Following its rings inward to the core, we saw the record of the great drought. Here were the very small rings that told of the hardships the tree had endured in 1299 and 1295. As we studied the rings further toward the center, 1288, 1286, 1283, and 1280 each told the same story we had found in other beams of lean years and hard living. Also, there were the years 1278, 1276, and 1275, the ring for each corroborating the diary entries other logs had given us.

Then came the years of the seventh decade of the 13th century, and the stories told by their rings agreed in every detail with those told by the rings for the same years in the Oraibi beam.

But whereas the Oraibi beam could tell us nothing back of 1260, Showlow's HH39 did not stop there. Here was its account of 1258, a hard year, and of 1254, an even harder one. Presently it told of 1251 and 1247. . . .

We were getting down close to the center now. But the rings were clear and easily understood. Finally came the one at the very core, and from its central ring we learned that this charred old stick began its life as a promising upright pine A.D. 1237, just ten years after the Sixth Crusade moved eastward to compel the Saracens to restore Jerusalem.

The history within that carbonized bit of beam held us spellbound; its significance found us all but speechless; we tried to joke about it, but failed miserably. We felt that here was the tie that would bind our old chronology to our new and bring before us undreamed-of historic horizons.

Later that evening we gathered under the spluttering old gasoline torch in the village hotel, and beneath its flickering light, by the use of my skeleton plots of prehistoric tree rings, we began to determine whether our historical chronology, now extended back from 1260 to 1237 by Beam HH39, might not overlap the old chronology.

As we studied these rings the answer came. The ring in our old chronology that represented its 551st year, matched perfectly with that of the ring for the year 1251 in Beam HH39. And then our big surprise! We had not a gap to bridge as we had thought, but one we had closed without knowing it!

Our two chronologies had covered an overlapping period. But those rings of the old series which overlapped the new at 1260 had been gathered from such small fragments that I had never been willing to accept their evidence as to this overlapping. To be sure, I had dwelt upon this possibility at times, but always rejected it as unconvincing. It was Beam HH39 that cleared away all doubt. . . .

It still remained to examine with even further care the rings recording the great drought in the late years of the 13th century to see if by any chance anything had been overlooked. It would be necessary to prepare a complete photographic record of rings from the beginning of Pueblo Bonito chronology down to the present time; also, a complete review must be made of some 5,000 beam fragments, charred and otherwise, to get the various building periods in the 40 ruins from which they had come.

But when I finally went to sleep it was with the consciousness that my old chronology had begun A.D. 700; that the earliest beam we had recovered from Pueblo Bonito had been cut A.D. 919 from a tree that was 219 years old when cut; that Pueblo Bonito had reached its golden age in 1067 and was still occupied in 1127.

The next morning I returned to our beams. More deliberate study added new strength to their story. The years between 1260 and 1295, the earliest in the historic chronology, had been dated by the Oraibi log alone; likewise the late years of the prehistoric sequence had many defective rings in the great drought period which ended it. It had been the uncertainties arising out of these conditions that had made impossible the determination of the overlap without additional beam material.

But when we found Beam HH39 it proved to be the bridge over which we could pass the deep chasm of remaining uncertainty. Its respective ends, figuratively speaking, rested upon staunch abutments in both the old and the new sequences.

Its inner rings overlapped the late decades of the old chronology by 49 years, the final ring resting on the year 537 of that sequence; its outer ones overlapped the earliest 120 years of the new, the last one reaching to 1380.

Thus the 26 years from 1260 to 1286, which had belonged to both chronologies, were definitely matched and their union confirmed by Beam HH39, which in American archeology is destined to hold a place comparable to Egypt's Rosetta Stone.

The successful dating of the many ruins of the pueblo area that this research has made possible enables us now to correlate the increases of rainfall that permitted these villages to expand and the drought years that placed upon them the heavy hand of starvation.

With careful archeological study we shall perhaps be able to trace the movements of clans and test tribal traditions which have been so often quoted as the early history of these people. In the combination of climatic conditions with tribal activities we have a rich field for studying the influence of climate on human history.

19. ANCIENT MAYA RUINS [4]

BY W. H. HOLMES

The Maya Race. At the period of conquest the Maya tribes, occupying the peninsula of Yucatan and considerable portions of neighboring territory to the south and west, are said to have comprised in the neighborhood of 2,000,000 souls. Today they are distributed over nearly the same area, but are reduced in numbers, it is estimated, to less than 500,000, half at least of whom continue to speak the Maya tongue in its purity. At the north where there has been much infusion of Spanish blood the race has been largely modified and an interesting and very homogeneous half-blood people has sprung up; but in the interior many of the tribes are of nearly pure blood and retain a strong spirit of independence. . . .

Monumental Remains. Maya architecture, with its associated sculpture and painting, constitutes the best remaining index of the achievements of the race. The 70,000 square miles of Maya territory are so dotted with the ruins of towns and cities that the traveler is seldom out of sight of some mound, pyramid or other massive structure. . . .

Building Materials. The nature of the materials at the disposal of a people inclined to building exerts a profound influence upon the results achieved. Stone of somewhat decidedly favorable qualities would seem almost essential to greatness in the art of architecture. The Mayas were especially favored in this respect. The peninsula of Yucatan is composed of massive beds of limestone, homogeneous in texture and easily cut, even with primitive tools. Nature had not only supplied the stone, but it had in some measure prepared it for building. Although the land is approximately a plain, it is still in a small way broken up by low ridges and steps, and by sinkage into underground channels. The forests, growing densely everywhere, have broken up the surface beds, giving great quantities of loose stone immediately available to the builder and directing the way to the opening and working of quarries. The presence of unlimited supplies of limestone together with timber made the burning of lime an easy task and this product was extensively employed. The Yucatec stone mason had, therefore, every necessary building material at hand, although he still lacked, in a great measure, materials suited to the manufacture of quarrying and cutting tools. Cherty seams or masses of indurated limestone, occurring in many

    [4] From pages 19-52 of W. H. Holmes, "Archæological Studies among the Ancient Cities of Mexico," Part I, *Field [Columbian] Museum of Natural History, Anthropological Series*, Volume 1, Number 1, 1895.

parts, served for the ruder tools, and picks and chisels of special hardness were probably brought in from a distance. . . .

Mortar, made of lime and sand, and cement-like mixtures composed of mortar tempered with gravel, pounded stone, etc., were extensively used, and their durability is remarkable. Numerous floors and roofs are still preserved, and many fine examples of stucco modeling have withstood the destructive effects of the weather for four hundred years or more. . . .

Masonry, Stucco Work, and Painting. The masonry comprises, in general, hearting and facing. The former consists of earth, mortar and stones variously combined and usually forming strong, well-compacted bodies. The latter consists of stone cut or uncut and laid up, with few exceptions, in excellent mortar. Where the stones were accurately cut, little mortar appears in the face of the wall, but it was freely used in the hearting, and when the facing stones were deep they were dressed somewhat smaller behind, and set back in the mortar as a tooth in its socket. In the facing of many walls, however, the stones were very shallow—often mere tile-like slabs—and had but slight hold upon the body of the hearting.

In those centers of building operations where the limestone was readily worked and of fine, even texture, the facing is well cut, and the wall surfaces are in general so even and true as to stand the test of the square and plumb line; but in localities where the stone is uneven in texture and quite hard, or in provincial sections where building was not carried to a high degree of perfection, the facing is rarely well dressed, save about the doorways, arches, corners and especially exposed parts. Rough surfaces were very generally evened up with plaster.

A remarkable feature of these structures is the great thickness of the walls, and especially the extraordinary massiveness of the masonry above the spring of the arches. This is clearly shown in several of the sections inserted in the following pages. Where, for example, the outer wall is three feet thick and the arch within is ten feet wide, the mass of masonry thickens upward from three feet at the base of the arch to eight feet at the ceiling level, and in an inner wall, widening both ways, to thirteen feet, so that two-thirds or more of the space included in the upper half of the structure is solid masonry. The roof is often very thick, thus greatly increasing the bulk, and it seems a marvel that collapse from mere weight has not been more frequent than seems to have been the case. To all this bulk were added, in many instances, massive false fronts or colossal roof-combs laden with ornament. So strongly knit is the masonry, however, that but for the decay of wooden lintels, most of the great façades now in ruins would have been very fully preserved.

I have computed that a single-chamber structure, with walls of usual thickness and with average arch space and roof mass, would have two-thirds of its bulk solid masonry, which looks like a lavish waste of space, material and labor. If we take the measurements of the Governor's Palace at Uxmal, given by Bancroft, we find by a rough computation that the structure occupies some 325,000 cubic feet of space, upwards of 200,000 of which is solid masonry, while only about 110,000 feet is chamber space. If the sub-structure be taken into account, the mass of masonry is to the chamber space approximately as 40 to 1.

Notwithstanding the success of these Maya masons in erecting buildings capable of standing for hundreds of years, they were yet ignorant of some of the most essential principles of stone construction, and are thus to be regarded as hardly more than novices in the art. They made use of various minor expedients, as any clever nation of builders would, but depended largely on mortar and inertia to hold their buildings together.

One of the most elemental essentials of good work is the systematic breaking of joints in laying one course of stones over another. This idea had hardly been grasped, as it not infrequently happens that a seam or succession of joints is connected almost directly from base to summit of a wall, and at corners, within and without, and about doorways the stones are not bonded at all and are free to fall out as soon as the mortar gives way. The only possible explanation of this condition of the work that occurs to me is that the habit of treating the stones of a wall as so many elements of a mosaic pattern has tended to retard progress in the direction of what is sometimes called scientific construction. It will readily be seen that in carving and laying the stones of a geometric design, as a line of fret-work or of snouted masks, it would be extremely inconvenient to adapt the shapes to any system of jointage, and indeed such a thing would be out of the question. . . .

Substructures. The ancient cities of Yucatan were built on plains or on comparatively level ground and were without the advantage of bold natural features, but art largely supplied this want, and no nation of builders, save possibly the Mound-builders of the Mississippi Valley, has ever equaled this people in the number, variety, and size of its terraces and pyramids; however, there appear to be no pyramids that are mere pyramids, no terraces that are mere terraces; all or nearly all were constructed to support buildings, altars, or idols, and their diversity of size, contour and position give striking and picturesque results. Usually the substructures are square or rectangular in plan. The largest reported in Yucatan is upward of 500 feet in length and width, and the height of the loftiest reaches nearly 100 feet. The sides slope at various angles and some are practically vertical in whole or in part; many rise in steps, the succeeding terraces or platforms being of equal or unequal height and of varying horizontal extent. As a rule they are or were faced with stone which was dressed smooth or plastered. In the finer structures the terrace faces were paneled in hewn stone or embellished with moldings or with sculptured or stucco reliefs. The corners were often rounded and formed of large and specially sculptured stones. They were ascended by substantial, generally steep and wide stairways on one or more of the sides. The interior mass was constructed of earth and stones or mortar and stones usually forming a solid or well compacted body. In cases, however, this pile was not depended upon as a sufficient support for the superstructure, and foundation walls were carried up from considerable depth or from the ground level. The upper surface was generally floored with cement, though paving with slabs is occasionally seen. No doubt these piles were in cases the result of a long period of growth, and it probably sometimes happened that when a loftier structure was desired ground floor apartments were filled in solid with rubble or masonry, giving firm foundations for a second story or superstructure. In some cases the exterior of vertical-walled substructures was enforced by abutting masonry entirely encasing the original nucleus and giving the effect of an ordinary sloped terrace or pyramid.

In Fig. 1 a few examples of terraces and pyramids are presented in outline. . . .

Stairways. The stairways of the Maya pyramids (see Fig. 1), share in a large measure the boldness and magnitude of the constructions with which they are associated and of which they form an essential part. A single stairway would have afforded all necessary access to the lofty summits, but it is not unusual to find two flights, and three or even four flights are known leading to the same temple, and each built on an equally grand scale and finished with like elaboration. All are exterior and centrally placed, leading directly up the face of the pyramid. Usually they are wide and bordered with some kind of solid balustrade. The favorite design for the rail is a colossal serpent, the head with wide open mouth and protruding tongue extended upon the ground, the body, appropriately carved, extending to the summit. In Yucatan the steps are neither high nor wide, averaging perhaps a foot in rise and a little less in tread. The pitch is thus 45 degrees or more. The stones used are generally rather small and not very smoothly dressed or well fitted, and it is probable that all important flights were finished in cement and color. . . .

Superstructures. I cannot undertake in this place to give more than

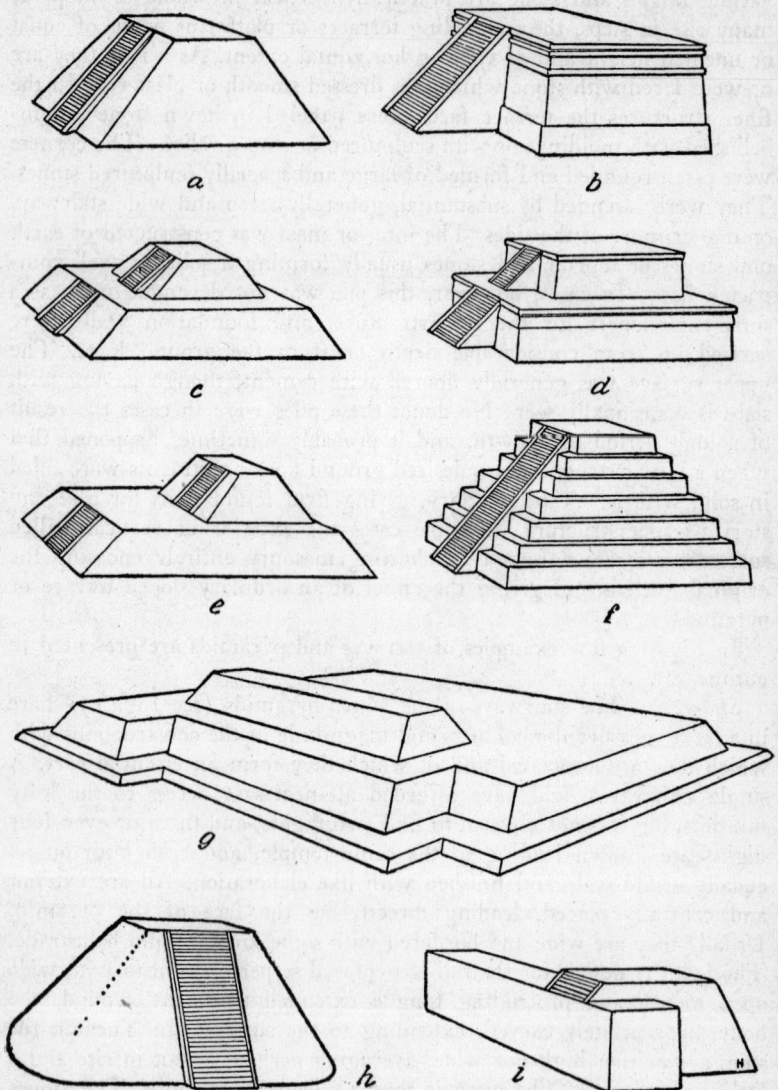

Fig. 1. Examples of terraces and pyramids, superstructures omitted.

a mere outline of the leading features and characteristics of the many buildings visited. . . .

The ground plan is usually rectangular, two or three examples only of round houses having been reported. Large buildings of independent position are mostly rather long and narrow, the width having been limited by the difficulty of widening the arch where one or two tiers of rooms are used, and of securing light in the inner chambers of multiple tiers, since the upper wall and roof are never perforated. In detail the plan of large buildings, even the most complex, shows little more than a mere multiplication of the simple rectangular cell unit. . . .

The buildings usually classed as temples are not large and are generally squarish in plan. They have from one to four rooms. When the rooms are multiple they are so arranged as to indicate pretty clearly a specialization of use. The two essential features in such cases are an

Fig. 2. Specialization of the ground plan of Maya temples.

outer chamber or vestibule and an inner chamber or sanctuary. . . . In Fig. 2 a series of temple plans is given, illustrating the remarks just made. . . .

The greater Maya buildings, though at times appearing complex in plan, are really exceedingly simple. The unit is the single cell or chamber seen standing alone in *a*, Fig. 3. The building shown in *b* consists of several units combined in one; variety is given to the plan in unsymmetrical structures by adding other units in less uniform ways and of varying size. The building shown in *d* differs from the preceding in having a sloped instead of a vertical entablature, the interior arrangement being much the same as in *b*. A sketch, intended as a restoration of the Caracol or Round Tower at Chichen, is presented in *c*. This edifice contains two circular, concentric chambers identical in construction principle with the rectangular forms. In *e* we have the Palenque type of temple, and *f* is the square tower of the Palace at Palenque, the plan and construction of which are peculiar in several respects. . . .

The illustration given in Fig. 4 will serve to indicate sufficiently the construction and relations of the various features of an ordinary Maya building. The upper part of the substructure or pyramid is included

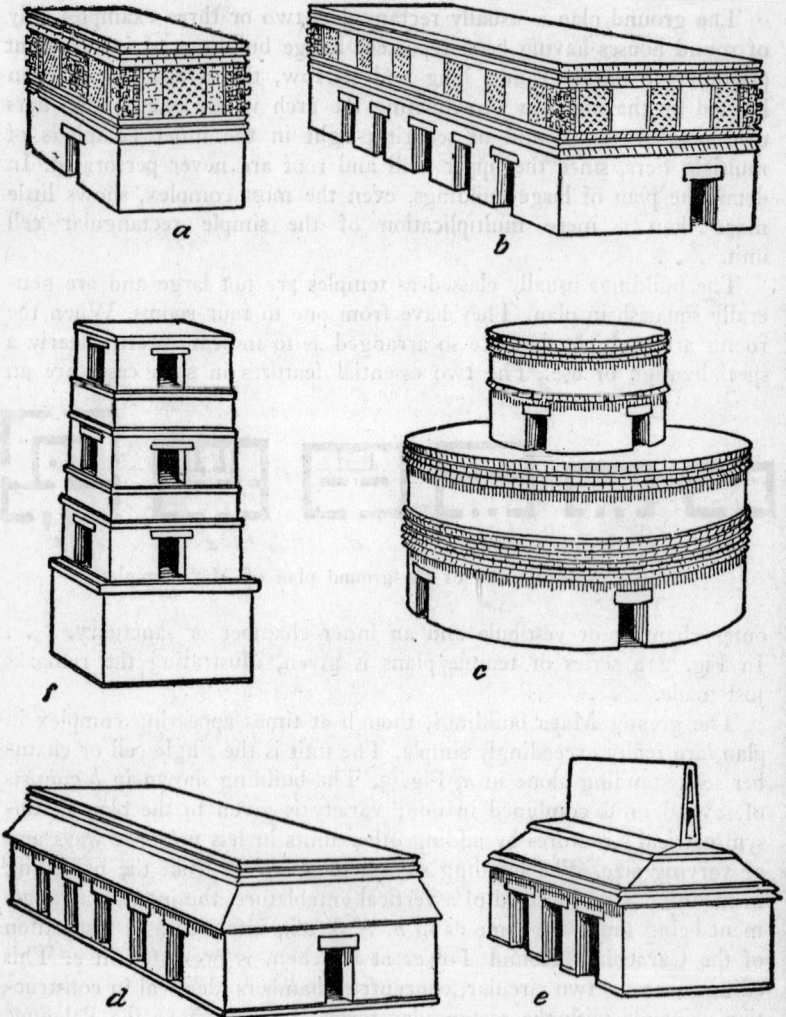

Fig. 3. Examples of Maya buildings.

and shows the stairway at the left, approaching the front doorway, and plain slope at the right. Details of the masonry of this mass are somewhat hypothetical, as I have not been able to determine whether or not it is the rule that a special foundation wall with vertical outer face

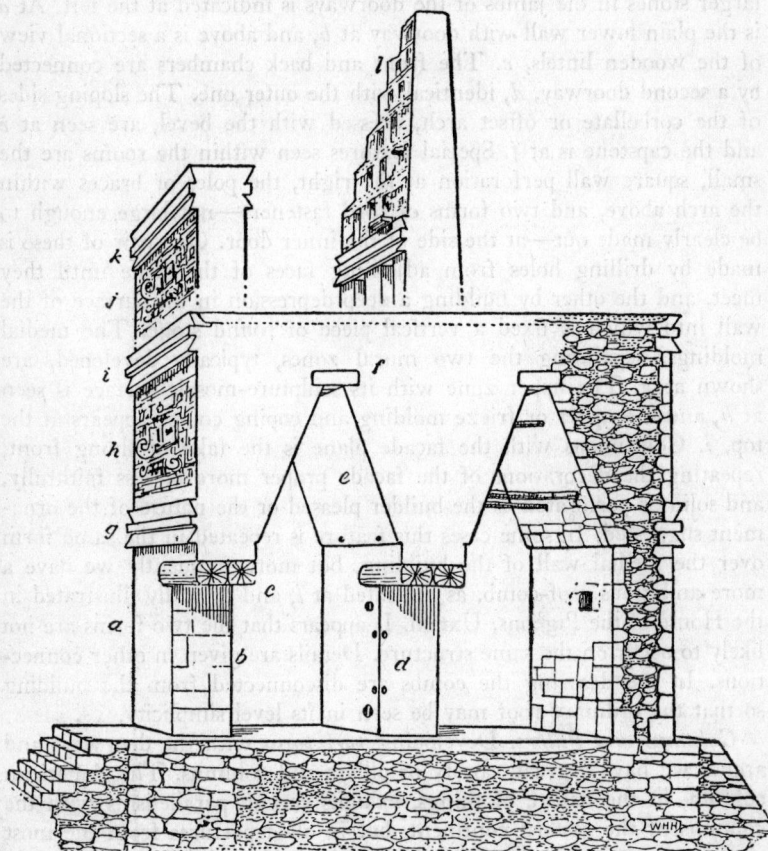

Fig. 4. Transverse section of an ordinary Yucatec building. The upper part of the pyramid is shown with the stairway at the left.

was built from the ground up, but it is certain that this was often the case, and that the stairway and abutting masonry were afterward added, as here shown, transforming the vertical-faced substructure into a sloping one. The floor is cemented as a rule, but occasionally is flagged, and the inner floor is in cases a step higher than the esplanade without. The superstructure here utilized, has two chambers, or two tiers of chambers, vaulted with the ordinary arch, and the walls are vertical without as is usual in Yucatan. The nature of the facing and hearting is shown in section in the back wall at the right, and the illy jointed and bonded masonry is correctly represented. The use of larger stones in the jambs of the doorways is indicated at the left. At *a* is the plain lower wall with doorway at *b,* and above is a sectional view of the wooden lintels, *c.* The front and back chambers are connected by a second doorway, *d,* identical with the outer one. The sloping sides of the corbellate or offset arch, dressed with the bevel, are seen at *e* and the capstone is at *f.* Special features seen within the rooms are the small, square wall perforation at the right, the poles or braces within the arch above, and two forms of cord fasteners—not large enough to be clearly made out—at the side of the inner door. One pair of these is made by drilling holes from adjoining faces of the stone until they meet, and the other by building a deep depression in the surface of the wall into which is fixed a vertical piece of round stone. The medial moldings, separating the two mural zones, typically developed, are shown at *g.* The upper zone with its sculpture-mosaic surface is seen at *h,* and the upper or frieze molding and coping course appears at the top, *i.* Continuous with the façade plane is the false or flying front, repeating the decorations of the façade proper more or less faithfully, and solid or perforated as the builder pleased or the nature of the ornament suggested. In some cases this feature is repeated in the same form over the medial wall of the building, but more frequently we have a more ambitious roof-comb, as indicated at *l,* and typically illustrated in the House of the Pigeons, Uxmal. It appears that the two forms are not likely to occur on the same structure. Details are given in other connections. In the drawing the combs are disconnected from the building so that the ordinary roof may be seen in its level simplicity. . . .

Columns and Pillars. Developing *pari passu* with the doorways and arches we have a great variety of pillars and columns. The American column, in the nature of things, exhibits certain parallelisms with the columns of the eastern continent, but in all departures from the most elementary treatment and use it may be said to be characteristically American. Square columns, most numerous in Chichen, and pillars or piers, typically developed in Palenque, were usually simple in form though often embellished with elaborate sculptures or plastic designs in low relief, whilst the round column had advanced beyond the more elemental form with its shaft and simple cap, and was given, in whole or in part, varied and remarkable life forms, the feathered serpent being the favorite motive embodied. Among the most striking features of the great buildings of Chichen-Itza are the massive serpent columns, and on the Island of Cozumel, in a diminutive temple, the life-sized figure of a human being or man-like ape is sculptured in high relief against the face of the column.

Columns were usually assembled in pairs, where introduced into doorways to support the entablature, but appeared in groups and rows numbering scores or hundreds where extended façades or large roof areas were supported. Few specimens are monolithic, save in the east, as at Cozumel, where the size was reduced to a minimum and the available stone was perhaps more than usually massive. The proportions are considerably varied, but all are short and heavy. The diameter is to the height, approximately, as 1 to 3½. The square column is always built up of a number of heavy blocks.

The round column had become such a familiar feature of the building art that it was employed outside of its normal range of functions, appearing very frequently in the field of pure embellishment. In many of the Yucatec buildings it was used, on a reduced scale, to decorate the façades, where it was effectively introduced in moldings and friezes, forming long rows set in contact side by side. Generally the form was rounded only in front, while the back was flat or uneven and set in mortar. The form was varied in cases by formal moldings encircling the shaft, giving the effect, in a simple way, of our turned balusters. . . .

The Arch. The Maya arch presents a number of interesting forms and phases, all, probably, directly traceable to the more primitive forms of chamber spans or vaults in common use all over America. Among these earlier forms we have, first, the beam of wood or slab of stone connecting two lateral supports or walls and forming part of the roof or serving to support it; second, the single lean-to, in which the parts are placed against some fixed vertical surface or support; third, the double lean-to, where opposing parts are set against each other with or without a ridge pole; and, fourth, the circular lean-to, in which the parts form a cone with or without a central supporting pole. All are equally elementary, and it will be impossible to determine just which varieties contributed most toward the development of the higher forms of vault in use among the Mayas. There are, however, but two principles of construction involved in all of these spans—the horizontal span and the lean-to. The latter is never used alone but occurs in combination with the former.

The prevailing form of Maya arch is based on the horizontal span, employing not single long slabs, but a series of short slabs so placed as to bridge the void by degrees. A course of stones is laid along the top of each of the opposing walls, projecting a little, a second course is laid in like manner, and others follow until by a series of offsets the sides have approached to within a foot or two, when a course of large well-squared slabs is laid across, completing the span.

In examples employing the lean-to principle, the construction is the same up to the point of connecting the closely approximate walls. Instead of laying a course of flat capstones across, two courses were employed, set on edge on the upper courses of the walls and inclined together at the top, continuing the pitch of the walls and forming the true cuneiform arch. The object of the off-setting is, of course, to reduce the span of the void, thus permitting the use of ceiling stones of small size instead of large and long stones which were hard to obtain and easily broken, or beams of wood which soon decayed. These arches really represent the emancipation of the Maya builder from the thraldom of the wooden beam. The prevailing variety was used in all forms of chambers and also in certain large vaulted passages, as in the Palace at Uxmal, and occasionally in smaller openings, as at Palenque, but the flat span or lintel remained in nearly universal use for ordinary doorways. A unique appearing arch is found at Palenque, the sides being curved in such a way as to give a somewhat trefoil effect to the opening. The principle of construction is, however, the same as in the prevailing form of the cuneiform arch, the profile being curved instead of straight.

It is evident that considerable difficulty was experienced in carrying up the long slopes of the larger vaults, and the high angle adopted was one means of lessening the tendency to collapse. The projecting stones were largely held in place by the masonry of the body of the wall, which was carried up at the same time, but even this, especially in cases where the outer surface was also inclined, could not have prevented the frequent falling of the work when approaching the apex. In meeting this difficulty it was a common practice to use timbers—generally poles of medium or small size—which were placed across and built into the masonry as it rose, holding the walls apart. These beams are preserved in hundreds of cases and nearly every vault shows by its numerous beam sockets that this device was extensively relied upon. I believe the theory is advanced by some writer that a core of masonry was first built of the proper shape, and the vault constructed over it. I doubt if the numerous examples of masonry-filled apartments observed are satisfactory proof of this, but a careful examination of the surface finish in a room so filled might readily settle the question.

In Fig. 5 I present sketches of six examples of the Maya arch. These do not cover the entire ground, but others so far as I have seen are merely variations of the two prevailing types, shown in *a* and *b*, the first, terminating above in two rows of inclined slabs, forming the apex, and the second closed with a course of horizontal slabs. The

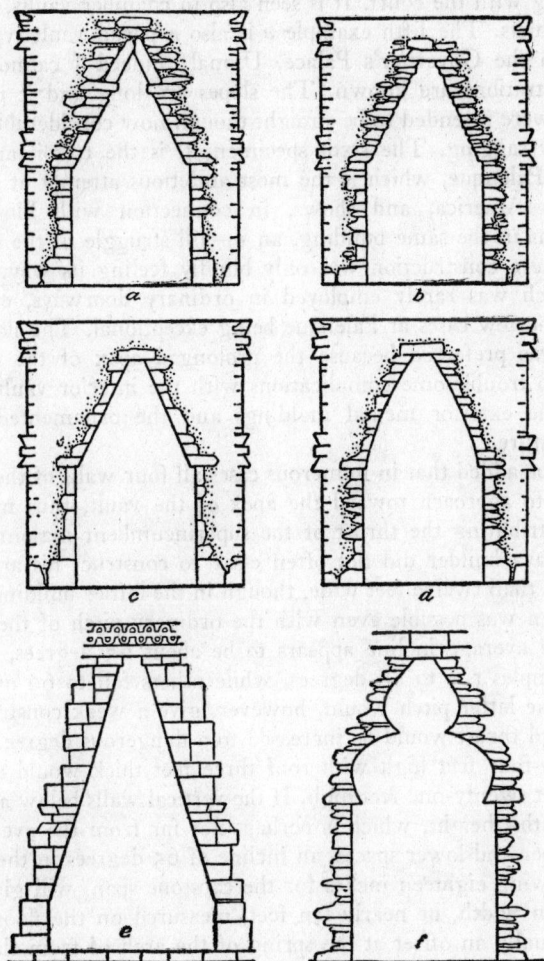

Fig. 5. Examples of Maya arches.

former is seen in Chichen-Itza, but is rare elsewhere, and the latter was almost universally used in chamber vaults. The specimen shown in *c* differs from *b* only in having the corbellate or offset margins of the stones dressed with the slope, making a plane surface. That given in *d* is identical with the preceding, save that its inclined faces are slightly curved; it is the form sometimes used in the portal vaults which open through one or more of the buildings of a quadrangular group communicating with the court. It is seen also in chamber vaults, in bridges and aqueducts. The fifth example *e* is also a portal vault typically developed in the Governor's Palace, Uxmal; indeed I cannot say that other illustrations are known. The slopes are long and it is probable that they were intended to be straight though now considerably warped, possibly by sagging. The sixth specimen, *f*, is the trefoil arch of the Palace in Palenque, which is the most ambitious attempt at arch elaboration in America, and shows, in connection with kindred wall perforations in the same building, an up-hill struggle of the esthetic in a field where construction was only blindly feeling its way.

The arch was rarely employed in ordinary doorways, exterior or interior, the few cases at Palenque being exceptional. The flat form of opening was preferred because the prolonged apex of the cuneiform arch led to troublesome complications with the interior vaults, as well as with the exterior medial moldings and the ornamented zone of the entablature.

It may be added that in numerous cases all four walls of the chamber are made to approach toward the apex of the vault, thus more thoroughly distributing the thrust of the superincumbent masonry.

The Maya builder did not often essay to construct his arch over a space more than twelve feet wide, though in the loftier buildings a much greater span was possible even with the ordinary pitch of the opposing walls. The average incline appears to be about 65 degrees, but occasional examples rise to 80 degrees, while others fall to 60 or even 55 degrees; the latter pitch would, however, give a weak construction, as the outward thrust would be increased to a dangerous degree. A building twenty-four feet high with roof three feet thick would accommodate a vault twenty-one feet high. If the vertical walls below are carried up to half this height, which is perhaps not far from the average relation of upper and lower spaces, an incline of 65 degrees in the opposing walls, allowing eighteen inches for the capstone span, will give a vault nine feet in width, or nearly ten feet, measured on the floor level, as there is usually an offset at the spring of the arch of from three to six inches on each side.

In the vaulted passageways through the Governor's Palace at Uxmal the incline of the arch begins within a few inches of the ground, so that in the long rise of twenty feet or more, even with the high pitch of 70 degrees, the width spanned is not far from eighteen feet. The highest arch met with in my own investigations is in the outer annular chamber or gallery of the Round Tower at Chichen. The height is about twenty-four feet, while the width is only six feet; the pitch of the vault walls is therefore unusually great, and the apex correspondingly sharp.

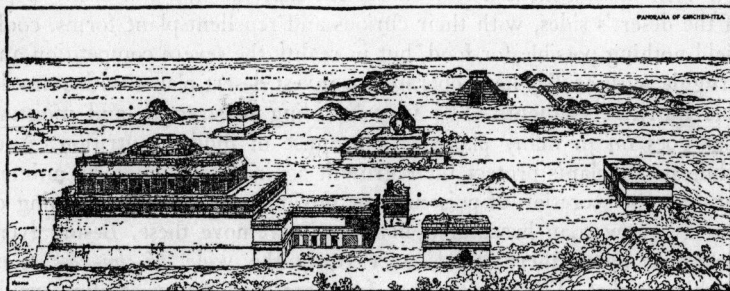

Subsistence and Material Culture

20. DESERT PLANT FOODS OF THE COAHUILLA [1]

BY DAVID PRESCOTT BARROWS

TO THE unsophisticated it would seem that the dry and rocky slopes of the desert's sides, with their curious and repellent plant forms, could yield nothing possible for food, but in reality the severe competition and struggle with aridity have operated to invest desert plants with remarkable nutritive elements. The very hoarding of strength and moisture that goes on in many plants is a promise of hidden nutrition. And, while many plants protect their growth against destruction by animals through the secretion of poisonous or noxious elements, the cunning of the savage woman has taught her how to remove these. Beside every Coahuilla home there stands ever ready the wide *pá-cha-ka-vel*, or leaching basket. The results prove far more than the expectation would warrant.

I cannot pretend to have exhausted the food supply of these Indians, but I have discovered not less than sixty distinct products for nutrition, and at least twenty-eight more utilized for narcotics, stimulants, or medicines, all derived from desert or semi-desert localities, in use among these Indians. . . .

On the desert the main reliance of the Coahuilla Indians is the algaroba or mesquite. This remarkable tree is well known to any one who has traversed the sandy Southwest. Its range is wide, from the desert slopes of the California mountains, eastward in southern latitudes to Texas. Of the Colorado basin it is the characteristic tree. It grows to a height of from thirty to forty feet. Its wood is close-grained and hard; its leaves small but abundant, and its branches well armored with spines. . . .

The fruit of the algaroba or honey mesquite (*Prosopis juliflora*) is a beautiful legumen, four to seven inches long, which hangs in splendid

[1] From pages 54-70 of David Prescott Barrows, *The Ethno-Botany of the Coahuilla Indians of Southern California*, University of Chicago Press, 1900. The name Coahuilla, now more generally written Cahuilla, is pronounced "Kah-wee-yah." By permission.

clusters. A good crop will bend each branch almost to the ground, and as the fruit falls, pile the ground beneath the tree with a thick carpet of straw-colored pods. These are pulpy, sweet, and nutritious, affording food to stock as well as to man.

Everywhere in the Colorado country, to the Mojave, Yuma, and Cocopah, as well as to the Coahuilla, they are the staple of life. The Coahuillas gather them in July and August in great quantities, drying them thoroughly and then packing them away in the basket granaries. The beans are never husked, but pod and all are pounded up into an imperfect meal in the wooden mortar. This meal is then placed in earthen dishes and thoroughly soaked. It is then ready to be eaten, and is called by the Coahuillas, *pé-chi-ta*, or *mén-yi-kish*, according as it is, or is not, sifted. A light fermentation, which shortly results, improves it. The mass itself, while requiring vigorous mastication, is sweet and wholesome. It is sometimes rolled into compact balls and carried for food on a journey.

According to Mr. Havard, this pulp contains "more than half its weight of assimilative principles, of which the most important is sugar, in the proportion of 25 to 30 per cent."

The "screwbean" or toŕnillo (*Prosopis pubescens*, Benth.) is less abundant than the algaroba. Its fruit is a cluster of little yellow spirals united at one point. It contains even more saccharine matter than the algaroba, and may be eaten with relish as plucked from the tree. A fermented beverage can be made from this meal and was once much drunk by the Indians of the Colorado river. Major Heinzleman described its use among the Yumas: "The pod mesquite begins to ripen in June, the screwbean a little later. Both contain a great deal of saccharine matter; the latter is so full it furnishes by boiling a palatable molasses, and from the former, by boiling and fermentation, a tolerably good drink may be made."

Along the overflowed banks of the New river, and elsewhere about the desert's edge, where cloudbursts or freshets send their sudden streams of muddy water out over the sand, there grows up luxuriantly an enormous species of Chenopodium. In the New river country I have seen the growth higher than a man's head as he sat on horseback. The stalks are sometimes six inches in diameter. The leaves are eaten readily by horses, and the plant is of much value to parties crossing the desert and to stockmen. Its local name is "careless weed." The seeds are eaten by the Indians and the leaves used for greens. Northward, in the Cabeson and Coyote, a smaller and probably distinct species, identified by Mr. Jepson as *Chenopodium Fremontii*, flourishes after freshets. Its dry branches are covered with seeds which are gathered by the Indians in large quantities, and ground into flour which is baked into little cakes. The Coahuillas call the plant *kit* or *ke-et*. After a good harvest of this Chenopodium the edge of the Coyote cañon will be fringed with granaries holding stores of this food. . . .

The most varied stores of food, however, do not come from the fluviatile plain of the Colorado, but from the forbidding mountains that rise high and abruptly on the westward. . . .

Most remarkable of all the plants that flourish in these wastes is the agave, perhaps the most unique and interesting plant of all America. It ranges widely throughout southwestern United States and Mexico with a large number of species, perhaps one hundred in all; and outside of Mexico, where it furnishes "pulque" and "vino mescale," it is used for food by Apaches, the Pah Ute family, and desert tribes in general. By all these Indians is it prepared for food in much the same way. Several species have become familiar, as the "century plants" of California gardens, but they are not handsome plants except when in bloom, though they give themselves most beautifully to the wants of the Indian.

The life history of all these species is much the same. They come up in little round heads or cabbages. For years this head enlarges, throwing out fibrous leaves armed with a spine at the point. Even in the hot air of the desert it is twelve to fifteen years before the period of flowering is reached. Then from the center of the plant there starts up a stalk, growing with great rapidity. In the larger species this stalk may be twenty to thirty feet high and eighteen inches through at the base. From this stalk clusters of pale yellow blossoms, thousands in number, open in the hot, quivering sunshine. This supreme act ends the life of the plant.

Within the territory of the Coahuillas there is but a single species, the *Agave deserti*, Engelm., which grows abundantly along the eastern base of the coast ranges in San Diego county, and southward into Baja California. It was first discovered by Lieutenant W. H. Emory, of the Mexican Boundary Survey, in 1846. It is a small species with leaves densely clustered, thick and deeply concave, only six to twelve inches long. The scape or stalk is from ten to twelve feet high and slender. The flowers are a bright yellow. From April on, the cabbages and stalks are full of sap and are then roasted. Parties go down from the mountain villages into Coyote cañon for the purpose. Great fire pits or ovens, called *na-chish-em*, are dug in the sands and lined with stones. Fire is kept up in the pit until the stones are thoroughly heated; the mescal heads are then placed in the hole and covered over with grass and earth and left to roast for a day or two. Mescal heads thus cooked consist of fibrous, molasses-colored layers, sweet and delicious to the taste and wonderfully nutritious. Pieces will keep for many years. The agave is called *a-mul,* the sections of the stalk, *u-a-sil,* which are also roasted and, though fibrous, are sweet and good, and the short leaves about the head, *ya-mil.* The yellow blossoms, *amu-sal-em,* are boiled and dried for preservation, and then boiled anew when ready to be eaten. The fibers from the leaves of the agave, *amu-pa-la,* are exceedingly important in manufactures. . . .

The *Yucca Mohavensis* (Coahuilla *hú-nu-vút*) grows abundantly on various hillsides and sandy cañons of the southern exposure of the San Jacinto range, as well as near the summits of the cañons on the desert slopes. The species is quite different in appearance from the *Yucca Whipplei,* Torr., which grows so abundantly nearer the coast and in the vicinity of Pasadena, and is known as the "Spanish bayonet" or *quijotes.* In the *Yucca Mohavensis* the clusters of spines are very dense about its foot, and its short, thick stump or caudex rises to a height sometimes of six feet from the ground. Its flower stalk or scape is short and thick, but clustered with the delicate waxy flowers of the yucca kind. The fruit, *nin-yil,* appears as plump, sticky, green pods, three or five inches long with big, black seeds filling the center in four rows. These are picked when green and roasted among the coals. They have a sweet, not unpleasant taste, slightly suggestive of roasted green apples. When ripe, the pods are eaten uncooked and are sweet and pleasant, though slightly puckering to the taste. . . .

Higher up on the mountains grow two species of wild plum or cherry. One, the *Prunus ilicifolia,* Walp., has an extensive range along the California coast and had a wide use among the California Indians. It is called by the Mexicans "yslay" and by the Coahuillas *chá-mish.* It grows abundantly in all the cañons of the San Jacinto mountains, its dark, handsome foliage crowding many a pass and hillside. Its fruit is of a reddish-yellow color, and resembles very small gage plums. The pulp is, however, very thin and puckery and the pit preposterously large. It is the kernel of the latter and not the pulp that is mostly utilized. These plums are gathered in very large quantities in August and are spread in the sun until the pulp is thoroughly shrunken and dried. The thin shells of the pits are then easily broken open and the kernels extracted. These are crushed in the mortar, leached in the sand basket, and boiled into the usual atole. The other plum tree has with some question been identified by Mr. Jepson as the *Prunus Andersonii,* Gray. I found it growing along the eastern summits of the San Jacinto range.

Its fruit somewhat resembles the *Zizyphus* and was formerly eaten by the Coahuillas, who called it *cha-wa-kal*. . . .

Before dismissing the truly desert plants that yield food, a word is merited by the palms. These have been referred to above. They grow in long, waving lines along the gorges leading into the desert wherever water stands in pools or seeps through the sandy bottoms. Beneath the wide fronds the dates grow in great clusters, supported by a strong but drooping stalk. These dates are very small and the seeds are disproportionately large, but early in the fall, when they ripen, the Coahuillas lasso the clusters and draw them down for food. Swarms of bees surround the fruit as it ripens, and in the fronds of the palms are multitudes of "yellow jackets'" nests. The Indians of Lower California cut out the heart or center of the top of young palms and eat them with great relish. I have not known the Coahuillas to indulge in these "palmitos."

In the valleys near the summit of the range and especially in the Piñon Flats are groves of the *Juniperus occidentalis*, Hook., low evergreen trees, with thin, shreddy bark. The fruit, a bluish-black drupe the size of a small marble, is eaten by the Coahuillas and called by them *is-wut*.

The acorn was one of the most generally used foods of the Indians of the Pacific coast. Its use was noticed by Cabrillo, the first white explorer to navigate these waters. "They eat acorns and a grain which is as large as maize and is white, of which they make dumplings. It is good food." Certain parts of the coast, the Upper San Joaquin valley and the mountains of the Coast Range are thickly covered with forests of this stately tree. There are no less than fourteen species of oaks in the whole of California and about eight are found in the southern part of the state. Their fruit contains "starch, fixed oil, citric acid, and sugar, as well as astringent and bitter principles." The largest and most palatable acorn is that of the white oak, or Mexican "roble" (*Quercus lobata*), "common throughout the state, on the plains and in the foothills, in the southern part of the state somewhat higher in the mountains." It was mostly from this tree that the Indians of the past supplied themselves. . . .

The *Quercus dumosa*, Nutt., which has a thick, large fruit, grows on the Coahuilla mountain and is gathered in considerable quantities by the Indians of Coahuilla valley. This acorn is called by them *kwin-yil*. It is ground in the mortar and leached in the sand basket. Dr. Havard reports that the sand mixed with the meal by washing has "a decided effect upon the teeth. My informant, a medical officer, tells me that he has seen an Indian forty-five years old with the crowns of his otherwise healthy teeth half gone, while in Indians sixty years old it is not uncommon to see all the teeth worn down even with the gums." Although the sand basket as a means for preparing food is in constant use among the Coahuilla Indians, I have never myself noticed any such effects.

The piñon or pine nut is a very important article of food. The lower limit of the pineries, in southern California, is, of course, high, being almost everywhere about 5,000 feet, and it is only by reason of the fact that the Coahuillas have penetrated into the mountains from the desert that this source of food is available to them at all. The summits of Torres and Coahuilla mountains and the higher San Jacinto peaks are covered with pines of several species; the gigantic sugar pine of the Pacific slope (*P. Lambertiaana,* Dougl.) with a cone a foot and a half in length, the Mexican nut pine (*P. Sembroides*), and (*P. Parryana,* Eng.), and also the single-leafed or Nevada nut pine (*P. Monophylla*), so precious to the Indians of the Great Basin. These nuts are gathered in large quantities, generally in the late fall of the year. Mr. B. H. Dutcher, of the Death Valley Expedition of 1891, has given a careful account of piñon gathering among the Panamints on the west side of Death Valley. The tree was the *P. Monophylla,* which has a small cone three inches long. These were pulled and beaten from the trees with a pronged stick and collected in light packing baskets while still sticky with gum. They were then piled on a heap of brush and roasted, which dried the pitch and spread the leaves of the cone. The nuts were then jarred out by a heavy blow from a stone on the apex of the cone. The nuts were winnowed from the chaff by tossing them from a flat basket in the breeze. The Coahuillas harvest the nuts in precisely the same manner. Sometimes in mid-summer the cones are beaten from the trees, before the ripened harvest time, thoroughly roasted in a fire, split open with a hatchet and the nuts extracted. Piñones are called by the Coahuillas *te-wat-em;* the cones *te-vat,* and the little almond-like cavities in which the nuts lie and which are exposed in section when the cone is split open are called *he-push* or the "eyes" of the *te-vat.* The pine most used is the *Pinus monophylla.* . . .

Perhaps the most important of the seed foods used by the Indians is the justly famed "chia" (*Salvia Columbariæ,* Benth.), called by the Coahuillas *pá-sal.* The plant is one of the smallest of the sage family. It grows up from an annual root with a slender branching stem, terminated by several curious whorls containing the seeds. These are dark, round, flat bodies, that have a slippery, uncertain feeling to the touch. The genus Salvia has an exceedingly wide range and use as a food plant. According to Dr. Havard the *Salvia polystarchia,* Ort., is largely cultivated in northern and central Mexico. These seeds are rich in mucilage and oil. "After careful roasting they are ground into meal, which, when thrown into water, expands to several times its bulk, the mucilage rapidly dissolving. By adding lemon and sweetening a very popular Mexican beverage is produced."

Chia was a staple food with the Indians of the Pacific coast. Large quantities, already parched, have been taken from graves on the Santa Barbara channel. The seeds are gathered by the Coahuillas with the seed fan and flat basket, and are parched and ground. The meal is then mixed with about three times as much wheat flour and the whole pounded up together. It makes a dark looking meal. This is "pinole," called by the Coahuillas *to-at*. It is an old and famous preparation. . . .

Pinole, by the Coahuillas, is sometimes baked into little cakes or biscuits. Either way chia is used, it is very good; has a pleasant, nutty flavor, and is exceedingly wholesome. . . .

Among the fruits most important to the Indian inhabitants of the Southwest stand those of the cactus family. There are over fifty species in the United States and a majority of these are found in California.

The Mexican prickly pear or "tuna" (*Opuntia tuna*, Mill) is said by Dr. Havard to have been brought to the Pacific coast from Mexico, where it had been cultivated from time immemorial. It was planted in hedges about the missions and ranch-houses, where it thrives still in picturesque clusters and is now thoroughly naturalized. Its fruit is the well-known "Indian fig." While it has not been planted anywhere on the reservations of the Coahuillas, they sometimes obtain the fruit from other Indians of the valleys. The cactus plant is called by the Coahuillas *na-vit* and the little bud-like fruit *na-vit-yu-lu-ku* or "the little heads of the cactus."

There are numerous species of cactus throughout the mountains down to the desert level. About a dozen yield fruit products utilized by the Coahuillas. In most cases it is the ripened fruit or "fig" that is eaten. In several cases it is the abundant seeds, in others, the buds and succulent joints of stalk. Except in a few instances I can do no more in the way of identification of these species than to give a description of the plant and state its uses and Indian name.

The *Opuntia basilaris* is an especially valuable cactus plant of the Coahuillas. It is one of the small varieties and has a tender slate-colored stem in flat joints. The young fruit in early summer is full of sweetness. These buds are collected in baskets, being easily broken off with a stick. The short, sparse spines are wholly brushed off with a bunch of grass or a handful of brush twigs. The buds are then cooked or steamed with hot stones in a pit for twelve hours or more. This cactus is called *má-nal*.

Mr. Coville describes exactly the same use of this plant by the Panamints. This cooked cactus is, he says, called *nä-vo*. I would call attention to the similarity of this word to the general Coahuilla word for cactus fruit, *na-vit*. No vocabulary of the Panamints has ever been published, but they are undoubtedly of the same great stock as the Coahuillas and such verbal similarities are to be expected.

Mu-tal is another of the opuntia, with flat, ugly jointed stems, growing low and spreading over the ground in the most arid stretches of the valleys. The flat joints, the size of one's palm, are crowded along their edges with buds as big as the last joint of a man's thumb. They are gathered in large quantities, brushed, and dried. They are often stored for subsequent use, and when needed for food are prepared by boiling in water with a little salt and lard. Very frequently also the fruit is allowed to ripen for its seeds. The figs, after being dried, are spread out on a hard, smooth, dirt floor and then the woman sits down beside the pile of cactus heads and with a flail, made from the leaf stem of the desert palm, thoroughly threshes out the seeds. These are then winnowed from the chaff and stored for winter use. Along through the winter, as needed for food, they are pounded into meal and cooked into an atole. These seeds are called *wi-al* and they are obtained from several species of cactus besides the *mu-tal*. . . .

Ko-pash is the famed "nigger head," the *Echinocactus cylindricis*. It appears above the sand simply as a round fluted globe, a little larger than a man's head. It is covered with spines and bears a small edible fig. But its chief value does not lie in its fruit, but in its succulent and thirst-relieving interior. No plant could be more admirably contrived as a reservoir, and the thick tough rind and protective spines enclose an interior that is full of water. This plant is often resorted to by thirsty travelers and, according to the stories told over the desert, frequently saves life.

A review of the food supply of these Indians forces in upon us some general reflections or conclusions. First, it seems certain that the diet was a much more diversified one than fell to the lot of most North American Indians. Roaming from the desert, through the mountains to the coast plains, they drew upon three quite dissimilar botanical zones. There was no single staple, on the production of which depended the chances of sufficiency or want. Any one of several much used products might be gathered in sufficient quantities to carry the entire tribe through a year of subsistence. There was really an abundant supply of wild food, far more than adequate, at nearly all times of the year, for the needs of the several thousand Indian inhabitants of former times, although hardly a score of white families will find a living here after all the Indians are gone. And the secret of this anomaly lies in the fact that the Indian drew his stores of food from hillsides and cañons, where the white man looks for nothing and can produce nothing. The territory is a very large one, perhaps 4,000 square miles of cañons and mountains, rough plains, and sandy deserts. In all of it, as we have seen, there are few spots of beauty; only the valleys of pines, the wonderful cañons of palms, and the green potreros about the springs; while over most broods the hot, throbbing silence of the desert. And yet this habitat, dreary and forbidding as it appears to most, is after all a generous one. It bears some of the most remarkable food plants of any continent. Nature did not pour out her gifts lavishly here, but the patient toiler and wise seeker she rewarded well. The main staples of diet were, indeed, furnished in most lavish abundance. Let us notice a few instances. The crops of legumens, that annually fall from the splendid mesquite groves of the Cabeson or the New river country, could not be wholly utilized by a population that numbered a hundred thousand souls. I have seen the mesquite beans fallen so heavily beneath the trees in the vicinity of Martinez as to carpet the sand for miles. Centals could be gathered about every tree. Hundreds of horses and cattle that ranged the valley, to say nothing of the busy women that had crowded their granaries full, effected no visible diminution of the supply. . . .

The road from Coahuilla valley down to Ahuanga creek descends along the bottom of a gorge. The sides of this cañon are covered with *Yucca Mohavensis*. In July or early August these palm-like trees, for so they almost are, are all crowded with stalks hung with heavy pods, more fruit drying in the sun than the entire tribe could devour. The groves of oaks and pines in the higher valleys of San Jacinto; the abundant crops of chia and other seed plants; the elder berry, so greatly enjoyed, that frequently families will live for weeks on little else; all of these can be found in inexhaustible quantities. Another fact very favorable to the Indians is the long season over which the gathering of these staples is distributed. The harvest time opens in April, with the budding out of agave and yucca stalks, and from this time until late fall there is no month without its especial product. The chia and other seed plants are ready for the fan in May and June, the wild plums in June and July, the mesquite and sambucus in August, and the piñons and acorns from September on. For only about four months of winter was it necessary to hoard food. The ollas and basket granaries were sufficient store-houses.

21. SUBSISTENCE AND SOCIETY AMONG THE HEIKUM BUSHMEN [2]

BY L. FOURIE

THE Hei-²om, or Heikum as they are called by people who are unable to pronounce the clicks of the Hottentot language, are generally believed to have resulted from the intermixture of Hottentots with a now extinct Bushman tribe which originally inhabited the greater portion of the Territory now known as Damaraland and Ovamboland. Among the Klip Kaffirs, on the other hand, there is a tradition that the Hei-²om and the Hottentots were descended from two Hottentot brothers, one of whom, the ancestor of the present day Hei-²om, preferred a hunter's life to the less interesting pastoral life of his tribe. The name Hei-²om is stated to have been applied to the ancestral tribe of Bushmen by the Hottentots because in by-gone days its members slept in trees as a protection against lions. It is derived from the Hottentot words heis denoting a tree and ²om to sleep, and thus means "tree sleeping."

A greater degree of racial intermixture is met with among the Hei-²om than among any of the other existing tribes of Bushmen. Their manner of life is still that of Bushmen but, unlike their neighbors of the Kalahari, they have no language of their own and speak a Nama [Hottentot] dialect. Except among the groups in the vicinity of the Etosha Pan every trace of their original organization has disappeared almost completely. . . .

It is with certain customs of the Hei-²om of the Etosha Pan region that I propose to deal in this paper.

These Hei-²om, like all other organized Bushman tribes, consist of a number of closely related family groups. Each group, ²gãub, has its own territory or hunting ground, known as ⁴hūb. The various groups are generally referred to among each other by a name which either indicates the locality in which they live or describes some physical or other characteristic of such locality or group. Hence there are the ³Goa-khoin or people residing in the country on the south bank of the Omuramba Ovambo around ³Goab; . . . the χomk-hoin, along the

---

[2] From "Preliminary Notes on Certain Customs of the Hei-//om Bushmen," in *Journal of the South West Africa Society*, Volume 1, pages 49-63, 1925-26. English equivalents have been substituted for the native terms of the original whenever possible. The small numbers ¹, ², ³, ⁴, represent the "clicks" of the Bushman and Hottentot languages, and replace respectively the following symbols in the original: single bar, double bar, double-crossed bar, exclamation.

southern border of the Etosha Pan, or people who χom or scrape together, the name indicating the method of collecting salt on the Pan; . . . and so forth.

I

At the head of each group is a chief or big man, gei-khoib. All the members of the group [²gãub] live in a common encampment or werft, called ²gãus or gei-²gãus according as to whether it is small or large. The huts of the married families are arranged in the form of an irregular circle. That of the chief is always situated in the east, facing but at some distance from the other huts. The right or north side of the encampment is reserved entirely for the sisters of the chief and their families. When the eldest sister visits the chief she is accommodated in a hut immediately to his right, and any other visiting sisters build their huts to the right of that of the eldest sister. Any daughter of the chief, when visiting him, is allowed to erect her hut directly opposite to his at the furthest extremity of the encampment. This is done on account of the parent-in-law taboo which exists among the Hei-²om in common with other Bushman tribes. The brothers of the chief live immediately to his left on the south side of the encampment, and beyond them are placed the other married families of the community. At or near the center of the encampment is situated a large tree known as the ⁴kheis which in the Nama language denotes a werft or encampment. Within the circle of huts towards the south is the hut of adolescent young girls, ³kham-khoidi or oa-χai-khoidi, and towards the north, that of the adolescent young men, aχarogu. Mature marriageable young women, ⁴gari-khoidi, occupy huts next to those of their parents in the circle. Old widows and widowers, as also visitors from any neighboring group, live outside the circle of married people. The dancing place is to the west within the circle. The general layout of the encampment is shown on the accompanying diagram.

Hutmaking is the work of the women. The husband does not interfere in any way with his wife's building operations. She selects the site within the limits prescribed by custom and makes the dwelling at her own leisure and pleasure. In the rainy season the huts are erected very quickly, most women completing the whole structure in a single day. The adolescent girls make their hut . . . themselves. The hut for the boys is made in coöperation by the mothers of the boys concerned, and during the dry season is an open structure without any roof. . . . In the wet season it is roofed over. . . . Huts are never placed immediately underneath trees on account of the risk of being struck by lightning.

Each family has two fires, namely, one inside the hut for light and warmth and one in front of the entrance to the hut for cooking purposes. Both fires are known as ¹ais. The fire within the hut of the chief is called om-¹ais and the one outside, or the principal fire, ⁴ou-¹ais.

The large tree in or near the center of the encampment is reserved as a meeting-place for men for ceremonial and other purposes. Women are entirely forbidden to approach it or to join the men when gathered underneath it. To this, however, there is one exception, namely, the wife of the chief may go to it to obtain fire for kindling the principal fire or for other menial purposes when required by her husband. With the exception of the chief nobody is permitted to live in close proximity to this tree. Under it is made the first fire (⁴hei-¹ais) on the establishment of a new encampment, and underneath it is deposited, for distribution, all meat killed in the chase.

Fire is looked upon as belonging to the chief and the fire kindled by him is regarded as the only real fire containing all the requisite properties for preserving the welfare of the community.

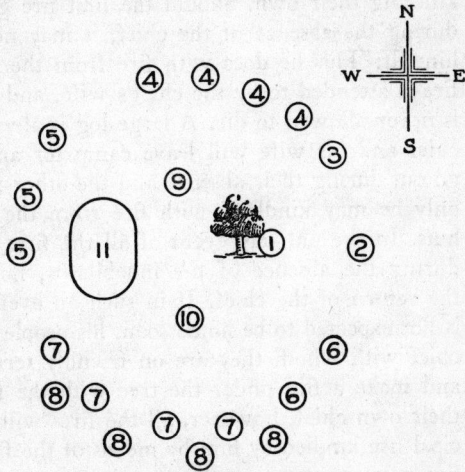

1, tree. 2, chief. 3, chief's oldest sister. 4, other sisters of chief. 5, daughters of chief. 6, brothers of chief. 7, other members of community. 8, visitors, widows, widowers. 9, adolescent young men. 10, adolescent girls. 11, dancing place.

Every Bushman knows how to use firesticks (hei-doros), but will not and may not kindle a fire with them in the encampment, as firemaking is a matter of serious import and the chief is the only person who is able to bring forth from it the magic properties which bring health and happiness and ward off evil. Hence when it becomes necessary to move camp, as for example, after a death has taken place, the whole community take up all their goods and chattels and, led by the chief, set off in search of a new site to be selected by the latter. Having found a suitable one, he places his belongings on the spot on which his own hut is to be erected. His followers, passing on his left, take up suitable places for their huts in like manner. The chief then proceeds to the tree and kindles a fire underneath it by means of the fire-sticks. Fire from the old encampment or any other source may not be used for this purpose. He next applies ³norab and dabas to the fire by scraping the roots of these plants with his knife into it. This is done to invest the fire with magical properties. He then lights his pipe with the "first fire" to show that the fire is now free for use by the other members of the community. This is next used by his wife for lighting the [principal] fire in front of his hut. The men may now come and light their pipes from the first fire and the women may fetch fire from the principal fire for kindling their own. Should the first fire go out, as sometimes happens during the absence of the chief, it may not be lit except by the latter himself. This he does with fire from the principal fire. The principal fire is attended to by the chief's wife, and under normal circumstances is never allowed to die. A large log is always placed upon it before the chief and his wife will leave camp for any length of time. Should it go out during their absence and the other fires remain burning, he and only he may kindle it with fire from the first fire or from the other huts. In the unlikely event of all the fires having become extinguished during the absence of the inhabitants, no fires may be kindled until the return of the chief. If in such an eventuality he has gone far and is not expected to be home soon, his people will approach a neighboring chief with whom they are on friendly terms and the latter will come and make a fire under the tree with the fire-sticks. On the return of their own chief, however, all the fires will be put out and a new principal fire kindled by him by means of the fire-sticks. The new principal fire now serves to supply the other members of the group. At times it may happen that some of the members of the community may not be living in the encampment but in some outside one. This is usually the case only in times of drought when the game have moved far afield and great difficulty is being experienced in obtaining veldkos. Further, people driven out by another group and seeking protection are sometimes allowed to live some distance away from the encampment. Such communities are not allowed to make their own fire or to obtain it from any other source but the principal fire of the chief with whom they have sought shelter.

Persistent ill-health among the members of the community or difficulty in obtaining veldkos or want of luck in the chase may cause the chief, either of his own accord or after consultation with his people, to proclaim that it is necessary to make a new fire. In such an event all fires, including the principal one, are extinguished by being covered over with ashes. The chief at the same time notifies all outside camps of his decision and the latter likewise extinguish their fires. He then kindles a new principal fire in front of his hut with the fire-sticks and applies [3]norab and dabas in the manner described above. The new fire is not made on the same spot as the old fire, but a few feet away from the place on which it had been.

II

Certain practices are observed in connection with the chase. Bow and poisoned arrow are the weapons used for hunting. The poison is obtained from the tuber of a plant (*Adenium* ? sp.) called [4]kores. In the preparation of the poison the tuber is sliced and the milky juice squeezed out into an old pot or other receptacle by means of an oval-shaped piece of flat bone made from the shoulderblade of big game. The juice is boiled until it is black and of so thick a consistence that the bubbling ceases. The finished poison is also known as [4]kores. While still warm in the pot it is rounded into balls with the bone and transferred to a little bag made from the thin belly skin of the zebra. Each person prepares his own poison. When required for use as much as is necessary is cut off with the bone, spat upon, and mounded on to the previously heated arrow head with the bone. After the poison has been applied to the arrow head it is referred to as [4]om. . . .

After an animal has been shot it is followed by the hunter until it expires or until nightfall when he returns to the encampment. The following morning the whole community takes part in the search for the carcass as the previous day's tracks had in all probability been effaced during the night by other animals. The searchers spread out on a wide front and keep a very sharp lookout for the presence of vultures. After the carcass has been found it is skinned by the men. The belly is then opened and the entrails removed and cleaned. Bags are made from the stomach and into these the blood is collected. The animal is next cut up and after this has been done the liver is roasted and eaten by the men. The skin, if suitable for the purpose, is cut into sandals, bowstrings, etc., on the spot. The meat is then removed to the encampment by the men, who may occasionally be assisted by the women. On arrival at the encampment all the meat is laid on the ground under the tree, either on the sticks which were used in carrying it or on branches. The chief now comes forward and if he finds that the first fire has gone out he returns to his hut, brings fire and wood and re-lights it. If he is absent when the meat is brought in he is immediately sent for, the meat in the meantime being hung on the tree. After having kindled the fire the chief instructs one of the men —the one who has shot the animal is excluded from doing any work— to open the bones and collect the marrow. The blood and the marrow are placed on the fire in separate pots and at the same time some of the meat for the men is also cooked. As soon as the latter is ready for eating, the chief removes a piece from the pot and "tastes" it. This is done by holding it between the teeth and fingers and cutting off and eating a morsel or two. The meat is now safe for the members of his group to eat. The cooked meat is then pounded with a stone, teased between the fingers and thrown into the pot containing the blood. The melted marrow is next stirred into the mixture of blood and meat. The resulting dish is known as [3]koms.

All meat killed with bow and arrow is soχa and may not be partaken of until it has been tasted by the chief. The liver, however, is eaten by the men immediately after the animal has been cut up, and is thus excluded from the scope of the soχa as far as men are concerned, but to the women it is soχa. All parts of the animal are eaten, but certain categories of people may eat only certain prescribed portions of the animal, the rest of the meat being soχa to them. For example, the wife of the man who killed the animal is entitled to the superficial covering of meat and fat of the hind quarters, the entrails, and the trotters. Her portion is known as the [3]noe-di and is the only meat which may be partaken of by women. The [3]noe-di is shared by her with the other women, including the adolescent girls, and with the young children. The [3]noe-di, however, may not be eaten until the chief has tasted the meat. It is cut on the spot where the carcass was found, by the person who shot the animal, and handed over to the latter's wife after arrival at the encampment. It is not brought under the encampment tree. It is cooked by the wife of the hunter on the fire in front of her hut, after which the other women come and get their portions and eat it in their own huts. The girls obtain their meat from their respective mothers, as also do young children still living with their parents. If women partake of any other meat than the [3]noe-di, the poison of the arrow will not act when an animal has been shot. The meat which may be eaten by the young men is known as [4]om-[2]gani and includes the flesh of the abdominal wall, kidneys, etc., and the genital organs such as udder, testicles, etc. It is prepared by the young men themselves over their own fire at their hut. The person who shot the animal receives the ribs and shoulder blade of one side. He may prepare his portion either under the tree or over his own fire. The ribs must be cooked and the shoulder blade roasted because they taste better when done in this manner. The rest of the meat is soχa to him and if he eats any other part he will not meet with success in hunting because the poison will weaken and refuse to act. The parts of the animal which go to the chief are known as the so-eis and include portions about two fingerbreadths in size from each quarter, from each

side of the back, and one rib from each side. These are strung on a
thong or cord and hung up for his sole use. So-eis may, however, be
shared by him with a visiting chief. The chief's wife receives her share
from the ³noe-di. The chief may also partake of the meat for the remainder of the men, called the so-²gani, under which is included the
³koms. The latter may be eaten only under the encampment tree.
After it has been prepared, each man brings his wooden bowl or other
receptacle and helps himself. Any man whose wife is menstruating will,
however, not partake of the ³koms as it contains blood. The rest of the
meat is divided among the men by the chief and is prepared and eaten
at their huts. . . .

Any want of success in the chase is generally attributed to some
chance incident. For example, a man, who has had bad luck in hunting while his wife had her periods, will not hunt again when she is
in that condition nor will she eat any of the ³noe-di at such times. The
meat of an animal killed by a dog may not be eaten by women or by
any men whose wives are menstruating. This prohibition is to prevent
bad luck befalling the dog in the pursuit of game. If, however, an
animal is killed with bow and arrow after having been brought at bay
by a dog, the meat is soχa and the women may eat the ³noe-di. The
remains of an animal killed by a lion are not soχa and may be partaken of by all individuals. Care, however, is taken not to offend the
lion, which likewise [is believed to] observe certain practices after each
kill. After having had his fill he buries the sacrum and haunch-bones
and covers them over with the stomach contents of the animal. If he
should be unsuccessful in hunting his prey he returns to the spot of
the last kill, digs up the buried parts and inters them in another place.
This he does to restore his luck and if he should find that the bones
have been taken away he will follow the person who removed them
right into the encampment.

Soχa applies only to meat killed with bow and arrow and as far
as is known at present this practice exists among the χom-khoin,
¹Koma-khoin and Go-gara-khoin. Among these groups the meat of
the following animals is soχa, namely, steinbuck, duiker, springbuck,
harte-beest, gemsbuck, kudu, wildebeest and giraffe. The eland, which
is a comparatively rare visitor to the parts occupied by these groups is
not killed at all by the χom-khoin who believe that harm will befall
any person who eats its meat. In other words the χom-khoin consider
the eland to be absolute soχa. Among other groups the man who shoots
an eland must, on returning to the encampment, sleep under the tree
as relations with his wife will prevent the poison from killing the
animal. The same applies to a person who shoots a giraffe.

Snakes, with the exception of the python, are not eaten by either men or women. The mole is not killed because its winter larder of öintjes (*Cyperus edulis* Dtr.) forms a valuable addition to the supplies of the Bushmen. The hyena, jackal, and other vermin as well as birds are relished by all sections of these communities.

Brief reference will now be made to a ceremony which is observed in connection with the collection of veldkos by the women. It is practiced when the fruit of the [3]huin ripens, generally after the onset of the big rainy season in the month of February. On a certain day, appointed by the chief, all the women, under the guidance of the chief's wife, set out to collect the first fruit of the [3]huin, the men in the meantime remaining in the encampment. The trees from which the fruit is to be gathered are indicated by the chief's wife. On the return of the women to the encampment they deposit the bags containing the fruit in front of the hut of the chief. His wife then fills four or five basins by taking a little from the bag of each woman and places them under the tree. Her husband now kindles the first fire, and after having applied [3]norab and dabas to appease the fire for a plentiful harvest, takes a handful or two of the fruit and eats it. The fruit is now free, and both men and women may eat it. . . .

III

As young girls approach the age of puberty they are placed in a hut in which they sleep at night. During the daytime they gather veldkos either by themselves or in company with the married women. Men, whether married or single, may not enter the girls' hut nor may they speak to the girls. The latter may, however, speak and be spoken to by the adolescent boys, but only at a distance so that no conversation of an intimate nature is possible without being overheard by the grownup people. A man may on occasion address a girl by saying, "You must grow up so that I may marry you," but she will not reply. When addressed by a man, say in the veld, she runs away to her companions, saying, "I dare not speak to you." The married women visit the girls' hut and instruct the inmates in various domestic matters, e.g. the way to clean and tidy their huts, to remain quiet when their husbands are cross, to prepare their husbands' food separately from their own, to pick up and beat the kudu skin on returning home in the evening so that the husband does not sleep on the previous day's dirt, etc. They further teach them to gather wood, to make the fire, to take away the ashes, and so forth. At the onset of the first menstruation the girl tells her mother or, in case she has no mother, her best friend, who then reports to one of the married women, not necessarily to the chief's wife. She is then isolated in a small round hut which is completely closed in except for a small entrance. It is known as the ¹hawa-omi (hut for waiting) and is situated close to the girls' hut. She is required to remain inside the ¹hawa-omi and dare not show herself outside. No fire is made in the hut. She is fed by her mother or in the absence of the latter by another married woman. She is not visited by anybody except the person who feeds her. . . . She may be given veldkos but is not allowed to partake of meat. No man, not even the girl's father, may pass close to the ¹hawa-omi or attempt to speak to her. She remains in the ¹hawa-omi as long as the condition lasts. When it has ceased she informs her mother or the woman who has been attending her. The latter tells the other married women, and they all prepare to dance the ¹hawa-³nab. This dance takes place during the day and men may not take part in it. They may, however, remain in the encampment while it is going on or enter it when returning from the veld. The adolescent girls are also excluded from it. The dance may be continued for three or four days. . . . Now two of the adolescent girls come forward and take her to fetch water. This is done at a run, the water being brought quickly and placed at the hut of the old woman who rubbed her down. Then two other girls take her to fetch wood. This is likewise done at a run, and after the wood has been deposited the ceremony is over. She is now a woman and known as a ⁴gari-khois (mature young woman). While the ceremony was in progress a new hut was built for her by her mother. In this she now takes up her residence until she marries.

The ⁴gari-khois is now eligible to marry, and she accompanies the married women on their various excursions for food, wood, etc., and associates with them. . . .

Marriage within the group (²gãub) is forbidden and is patrilocal. When, however, the parents of the bride are very old and poor in the primitive sense of the word the husband may be required to remain with the group of his parents-in-law. Further, a chief may under exceptional circumstances require a son-in-law to remain with him. . . . As a rule men do not go far for wives, and intermarriage takes place between neighboring groups. . . . A man may, however, not marry his own sister, his cousins on either side, or his brother's or sister's daughter. The same prohibition applies to women. Among all the groups each man has two wives as a rule. The wives may or may not be related. The second wife is taken some time after the first. The wife taken first is looked upon as the principal wife, who exercises a certain amount of authority over the second wife. Each wife has a hut of her own and the husband lives with the principal wife, only visiting the second. . . .

A young man eligible for marriage is known as a ⁴gari-khoib. When he desires to marry he first speaks about the matter to his best friend, who then approaches the parents of the prospective bride. The latter will reply, "We are poor, we cannot afford to give our daughter away." Thereupon the friend returns to the suitor and tells him to go and speak to the mother himself. The suitor then proceeds to the encampment of the girl's mother, taking his bow and arrows with him. On arrival at her hut he sits down some distance away and says, "I want your daughter." The mother replies, "We are too poor to give our daughter away," to which the suitor responds, "I have come myself to speak to you. If you die I will bury you, if your husband dies I will bury him," thereby implying that he has become one of the family and prepared to share their sorrows and sufferings. The mother then replies, "You are right, you may take her. I will do as you say and see whether you will carry out your promises," and, taking his bow and arrows, proceeds to her daughter's hut and places them in the hut. Then, without speaking to her daughter, she returns to her own hut. The daughter knows to whom the bow and arrows belong. The suitor goes to the girl's hut towards dusk but does not speak to her. Being still shy and afraid of men, she may run away, but does not go to her mother's hut, as she is afraid of being punished. He remains in her hut, sleeping in it at night and hunting during the day. If, after two or three days, she does not come back, he returns to his encampment and, after obtaining some beadwork from his mother and sister, presents it to his mother-in-law through his sister. He returns to his bride's hut in the meantime. The mother-in-law must accept the present (²ama-χun), as the marriage was completed when she took his bow and arrows and placed them in her daughter's hut. Towards midnight the mother takes her daughter to the daughter's own hut and, if necessary, removes her there by force. The bride and bridegroom do not speak to each other nor, under normal circumstances, are the presents sent to her mother by the bridegroom until they have slept together. After the marriage has been consummated, the husband goes out hunting to obtain meat for the ⁴gū-³a-³nab or the dance after an animal was killed for the purpose of making a wife's leather skirt. The young couple continue to live in the bride's hut for some months before taking up residence with the husband's group. On arrival in his own encampment his mother builds a hut for them. The son-in-law neither looks at nor speaks to his mother-in-law, nor will he mention her name or enter her hut even in case of sickness or during her absence. When in the absence of his mother-in-law it is necessary to speak to any-body in her hut he will keep at a distance and depart as soon as he sees her approaching. They never refer to each other by name but always as my son-in-law or my mother-in-law. The son-in-law does not associate with his father-in-law either, but similarly avoids him; and should they meet accidentally, they may exchange greetings, but no general conversation will take place nor will they look each other in the face.

A woman seldom has more than five children but as a rule only two or three. The child suckles until it is able to walk well. The children are looked upon as belonging to the father, but if husband and wife should separate, the girls are taken by the father and the sons by the mother. Illegitimate children are unknown. When a wife is deserted by her husband the fatherless children are known as ²gu-o-¹gōai. Sep-aration of husband and wife may take place under various circum-stances, for example, when a woman is childless, but this is entirely a matter for adjustment between husband and wife. The wife on separa-tion returns to her own group. Orphans are adopted by their maternal grandparents. A childless wife is as a rule sent back to her people. The present made to her mother is not returned to the husband. Child murder is not practiced. . . .

The chief is succeeded by his eldest sister's son and not by his own son, brother, etc. If, on his death, his successor is a minor, the eldest sister has the right to tell her husband to make the fire, but as long as she does not exercise this right the eldest brother of the deceased chief is entitled to do so. If both her husband and the eldest brother of the late chief are comparatively young men or refuse to make the fire, she may call upon one of the old men in the group to do so, but the ³norab and dabas she applies to the fire herself.

Owing to the marriage customs of the Hei-²om the eldest sister of the chief does not live in his encampment. As soon as he takes ill she is sent for, or, if he should die suddenly, she is summoned immediately, as he may not be buried before she arrives. Her whole household comes with her. After the burial the fire is kept going until they move to an-other camp, when the whole group will set off to look for a new site which is indicated by her. They move the day after the burial. She places her hut in the east and her son lives either to her immediate right or left, away from the other young men in the encampment. If the eldest sister is without issue then her next sister's eldest son succeeds, no matter in which group she may be living.

22. TERRACE AGRICULTURE IN THE PHILIPPINES [3]

BY A. E. JENKS

IN ALL of Igorot culture the most apparent and strikingly noteworthy fact is its agriculture. In agriculture the Igorot has reached his highest development. On agriculture hangs his claim to the rank of barbarian —without it he would be a savage.

Igorot agriculture is unique in Luzon, and, so far as known, throughout the Archipelago, in its mountain terraces and irrigation.

There are three possible explanations of the origin of Philippine rice terraces. First, that they (and those of other islands peopled by primitive and modern Malayans, and those of Japan and China) are indigenous —the product of the mountain lands of each isolated area; second, that most of them are due to cultural influences from one center, or possibly more than one center, to the north of Luzon—as influences from China or Japan spreading southward from island to island; third, that they, especially all those of the islands—excluding only China—are due to influences originating south of the Philippines, spreading northward from island to island.

Terracing may be indigenous to many isolated areas where it is found, and doubtless is to some; it is found more or less marked wherever irrigation is or was practiced in ancient or modern agriculture. However, it is believed not to be an original production of the Philippines. . . .

The historic cultural movements in Malaysia have been not from the north southward but from Sumatra and Java to the north and east; they have followed the migrations of the people. It is believed that the terrace-building culture of the Asiatic islands for the production of mountain rice by irrigation during the dry season has drawn its inspiration from one source, and that such terraces where found today in Java, Lombok, Luzon, Formosa, and Japan are a survival of a very early culture which spread from the nest of the primitive Malayan stock and left its marks along the way—doubtless in other islands besides these cited. If Japan, as has Formosa, had an early Malayan culture, as will probably be proved in due time, one should not be surprised to find old rice terraces in the mountains of Batanes Islands and the Loo Choo Islands which lie between Luzon and Japan.

It must be noted here that all Bontoc agriculture labors, from the

[3] From pages 88-93 of A. E. Jenks, "The Bontoc Igorot," *Philippine Islands Ethnological Survey Publications*, Volume 1, 1905. The Bontoc Igorot live in the interior of the northern part of the Island of Luzon.

building of the sementera to the storing of the gathered harvest, are accompanied by religious ceremonials. They are often elaborate, and some occupy a week's time. These ceremonials are left out of this chapter to avoid detail; they appear in the later chapter on religion.

There are two varieties of sementeras—garden patches, called "pay-yo' "—in the Bontoc area, the irrigated and the unirrigated. The irrigated sementeras grow two crops annually, one of rice by irrigation during the dry season and the other of camotes, "sweet potatoes," grown in the rainy season without irrigation. The unirrigated sementera is of two kinds. One is the mountain or side hill plat of earth, in which camotes,[4] millet, beans, maize, etc., are planted, and the other is the horizontal plat (probably once an irrigated sementera), usually built with low terraces, sometimes lying in the pueblo among the houses, from which shoots are taken for transplanting in the distant sementeras and where camotes are grown for the pigs. Sometimes they are along old water courses which no longer flow during the dry season; such are often employed for rice during the rainy season.

The unirrigated mountain-side sementera, called "fo-ag'," is built by simply clearing the trees and brush from a mountain plat. No effort is made to level it and no dike walls are built. Now and then one is hemmed in by a low boundary wall.

The irrigated sementeras are built with much care and labor. The earth is first cleared; the soil is carefully removed and placed in a pile; the rocks are dug out; the ground shaped, being excavated and filled until a level results. This task for a man whose only tools are sticks is no slight one. A huge bowlder in the ground means hours—often days— of patient, animal-like digging and prying with hands and sticks before it is finally dislodged. When the ground is leveled the soil is put back over the plat, and very often is supplemented with other rich soil. These irrigated sementeras are built along water courses or in such places as can be reached by turning running water to them. Inasmuch as the water must flow from one to another, there are practically no two sementeras on the same level which are irrigated from the same water course. The result is that every plat is upheld on its lower side, and usually on one or both ends, by a terrace wall. Much of the mountain land is well supplied with bowlders and there is an endless water-worn supply in the beds of all streams. All terrace walls are built of these un-dressed stones piled together without cement or earth. These walls are called "fa-ning'." These are from 1 to 20 and 30 feet high and from a foot to 18 inches wide at the top. The upper surface of the top layer

---

[4] Sweet potatoes.

of stones is quite flat and becomes the path among the sementeras. The toiler ascends and descends among the terraces on stone steps made by single rocks projecting from the outside of the wall at regular intervals and at an angle easy of ascent and descent.

These stone walls are usually weeded perfectly clean at least once each year, generally at the time the sementera is prepared for transplanting. This work falls to the women, who commonly perform it entirely nude. At times a scanty front and back apron of leaves is worn tucked under the girdle.

In the Banawi [Ifugao] district, south of the Bontoc area, there are terrace walls certainly 75 feet in height, though many of these are not stones, since the earth is of such a nature that it does not readily crumble.

It is safe to say that nine-tenths of the available water supply of the dry season in the Bontoc area is utilized for irrigation. In some areas, as about Bontoc pueblo, there is practically not a gallon of unused water where there is space for a sementera.

A single area consisting of several thousand acres of mountain side is frequently devoted to sementeras, and I have yet to behold a more beautiful view of cultivated land than such an area of Igorot rice terraces. Winding in and out, following every projection, dipping into every pocket of the mountain, the walls ramble along like running things alive. Like giant stairways the terraces lead up and down the mountain side, and, whether the levels are empty, dirt-colored areas, fresh, green-carpeted stairs, or patches of ripening, yellow grain, the beholder is struck with the beauty of the artificial landscape and marvels at the industry of an otherwise savage people.

By irrigation is meant the purposeful distribution of water over soil by man by means of diverting streams or by the use of canals in the shape of ditches or troughs for conveying and directing part of a water supply, or by means of some other man-directed power to raise water to the required level.

The Igorot employ three methods of irrigation: One, the simplest and most natural, is to build sementeras along a small stream which is turned into the upper sementera and passes from one to another, falling from terrace to terrace until all water is absorbed, evaporated, or all available or desired land is irrigated. Usually such streams are diverted from their courses, and they are often carried long distances out of their natural way. The second method is to divert a part of a river by means of a stone dam. The third method is still more artificial than the preceding—the water is lifted by direct human power from below the sementera and poured to run over the surface.

The first method is the most common, since the mountains in Igorot land are full of small, usually perpetual, streams. There are practically no streams within reach of suitable pueblo sites which are not exhausted by the Igorot agriculturist. Everywhere small streams are carefully guarded and turned wherever there is a square yard of earth that may be made into a rice sementera. Small streams in some cases have been wound for miles around the sides of a mountain, passing deep gullies and rivers in wooden troughs or tubes.

Much land along the river valleys is irrigated by means of dams, called by the Igorot "lung-ud'." During the season of 1903 there was one dam across the entire river at Bontoc, throwing all the water which did not leak through the stones into a large canal on the Bontoc side of the valley. Half a mile above this was another dam diverting one-half the stream to the same valley, only onto higher ground. Immediately below the main dam were two low piles of stones jutting into the shallow stream from the Bontoc side, and each gathering sufficient water for a few sementeras. Within a quarter of a mile below the main dam were three other loose, open weirs of rocks, two of which began on a shallow island, throwing water to the Samoki side of the river. In the stream a short distance farther down a shallow row of rocks and gravel turned water into three new sementeras constructed early in the year on a gravel island in the river.

The main dam is about 12 feet high, 2 feet broad at the top, 8 or 10 at the bottom, and is about 300 feet long. It is built each year during November and December, and requires the labor of fifteen or twenty men about six weeks. It is constructed of river-worn bowlders piled together without adhesive. The top stones are flat on the upper surface, and the dam is a pathway across the river for the people from the time of its completion until its destruction by the freshets of June or July.

The upper dam is a new piece of primitive engineering. It, with its canal, has been in mind for at least two years; but it was completed only in 1903. The dam is small, extending only halfway across the river, and beginning on an island. This dam turns water into a canal averaging three feet wide and carrying about five inches of water. The canal, called "a'lak," is about 3,000 feet long from the dam to the place of discharge into the level area. For about 530 feet of this distance it was impossible for the primitive engineer to construct a canal in the earth, as the solid rock of the mountain dips vertically into the river. About fifty sections of large pine trees were brought and hollowed into troughs, called "ta-la'kan," which have been secured above the water by means of buttresses, by wooden scaffolding, called "to-kod'," and by attachment to the overhanging rocks, until there is now a continuous artificial waterway from the dam to the tract of irrigated land.

Considerable engineering sense has been shown and no small amount of labor expended in the construction of this last irrigating scheme. The pine logs are a foot or more in diameter, and have a waterway dug in them about ten or twelve inches deep and wide. These trees were felled and the troughs dug with the wasay, a short-handled tool with an iron blade only an inch or an inch and a half wide, and convertible alike into ax and adz.

There seems to be a fall of about twenty-two feet between the upper dam and the discharge from the troughs. This fall in a distance of about 3,000 feet seems needlessly great; however, the primitive engineer has shown excellent judgment in the matter. First, by putting the dam (upper dam) where it is, only half the stream had to be built across. Second, there is a rapids immediately below the dam, and, had the Igorot built his dam below the rapids, a dam of the same height would have raised the water to a much lower level; this would have necessitated a canal probably ten or twelve feet deep instead of three. Third, the height of the water at the upper dam has enabled him to lay the log section of the waterway above the high-water mark of the river, thus probably insuring more or less permanence. Had the dam been built much lower down the stream the troughs would have been near the surface of the river and been torn away annually by the freshets, or the people would be obliged each year to tear down and reconstruct that part of the canal. As it now is it is probable that only the short dam will need to be rebuilt each year.

All dams and irrigating canals are built directly by or at the expense of the persons benefited by the water. Water is never rented to persons with sementeras along an artificial waterway. If a person refuses to bear his share of the labor of construction and maintenance his sementeras must lie idle for lack of water.

All sementera owners along a waterway, whether it is natural or artificial, meet and agree in regard to the division of the water. If there is an abundance, all open and close their sluice gates when they please. When there is not sufficient water for this, a division is made— usually each person takes all the water during a certain period of time. This scheme is supposed to be the best, since the flow should be sufficient fully to flood the entire plat—a 100-gallon flow in two hours is considered much better than an equal flow in two days.

During the irrigating season, if there is lack of water, it becomes necessary for each sementera owner to guard his water rights against other persons on the same creek or canal. If a man sleeps in his house during the period in which his sementeras are supposed to receive water, it is pretty certain that his supply will be stolen, and, since he was not on guard, he has no redress. But should sleep chance to overtake him in his tiresome watch at the sementeras, and should some one turn off and steal his water, the thief will get clubbed if caught, and will forfeit his own share of water when his next period arrives.

The third method of irrigation—lifting the water by direct human power—is not much employed by the Igorot. In the vicinity of Bontoc pueblo there are a few sementeras which were never in a position to be irrigated by running water. They are called "pay-yo' a kao-u'chan," and, when planted with rice in the dry season, need to be constantly tended by toilers who bring water to them in pots from the river, creek, or canals.

23. THE ORIGIN AND DISTRIBUTION OF AGRICULTURE IN AMERICA [5]

BY H. J. SPINDEN

AGRICULTURE may be named as the antecedent condition for all the high cultures of the New World. The concept of agriculture may have had several points of origin, but this does not seem likely, since maize, beans, and squashes were common products wherever agriculture was practiced in America. Other plants, fitted for special environments, had a more limited distribution, examples being manioc (*Manihot utilissima*, etc.) of the humid lowlands of the Amazon basin and of the West Indies, and the potato (*Solanum tuberosum*) that was cultivated most extensively in the rather arid highlands of Peru. Wild stocks for some of the aboriginal food plants of America are often difficult to obtain, but botanical knowledge is far from complete for some of the most significant areas. We have proof of the migration of the agricultural complex from Mexico into the United States. In both the Mound Area and the Pueblo Area, the comparatively high state of society and art was directly dependent on agriculture, yet in these areas not one food product is known to have been locally developed from an indigenous plant. While the concept and the complex of agriculture undoubtedly migrated from Mexico into the southern and eastern parts of the United States we must be careful not to confuse this phenomenon with an actual migration of peoples. There is no reason to doubt that the plant culture

[5] From H. J. Spinden, "The Origin and Distribution of Agriculture in America," in *Proceedings of the 19th International Congress of Americanists* (held in Washington, 1915), pages 269-276, 1917.

spread as rapidly and as easily across tribal barriers in ancient times as horse culture in modern times.

There are arts that seem in a general way to be dependent on agriculture or at least concomitant with it. The most important of these is pottery. Pottery is of little use to people who are not stationary, and stationary people are usually (but not necessarily) agriculturists. In the New World we find that the boundaries of pottery distribution closely parallel the boundaries of agriculture distribution, extending in some regions slightly beyond them. Now pottery, with its infinite variation in form and ornament, furnishes us evidence of cultural connections and cultural developments that can be considered profitably along with problems of ancient American food plants.

If we could be certain that the early Mexican culture, now called the Archaic, was the direct outgrowth of the invention of agriculture and the subsequent stabilization of society, our position in regard to certain fundamentals of ancient American history would be very strong indeed. This Archaic Culture, studied best in its ceramic remains, seems to have had its birth on the highlands of Mexico and to have spread without much change as far as the Isthmus of Panama. Maize (*Zea mays*) seems to have been developed from a wild grass which may be the teosintli (*Euchlæna mexicana*) of the Mexican highlands. When we consider the geographical and climatic range of the adaptation of maize we must admit that the Mexican plateau is an intermediate and very likely home for the wild progenitor of this great food plant. On the north its cultivation had been extended in pre-Columbian times to the mouth of the St. Lawrence and on the south to the mouth of the Rio de la Plata. The plant had been accultured to extreme conditions of heat and cold, drought and moisture. To be sure there is in artificial cultivation, even when practiced by primitive people, an obvious selective character that might rapidly lead to a differentiation of plant types. The saving of seed stock after any harsh condition has operated to cut down the yield naturally breeds immunity to that condition. Still it is much more reasonable to suppose that modification would take place from a mean toward each extreme of adaptation rather than from one extreme to the other. . . .

Irrigation is often looked on as a remarkable sequel of the introduction of agriculture into an arid country. But from the best historical evidence at our command we should rather regard it as an invention which accounts for the very origin of agriculture itself. The earliest records of cultivated plants are seen in Mesopotamia, Egypt, Mexico, and Peru, where irrigation was practiced, and in each region are likewise seen the earliest developments of the characteristic arts of sedentary peoples, namely, pottery and weaving, and the elaborate social and religious structures that result from a sure food supply and a reasonable amount of leisure.

Quite aside from these known facts in the case, there are several reasons why we should look for the first appearance of agriculture in an arid environment. The press of population on food supply is greater there than in free-and-easy lands where nature is bountiful but where an insidious competition works behind the screen of plenty and cuts down life. In the desert the clearing of the field is less laborious than in the jungle and the control of the life-giving water makes man the master of the entire situation. As for the intermediate type of environment, where agriculture is possible without irrigation and where it normally spreads with the rise of human culture, there is usually such a supply of wild game, of berries, of edible roots, etc., that the advantage of tilling the soil does not at first appear. Even when agriculture is known in such favorable country, the indigenous plants are seldom found in cultivation. The abundant harvests of wild acorns in California, of wokas in southern Oregon, of wappato along the Columbia, of camas and kous in the pleasant uplands of Idaho, and of wild rice in the lake region of Minnesota and southern Canada, were effectual barriers against the invention or spread of agriculture among the tribes inhabiting these regions. . . .

Map 1 shows the final distribution of pottery in the New World. Aside from the independent development of crude ceramic art among the Alaskan Eskimo, the whole grand area may show the result of a spreading-out of the pottery concept from a single point of origin. Everywhere in this great stretch of territory the use of pottery is practically limited to agricultural peoples. The area is, to be sure, somewhat larger than that held by the agricultural tribes of today. The oversize can be explained on two grounds. In some regions the pottery remains are scanty and sporadic and may be ascribed to nomadic Indians who made a slight use of the pottery objects manufactured by their sedentary neighbors. In other outside regions the pottery remains are so plentiful as to indicate that agriculture was once practiced there but has now been given up. For instance, there was never more than a slight use of pottery in the western stretches of Kansas, Oklahoma, and Texas, where the nomadic Kiowa and Comanche dwelt, at least in later times; while in southern Colorado and southeastern Utah, a rather high type of agriculture was once established but has long since given way to a ruder manner of life. . . .

Map 2 gives the limits of the distribution of agriculture in the New World and makes a rough distinction between three general types of agriculture.

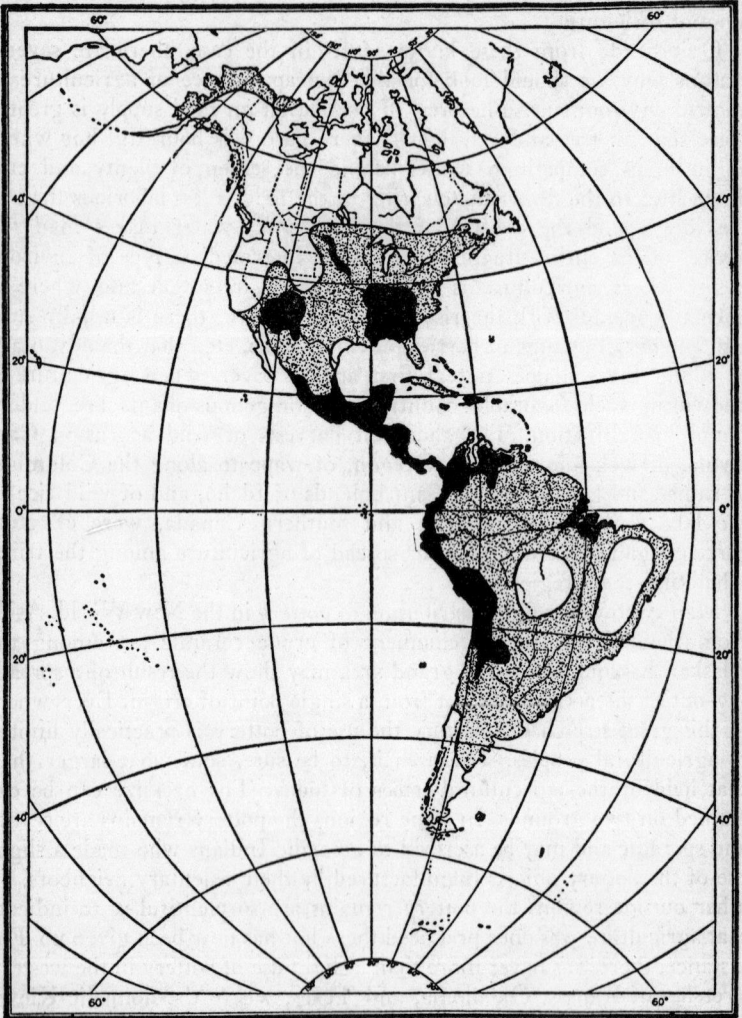

Map 1. Pottery in the New World. Intensive regions in black; non-pottery
regions in white.

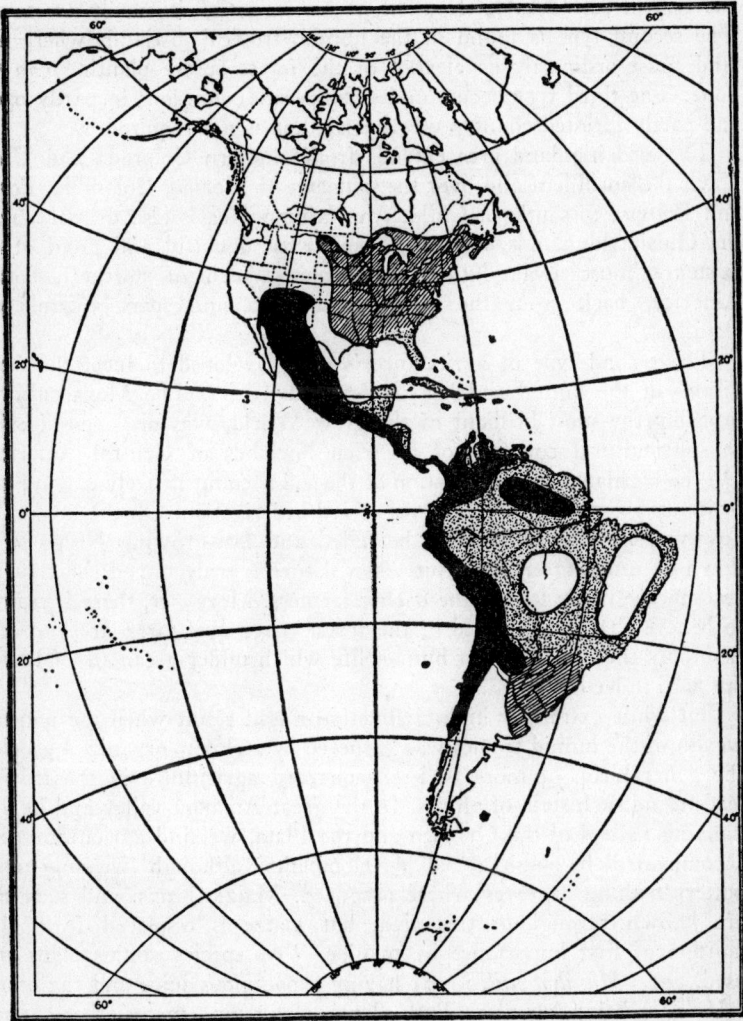

Map 2. Agriculture in the New World. Mountainous and mostly **arid regions in black**; lowland humid regions stippled; temperate region in lines.

The first and apparently oldest type occurs in open and rather arid territory of considerable elevation, where irrigation is usually necessary. The second type is found in the humid, tropical lowlands where the land must ordinarily be cleared of the forest before planting can be done. The third type occurs under temperate conditions in partly open and partly forested country where irrigation is not required.

The arid highland area extends from southern Colorado and Utah down the cordillera and over the plateaux of Mexico, Colombia, Peru, and Bolivia, to southern Chile. An outlying area is also drawn across the Guiana highlands, but this is somewhat doubtful and proof of its existence must await future exploration. Much of northern South America, back from the coast, is savanna and sparsely timbered plain. . . .

The second type of agriculture is that developed to meet the conditions of the humid and heavily forested tropics. The Maya culture, probably the most brilliant of the New World, was made possible by the agricultural conquest of the rich lowlands of Central America. On the highlands the preparation of the soil is comparatively easy owing to scanty vegetation and a control vested in irrigation. On the lowlands, however, great trees have to be felled and fast-growing bushes kept down by untiring energy. But when nature is truly tamed she returns recompense many fold to the daring farmers. Moreover, there is reason to believe that the removal of the forest cover over large areas affects favorably the conditions of human life which under a canopy of leaves are hard indeed. . . .

But while extremely high civilization might result when the natural wealth of the humid tropics was garnered by a closely organized people, the general run of more or less haphazard agriculture in the tropics leads to no such state of affairs. In the great Amazon valley and in the flanking valleys of the Orinoco and the Plata, we find agriculture unaccompanied by high social developments, although weaving and pottery-making are everywhere practiced. Maize, beans, and squashes are known throughout this area, but maize is displaced from the position of first importance by manioc. Two species of this plant are used, one (*Manihot utilissima*) having a poisonous juice and the other (*M. aipi*) being harmless. Both plants, along with many other species of the same family, are said to grow wild in Brazil, and there is little doubt that domestication first took place in this area. A single technical process of extracting the poisonous juice of the favorite manioc is found wherever the plant is cultivated, and similar types of clay griddles are used in making the cassava cakes. . . .

While the general classification of tropical agriculture into arid highland and humid lowland types is hardly to be disputed, still there are many domesticated plants that cannot be definitely ascribed to the one environment as opposed to the other. . . .

The third type of agriculture was adapted to temperate conditions. It is most completely exemplified in the eastern half of the United States, but seems also to have been developed, though to a much less extent, in parts of the Argentine and Uruguayan pampas. Maize is again the staple, with beans and squashes as associated crops. Among the Mandan of North Dakota maize was modified to meet the conditions of a very short summer and ripen within sixty or seventy days of planting. Among the Iroquois agriculture was also brought to a high plane, especially when we consider that all the plants under cultivation were indigenous to the tropics.

24. THE DOMESTICATION OF ANIMALS [6]

BY FRANCIS GALTON

THE few animals that we now possess in a state of domestication were first reclaimed from wildness in prehistoric times. Our remote barbarian ancestors must be credited with having accomplished a very remarkable feat, which no subsequent generation has rivaled. The utmost that we of modern times have succeeded in doing, is to improve the races of those animals that we received from our forefathers in an already domesticated condition.

There are only two reasonable solutions of this exceedingly curious fact. The one is, that men of highly original ideas, like the mythical Prometheus, arose from time to time in the dawn of human progress, and left their respective marks on the world by being the first to subjugate the camel, the llama, the reindeer, the horse, the ox, the sheep, the hog, the dog, or some other animal to the service of man. The other hypothesis is that only a few species of animals are fitted by their nature to become domestic, and that these were discovered long ago through the exercise of no higher intelligence than is to be found among barbarous tribes of the present day. The failure of civilized man to add to the number of domesticated species would on this supposition be due to the fact that all the suitable material whence domestic animals could be derived has been long since worked out.

I submit that the latter hypothesis is the true one for the reasons

[6] First published in *Transactions of the Ethnological Society*, 1865; included in his *Inquiries into Human Faculty and its Development*, Macmillan, 1883.

about to be given; and if so, the finality of the process of domestication must be accepted as one of the most striking instances of the inflexibility of natural disposition, and of the limitations thereby imposed upon the choice of careers for animals, and by analogy for those of men.

My argument will be this: All savages maintain pet animals, many tribes have sacred ones, and kings of ancient states have imported captive animals on a vast scale, for purposes of show, from neighboring countries. I infer that every animal, of any pretensions, has been tamed over and over again, and has had numerous opportunities of becoming domesticated. But the cases are rare in which these opportunities have led to any result. No animal is fitted for domestication unless it fulfills certain stringent conditions, which I will endeavor to state and to discuss. My conclusion is, that all domesticable animals of any note have long ago fallen under the yoke of man. In short, that the animal creation has been pretty thoroughly, though half unconsciously, explored, by the every-day habits of rude races and simple civilizations.

It is a fact familiar to all travelers, that savages frequently capture young animals of various kinds, and rear them as favorites, and sell or present them as curiosities. Human nature is generally akin: savages may be brutal, but they are not on that account devoid of our taste for taming and caressing young animals. . . .

In proving this assertion, I feel embarrassed with the multiplicity of my facts. I have only space to submit a few typical instances, and must, therefore, beg it will be borne in mind that the following list could be largely reënforced. Yet even if I inserted all I have thus far been able to collect, I believe insufficient justice would be done to the real truth of the case. Captive animals do not commonly fall within the observation of travelers, who mostly confine themselves to their own encampments, and abstain from entering the dirty dwellings of the natives; neither do the majority of travelers think tamed animals worthy of detailed mention. Consequently the anecdotes of their existence are scattered sparingly among a large number of volumes. It is when those travelers are questioned who have lived long and intimately with savage tribes that the plenitude of available instances becomes most apparent. . . .

[North America.]—The traveler Hearne, who wrote towards the end of the last century, relates the following story of moose or elks in the more northern parts of North America. He says:

"I have repeatedly seen moose at Churchill as tame as sheep and even more so. . . . The same Indian that brought them to the Factory had, in the year

1770, two others so tame that when on his passage to Prince of Wales's Fort in a canoe, the moose always followed him along the bank of the river; and at night, or on any other occasion when the Indians landed, the young moose generally came and fondled on them, as the most domestic animal would have done, and never offered to stray from the tents."

Sir John Richardson, in an obliging answer to my inquiries about the Indians of North America, after mentioning the bison calves, wolves, and other animals that they frequently capture and keep, said:

"It is not unusual, I have heard, for the Indians to bring up young bears, the women giving them milk from their own breasts."

He mentions that he himself purchased a young bear, and adds:

"The red races are fond of pets and treat them kindly; and in purchasing them there is always the unwillingness of the women and children to overcome, rather than any dispute about price. My young bear used to rob the women of the berries they had gathered, but the loss was borne with good nature."

I will again quote Hearne, who is unsurpassed for his minute and accurate narratives of social scenes among the Indians and Esquimaux. In speaking of wolves he says:

"They always burrow underground to bring forth their young, and though it is natural to suppose them very fierce at those times, yet I have frequently seen the Indians go to their dens and take out the young ones and play with them. I never knew a Northern Indian hurt one of them; on the contrary, they always put them carefully into the den again; and I have sometimes seen them paint the faces of the young wolves with vermilion or red ochre."

[South America.]—Ulloa, an ancient traveler, says:

"Though the Indian women breed fowl and other domestic animals in their cottages, they never eat them: and even conceive such a fondness for them, that they will not sell them, much less kill them with their own hands. So that if a stranger who is obliged to pass the night in one of their cottages offers ever so much money for a fowl, they refuse to part with it, and he finds himself under the necessity of killing the fowl himself. At this his landlady shrieks, dissolves into tears, and wrings her hands, as if it had been an only son, till seeing the mischief past mending, she wipes her eyes and quietly takes what the traveler offers her."

The care of the South American Indians, as Quiloa truly states, is by no means confined to fowls. Mr. Bates, the distinguished traveler and naturalist of the Amazons, has favored me with a list of twenty-two species of quadrupeds that he has found tame in the encampments of the tribes of that valley. It includes the tapir, the agouti, the guinea-pig, and the peccari. He has also noted five species of quadrupeds that were in captivity, but not tamed. These include the jaguar, the great ant-eater, and the armadillo. His list of tamed birds is still more extensive.

[North Africa.]—The ancient Egyptians had a positive passion for tamed animals, such as antelopes, monkeys, crocodiles, panthers, and hyenas. Mr. Goodwin, the eminent Egyptologist, informed me that "they anticipated our zoölogical tastes completely," and that some of the pictures referring to tamed animals are among their very earliest monuments, viz. 2000 or 3000 years B.C. . . .

[Equatorial Africa.]—The most remarkable instance I have met with in modern Africa is the account of a menagerie that existed up to the beginning of the reign of the present king of the Wahumas, on the shores of Lake Nyanza. Suna, the great despot of that country, reigned till 1857. Captains Burton and Speke were in the neighborhood in the following year, and Captain Burton thus describes the report he received of Suna's collection:

"He had a large menagerie of lions, elephants, leopards, and similar beasts of disport; he also kept for amusement fifteen or sixteen albinos; and so greedy was he of novelty, that even a cock of peculiar form or color would have been forwarded by its owner to feed his eyes. . . ."

[Australia.]—Mr. Woodfield records the following touching anecdote in a paper communicated to the Ethnological Society, as occurring in an unsettled part of West Australia, where the natives rank as the lowest race upon the earth:

"During the summer of 1858-9 the Murchison River was visited by great numbers of kites, the native country of these birds being Shark's Bay. As other birds were scarce, we shot many of these kites, merely for the sake of practice, the natives eagerly devouring them as fast as they were killed. One day a man and woman, natives of Shark's Bay, came to the Murchison, and the woman immediately recognizing the birds as coming from her country, assured us that the natives there never kill them, and that they are so tame that they will perch on the shoulders of the women and eat from their hands. On seeing one shot she wept bitterly, and not even the offer of the bird could assuage her grief, for she absolutely refused to eat it. No more kites were shot while she remained among us. . . ."

We will now turn to the next stage of our argument. Not only do savages rear animals as pets, but communities maintain them as sacred.

The ox of India and the brute gods of Egypt occur to us at once; the same superstition prevails widely. . . .

It would be tedious and unnecessary to adduce more instances of wild animals being nurtured in the encampments of savages, either as pets or as sacred animals. It will be found on inquiry that few travelers have failed altogether to observe them. If we consider the small number of encampments they severally visited in their line of march, compared with the vast number that are spread over the whole area, which is or has been inhabited by rude races, we may obtain some idea of the thousands of places at which half-unconscious attempts at domestication are being made in each year. These thousands must themselves be multiplied many thousandfold, if we endeavor to calculate the number of similar attempts that have been made since men like ourselves began to inhabit the world.

My argument, strong as it is, admits of being considerably strengthened by the following consideration:

The natural inclination of barbarians is often powerfully reënforced by an enormous demand for captured live animals on the part of their more civilized neighbors. A desire to create vast hunting-grounds and menageries and amphitheatrical shows, seems naturally to occur to the monarchs who preside over early civilizations, and travelers continually remark that, whenever there is a market for live animals, savages will supply them in any quantities. The means they employ to catch game for their daily food readily admits of their taking them alive. Pit-falls, stake-nets, and springes do not kill. If the savage captures an animal unhurt, and can make more by selling it alive than dead, he will doubtless do so. He is well fitted by education to keep a wild animal in captivity. His mode of pursuing game requires a more intimate knowledge of the habits of beasts than is ever acquired by sportsmen who use more perfect weapons. A savage is obliged to steal upon his game, and to watch like a jackal for the leavings of large beasts of prey. His own mode of life is akin to that of the creatures he hunts. Consequently, the savage is a good gamekeeper; captured animals thrive in his charge, and he finds it remunerative to take them a long way to market. The demands of ancient Rome appear to have penetrated Northern Africa as far or farther than the steps of our modern explorers. The chief centers of import of wild animals were Egypt, Assyria (and other Eastern monarchies), Rome, Mexico, and Peru. . . .

I conclude from what I have stated that there is no animal worthy of domestication that has not frequently been captured, and might ages ago have established itself as a domestic breed, had it not been deficient in certain necessary particulars which I shall proceed to discuss. These are numerous and so stringent as to leave no ground for wonder that out of the vast abundance of the animal creation, only a few varieties of a few species should have become the companions of man.

It by no means follows that because a savage cares to take home a young fawn to amuse himself, his family, and his friends, that he will always continue to feed or to look after it. Such attention would require a steadiness of purpose foreign to the ordinary character of a savage. But herein lie two shrewd tests of the eventual destiny of the animal as a domestic species.

Hardiness.—It must be able to shift for itself and to thrive, although it is neglected; since, if it wanted much care, it would never be worth its keep.

The hardiness of our domestic animals is shown by the rapidity with which they establish themselves in new lands. The goats and hogs left on islands by the earlier navigators throve excellently on the whole. The horse has taken possession of the Pampas, and the sheep and ox of Australia. The dog is hardly repressible in the streets of an Oriental town.

Fondness of Man.—Secondly, it must cling to man, notwithstanding occasional hard usage and frequent neglect. If the animal had no natural attachment to our species, it would fret itself to death, or escape and revert to wildness. It is easy to find cases where the partial or total non-fulfillment of this condition is a corresponding obstacle to domestication. Some kinds of cattle are too precious to be discarded, but very troublesome to look after. Such are the reindeer to the Lapps. Mr. Campbell of Islay informed me that the tamest of certain herds of them look as if they were wild; they have to be caught with a lasso to be milked. If they take fright, they are off to the hills; consequently the Lapps are forced to accommodate themselves to the habits of their beasts, and to follow them from snow to sea and from sea to snow at different seasons. The North American reindeer has never been domesticated, owing, I presume, to this cause. The Peruvian herdsmen would have had great trouble to endure had the llama and alpaca not existed, for their cogeners, the huanacu and the vicuña, are hardly to be domesticated.

Zebras, speaking broadly, are unmanageable. The Dutch Boers constantly endeavor to break them to harness, and though they occasionally succeed to a degree, the wild mulish nature of the animal is always breaking out, and liable to balk them.

It is certain that some animals have naturally a greater fondness for man than others; and as a proof of this, I will again quote Hearne about the moose, who are considered by him to be the easiest to tame and domesticate of any of the deer tribe. Formerly the closely allied European elks were domesticated in Sweden, and used to draw sledges, as they are now occasionally in Canada; but they have been obsolete for many years. Hearne says:

"The young ones are so simple that I remember to have seen an Indian paddle his canoe up to one of them, and take it by the poll, without experiencing the least opposition, the poor harmless animal seeming at the same time as contented alongside the canoe as if swimming by the side of its dam, and looking up in our faces with the same fearless innocence that a house lamb would."

On the other hand, a young bison will try to dash out its brains against the tree to which it is tied, in terror and hatred of its captors.

It is interesting to note the causes that conduce to a decided attachment of certain animals to man, or between one kind of animal and another. It is notorious that attachments and aversions exist in nature. Swallows, rooks, and storks frequent dwelling houses; ostriches and zebras herd together; so do bisons and elks. On the other hand, deer and sheep, which are both gregarious, and both eat the same food and graze within the same enclosure, avoid one another. The spotted Danish dog, the Spitz dog, and the cat, have all a strong attachment to horses, and horses seem pleased with their company; but dogs and cats are proverbially discordant. I presume that two species of animals do not consider one another companionable, or clubable, unless their behavior and their persons are reciprocally agreeable. A phlegmatic animal would be exceedingly disquieted by the close companionship of an excitable one. The movements of one beast may have a character that is unpleasing to the eyes of another; his cries may sound discordant; his smell may be repulsive. Two herds of animals would hardly intermingle, unless their respective languages of action and of voice were mutually intelligible. The animal which above all others is a companion to man is the dog, and we observe how readily their proceedings are intelligible to each other. Every whine or bark of the dog, each of his fawning, savage, or timorous movements is the exact counterpart of what would have been the man's behavior, had he felt similar emotions. As the man understands the thoughts of the dog, so the dog understands the thoughts of the man, by attending to his natural voice, his countenance, and his actions. A man irritates a dog by an ordinary laugh, he frightens him by an angry look, or he calms him by a kindly bearing; but he has less spontaneous hold over an ox or a sheep. He must study their ways and tutor his behavior before he can either understand the feelings of those animals or make his own intelligible to them. He has no natural power at all over many other creatures. Who, for instance, ever succeeded in frowning away a mosquito, or in pacifying an angry wasp by a smile?

Desire of Comfort.—This is a motive which strongly attaches certain animals to human habitations, even though they are unwelcome: it is a motive which few persons who have not had an opportunity of studying animals in savage lands are likely to estimate at its true value. The life of all beasts in their wild state is an exceedingly anxious one. From my own recollection, I believe that every antelope in South Africa has to run for its life every one or two days upon an average, and that he starts or gallops under the influence of a false alarm many times in a day. Those who have crouched at night by the side of pools in the desert, in order to have a shot at the beasts that frequent them, see strange scenes of animal life; how the creatures gambol at one moment and fright at another; how a herd suddenly halts in strained attention, and then breaks into a maddened rush, as one of them becomes conscious of the stealthy movements or rank scent of a beast of prey. Now this hourly life-and-death excitement is a keen delight to most wild creatures, but must be peculiarly distracting to the comfort-loving temperament of others. The latter are alone suited to endure the crass habits and dull routine of domesticated life. Suppose that an animal which has been captured and half tamed received ill-usage from his captors, either as punishment or through mere brutality, and that he rushed indignantly into the forest with his ribs aching from blows and stones. If a comfort-loving animal, he will probably be no gainer by the change; more serious alarms and no less ill-usage awaits him; he hears the roar of the wild beasts and the headlong gallop of the frightened herds, and he finds the buttings and the kicks of other animals harder to endure than the blows from which he fled. He has the disadvantage of being a stranger, for the herds of his own species which he seeks for companionship constitute so many cliques, into which he can only find admission by more fighting with their strongest members than he has spirit to undergo. As a set-off against these miseries, the freedom of savage life has no charms for his temperament; so the end of it is, that with a heavy heart he turns back to the habitation he had quitted. When animals thoroughly enjoy the excitement of wild life, I presume they cannot be domesticated, they could only be tamed, for they would never return from the joys of the wilderness after they had once tasted them through some accidental wandering.

Gallinas, or guinea-fowl, have so little care for comfort, or indeed for man, that they fall but a short way within the frontier of domestication. It is only in inclement seasons that they take contentedly to the poultry-yards.

Elephants, from their size and power, are not dependent on man for protection; hence, those that have been reared as pets from the time they were calves, and have never learned to dread and obey the orders of a driver, are peculiarly apt to revert to wildness if they once are allowed to wander and escape to the woods. I believe this tendency, together with the cost of maintenance and the comparative uselessness of the beasts, are among the chief causes why Africans never tame them now; though they have not wholly lost the practice of capturing them when full-grown, and of keeping them imprisoned for some days alive. Mr. Winwood Reade's account of captured elephants, seen by himself near Glass Town in Equatorial Western Africa, is very curious.

Usefulness to Man.—To proceed with the list of requirements which a captured animal must satisfy before it is possible he could be permanently domesticated: there is the very obvious condition that he should be useful to man; otherwise, in growing to maturity, and losing the pleasing youthful ways which had first attracted his captors and caused them to make a pet of him, he would be repelled. As an instance in point, I will mention seals. Many years ago I used to visit Shetland, when those animals were still common, and I heard many stories of their being tamed: one will suffice: A fisherman caught a young seal; it was very affectionate, and frequented his hut, fishing for itself in the sea. At length it grew self-willed and unwieldy; it used to push the children and snap at strangers, and it was voted a nuisance, but the people could not bear to kill it on account of its human ways. One day the fisherman took it with him in his boat, and dropped it in a stormy sea, far from home; the stratagem was unsuccessful; in a day or two the well-known scuffling sound of the seal, as it floundered up to the hut, was again heard; the animal had found its way home. Some days after the poor creature was shot by a sporting stranger, who saw it basking and did not know it was tame. Now had the seal been a useful animal and not troublesome, the fisherman would doubtless have caught others, and set a watch over them to protect them; and then, if they bred freely and were easy to tend, it is likely enough he would have produced a domestic breed.

The utility of the animals as a store of future food is undoubtedly the most durable reason for maintaining them; but I think it was probably not so early a motive as the chief's pleasure in possessing them. That was the feeling under which the menageries, described above, were established. Whatever the despot of savage tribes is pleased with becomes invested with a sort of sacredness. His tame animals would be the care of all his people, who would become skillful herdsmen under the pressure of fear. It would be as much as their lives were worth if one of the creatures were injured through their neglect. I believe that the keeping of a herd of beasts, with the sole motive of using them as a reserve for food, or as a means of barter, is a late idea in the history of civilization. It has now become established among the pastoral races of South Africa, owing to the traffickings of the cattle-traders, but it was by no means prevalent in Damara-Land when I traveled there in 1852. I then was surprised to observe the considerations that induced the chiefs to take pleasure in their vast herds of cattle. They were valued for their stateliness and color, far more than for their beef. They were as the deer of an English squire, or as the stud of a man who has many more horses than he can ride. An ox was almost a sacred beast in Damara-Land, not to be killed except on momentous occasions, and then as a sort of sacrificial feast, in which all bystanders shared. The payment of two oxen was hush-money for the life of a man. I was considerably embarrassed by finding that I had the greatest trouble in buying oxen for my own use, with the ordinary articles of barter. The possessor would hardly part with them for any remuneration; they would never sell their handsomest beasts. . . .

Breeding freely.—Domestic animals must breed freely under confinement. This necessity limits very narrowly the number of species which might otherwise have been domesticated. It is one of the most important of all the conditions that have to be satisfied. The North American turkey, reared from the eggs of the wild bird, is stated to be unknown in the third generation, in captivity. Our turkey comes from Mexico, and was abundantly domesticated by the ancient Mexicans.

The Indians of the Upper Amazon took turtle and placed them in lagoons for use in seasons of scarcity. The Spaniards who first saw them called these turtle "Indian cattle." They would certainly have become domesticated like cattle, if they had been able to breed in captivity.

Easy to tend.—They must be tended easily. When animals reared in the house are suffered to run about in the companionship of others like themselves, they naturally revert to much of their original wildness. It is therefore essential to domestication that they should possess some quality by which large numbers of them may be controlled by a few herdsmen. The instinct of gregariousness is such a quality. The herdsman of a vast troop of oxen grazing in a forest, so long as he is able to see one of them, knows pretty surely that they are all within reach. If oxen are frightened and gallop off, they do not scatter, but remain in a single body. When animals are not gregarious, they are to the herdsman like a falling necklace of beads whose string is broken, or as a handful of water escaping between the fingers.

The cat is the only non-gregarious domestic animal. It is retained by its extraordinary adhesion to the comforts of the house in which it is reared.

An animal may be perfectly fitted to be a domestic animal, and be peculiarly easy to tend in a general way, and yet the circumstances in which the savages are living may make it too troublesome for them to maintain a breed. The following account, taken from Mr. Scott Nind's paper on the Natives of King George's Sound in Australia, and printed in the first volume of the *Journal of the Geographical Society*, is particularly to the point. He says:

"In the chase the hunters are assisted by dogs, which they take when young and domesticate; but they take little pains to train them to any particular mode of hunting. After finding a litter of young, the natives generally carry away one or two to rear; in this case, it often occurs that the mother will trace and attack them; and, being large and very strong, she is rather formidable. At some periods, food is so scanty as to compel the dog to leave his master and provide for himself; but in a few days he generally returns."

I have also evidence that this custom is common to the wild natives of other parts of Australia. . . .

Selection.—The irreclaimably wild members of every flock would escape and be utterly lost; the wilder of those that remained would assuredly be selected for slaughter, whenever it was necessary that one of the flock should be killed. The tamest cattle—those that seldom ran away, that kept the flock together and led them homewards—would be preserved alive longer than any of the others. It is therefore these that chiefly become the parents of stock, and bequeath their domestic aptitudes to the future herd. I have constantly witnessed this process of selection among the pastoral savages of South Africa. I believe it to be a very important one, on account of its rigor and its regularity. It must have existed from the earliest times, and have been in continuous operation, generation after generation, down to the present day.

Exceptions.—I have already mentioned the African elephant, the North American reindeer, and the apparent, but not real exception of the North American turkey. I should add the ducks and geese of North America, but I cannot consider them in the light of a very strong case, for a savage who constantly changes his home is not likely to carry aquatic birds along with him. Beyond these few, I know of no notable exceptions to my theory.

SUMMARY

I see no reason to suppose that the first domestication of any animal, except the elephant, implies a high civilization among the people who established it. I cannot believe it to have been the result of a preconceived intention, followed by elaborate trials, to administer to the comfort of man. Neither can I think it arose from one successful effort made by an individual, who might thereby justly claim the title of benefactor to his race; but, on the contrary, that a vast number of half-unconscious attempts have been made throughout the course of ages, and that ultimately, by slow degrees, after many relapses, and continued selection, our several domestic breeds became firmly established.

I will briefly restate what appear to be the conditions under which wild animals may become domesticated: 1, they should be hardy; 2, they should have an inborn liking for man; 3, they should be comfort-loving; 4, they should be found useful to the savages; 5, they should breed freely; 6, they should be easy to tend.

It would appear that every wild animal has had its chance of being domesticated, that those few which fulfilled the above conditions were domesticated long ago, but that the large remainder, who fail sometimes in only one small particular, are destined to perpetual wildness so long as their race continues. As civilization extends they are doomed to be gradually destroyed off the face of the earth as useless consumers of cultivated produce. I infer that slight differences in natural dispositions of human races may in one case lead irresistibly to some particular career, and in another case may make that career an impossibility.

25. FLINT WORKING BY ISHI [7]

BY NELS C. NELSON

INTRODUCTORY

THE very ancient art of producing implements from flint and allied stone substances by means of a fracturing process, though practiced almost the world over, seems to have reached a really high state of perfection in only three localities, namely, Egypt, Denmark with adjoining parts of Scandinavia, and the Pacific coast of the United States. To be sure, choice bits of workmanship are to be found elsewhere, as for

[7] Originally printed in the *Holmes Anniversary Volume*, Washington, 1916, pages 397-402.

example in France and in Mexico, but these appear to be exceptions rather than the rule.

Just why these seemingly sporadic occurrences of excelling technique should be localized as they are is an interesting question because the manual dexterity implied might with reason have been looked for elsewhere, unless we at once yield the point that such dexterity is not a gift peculiar to any branch of mankind or, in other words, that the human factor is not the only factor concerned. For the present therefore the archæologist in attempting to explain these isolated appearances of highly cultivated flint technique can do little more than suggest that they were conditioned to some extent at least by two interdependent factors, the first being the presence of unlimited amounts of raw material and the other a grand scale of manufacture. The larger the output and the larger the number of artisans at work the greater the possibility of an expert—an artist—whose technique, once perfected, stood some chance of being copied and handed down. . . .

ISHI AND HIS WORK

During the early part of 1912, while connected with the University of California Museum of Anthropology, I had opportunity to observe and in a measure to direct the activities of Ishi, the lately rescued survivor of the Yahi or Southern Yana Indians. Among other things suggested to him, partly to satisfy the interest of the visiting public, was that of chipping arrowpoints, and probably nothing else that he undertook proved of equal interest and satisfaction to visitors as well as to himself. He still keeps up the work and is not at all averse to having it inspected. Whether or not Ishi is an artist might be a matter for debate, but no one will deny that he is an experienced workman. This conclusion is based partly on a comparison of his productions with the best to be found in California and also on what the English flint workers at Brandon tell us as to the time normally required to master the art.

Unfortunately, what might perhaps be considered strictly scientific procedure was sacrificed at the beginning. In the first place, no considerable amount of raw obsidian being at hand, bits of heavy plate-glass were furnished, and Ishi, finding this substance somewhat less refractory than obsidian and much more easily worked than chalcedony, agate, and the like, soon offered mild objections to using any medium except glass. This does not mean, however, that he could not be prevailed upon to work obsidian and other rocks. In the second place, Ishi, whether as a result of outside suggestions or his own intelligence I do not recall, found tools made of iron preferable to the old-fashioned implements of Indian manufacture. But while these facts might be urged as objections to the genuineness of his art, it still remains a fact that Ishi's method is his own and was mastered by him years before, probably with tools of the same general size and shape, if not actually of iron.

That iron tools are the best, considered from the point of view of the finished product made with them, is very doubtful; it is so hard and unyielding in comparison with bone or antler as to tend to bruise the edge of the obsidian; but, on the other hand, it keeps the point better and in that way saves time. With these facts in mind let us briefly consider what actually takes place when Ishi goes to work.

THE TOOLS EMPLOYED

Given a nodule of flint or a lump of obsidian, Ishi, in making a notched arrowpoint, let us say, employs three distinct processes, for each of which special tools ordinarily are required. The first process involves the division or breaking up of the obsidian mass to obtain suitable thin and straight flakes; the second process consists in chipping the selected flake to the size and shape of the arrowpoint desired; and the third and final process embodies, among other things, the notching of the base of the point to facilitate its attachment to the arrowshaft.

For the first process, that of dividing the obsidian mass, an ordinary hard, water-worn bowlder may do, especially if only small flakes are wanted, the obsidian being broken up or a flake struck from it by a direct blow. But if a large spearpoint or knife-blade is ultimately desired, an intermediate tool is needed. This is apparently (Ishi never made one for me to see) a short, stout, blunt-pointed piece of bone or wood serving as a sort of punch and sometimes as a lever. As a matter of fact, what is wanted in the case of producing a large implement is not the division of the obsidian mass but the trimming down of this mass by the detachment from it of all unnecessary portions. A direct blow with a hammerstone might be fatal to the obsidian core being thus shaped, while an indirect blow, delivered through this punch, the same being held at a selected spot and angle, has some chance of success in removing the superfluous portions without shattering the whole piece to bits. A hammerstone then, or a hammerstone together with a punch, are the tools required for the preliminary rough work, namely, the production of flakes or of a flaked core.

For the secondary flaking or, as it will be termed in this paper, *chipping*, a tool was made as follows: Ishi on one occasion took a common spike and at another time a piece of iron rod about the size of a lead pencil. He ground one end down about equally on two opposing sides, making a curving, chisel-like cutting edge, lenticular in cross-section—a tool of a nature halfway between an awl and a chisel. Around the butt-end a bit of cloth was wrapped to ease the handhold, and the chipping tool was finished. The notching tool was practically a duplicate of the preceding, but much smaller. A slender nail was sharpened as before and, being too small to be held in the hand as it was, the butt-end was inserted into an improvised wooden handle. The whole tool was nothing more nor less than a common awl.

Another necessary item was a piece of leather or hide with which to protect the hand holding the obsidian during the chipping and notching processes.

Five things therefore seem to constitute the full complement of tools and accessories used in making the average chipped artifact. But more or fewer tools may no doubt be employed under extreme conditions.

METHODS OF WORK

Preliminary Flaking.—Unfortunately, while Ishi went through the motions of this process a number of times for me, I never photographed it, wishing first to be convinced of its feasibilities. But for reasons which I did not comprehend at the time, Ishi always refused to execute the process. Professor Kroeber has since been partly successful with him, and from his report I judge that Ishi's reluctance was due in all probability to the element of danger involved. Thus it appears that the first time Ishi was induced to try flake production he was cut about the face by flying bits of the glass-like substance and bled profusely. Quite naturally therefore the accompanying illustration of the act (Fig. 1), furnished by Professor Kroeber, shows Ishi with his eyes closed. This photograph, it should be explained, is not a mere pose; it is a selected view of the workman in action and as such tells a better story than words could do. Ishi holds a water-worn bowlder in the right hand and a lump of obsidian in the left, and is attempting to break up the latter or to dislodge flakes from it by means of repeated direct blows. From among the resulting fragments he will pick out those most readily adapted to the purpose needed, let us say arrowpoints, and proceed at once to shape them.

Secondary Flaking or Chipping.—Having selected a suitable flake, Ishi assumes a new pose. The actual disposition of flake and tool is indicated in the detail views of Fig. 2. The flake to be worked will be observed resting on a bit of leather and placed transversely across the proximal fleshy part of the left palm and there held by one or more of the finger-tips. The chipping tool, grasped firmly with the right hand, is placed on the upper side of the flake, very close to the edge, and by a quick, downward pressure a chip is removed from the under-side of the flake. That much of this seemingly simple act will be noticed by any casual observer, but it may be well to analyze the act a little so as to show that it is after all not so simple as it looks. There is, so to speak, some knack about it. First of all we may note the fact, well shown in the illustration, that the axis of the tool used and the edge of the obsidian to be worked do not meet at a right angle, although they are in nearly the same plane. Secondly, and this does not show well in the illustration, the chipping tool is so turned on its axis that the plane of its cutting edge meets the plane of the flake to be worked at nearly, if not quite, a right angle. That this turn of the chipping tool is necessary or at least deliberate is certain because Ishi employs it invariably in the later stages of the chipping process, but not at all regularly in the early stages. Not having experimented very much, I am unable to say why Ishi proceeds as he does, but he gets results which I cannot imitate, try as I will. Ishi removes thin and fairly slender chips that extend two thirds or more across the face of the flake, while my chips are thick and short. Consequently his arrowpoints when finished are thin and shapely, while mine, much to his disgust, are thick and clumsy affairs. My work resembles the abrupt Mousterian retouch, while Ishi's is the true Solutrian technique.

As to the actual movements involved in chipping, these would be rather difficult to describe. The pressure exerted, if not too great, comes mostly from a wrist action; but if greater weight is needed the leverage is thrown back to the elbow and shoulder. The precision of the movement in the later and more delicate stage of the work is guided by placing the index finger of the tool against the edge of the palm on which the flake lies. The pressure is down, of course, rather than up, mainly in order to avoid the flying chips, and the chips being left in the palm of the hand absolutely necessitates the leather pad. Ishi works rapidly, reversing the flake often or not as conditions require. He begins chipping at the point on the flake nearest the tool and gradually works toward the farther end, and his best work appears to be done when he is chipping in a direction from the point end of the arrowpoint toward the base rather than when, on reversal, he must work in the opposite direction, i.e. from the base of the arrowpoint toward the point. Working in this manner Ishi can finish an arrowpoint of average size in half an hour, more or less, according to the nature of the substance he is working and also according to the adaptability of the flake originally selected. Having finished he proceeds to the final step.

Fig. 1. The primary process—dislodging flakes.

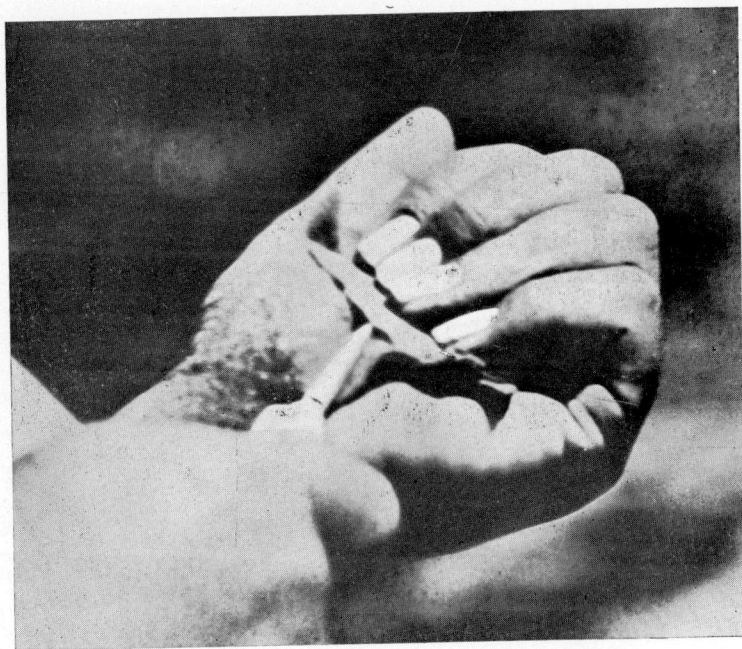

Fig. 2. The secondary process—chipping.

Notching and Serrating.—First of all, Ishi takes his leather pad, doubles it over the end of his left thumb, and ties it in place with a string. Then he grips the arrowpoint near the base, holding it firmly between the end of the protected thumb and adjoining index finger. With the right hand he directs the point of the notching tool against the edge of the arrowpoint at the place where the notch is to be, and by a slight pressure removes a small chip. The tool is held perpendicular to the plane of the arrowpoint and is pushed forward as if to be driven into the end of the thumb. For each minute chip thus removed the arrowpoint is reversed until the notch is of the depth desired. The successful act requires some deftness, or the stem is sure to be severed from the blade of the arrowpoint. Ishi seldom fails, however, especially when working with glass, and he completes the two notches often in about half a minute's time. If the edge of the arrowpoint was to be surrated, Ishi would doubtless proceed in the same way, although I never asked him to try.

26. TYPES OF BASKET WEAVES [8]

BY OTIS T. MASON

As you gaze on the Indian basket maker at work, herself frequently unkempt, her garments the coarsest, her house and surroundings suggestive of anything but beauty, you are amazed. You look about you, as in a cabinet shop or atelier, for models, drawings, patterns, pretty bits of color effect. There are none. . . . Her tools are more disappointing still, for of these there are few—a rude knife, a pointed bone, that is all. Her modeling block is herself. Her plastic body is the repository of forms. Over her knee she molds depressions in her ware, and her lap is equal to all emergencies for convex effects. She herself is the Vishnu of her art, the creator of forms. . . .

In all types of weave the working strands are constantly dampened by dipping the fingers into a basket or cup of water close at hand, or, in the case of embroidery, by drawing the section of grass stem through the lips. . . .

The various processes of manufacture will now be definitely explained. In technic, basketry is either hand-woven or sewed. The hand-woven basketry is further divisible into (A) *Checkerwork*, (B) *Twilled-work*, (C) *Wickerwork*, (D) *Wrappedwork*, and (E) *Twinedwork*,

[8] Selected from pages 221-258 of Otis T. Mason, "Aboriginal American Basketry," *U. S. National Museum Report* for 1902, pages 171-548 (1904).

in several varieties. The sewed work goes by the name of coiled basketry, and is classed both by the foundation and the fastening. In addition to these technical methods on the body, special ones are to be found in the border.

(A) *Checkerwork.*—This occurs especially in the bottoms of many North Pacific coast examples, and also in the work of eastern Canadian tribes; in matting its use is well-nigh universal.

In this ware the warp and the weft have the same thickness and pliability. It is impossible, therefore, in looking at the bottoms of the

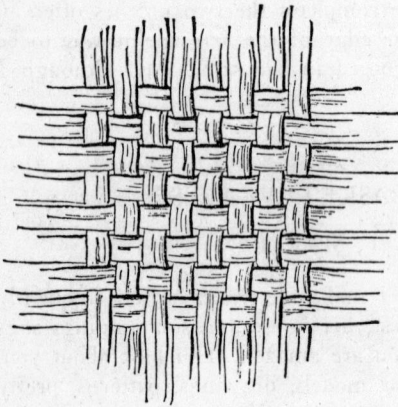

Fig. 1. Fine checkerwork.   Fig. 2. Twilledwork.

cedar-bark baskets and the matting of British Columbia (Fig. 1) or Eastern Canada to tell which is warp and which is weft. In very many examples the warp and weft of a checker bottom are turned up at right angles to form the warp of the sides, which may be wicker or twined work. . . . When warp and weft are fine yarn or threads the result is the simplest form of cloth in cotton, linen, piña fiber, or wool. The cheap fabrics of commerce are of this species of weaving. In art and industry lattice-work frequently shows the bars intertwined as in checker basketry. . . .

(B) *Twilledwork.*—This is seen especially in those parts of the world where cane abounds. In America it is quite common in British Columbia, Washington, Southern United States, Mexico, and Central America, and of excellent workmanship in Peru, Guiana, and Ecuador. The fundamental technic of diagonal basketry is in passing each element of the weft over two or more warp elements, thus producing either diagonal or twilled, or, in the best samples, an endless variety of diaper patterns. . . . (See Fig. 2.)

Twill, or *tweel*. A diagonal appearance given to a fabric by causing the weft threads to pass over one warp thread, and then under two, and so on, instead of taking the warp threads in regular succession, one down, one up. The next weft thread takes a set oblique to the former, throwing up one of the two deposed by the preceding. In some twills it is one in three, or one in four. The Latin *trilix*, a certain pattern in weaving, became *drillich* in German, and hence our word *drill*. *Twill* is derived from *zwillich*, which answers to the Latin *bilix*, and the Greek *dimitos*. The latter survives in *dimity*. See also *samite*, derived from Greek *hexamiton*, six thread.

The French *touaille* has also been suggested as the etymological source of the word.

The fabrics thus woven are very numerous—satin, blanket, merino, bombazine, kerseymere, etc. When the threads cross each alternately in regular order it is called *plain weaving;* but in *twill* the same thread of weft is *flushed*, or separated from the warp while passing over a number of warp threads, and then passes under a warp thread.

The points where the threads of the warp cross form diagonal lines, parallel to each other, across the face of the cloth. In *blanket twill* every third thread is crossed. In some fabrics 4, 5, 6, 7, or 8 threads are crossed. In *full satin twill* there is an interval of 15 threads, the warp (*organzine silk*) being floated over 15 threads of the woof (*tram*), giving the glossy appearance. . . .

Excellent variety was also produced in this kind of weaving by means of color. Almost any textile plant when split has two colors, that of the outer, or bark surface, and that of the interior woody surface or pith. Also the different plants used in diagonal basketry have great variety of color. By the skillful manipulation of the two sides of a splint, by using plants of different species, or with dyed elements, geometric patterns, frets, labyrinths, and other designs in straight line are possible. . .

(c) *Wickerwork.*—The name is from the Anglo-Saxon *wican*, to bend. Common in Eastern Canada, it is little known on the Pacific coast and in the Interior Basin, excepting in one or two pueblos, but is seen abundantly in Southern Mexico and Central America. It consists of a wide or a thick and inflexible warp and a slender flexible weft (Fig. 3). The weaving is plain and differs from checkerwork only in the fact that one of the elements is rigid. The effect on the surface is a series of ridges. It is possible also to produce diagonal effects in this type of weaving.

Wickerwork must have been a very early and primitive form of textile. Weirs for stopping fish are made of brush, and wattled fences for game drives are set up in the same manner. A great deal of the coarse basketry in use for packing and transporting is made in this fashion. The Zuñi Indians make gathering baskets of little twigs after the same technic, the inflexible warp being made up of a small number of twigs of the same plant, laid side by side. The transition from checker to

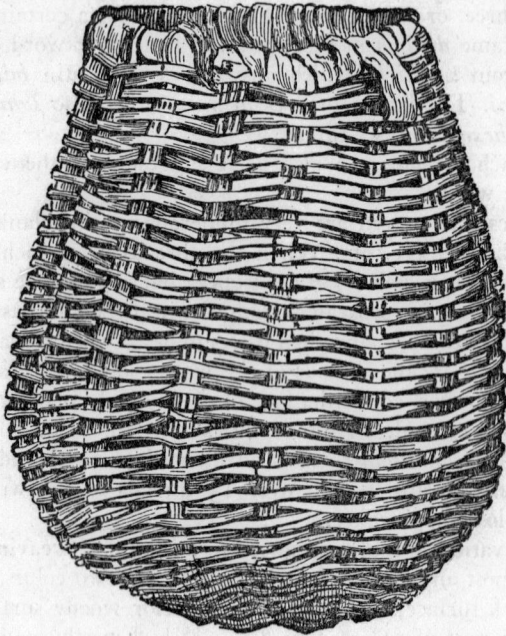

Fig. 3. Wicker basket. Zuñi, New Mexico.

wicker in some examples is easy. The moment one element, either warp or weft, is a little more rigid than the other, the intersections would naturally assume a wicker form. . . .

Wickerwork has pleasing effects combined with diagonal and other work. Fig. 4 is a square Hopi plaque, having twilled weaving in the middle and a band of wicker outside of this, the whole finished with rough, coiled sewing on the border.

It has passed into modern industry through the cultivation of osiers, rattan, and such plants for market baskets, covers for glass bottles, and in ribbed cloth, wherein a flexible weft is worked on a rigid warp.

Also, good examples are now produced by the Algonkin tribes of New England and Eastern Canada. . . .

(D) *Wrappedwork.*—Wrapped basketry consists of flexible or rigid warp and flexible weft. Examples of this technic are to be seen in America at the present time among the Indians of Southern Arizona for their carrying frames.

The warp extends from the rigid hoop, which forms the top, to the bottom where the elements are made fast. Firmness is given to the

Fig. 4. Twilled and wicker mat. Hopi Indians, Arizona.

structure by means of two bowed rods crossing at right angles at the bottom and securely lashed at the top. The weft, usually of twine, is attached to one of the corner or frame pieces at the bottom and is wrapped once around each warp element. This process continues in a coil until the top of the basket is reached. In some of its features this method resembles coiled work, but as a regular warp is employed and no needle is used in the coiling, it belongs more to the woven series. Hudson mentions the same among the Pomos for holding roof poles in place. The wrapping is very close where the rafters come to a point. As they widen the weft comes to be farther apart, being quite open on the outer margin. This method of weaving was employed by the Mound Builders of the Mississippi Valley. Markings of wrapped weaving pressed on ancient pottery taken from a mound in Ohio are to be seen in the Third Report of the Bureau of Ethnology. (See Fig. 5.)

This style of weaving had not a wide distribution in America and is used at the present day in a restricted region. When the warp and the weft are of the same twine or material and the decussations are drawn tight, the joint resembles the first half of a square knot. The Mincopies of the Andaman Islands construct a carrying basket in the same technic. Specimens of their work were collected and presented to the U. S. National Museum by Dr. W. L. Abbott. These baskets resemble most closely the Mohave specimens, only they are smaller and more attractive. The Mincopies and their neighbors far and near have the incomparable rattan for warp and weft, which combines the strength and

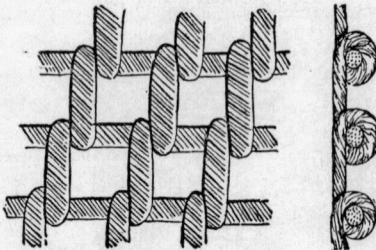

Fig. 5. Wrapped weaving, from mound in Ohio.

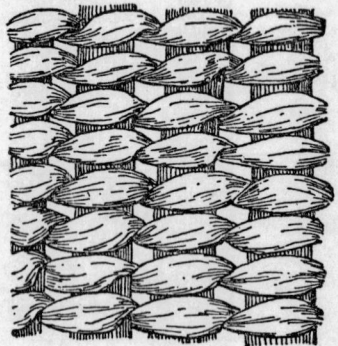

Fig. 6. Plain twined weaving.

flexibility of copper wire. The distribution of this wrapped weaving has not been studied. . . .

(E) *Twinedwork.*—This is found in ancient mounds of the Mississippi Valley, in bagging of the Rocky Mountains, down the Pacific coast from the Island of Attu, the most westerly of the Aleutian chain, to the borders of Chile, and here and there in the Atlantic slope of South America. Indeed, it is found among savages throughout the world. It is the most elegant and intricate of all in the woven or plicated series. Twined work has a set of warp rods or rigid elements as in wickerwork, but the weft elements are commonly administered in pairs, though in three-strand twining and in braid twining three weft elements are employed. In passing from warp to warp these elements are twisted in half-turns on each other so as to form a two-strand or three-strand twine or braid and usually so deftly as to keep the smooth, glossy side of the weft outward. . . .

According to the relation of the weft elements to one another and to the warp, different structures in twined weaving result as follows:

1. Plain twined weaving over single warps.

2. Diagonal twined weaving or twill over two or more warps.

3. Wrapped twined weaving, or bird-cage twine, in which one weft element remains rigid and the other is wrapped about the crossings.

4. Lattice-twined weaving, tee or Hudson stitch, twined work around vertical warps crossed by horizontal warp element.

5. Three-strand twined weaving and braiding in several styles.

1. *Plain twined weaving.*—Plain twined weaving is a refined sort of wattling or crating. The ancient engineers, who built obstructions in streams to aid in catching or impounding fish, drove a row of sticks into the bottom of the stream, a few inches apart. Vines and brush were woven upon these upright sticks which served for a warp. In passing each stake the two vines or pieces of brush made a half turn on each other. This is a very primitive mode of weaving. Plain twined basketry is made on exactly the same plan. There is a set of warp elements which may be reeds, or splints, or string, arranged radially on the bottom and parallel on the body. The weft consists of two strips of root or other flexible material, and these are twisted as in forming a two-strand rope passing over a warp stem at each halfturn. (See Fig. 6.) Many wastebaskets are woven on this plan. . . .

In this connection must not be overlooked a variety of twined weaving in which the warp plays an important part. It is a transition between the plain twine and the next type, the halves of the double warp standing for the independent warp stems of the diagonal weave. If the weft be administered in open work with the rows from a fourth to a half an inch apart and the warp elements be flexible under the strain of weaving, they will assume a zigzag shape.

Pleasing varieties of this type of twined weaving will be found in the Aleutian Islands. It resembles hemstitching. The Aleuts frequently use, for their warp, stems of wild rye or other grasses, in which the straws are split, or a pair used, and the two halves pass upward in zigzag form. Each half of a warp is caught alternately with the other half of the same straw and with a half of the adjoining straw, making a series of triangular instead of rectangular spaces. (See Fig. 7.)

A still further variation is given to plain twined ware by crossing the warps. In bamboo basketry of eastern Asia these crossed warps are also interlaced or held together by a horizontal strip of bamboo passing in and out in ordinary weaving. In such examples the interstices are triangular, but in the twined example here described the weaving passes across between the points where the warps intersect each other, leaving hexagonal interstices. (See Fig. 8.) This combination of plain twined weft and crossed warp has not a wide distribution in America, but examples are to be seen in southeastern Alaska and among relics found in Peruvian graves.

2. *Diagonal twined weaving.*—In diagonal twined weaving the twisting of the weft filaments is precisely the same as in plain twined weaving. The difference of the texture is caused by the manner in which the weft crosses the warps. This style abounds among the Ute Indians and the Apache, who dip the bottles made in this fashion into pitch and thus produce a water-tight vessel, the open meshes receiving

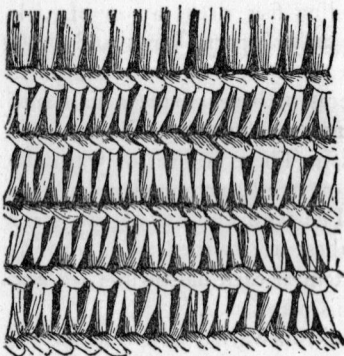

Fig. 7. Twined openwork. Aleutian Islands.

Fig. 8. Crossed warp, twined weave. Makah Indians, Washington.

the pitch more freely. The technic of the diagonal weaving consists in passing over two or more warp elements at each turn, just as in weaving with a single element. But the warp of the diagonal twined weaving never passes over or under more than one weft as it does in twilled weaving. There must be an odd number of warps, for in the next round the same pairs are not included in the half turns. The ridges on the outside therefore are not vertical as in plain weaving, but pass diagonally over the surface, hence the name. (See Fig. 9.) . . .

3. *Wrapped twined weaving.*—In wrapped twined weaving one element of the twine passes along horizontally across the warp stems, usually on the inside of the basket, forming a lattice. The binding element of splint, or strip of bark, or string, is wrapped around the crossings of the horizontal element with the vertical warp.

On the outside of the basket the turns of the wrapping are oblique; on the inside they are vertical. It will be seen on examining this figure that one row inclines to the right, the one above it to the left, and so on alternately. This was occasioned by the weaver's passing from side to side of the square carrying basket, and not all the way round as usual. The work is similar to that in an old-fashioned bird cage, where the upright and horizontal wires are held in place by a wrapping of finer soft wire. The typical example of this wrapped or bird-cage twine is to be seen among the Makah Indians of the Wakashan family living about Neah Bay, Washington, and in the soft hats of Salish and Shahaptian. (See Fig. 10.)

In this type the warp and the horizontal strip behind the warp are both in soft material. The wrapping is done with a tough straw-colored

Fig. 9. Diagonal twined weaving. Ute Indians, Utah.

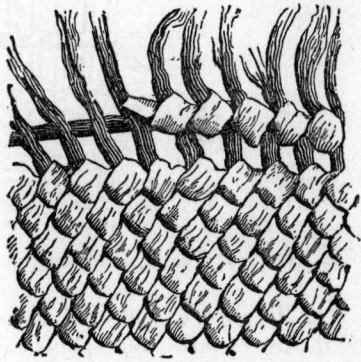

Fig. 10. Wrapped twined weaving. Makah Indians, Washington.

grass. When the weaving is beaten home tight the surface is not unlike that of a fine tiled roof, the stitches overlying each other with perfect regularity. Such a simple style of fastening warp and weft together would seem to have occurred to tribes of savages in many parts of the world. Strange to relate, however, excepting in Washington and the ocean side of Vancouver Island, the process is not known. The exception to this statement is to be found in a few sporadic cases where, perhaps, Nutka and Makah women had married into adjoining tribes. . . .

4. *Lattice-twined weaving.*—The lattice-twined weaving, so far as the collections of the National Museum show, is confined to the Pomo Indians, of the Kulanapan family, residing on Russian River, California. It is so called because it has a vertical and a horizontal warp resembling latticework. Dr. J. W. Hudson calls this technic tee. This is a short and convenient word, and may be used for a specific name. The tee-twined weaving consists of four elements, (*a*) the upright

warp of rods, (*b*) a horizontal warp crossing these at right angles, and (*c, d*) a regular plain-twined weaving of two elements, holding the warps firmly together. (See Fig. 11.)

In all these examples in the National Museum the horizontal or extra warp is on the exterior of the basket. On the outside the tee basket does not resemble the ordinary twined work but on the inside it is indistinguishable. Baskets made in this fashion are very rigid and strong, and frequently the hoppers of mills for grinding acorns, and also watertight jars, are thus constructed. The ornamentation is confined to narrow bands, the artist being restricted by the technic. . . .

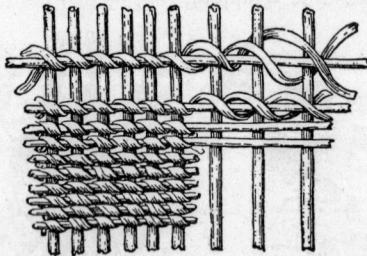

Fig. 11. Tee or lattice-twined weaving. Pomo Indians, California.

5. *Three-strand twined weaving.*—Three-strand twined weaving is the use of three weft splints and other kinds of weft elements instead of two, and there are four ways of administering the weft:

(*a*) Three-strand twine.
(*b*) Three-strand braid.
(*c*) Three-strand, false embroidery, Tlinkit.
(*d*) Wrapped twine, Thompson River.

It will be seen in studying these four methods that they are partly structural and partly ornamental, especially the last two. Inasmuch, however, as the Indian woman makes her ornamental work a part of her industrial work, the four methods may be all studied here. Very little was known among the American aborigines concerning additional ornaments given to the textile after the foundation was woven. The part which furnishes strength to the fabric and that which gives decoration were in technic one and the same process.

(*a*) *Three-strand twine.*—In this technic the basket-weaver holds in her hand three weft elements of any of the kinds mentioned. In twisting these three, each one of the strands, as it passes inward, is carried behind the warp stem adjoining, so that in a whole revolution the three weft elements have in turn passed behind three warp ele-

ments. After that the process is repeated. By referring to the lower
halves of Figs. 12 and 13, the outside and the inside of this technic
will be made plain. On the outside there is the appearance of a three-
strand string laid along the warp stems, while on the inside the texture
looks like a plain twined weaving. The reason for this is apparent,
since in every third revolution one element passes behind the warp
and two remain in front. Three-strand twined work is seldom used
over the entire surface of a basket. . . .

(*b*) *Three-strand braid.*—In three-strand braid the weft elements
are held in the hand in the same fashion, but instead of being twined
simply they are plaited or braided, and as each element passes under one
and over the other of the remaining two elements, it is carried behind

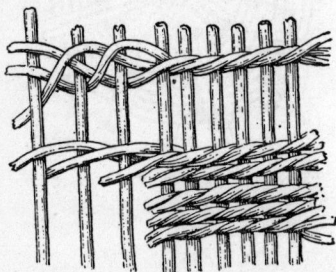

Fig. 12. Three-strand braid and
twined work. (Outside.)

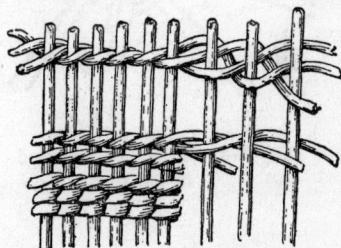

Fig. 13. Three-strand braid and
twined work. (Inside.)

a warp stem. . . . On the surface, when the work is driven home, it is
impossible to discriminate between three-strand twine and three-strand
braid. The three-strand braid is found at the starting of all Pomo
twined baskets, no matter how the rest is built up. . . .

Something should be said in this connection about the manner of
laying the foundation for weaving baskets. In many of the specimens
illustrated in this work it will be seen that very little tasteful care has
been bestowed upon this part of the work. The Eskimos, for instance,
do not know how, seemingly, but use a piece of rawhide, and it is said
that the Indians of British Columbia formerly inserted a piece of
board or wood at the bottom of their coiled baskets and sewed the
coils around an edge of it, but there is method in much of the basket
weaving in this point, as will be seen on examining the plates. Miss
Mary White, in her book, More Baskets and How to Make Them,
has worked this subject out very carefully.[9]

[9] *How to Make Baskets*, New York, 1902, also *More Baskets and How to
Make Them*, 1903.

Figs. 14 to 17, inclusive, show the result of her studies.

Fig. 14 is the simplest form of starting the bottom of a basket. Four warp stems are arranged in pairs and crossed at the center. A strip of wood or a flexible stem is wound twice around the intersection. The figure also shows how additional warp stems may be introduced into

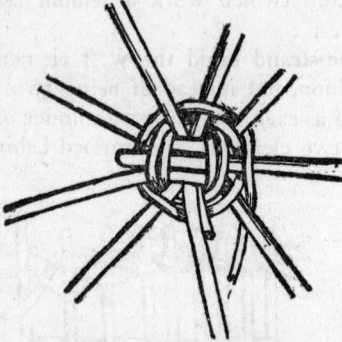

Fig. 14. Warp stems crossed in pairs.

Fig. 15. Warp stems crossed in fours.

Fig. 16. Sixteen stems woven in fours.

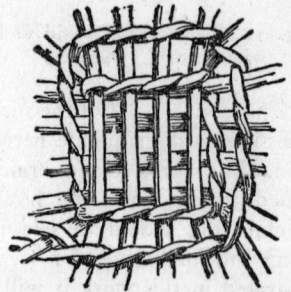

Fig. 17. Warp stems crossed in fours and twined.

this pattern, being thrust between the regular stems. Once they are held firmly in place by two or three rows of common basket weaving, additional warp stems are added, and they are bent out radially as a foundation for the work.

Fig. 15 shows how a start may be made with 16 warp stems crossing in groups of four at the center. Two sets begin at once to divide and radiate, and after they are held together by three rows of weft the other eight are spread out in the same way. The drawing illustrates exactly the manner in which this is done.

Fig. 16 shows another method of beginning with 16 warp stems, plaiting them into checker pattern at first, then afterwards spreading them out radially.

Fig. 17 brings us into the Hopi Indian type of twined weaving. Here four stems in one direction cross the same number at right angles and are held in place by a row of twined weaving, additional warp stems being inserted at the corners, which spread out radially. . . .

COILED BASKETRY

Coiled basketry is produced by an over-and-over sewing with some kind of flexible material, each stitch interlocking with the one immediately underneath it. . . .

Coiled basketry in point of size presents the greatest extreme. There are specimens delicately made that will pass through a lady's finger ring, and others as large as a flour barrel; some specimens have stitching material one-half inch wide, as in the Pima granaries, and in others the root material is shredded so fine that nearly 100 stitches are made within an inch of space. In form the coiled ware may be perfectly flat, as in a table mat, or built up into the most exquisite jar shape. In design the upright stitches lend themselves to the greatest variety of intricate patterns.

Coiled basketry may be divided into ten varieties, based on structural characteristics.

The foundation of the coil may be (1) a single element, either splint, or stem, or rod; (2) a stem or other single element, with a thin welt laid on top of it; (3) two or more stems one over another; (4) two stems or other elements laid side by side, with or without a welt; (5) three stems in triangular position; (6) a bundle of splints or small stems; (7) a bundle of grass or small shreds.

The stitches pass around the foundation in progress (1) interlocking with and sometimes splitting stitches, but not inclosing the foundation underneath; (2) under one rod of the coil beneath, however many there may be; (3) under a welt of the coil beneath; (4) through splints or other foundation, in some cases systematically splitting the sewing material underneath. With these explanations it is possible to make the following ten varieties of coiled basketry, matting, or bagging:

A. Coiled work without foundation.
B. Simple interlocking coils.

C. Single-rod foundation.
D. Two-rod foundation.
E. Rod and welt foundation.
F. Two-rod and splint foundation.
G. Three-rod foundation.
H. Splint foundation.
I. Grass-coil foundation.
K. Fuegian coiled basketry.

These will now be taken up systematically and illustrated. (See Fig. 18.)

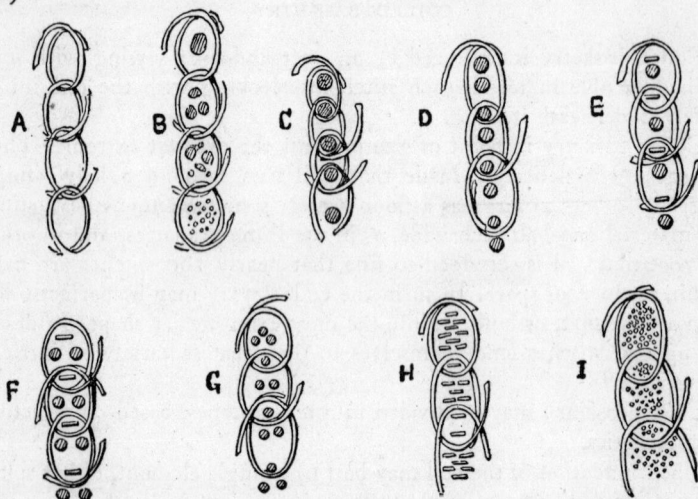

Fig. 18, A-I. Cross sections of varieties in coiled basketry.

A. *Coiled work without foundation.*—Specimens of this class have been already mentioned. The sewing material is babiche or fine rawhide thong in the cold north, or string of some sort farther south. In the Mackenzie Basin will be found the former, and in the tropical and subtropical areas the latter. If a plain, spiral spring be coiled or hooked into one underneath, the simplest form of the open coiled work will result. An improvement of this is effected when the moving thread in passing upward after interlocking is twined one or more times about its standing part. (See Fig. 18A.) . . .

B. *Simple interlocking coils.*—Coiled work in which there may be any sort of foundation, but the stitches merely interlock without catching under the rods or splints or grass beneath. This form easily passes into those in which the stitch takes one or more elements of the foundation, but in a thorough ethnological study small differences cannot be overlooked. (See Fig. 18B.) . . .

c. *Single-rod foundation.*—In rattan basketry and Pacific coast ware, called by Dr. J. W. Hudson tsai in the Pomo language, the foundation is a single stem, uniform in diameter. The stitch passes around the stem in progress and is caught under the one of the preceding coil, as in Fig. 18c. In a collection of Siamese basketry in the U. S. National Museum the specimens are all made after this fashion. The foundation is the stem of the plant in its natural state; the sewing is with splints of the same material, having the glistening surface outward. As this is somewhat unyielding it is difficult to crowd the stitches together, and so the foundation is visible between. California is not far behind the East in the quality of material, willow for the basis of the coil, and plants in a variety of colors for the sewing. The Siamese coiled basketry has little of design on its surface, but the American basketmaker may fix whatever her imagination may suggest. The effect of the plain stitching is pleasing to the eye by reason of the regular broken surface. In America single-rod basketry is widely spread. Along the Pacific coast it is found in northern Alaska and as far south as the borders of Mexico. The Pomo Indians use it in some of their finest work. The roots of plants and soft stems of willow, rhus, and the like are used for the sewing, and being soaked thoroughly, can be crowded together so as to entirely conceal the foundation. (See Fig. 19.) . . .

D. *Two-rod foundation.*—One rod in this style lies on top of the other; the stitches pass over two rods in progress and under the upper one of the pair below, so that each stitch incloses three stems in a vertical series. A little attention given to Fig. 18D will demonstrate that the alternate rod, or the upper rod, in each pair will be inclosed in two series of stitches, while the other or lower rod will pass along freely in the middle of one series of stitches and show on the outer side. . . .[10]

F. *Two-rod and splint foundation.*—In this style the foundation is made thicker and stronger by laying two rods side by side and a splint or welt on top to make the joint perfectly tight. The surface will be corrugated. Tribes practicing this style of coiling generally have fine material and some of the best ware is so made up. (See Fig. 18F.) . . .

G. *Three-rod foundation.*—This is the type of foundation called by Carl Purdy bam shi bu, from bam, sticks, and sibbu, three. Among the Pomo and other tribes in the western part of the United States the most

[10] The rod and welt foundation, which is illustrated in figure 18E, but whose description is not included here, passes easily into forms C, D, and F.

delicate pieces of basketry are in this style. Dr. Hudson calls them "the jewels of coiled basketry." The surfaces are beautifully corrugated, and patterns of the most intricate character can be wrought on them. The technic is as follows: Three or four small willow stems of uniform thickness serve for the foundation, as shown in Fig. 20; also in cross section in Fig. 18G. The sewing, which may be in splints of willow, black or white carex root, or cercis stem, passes around the three stems constituting the coil, under the upper one of the bundle below, the stitches interlocking. In some examples this upper rod is replaced by

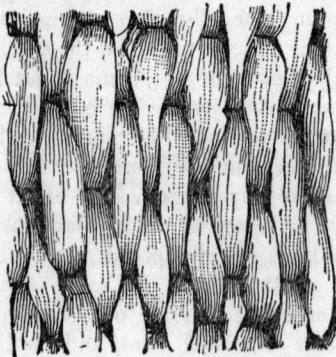

Fig. 19. Detail of single-rod coil in basketry.

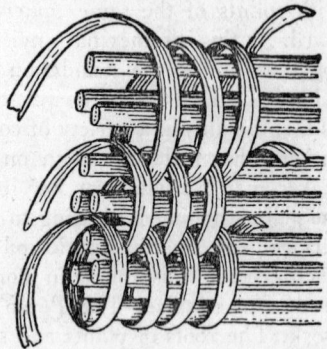

Fig. 20. Foundation of three rods, stitches catching rod underneath.

a thin strip of material serving for a welt (see Fig. 18F). In the California area the materials for basketry are of the finest quality. The willow stems and carex root are susceptible of division into delicate filaments. Sewing done with these is most compact, and when the stitches are pressed closely together the foundation does not appear. On the surface of the bam shi bu basketry the Pomo weaver adds pretty bits of bird feathers and delicate pieces of shell. The basket represents the wealth of the maker, and the gift of one of these to a friend is considered to be the highest compliment. . . .

H. *Splint foundation.*—In basketry of this type the foundation consists of a number of longer or shorter splints massed together and sewed, the stitches passing under one or more of the splints in the coil beneath. In the Pomo language it is called chilo, but it has no standing in that tribe. In the Great Interior Basin, where the pliant material of the California tribes is wanting, only the outer and younger portion of the stem will do for sewing. The interior parts in such examples are made up into the foundation. All such ware is crude, and the sewing frequently passes through instead of around the stitches below. In the Klikitat basketry the pieces of spruce or cedar root not used for sewing material are also worked into the foundation. (See Fig. 18H.)

In a small area on Fraser River, in southwestern Canada, on the upper waters of the Columbia, and in many Salishan tribes of northwestern Washington, basketry, called imbricated, is made. The foundation, as said, is in cedar or spruce root, while the sewing is done with the outer and tough portion of the root; the stitches pass over the upper bundle of splints and are locked with those underneath. On the outside

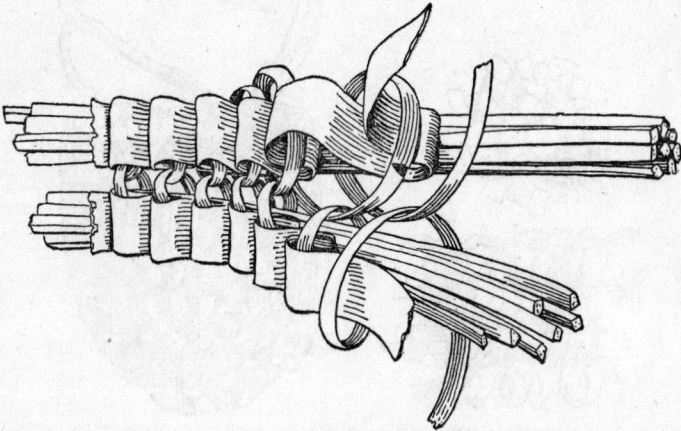

Fig. 21. Imbricated work detail, called Klikitat. Showing method of concealing coil stitches.

of these baskets is a form of technic, which also constitutes the ornamentation. It is not something added, or overlaid, or sewed on, but is a part of the texture effected in the progress of the manufacture. (See Fig. 21.)

The method of adding this ornamentation in strips of cherry bark, cedar bast, and grass stems, dyed with Oregon grape, is unique, and on this account I have applied the term "imbricated" to the style of weave here shown.

The strip of colored bark or grass is laid down and caught under a passing stitch; before another stitch is taken this one is bent forward to cover the last stitch, doubled on itself so as to be underneath the next stitch, and so with each one it is bent backward and forward so that the sewing is entirely concealed, forming a sort of "knifeplaiting." . . .

1. *Grass-coil foundation.*—The foundation is a bunch of grass or rush stems, or small midribs from palm leaves, or shredded yucca. The

effect in all such ware is good, for the reason that the maker has perfect control of her material. Excellent examples of this kind are to be seen in the southwestern portions of the United States, among the Pueblos and Missions, and in northern Africa. The sewing may be done with split stems of hard wood, willow, rhus, and the like, or, as in the case

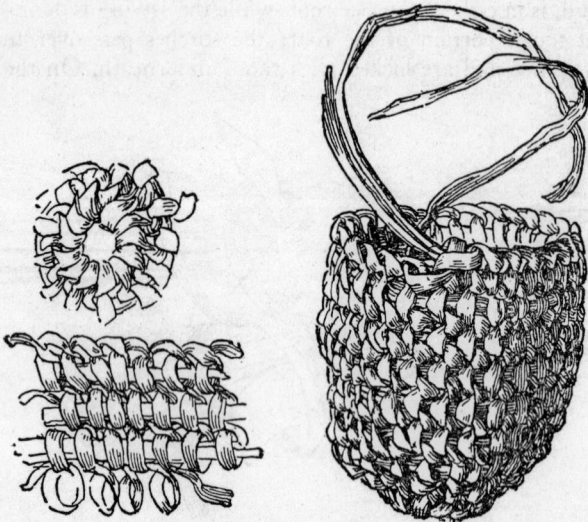

Fig. 22. Fuegian coiled basket, and details.

of the Mission baskets in southern California, of the stems of rushes (*Juncus acutus*) or stiff grass (*Epicampes rigens*). (See the cross section given in Fig. 18.) In the larger granary baskets of the Southwest a bundle of straws furnishes the foundation, while the sewing is done with broad strips of tough bark. . . .

κ. *Fuegian coiled basketry.*—In this ware the foundation is slight, consisting of one or more rushes; the sewing is in buttonhole stitch or half hitches, with rush stems interlocking. The resemblance of this to Asiatic types on the Pacific is most striking. (See Fig. 22.)

Social Culture

27. SOCIAL ORGANIZATION OF THE KARIERA OF AUSTRALIA [1]

BY A. RADCLIFFE BROWN

THE Kariera tribe occupies the coast of Western Australia from a point to the east of the Sherlock River to a point east of Port Hedland, extending inland for about 50 miles. . . .

TRIBAL AND LOCAL ORGANIZATION

The tribe is distinguished from its neighbors by the possession of a name, a language and a defined territory. There is no tribal chief, nor any form of tribal government. The fights that formerly took place were not wars of one tribe with another, but of one part of one tribe with one part of another, or at times of one part of a tribe with another part of the same tribe. Thus there was no unity of the tribe in warfare.

The extent of the territory of the tribe is between 3,500 and 4,000 square miles. . . .

The tribe is divided into a number of local groups, each with its own defined territory. Membership of the local group is determined by descent in the male line; that is to say, a child belongs to the local group of its father and inherits hunting rights over the territory of that group. There are no distinctive names for the local groups. To the question "Where is your country?" (*Wanja nyinda ngura?*), a native replies by naming one of the more prominent camping places of his local group, or in some cases the place where he was born. . . .

In default of an actual survey, it is impossible to do more than give a rough estimate of the extent of the territory belonging to each local group. Along the coast there are seven local groups, occupying altogether a strip of land about 80 miles long and a little less than 10 miles wide. This gives the area occupied by each as about 100 square miles

[1] From "Three Tribes of Western Australia," in *Journal of the* [*Royal*] *Anthropological Institute,* Volume 43, pages 143-194, 1913.

or a little more. The inland local groups seemed to me to occupy each a somewhat larger country, between 150 and 200 square miles. This is what we might expect, since the coast natives have both the land and the sea from which to obtain their food-supply. As a rough estimate, therefore, but the best that our knowledge permits, we may suppose that the tribe consisted of between twenty and twenty-five local groups. It is impossible at this time to obtain any accurate information as to the former volume of the local groups, that is the number of individuals belonging to each. My own estimate is that each group contained not less than 30 individuals, giving the minimum for the tribe at about 750 with a density of about 2 per square mile. This, however, is a very rough estimate, and no reliance must be placed upon it.

The country of a local group, with all its products, animal, vegetable, and mineral, belongs to the members of the group in common. Any member has the right to hunt over the country of his group at all times. He may not, however, hunt over the country of any other local group without the permission of the owners. A single exception to this rule seems to have existed where a man was following a kangaroo or emu and it crossed the boundary into the country of his neighbors, when he might follow it and kill it. Hunting, or collecting vegetable products on the country or another local group constitutes an act of trespass and was in former times liable to be punished by death. The importance attached to this law seems to have been so great that offenses against it were very rare. In the early days of the settlement of the whites in the country of this and neighboring tribes, the squatters made use of the natives as shepherds, and I have been told on several occasions that they found it at first impossible to persuade a native to shepherd the sheep anywhere except on his own country. I could not find any evidence of the individual ownership of any part of the soil or any of its products. The whole territory of the group and everything on it seem to belong equally to all the members of the group.

It is impossible for a man to leave his local group and become naturalized or adopted in another. Just as the country belonged to him, so he belonged to it. If he left it he became a stranger, either the guest or the enemy of the men in whose country he found himself. He might pay visits to other groups, and such visits were apparently of very frequent occurrence, but his "home" was his own country, the country of his father and his father's father. . . .

In their original condition of life the natives never stayed long in one place. They shifted from one camping ground to another perpetually. It does not seem that the whole local group always lived and moved about as one body. A single family, that is a man and his wife or wives and their children, often traveled and hunted by themselves. A single individual, or a family, or several families, might pay a visit to a neighboring group, during which time they hunted in the country of their hosts. When some particular article of food became very plentiful in the country of one group they invited their neighbors to come and stay with them. Thus the inland natives visited those on the coast when fish was plentiful. On the occasion of the performance of a ceremony, members of different local groups might be found camped together often for weeks at a time. There was thus a perpetual shifting to and fro both within the country of the group and from one group to another.

This state of things shows very clearly that the unit of social life in the Kariera tribe was the family, consisting of a man and his wife or wives and their children. Such a unit might move about by itself without reference to the movements of the other families of the local group. In the camp each family had its own hut or shelter with its own fire. The family had its own food supply which was cooked and consumed by the family. The man provided the flesh food and his wife provided the vegetable food and such things as small mammals or lizards.

A native camp is composed of two parts, the married people's camp and the bachelors' camp. The latter contains all the unmarried men, including widowers; unmarried women and widows live with one or other of the families of the married people. If a visitor comes to the camp and brings his wife with him, he puts his fire and shelter near the married people, on the same side as his own country lies. If he is unmarried, or if he has not brought his wife with him, he goes to the bachelors' camp.

It will be shown later that a man is not permitted to marry a woman of his own local group. The result of this was that in the camp of a local group would be found only men and unmarried women and children who belonged to the group by birth, the married women all belonging by birth to other groups. A woman seems to have retained a sort of right over the country of her birth, so that a man and his wife were generally welcome to visit the wife's local group whenever they wished. A man seems also to have a sort of secondary right over the country of his mother, that is the country to which she belonged by birth. In a large number of cases this was the same as the country of his wife. In both cases, however, it seems to have meant no more than that a man was sure of a welcome in the country of his wife or his mother.

RELATIONSHIP AND MARRIAGE

The Kariera tribe is divided into four parts that I shall speak of as *classes*. The names of these are Banaka, Burung, Palyeri, and Karimera. No meanings were found for these names. To the natives of the present day they are simply the names of social divisions, and have no further meanings. These classes regulate the marriages of the natives. A man of any given class is restricted in his choice of a wife to one of the other classes. Thus a Banaka man may only marry a Burung woman and a Burung man may only marry a Banaka woman. The two classes, Banaka and Burung, thus form what will be spoken of as an *intermarrying pair* or simply a *pair*. This does not imply that a Banaka man may marry *any* Burung woman, but only that he may not marry a woman of any other class. The child of a Banaka man and a Burung woman is neither Banaka nor Burung but Palyeri, while the child of a Burung man and a Banaka woman is Karimera. The rules of marriage and descent of the Kariera tribe are shown in the following table:—

Father	Mother	Child
Banaka	Burung	Palyeri
Burung	Banaka	Karimera
Palyeri	Karimera	Banaka
Karimera	Palyeri	Burung

This may be expressed more concisely by means of a diagram.

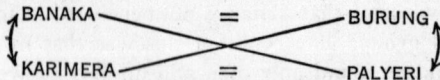

The sign = connects the two classes of an intermarrying pair, and therefore shows the relation of husband and wife. The sign $\big\rbrace$ connects the class of a mother with the class of her child. I propose to speak of the classes so related as together forming a *cycle*. In the Kariera tribe Banaka and Karimera form one cycle and Burung and Palyeri the other. The children of a woman always belong to the same cycle as herself, but to the other class of the cycle. The sign / connects the class of a father with the class of his child. I propose to speak of the two classes so connected as together forming a *couple*. In the Kariera tribe Banaka and Palyeri form one couple and Karimera and

Burung form the other. The children of a man always belong to the same couple as himself, but to the other class of the couple. There are no names in the Kariera tribe for the cycles, couples, or pairs.

This class system can only be understood by a study of the system of reckoning the relationships of consanguinity and affinity. The following is a list of the terms used to denote these relationships. M. stands for "Male speaking," F. for "Female speaking," and M.F. for "Male or Female speaking":

Maeli.—Father's father M.F., father's father's brother M.F., mother's mother's brother M.F., consort's mother's father M.F., son's son and daughter M.

Kabali.—Father's mother M.F., father's mother's sister M.F., mother's father's sister M.F., consort's mother's mother M.F., son's son and daughter F.

Tami.—Mother's father M.F., mother's father's brother M.F., father's mother's brother M.F., consort's father's father M.F., daughter's son and daughter M.

Kandari.—Mother's mother M.F., mother's mother's sister M.F., father's father's sister M.F., consort's father's mother M.F., daughter's son and daughter F.

Mama.—Father M.F., father's brother M.F., mother's sister's husband M.F., consort's mother's brother M.F.

Nganga.—Mother M.F., mother's sister M.F., father's brother's wife M.F., consort's father's sister M.F.

Kaga.—Mother's brother M.F., father's sister's husband M.F., consort's father M.F.

Toa or Yumani.—Father's sister M., mother's brother's wife M., wife's mother M., brother's son F., daughter's husband F., husband's sister's son F.

Yuro.—Father's sister F., mother's brother's wife F., husband's mother F.

Kaja.—Older brother M.F., father's brother's son and mother's sister's son if older than the speaker.

Turdu.—Older sister M.F., father's brother's daughter and mother's sister's daughter if older than the speaker.

Margara.—Younger brother M.F., father's brother's son and mother's sister's son if younger than the speaker.

Mari.—Younger sister M.F., father's brother's or mother's sister's daughter if younger than the speaker.

Ñuba.—Mother's brother's daughter M., father's sister's daughter M., mother's brother's son F., father's sister's son F., wife M., husband F., brother's wife M., wife's sister M., sister's husband F., husband's brother F.

Kumbali.—Mother's brother's son M., father's sister's son M., sister's husband M., wife's brother M.

Bungali.—Mother's brother's daughter F., father's sister's daughter F., brother's wife F., husband's sister F.

Mainga.—Son M.F., brother's son M., sister's son F.
Kundal.—Daughter M.F., brother's daughter M., sister's daughter F.
Kuling or Yaraija.—Sister's son M., daughter's husband M.
Ngaraia or Bali.—Sister's daughter M., son's wife M.
Ngaraia.—Brother's daughter F., son's wife F.
Nguranu.—Wife M. (specific).
Yarungu.—Brother's wife M.

As shown in the above list, each term is applied to a number of different relatives. Only some of those to whom the term is applied are mentioned in the list. Thus the term *mama* is also applied to a mother's brother's wife's brother, to a sister's husband's mother's brother, and to many other relatives. The list of relatives denoted by any one term could be extended indefinitely.

At the same time each of the terms in the above list is used by the natives in a sense corresponding to our own use in English of the terms "father," "mother," etc. Thus, although a given person applies the name *mama* to a large number of individuals, if he is asked "Who is your *mama?*" he immediately replies by giving the name of his actual father, unless his own father died during his infancy, in which case he gives the name of his foster father. In the same way, if asked for his *maeli* he gives the name of his own father's father, although there are a number of other men to whom he applies the same term. Each term, therefore, has, what we may call, a primary or specific meaning. The primary meaning of *mama* is "father," and that of *maeli* "father's father." The primary meaning of the native term corresponds very closely to our own use of relationship terms in English. In West Australia I collected a large number of genealogies, and in questioning the natives I always used the native terms of relationship in their primary meanings. I never experienced any difficulty except in such cases as the one I have mentioned, where the name of a foster parent was substituted for that of the true parent.

In English we use the one word "cousin" to denote a number of persons standing in different relations to the one person. We distinguish between near and distant cousins, and have developed a somewhat complicated terminology to denote these distinctions. Just as we use the word "cousin" so the Kariera native uses his word *mama* (father), speaking of a large number of different related persons by the one name, but distinguishing in thought, though not in words, those of his "fathers" who are more nearly related to him from those who are more distantly related. In the modern blackfellow English he speaks of his "close-up" and his "far-away" "fathers." The same is the case with every other term of relationship. With regard to the term for "father," a man's nearest relative of this kind is not necessarily the man who gave him birth, but the man under whose care he lived as a child. This is, of course, his own physiological father in most cases, and in cases where the real father dies the child is, in most cases, adopted by a brother of the father. This distinction between nearer and more distant relatives of the same kind (that is, denoted by the same term) is of the greatest importance in the social life of the Kariera tribe. It seems probable that it is equally important in other tribes of Australia, though I do not know that it has been specifically pointed out by previous writers.

Although the use of the terms of relationship is based on actual relations of consanguinity and affinity, it is so extended as to embrace all persons who come into social contact with one another. If we take any single member of the tribe, then every person with whom he has any social dealings whatever stands to him in one or other of the relations denoted by the terms in use and may be addressed by that term. In this way the whole society forms a body of relatives. In the Kariera tribe, a man or woman never addresses any one, except young children, by a personal name, but used the appropriate relationship term. The method of determining the relationship of two individuals is extremely simple. Let us suppose, as an example, that two men, A and B, meet each other for the first time. The man A has a relative C who is his *mama*. At the same time C is the *kaga* of B. It immediately follows that A and B are *kumbali* to each other. Yet in all this system of widely extended relationships the real relations of consanguinity are never lost sight of. The natives preserve their genealogies carefully in their memories, though in these degenerate days the younger men and women neglect such knowledge. With the help of the genealogical knowledge of the older men and women it is possible to trace out some relationship, however distant it may be, between any two members of the same tribe. When a stranger comes to a camp that he has never visited before, he does not enter the camp, but remains at some distance. A few of the older men, after a while, approach him, and the first thing they proceed to do is to find out who the stranger is. The commonest question that is put to him is "Who is your *maeli*?" (father's father). The discussion proceeds on genealogical lines until all parties are satisfied of the exact relation of the stranger to each of the natives present in the camp. When this point is reached, the stranger can be admitted to the camp, and the different men and women are pointed out to him and their relation to him defined. I watched two or three of these discussions in West Australia. I took with me on my journey a native of the Talainji tribe, and at each native camp we came to,

the same process had to be gone through. In one case, after a long discussion, they were still unable to discover any traceable relationship
between my servant and the men of the camp. That night my "boy"
refused to sleep in the native camp, as was his usual custom, and on
talking to him I found that he was frightened. These men were not
his relatives, and they were therefore his enemies. This represents the
real feeling of the natives on the matter. If I am a blackfellow and meet
another blackfellow, that other must be either my relative or my
enemy. If he is my enemy I shall take the first opportunity of killing
him, for fear he will kill me. This, before the white man came, was the
aboriginal view of one's duty towards one's neighbor, and it still remains at the back of his mind at the present day in spite of the new
conditions brought about by the coming of the white man.

In order to explain the Kariera system of relationship, I have made
out the two accompanying genealogical tables, by means of which it is
possible to trace out the relation of a man or a woman to any other
member of the same society. . . .

TABLE I.[2] MALE SPEAKING

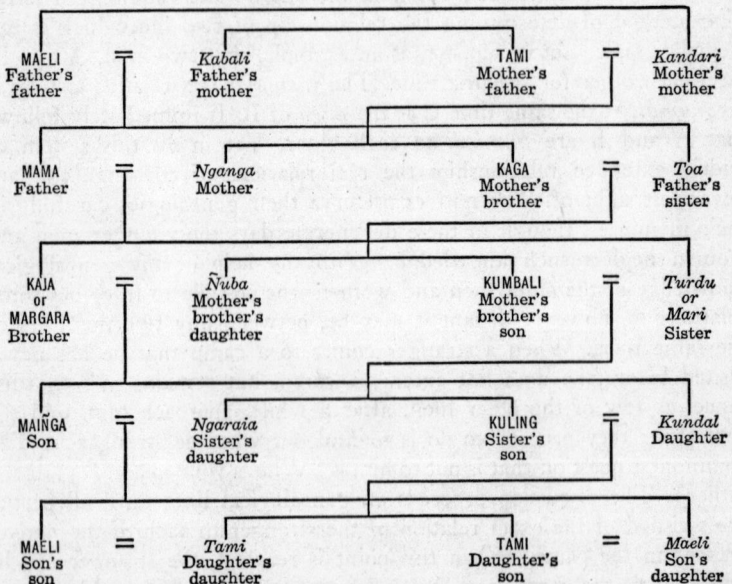

[2] In these tables the sign = connects a husband and a wife. The husband is
on the left of the sign and is denoted by capitals (MAMA), the wife is to the
right, and is denoted by italics (*Nganga*). The descendants of a married pair
are shown by the lines from the sign =.

TABLE 2. FEMALE SPEAKING

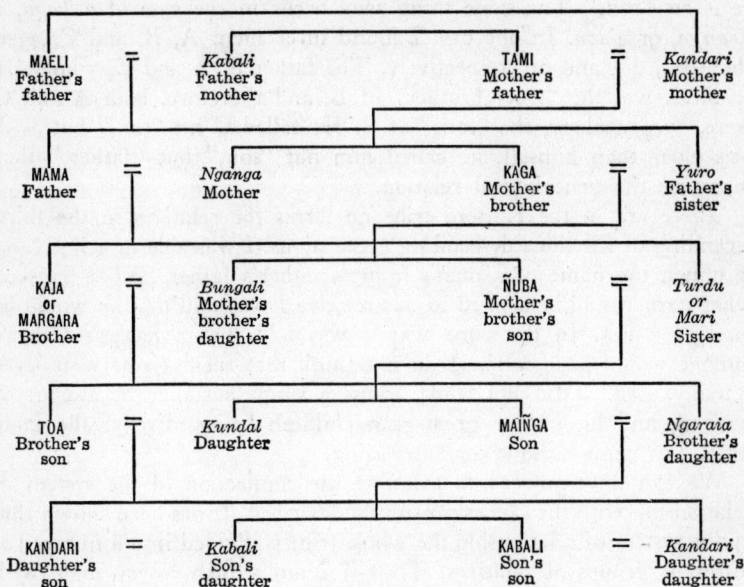

MAELI Father's father	=	*Kabali* Father's mother		TAMI Mother's father	=	*Kandari* Mother's mother
MAMA Father	=	*Nganga* Mother		KAGA Mother's brother	=	*Yuro* Father's sister
KAJA or MARGARA Brother	=	*Bungali* Mother's brother's daughter		ÑUBA Mother's brother's son	=	*Turdu* or *Mari* Sister
TOA Brother's son	=	*Kundal* Daughter		MAIÑGA Son		*Ngaraia* Brother's daughter
KANDARI Daughter's son	=	*Kabali* Son's daughter		KABALI Son's son	=	*Kandari* Daughter's daughter

. . . In the second descending generation the children of *maiñga* and *ngaraia* are *maeli* without distinction of sex, and the children of *kuling* and *kundal* are *tami*. This last feature is due to the reciprocal use of the terms for grandparents. Thus I am *maeli* (father's father) to my son's son and he is *maeli* to me. Similarly I am *maeli* to my son's daughter and she is *maeli* to me. If a woman is speaking she is *kabali* (father's mother) to her son's son and he is therefore *kabali* to her. The following table shows how the terms for grandparents and grandchildren are used reciprocally:—

Father's father M.F. = Son's son and daughter M.
Father's mother M.F. = Son's son and daughter F.
Mother's father M.F. = Daughter's son and daughter M.
Mother's mother M.F. = Daughter's son and daughter F.

By means of the laws enumerated above, which are expressed in a concrete form in the genealogical tables, it is possible to find immediately the relation of any two persons by considering the relation of them to a third. There is, however, one important point that has so far been omitted. It may happen that a man B is by genealogy the "father" of a man A, but is younger than A. In such a case A calls B not "father," but "son," and B calls A "father," although by genealogy he is his "son." The same thing may occur in the case of a *kaga*, a *nganga*, or a *toa*. In one case I found three men, A, B, and C, aged about 65, 63, and 60, respectively. The father of A and C, who were brothers, was the "elder brother" of B, and therefore, both A and C were, by genealogy, the "sons" of B. He called C his "son," but as A was older than himself, he called him not "son," but "father," thus reversing the genealogical relation.

There are in the Kariera tribe no terms for relatives in the third ascending or the third descending generations. I was able in a few cases to obtain the name of a man's father's father's father. When I asked what term would be applied to this relative I was told that he would be *maiñga* (son). In the same way I was told that a father's father's mother would be *ngaraia*. I do not think that these terms were ever actually used. I did not come across a single instance of a man or woman, and his or her great-grandchildren being alive at the same time. The point is, however, interesting.

We can now proceed to examine the connection of the system of relationship with the classes previously described. It has been shown that by the system of relationship the whole tribe is divided into a number of different groups of relatives. Thus if I am a man, every male with whom I have any social relations is either (1) my *maeli*, (2) my *tami*, (3) my *mama*, (4) my *kaga*, (5) my *kaja* or *margara*, (6) my *kumbali*, (7) my *maiñga*, or (8) my *kuling*. . . . These male relatives may be arranged in the following diagram, a horizontal line separating those older from those younger than the speaker:

A	D	B	C
Maeli Kaja	Mama	Tami Kumbali	Kaga
Margara Maeli	Maiñga	Kumbali Tami	Kuling

Thus I belong to the column A, and every person represented in that column is either my *maeli*, my *kaja*, or my *margara*. Every person in column D is either *mama* or *maiñga* to me, and is either *mama* or *maiñga* to every person in column A. But a man who is *mama* to me may be *maiñga* to my *kaja*, and one who is *maiñga* to me may be *mama* to my *margara*. Inversely every person in column A is either *mama* or *maiñga* to every person in column D. Similarly the men of column B are *tami* and *kumbali* to those of A, and inversely those of A are *tami* or *kumbali* to those of B.

The four columns in the diagram correspond to the four classes which have been described earlier. Thus if I belong to the class Banaka all the men of that class are, by genealogy, either *maeli, kaja,* or *margara* to me; the men of the Palyeri class are my *mama,* and my *maiñga;* those of the Burung class are my *tami* or my *kumbali;* and the Karimera men are my *kaga* and *kuling.*

It was stated earlier that a man of the Banaka class can only marry a woman of the Burung class. We are now able to explain what this rule means. In the Kariera tribe a man may only marry a woman who stands to him in the relation of *ñuba.* If the man is Banaka his *ñuba* is Burung, and therefore in saying that he must marry a *ñuba,* we are saying that he must marry a Burung woman. But amongst the Burung women there are some who are not his *ñuba,* namely, his *kabali* and his *tami,* and these women he may not marry. A man's *kabali* must be only a few years older than himself, so that marriage would be quite possible. It is, however, in the Kariera tribe, forbidden. The marriage rule of the Kariera is simplicity itself: a man may marry a woman who is his *ñuba,* but he may marry no one else. Thus we may say that in the Kariera tribe marriage is regulated by relationship, and by relationship alone.

A man applies the term *ñuba* to the daughter of any *kaga* and any *toa.* He applies the term *kaga* to his mother's brother and the term *toa* to his father's sister. Therefore it is obvious that by the above-stated marriage rule a man may marry the daughter of his own mother's brother, or of his own father's sister. Such marriages of the children of a brother with those of his sister are common in this tribe. Indeed we may say that the proper person for a man to marry, if it be possible, is his own first cousin. In the genealogies collected by me I found that in nearly every case where such a marriage was possible it had taken place.

A common custom in this as in most Australian tribes is the exchange of sisters. A man, A, having one or more sisters finds a man, B, standing to him in the relation of *kumbali* who also possesses a sister. These men each take a sister of the other as wife. As a result of this practice it often happens that a man's father's sister is at the same time the wife of his mother's brother. If these two have a daughter she will in the ordinary course of events become the man's wife.

As the natives themselves put it to me, a man must look to his *kaga* to provide him with a wife by giving him one or more of his daughters.

The relative who is most particularly his *kaga*, in the same sense that his own father is most particularly his *mama*, is his mother's brother, who may or may not be at the same time the husband of his father's sister. It is to this man that he looks first for a wife. If his own mother's brother has no daughter, or if she is already disposed of, he must apply to other persons who stand to him in the relation of *kaga*, to the husband of his father's sister for example. He may have to go much further afield and apply to some distant *kaga*, but this is only the case when there are available no nearer relatives. Thus we may say that the man who is preëminently *kaga* (as his own father is preëminently *mama*) is his mother's brother; the woman who is preëminently *toa* is his own father's sister who should be the wife of the *kaga*; consequently the woman who is preëminently a man's *ñuba* is the daughter of his own mother's brother, or failing this, of his own father's sister. It is this woman to whom he has the first right as a wife.

The arrangement of marriages, as in other Australian tribes, is managed by the older people. While the children are quite small it is arranged which ones are to marry. The death of one or other of them may, of course, necessitate a new arrangement. Thus, when a boy is growing up he learns which girl is to be his wife. To the father of this girl he owes certain duties, the chief being that he must make him presents from time to time. This man is his father-in-law, and, as has been said, is in some cases his mother's brother. At the same time the man has a secondary right to a number of other girls. If the girl betrothed to him should die, he will have to try to obtain one of these, and therefore he must devote some attention to their fathers, making them presents from time to time, and going to visit them. It is this fact that seems to determine the social relations of a man with his various *kaga*. They are all prospective fathers-in-law. A man owes the same sort of duties to all the men whom he calls *kaga*, but the recognition of these duties is more intense in some cases than in others.

A man applies the name *toa* to his father's sister and to the wife of any *kaga*, that is to any woman who might be his mother-in-law. He may not speak to any of these women, nor have any social dealing whatever with them. If for any reason he is obliged to be near one of his *toa* he must take care that he does not look at her. He will, if possible, interpose a hut or bush between himself and her, or else he will sit with his back to her. This rule breaks down when a man gets on in years and has been long married with children of his own. He then ceases to speak of these women as *toa*, calling them *yumani* instead, and he is permitted to speak to them if he wishes, although the old habit still shows itself, and he has very little to do with them. I was not able to make out that the necessity of avoidance was more intense in respect to the actual mother-in-law. A man must avoid all his *toa*, and must apparently avoid them all to an equal degree, until the time comes when they can be regarded as *yumani,* and the necessity for avoidance ceases.[3]

There is no similar avoidance in the case of a woman, that is to say, she does not need to avoid her father-in-law or her mother-in-law, but only her son-in-law. A woman calls her husband's mother not *toa* or *yumani* but *yuro.*

We may resume briefly the chief points of the above description:

(1) The relationship system of the Kariera tribe is not only a system of names or terms of address, but is preëminently a system of reciprocal rights and duties. A man owes the same duties (though not in the same degree) to all the persons to whom he applies the same term. Thus the relationship system regulates the whole social life of the people.

(2) It is based on actual relations of consanguinity and affinity that can be traced by means of the genealogical knowledge preserved by the old men and women.

(3) The recognition of relationships is so extended that every one with whom an individual comes in contact in the ordinary course of social life is his relative. It is impossible for a man to have any social relations with any one who is not his relative because there is no standard by which two persons in this position can regulate their conduct towards one another. I am compelled to treat a person differently according as he is my "brother," "brother-in-law," "father," or "uncle." If I do not know which of these he is, all intercourse is impossible.

(4) Within the body of relatives of a given kind distinctions are made between nearer and more distant relatives, just as in English we distinguish between nearer and more distant "cousins" though still calling them all by the same name. These distinctions are not of kind but of degree, if we may use the phrase. Thus though a man owes certain duties to all the men he calls "father" he must observe them more particularly in regard to his own father or his father's brothers than in regard to a distant cousin of his father. The same is the case with every other relationship.

(5) In Australia, much more than in civilized communities, a great deal of attention is paid to actual relationship by blood and marriage.

[3] I believe that the matter is settled by the older men and women, who decide that two persons who are *toa* to each other shall be made *yumani.* There may be some sort of ceremony on such occasions, but I could not ascertain any details about it.

Thus the Australian system is characterized, not by a less intense, but by a more intense recognition of actual relationships of consanguinity.

(6) The classes of the Kariera tribe are groups of related persons. The rule that a man of one class may only marry a woman of one of the other classes is the result of the more fundamental rule that a man may only marry a woman bearing to him a certain relation of consanguinity, namely, the daughter of his mother's brother. Marriage is regulated by consanguinity and by consanguinity alone.

When a girl is old enough to be claimed as a wife she is handed over by her father to the husband, who takes her away to his own camp. There does not seem to be any ceremony on such an occasion. Polygyny is practiced. In the genealogies I did not find a case of a man having more than three wives alive at the same time. Where there are several sisters in a family they are all regarded as the wives of the man who marries the eldest of them. He may, if he chooses, waive his right in favor of his younger brother, with the consent of the father of the girls. If a family contained four girls and a man took the two oldest, but permitted his younger brother to marry the third, the youngest daughter thereby also becomes the wife of the younger brother, and the older brother cannot claim any right to her. When a man dies his wives pass to his younger brother or to the man who stands nearest to him in the relation of *margara*. This man marries the widow and adopts the children.

There is no polyandry; that is to say, a woman is always the wife of one man alone. The word *nguranu* is used by a man to distinguish his own wife from other women whom he might have married but who are actually the wives of his own or tribal brothers, the latter being called *yarungu*. In this and the neighboring tribes there are certain customs of sexual license on ceremonial occasions when men who stand in the relation of brother to one another lend each other their wives. I was not able to witness one of these ceremonies and what little information I obtained in answer to questions is too unreliable to allow me to speak definitely on the subject.

A woman who is promised or married to a given man may run away with another. If the two who thus elope are not *ñuba* to each other they are separated by the tribe and punished, the woman being beaten by her female relatives and the man speared through the thigh. If they are of the proper relation, that is, if they are *ñuba* to each other, it rests with the husband of the woman to get her back if he can. This often leads to a fight in which one or other gets killed. Practically all the quarrels amongst the natives are about the women.

In many Australian tribes what we may call irregular marriages are in some instances permitted, that is, a man is permitted by the tribe to marry a woman who by the tribal law is forbidden him. I have obtained good evidence, by means of genealogies, that in a number of tribes of Western Australia such irregular marriages took place before the country was occupied by white men. In the Kariera tribe one or two such marriages have taken place in recent years, but have been viewed with great disapproval, and in the genealogies I collected, there is not a single instance of such a marriage taking place before 1860.

Having described the relationship organization of the Kariera tribe it is necessary to consider the relation of that system to the local organization previously described. The whole tribe is divided into two couples of classes, Banaka-Palyeri and Karimera-Burung. Each local group, however, that is, each of the local subdivisions of the tribe, consists of members of one couple only. Thus one local group consists of men and women of the classes Karimera and Burung, while another consists of Banaka and Palyeri men and women. . . .

It is obvious from the above account that a man can never marry a woman of his own local group, since such women are either *kandari*, *toa*, *turdu*, *mari*, *kundal*, or *maeli* to him. We therefore find in this tribe the condition often called "local exogamy" by ethnologists. On analysis, however, we see that this local exogamy is simply the result of the regulation of marriage by relationship, together with the peculiar constitution of the local group.

I propose in this and future publications to use the word "clan" to denote a social division of this kind, of which the Kariera local group is an example. A clan by this definition consists of a body of persons who are closely related to one another in one line (that is, either in the male line or in the female line) and who are clearly marked off in some way from the similar divisions of the same society. In the Kariera tribe we have clans with descent in the male line. Each clan includes a number of men who are, by the relationship system, father's father, father, brother, son, or son's son to each other. Each clan is marked off from every other by the possession of its own territory, and as we shall see later, by other features also.

A man's own clan contains only men who are his *maeli*, *mama*, *kaja*, *margara*, and *mainga*, and it contains all his nearest relatives of these kinds, thus serving to mark off those most nearly related to him from those more distantly related. This is the essential feature of a clan in Australia, that it provides this distinction between near and distant kindred.

TOTEMISM

We have seen that the Kariera tribe is divided into a number of local groups each with its own defined territory, with descent in the male line, and that each local group belongs to one of the two couples into which the tribe is divided. It has been shown that the local group thus forms what we may call a "clan," with male descent, all the male members of the clan being "father's father," "son's son," "father," "son," or "brother," to each other.

Each of these clans forms a single totemic group, possessing a number of totems. All the totems of the clan are equally the totems of every member of the clan. For each totem belonging to the clan there is within the territory of the clan a ceremonial ground or totemic center for which the name is *talu*. The *talu* is a spot set apart for the performance of totemic ceremonies. Thus the *Pidira talu* is the spot set apart for the performance of ceremonies connected with the *pidira*, white cockatoo. The *talu* belongs to the men of the local group in whose territory it is found, and the ceremonies connected with the *talu* belong to them at the same time. If a *talu* lies within the territory of a certain local group, only the members of that local group can perform the ceremony connected with it.

The totemic ceremonies of the Kariera tribe have been discontinued for many years. I was therefore unable to see any of them performed and had to rely entirely on what the natives told me about them. Information of this kind is of course very unsatisfactory. The purpose of the ceremonies is said to be to increase the supply of the animal, plant, or other object with which it is connected. Thus the purpose of the *mungu* or white ant ceremony is to increase the white ants, which are eaten by the aborigines. At many of these totemic ceremonial grounds there is either a single bowlder or a heap of small stones and these play a part in the ceremony connected with the place. In some cases it would seem that the stone or heap is struck with clubs or with stones held in the hand. The performers of these ceremonies are painted, and decorated with feathers and birds' down. The women of the clan take part in the ceremonies as well as the men. In some cases songs are sung, in others one of the performers calls out the names of different parts of the country. The head man of the clan, unless he be too old, takes the leading part in the ceremonies of his clan.

There is no prohibition whatever against a man or woman killing any one of his or her totems, if it be an animal, or against eating it if it be edible. . . .

Most of the totems are of an edible nature. Among the clans of the coast various species of fish preponderate. There is not a large number of vegetable species in the list of totems. I think it is probable that if the list were complete a larger number would be found. I did not find in the Kariera tribe either a kangaroo totem or an emu totem, nor was there a rain totem, unless we include in this tribe a clan at Pilbara, which more probably belongs to the Injibandi tribe. The absence of these totems in the Kariera tribe is of some interest when we compare that tribe with others, for example, with the tribes on the Ashburton River, to be described later. . . .

As regards many of the totems, it would seem that the totemic center or ceremonial ground is in a part of the country where the totem species is naturally plentiful. Thus the ceremonial grounds of the white cockatoo and the March fly are in the creek at Balla-balla, where these two species are plentiful. In a number of cases, not only in this but also in other tribes, I was able to satisfy myself that the totem animal or plant is actually more abundant near the ceremonial ground belonging to it than in other parts of the country. In a large proportion of cases the place where the ceremony is performed is called by a name formed by adding the suffix *na* to the name of the totem. Thus there are two totemic centers for *murumbari*, and in both cases the name of the totem center is Murumbarina. Many other examples may be found in the list of totems given above. Similar place names, that is, consisting of the name of some species of animal or vegetable species with the suffix *-na*, are also given to spots where there is no totemic center, but where the species in question is more abundant than elsewhere. . . .

THE BIRTH OF CHILDREN

When a woman conceives, her condition is said to be due to the action of some particular member of her tribe, who is spoken of as the *wororu* of the child after it is born. If a man of the right relationship gives a woman some food and after eating it she becomes pregnant, this man becomes the *wororu* of the woman's child. Sometimes the *wororu* does not gives the woman food to eat, but when he is hunting and has speared a kangaroo or an emu, as he is killing it he speaks to the spirit of the kangaroo and tells it to go to a certain woman. The spirit of the kangaroo follows the man home to the camp and goes inside the woman indicated, who thereby becomes pregnant. The man who sent the kangaroo or other spirit is recognized as the *wororu* of the child. In one case I was told that a man had "made" his own child, having killed an emu and sent the spirit into his own wife. Such a case is, however, an exception. The *wororu* of a child in every case (except this one) that I examined in the Kariera tribe is a man standing in the relation of "brother" to the actual father of the child, and therefore stands in the relation of *mama* (father or father's brother) to the child itself. In most of the cases that I examined the child had its origin in the spirit of a kangaroo killed by the *wororu*. In one case the man showed me a birth-mark on his thigh which he said was where his *wororu* had speared the kangaroo.

I did not find that there were any specific duties that a man or woman owes to his *wororu*. All that the natives told me was that a man "looks after" his *wororu*, that is, he attends to his wants, gives him food when there is an opportunity, and treats him much as he does his own father. It is possible, however, that there are some more specific duties that I did not discover.

The animal from whose spirit the child arises, or the animal or vegetable eaten by the mother and causing conception, is not in any way sacred to the individual thus connected with it by birth. He treats it just as he does every other animal or plant.

28. BÁNARO SOCIETY [4]

BY RICHARD THURNWALD

EACH of the villages has a name of its own. Different localities, such as parts of the forest, of the grassland, big trees, creeks, hunting grounds, fishing pools, sago swamps, etc., are provided with special designations or proper names. These appellations are used as village-names. However, the name of the settlement must be carefully distinguished from that of the tribe. The tribe-name is the designation given to a tribe by its neighbors. . . .

Each of its villages is composed of from three to six hamlets, each hamlet in turn consisting of from three to eight houses. Every hamlet boasts of a special communal structure, as a religious center called *bū'ek*, but there is no such common "goblin-hall" for the village as a whole. . . .

The social unit of the settlement is the hamlet. The hamlet, together with its inhabitants, derives its name from that of the goblin-hall; the name of the goblin-hall, as well as the name of the tribe, remains

[4] From monograph of the same name, in *Memoirs of the American Anthropological Association*, Volume 3, Number 4, 1916. The Bánaro live on the Keram River, in the northern part of what was German New Guinea.

constant. If the location of the hall should be changed on account of the migration of the tribe, or if a new hall should be built in the same village, the name would still be retained. So, in the example of the . . . Tjímundo tribe the names of the two goblin-halls, which with their surrounding houses constitute the village, have always been the same—Yuórmua and Nangúndumbir. Not only have the names of the goblin-halls been retained, but also their position in relation to the river in the different localities the tribe has occupied, the first being always farther downstream than the other. Yuórmua, the natives say, "goes first," and Nangúndumbir "follows," the whole village being imagined as floating down the river. Thus, the designation of the hall is in no way connected with the locality, but with the group of people belonging to the goblin-hall. I propose to call such a group a "gens." Thus, there are as many "gentes" as hamlets.

As one enters a goblin-hall, he is immediately impressed by its symmetrical plan. This is especially noticeable in the arrangement of the fireplaces, of which there are four, two on each side of the hall, directly opposite each other. . . .

The two symmetrical rows of fireplaces in the goblin-hall correspond to a division of the gens into two halves. It might perhaps be allowed to use the word "sib" in a narrower sense to indicate these halves. The sibs themselves have no special names, other than "the left," *bon*, and "the right," *tan*, drawn from their place in the goblin-hall. These terms refer to their relative positions as one faces the entry. The term for the left side, *a bòn areán*, is derived from the name for bamboo pipes, *bon-moróm*, meaning literally "bamboo-goblin." The designation for the right side, *tan*, probably has some connection with the big wooden drums. Although the word for drum is not involved, the appellation for iron-wood, out of which the drums are cut, is *tan*.

The external form of the settlement reflects precisely the internal organization of the tribe; for the goblin-hall, with adjacent houses in the same clearing, mirrors the social unit, the gens, just as the symmetric partition of the goblin-hall into two parts, the division of the gens into halves [sibs].

The symmetry in the arrangement of the goblin-hall is the expression in space-terms of the principle of social reciprocity or the "retaliation of like for like."

EXCHANGE SYSTEM

Among the Bánaro we find the exchange system in full operation, elaborately worked out in every detail. When a girl has reached the age of puberty and gone through the initiation ceremonies, she consults with her mother as to which of the marriageable youths suits her best. Of course, she often has an understanding with the boy beforehand. She may choose from among the boys of the several gentes of which her tribe is composed. Marriage within the gens is not permitted. It is only in exceptional cases that marriage into another tribe takes place, as an examination of native pedigrees proves. For this reason we may call the gens exogamic, the tribe endogamic.

The girl's mother discusses the matter with her husband, and if they agree, she prepares a pot of boiled sago, which they then carry in a basket to the parents of the chosen bridegroom. The families concerned confer with each other and come to a formal agreement. As compensation for the girl the sister of the bridegroom must be married to the bride's brother. But the sago is offered under the pretext of asking the bridegroom's sister in marriage for the bride's brother. If the other parents accept the sago, the case is settled, as far as the two sets of parents are concerned.

But the situation is now complicated further. We noticed above that each gens is divided into two sibs. These two sibs are united by a bond of friendship for mutual protection and pleasure, as well as for purposes of revenge against outsiders. The two sibs are considered to be the best of friends. They "can never fight" against each other. It seems required, therefore, by a kind of active sympathy, that if one sib is going to celebrate a marriage, the other sib shall also have an opportunity for a feast. Moreover the principle of requital implies that the other sib shall participate, as we shall see later on. Accordingly a bridegroom of the right side (*tan*) of the sib must take his bride from the same side of the other gens; a bridegroom of the left side (*bon*) takes his bride from a left sib.

After the parties have mutually agreed, each pair of parents confers with the paternal grandfather of each bridegroom. Each grandfather consults with his *mundū*, his special friend in the corresponding sib. If the grandfather is dead, his brother takes his place.

The *mundūs* of the grandfathers now confer with their sons, and the sons with their children, in order to arrange for two corresponding marriages further in the parallel sib. Thus we may count four pairs to be united by marriage. Two gentes each exchange one girl for a girl of the other gens, and this pair of girls is doubled by the parallel exchange in the corresponding sib of each gens.

This is the ideal system, but in reality it cannot always be carried out to its fullest extent. . . .

GIRLS' INITIATION

The marriage ceremony, as was mentioned above, is connected with the initiation ceremony of the girls. Girls are provided with husbands on reaching the age of puberty. It would lead us too far to give a detailed account of the rather complicated festivities here. The following, however, are some of their principal features.

Wild pigs are hunted, and domestic pigs slaughtered on different occasions, once by the fathers of the girls, once by their mothers' brothers. During a lapse of altogether nine months, the girls are confined to a cell in the family house, getting sago soup instead of water throughout that time. For the whole period their fathers are obliged to sleep in the goblin-house. At last their cell is broken up by the women, the girls released and allowed to leave the house. The women get cocoanuts laid ready beforehand, and throw them at the girls, whom they finally push into the water, again pelting them with cocoanuts. The girls crawl out of the water on to the bank, receive portions of sago and pork, and are now dressed, and adorned with earrings, nosesticks, necklaces, bracelets, and aromatic herbs. After this a dance of the women takes place.

That same evening the orgies begin. When dusk breaks in, the men assemble on the streets of the village. The old men consult with each other, agreeing to distribute the girls according to their custom. This custom was explained to me in the following way. The father of the chosen bridegroom really ought to take possession of the girl, but he is "ashamed" and asks his sib friend, his *mundū*, to initiate her into the mysteries of married life in his place. This man agrees to do so. The mother of the girl hands her over to the bridegroom's father, telling her that he will lead her to meet the goblin.

The bridegroom's father takes her to the goblin-hall and bids her enter. His *mundū* has already gone into the goblin-hall, and awaits her within. When she comes in, he, in the rôle of the goblin, takes her by the hand and leads her to the place where the big bamboo pipes (three to six meters long) are hidden.

These musical pipes, by the way, play a most important part in many ceremonies, and their voice is supposed to be that of the goblin himself. Sight of them is forbidden to women, on pain of death.

Before these hidden gods the couple unite. Afterwards the girl is led out of the goblin-hall, where her bridegroom's father awaits her and brings her back to her mother. The *mundū* returns home in a roundabout way, for he is "ashamed" to meet anybody on his way back.

The bridegroom's father goes back to the goblin-hall, and it is now his turn to perform the rôle of goblin, his *mundū* bringing him his son's bride.

After that, the same rite is performed with the other two girls.

The bridegrooms and the other boys, in the meantime, are confined in a house, set apart for this purpose, and watched by their mothers' brothers.

The fathers in their capacity of goblins are allowed to have intercourse with the brides on several subsequent occasions, but only in the goblin-hall.

The bridegroom is not allowed to touch her until she gives birth to a child. This child is called the goblin's child. When the goblin-child is born, the mother says, "Where is thy father? Who had to do with me?" The bridegroom responds, "I am not his father; he is a goblin-child." And she replies, "I did not see that I had intercourse with a goblin."

After the birth of the child, the bridegroom is expected to have finished building a new house, and the bride, the plaiting of the big sleeping bag, used on the banks of the Kerám River, as well as on the Sepík River, as a shelter from mosquitos. Then the couple are finally permitted to begin married life, without any further ceremonies, in the new house. On solemn occasions the goblin-father continues to exercise his "spiritual" function in the goblin-hall. . . .

When the first child, say a boy, comes to the age of puberty, and becomes a *guli*, as a child of about twelve years is called, he goes through initiation ceremonies which are somewhat similar to those of the girls described above.

BOYS' INITIATION

These ceremonies are also connected with the *mundū* institution. Boys of the two sibs are initiated together. First their fathers consult with each other. The grandfathers, who acted reciprocally as goblin-fathers of the firstborn, confer with the brothers of the respective mothers, in order to plan for a hunt of wild pigs in the forest. The two goblin-fathers go in one party, the two mothers' brothers in another. After the hunt, the two parties meet outside the village, and now the respective fathers and uncles of the boys return home together with the pigs. The goblin-father cuts the pig into two halves, giving one side to the adopted father of the goblin-child, and retaining the other for himself. The mothers boil the pork and prepare sago. The next morning the men bring the head of the pig to the goblin-hall, and deposit it before the bamboo pipes. Later on, the two mothers' brothers and the two legal fathers eat the head of the pig. The other women of the village bring baked sago to the goblin-hall, where the men are assembled. After sunset a *mundū*-festival takes place.

At this time the goblin-father ceases to exercise his right as representative of the goblin, ceding his power to his son, a man of the same age as the initiated woman's husband. The goblin-father, however, is formally invited, but he scratches his head and refuses. He might, for example, say, "No, I am too old now; my son had better take over the *mundū*-rights." These rights are, as a matter of fact, usually inherited.

From this time forth the husband's sib-friend, his *mundū*, acts as goblin on festive occasions.

The initiation ceremony coincides in time with the refusal of the goblin-father to continue in his goblin rights towards his sib-friend's daughter-in-law. This indicates that the goblin-father is entering into another age-class, paralleled by the permission of his son to enter into the full privileges of sex life, and by the arrival of his own goblin-child at the age of puberty. The latter stage is used as a means of grading the age-class.

During these ceremonies in the goblin-hall, the boys are brought to another house, and there watched over by their mothers' brothers. When the father returns, he brings a burning brand from the goblin-hall with him, goes to his son and describes a circle of fire around the head of his boy.

The fathers and the mothers' brothers now pick up the boys and carry them on their shoulders to the goblin-hall. Here they wait outside on the veranda until all the men have entered. The men form a line across the hall and begin to dance. The other men blow the pipes from behind the row of dancers. The boys are now brought inside the hall. At this, the pipers break through the line of rhythmically dancing men, and press the pipes upon the navels of the boys.

After further ceremonies, the boys are placed upon a piece of sago bark, and the fathers and mothers' brothers now take the bamboo pipes and blow upon them. Then they hand over the instruments to the boys and show them how to play them. After this, the boys continually practice playing the pipes.

Thereupon the boys are confined in cage-like cells (*momúnevem*), built for that purpose in the goblin-hall. The goblin-hall itself is surrounded during that time with a fence of sago leaves.

A good many other ceremonies are performed during the period the boys are interned, for instance a ceremony connected with the bull-roarer. They also insert in the urinary passage two or three stems of *Coix lacrima*, a barbed grass. These stems they pull out suddenly, so

that the walls of the passage are cut. After three months of confinement
the initiates are "shown" the phenomena of the world that surrounds
them—animals, plants, high water, thunder and lightning—which are
presented as spirits in the shape of wooden idols. They are also introduced to the goblins of this world and the spirits of their ancestors.

Five months later, during new moon, the father and the mother's
brother slaughter domestic pigs, as is usual at the conclusion of ceremonies. The mother now roasts the pork and cooks sago. The other
women of the gens also prepare sago. The men of the related gentes
bring taro, yams, bananas, sugar cane, tobacco, betel nut, and betel
pepper. Then they sing and dance, day and night.

Finally the boys are girded, clothed in a kind of fringed sago-leaf
skirt, belted with hoops of rattan, and adorned with plaited bracelets,
nose sticks, and ear ropes. Their waists are tightly bound with a wide
band of rattan wickerwork, drawn so firmly together that they can
hardly eat. It is the pride of the boys to have a slender waist.

Their father then offers them betel nut and betel pepper, and washes
them in the water left from the filtration of the sago. The mothers'
brothers shave their temples and the back of their heads, leaving a kind
of crest.

The fathers in the meantime have carved small human figures
(*bukámorom*, on the lower Sepík called *kandímboan*) as a gift of
mutual friendship between the intermarrying gentes. With these figures
a particular charm is performed. The father goes with the boy into
the forest to search for a water liana, a particular species containing
water in its stem. This liana is cut and the water allowed to flow over
the figure, betel nut and betel pepper are laid upon it, and it is then
wrapped up in bark. The figure is used as a love charm. If the boy
should go into the bush with this, he would expect to meet a woman.
When the women hear that such a charm has been executed, one of
them, ordinarily the wife of the mother's goblin-initiator, i.e. the wife
of his grandfather's sib friend, complies with the wish expressed in
the charm. This is the boy's initiation into sexual life.

At sunset the fathers and mothers' brothers carry the boys with the
pipes to the banks of the river, where they line up along the shore, the
boys still on their shoulders. The other men stand in a line behind
them, dancing and singing. The goblin-fathers, stationed at the two
ends of the line, hold a rattan rope in their hands, with which they
finally force the boys into the water, so that they may have a bath with
the pipes. Afterwards the boys return to the goblin-hall. Meanwhile the
women are sent to the forest, lest they should get a glimpse of the pipes.

The next morning another bathing ceremony takes place among

the adults of the community. First the men, singing and dancing, form a line along the bank of the river; the women line up behind them. The mothers of the boys who are being initiated make a fire by rubbing a cord of rattan on fire wood. The women begin to dance, the mothers drawing taut a long rope of rattan behind the men, by means of which they finally push them into the water. After this the women throw at the men cocoanuts previously laid ready. The men, in return, shoot back with bow and arrow, each man trying to hit his *mundū's* wife. The men now climb out of the water, and the reverse of the above ceremony takes place, the men pushing the women into the water with the rattan rope. This time the women shoot back from the water with arrows, aiming at their goblins.

While the bathing ceremony is going on, the boys are kept apart and watched over by their mothers' brothers.

On the same evening the festival in the goblin-hall is repeated, but this time is extended to the mothers' brothers and their *mundūs*. The latter also meet in the goblin-hall of the initiated boys.

After this the boys are brought home to their mothers. Here their hands are extended over a fire, and the joints of their fingers cracked over the flame.

These ceremonies conclude the festivities, and the boy is finally allowed to associate with women.

The initiation ceremonies, as we have seen, introduce the marriage rites and are intimately connected with them.

I should like to call attention to the fact that marriage ceremonies are not differentiated from the ceremonies associated with puberty. The maturing of sex is ritually identified with the functioning of sex, and the possibility of the function with its practical employment. This employment however is restricted to a definite group of persons and to certain fixed occasions, in the manner shown above. . . .

THE SYSTEM AT WORK

If we try to sum up the system that results from these various customs, we come to the following conclusions:

Each woman, as time goes on, has regular intercourse with three men: (1) With the sib-friend of her bridegroom's father; (2) with her husband; (3) with her husband's sib-friend. And each man also has legal intercourse with three women: (1) With his wife; (2) with his sib-friend's wife; (3) with the bride of his sib-friend's son. This holds true if we leave out of consideration the old woman who initiates the boy.

There is no doubt that this results in greater probability of conception, and that sterile marriages are prevented in a higher degree. But I doubt whether this eugenic reason had any influence in establishing these customs. However, in case a marriage should prove to be sterile, the man is allowed to take another wife; but then there are no ceremonies.

It must be borne in mind that if a child's extramarital father is its mother's sib-friend, this man is the son of its mother's goblin initiator. Thus the three men of the other sib with whom the woman has to deal, besides her husband, are a father and his son, and eventually this latter person's grandson. A man, however, has to do first with a woman of his grandmother's generation, hereafter with his female sib-friend of his wife's age-class, later with this woman's son's wife. A woman has intercourse with males who are lineal descendants, a man with females who are not direct offsprings in successive generations. A male will have union—besides his initiation—with two persons of his age-class and one of the following one, a female with one of the preceding age-class and two of her own, and eventually with her grandchildren's generation. It will be noticed that intercourse is avoided on the female side with the son's generation and correspondingly on the male side with the mother's age-class.

The offspring of the union with the goblin is called the "goblin's child," *mòro-me-mán*. Although the child remains with the mother, we cannot speak of a female line of descent, for the child is adopted by his mother's husband, who cares for his further education, and practically acts as his foster father. . . .

Whether the husband happens to be the children's father or not, is of no importance in this scheme; he is the foster father of his wife's goblin-child, and of any children his wife might have with his own *mundū*, as well. These children of his wife may, perhaps, originate entirely from fathers of the other sib of the gens. But the man is the head of his wife's family. The family relation and the sexual relation rest each upon a different basis, as has been shown above.

It will be seen that each of the four simultaneously intermarrying couples has a different pair of parents, if the first pair of mates is a pair of goblin-children. This first pair is paralleled by a second corresponding pair of goblin-children in the other sib. Each of the two pairs of goblin-children, as shown above, is "complemented" by another pair of ordinary children. The goblin-child and the corresponding ordinary child have each the same mother, but different fathers. The four pairs of intermarrying mates possess four mothers and eight fathers, each of the eight children belonging to another father.

DEFECTIVE CASES

We shall now turn to consider the cases where, for some reason or other, the system cannot be carried out to its fullest extent.

As we have seen, the marriage of one couple is always balanced by the counter-marriage of another couple of the opposite sib. Thus, it is necessary that each girl should have a brother and each boy a sister.

Nature, however, does not dispose of the distribution of sexes to one couple in such a systematic way. Therefore, the natives attempt to improve upon nature by killing the children of the undesirable sex in the succession of births. Thus, if two boys or two girls are born in succession, the second one is generally killed.

A second wife is taken, if the marriage with the first wife remains without issue, or if later the first wife does not give birth to a further child, if such is wanted to fill up the required even number of children.

Nevertheless, the standard of equal numbers in the distribution of the sexes cannot be maintained, because of possible deaths occurring in infancy or childhood. It may always happen that out of the four couples one person may be wanting. In such case the gaps may be filled by the substitution of cousins for brothers or sisters.

If conditions for a complete *mundū* marriage cannot be fulfilled a simple exchange marriage of two couples of corresponding gentes is arranged. On such an occasion the *mundū* is freely chosen from members of the opposite sib.

Where two sisters are to be exchanged for two sisters of another gens, and the elder sister of one family dies, the older brother of the corresponding family has the right to take the remaining sister, and the younger brother is left without a bride (and *vice versa* if the elder brother should die). In such a case a quarrel between the two brothers is likely to result. Later on, if the elder brother should die, the younger would succeed to the right to his brother's widow. . . .

In case the number of persons needed in the exchange system should prove uneven, the person left from one system is allowed to take a person remaining from another system. Should such an occasion occur, there would be no *mundū*.

THE BUYING OF WOMEN

The man, however, is then supposed to give presents for the woman he takes. If it should happen that a woman is obtained from another tribe, she is paid for with pots, usually ten in number. This case appears

to me to be significant and to hint at the way in which in other parts of
New Guinea the institution of buying the women may have arisen. . . .

SOCIALIZING INFLUENCE OF THE SYSTEM

The exchange system maintains a great socializing influence, for
by its means all members of the tribe are connected with, and dependent
on, each other. This appears in the different ceremonials where persons
are assigned special functions, as well as in the marriage system, which
has spread a network of all kinds of relationships, not only over the gens,
but over the tribe itself.

The working of this system of ties could well be felt when I tried
to recruit a boy from the Bánaro tribe for service with the expedition.
Of the boys who served me as informants, one (Yómba) was a single
man from a gens of the Bánaro tribe, the other (Mánape) from the
Rámunga tribe. It was impossible, however, to get another boy, in spite
of friendly relations, for there was no one to spare, each man having his
special part to play in the social system. . . .

Among the Bánaro the economic unit is the sib. It is the sib that has
definite claims to the sago places, hunting districts and plantation
grounds. These localities are identified by certain names and the
boundaries marked by creeks, swamps, big trees, grass limits, ravines,
bends of the river, etc. The owners as well as the other members of
the tribe know these localities and are aware of the traditional rights
to them.

The ties of kinship are associated with the common holding of the
land. The *connubium* tends to preserve the claims on a certain territory
within a restricted number of people. In consequence of the marriage
prescriptions the origin of the persons entitled to exploit the land is
limited, so that the offspring derives its rights through kinship to members of the community. Individuals have no claim of ownership or
rights of disposal over the ground. Therefore we cannot speak of a
transmission by inheritance, as the sib is not like a person, capable of
death. The right of a person depends on his situation in the social
complex. Hence the importance of stating the relationship.

Even the earnings of a boy recruited for service with the white
man fall to his sib as a requital for the absence of his working power
claimed by his sib. Whatever he brings home is distributed among his
kinsfolk.

Individual property is confined to the products of the labor of the
individual. The tree, for instance, that a man plants, or the fish that a
man catches, or the weir that a man weaves, or the stone ax he puts

together, belong to him as the fruit of his labor. This individual property is of a very temporary character, for the crops of the plantation are consumed when they are ripe, and the few tools are used up after a relatively short time. If a man should die, they are burned and buried with him, for they are considered as a sort of personal appurtenance. . . .

GERONTOCRACY AND MAGIC

The essential features of the system we have to deal with here, are as follows:

1. The exchange of women between two groups, based on the psychological principle of requital, a principle that regulates the social relations of a community among such of its members as are equal in age or sex. It may also be applied to the making of peace with formerly hostile communities, or the socialization of foreign groups.

2. This special kind of system has been brought about by the political form of the gerontocracy. The old men are the determining factor for external relations (war and peace) and internal life (e.g. the repartition of land for plantation purposes, hunting-grounds, etc.). They derive their power from the real or asserted knowledge they possess.

Ceremonies, especially such as are in connection with the materialization of the goblins, are kept secret. The arranging of the dances, the making and ornamenting of the masks, and, above all, the whirring of the bullroarer and the fluting of the bamboo pipes, are hidden from the people. In these are contained the charms for securing the help of the superhuman powers, on which success in life depends. Only with the lapse of time are the male members of the community successively initiated into the magico-religious ceremonies.

These secret ceremonies contain the sum total of the people's knowledge, representing a kind of primitive science adapted to the supposed pleasing of the goblin. Disease and suffering, defeat in the fight, are considered as consequences of the willful malice of the capricious goblins, and must therefore be prevented or remedied in connection with the supposed cause.

This knowledge, by the way, is often of what we should term a magical kind. We, from our point of view, discriminate between magical and, say, therapeutic means. To them, in general, medical science and magic are one and the same thing. It is we, who, according to the level of our experience, make a distinction between the two which is not felt by the native.

Difference in point of view ought also to be taken into account in a consideration of the exchange system, which must in no way be regarded as debauchery, but as the outcome of a moral and religious creed for the regulation of the most important problems of social and individual life.

The gerontocracy exercises its influence by theocratic means. But its power must not be overrated. The sway of the old men is not absolute. They exercise their power, not by command, but by advice. The boy or young man may or may not obey. The outcome of each particular case is the resultant of two forces: the authority of the particular old man concerned, and the relative courage of the younger man. But practically, the community is dominated by the influence of a few old men, to whose decisions the people consent.

This, in brief, is their political system: The old men give their tutorage in magic, etc., to the people, demanding a certain amount of deference and allegiance from them in return. On this basis are built up nearly all primitive political systems in the South Seas.

29. SOCIAL ORGANIZATION OF THE NAMA HOTTENTOT [5]

BY A. WINIFRED HOERNLÉ

THE people with whom this paper deals live in the territory known today as the Protectorate of Southwest Africa. They form one branch of the people known generally as the Hottentots, but from the very earliest days of the Dutch settlement at the Cape this branch of the Hottentot peoples has been called the Namaqua, and Nama is the name by which they call themselves today. The meaning of the word is unknown, but it is, according to tradition, the name of a remote ancestor of all the tribes calling themselves by the name. The old form, Namaqua, is probably derived from the dual form, Namakha, Namab being the masculine singular, Namas the feminine singular, and Naman the common plural. . . .

The indigenous people were in historical times divided into seven main groups, with one or two subsidiary ones which are known to have been late offshoots from these main groups. According to the

[5] In *American Anthropologist*, New Series, Volume 27, pages 1-24, 1925: "The Social Organization of the Nama Hottentots of Southwest Africa." The small numbers [1], [2], [3], [4], represent "click" sounds and replace respectively a single bar, double bar, double-crossed bar, and exclamation, in the original—as in the case of Selection 21.

traditions of these people they are all descendants of one line of ancestors. . . .

All these groups which I have enumerated I propose to speak of as "tribes," for, in spite of their claim to a common ancestry, these groups have been for a long time independent of one another. Each group has its acknowledged chief and its acknowledged fountains, though before the coming of the white man and of the Orlams the boundaries between the different groups were not marked in any clear manner. In an old document, translated in the Rhenish Missionary Record for 1854, the chief of the Rooi Natie complains that the Berseba Hottentots have taken possession of one of his fountains. He gives them permission to stay, but states specifically that this does not mean that he gives over the fountain to them; "the water is my water," he says again and again. We shall also see a little later that the different water holes, or fountains, in the country were always thought of as belonging to certain specific groups. This did not mean that other people could not use this water, but that one group had a prior claim to it established by habit, and had the right to expect that any other group intending to camp there for long would ask permission to do so. . . .

At the present day some of these tribes are extinct; that is to say, the tribal unity is totally destroyed, though one may still come across individuals claiming to belong to one or other of these tribes. But even where there is still a small remnant of people holding together under the leadership of a man whom they regard as a headman, or chief, the whole culture and power of the Nama is hopelessly destroyed. The history of all these tribes for the last 150 years has been one of incessant strife, first among themselves, owing to the dislocation caused by the incoming of the tribes from the south; next with the Hereros, a Bantu tribe advancing on them from the north; and last with the Germans who finally broke down the tribal cohesion completely, except in the case of the Berseba Hottentots, who remained loyal to their contract with the Germans and never fought against them. . . .

The social organization which I am about to describe, therefore, relates almost entirely to the past. The details of it have been gathered with great difficulty from the old headmen of the tribes, and much of it is little known to most of the younger generation.

If we study what I have called a tribe more closely, we shall find that in all cases it is composed of a number of patrilineal sibs, that is, of groups of people claiming to be related in the male line; and that one of these sibs claims seniority. The chieftainship is hereditary in this senior sib and is inherited in the male line. In some cases I have been given traditions of the formation of the tribe, the various sibs claiming relationship with one another in the far distant past, but in no case has it been possible to trace this relationship genealogically. Each sib names itself eponymously from its first known ancestor, or from the ancestor under whom it first claimed independence. The Nama themselves recognize these divisions into tribes and sibs, the tribe being called ⁴haus, and the sibs ⁴hau ⁴nati, that is, things within the tribe. . . .

When the tribe was first formed, the chieftainship was in the ¹Gari Gein sib, as one would expect, but nowadays the chieftainship has passed to the second branch, the ¹Gari ⁴Nagaman. According to the headmen of the tribe, who corroborate what the present chief, David Swartbooi, told me, the chieftainship passed from the one sib to the other when the elder branch became almost extinct. There are today only two or three people represented in this sib. . . .

There is no name for the families which together go to form a sib. They are also called ⁴hau ⁴nati. These families today have Dutch, or at any rate European, surnames, and though they claim to be blood kinsmen and in former days would not have intermarried, it is not now possible to trace any genealogical connection between these families. All the members of the chief's sib call themselves Swartboois, a name which seems to have been applied in the first instance to William Swartbooi whose Nama name, ⁴Huisib, however, means the root of a special kind of acacia. . . .

The analysis of the sib structure of this tribe shows, I think, the whole mechanism by which sibs and tribes are formed among the Nama. A large and flourishing family will very often have its own favorite pasturing grounds and be so large as to exclude members of other families or sibs. In course of time they become sufficient unto themselves, and the headman begins to play the part of chief. They arrange their migrations to suit themselves independently of the other members of the tribe, and in course of time are acknowledged to be independent. Then, as the families increase, descendants of the different brothers group themselves together more closely and form sibs and subsibs. In this way a new tribe develops from a sib, or a part of a sib, of the parent tribe. . . .

The families claiming to belong to a sib still tend to live together, though the old original camping order has long been given up. Information from many sources, however, enables one to reconstruct the old encampment, and this reconstruction agrees with information given to us by the early travelers among the Hottentots.

In the old days a Nama encampment was in the form of a great circle. The whole was enclosed with a great fence of thorn in which there were two gateways, one to the north, the other to the south.

Within this fence, round the circumference, were the huts of the ⁴haus, or tribe. There might on certain occasions be a whole tribe encamped in such a manner, and, in any case, there were usually some representatives of each of the sibs at the chief's headquarters, though there might be other encampments in other parts of the tribal territory. In the great open space in the center the cattle were herded at night. Special kraals were made for the calves and the lambs, but neither now nor in the past did the Hottentots make kraals for the cattle or the sheep. These animals just lie in front of the owner's hut for the night.

The following is the order in which the sibs of the Swartboois camped. In the western portion of the circle stood the huts of the chief's sib, facing east. On his left, as one faces east, came in order the ⁴Oa Gaon, the ²Naigaman, the ⁴Gurusin, the ¹Gari Karin, the ⁴Neise ein. On his right in order came the Goamun, the ²Khau Tanasen, the ¹Gari Gein, and the ⁴Ga ei Tanasen, meeting the ⁴Neise ein in the east of the circle. The Topnaars encamped in the order ²Hornibin Gein, ²Hornibin ¹Goan, ⁴Noraban, ¹Ubuxan, ¹Heibin, starting from the ²Hornibin Gein in the west and continuing round the circle to the left.

Through the whole course of Nama history the sib was the strongest social unit the Nama ever attained. Time and time again a strong sib would go off on its own, asserting its independence of the others, and sib loyalty was always stronger than tribal loyalty. It is no wonder, then, that the chief among the Hottentots was little more than *primus inter pares*. He was acknowledged to be the head of the senior sib and, if a person of fine character, was accorded a great deal of respect, but the heads of the other sibs acted as his council and he could not do much without their coöperation. The whole conduct of affairs, then, in a Nama tribe was, and is, the concern of the older men of the tribe.

The sib loyalty was very strong. Members of a sib all considered themselves to be blood relatives, and marriage in the sib was strictly forbidden. . . .

Membership of a sib guaranteed to a person a very strong measure of protection, for he could always count on the support of his fellow sib members. We know from accounts left to us by travelers among the Nama in the early part of last century that at that time the vendetta was still in full force among them; that is, the chief was unable in the interests of the whole people to prevent two sibs from carrying out revenge one on the other, or to force them to accept compensation. . . .

Though the old camping order of the sibs has long been given up, the order of camping of the families within the sib is still maintained in many instances, and could be studied among the Swartboois even in 1923. It has already been stated that among all the Hottentots all the sons of one woman are called by her big name, her gei khoi ¹ons, while all the daughters are similarly called after the gei khoi ¹ons of the father. In a settlement, therefore, we should expect to find the huts of a number of men called by the same name. This is exactly what we do find, and they are ranged in order of seniority, the eldest brother furthest to the right, the youngest furthest to the left, as we stand, facing outwards, at the doorway of any hut.

In the past the Hottentots were polygynists, but never to the same extent as the Bantu tribes around them. Nowadays they are ostensibly monogamists, but the standard of morals is extremely low among them. Each family has its own mat hut where the children remain until they marry. I have found a number of young girls sharing a hut together, and it may happen that a number of boys also share a hut, but this is not the general rule among the Nama. It is much more usual for the family to remain together until a new household is formed after marriage. Near each of the brothers in a family would be grouped his immediate dependents; his married sons on his right, the eldest furthest to the right, the youngest nearest to his father's hut, while on the left would be any married daughter who had not yet removed to her husband's people and any widowed sister who had come home to live with him. Other dependents of various kinds would also be camped to the left of a man's hut. Chief among these would be the ⁴gan, or servants, hardly to be called slaves, who were generally of the Berg Damara race, a people of negro affiliations which has long been in subjection to the Hottentots. Many Berg Damara even now are attached to Hottentot families as dependents. These people are free to marry as they will, and are never bought or sold, but they generally remain attached to the same family for long periods. Family servants is perhaps the best name for them. Many of those whose history I have studied were taken, or picked up, as small children by the Hottentots after one of the numerous wars when families were scattered and the children were left helpless in the veld, and they were then brought up in the family, acting as herdboys and in general counting themselves as members of the family. Intermixture of this black race with the Nama is now taking place, but there is little trace of its having been frequent in the past.

It remains now to describe the conduct of the people towards one another in the society, and this depends to a very large extent upon the kinship system, though relative age is also an important factor.

The kinship system of the Hottentots is a classificatory one with many similarities to the kinship systems found among the Bantu. The relative ages of the person speaking and of the person spoken of are very carefully recognized in these kinship terms. There is a special term for the mother's brother who stands in a very close relation to his sisters' children, and there are special terms for cross cousins, corresponding to the special relation in which these people stand to one another. . . .

Practically all the old regulations with regard to marriage have broken down among the Hottentots. Marriage with any first cousin is now permitted, though on the other hand the older people are resisting the marriages of first cousins at all, whether direct or cross cousins. There is a difference here from tribe to tribe, some of them being more influenced by European contacts than others but the tendency in all is the same. All my older informants are agreed that the marriage of direct cousins was out of the question in the old days. With regard to the cross cousins there is some difference between the tribes. In some of them, . . . marriage with the mother's brother's daughter is said to have been far more usual than marriage with the father's sister's daughter. The terminology for these relatives seems, however, to show that in the past marriage with both the mother's brother's daughter and the father's sister's daughter was allowed, and the behavior towards these relatives confirms this. In addition, I have illustrations of both kinds of cross cousin marriage in genealogies.

The duties and privileges of relatives. The chief consideration in the behavior of Nama to one another is the relative ages of the people concerned. Respect for age is inculcated in every possible way, and the whole social organization of the people is an illustration of the fact. In the family deference and respect must always be paid to elders. Thus, of a number of brothers the eldest always has the honored place and the first voice in any debate. Family feeling is strong, however, and brothers generally hold together. The behavior proper to brothers is due to all those people called by the name "brother," and little difference is made by the fact that they are often sons of fathers who are brothers and not sons of one man. Similarly, all women who are called "sisters" must be treated as sisters, and it would have been in the old days a most heinous offense for a man to have married such a woman. . . . In the old days the behavior of a brother and a sister was very strictly regulated. As tiny children they ran about together, but once they were grown up, they had to avoid one another completely. A brother was not allowed to speak to a sister directly, he must never be alone with her in the hut, he must never speak of her except in the most respectful terms. A sister was a *tàras*, that is, a person to be respected, not to be spoken to or of lightly. In the old days an oath by a sister was one of the greatest oaths a man could take, and a

sister could generally be relied on to stop any fight in which her
brother was taking part. The brother is said to be shy (*sou*) in the
presence of his sister, and the same is true of all the men a woman
would call brother. Should one of these men use bad language in her
presence a woman could demand a sheep from him with which to
purify herself of the pollution. It is a gei ⁴Keis, a great offense. Even
at the present day a man will not sleep in his sister's hut when he
visits her as a married woman. The eldest sister of a man is his gei
tàras, his great respected one.

Quite different is the behavior of a man to those of his own generation whom he calls ²Núrin. These women are his companions, his
playmates. All is possible with them, free speech and horse play. Even
sexual intercourse would not have been considered wrong. It was frequently one of these women that a man married in the old days.

The relation of a woman to her brother's children was one of great
restraint. Just as the father himself had to behave with much circumspection towards this woman, so his children had to treat her with the
greatest deference and respect.

The relation of a man to his sister's children was one of the
greatest indulgence and good will. A boy could do almost anything at
his maternal uncle's ⁴hèis, or home, without being blamed for it. He
could take, without asking, any of the specially fine animals among his
uncle's herds, and the uncle had no redress but to take misformed ugly
animals from his nephew's herds. This exchange was called ²núri
²as, and it is still practiced by the Nama today.

The only other relationship calling for special notice is that of a man
to his relatives by marriage. To his wife's sisters, a man behaved much
as he would to his wife, and even at the present day intercourse with
them is common, if they are unmarried or widowed. Such relations
are the cause of much trouble. A woman considered her husband's
younger brothers as her husbands, and used in the old days to be inherited by one of them. In the early missionary records there are
numerous instances of a younger brother taking over his elder brother's
widow. This practice is, of course, strongly condemned by the missionaries who report these things, and it is interesting to note that the
women seem to have taken advantage of the objection on the part of
the missionaries to avoid this relationship in some instances.

His wife's mother had always to be treated with the greatest deference
by a husband. They were said to be "shy" of one another, and the man
might never look at her when speaking to her. There used in the past
to be a special form of address between all relatives-in-law, the formal

"You" being applied both to the mother-in-law, to the brothers of a man's wife, and to her father, but it is not so used nowadays.

In addition to the strict prohibition against marriage in the sib, a man was not allowed to marry a woman of the same great name as himself, even though she might come from a tribe different from his own. Such a woman would be regarded either as a mother if much older, or as a daughter if younger than the man. Nowadays, this prohibition, too, has ceased to be observed. I have instances in the genealogies, though not many, of such marriages having taken place.

It will be seen from the account given of the kinship system and the "behavior patterns" accompanying kinship terms that the type of behavior which is expected of a person by another is directly indicated by the kinship term in use between them, so that a knowledge of these relationships is essential for an understanding of the whole moral regulation of the lives of the people.

There is just one other subject on which a few remarks may be appropriate. The relation of the tribes towards one another has been throughout the history of the Hottentots most capricious. On the one hand, one finds a great deal of intermarriage taking place between those tribes which happen to be near one another, and a great deal of visiting between the members of families so connected is always going on. Yet, on the other hand, there has never been sufficient feeling of solidarity between the tribes, for the Nama, or for the Hottentots in general, to organize themselves against a common enemy even when the danger was exceedingly great. Always one tribe has been played off against the others by all other peoples with whom they have come in conflict. There are many instances in their history in which two tribes have made an agreement with one another for some common object, but such agreements have always come to naught. There is even an interesting document, signed by most of the Nama and Orlam chiefs, agreeing to sink all differences and to unite against the common enemy, the Herero, but the agreement was never actually put into practice. So the Nama, and the Hottentots in general, are coming to be a people whose history lies all in the past, whose tribal organization is totally disrupted, and whose distinctive culture is becoming a thing unknown even to themselves, because of their failure to hold together, and to face the incoming cultures with a strong feeling of group solidarity.

30. MARRIAGE AND SOCIETY AMONG THE CROW INDIANS [6]

BY ROBERT H. LOWIE

MARRIAGE

A MAN had a preëmptive right to the younger sisters of a woman he had bought in marriage. Some men married a brother's widow; this was called "keeping a brother's wife."

As explained in my previous paper, there was abundant opportunity for philandering on such occasions as berry-picking and it happened that young people would form a permanent attachment on such occasions without further ceremony. This type of union was called "taking each other." Sometimes a young man used a go-between to make an offer to a young woman, and this was designated as "talking towards a woman."

The most honorable form of marriage was buying a wife, "paying for her." That is, a man would give horses to her male relatives and meat to her mother. It was usually a young, good-looking and virtuous woman who was purchased but it did not matter whether she had been previously married. "Men," said Gray-bull, "would buy a woman who was not crazy. The Lumpwoods never came to the door of my tipi to take away my last wife. That is the sort of wife we paid for." This is an allusion to the custom by which a member of the Lumpwood or rival Fox organization might carry off the wife of a member of the other society provided he had ever been on terms of intimacy with her.

Women stolen in this fashion were not usually kept for any length of time. Shell-necklace abducted three women in this manner but did not live with any of them longer than twenty days. He let them stay in a lodge other than his real wife's. There were some men who would keep these stolen women but the majority sent them away with such words as, "I have done marrying you, go away!" After this any man might marry her without being disgraced, except the husband from whose lodge she had been stolen.

When a woman abandoned a man she disliked, this was called "disliking a man." Shell-necklace said, contrary to Gray-bull's earlier statement, that in such a case the husband recovered the property he

[6] From pages 74-82 of Robert H. Lowie, "Notes on the Social Organization and Customs of the Mandan, Hidatsa, and Crow Indians," *Anthropological Papers of the American Museum of Natural History*, Volume 21, Part 1, New York, 1917.

had paid for her. A woman's relatives sometimes tried to dissuade her from running away from her husband.

The attitude of divorced spouses towards each other in later life naturally differed with different individuals. One interpreter told me that his father and mother hated each other and never had any social intercourse. Correspondingly, Young-crane informed me that she at first refused to be adopted into the Tobacco society by her former husband, Hunts-the-enemy, but was finally persuaded by her then husband, Crazy-dog. On the other hand, there are cases of divorced mates who converse on amicable terms.

Some concrete data as to married life are of considerable interest.

Young-crane married . . . a chief. . . . He had already married her elder sister and at the time of his death had two other wives,—one of them a relative. . . . The three related women inhabited the same lodge, while the fourth wife lived in a separate tipi; but sometimes all the wives of a man, even if unrelated, lived together. This first husband had been married to a wife whom he divorced and by whom he had four children. When he took to wife Young-crane, he gave her elder brother two horses and other presents. She had no children by him, but her eldest sister had three, of whom Packs-hat is the oldest. He has always called Young-crane "mother"; when she later married Hunts-the-enemy, Packs-hat called him "father," as he also did his own mother's second husband; he continued to address Hunts-the-enemy in this way even after Young-crane's divorce from him, and later when she married Crazy-head called him "father" also. Young-crane's first husband was killed and after a while she had Hunts-the-enemy for a lover and accordingly married him without purchase. However, he also took to wife a relative of Young-crane's whom she designated as her grandchild and who called her husband "father." This angered her. All the people thought Hunts-the-enemy had done something wrong in marrying a girl who called him "father" and said he was crazy. Accordingly, Young-crane separated from him. Later Crazy-head wished to marry her, and since he was a chief her brothers advised her to take him, and so she did without being purchased.

When Gray-bull was about twenty-two, he married for the first time. He had been out on a war party and when he came back he found a young woman who had come to his home, so he married her. She had a son by him, but the boy died. After about four years of marriage, she discovered that her husband had been out berry-picking with another young woman, so she got angry and told him to marry her rival. Accordingly, Gray-bull threw all her belongings out of the tent, and she left him. Then Gray-bull went to where his sweetheart was and married her without purchase. She was stolen by the Lumpwoods and Gray-bull never went near her for a year, and even then he did not seek her but she came to him. However, he did not keep her permanently. It was only for his last wife that property was paid. She was a virtuous woman, the widow of a brother of Gray-bull's, who had been killed. When Gray-bull's mother urged him to marry this woman, he at first declined, but at last consented. Then another brother of his took a horse and some property to the widow's mother, the horse being for the widow's father and the other gifts for her brothers. Some time after this one of the woman's brothers bade him stay in his lodge. Then one of her brothers came, stood outside the tipi, and called Gray-bull. Then he went with them and two of his own brothers to the woman's lodge. She was seated on a fine bed and had a backrest there. Gray-bull's brothers went to the rear and sat down, and all of them received food. When they had eaten, the brothers went home and Gray-bull remained and lay with his wife. He felt bashful because she had not been his mistress before.

POSITION OF WOMEN

The fact that the women certainly perform all the menial household duties and are ordered about by their husbands in regard to bringing water and the like is likely to convey the idea that the position of women was a very inferior one in Crow society. Random references to women in myth and song, and indeed the deliberate bravado with which the ideal Crow man might discard his wife at a dance or allow her to be abducted by a rival organization, tend to confirm this impression.

Nevertheless, as in the case of sexual morality, superficial appearances are in a measure deceptive as to the real native point of view. In the first place, it is worth noting that a woman exercises definite property rights. In buying specimens I noticed repeatedly that husbands did not attempt to influence, let alone force, wives in regard to the sale of their belongings. It is further noteworthy that while women were naturally barred from the distinctively military men's clubs they play an important part in the sacred Tobacco society. Women secured visions, though less frequently than men; and some of them were medical practitioners and exercised supernatural powers. As the Crow had a very definite conception of ideal manhood, so they have a clear notion of what a woman should be,—virtuous, skilled in feminine accomplishments, physically attractive. This complex is summed up in the expression "She is a good woman," which perhaps corresponds to our "perfect lady" with the addition of good looks. A woman of this type was certainly well thought of and might exert considerable influence on her husband.

It is further clear that the bold face put on when a woman was abducted often merely served as a mask for profound grief. Indeed the stoical decorum so emphatically demanded by tribal etiquette indicates how difficult an achievement this triumphing over one's emotions was considered. When Gray-bull lost his wife in the spring contest of the Foxes and Lumpwoods he bravely bade her go with his rival, but interrupting his narrative at this point he said to me, "If you have ever been married, you know how this felt."

Whether what has been called "romantic love" is less common among the Indians than in our own everyday life, it would be difficult to say. An educated interpreter ridiculed the notion of a man's committing suicide because of unrequited affection, but Werthers are not so common among us as he seems to have inferred from a reading of novels. At all events, Crow literature also comprises narratives of a hero undergoing dangers and achieving arduous tasks "all for the love of a lady," while one story recounts how a young woman braved all the perils and privations of a long overland journey through hostile territory in order to reach her disabled sweetheart.

SEXUAL MORALITY

In his discussion of the social life of the Yukaghir, Mr. Jochelson emphasizes the difference between theory and practice as regards the sexual relations of this people. Exactly the same point may be made with regard to the Crow. In practice there is a great looseness of manners, though the established rules of propriety are strictly observed.[7] War and love are described as the old Crow men's principal occupations, and the mythology, the reminiscences of informants, and ancient songs are all surcharged with evidence of the tendency to apparently unlimited philandering. To a superficial observer it would appear as though this masculine license were even today extended to the female sex. Young women of notorious immorality are not only not regarded as outcasts but in some instances are even taken to wife by young men who to all appearances might have made better matches. Their outward treatment, whether they are married or not, seems to differ not one whit from that accorded to other women.

Nevertheless, as already explained, the Crow have very definite ideals of feminine purity. A man certainly prides himself on being married to a woman of irreproachable chastity, and a wife of this type

[7] Thus, my interpreter twitted me with the fact that while whites censured the Indian's immorality a brother would not hesitate to speak freely with his sister, which no decent Crow would do.

enjoys a very different reputation and social status from that of a "crazy" one, as unchaste women are usually described. On public occasions precedence was yielded to the virtuous women. When Young-jack-rabbit had distinguished himself in battle, his grandmother, who "had never done anything wrong," led him about camp and sang his praises. During the Sun dance the highly honorary office of tree-notcher was bestowed on a woman who had been taken to wife in the most honorable way, i.e. one who had not run away with her lover but had been decently married by purchase, and who had been uniformly faithful to her husband. Chastity was likewise a prerequisite for another office in the same ceremony.

There can be no doubt that even theoretically there was a double standard of morality. No one thought any the worse of a man of prominence for having indulged in numerous love affairs: these were rather regarded as his rightful share of the good things of life. When a young man had assumed the especially dangerous office of a Crazy Dog, an old man would lead him through camp, announcing that since he was going to die the girls of the tribe who wanted to become his sweet-hearts must hasten to make overtures to him. One of my youngest interpreters, who had recently been married, would speak quite freely of the possibility of amours with other women, but he became grave in considering the case of his wife being disloyal. "Do you know what I should do?" he asked me; "I should never look at her or have anything more to do with her."

That, however, a certain preferential respect was accorded to a man of virtue is shown by another Sun dance usage. An expedition for the purpose of bringing white clay was always led by a man who had never taken liberties with any women but his own wife, even in the case of licensed privileges.

ETIQUETTE

When a visitor comes to a tipi, the host may say *kahé* by way of greeting, and this interjection is also used in addressing supernatural beings in prayer. If the inmates of the lodge happen to be outside they may say to the guest, *birē'ri'*, "Enter." He is made to sit in the rear of the lodge, the place of honor. If a woman is visited by her husband's wife or an adopted child, she bids them sit in the rear; other female visitors sit anywhere.

A man does not enter a lodge if his sister or brother-in-law or any of the wife's relatives comprised under the term *usu'a* is there alone. If he finds any woman alone in a lodge, he is not likely to enter unless she is a sister-in-law; and correspondingly a woman does not enter a lodge where she sees a man by himself unless he be a lover or a relative other than a brother.

If a visitor comes with his wife, they take seats opposite to the host and his wife, but if that side is occupied they go to the rear. When they have no visitors, a couple usually occupies the place where the blankets are spread for sleeping, generally on the sides. . . .

No matter at what time of day a visitor arrives, food of some sort is at once offered to him or her. In the old days this consisted mainly of pounded meat or something of the sort. It was not obligatory to eat up everything; sometimes a visitor would take home what was left. This was considered perfectly proper: "It did not matter." Sometimes a guest would ask for a container in which to take the food home. The hosts do not have to eat at the same time with their visitors. In the old days the people ate when they were hungry.

I have myself had occasion to observe again and again that guests do not usually eat in the immediate company of their hosts even if all partook of food at the same time. The usual arrangement is for each family to eat by themselves. Sometimes my interpreter and I ate separately from the other people; and almost always every man formed a distinct group with his wife and children, so that on some occasions there were as many as four groups. Once Bright-wing was seen to join Magpie and his wife, which Gray-bull explained by saying the former was Magpie's brother.

When people meet outdoors, they do not use any expression corresponding to our passing the time of day but will probably ask, "Where do you come from?" or "What are you doing?" On my return to the Crow Reservation one summer, an Indian greeted me with the remark: "I am glad to see you" (literally, I see you, I am better). On a similar occasion a Crow said, "This dear man has come, it seems."

Crow men do not kiss their wives or sweethearts publicly; only young children are kissed in the presence of other people. However, I have seen a newly married young man caressing his wife though without kissing her.

In referring to a deceased person, particularly if related to one present, it is customary to use a euphemism, saying not "He is dead," but "He is not here." Thus, my interpreter designated Gray-bull's dead wife in speaking to her husband.

A man often refers deprecatingly to his own achievements, but this is mock-modesty and he knows perfectly well that his audience is perfectly aware of the facts. Once Gray-bull, in spite of his excellent war record, adopted this tone, saying, "I have never done anything in war." Young-crane, his son's mother-in-law, fearing that I might misunderstand, at once explained that Gray-bull was a very brave man indeed.

31. MIWOK MOIETIES [8]

BY EDWARD WINSLOW GIFFORD

INTRODUCTION

THE Miwok Indians of the Sierra Nevada of California are divided by anthropologists into three dialectic groups, termed Northern or Amador, Central or Tuolumne, and Southern or Mariposa. These three groups occupy the western slope of the mountains from El Dorado County in the north to Madera County in the south. Their social organization takes the form of totemic exogamic moieties with paternal descent. . . .

MOIETIES

As already related, the Central Sierra Miwok are divided into exogamic moieties with paternal descent, usually spoken of as *kikua* (water side) and *tunuka* (land, or dry, side). Frequently the former are referred to as "bull-frog people" (*lotasuna*) and the latter as "bluejay people" (*kosituna*). The presence of two exogamic divisions with animal nicknames has at least a superficial analogy to a case mentioned by Dr. W. H. R. Rivers as occurring on the island of Raga or Pentecost in the northern New Hebrides.

With the Miwok the moiety has no subdivisions. At first glance the fact that 16 per cent. of the Central Sierra Miwok are named after bears, and the remainder after numerous other animate and inanimate objects and phenomena, would seem to suggest a phratral system, with numerous totemic gentes, gone into decay. The Indians, nevertheless, positively deny the existence of smaller divisions. They in no way regard the people with bear names, for example, as forming a special group. Nothing in the information obtained points to a phratral system ever having been in operation. . . .

EXOGAMY

The exogamic rules of the moieties were not rigidly adhered to even before the coming of the whites. Out of a series of 413 individuals, whose names were obtained, 184, or 45 per cent., belonged to the water moiety, and 229, or 55 per cent., to the land moiety. The greater number of these 413 individuals were either of the generation of the

[8] From monograph of the same name in *University of California Publications in American Archæology and Ethnology,* Volume 12, pages 139-194, 1916.

oldest Indians of today or of the preceding generation. Had the exogamic rules been strictly enforced it would have meant that ten people out of every hundred went unmarried or else married late in life. The natural result of this preponderance of one moiety over the other would be the breaking down of strict exogamy in actual practice, especially in a case like the present, where the system lacks the rigidity of the Australian marriage-class system. Informants stated that strenuous efforts were never made to prevent improper marriages. The relatives merely objected and pointed out the impropriety of such marriages. Under the heading "Marriages" are listed the recorded Miwok marriages, of which actually 25 per cent. are improper.

The figures in the last paragraph show the division into moieties of the Central Sierra Miwok as a whole, at least so far as the data go. A list of the inhabitants of only one village was obtained. This village was located on Big Creek near Groveland. The total number of individuals listed is one hundred and two and includes people of all generations within the knowledge of the informant. Out of this total, 56 per cent. belonged to the water moiety and 44 per cent. to the land moiety. This is the reverse of the situation among the Central Sierra Miwok exclusive of the Big Creek people. A table will perhaps make the situation clearer.

	Percentage of water moiety	Percentage of land moiety
Central Sierra Miwok in general	45	55
Village at Big Creek	56	44
Central Sierra Miwok, except Big Creek people	41	59

Unfortunately no other village censuses have been taken, so that in comparing the Big Creek people with the remainder of the Central Sierra Miwok we are comparing with a very miscellaneous and scattered lot of individuals. Roughly stated, however, they may be said to be mainly Jamestown and Knights Ferry people. At Big Creek twelve people out of a hundred were ineligible for monogamic marriage within the village, if strict exogamy were enforced. In the region outside of Big Creek, however, eighteen people out of a hundred were ineligible.

TOTEMISM

That totemic symptoms of one sort or another are present in the Miwok organization cannot be denied; yet, on the other hand, it must be acknowledged that the classing of the Miwok with totemic peoples is based on a rather weak foundation. The claims for such classification rest on three well established facts.

First, all nature is divided between land and water, in a more or less arbitrary manner, to be sure, as shown by the classing of such animals as the coyote, deer, and quail on the "water" side.

Second, the exogamic moieties are identified respectively with land and water.

Third, an intimate connection exists between the land and water divisions of nature and the land and water moieties. This connection is through personal names, which usually have an implied reference to animate or inanimate natural objects or phenomena, although not infrequently to manufactured objects instead. The objects or phenomena referred to in personal names belong, as a rule, either to the water or to the land side of nature. The names are applied according as the individual is of the water or of the land moiety. Hence, it may be said that each moiety is connected through the personal names of its members with a more or less definite group of objects and phenomena.

The ensuing very incomplete lists, the contents of which were spontaneous on the part of informants, give some idea of the dual classification of nature. The reason for placing on the "water" side certain creatures which are actually land animals is hard to understand. An informant explained two of the cases to me as follows: The quail is placed on the water side because a turtle once turned into a quail; while the coyote is placed on the water side because Coyote won a bet with the creator and the latter had to go to the sky and take a land-side name, while Coyote remained on earth and took a water-side name.

On the water side are coyote, deer, antelope, beaver, otter, quail, dove, kingbird, bluebird, turkey, vulture, killdeer, jacksnipe, goose, crane, kingfisher, swan, land salamander, water snake, eel, whitefish, minnow, katydid, butterfly, clouds, and rainy weather.

On the land side are tree squirrel, dog, mountain lion, wildcat, raccoon, jay, hawk, condor, raven, California woodpecker, flicker, salmon-berry, "Indian potato," sky, and clear weather. . . .

The Central Sierra Miwok as a whole do not believe that they are descended from animals. They do believe, however, that they succeeded the animals on earth, which is the belief common to the typical central Californian stocks. This belief, that before the coming of the Indians animals possessed the world, is very different from the idea of descent from the totem.

Informants stated that in former days it was customary for people to "show respect" to the bear, the eagle, and the falcon after any of these had been killed. This was done by laying the body of the slain creature on a blanket and having a little feast in honor of it when it was brought to the hunter's home. So far as I could ascertain, this was not a ceremony connected with moieties or with totemism. It was no different in import from the offerings made by the Miwok when a condor was killed or when the young of a certain hawk were taken from the nest. This type of ceremony was common to a large part of California. The purpose was to appease the animal or its spirit. The ceremony was based on the belief that the animals possessed dangerous supernatural power. Obviously the three cases in question are no different in motive from the above, or from the practices of other stocks, of which a notable example is the Maidu treatment of bears.

The supernatural powers obtained by shamans from animals were not received, except by coincidence, from the animal after which the shaman was named. A man of the water moiety might become a bear shaman just as readily as a man of the land moiety, even though bears and bear names are associated only with the latter moiety. Apparently a man's moiety and his personal name had no influence on his acquisition of supernatural power. The animal he was named after did not become his familiar or guardian spirit, except, as I have said, by coincidence.

CEREMONIES

The participation of the moieties as such in games and ceremonies was unimportant. Out of forty-four known ceremonies, the moieties took part as such in only four—the funeral, the mourning ceremony, the girl's puberty ceremony, and a dance known as the ahana. At least at Big Creek the moieties had reciprocal funerary functions, it being the duty of one moiety to care for the dead of the other. In the washing of the people which terminated the mourning ceremony washers of the water moiety tended one basket and washed people of the land moiety, while washers of the land moiety tended another basket and washed people of the water moiety. This custom, together with that of the moieties taking sides in games, obtained regularly at Big Creek, but not to such an extent elsewhere. This perhaps points to Big Creek as a place in which the moiety system was more firmly established.

In the girl's puberty ceremony it was customary for some girl, for whom the rites had previously been performed, to exchange dresses with the initiate. In all cases the two girls belonged to opposite moieties; if the initiate was of the water moiety, the girl who exchanged dresses with her must be of the land moiety. In the ahana dance the spectators, who made gifts to the dancers, were always of the opposite moiety but of the same sex as the dancers to whom they gave presents. . . .

PERSONAL NAMES

A child was named shortly after birth, preferably by a grandfather, but not infrequently by any one of the near relatives. The name received at that time was kept throughout life. Names of men and women did not differ. Occasionally a person received a nickname later in life.

The literal meanings or derivations, in part at least, as well as the connotations, of 144 personal names were obtained. Thirty-four of these names prove to be nouns or derivatives of nouns, and 102 verbs or derivatives of verbs. . . .

To a strange Indian, not acquainted with the individual whose name is mentioned, verb names have only their literal meaning. To the friends and acquaintances of the individual, however, the name has more than its literal meaning. It has an implied meaning, which usually brings in a reference to an animate or inanimate object. For example, the personal name Wüksü is a form of the verb meaning "to go." Yet to the friends and relatives of the man his name meant "sun going down." Another interesting case is found in the personal names Hausü and Hautcu, both derived from *hausus*, to yawn, or to gape. The former is a land moiety name and a bear is implied; the latter is a water moiety name and a salmon is implied. An extreme case, but one which throws light on the mental attitude of the name-giver, is that of the name Kuyunu. This name, according to the informant, had the connotation, "Dog wagging its tail." Kuyunu contains the same root as *kuyage*, to whistle. Apparently the name-giver thought of the whistling of a man to a dog as the cause of the dog wagging its tail, and, instead of naming the child after the action of the dog, named it after the cause of the dog's action; namely, whistling. Without knowledge of the individual, a Miwok, on hearing any of the above names, would be unable to decide as to the person's moiety or as to the animal or object implied. In the seventy bear names obtained, the word for bear is actually used in only one case.

In other words, among the Miwok there is absolutely nothing in the literal meanings of over 70 per cent. of the personal names even to suggest totemism. It is only in the implied meanings that the totemic element appears. In this respect there is a striking resemblance to the Mohave custom of calling women by names which have only an implied and perhaps esoteric reference to natural objects or phenomena, the coyote, for instance. . . .

Half-breeds born of Miwok mothers and white fathers are always considered as belonging to the moiety of which the mother is not a member. For example, if the mother is of the land moiety, the half-breed child will be of the water moiety and his or her name will refer to an animal or object identified with the water side of nature.

MARRIAGES

Ninety-nine marriages were recorded among the Central Sierra Miwok, thirty-two of these being from Big Creek alone. In the following table proper marriages, that is, between individuals of different moieties, are indicated by W-L; improper marriages, that is, between individuals of the same moiety, are indicated by W-W for the water moiety and L-L for the land moiety.

	W-L	W-W	L-L	Percentage of proper marriages	Percentage of improper marriages
Village at Big Creek.........	26	5	1	81	19
Central Sierra Miwok, except Big Creek people.........	48	1	18	72	28
Central Sierra Miwok in general	74	6	19	75	25

GENEALOGIES

In the genealogical information obtained there are forty-eight male lines of descent. Some of these are rather long, covering four or five generations. Others consist merely of two generations—a man and his offspring. Of these lines of descent only nine show complete transmission of the eponym of the paternal ancestor to the descendants. In other words, less than one-fifth of the Central Sierra Miwok families named all their children after the eponym of the father or other male ancestor of the group. Plainly, there is no rule of transmission of the eponym of the male ancestor, and consequently no widespread belief in descent from the eponymous animal. . . .

CROSS-COUSIN MARRIAGE

When asked if it were proper for a man to marry a cousin, Miwok informants always replied in the negative. In obtaining genealogical information, however, cases came up in which a man married his mother's brother's daughter. I called my informant's attention to this fact and received the reply that the individuals concerned were not regarded as cousins, for they stood in the relation of *añsi* and *anisü* to each other, which translated into English would be son and aunt, or potential stepmother. This affords an excellent example of the futility of using English terms of relationship with natives when discussing native customs.

Every Miwok to whom the question was put stated that the proper mate for a man was a woman who stood in the relation of *anisü* to him, providing she was not too closely related to him. Although a man might marry his *anisü* cross-cousin, who was the daughter of his mother's brother, he could under no circumstances marry his *lupuba* cross-cousin, who was the daughter of his father's sister. This one-sidedness of cross-cousin marriage among the Miwok in no way affected its popularity, or, to be more exact, the popularity of *anisü-añsi* marriages, of which the cross-cousin marriage is one form. In many cases my informants would state that a certain man and his wife stood in the relation to each other of *añsi* and *anisü*. Although these instances were not substantiated, except in four cases, by genealogical proof, they show the popularity of this form of marriage. At Big Creek six of the listed marriages are of this type, eight are not, and on the remaining eight I have no information. Cases were encountered in which a husband and wife claimed to stand in the *añsi-anisü* relation to each other, but, when asked to demonstrate the relation, were unable to trace the connecting links. This state of affairs shows clearly that *añsi-anisü* marriages must have been the vogue, otherwise married people who could not prove such a relationship would not lay claim to it. Even among the Northern Sierra Miwok at Elk Grove, among whom the moiety system does not seem to exist, *añsi-anisü* marriages were the custom. The Southern Sierra Miwok of Madera County state that these marriages were proper, but that the contracting parties must be only distantly related.

Informants at Jamestown, while stating that *anisü-añsi* marriages were prevalent there as elsewhere, said that marriages between first cousins, who stood in this relation, were commoner higher in the mountains than at Jamestown. The men at Jamestown and lower in the foothills were inclined to marry an *anisü* further removed than a first cousin. There seems to have been a sentiment at Jamestown against the marriage of first cousins. One woman was asked if she would consider it proper for her son to marry her brother's daughter. She replied, "No, she is too much like his mother," meaning herself. Her reply may have been engendered by the Miwok custom of a man marrying his wife's brother's daughter. By this marriage his new wife, who is also his son's *anisü* cross-cousin, would become his son's stepmother; hence perhaps the woman's statement with regard to her son's *anisü* cross-cousin, "too much like his mother."

32. THE SOCIAL ORGANIZATION OF THE WEST COAST TRIBES [9]

BY EDWARD SAPIR

. . . ALL these tribes are characterized by a clear development of the idea of rank; indeed, it may be said that nowhere north of Mexico is the distinction between those of high and those of low birth so sharply drawn as in the West Coast tribes. Three classes of society may be recognized—the nobility, the commoners, and the slaves. It is not practicable to distinguish between chiefs and nobles, as has been done for instance by Hill-Tout for the Coast Salish, as the lesser chiefs or nobles grade right in continuously with the head chiefs. Intermarriages between nobles and commoners or slaves, and between commoners and slaves, were in theory quite impossible, and in earlier days could at best have been but rare. We learn here and there from their legends that individuals of low rank were sometimes raised to a higher rank by marriage into a chief's family; but the very point made in such cases serves to emphasize the essential differences of rank. High rank is determined primarily by descent—whether in the male or female line depends on the tribe. A very important factor, furthermore, in determining rank is wealth, as illustrated more particularly by the distribution of great quantities of property at ceremonial feasts generally known as potlatches. It is not enough for one of high birth to rest in his hereditary glory. If he wishes to preserve the respect of his fellow tribesmen, he must at frequent intervals reassert his rank by displays of wealth, otherwise he incurs the risk of gradually losing the place that properly belongs to him on the score of inheritance. We read, indeed, of cases in which men of lower rank have by dint of reckless potlatching gained the ascendancy over their betters, gradually displacing them in one or more of the privileges belonging to their rank. Among the West Coast Indians, as in Europe, there is, then, opportunity for the unsettling activities of the parvenu.

A necessary consequence of the division of the village community into a number of large house-groups is that, associated with each chief, there is, besides the immediate members of his own family, a group of commoners and slaves, who form his retainers. The slaves are immediately subject to his authority and may be disposed of in any manner that he sees fit. The commoners also, however, while possessing a much

[9] From the article of the same name in *Transactions of the Royal Society of Canada*, Section II, Series III, Volume 9, pages 355-374, 1915.—"West Coast" refers to Canada; but the Tlingit of southernmost Alaska are included.

greater measure of independence, cannot be considered as unattached. Everything clustered about a number of house-groups headed by titled individuals, and in West Coast society, as in that of medieval feudalism, there was no place for the social freelance. If the number of commoners and slaves connected with a chief's family grew too large for adequate housing under a single roof, one or more supplementary houses could be added on to the first; but they always remained under its sphere of influence. In this way we can understand how even a group of houses forming an outlying village might be inhabited entirely by people of low birth, who were directly subject to one or more chiefs occupying houses in the mother village. From this point of view the whole tribe divides into as many social groups as there are independent chiefs.

The rank of chief or noble is connected in most cases with a certain degree of personal power, but real communal authority is naturally vested in only the highest chief or chiefs of the village, and then not always as absolutely as we might be inclined to imagine. Even the highest chief is primarily always associated with a particular family and house, and if he exercises general authority, it is not so much because of his individual rank as such, as because the house group that he represents is, for one reason or another, the highest in rank in the community. In legendary terms this might be expressed by saying that the other groups branched off from or attached themselves to that of the head chief.

Fully as characteristic of high rank as the exercise of authority is the use of a large variety of privileges. The subject of privileges among the West Coast Indians is an exceedingly complex one and cannot be adequately disposed of here. Privileges include not only practical rights of economic value, such as the exclusive or main right to a particular fishing ground or the right to receive a certain part of a whale which has drifted onto the tribal shore; but also, and indeed more characteristically, many purely ceremonial or other non-material rights. It is these which form the most important outward expression of high rank, and their unlawful use by those not entitled to them was certain in every case to bring about violent friction and not infrequently actual bloodshed. One of the most important of these privileges is the right to use certain carvings or paintings, nearly always connected with the legendary history of the family which the chief represents. We shall have somewhat more to say of these crests later; here I wish to point out that from our present point of view the crests are but one of the many privileges that are associated with high rank. A further indication of such rank is the right to use certain names. The right to the use of any name is, properly speaking, determined by descent, and the names which have come to be looked upon as higher in rank than others naturally descend only to those that are of high birth. These names comprise not only such as are applied to individuals and of which a large number, some of higher, others of lower rank, are at the disposal of the nobleman; but also names that he has the exclusive right to apply to his slaves, to his house, very often to particular features of his house, such as carved posts and beams, and in some cases even names applied to movable objects such as canoes or particularly prized harpoon-heads or other implements. Further indicative of rank is the right to perform particular dances both in secular feasts or potlatches and, though perhaps to a somewhat less extent, also at ritualistic performances.

Perhaps the clearest outward manifestation of rank is in the place given a chief whenever it is necessary to arrange in some order the various participants in a public function. Thus, in a public feast or potlatch, those of high rank are seated in certain parts of the house that are preserved exclusively for the nobility. These are the rear of the house and the halves of the sides which are nearest the rear. These seats are graded as to rank, and it is perhaps not too much to surmise that the obvious grading made visible to the eye by a definite manner of seating at feasts was in a large measure responsible for the extension of the idea of grading of ranks and privileges generally. The exact seat of honor differed somewhat with the different tribes. In some it was the centre of the rear; in others that seat on the right side of the house, as one faces the door, which was nearest the corner. Other arrangements into series which could give a concrete idea of the rank-ing enjoyed by an individual are the order in which gifts are distributed to the chiefs at a potlatch; furthermore, the order in which they are called out when invited by a representative of another tribe to attend a feast which is to be given some time in the near future by the latter. The ranking orders thus arrived at by seating, distribution of gifts, invitations to feasts, and in various other ways that it is not necessary to enter upon here, might be expected to coincide. To a certain extent they do tend to approximate, and the highest in rank in a community will nearly always be found to head any such list that might be con-structed. In practice, however, one finds that the various orders do not necessarily strictly correspond, in other words, that a person might individually be of lesser rank than another from the point of view of seating, but would have a prior claim to be invited, say. This curious state of affairs shows clearly enough that at last analysis rank is not a permanent status which is expressed in a number of absolutely fixed ways, but is rather the resultant standing attained by the inheritance of a considerable number of theoretically independent privileges which do, indeed, tend in most cases to be associated in certain ways, but may nevertheless be independently transmitted from generation to generation.

Nowhere in America is the idea of the grading of individuals carried to such an extent as among the West Coast Indians. It applies, however, only to the nobility, the commoners and the slaves not being differentiated among themselves with regard to rank. It has already been indicated how the ceremonial seating, for instance, of the nobility is expressive of their higher or lower status relatively to each other. In those tribes, like the Haida and Tlingit, that are subdivided into phratries and clans, a matter that we shall take up presently, this grading of chiefs represents something of a political or administrative basis, inasmuch as subsidiary to the town chief we have a number of clan heads. Subordinate to these, in turn, are the heads of the various house groups. Here again, however, it is important to notice that the town chief is always at the same time the chief of the particular clan that is dominant in that village and that the clan chief is at the same time the head of the particular house group that forms the nucleus of, or is the highest in rank in, the clan. In other words, ranking is not so much of a political or administrative character as it is determined by the handing down of status and privilege from holder to heir. It follows that the political organization, such as it is, impresses one as superimposed on the house group or family organization by inner growth of the latter. So strong a hold has the idea of ranking taken upon the Indians that we find it operative even in cases where it would naturally not be expected to find application. Thus, it is often customary for a number of invited tribes as such, as represented of course by certain chiefs, to be assigned definite ceremonial seats and thereby by implication to be ranked relatively to each other—at times a somewhat risky proceeding. Furthermore, in some tribes it is even customary for medicine men to be organized on the basis of rank, such ranking not necessarily depending entirely on the individual supernatural powers displayed by the medicine men as on the fact that they are entitled by inheritance of medical lore to such and such honors.

As already indicated, the subject of privileges is a vast one, and a complete enumeration of all the economic, ceremonial, and other privileges of one high in rank would take a long time. To a certain extent a man has the right to split his inheritance, in other words, to hand down to one of his sons or nephews, as the case might be, certain privileges, to another certain others. Very often such a division is reducible to the association of privileges with definite localities, a point which is of primary importance in connection with the village community as the fundamental unit in West Coast organization. Thus, if one by the accidents of descent has inherited according to one line of descent a number of privileges associated with village A, in which he is no longer resident, and a number of other privileges according to another line of descent originally associated with village B, in which he is resident, it would be a quite typical proceeding for him to bring up one of his heirs, say the one naturally highest in rank, to assume control of one set of privileges, a younger heir of the other. If the privileges originally connected with village B, let us say, tend to give one a higher place in the tribe than those connected with village A, the chances are that the first heir will be induced to take up his permanent residence in that village, while the transmitter may take the younger heir down to the more distant village and take up residence for a period in order to introduce his heir, as it were, to the privileges designed for him. In other words, there is a more or less definite tendency to connect honors with definite villages and, indeed, no matter how much rights of various sorts may become scattered by the division of inheritances, by the changes of residence due to inter-marriage, and by other factors which tend to complicate their proper assignment, a West Coast Indian never forgets, at least in theory, where a particular privilege originated or with what tribe or clan a particular right, be it name, dance, carving, song, or what not, was in the first instance associated. In short, privileges are bound to the soil.

This brings us to what I believe to be one of the most fundamental ideas in the social structure of these Indians, that is, the idea of a definite patrimony of standing and associated rights which, if possible, should be kept intact or nearly so. Despite the emphasis placed on rank, I think it is clear that the individual as such is of very much less importance than the tradition that for the time being he happens to represent. The very fact that a man often bears the name of a remote ancestor, real or legendary, implies that the honors that he makes use of belong not so much to him individually as to his glorious ancestry, and there is no doubt that the shame of falling behind, in splendor and liberality, the standard set by a predecessor, does much to spur him on to ever greater efforts to increase his prestige and gain for himself new privileges. There is one interesting fact which clearly shows the importance of the family patrimony or of the standing of a particular line of descent as such, as distinct from the individual who happens to be its most honored representative. This is the merging of various persons belonging to three or four generations into a single unit that need not be further differentiated. Among the Nootka Indians, for instance, an old man, his oldest son say, the oldest son of the son, and, finally, the infant child of the latter, say a daughter, form, to all intents and purposes, a single sociological personality. Titularly the highest rank is accorded, among the Nootka, to the little child, for it is always the last generation that in theory bears the highest honors. In practice, of course, the oldest members of the group get the real credit and do the business, as it were, of the inherited patrimony; but it would be difficult in such a case to say where the great-grandfather's privileges and standing are marked off against those of his son, or grandson, or great-granddaughter. In some cases even a younger son, who would ordinarily be considered as definitely lower in rank than his elder brother, might represent the standing of his father by the exercise of a privilege, say the singing of a particular song in a feast, that belongs to the patrimony of the family. "For men may come and men may go," says the line of descent with its distinctive privileges, "but I go on for ever." This is the Indian theory as implied in their general attitude, though there is no doubt that tremendous changes have in many instances gradually evolved by the dying out of particular lines of descent and the taking over of their privileges by other groups only remotely perhaps connected with them by kin, by the introduction of a new privilege gained say as a dowry, and by numerous other factors. The best way to gain a concrete idea of such a structure of society is to think of the titled portion of the tribe as holding up a definite number, say 15 or more, honored names, or occupying that number of seats, that have descended from the remote past. The classification of the tribe according to kin intercrosses with that based on rank, as by it individuals are brought together who, from the latter point of view, would have to be kept apart. It is clear that not all the members of a large family group can inherit the standing and all the privileges that belong to it. There must be a large number, particularly the younger sons and daughters and those descended from them, who are less favored than their elders and who will inherit only some, probably the lesser, privileges. In the course of time, as their relationship to the heads of the family or clan becomes more and more remote, they must be expected to sink lower and lower in the general social scale, and there is no doubt that a large proportion of the commoners are to be considered as the unprivileged kinsmen of the nobles. This is no doubt the attitude of at least some of the Indian tribes, such as the Nootka, among whom such a notion of the relation between the classes of society as we find among the castes of India, say, is certainly not found. There is no doubt, however, that with the growth of power attained by the chiefs and with the increasing remoteness of the ties of kinship binding them with most of the commoners, the chasm between the two would gradually widen. The slaves must be left out of account in this connection. They do not enter into the genealogical framework of the tribe, but seem to a large extent to have been recruited from captives of war.

Indian legend, at least among the Nootka and Kwakiutl, generally conceives of the village community as having grown up out of the small family immediately connected in the remote past with a legendary ancestor. All the members of the village community are therefore looked upon as direct descendants of a common ancestor and must therefore, at least in theory, bear definite degrees of relationship to one another. Whether or not the members of a village are actually so connected is immaterial, the essential point being that even in those tribes where there is no clan organization properly so-called, there is, nevertheless, a distinct feeling of kinship among all or most of the members of each of its village communities. This is borne out by the fact that individuals are taught to address each other by certain terms of relationship, even where the appropriateness of such terms is not obvious to them. Thus, a man well advanced in years might call a little child his older brother, for the reason that they are respectively descended from ancestors who stood to each other in that relation. Naturally intermarriages would bring about intercrossings of all sorts, and in course of time the more remote degrees of relationship would be forgotten and new ones, brought nearer home by more recent marriages, take their place.

Let us suppose that a village community is strictly homogeneous in structure, that is, contains no members that cannot count their descent in either the male or female line from the common ancestor. It is obvious that this state of affairs cannot last indefinitely. The accidents of war will doubtless bring it about that sooner or later some neighboring village community, that has suffered considerably at the hands of an enemy and that finds itself subject to extermination at their hands, will seek protection from the first village community and, in order to gain this end, will receive permission to take up residence with it. It is immediately apparent that the new enlarged village community, provided it is permanent, will have increased in complexity of structure. Their adherence to their respective traditions will be such that neither of the former village communities will give up its peculiar set of privileges, so that a twofold division of the community, as accentuated by these privileges, will persist. If we imagine this process to have occurred several times, we will gradually arrive at a community which is subdivided into several smaller units which we may call septs or bands, or perhaps even clans, each of which has its distinct stock of legendary traditions and privileges exercised by its titled representatives and whose former connection with a definite locality is still remembered. The growth of the village community does not need, of course, to have taken place only in this fashion. Many other factors may be at work. The group added to the original community may be the survivors of a conquered village who are given a subordinate place. Furthermore, a member of another tribe or community that has married into the community may, if he (or she) has sufficient prestige, be able to assert the higher rank that he (she) brings with him (her) and found a new line of descent which will take its place side by side with those already represented. We see, then, a number of ways in which the typical division of a tribe into clans, such as we find among the Haida, may be expected to originate. Such a clan, from the point of view of West Coast conditions, may be defined as a group of kinsmen, real or supposed, who form one of the sub-divisions of a village community and who inherit a common stock of traditions associated with a definite locality, the original home of the group.

Clans in this sense we have among the southern tribes that we have enumerated; but it is not until we reach the more northern tribes, such as the Tlingit, Haida, and Tsimshian, that the clan becomes a clearly defined and perfectly solidified unit. This is brought about primarily by the restriction of inheritance. Among the Nootka Indians, for instance, it is possible to inherit privileges in both the male and female lines, preference, where possible, being given to the former. This being the case, it is often hard to see exactly to which sept or clan a person properly belongs, and the decision is generally based on the character of the privileges that are transmitted to him, for, as we have seen, a privilege is always connected with a definite locality, sept, or original village community. In other words, a person steps into certain rights to which he has a claim by descent, and in the exercise of these becomes identified with the particular sept or clan with which they are associated. As the septs have their definite seating at feasts, it is easy to see how the identification of an individual with one sept rather than with another can be made visible. This will indicate also that there are certain natural limitations to the inheritance of all privileges that one has a theoretical claim to. This sort of clan division, however, for the reason that it is too ill-defined and vacillating, can hardly be considered as typical of what we ordinarily understand by clan organization. If, however, we once limit the inheritance of status and privileges to either the male or female line, to the absolute exclusion of the other, we obtain a series of septs or clans that are once and for all rigidly set off against each other. Among the more northern tribes, then, who inherit through the female line alone, there can never be the slightest doubt as to what clan a person is to be identified with.

Furthermore, among the more southern tribes intermarriage is prohibited only between such as are demonstrably related by blood, even if fairly remotely so. Owing to the structure of the village community, this would in many cases mean that there are few persons in a village that one is legally entitled to marry; but it is important to note that the village community as such need not be exogamous, that is, does not specifically prohibit intermarriage among its members. The clan of the northern tribes, which is more rigidly defined by descent and which therefore gains in solidarity, is further accentuated by strict exogamy. Whether such exogamy is a primary feature of the clan itself or is only a necessary consequence of the exogamy of certain larger groups known as phratries, which we shall take up in a moment, is a question which I would not venture to decide and which need not occupy us here. We spoke before of the fact that the original village communities, before amalgamating, each had its peculiar privileges. Certain of these privileges, particularly the crest paintings and carvings, are emblematic of the communities and may be said to give the septs or clans a totemic character. Among the southern tribes, however, it would seem that the crests, which are generally animals or supernatural beings, are employed exclusively by the nobles and that a commoner, even though identified with a particular sept, cannot be said to be in any sense associated with the crest. To what extent the crests are characteristic of the clan generally in the north and to what extent they are more especially in the nature of privileges enjoyed by the nobles, has not been made perfectly clear. It would seem that certain crests, whose origin is particularly remote, have lost such individual value as they may have had and have become clan emblems properly speaking, whereas others are more restricted in their use and would seem to be the peculiar privilege of certain titled individuals or families.

We shall now briefly review the main facts of clan organization among the Tlingit, Haida, Tsimshian, and Kwakiutl, concerning whom our published information is fullest. The Tlingit are divided into two main divisions, known respectively as Ravens and Wolves, the latter being in some of the villages referred to also as Eagles. In at least one of the southern Tlingit tribes, the Sanya, there is a division which stands outside of the grouping into two phratries, and the members of which may intermarry with either the Ravens or the Wolves. The Ravens and Wolves are respectively debarred from intermarriage within their own ranks. A Raven man must marry a Wolf woman, a Wolf man a Raven woman, while the children of the pair belong to the phratry of the mother. It is important to bear in mind that this dual division of the Tlingit Indians is not associated with particular villages or even tribes, but applies to all the Tlingit tribes. A Raven, for instance, from Tongas, the southernmost Tlingit village, is as strictly debarred from marrying a Raven woman of Yakutat, in the extreme north, as a Raven woman of his own village. When we remember that he may never have been within miles of Yakutat and may know few or no Indians from that region, we see clearly that whether or not phratric exogamy is in origin an outgrowth of an interdict against marriage of those of close kin, an interdict which we find to be practically universal, it is certainly rather different from it psychologically. The leading crest or emblem of the Raven people is the raven, who is at the same time the most important mythological being in the beliefs of the Tlingit Indians. The main crest of the Wolf people is the wolf. The phratries stand to each other as opposites that do each other mutual services. Thus, the Wolves conduct the funeral ceremonies of the Ravens and, when they give a feast, distribute the property to the Ravens.

Each phratry is subdivided into a considerable number of clans, each with its own distinctive crest or crests, generally in addition to the general crest of the phratry to which it belongs. Unlike the two main phratries, the clans are not found in all the villages of the Tlingit, though many of them are found represented in more than one village. If we assume, as I believe to be the case, that the clans were originally nothing but village communities, it follows that the present distribution of clans is secondary and due to migrations or movements of part of the clansmen away from the main body of their kinsmen. Should a number of clansmen of the original clan village be induced for one reason or another to take up residence in another village, the home primarily of another clan, it is clear that they would, to begin with, be an intrusive element in their new home; but would in course of time be looked upon as forming an integral part of the village community, though of lesser importance than the dominant clan. The legends of the Indians themselves clearly indicate that such whole or partial clan movements have frequently taken place. Many of the names of the clans themselves plainly indicate their local origin. Thus, the Kiksadi are a Raven clan that are found represented in several Tlingit tribes, such as the Sanya, the Stikine people, and the Sitka Indians. The name means nothing more than People-of-the-Island-Kiks and clearly implies that the clan was, to begin with, at home in a particular locality and gradually became distributed over a large area by various movements of population. The force of tradition would always be strong enough to keep up the old clan crests and other clan privileges, wherever the clansmen moved. In course of time the appearance is attained of a clan distribution which has nothing to do with local communities as such.

Very similar conditions prevail among the Haida Indians. Here again we have two main phratries, subdivided into a large number of clans. As among the Tlingit, the Haida phratries are exogamous and descent in them is reckoned through the female line. One of them is termed Raven, though, curiously enough, the main crest of this phratry is not the raven but the killer-whale. The opposite phratry is termed Eagle, this animal being the chief crest of the phratry. Among the Haida, as among the Tlingit, the native legends indicate that the clans were originally confined to certain definite localities, but that in course of time the clansmen moved about in various ways until now, when they are represented in a number of villages. One concrete instance will serve to illustrate the actual state of affairs. In the town of Skidegate there were represented in earlier times three distinct Eagle clans, and three distinct Raven clans, each of these six clans occupying its own houses. Of the six clans the dominant one was an Eagle clan known as People-of-the-great-house, claiming as their crests the Raven (this in spite of the fact that they do not belong to the Raven phratry), a supernatural being known as *wāsgo*, the dog-fish, the weasel, the eagle, the sculpin, and the halibut. Presumably this clan formed the original nucleus of the present town of Skidegate about which the other clans in course of time clustered. The Haida clan names are generally either local in character, like most of the Tlingit names, or of an honorific character, like the one that we have just quoted.

The Tsimshian are organized similarly to the Tlingit and Haida, except that their clans are grouped into four phratries: the Raven, Eagle, Wolf, and Grizzly Bear.

Among the southern Kwakiutl also the single tribes are sub-divided into a number of clans, each of which, there is reason to believe on legendary and other evidence, originally formed a separate village community. These have chiefly honorific titles, such as "The-chiefs," "Those-who-receive-first," and "Having-a-great-name." Some of these names occur in more than one of the Kwakiutl tribes; but it seems more likely that these correspondences in name are due to imitations rather than to a genealogical connection between the clans of like name. The social structure of the Kwakiutl Indians differs from that of the Tlingit and Haida in that the clans are not grouped into phratries, and that they do not seem to be exogamous. As to descent, it seems that at least the most important privileges are regularly transmitted as a dowry to the son-in-law, who holds them in trust for his son. This method of inheritance has been explained as a peculiar

Kwakiutl adaptation of an originally paternal system of inheritance to the maternal system in vogue among the more northern tribes, by whom the Kwakiutl were presumably influenced. There are, however, some difficulties in the way of this explanation, one of which is the fact that the Nootka Indians to the south are not organized on a purely paternal basis, but allow many privileges to descend through the female line. Among them also such privileges may be handed over as a dowry, though this system has not been standardized among them to the same extent as among the Kwakiutl.

There are two important peculiarities of the West Coast crests which make them contrast with the totems of such typical totemic communities as the Iroquois Indians of the east or the Pueblos of the southwest. Among these latter, who, like the Haida and Tlingit, are organized into exogamous clans of maternal descent, a clan has a single crest or totem after which it is named. Moreover, no other clan can use this totem. The West Coast clans differ in both these respects. As we have already shown in the case of one of the Haida Eagle clans, a group of clansmen generally lay claim to more than one crest; further, only certain crests are confined to single clans, the more important ones being generally represented in several. Thus, the grizzly-bear is claimed as a crest by no less than twelve distinct Haida clans of the Raven phratry, the rainbow by eight, the sea-lion by five, the beaver by twelve Eagle clans, the whale by seven, the humming-bird by three, and so on. In some cases, a clan even makes use of a crest which primarily belongs to the opposite phratry. Evidently there is not the same intimate and clear-cut association between totem and clan, as such, that is typical of the Iroquois and Pueblo Indians.

It is probable that the duplication of crests is to be explained chiefly on the theory that many clans arose as subdivisions of other clans. Such a clan offshoot would keep the old crest or crests, but might in time add one or more to its stock, without sharing them with the mother clan. The clan can, indeed, be arranged in the form of a genealogical tree and the crests stratified. The older the crest, the greater number of times is it found in the various clans; on the other hand, a crest found in only one clan may be suspected to be of recent origin, as it probably does not antedate the severance of its clan from the older group originally including it.

Whatever may have been its origin, the crests seems to have become, to a large extent, a symbol of greatness, and it became the desire of the chiefs to add to their prestige by the acquisition of new crests. They were not only obtained by inheritance, but could be secured as gifts, or even by forcible means in war. The fact that the name of the clan does not as a rule refer to a totem also seems to indicate that the clan may not, to begin with, be organically connected with a particular crest. That the clansmen are not conceived of as descended from one of their crest animals, and that there seem to be no taboos in force against the eating or killing of the crest animals, need not matter, for these are by no means constant features of even typical totemic societies.

There is another feature of the crests of the West Coast Indians which accentuates their difference from typical clan totems. This is the tendency they have to be thought of in very concrete terms, as carvings or paintings. It would in many cases, for instance, be more correct to say that a certain chief uses a ceremonial hat representing the Beaver, or that he has the right to paint the Thunder-bird on the outside of his house, than that he possesses the Beaver or Thunder-bird crest or totem. His justification for the use of these would be a legend, telling of how one of his ancestors gained the privilege by contact with the crest animals—a type of legend which is told to account for the use of nearly all crests. We see more clearly now why earlier in this paper I referred to crests as a particular type of an inheritable privilege. Incidentally, it is interesting to note that the Kwakiutl term for crest seems to denote primarily a carving.

Crests are shown or utilized in different ways. They may be painted on movable boards used as screens or otherwise, painted on the outside of the house or along the bed platform, carved on the house-posts or beams, or on memorial columns, or on the outside house-posts popularly known as totem poles, tattooed on the body, painted on the face during feasts, represented in dance-hats, masks, staffs, or other ceremonial paraphernalia, woven in ceremonial robes, referred to in clan legends, dramatically represented at potlatches in performances based on such legends, referred to in songs owned by the clan or clan-chiefs, and in individual or house names. Not all house names, however, refer to a crest. The village and clan names are also, as a rule, unconnected with crests. So accustomed have the West Coast Indians, particularly those of the north, become to the representation of crest animals in carving and painting, that they introduce them even in objects that are not as a rule connected with the exercise of privileges. Among such objects are the beautifully ornamented dishes, boxes, batons, spoons, rattles, clubbers, and gambling-sticks that are so often admired in ethnological museums. We see here how the elaboration of the crest system has fostered among these Indians the development of plastic art. It has also been suggested, and I believe with justice, that the tendency to artistic and dramatic representation in turn reacted upon the development of the crest system, a development that was strengthened by the ever-present desire for new privileges and for novel ways of exhibiting the old ones.

The origin of the crests need not have been the same in all cases. In some cases, for instance, it can be shown that they were obtained by marriage or as gifts in return for a service. These new crests would of course be handed down along with the old inherited ones. Such methods of obtaining crests, however, must be considered as purely secondary, and the real problem of accounting for their origin still remains. The most plausible explanation that has been offered is, on the whole, that which considers the clan crest as an extension of the personal manitou or tutelary being. Among practically all Indians we find the practice of seeking supernatural protection or power by fasting and dreaming of certain animals or objects that are believed to be endowed with such power. If we suppose that a personal guardian thus obtained is handed down by inheritance, we can readily understand how the manitou of an ancestor may gradually become transformed into a clan totem or crest. The main difficulty with this theory is that personal guardians or medicines do not normally seem to be inheritable. On the other hand, the legends related by the West Coast Indians to account for the origin of crests do bear an unmistakable resemblance to tales of the acquisition of supernatural guardians. It is not difficult to understand how the religious element, which must have been strongly emphasized in the manitou, gradually faded away as the manitou developed (or degenerated) into a crest. At any rate, the problem is far from being satisfactorily solved.

Even more fundamental than the clans are, among the northern tribes, the phratries which include them. Their origin also is far from clear. Whether they resulted from the amalgamation of a number of clans into larger units, or whether, on the contrary, the clans within the phratry are to be considered as local offshoots from it, is often difficult to decide. On the whole, however, the latter alternative seems the more typical one. This is indicated, first of all, by the fact that each of the two main phratries is represented in every village, though, on the other hand, the necessary intermarriages between the phratries might soon bring about this state of affairs under any circumstances. More important is the fact that the phratric crest is shared by all or practically all the clans of the phratry; this seems to imply that the phratry with its crest is a fundamental unit antedating the rise of the separate clans. The fundamental importance of the two phratric divisions of the Haida is beautifully illustrated by their belief in the validity of this social arrangement in the supernatural world. Thus, every being of the sea was conceived of as belonging from the beginning of time to either the Raven or Eagle phratry. It is conceivable that the phratries are sociologically reinterpreted forms of originally distinct tribal units. Apropos of this possibility, it may be noted that in many tribal organizations certain clans, gentes, camp-circle units, or other social units are, either in fact or origin, a group of aliens incorporated into the main tribe. According to Tlingit legend, indeed, the Ravens were originally Coast people, the Wolves inland people. This may, however, be a mere rationalization of an obvious fact of zoölogical distribution, the raven being common on the coast while the wolf is chiefly confined to the woods.

So much for social organization according to rank and kinship. The third type of organization, the local, we have had to take up in connection with the other two. Local classifications as distinct from kin classifications arise only when the clan ceases to be confined to a single locality. When this happens, the kin and local groupings necessarily intercross and town administration arises, which provides for more than the needs of a clan or group of kinsmen.

The ritual organization which we have listed as a fourth type of social organization is best developed among the Kwakiutl Indians. Among these Indians the clan system which is operative during the greater part of the year, the so-called profane season, gives place during the winter to a ritualistic organization based on the right to the performance of religious dances. The dancers impersonate various supernatural beings from whom they are supposed to have received manitou power. In actual practice the performance of the dances is conditioned by the inherited right to them. Such rights are justified in legends accounting for the introduction of the dance by an ancestor, supposed to have come in contact with the supernatural being himself and to have been instructed by him. In a sense all those who perform the same dance form a secret society, though this term, which has been often used, does not seem particularly appropriate to me. The dances are graded into two series—a lower and a higher one. The dancers of the lower series are collectively known as Sparrows,[10] those of the higher as Seals. One may pass in successive seasons from one so-called society to another, up to the point allowed by his or her particular inheritance. The most important of the dance-societies are the Ghosts, the Fool-dancers, the Grizzly-bears, and the Cannibals. While there are certain external resemblances between the ritual and clan organizations of the Kwakiutl, I believe it would be erroneous to consider the

[10] Or some other small bird.

former as specialized forms of the latter. I consider it far more likely that the ritualistic activities were simply patterned on the normal clan organization, the ever-present tendency to ranking finding expression in both. The other tribes of this region have borrowed much of the Kwakiutl rituals, but do not seem to share their elaborate ritual organization.

The space at our disposal will not permit us to go more deeply into the intricacies of West Coast social organization. It is difficult to render clear in a few strokes what seems an essentially involved set of social phenomena and I am not at all certain that I have succeeded in my object. The main points that I have tried to bring out are the fundamental importance of inherited privileges as such, the growth of the village community into a clan, the peculiar character of the crest system of these Indians when compared with typical totemism elsewhere, and the almost exaggerated development of the idea of grading of individuals and privileges.

33. THE POTLATCH OF THE KWAKIUTL INDIANS [11]

BY FRANZ BOAS

BEFORE proceeding any further it will be necessary to describe the method of acquiring rank. This is done by means of the *potlach*, or the distribution of property. This custom has been described often, but it has been thoroughly misunderstood by most observers. The underlying principle is that of the interest-bearing investment of property.

The child when born is given the name of the place where it is born. This name (*gi'nLaxLē*) it keeps until about a year old. Then his father, mother, or some other relative, gives a paddle or a mat to each member of the clan and the child receives his second name (*nā'ma'p'axLēya*). When the boy is about ten or twelve years old, he obtains his third name (*gōmiatsExLä'yē*). In order to obtain it he must distribute a number of small presents such as shirts or single blankets among his own clan or tribe. When the youth thus starts out in life he is liberally assisted by his elders, particularly by the nobility of the tribe.

I must say here that the unit of value is the single blanket, now-a-

[11] From "The Social Organization and the Secret Societies of the Kwakiutl Indians," Report of the U. S. National Museum for 1895, Washington (1897). Pages 341-346, 358-359 have been used. The Kwakiutl live on Vancouver Island, British Columbia.

days a cheap white woolen blanket, which is valued at fifty cents. The double blanket is valued at three single blankets. These blankets form the means of exchange of the Indians, and everything is paid for in blankets or in objects the value of which is measured by blankets. When a native has to pay debts and has not a sufficient number of blankets, he borrows them from his friends and has to pay the following rates of interest:

For a period of a few months, for five borrowed blankets six must be returned (*Lē'k·ō*); for a period of six months, for five borrowed blankets seven must be returned (*mā''Laxsa Lēk.ōyō*); for a period of twelve months or longer, for five borrowed blankets ten must be returned (*dē'ida* or *gē'La*).

When a person has a poor credit, he may pawn his name for a year. Then the name must not be used during that period, and for thirty blankets which he has borrowed he must pay 100 in order to redeem his name. This is called *q'ā'q'oaxō* ("selling a slave").

The rate of interest of the *Lē'k·ō* varies somewhat around 25 per cent., according to the kindness of the loaner and the credit of the borrower. For a very short time blankets may be loaned without interest. This is designated by the same term.

When the boy is about to take his third name, he will borrow blankets from the other members of the tribe, who all assist him. He must repay them after a year, or later, with 100 per cent. interest. Thus he may have gathered 100 blankets. In June, the time set for this act, the boy will distribute these blankets among his own tribe, giving proportionately to every member of the tribe, but a few more to the chief. This is called *Lā'X'uit*. When after this time any member of the tribe distributes blankets, the boy receives treble the amount he has given. The people make it a point to repay him inside of a month. Thus he owns 300 blankets, of which, however, he must repay 200 after the lapse of a year. He loans the blankets out among his friends, and thus at the close of the year he may possess about 400 blankets.

The next June he pays his debts (*quoana'*) in a festival, at which all the clans from whom he borrowed blankets are present. The festival is generally held on the street or on an open place near the village. Up to this time he is not allowed to take part in feasts. But now he may distribute property in order to obtain a potlatch name (*p'ä'tsaxLäyē*). This is also called *Lā'X'uit*.

At this time the father gives up his seat (*Lä'Xoē*) in favor of his son. After the boy has paid his debts, the chief calls all the older members of the tribe to a council, in which it is resolved that the boy is to receive his father's seat. The chief sends his speaker to call the boy, and his clan go out in company with the speaker. The young man—for henceforth he will be counted among the men—dresses with a black headband and paints long vertical stripes, one on each side of his face, running down from the outer corners of the eyes. The stripes represent tears. He gives a number of blankets to his friends who carry them into the house where the council is being held. The speaker enters first and announces his arrival. The young man follows and after him enter his friends, carrying blankets. He remains standing in front of the fire, and the chief announces to him that he is to take his father's seat. Then the boy distributes his blankets among the other clans and sells some for food, with which a feast is prepared. His father gives up his seat and takes his place among the old men (*Nō'matsēiL*). The blankets given away at this feast are repaid with 100 per cent. interest. In this manner the young man continues to loan and to distribute blankets and thus is able with due circumspection and foresight to amass a fortune. Sometimes it happens that the successor to a man's name (*Lawu'lqame*) already has a name of his own. In all such cases (also when the name is acquired by inheritance) the successor gives up his name and his property to his own successor.

Possession of wealth is considered honorable, and it is the endeavor of each Indian to acquire a fortune. But it is not as much the possession of wealth as the ability to give great festivals which makes wealth a desirable object to the Indian. As the boy acquires his second name and a man's estate by means of a distribution of property, which in course of time will revert to him with interest, the man's name acquires greater weight in the councils of the tribe and greater renown among the whole people, as he is able to distribute more and more property at each subsequent festival. Therefore boys and men are vying with each other in the arrangement of great distributions of property. Boys of different clans are pitted against each other by their elders, and each is exhorted to do his utmost to outdo his rival. And as the boys strive against each other, so do the chiefs and the whole clans, and the one object of the Indian is to outdo his rival. Formerly feats of bravery counted as well as distributions of property, but nowadays, as the Indians say, "rivals fight with property only." . . .

I referred several times to the distribution of blankets. The recipient in such a distribution is not at liberty to refuse the gift, although according to what I have said it is nothing but an interest-bearing loan that must be refunded at some future time with 100 per cent. interest. This festival is called *p'a'sa*, literally, "flattening something" (for instance, a basket). This means that by the amount of property given the name of the rival is flattened.

There is still another method of rising in the social scale, namely, by showing one's self superior to the rival. This may be done by inviting the rival and his clan or tribe to a festival and giving him a considerable number of blankets. He is compelled to accept these, but is not allowed to do so until after he has placed an equal number of blankets on top of the pile offered to him. This is called *dāpEntgala* and the blankets placed on top of the first pile are called *dā'pEnō*. Then he receives the whole pile and becomes debtor to that amount, i.e., he must repay the gift with 100 per cent. interest.

A similar proceeding takes place when a canoe is given to a rival. The latter, when the gift is offered to him, must put blankets to the amount of half the value of the canoe onto it. This is called *dā'g·ot*, "taking hold of the bow of the canoe." These blankets are kept by the first owner of the canoe. Later on, the recipient of the canoe must return another canoe, together with an adequate number of blankets, as an "anchor line" for the canoe. This giving of a canoe is called *sā'k·a*.

Still more complicated is the purchase or the gift, however one chooses to term it, of a "copper." All along the North Pacific Coast, from Yakutat to Comox, curiously shaped copper plates are in use, which in olden times were made of native copper, which is found in Alaska and probably also on Nass River, but which nowadays are worked out of imported copper. . . . These coppers have the same function which bank notes of high denominations have with us. The actual value of the piece of copper is small but it is made to represent a large number of blankets and can always be sold for blankets. The value is not arbitrarily set but depends upon the amount of property given away in the festival at which the copper is sold. On the whole, the oftener a copper is sold the higher its value, as every new buyer tries to invest more blankets in it. Therefore the purchase of a copper also brings distinction, because it proves that the buyer is able to bring together a vast amount of property.

Each copper has a name of its own, and from the following list of coppers, which were in Fort Rupert in 1893, the values attached to some of them may be seen:

Mā'xts'ōlem ("all other coppers are ashamed to look at it"), 7,500 blankets.

L'ā'xolamas ("steel-head salmon," i.e. it glides out of one's hands like a salmon), 6,000 blankets.

Lō'pēLila ("making the house empty of blankets"), 5,000 blankets.

De'nt'alayō ("about whose possession all are quarreling").

Mau'ak·'a ("sea-lion").

Qau'lō'ma ("beaver face").

Lē'ita ("looking below"; namely, in order to find blankets with which to buy it).

Nū'sē ("moon"; its engraving represents the half-moon, in which a man is sitting).

G·ā'waqa ("a spirit." He'iltsuq dialect, corresponding to the Kwakiutl Ts'ō'nōqoa).

Ne'lqEmāla ("dry face").

Ne'nqEmāla ("bear face").

K·'ā'na ("crow"; Hē'iltsuq dialect).

Qoayî'm ("whale").

Ma'x'ēnōx ("killer whale").

Qoayî'mk.în ("too great a whale").

Wī'na ("war," against the blankets of the purchaser).

The purchase of a high-priced copper is an elaborate ceremony, which must be described in detail. The trade is discussed and arranged long beforehand. When the buyer is ready, he gives to the owner of the copper blankets about one-sixth of the total value of the copper. This is called "making a pillow" for the copper (*qē'nulīLa*); or "making a feather bed" (*ta'lqoa*) or "the harpoon line at which game is hanging" (*dō'XsEmt*), meaning that in the same manner the copper is attached to the long line of blankets; or "taken in the hand, in order to lift the copper" (*dā'g·ilēlEm*). The owner of the copper loans these blankets out, and when he has called them in again, he repays the total amount received, with 100 per cent. interest, to the purchaser. On the following day the tribes assemble for the sale of the copper. The prescribed proceeding is as follows: The buyer offers first the lowest price at which the copper was sold. The owner declares that he is satisfied, but his friends demand by degrees higher and higher prices, according to all the previous sales of the copper. This is called *g·i'na*. Finally, the amount offered is deemed satisfactory. Then the owner asks for boxes to carry away the blankets. These are counted five pairs a box, and are also paid in blankets or other objects. After these have been paid, the owner of the copper calls his friends—members of his own tribe—to rise, and asks for a belt, which he values at several hundred blankets. While these are being brought, he and his tribe generally repair to their house, where they paint their faces and dress in new blankets. When they have finished, drums are beaten in the house, they all shout "hi!" and go out again, the speaker of the seller first. As soon as the latter has left the house he turns and calls his chief to come down, who goes back to where the sale is going on, followed by his tribe. They all stand in a row and the buyer puts down the blankets which were demanded as a belt, "to adorn the owner of the copper." This whole purchase is called "putting the copper under the name of the buyer" (*Lā'sa*).

In this proceeding the blankets are placed in piles of moderate height, one pile close to the other, so that they occupy a considerable amount of space. In Fort Rupert there are two high posts on the beach bearing carved figures on top, between which the blankets are thus piled. They stand about forty steps apart.

On the following day all the blankets which have been paid for the copper must be distributed by the owner among his own tribe, paying to them his old debts first, and, if the amount is sufficient, giving new presents. This is called "doing a great thing" (*wā'lasila*).

Coppers are always sold to rivals, and often a man will offer his copper for sale to the rival tribe. If it is not accepted, it is an acknowledgment that nobody in the tribe has money enough to buy it, and the name of the tribe or clan would consequently lose in weight. Therefore, if a man is willing to accept the offer, all the members of the tribe must assist him in this undertaking with loans of blankets. Debts which are repaid in the *wā'lasila* were mostly contracted in this manner.

MARRIAGE

Marriage among the Kwakiutl must be considered a purchase, which is conducted on the same principles as the purchase of a copper. But the object bought is not only the woman, but also the right of membership in her clan for the future children of the couple. I explained before that many privileges of the clan descend only through marriage upon the son-in-law of the possessor, who, however, does not use them himself, but acquires them for the use of his successor. These privileges are, of course, not given as a present to the son-in-law, but he becomes entitled to them by paying a certain amount of property for his wife. The wife is given to him as a first installment of the return payment. The crest of the clan, its privileges, and a considerable amount of other property besides, are given later on, when the couple have children, and the rate of interest is the higher the greater the number of children. For one child, 200 per cent. of interest is paid; for two or more children, 300 per cent. After this payment the marriage is annulled, because the wife's father has redeemed his daughter. If she continues to stay with her husband, she does so of her own free will (*wūle'L*, "staying in the house for nothing"). In order to avoid this state of affairs, the husband often makes a new payment to his father-in-law in order to have a claim to his wife.

The law of descent through marriage is so rigid that methods have developed to prevent the extinction of a name when its bearer has no daughter. In such a case a man who desires to acquire the use of the crest and the other privileges connected with the name performs a sham marriage with the son of the bearer of the name (*Xuē'sa;* Newettee dialect: *dā'xsitsEnt*, "taking hold of the foot"). The ceremony is performed in the same manner as a real marriage. In case the bearer of the name has no children at all, a sham marriage with part of his body is performed, with his right or left side, a leg or an arm, and the privileges are conveyed in the same manner as in the case of a real marriage.

It is not necessary that the crest and privileges should be acquired for the son of the person who married the girl, but they may be transferred to his successor, whoever that may happen to be.

34. SHELL-MONEY OF NEW BRITAIN [12]

BY BENJAMIN DANKS

The shell-money of New Britain is a very important factor in the life of a New Britain savage. Any account of the New Britain people, their lives and their customs, will fall short of what it should be if this important currency is not discussed.

The name of this money on the Duke of York group and New Ireland is Diwára. On New Britain it is called Tambu. . . .

The shell of which Tambu is made is very small. It is procured from the people who live on the N. W. coast of New Britain. I have not been able to ascertain the exact part of the coast. In company with the Rev. G. Brown and others I went to the place where the people from the Gazelle Peninsula purchase it. When we asked the people where it was obtained they pointed us still further west. I have seen ornaments from the east coast of New Guinea, and from that fact think that possibly the shell may be found on Brooks Island between New Britain and New Guinea. When purchased at Nakanai the shells are just as they are found upon the beach or dug from the earth. They are done up in packets varying in size, and consequently in value also. The secret as to where they are obtained is very jealously kept by the Nakanai people. I have never found one man in the Gazelle Peninsula who had the faintest idea as to its whereabouts. It is evidently a trade secret,

[12] From "On the Shell-Money of New Britain," in *Journal of the [Royal] Anthropological Institute [of Great Britain and Ireland]*, volume 17, pages 305-317, 1888.

kept close by the Nakanai people in order to prevent the Pele and other trade from passing their country.

When brought from Nakanai, each man sits down and threads his shells on long strips of cane. A hole is first punched through the back of the shells. The strips of cane, which are about two feet six inches in length, are scraped or pared down to the required size, and the shells are then strung. To join these pieces of cane one end of one piece is made wedge-shape. One end of another piece is split a little down the center. The wedge end of the one piece is put between the two halves of the split end of the other piece, and a few shells are drawn over the splice, binding the two sides of the one piece on the wedge of the other. This process is repeated until all the shells are strung into one long length, which is then rolled up into coils ranging from sixty to four and five hundred fathoms. The coil is then carefully and neatly wrapped up in banana leaves and suspended in the treasure-house until required.

The money thus prepared is the national currency. By it trade is carried on and it enters largely into every custom and ceremony of the land. It can be, and is, divided as easily as we divide our pounds into shillings and shillings into pence. For the sake of illustration let their fathom of Tambu be represented by our £. Then half fathom = 10s. Quarter fathom = 5s., and lowest of all two shells may represent our farthing. The length we have called a fathom is the distance between the two hands, when they are stretched out straight in opposite directions. A man is praised according to the good full measure he gives, and execrated according to the short measure he may give. The word for purchasing a thing is *kul*. The word for barter, i.e. exchange of produce, is *buapa*, thus showing that the two ideas are as distinct in the minds of the natives as they are in our own.

There are fixed prices for some things. Prices for other things differ, as with us, according to the law of supply and demand. All articles of food remain at much about the same price. The following is a list of prices obtaining in New Britain:—

Salmon, large.......................½ fathom Tambu.
Fowls according to size...............½ to ¼ fathom Tambu.
Breadfruit, sixty for..................1 fathom Tambu.
Taro [13] and yams according to state of
   crop, if plentiful, sixty for..........1 fathom Tambu.

[13] In purchasing vegetable food, it often happens that a man will buy the whole of a neighbor's crop before it is dug, for a greater or smaller sum according to the size of the plantation and yield. I have purchased crops thus at from ten fathoms to twenty and twenty-five fathoms of Tambu.

```
If scarce, fifty for...................1 fathom Tambu.
Betel-nuts, a large bunch..............¼ fathom Tambu.
Twelve betel-nuts.....................4 shells only.
Canoes, large.........................20, 25, 30, 50 fathoms Tamou.
Canoes, small.........................7 fathoms and upwards Tambu.
Pigs according to size, from............7 to 10 fathoms Tambu.
Dogs according to size, from...........2 to 3 fathoms Tambu.
Cockatoos ...........................2 to 5 fathoms Tambu.
2 yards print.........................1 fathom Tambu.
1 tomahawk (good)...................3 to 4 fathoms Tambu.
Large plantation knife................3 fathoms Tambu.
Large fishing nets....................40 to 50 fathoms Tambu.
Small fishing nets....................1, 2, 3, 4 fathoms Tambu.
```

Husband and wife possess this money quite independently of each other. The children also, almost as soon as they can understand anything, are taught that the acquisition and retention of wealth is an important, if not the most important, duty of life. To let money go for nothing in return or to pay a shell more than is necessary for an article is considered the height of folly. Consequently little boys and girls have their little store and bank, and are keen traders. A wife, however, is often despoiled of her money by her husband. Not indeed by force. That would be an invasion of the rights of property, and an offense against the public conscience. The husband perhaps gets up a charge of adultery against his wife, he becomes very angry and threatens to do her bodily harm unless she pays him so much money. Often she is charged with saying something derogatory to him. She is then made to pay for "defamation of character." She pays in order to escape bodily harm at the hands of husband. Often enough the charge is true, but often it is not. In either case he gets money from her.

Money is lent at the uniform rate of ten per cent. It is the custom on Duke of York, that when a person wishes to borrow money he must return eleven fathoms for ten fathoms borrowed. The word for interest there is *wawaturu*, thus showing that the idea of usury is perfectly understood. On New Britain the idea is not so fully developed. I have not found on New Britain a word equal to the Duke of York word *wawaturu*. *Kumbika* is the New Britain word which most resembles the Duke of York word. Its literal meaning is either a present, or to present, to give, to pay. When money is borrowed, however, it is never returned without a fathom for every ten fathoms borrowed, but the idea in the native mind does not seem to be so much interest, as an expression of thanks for the favor. It amounts practically to the same thing, but there is a difference in the native mind.

A New Britain native has an aversion to breaking in upon his capital. If a man has a coil of money but no "change," and requiring for his present need only a few fathoms, he will take his coil and pawn it for as many fathoms as he requires. The coil is kept by the lender until the sum is repaid with interest, upon which the coil is returned to its owner. This custom is called the *vuvuring.*

The people greatly deplore the loss of this wealth from the community and will do much to avert it. If a rich man is offended and threatens to remove to another town, his friends and sometimes many of the leading men of the place will pay him something to remain with them.

One man often becomes a banker for a number of men. He is generally a man who is feared and who has a reputation for valor and a good following. His house then forms a rallying point in times of trouble for all those who have lodged money there. He thus becomes a person of influence and power, because, no matter what villainy he may perpetrate, the depositors rally round their money to defend it, and in so doing defend him. I do not know that he is held responsible for anything which may be missing. I have known cases where the banker has been offended by one of the depositors, and he has refused to give back the deposit, claiming it as compensation for the offense. Being feared by the offender, nothing has been done. I have also known young men deposit money with their uncle, i.e. their mother's brother, and the uncle has used the money as his own. There seems to be no redress in that case. I have never heard of any banker using or making away with or retaining money belonging to others except in the above cases.

A borrower comes more or less under the influence and power of the lender. If the borrower is a young man and has borrowed money to purchase a wife, or if a person has purchased a wife for him, he is then more or less at the bidding of the lender until the loan is repaid. All initiation fees into various clubs or societies are, as a rule, paid by the elders or chiefs, thus bringing the boys and young men under their influence. If a borrower shows a disposition to be restive, he is at once reminded of his obligation to pay, and the "screw" is as powerfully applied as with us. If a man refuses to repay a loan, he is thenceforth a marked man. His character is gone. He is called a *"watukum,"* meaning an embezzler. None will lend him money in the future. Some young men cannot marry for the simple reason they cannot purchase a wife, and no one will lend them money because they are lazy, or have not been able to make money in the past, and there is a doubt as to whether they will be able to make it in the future.

Partnerships are entered into by the people. Two or three will own a fishtrap or a number of them, or perhaps a large fishing net. The proceeds of the sale of the produce are carefully counted at the conclusion of the day's work and equally divided, or it may be the profits are divided at the end of a season. Trading and other ventures are jointly carried on and strict accounts kept, each partner being a check on the others. The strength of their memory in money matters is astonishing. Large plantations are made by a number of people and the produce sold. The greatest source of wealth to the coast tribes lies in their trading for the shell of the Tambu, and in the products of their fishtraps and plantations.

Atonement of Wrong is made by the payment of Tambu, the amount fixed being according to the wrong done. This fact has a great restraining influence upon New Britain society. Thus:

When war has been carried on for any length of time, and persons have been killed or injured, no peace can be made until the friends of the killed and wounded, in the latter case the wounded themselves, have received compensation from the enemy. Each side must pay the other for damage inflicted. This reciprocal payment, if I may so call it, is shown in the word used to express both the act and the action. On Duke of York it is *wekul*. On New Britain it is *warakul*. *Kul* = buy, pay: the *we* on Duke of York, and the *wara* on New Britain denotes reciprocal action. Thus, *wekul* and *warakul* literally mean paying each other. The side which was originally wronged receives any sum mutually agreed upon in satisfaction of the original wrong out of which the war sprang, in addition to payment for whatever injury may have been inflicted during the fighting. This money is paid, not out of any public fund, but by the parties principally concerned. While so much as a single wound is not atoned for, peace cannot be considered likely.

Because of the lack of all constituted authority among the people, simple and ordinary quarrels lead to serious ones. There is no one man vested with power or authority who can say "cease," when any quarrel has reached a certain stage. All peace is arranged by common agreement, mutual consent, not by personal authority. Take the following example:—

To Meli and To Delu were two boys. To Meli put an iron ramrod into the fire, and when it was hot he drew it across To Delu's bare back. To Delu was incensed at this, and at once ran to the beach and cut down some crotons belonging to To Rumu. To Rumu was angry at the loss of his crotons, and he went along the beach and smashed a canoe belonging to another man. The owner of the canoe went and broke two canoes belonging to another man. The owner of the two canoes burnt down another man's house, and even more mischief still sprang out of To Meli's practical joking. All now thought that the matter should be settled. To Meli had to pay To Rumu for the crotons which To Delu had cut down, because by burning To Delu he had been the cause of the crotons being cut down. To Delu who had been burnt, had to pay for the broken canoe, because he, by cutting down the crotons, had caused the canoe to be broken. To Rumu by breaking the one canoe had caused the two canoes to be broken, and so he had to pay for them. The man who smashed the two canoes caused the house to be burnt down so he had to pay for that. So every account had to be settled until they found a man whose property had been injured, but who had injured none in return. His claim would then be paid and the matter ends. It will be seen that the boy who was burnt got nothing for the injury done to him. However, by cutting down the crotons he had forced To Meli to pay for them, and in causing him to lose money by such payment he found a little satisfaction; he had also involved others in loss of property which caused them to be angry with To Meli, whose position was an unenviable one for some time after. . . .

All claims are adjusted by the popular voice, i.e. all have a voice in the settlement. A violent man however, may frighten an offender into paying an extravagant price. As a rule, when atonement is made, the price of an article destroyed is fairly met. It sometimes happens that the injured suffer considerable loss. Women and young people who are not well backed by their friends will nearly always lose. Apart from force, there is little or no justice. Public opinion is a great factor in the adjustment of all disputes, but, as already shown, a violent man may over-ride all public opinion.

The manner in which public opinion is appealed to is as follows:—

The people live in families, i.e. father and mother with their children, and as many of their kinsmen who may wish to live with them; each family or kinsmen having separate houses of their own, and all the houses may be enclosed by one fence, or each house may have its own fence, but erected very close to each other. Hence if one member is injured, all the family know it at once. If kinsmen are living at a distance they are informed as soon as possible of the occurrence. A man's own kin are bound to stand by him even though he be altogether in the wrong. They gather together and make a great noise, shouting and threatening the wrong-doer. This attracts the attention of the neighbors who run together to see what is the matter. The injured man and his kinsmen, together with their following, which may include as many as like to see a row, go near the place where the offender lives, and send one of their number to him and his friends (who have gathered together, on the first sign of a disturbance) with terms of settlement. It may take hours to arrange the terms, two or three messengers continually going to and fro between the parties, until the affair is settled. There is no lack of communication. All the townsfolk, not personally concerned in the quarrel, are ready for the office of go-between, and seem very happy in being so employed. One, or perhaps two or three of them, may be selected, but these are recognized by both parties as fully accredited; but they have no power to dictate terms of peace. They are simply messengers from one party to the other, and the parties themselves must decide whether the terms proposed are to be accepted or rejected. The initiative is always taken by the injured person if he is able, if not then by the nearest kinsman who may be present. In the case of a woman or a child being injured, the husband, uncle (i.e. mother's brother), father, or nearest kinsman or kinsmen present, take the matter up on their behalf.

The principal parties on either side are, of course, the injured person and the wrong-doer, but they are considerably influenced by their friends and following, though if the offended man chooses to accept the compensation offered, he may do so even against the advice of his friends. The affair generally takes the form of a haggling bargain. A is injured by B. He sends a go-between to B with the message that he will be satisfied with, say, ten fathoms of Tambu. B gives the messenger five fathoms. This is rejected and the money goes back. B adds a little more, and this is repeated until he sends his ultimatum, that he will not give another shell. This is generally accepted, but if not, any of the methods of redress already mentioned may be resorted to.

If the quarrel cannot be settled without a fight, either party can obtain the help of a number of men by paying them for it, while the neutrality of any influential man, who is supposed to be likely to favor the other side, may be secured by a sufficient bribe. This is called *vitar ia* = "tying or binding him." . . .

The possession of Tambu has a very important influence on the lives of the New Britain people. Thus:

It establishes personal right to property, and the right to alienate that property by sale or gift independent of any one else. The whole town or family may be against the sale or gift, but has only the power to protest and cannot prevent it if the person is determined to sell. This right extends even to women and children. The writer has purchased land (for mission purposes) from women who insisted upon selling even against the wish of their friends. The sale completed, its validity has been recognized. I have known persons who have objected to the sale of a thing make a present to the owner of a fathom, and sometimes more, of Tambu to induce the owner not to sell. A native generally listens to that argument.

It makes the people frugal and industrious. No man is held in greater contempt than a spendthrift. In point of fact such a person is scarcely known. Nothing is wasted. In purchasing, a man will only buy just as much of anything as he requires for the time being. Hence we see no wholesale business done. One venture at a time is the business maxim of the New Britain people. Plantation produce is the one source of wealth for the inland people. A bunch of bananas will bring, according to size, from a quarter to a whole fathom of Tambu. Cocoa-nuts from sixty to one hundred per fathom. Hence the inland people are nearly always at work at their plantations. They are either in them, or preparing something in connection with them, or selling the produce. Market is held on the coast every third day in a large number of places. Those who live very far back inland have their inland markets where they sell to those nearer the beach, who in turn sell what they buy to the coast people. These markets are so arranged that two are seldom held near each other on the same day. A man taking his produce to one market today, may take more to another tomorrow if he is so disposed, and it is safe for him to do so. The coast people meet the inland people at these markets with their fish and articles of European manufacture, and either sell them for Tambu or barter for food and other things only obtainable in the country.

On the coast, fishing, in addition to plantations, is a source of income. The fishtrap is unique, and takes two or three weeks to make, and when finished it is quite a work of art. It costs in all, including the cost of food and wages for those who assist, and the cable to anchor it by— often 500 fathoms long—about six or seven fathoms. Men work from early morning till late at night making these traps. By the time the traps are made plantations require attention. Only those who know nothing about the New Britain people will call them lazy. After a residence of nearly eight years among them the writer has arrived at the conclusion that, comparatively speaking, they are as busy as Europeans are. There are and have been parts of Duke of York, New Ireland, and New Britain where enforced idleness and therefore want and wretchedness existed in the most debasing degree. But when Christianity has stepped in and made peace where peace was scarcely ever known, idleness gave place to industry and wretchedness to comparative comfort and wealth. The innate industry of the people shone forth the moment property and life became in any degree safe. I have known a man make fifty fathoms of Tambu during the fishing season, and ten or twelve fathoms from his plantations.

It makes them a commercial people. By the aid of intermediaries their commercial transactions extend to places they have never visited. But they never, or very seldom, trust their money with the intermediary. He buys the article with his own money and sells it to them for theirs, making what profit he can by the transaction. In the old heathen days Kinawanua people, a town on Duke of York Island, could go to one town on New Ireland and there trade for goods from that place and sell their own. Waira, another town, had its place also. Nakukuru people could cross over to three places on New Britain and do their trading. It is needless to say that through the establishment of mission stations in each town, trade is now carried on between New Britain and other parts of the group with almost perfect freedom. A bargain once made and concluded is seldom or never disputed. All disputation and haggling is done previous to the conclusion of the bargain.

While Tambu has brought some benefit to the New Britain people it has not been an unmixed blessing. To it, or rather to love for it, may be attributed in no small degree their intense selfishness and their glaring ingratitude. The expression of gratitude often leads to a little expense. Hence gratitude is too expensive a luxury for a New Britain man to be acquainted with. A spirit and life which is unselfish must often suffer loss. A New Britain man cannot afford that. A people whose greatest love is reserved for money, and whose highest aim is to get money, is an exceedingly hard-hearted and an intensely selfish people.

There are other matters closely connected with this shell-money. Its influence is supposed to extend even to the next life. There is not a custom connected with life or death in which this money does not play a great and a leading part.

35. IFUGAO LAW [14]

BY R. F. BARTON

SOURCES AND STATUS OF IFUGAO LAW

THE Ifugaos have no form of writing: there is, consequently, no written law. They have no form of political government: there is, therefore,

[14] Extracted from pages 11 to 105 of "Ifugao Law," *University of California Publications in American Archæology and Ethnology,* volume 15, part 1, 1919.

no constitutional or statutory law. Inasmuch as they have no courts or judges, there is no law based on judicial decisions.

Ifugao law has two sources of origin: taboo (which is essentially religious) and custom. The customary law is the more important from the greater frequency of its application.

Relation of taboo to law.—The Ifugao word for taboo is *paniyu*. The root, which appears under the varying forms *iyu, iho, iyao,* and *ihao,* means in general "evil" or "bad." The prefix *pan* denotes instrumentality or manner. The word *paniyu* means both by derivation and in use, "bad way of doing," or "evil way." By far the greater number of taboos have their origin in magic. A very large number of them concern the individual, or those closely related to him by blood ties, and for this reason have no place in a discussion of law. Thus a pregnant woman may not wear a string of beads, since the beads form a closed circle and so have a magic tendency to close her body and cause difficult childbirth. This, however, is not a matter that concerns anybody else, and so could be of no interest at law. It is taboo for brothers to defecate near each other, but only they are harmed thereby, and the matter is consequently not of legal interest.

The breaking of a taboo that concerns the person or possessions of an individual of another family is a crime. The following instances will illustrate:

In nearly all districts of Ifugao it is taboo for persons of other districts to pass through a rice field when it is being harvested. It is also taboo for foreigners to enter a village when that village is observing its ceremonial idleness, *tungul*, at the close of harvest time. One who broke this taboo would be subject to fine. In case it were believed that the fine could not be collected, he would be in danger of the lance.

It is taboo to blackguard, to use certain language, and to do certain things in the presence of one's own kin of the opposite sex that are of the degrees of kinship within which marriage is forbidden or in the presence of another and such kindred of his, or to make any except the most delicately concealed references to matters connected with sex, sexual intercourse, and reproduction. Even these delicately concealed references are permissible only in cases of real necessity. The breaking of this taboo is a serious offense. One who broke the taboo in the presence of his own female kin would not be punished except in so far as the contempt of his fellows is a punishment. In Kiangan, before the establishment of foreign government, breaking the taboo in the presence of another and of his female kin of the forbidden degrees is said to have been sometimes punished by the lance.

It is taboo for one who knows of a man's death to ask a relative of the dead man if the man is dead. The breaking of this taboo is punishable by fine. . . .

A third person may make no remark in the presence of kin of the opposite sex as to the fit of the girl's clothing; as to her beauty; nor may he refer to her lover, nor play the lover's harp. Many ordinary things must be called by other than their ordinary names. Even the aged priests who officiate at a birth feast must refer in their prayers to the fœtus about to be born as "the friend" and to the placenta as "his blanket." A great number of things are forbidden in the presence of kindred of opposite sex that would not shock even the most prudish of our own people. The third taboo seems to be aimed against the bandying or the taking in vain of the name of the dead. . . .

General principles of the Ifugao legal system.—Its personal character. Society does not punish injuries to itself except as the censure of public opinion is a punishment. This follows naturally from the fact that there is no organized society. It is only when an injury committed by a person or family falls on another person or family that the injury is punished formally.

Collective responsibility.—Not only the individual who commits an act but his kin, in proportion to the nearness of their kinship, are responsible for the act. Their responsibility is slightly less than his. This applies not only to crimes but to debts and civil injuries.

Collective procedure.—Legal procedure is by and between families; therefore a family should be "strong to demand and strong to resist demands." *A member of an Ifugao family assists in the punishment of offenders against any other member of his family, and resists the punishment of members of his family by other families.* A number of circumstances affect the ardor with which he enters into procedures in which a relative is concerned and the extent to which he will go into them. Among these are: (*a*) the nearness or remoteness of his relationship to the relative concerned in the action; (*b*) relationship to the other principal in the action; (*c*) the loyalty to the family group of the relative principally concerned in the procedure and the extent to which this relative discharges his duty to it; (*d*) evidence in the case bearing on the correctness of the relative's position in the controversy.

A corollary of the above principle.—Since legal procedure is between families, and never between individuals, nor between a family and an individual, crimes of brother or sister against brother or sister go unpunished. The family of the two individuals is identical. *A family cannot proceed against itself.* But in the case of incest between a father and a daughter the father might be punished by the girl's mother's family on the ground that he had committed a crime against a member of that family. It is true that just as great an injury would have been committed against the family of the father, since the relationship of the daughter to that family is the same as to her mother's family. But the father, the perpetrator of the crime, being a nearer relative of his own family than his daughter, his family certainly would not take active steps against him. Were the crime a less disgraceful one, the father's kin would probably contest his penalty.

The family unity must at all hazards be preserved.—Clemency is shown the remoter kin in order to secure their loyalty to the family group. A large unified family group is in the ideal position of being "strong to demand and strong to resist demands." The family is the only thing of the nature of an organization that the Ifugao has, and he cherishes it accordingly.

Collective recipiency of punishment.—Just as the family group is collectively responsible for the delinquencies of its members, but in less degree than the delinquent himself, so may punishment be meted out to individuals of the group other than the actual culprit, although naturally it is preferred to punish the actual culprit; and so may debts or indemnities be collected from them. But only those individuals that are of the nearest degree of kinship may be held responsible; cousins may not *legally* be punished if there be brothers or sisters. . . .

GO-BETWEENS

The go-between.—No transaction of importance of any sort between persons of different families is consummated without the intervention of a middle man, or go-between, called *monbaga* (bespeaker) in civil transactions; and *monkalun* (admonisher) in criminal cases.

Go-betweens are used commonly in (*a*) buying and selling of family property of whatever kind or value; (*b*) buying and selling of animals and the more valuable personal property, except chickens, and in some cases pigs; (*c*) the borrowing of money or other wealth; (*d*) marriage proposals and the negotiating of marriage contracts; (*e*) collection of debts; (*f*) all steps connected with the *balal*, such as pawn of rice fields, or their redemption; (*g*) demands for damages to property or persons; (*h*) the buying back of heads lost in war, the ransoming of the kidnaped, or the making of peace.

The go-between is the principal witness to a transaction. For his services he receives pay which is fixed to a fair degree of exactness for a particular service. This pay ranges from a piece of meat to a fee of twenty or twenty-five pesos.

Responsibility of go-betweens.—Go-betweens are responsible to both parties to a transaction, for the correct rendering of tenders, offers, and payments. Their word binds only themselves, however—not their principals. Go-betweens are not agents of one party more than another. They are supposed to be impartial, and interested only in consummating the transaction involved in order to get their fee.

Thus, suppose that A sends B as a go-between to sell a field to C, a man of another district. B finds that he cannot sell the field for the price A asked for it, and, anxious to consummate a sale and so collect his fee, he agrees to sell the field to C for a lower price than that asked by A.

In such a case as this, B is responsible to C in case A refuses to abide by C's agreement to sell. C has the right to collect damages.

The oriental propensity to "squeeze" is proverbial. It is condoned in law—one might almost say legitimized, provided it be not found out. Thus:

A sends B to Nueva Vizcaya to buy a carabao. The regular commission for this service is ten pesos, the agent to deliver a living carabao to the principal, and to be responsible for the value if the carabao die on the route. This, the usual agreement, holds between them. A furnishes B with eighty pesos with which to purchase the animal. B returns with the animal, representing that he paid seventy pesos for it, when, as a matter of fact, he paid out sixty pesos, thus gaining ten pesos "squeeze."

If A finds out that B paid only sixty pesos for the carabao, the only thing he can do is to collect the ten pesos difference between what A paid and what he said he paid. He cannot assess punitive damages.

Conditions relieving a go-between of responsibility.—An act of God or the acts of a public enemy relieve a go-between or an agent from responsibility. Thus an agent sent to purchase an animal in *baliwan* (the stranger country) is under obligation to deliver it alive. But if it be struck by lightning, or if the carabao be taken away from him by enemies, and he has a wound to bear witness that he offered due resistance to them; or, in case he has no wound, if he has witnesses or good proof of the fact that the enemy was so superior in force as to make resistance foolhardy, he cannot be held for payment of the animal. . . .

PENALTIES

The Ifugaos have two punishments for crime: the death penalty and fine. These punishments are inflicted and executed by the offended person and his kin.

Nature and reckoning of fines.—Fines are of two sorts: fines of "tens," *bakid*, and fines of "sixes," *na-onom*, each unit of the ten or six being a portion of the whole fine. The different parts of the fine go to different people. Oftentimes sticks, knots, or notches are used to assist in calculation. In Banaue and neighboring districts these aids to calculation are also kept as a record. The unit payments grow successively smaller from the first to the last.

The first unit of any series is called *pu-u*, meaning "base." It is of the greatest value, and goes to the injured individual. The second payment, sometimes, goes to the go-between. In that case, the kin of the injured man take all the rest. If the fee of the go-between be provided for outside of the fine, the kin of the injured man take all except the *pu-u*, the first unit. This is but just, since they have backed their kinsman in his action against the offender, have perchance risked their lives in his cause, and also stand ready at all times to help pay any fines that others may assess against him.

The second, and sometimes the third and fourth units, are called *haynub di pu-u*, meaning "followers of the base." They are of less value than the *pu-u*. Then follow units consisting, each, of four irons (spear-heads, axes, knives). These units are called *natauwinan*. Then come units of three irons each, called *natuku;* then units of two irons each, called *nunbadi;* then units of one iron each, called *na-oha.* In the case of fines composed of six units, there is usually no *haynub*.

The Malay does nothing without first thoroughly talking it over. After a payment has been tentatively consented to by the offender and his family, there yet remain many conferences with the go-between before everything is arranged. An uninitiated white man on seeing a group of these people, squatted in a circle, moving little sticks about, and in heated discussion, might think they were playing some primitive but absorbing native game. And, I am not sure that the attitude of their minds is very different! . . .

CIRCUMSTANCES WHICH AFFECT PENALTY

Certain circumstances, namely, criminal responsibility, alienship, kinship, confession, and the relative rank of offender and offended, affect penalty, either as to its severity or as to the likelihood of its being inflicted at all.

Moral turpitude not a factor.—Moral turpitude, which plays no small part in our own law in determining punishment, seems not to enter into the consideration of Ifugao law. Thus, such crimes as incest between brother and sister, parricide, matricide, fratricide, and treason against one's family, all go unpunished. Even the betrayal of a co-villager into the hands of the enemy subjects the offender to only a third degree of likelihood of being punished. These crimes probably go unpunished in accordance with the following correlated fundaments of Ifugao society: Legal procedure is conducted by and between families; the family unit is the most precious thing in Ifugao social life; *family unity must, at all hazards, be preserved.* In the case of a murder accomplished by treachery, as for example, the killing of a guest, the moral turpitude involved might perhaps hasten punishment—it might even increase its severity in that the kin of the murdered person might retaliate on a greater number of those concerned in the murder. But such an abuse of hospitality appears never to have occurred.

Another reason why what we consider moral turpitude does not enter into punishment is that treachery, ambush, and accomplishment by superior force are the rule, not only in commission of crime, but also in perfectly legal capital executions and seizures of property.

PENAL RESPONSIBILITY

As between principals and their accomplices and accessories, Ifugao law recognizes only gradations in likelihood of punishment. The penalty is the same for all of them; but very frequently the offense is considered as having been expiated by the punishment of those whose responsibility for it is greatest, and the rest go free.

The nungolat, or principal.—The *nungolat* (he who was strong) is the conceiver, planner, and director of an offense. He may or may not take an active part in its commission. Whether or not he does so, he is considered to be responsible for it in the highest degree. He is, of all who take part in the offense, the most likely to be punished.

The following example, continued through several succeeding sections, shows the various degrees of criminal responsibility, and the corresponding degrees of likelihood of punishment:

A decides to avenge the death of a kinsman. He consequently calls a number of his kinsmen and proposes a war expedition to take the head of Z, an enemy concerned in the death of the murdered kinsman, in another village. They agree. A calls the family priests to his house to perform the necessary religious preliminaries to setting out on a head-hunting expedition. The ceremonies are performed, and the omen of the bile sac promises well. But, just before starting, some accident happens to A, which the priests attribute to the sorcery of the enemy. A consequently does not accompany the expedition. He is, notwithstanding, the *nungolat*, and is more likely to be the object of vengeance than any other, should the crime be accomplished.

The tombok, or "thrower."—In offenses in which a spear is thrown, he who throws the effective spear is called the *tombok*. His responsibility for the crime is second to that of the *nungolat*, as is also his likelihood of being punished.

Iba'n di nungolat, the *"companions of the one who was strong."*— Those who assist in the commission of a crime by reënforcing, accompanying, assisting, backing, giving aid and comfort to the committer thereof, or furnishing anything needful to the consummation of the crime incur the next lesser degree of criminal responsibility and of likelihood of being punished to those of the conceiver and committer of the crime.

The montudol, *"shower,"* or *informer*.—One who gives a person in the act of committing a crime information necessary to the successful carrying out of his intent, is guilty in the same degree as are persons of the preceding paragraph.

Thus, continuing the illustration started above, suppose that B, C, D, E, F, G, H, and I go to take the head of A's enemy and theirs. They meet O, a co-villager of Z, the man whose head they want to take, and ask him regarding Z's whereabouts. The fact could not be otherwise than patent to O, that a head-hunting party was addressing him. He answers truthfully that Z is in his sweet-potato field, and that the party may reach the field by such and such by-path, without their being seen by Z's kin or co-villagers. The party follows O's directions. B spears Z.

B is the *tombok*; C, D, E, F, G, H, and I are the "companions of the one who was strong," and O is the *montudol*. . . .

The relation of intent to criminal responsibility.—*Gulad*, or intent, is probably the greatest single factor in determining penal responsibility. Thus:

A deed committed without intent, and without carelessness, is excused. One has not, usually, even to make restitution for the injury done. Thus, in the case of a bolo flying out of a man's hand, and putting out the eye of another, no damages were assessed. An enormous number of men, every year, are injured in the free-for-all scrambles over sacrificed carabaos. Many of these injuries result in stiff joints; some of them in deaths. In no case, not even in the case of death, is a payment demanded. Suppose that in the chase a number of hunters have surrounded a wild boar. The boar charges one of them. This man leaps backward, and, at the same time, draws back his spear to throw it at the boar. In so doing, he stabs a companion behind him with the shod end of the spear handle. This is not an uncommon accident. The others of the party are witnesses that the killing was purely accidental (*naloktat*). No fine is assessed; but the killer, to show that he is sorry, usually assists in the funeral feast. Of course, if there were no witnesses, and if there were a possible motive to complicate matters, the ending of the case might not be so happy.

Suppose that a number of men are throwing at a target with their spears. A child runs in the way, and is killed. One-half the usual fine for manslaughter is assessed on the ground that the thrower was careless in that he did not make sure before he threw the spear that such an accident could not occur. In this case there was an absence of intent; but carelessness was present.

A man kills a neighbor at night, acting under the impression that he is killing an enemy seeking his life. He is subjected to a much heavier fine than if he had killed him through carelessness, since there is present both the intent to kill, although not criminal, and carelessness in that he did not make sure at whom he was casting his spear. . . .

Rank and standing in the community.—This is probably the greatest single factor in determining the severity of punishment in cases where a crime is punishable by fine. But the aggressiveness and the war footing of the two parties to the controversy enter even here to an astounding degree.

In the Kiangan-Maggok area, there are three grades of fines—the highest for the punishment of crimes of one *kadangyang*, or rich man, against another; a medium grade for crimes of persons of the *tumok*, or middle class, against each other; and a third and lowest grade for the *nawatwat*, the poverty stricken. Each lower grade of fine is a little more than half the next higher one.

In the Kababuyan area, there are five grades of fines—one for the very rich, one for the fairly rich, one for the middle class, one for the poor, one for the poverty stricken. In Sapao and in Asin, there are four grades.

So long as both offender and offended are of the same class, there is no trouble about determining the fine proper in a given case. But when they are of different classes, the case is not so simple, and the factors of fighting strength and personality enter.

Suppose that R, a rich man, commits adultery against P, a poor man. P sends a go-between to demand the highest grade of fine for this crime—that is, the grade which *kadangyang* pay. R does not deny the crime, but states that he considers the payment of the fine that is due one rich man from another preposterous. He states that he is willing to pay the fine proper to the poorer class. To this P replies that he did not begin this action for the purpose of getting money, but for the purpose of so punishing R as to make a repetition of the crime improbable. There are three possible endings in such a case:

(*a*) P's kin represent to him that they cannot afford to have war with R;

that R's people hold a lot of debts over their heads; that should R prove obdurate, and should the affair end in a lance throwing, R's people would wipe them off the earth. They advise P to be satisfied with the lowest grade of fine. He agrees.

(*b*) P and R compromise on the grade of fine that is midway between their stations; that is, the fine of the middle class. In Kiangan this is the usual settlement.

(*c*) P shows such *bungot* (wrath and ferocity) that R's kin advise him to pay the larger fine. They point out that the fine is a small matter as compared with the loss of life, and state that there is no telling what this poverty-stricken but rampant dog will do. This settlement is not uncommon in the Kiangan area, where the poor people have a great deal of pride and bravery, but rare in other parts of Ifugao.

Aside from other matters, the diplomacy and tact of the go-between would have a great deal to do toward determining which of these contingencies would result.

It is extremely hard to make a general statement as to fines when offender and offended are of different classes. It may safely be said that the fines assessed average the amount midway between the fines proper to the two classes concerned. Thus, when a poor man offends a rich man, and when a rich man offends a poor man, the average of the fines assessed equals approximately the fine assessed for injuries within the middle class. In questions in which rich and middle class persons are involved, the fines approximate an amount half way between the fines of the rich and of the middle classes.

Importance of influential position and personality.—The fact has already been mentioned that Ifugao administration of justice is remarkably personal in nature. We have just seen to what an extent personality and war-footing enter into the infliction of fines when offender and offended are of different classes. Nowhere can a man of magnetism and force reap greater benefit from these qualities, relatively speaking, than in an Ifugao controversy. The fact stares us in the face in every phase of Ifugao law, especially in procedure. . . .

THE TAKING OF LIFE

The Ifugao has one general law, which with a few notable exceptions he applies to killings, be they killings in war, murders, or executions which public opinion would pronounce justifiable and legal. That law is: *A life must be paid by a life.* Let us pass now to a consideration of various classes of the takings of human life.

Executions justifiable by Ifugao law.—Public opinion or custom, or both, justify the taking of a life in punishment for the following crimes:

sorcery; murder; persistent and willful refusal to pay a debt when there is the ability to pay; adultery discovered *in flagrante;* theft by one of a foreign district; refusal to pay a fine assessed for crime or for injury suffered. But even though custom and public opinion justify the administration of the extreme penalty in these cases, the kin of the murdered man do not, in most cases, consider the killing justified. There are innumerable circumstances that complicate a given case. Was the sorcery proven or only suspected? Was it a murder that the man committed; or was he justified in the killing? Would not the debtor have come to his right mind had his creditor waited a little longer; and did the creditor approach him in the right way with reference to the debt? Did not the woman make advances in the adultery case that no self-respecting male could turn down? Was not the indemnity assessed too large or otherwise improper; or did the injured party wait long enough for the payment? These and a thousand other questions may arise with respect to the various cases.

If the death penalty be inflicted by persons of a foreign district, it is sure to be looked upon as a murder.

At feasts and gatherings about the "bowl that cheers" and especially in drunken brawls, an unavenged killing, no matter what the circumstances, is likely to be brought up as a reflection upon the bravery or manhood of the living kin, and so urge them to the avenging of what was really a justified execution.

Murder, sorcery, and a refusal to pay the fine for adultery justify the infliction of the death penalty even on a kinsman if he is not too close a relative. An execution of one kinsman by another is not so likely to be avenged as is justifiable execution by one outside the family. . . .

Hibul or homicide.—The Ifugao law clearly recognizes several grades of homicide.

(*a*) The taking of life when there is an entire absence of both intent and carelessness. As for example, in the case already cited, when a party of hunters have a wild boar at bay. The boar, as there stated, charges the most advanced of the hunters, and in retreating backwards, the latter jabs one of his companions with the shod point of his spear handle. There is no penalty for such a taking of life.

(*b*) The taking of life when there is clearly an absence of intent, but a degree of carelessness. For example, a number of men are throwing spears at a mark. A child runs in the way, and is killed. The penalty is a fine varying from one-third to two-thirds the amount of the full fine for homicide according to the degree of carelessness.

(*c*) Intentional taking of the life of another, under the impression that he is an enemy when in reality he is a co-villager or a companion. In case the killer can make the family of the slain understand the circumstances, only a fine is assessed. This fine is called *labod*. If the killer be unrelated to the slain, the full amount of the *labod* is demanded; if related, the amount is usually lessened.

Example: Dumauwat of Baay was irrigating his fields at night. Some of his companions told him that there were some head-hunters from an enemy village near. In the darkness, Dumauwat encountered another man, Likyayu, the betrothed of his daughter. He asked him who was there. On account of the noise of water falling from the rice fields, Likyayu did not hear the inquiry, and said nothing. Dumauwat speared him. Likyayu cried out. Dumauwat recognized his voice, and carried him home. He furnished animals for sacrifice to secure Likyayu's recovery. Likyayu recovered. Had he died, Dumauwat would have been called on for the full amount of the fine; but had Likyayu been *firmly* engaged to Dumauwat's daughter, that is, had the *bango* ceremony been performed, the full amount of the *labod* fine would not have been demanded, since the relationship would have been an extenuating circumstance.

(*d*) The taking of life by persons in a brawl or by an intoxicated or insane person. In case the slain died before his slayer could agree to provide animals for sacrifice, the latter would probably be killed by the kin of the slain if he were of a foreign district. He might be killed if a non-related co-villager. He would be fined the *labod* if a kinsman. He would probably go scot free if a brother or uncle.

Example: A of Longa became insanely drunk at a feast at the house of his brother Gimbungan. He attempted to embrace the comely daughter of Gimbungan, his niece. Gimbungan tried to quiet him, and in so doing aroused his ire. He drew his spear menacingly, and in so doing pierced the girl— who was at his back—with the shod point at the end. She died. A was properly penitent when he sobered, and furnished animals for sacrifice. The fine of *labod* was not, however, demanded of him. This was about thirty-five or forty years ago. Considerable feeling exists between the two branches of the family to this day, owing to this occurrence.

The burden rests upon the slayer in the above cases to show that the killing was accidental or that he was so drunk as to have utterly lost his reason. The absence of a motive is a great help to him in this. If he has ever had a serious altercation with the slain, in the absence of controverting evidence, the presumption is likely to be that the killing was intentional, and that he has been "feigning friendship in order to kill by *ugâ* (treachery)." . . .

Special liability of the givers of certain feasts.—The givers of *uyauwe* or *hagabi* feasts (glorified general welfare feasts to which great numbers of people come) are responsible for wounds or deaths that occur at these feasts. When a man decides to initiate himself and his wife into the ranks of the *kadangyang* by giving one of these feasts, he appoints one of the old priests of his family to perform the *tikman* ceremonies. These ceremonies are sacrifices to the various classes of deities whose special function is the "tying up" of men's stomachs and passions. Prayers are addressed to these deities that a little food satisfy the guest that attends the feast, to the end that the giver be not eaten out of house and home; that a little rice wine suffice to intoxicate the people; that the passions of men be tied up to the end that no quarrels or frays occur; that no rice-wine jars or gongs be broken; that no accidents occur—in short, that the whole feast pass off smoothly. The duties of the *manikam* (the priest who performs these ceremonies) are rather arduous. To say nothing of the ceremonies he conducts, he must fast for a number of days and must observe a number of taboos. He receives rather a large fee for these services. And, indeed, their importance, in the eyes of the Ifugaos, and the legal responsibility he incurs, certainly justify a large fee.

The *manikam* priests are jointly responsible with the giver of the feast for accidents or violence that may occur. This liability of the giver of the feast for wounds or loss of life is based on the supposition that if he had not given the feast the wound would not have occurred; and possibly that he gave the feast with the motive of bringing about such an occurrence. The liability of the *manikam* is based on the supposition that there must have been a remissness on his part in his religious duties, else the accident or loss would never have occurred. The following is an actual instance that would indicate that this provision of the law is an incipient employer's liability provision.

Malingan of Pindungan, many years ago, gathered together his kin and friends, performed the preliminary feasts, and went to Payauan to make a *hagabi* (lounging bench, the insignium of the *kadangyang* class). They made a very large *hagabi* that weighed nearly a ton. In helping to carry it across the river two men were carried downstream by the current and drowned. Demand was made on Malingan and the *manikam* of the feast for the *labod* fine. It was paid, and that is the reason Malingan's descendants are not wealthier today, for formerly Malingan was one of the wealthiest men of the district. . . .

The labod, fine assessed for homicide.—This fine is paid to the family of the slain. For the *kadangyang*, or wealthy class, the full fine consists of ten portions or divisions, totaling 975 pesos in the case tabulated below. . . .

PUTTING ANOTHER IN THE POSITION OF AN ACCOMPLICE

The tokom, or fine for compromising another.—He who, voluntarily or involuntarily, puts another in the position of an accomplice, or in such a light that he might be regarded as being an accomplice in the commission of a crime, and so be liable to punishment as such, must pay the person so injured a fine, called *tokom*. It may almost be said that he who causes another person's name to be prominently mentioned or bandied in connection with a crime must pay this fine.

The following are instances in which a *tokom* would be demanded:

A of another district comes to the house of B, and is received by B as a guest. While he is going home and while he is in the outskirts of the district he is speared by C, a neighbor of B's or a resident of the same district. B must force C to pay a *tokom*.

B steals or illegally confiscates property belonging to A. C sees B in the act. He demands a *tokom*—in this case it may be the bolo or spear that B is carrying—and so puts himself "on record" as not having been an accomplice. But he says nothing about the crime unless it come to light that he was a witness of it. In this case he proves by the *tokom* that he received that he had no connection with it. As a matter of practice it would seem that a gift received from the thief would tend to lead the witness to conceal the crime.

A gives an *uyauve* feast. At the attendant drink feast B in a drunken brawl kills C. A and the *manikam* D must demand a *tokom* from B in order to clear their reputations. . . .

One who is put in a position in which a *tokom* is due him must collect the *tokom*. It is not sufficient that he demand the payment of it—he must enforce the payment. Otherwise he will be considered by the kin of the injured as having been an accomplice, and liable to punishment accordingly. . . .

THE MONKALUN OR GO-BETWEEN

Nature of his duties.—The office of the *monkalun* is the most important one to be found in Ifugao society. The *monkalun* is a whole court, completely equipped, in embryo. He is judge, prosecuting and defending counsel, and the court record.[15] His duty and his interest are for a peaceful settlement. He receives a fee, called *lukba* or *liwa*. To the end of peaceful settlement he exhausts every art of Ifugao diplomacy. He

[15] The word *monkalun* comes from the root *kalun*, meaning *advise*. The Ifugao word has the double sense, too, of our word *advise*, as used in the following sentences, "I have the honor to advise you of your appointment" and "I advise you not to do that."

wheedles, coaxes, flatters, threatens, drives, scolds, insinuates. He beats down the demands of the plaintiffs or prosecution, and bolsters up the proposals of the defendants until a point be reached at which the two parties may compromise. If the culprit or accused be not disposed to listen to reason and runs away or "shows fight" when approached, the *monkalun* waits till the former ascends into his house, follows him, and, *war-knife in hand*, sits in front of him and compels him to listen.

The *monkalun* should not be closely related to either party in a controversy. He may be a distant relative of either one of them. The *monkalun* has no authority. All that he can do is to act as a peace making go-between. His only power is in his art of persuasion, his tact and his skillful playing on human emotions and motives. Were he closely related to the plaintiff, he would have no influence with the defendant, and *mutatis mutandis* the opposite would be true.

Ultimately in any state the last appeal is to a death-dealing weapon. For example, in our own society a man owes a debt which he does not pay. Action is brought to sell his property to pay the debt. If he resists, he is in danger of death at the hands of an agent of the law. Much more is he in danger if he resists punishment for crime. The same is true in the Ifugao society. The lance is back of every demand of importance, and sometimes it seems hungry.

An Ifugao's pride as well as his self-interest—one might almost say his self-preservation—demands that he shall collect debts that are owed him, and that he shall punish injuries or crimes against himself. Did he not do so he would become the prey of his fellows. No one would respect him. Let there be but one debt owed him which he makes no effort to collect; let there be but one insult offered him that goes unpunished, and in the drunken babbling attendant on every feast or social occasion, he will hear himself accused of cowardice and called a woman.

On the other hand, self-interest and self-respect demand that the accused shall not accept punishment too tamely or with undue haste, and that he shall not pay an exorbitant fine. If he can manage to beat the demands of the complainant down below those usually met in like cases, he even gains in prestige. But the *monkalun* never lets him forget that the lance has been scoured and sharpened for him, and that he walks and lives in daily danger of it.

The accuser is usually not over anxious to kill the accused. Should he do so, the probabilities are that the kin of the accused would avenge the death, in which case he, the slayer, would be also slain. The kin of each party are anxious for a peaceable settlement, if such can be honorably brought about. They have feuds a-plenty on their hands already.

Neighbors and co-villagers do not want to see their neighborhood torn by internal dissension and thus weakened as to the conduct of warfare against enemies. All these forces make for a peaceful settlement.

It is the part of the accused to dally with danger for a time, however, and at last to accede to the best terms he can get, if they be within reason.

TESTIMONY

Litigants do not confront each other.—From the time at which a controversy is formally entered into, the principals and their kin are on a basis of theoretical—perhaps I ought to say religious—enmity. A great number of taboos keep them apart. Diplomatic relations between the two parties have been broken off and all business pertaining to the case is transacted through the third party, the *monkalun*. He hears the testimony that each side brings forward to support its contention. Through him each controversant is confronted with the testimony of the other. It is greatly to the interest of the *monkalun* to arrange a peaceful settlement, not only because he usually receives a somewhat larger fee in such case, but because the peaceful settlement of cases in which he is mediator builds up a reputation for him, so that he is frequently called and so can earn many fees. To the end of arranging this peaceful settlement, the *monkalun* reports to each party to the controversy the strong points of the testimony in favor of the other party, and oftentimes neglects the weaknesses.

There are no oaths or formalities in giving of testimony.

ORDEALS

Cases in which employed.—In criminal cases in which the accused persistently denies his guilt, and sometimes in case of disputes over property the ownership of which is doubtful, and in cases of disputes over the division line between fields, ordeals or trials are resorted to. The challenge to an ordeal may come from either the accuser or the accused. Refusal to accept a challenge means a loss of the case, and the challenger proceeds as if he had won the case.

If the accused comes unscathed from the ordeal, he has the right to collect from his accuser the fine for false accusation.

If two people mutually accuse each other, *panuyu*, they are both tried by ordeal. If both be scathed, they are mutually responsible for the indemnity to the injured person. If only one be scathed, he is responsible for the indemnity to the injured person and for a payment of the fine for false accusation to the one whom he accused.

The hot water ordeal.—A pot, a foot or more in depth, is filled with water and heated to a furious boiling. A pebble is dropped into it. The accused must reach his hand into the water without undue haste, extract the pebble, and then replace it. Undue haste is interpreted as a confession of guilt. This ordeal is used in certain sections of Ifugao, while in others the hot bolo test is used. It is interesting to note that neither of them is efficacious in determining accusations of adultery. This is for the reason that the gods of animal fertility and growth do not permit an accused to receive an injury for that act which is so eminently useful in their particular sphere of activity. Thus, Ifugao religion looks with the greatest disfavor upon things which tend to restrict population, just as our law frowns upon statutes in restriction of marriage.

The hot bolo ordeal.—In this, if two persons mutually accuse each other, their hands are placed side by side. The *monkalun* lowers a hot knife on their hands. The knife burns the guilty person much more seriously than the guiltless one. If only one person be put to the test, it is said that the knife bends away from the hands of an innocent person. The *monkalun*, with all his might, it is said, cannot put the knife down on the hand: the gods of war and justice will not permit it. But if the person be guilty, the knife grips the hand in its eagerness. If the accused show fear and try to withdraw, the kin of the accuser may catch him and burn him well. I know a man whose fingers were burned off in this way, the thumb adhering to and coalescing with the palm.

The alao or duel.—Eggs, *runo* stalks, or spears are used in trials, the accused facing each other and, at the word of the *monkalun*, hurling their missiles. The duel is not without its dangers. Even though eggs or *runos* be used, the one struck is likely to return a stone; and from throwing stones to throwing spears is an easy step. The two parties of kin are likely to take a hand. How much more likely are they to take a hand and avenge their kinsman if spears be the missiles and he be wounded!

The duel is used in cases of adultery, sorcery, and in some disputes over rice fields, everywhere in Ifugao. In adultery cases, only eggs are used in the duel.

Trial by bultong or wrestling.—This ordeal is used throughout Ifugao, preëminently to settle cases of disputed rice-field boundaries.

The Ifugao clearly recognizes that the processes of nature—landslides, the erosion of rainfall in wet weather, and caking and crumbling in dry weather—tend to wear away a terrace not maintained by a stone wall. A terrace maintained by a stone wall is a rarity in the

Kiangan district. Should the boundary not be well marked by *paghok* a dispute is nearly sure to result sooner or later. These disputes are usually settled by wrestling matches. The wrestling matches are usually friendly. The Ifugao believes that the ancestral spirits of the controversants know which party is in the right, that they know just where the true boundary is, and that they see to it that he who is right shall win, provided always that they be invoked with the proper sacrifices; and that they "hold up" even the weaker of the wrestlers, and cause him to win, provided his cause be just. Notwithstanding this belief, the people are sufficiently practical to demand that the wrestlers be approximately evenly matched. The owners of the adjacent fields may themselves wrestle, or they may choose champions to represent them. Between kinsmen these matches are presumably friendly; and only sacrifices of dried meat are offered the ancestral spirits. But between those not related, there is often a great deal of unfriendly feeling. In this latter case numerous chickens and two or three pigs are sacrificed, and ceremonies like those against enemies are performed.

On the appointed day the two parties meet at the disputed boundary and occupy opposite ends of the disputed land. A party of mutual kin follows along and occupies a position midway between the adversaries. With each party is one of the family priests. Taking betels and dried meat (presuming the contest to be a friendly one) from a headbasket, the priest prays very much as follows: "Come, Grandfather Eagle, Grandfather Red Ant, Grandfather Strong Wind, Grandfather Pangalina; come, Grandmother Cicada, Grandmother Made Happy, Grandmother Ortagon; come, Grandfather Gold, etc. [throughout a list of perhaps a hundred ancestors]. Here are betels and meat; they are trying to take our field away from us. And was it here, Grandmother Grasshopper, that the boundary of the field was? No, you know that it was a double arm's length to the right. Hold us up, you ancestors, in order that *we* may be the wearers of gold neck-ornaments; in order that *we* may be the ones who give expensive feasts. Exhort [here the priest names over the gods of war and justice] to hold us up. Was it here, Grandfather Brave, that the boundary was when you bought the field? Do not let them take our land away from us, for we are to be pitied. We are sorely tried!"

After the prayers of the priest, each champion is led by one of his kinsmen to the place where the first wrestling is to occur. This leading is very ceremoniously done, and suggests the heralding of the champions in feudal days. The dike of the upper terrace has been cleaned off at intervals of fifteen to twenty-five feet in order that the owner of the upper field may have no advantage. The champions frequently work themselves down half-thigh deep in rice-field mud, water, and slime. Catching fair and even holds, they begin to wrestle, encouraged each by the shouts and cries of his kinsmen and by the calling of the old men and old women on the spirits of the ancestors. Each wrestler tries to push his opponent into the territory that that opponent is defending and to down him there. If A throws B in B's field, ten feet from the line on which they wrestle, A wins ten feet of the rice field at that point. Finally, there is a fall that more than likely capsizes one or both of them in the black mud. One point in the boundary is determined. Frequently the lower terrace is eight or ten feet lower than the upper one, but there are no injuries for the reason that the mud is at least two feet deep and is a soft place in which to fall.

At every fifteen or twenty feet along the disputed boundary there is another wrestling match. Sometimes the champions are changed. The new boundary runs through every point at which there has been a fall.

The umpire and the decision.—The *monkalun* is the umpire in trials by ordeal. He interprets undue haste or a faulty performance as a confession of guilt. On the day following the trial by fire or hot water he goes to the house of the accused and examines the hand and forearm. If he finds white inflamed blisters, he pronounces him guilty. In the case of a duel, he pronounces the one struck by the missile guilty. The Ifugaos believe that the gods of war and justice turn missiles aside from the innocent in these duels. For the umpire to be manifestly unfair, would be for him seriously to imperil his own life.

As a matter of fact, a person whose skin is rough, dry, and horny has a great advantage in these ordeals. Since sword climbing and the walking on hot stones and live coals have occurred in other parts of the world, it would seem that a question might be raised whether *state of mind*, or other factors as yet unexplained, may not enter these affairs. . . .

Seizure of chattels.—If a kinsman of remoter kinship than that existing between brothers commit a crime punishable by death, except sorcery or murder, and obstinately refuse to pay the fine assessed, seizure of his property or part of it is made.

Seizures are made from unrelated persons to cover fines due in punishment of theft, malicious killing of animals, arson, and the minor crimes, also to secure payment of a debt.

The following is a list of the things usually seized: gongs, rice-wine jars, carabaos, gold beads, rice fields, children, wives.

A seizure may be made by fraud or deceit, or it may be made in the absence of the owner of his household, or it may be made by superior force. Considering only the manner of the seizure, there is but one law to be followed: the seizure must be made in such a manner as to leave no doubt as to the identity of him who seizes. Thus if B persistently refuses to pay a fine owed to A, A may go to B's house when there is nobody at home and may run away with a gong. If he leaves his bolo, his scabbard, his blanket or some other personal effect in the house as a sort of a visiting card, his seizure is legal. Or A may go to B's house, and, pretending friendship, borrow the gong, representing that he wants to play it at a feast and, having secured possession of it, refuse to return it till the fine be paid. Or suppose that an agent of B's is bringing a carabao up from Nueva Vizcaya, and that the agent has to travel through A's village. A and his friends stop the agent and take the carabao away from him, telling him to inform B that the carabao will be delivered to him when the fine is paid. . . .

Seizure of rice fields.—The seizure of rice fields is practicable only in case the fields are near the village of him who seizes them. For if located in a distant district, the working of the field would be extremely hazardous, and its protection and continuous holding impossible.

Fields may properly be seized for collection of debt or for refusal to pay fines or indemnities. Portions of fields are seized sometimes in disputes as to ownership or boundaries.

Disputes over ownership and boundary come to a head during spading time. One party begins to spade for the next year's crop the land claimed by the other. The other party sticks up *runos,* tied "ethics lock" fashion (*alpud*), along the line which he claims to be the true boundary. The first party then pulls up these *runos,* and sticks down others along the line claimed by it as the true boundary. The issue is joined. The defendant has made his "rejoinder." A *monkalun* is now selected by the plaintiff party, and tries to arrange—and in case of disputed boundaries nearly always does arrange—a means of peaceful settlement, either by compromise or through trial by wrestling. Sometimes the ownership of a field itself is in question. Usually the question is one of inheritance; although there are a number of other causes that may give rise to dispute. Ownership is usually peaceably settled by means of a wrestling match. . . .

Enforced hospitality.—Sometimes a creditor and a numerous and powerful following of kinsmen descend upon a debtor's house as unwelcome guests, consume his stores of food, and force his hospitality until appeased by the payment of the debt.

This form of collection can only be used in the case of debts, for in all other controversies, taboos forbid the eating of the adversary's food, drinking his water, chewing his betels, etc. Even in the case of debt, if a go-between has been sent to the debtor, this means may not be used. It can only be used in a case where "diplomatic relations" have not been ruptured. . . .

Cases illustrating seizure and kidnaping.—Kodamon of Pindungan and Katiling of Ambabag had a dispute over the boundary of a field. There were *paghok* to mark the boundary, but Kodamon contended that all memory of the planting of the *paghok* was absent, and that they were, consequently, without significance in the matter of dispute. They wrestled, and Kodamon lost a little ground, but Katiling tried to take more than was due him according to the verdict of the wrestling matches. Katiling sent men to spade the disputed territory, and led an armed force out to support them. Kodamon led an armed force to the field. At the same time and at a safe distance, the mutual kin of the two parties and a goodly number of neighbors gathered. Kodamon was armed with a Remington rifle whose trigger was broken; Dulinayan, a kinsman of Katiling, with a revolver for which he had no ammunition. The other members of each force however were substantially, if less spectacularly, armed with spears which they well knew how to use. Women rushed in between the two parties, and catching the warriors by the waist tried to lead them away. One can well believe that the air was riven by curses, threats, accusations, upbraidings, imprecations, invocations. The male neutral kin shouted from their safe distance that if Kodamon killed Katiling, they would kill Kodamon (as a vengeance for the death of their kinsman) while if Katiling killed Kodamon, they would avenge their kinsman's death by killing Katiling. "What kind of a way is this for co-villagers to settle a dispute," they shouted. "Go back home and beget some children, and marry them to each other, giving them the two fields, and then it will make no difference where the division line is!" There was an exchange of spears in which Buaya, a kinsman of Kodamon's, was wounded slightly. The matter was then left in abeyance with the understanding that as soon as possible, the two families be united by a marriage, and the two fields given the married couple.

It happened, however, that on account of the sexes of the unmarried children of the families, a union between them was impossible. Accordingly, Kodamon gave his field to his son Dulnuan, and Katiling traded his field to Pingkihan, his brother. Both of these young men had pregnant wives. Pingkihan's wife gave birth first, the child being a girl. Shortly afterward, Dulnuan's wife gave birth. I met Dulnuan, and not knowing of the event, and noticing that he seemed downcast, asked him why he was so sad. "My wife has given birth to a *girl* baby," he said. The quarrel over the boundary is as yet unsettled.

36. WARFARE OF THE PLAINS INDIANS [16]

BY GEORGE BIRD GRINNELL

IN EARLY days, after subsistence, the first requirement of life, had been attended to, war was the most important pursuit of certain plains tribes. Among the war customs, two of those best known and most written about are scalping and counting coup. These are very generally misunderstood and are ill defined in the books. It seems the more important to correct existing errors because these customs are no longer practiced and are now known only to old men.

In a periodical, which recently described a collection of Indian clothing and implements, the following words occur:

"In former times, the most notable achievement of an Indian was the taking of a scalp, but with the introduction of rifles the killing of a man became so easy and there were usually so many scalps taken after a battle that this trophy began to lose its importance. The Indians considered it a much braver act to touch the body of a fallen foe with a coup stick under fire of the enemy."

In the Handbook of Indian Tribes it is said, "Coups are usually 'counted'—as it was termed—that is, credit of victory was taken for three brave deeds, viz. killing an enemy, scalping an enemy, or being the first to strike an enemy either alive or dead. Each one of these entitled a man to rank as a warrior and to recount the exploit in public; but to be first to touch the enemy was regarded as the greatest deed of all as it implied close approach during battle."

The first of these quotations is—except the last sentence—fantastically untrue, while the second is also misleading, since the killing or scalping of an enemy seems to be given equal rank with touching the enemy. Among the plains tribes with which I am well acquainted—and the same is true of all the others of which I know anything at all—coming in actual personal contact with the enemy by touching him with something held in the hand or with a part of the person was the bravest act that could be performed.

To kill an enemy was good in so far as it reduced the numbers of the hostile party. To scalp an enemy was not an important feat and in no sense especially creditable. Enemies were not infrequently left unscalped. If scalped, the skin of the head was taken merely as a trophy,

[16] From "Coup and Scalp Among the Plains Indians," *American Anthropologist*, New Series, Volume 12, pages 296-310, 1910.—The tribes in question are the Pawnee, Cheyenne, Arapaho, Kiowa, Comanche, Crow, Blackfoot, Sioux or Dakota, etc.

something to show, something to dance over—a good thing but of no great importance; but to touch the enemy with something held in the hand, with the bare hand, or with any part of the body, was a proof of bravery—a feat which entitled the man or boy who did it to the greatest credit.

When an enemy was killed, each of those nearest to him tried to be the first to reach him and touch him, usually by striking the body with something held in the hand, a gun, bow, whip, or stick. Those who followed raced up and struck the body—as many as might wish to do so. Any one who wished to might scalp the dead. Neither the killing nor the scalping was regarded as an especially creditable act. The chief applause was won by the man who first could touch the fallen enemy. In Indian estimation the bravest act that could be performed was to count coup on—to touch or strike—a living unhurt man and to leave him alive, and this was frequently done. Cases are often told of where, when the lines of two opposing tribes faced each other in battle, some brave man rode out in front of his people, charged upon the enemy, ran through their line, struck one of them and then, turning and riding back, returned to his own party. If, however, the man was knocked off his horse, or his horse was killed, all of his party made a headlong charge to rescue and bring him off.

When hunting, it was not unusual for boys or young men, if they killed an animal, especially if it was an animal regarded as dangerous, to rush up and count coup on it. I have been told of cases where young men, who, chasing a black bear on the prairie, had killed it with their arrows, raced up to it on foot to see who should count the first coup.

It was regarded as an evidence of bravery for a man to go into battle carrying no weapon that would do any harm at a distance. It was more creditable to carry a lance than a bow and arrow; more creditable to carry a hatchet or war club than a lance; and the bravest thing of all was to go into a fight with nothing more than a whip, or a long twig —sometimes called a coup stick. I have never heard a stone-headed war club called coup stick.

It was not an infrequent practice among the Cheyenne—as indeed among other plains tribes—for a man, if he had been long sick and was without hope of recovery, or if some great misfortune had happened to him and he no longer wished to live, to declare his purpose to give his body to the enemy. In practice this meant committing suicide by attacking enemies without any suitable means of offense or defense, doing some very brave thing, and being killed while doing it. This, of course, was a most honorable way of dying, far more so than to kill one's self by shooting, by knife, or by the rope, though there was no disgrace in self-destruction. Suicide by hanging, however, was usually confined to girls who had been crossed in love.

There is still living in Montana a man who, when seventeen or eighteen years of age, after a long illness to which there seemed no end, declared to his father that he wished to give his body to the enemy. The father assented, fitted out the son with his strongest "medicine," and sent the boy off with a party to the south, armed only with a little hatchet. After the party had reached the country of the enemy, two of these, who were Omaha, were discovered returning from the hunt. Both had guns. The Cheyenne charged on them, and the boy, Sun's-road, having been provided with his father's best war horse, led. He overtook one of the enemy who turned and tried to shoot at him, but the gun snapped. Sun's-road knocked the man off his horse with his little hatchet and riding on overtook the other man, who turned and shot at him; but Sun's-road dropped down on his horse, avoided the bullet, and knocked the Omaha off his horse. Both enemies were killed by the Cheyenne who were following Sun's-road. The young man had now fulfilled his vow. He received from the members of the war party, and from the tribe when he returned to the village, the greatest praise. He recovered his health, and now at the age of seventy-four or seventy-five years still tells the story of his early adventures.

The Cheyenne counted coup on an enemy three times; that is to say, three men might touch the body and receive credit, according to the order in which this was done. Subsequent coups received no credit. The Arapaho touched four times. In battle the members of a tribe touched the enemy without reference to what had been done by those of another allied tribe in the same fight. Thus in a fight where Cheyenne and Arapaho were engaged the same man might be touched seven times. In a fight on the Rio Grande del Norte, where Cheyenne, Arapaho, Comanche, Kiowa, and Apache defeated the Ute, the counting the coups by the different tribes resulted in tremendous confusion.

When a Cheyenne touched an enemy the man who touched him cried, "Ah haih' " and said, "I am the first." The second to touch the body cried, "I am the second," and so the third.

It is evident that in the confusion of a large fight, such as often took place, many mistakes might occur, and certain men might believe themselves entitled to honors which others thought were theirs. After the fight was over, then, the victorious party got together in a circle and built a fire of buffalo chips. On the ground near the fire were placed a pipe and gun. The different men interested approached this fire, and, first touching the pipe called out their deeds, saying, "I am the first," "second," or "third," as the case might be. Some man might dispute another and say, "No, I struck him first," and so the point would be argued and the difference settled at the time.

Often these disputes were hot. I recall one among the Pawnee about which there was great feeling. A Sioux had been killed and Baptiste Bahele, a half-breed Skidi and sub-chief, and a young man of no special importance, were racing for the fallen enemy to secure the honor of touching him first. Baptiste had the faster horse and reached the body first, but, just as he was leaning over to touch it, the animal shied and turned off, so that what he held in his hand did not actually touch the body, while the boy who was following him rode straight over the fallen man and struck him. Baptiste argued plausibly enough that he had reached the body first and was entitled to be credited with the coup, but acknowledged that he did not actually touch the body, though he would have done so had his horse not shied. There was no difference of opinion among the Indians, who unanimously gave the honor to the boy.

Once two young Cheyenne were racing to touch a fallen enemy. Their horses were running side by side, though one was slightly ahead of the other. The man in advance was armed with a saber, the other, almost even with him, was leaning forward to touch the enemy with his lance. A saber being shorter than a lance, the leading man was likely to get only the second coup, but he reached down, grasped his comrade's lance, and gave it a little push, and it touched the enemy as they passed over him. Although the owner of the lance still held it, yet because his hand was behind the fellow's on its shaft, he received credit only for the second coup. If a man struck an enemy with a lance, any one who touched or struck the lance while it was still fixed in or touching the enemy's person, received credit for the next coup.

A man who believed he had accomplished something made a strong fight for his rights and was certain to be supported in his contention by all his friends, and above all by all his relatives. When disputes took place, there were formal ways of getting at the truth. Among the Cheyenne a strong affirmation, or oath, was to rub the hand over the pipe as the statement was made, or to point to the medicine arrows and say, "Arrows, you hear me; I did (or did not do) this thing." The Blackfeet usually passed the hand over the pipe stem, thus asseverating that the story was as straight as the hole through the stem.

With the Cheyenne, if there was a dispute as to who had touched an enemy, counting the first coup, a still more formal oath might be exacted. A buffalo skull, painted with a black streak running from between the horns to the nose, red about the eye sockets, on the right-hand cheek a black, round spot, the sun, and on the left a red half-moon, had its eye sockets and its nose stuffed full of green grass. This represented the medicine lodge. Against this were rested a gun and four arrows, representing the medicine arrows. The men to be sworn were to place their hands on these and make their statements. Small sticks, about a foot long, to the number of the enemies that had been killed in the fight which they were to discuss, were prepared and placed on the ground alongside the arrows and the gun.

In a mixed fight where many people were engaged there were always disputes, and this oath was often—even usually—exacted. A large crowd of people, both men and women, assembled to witness the ceremony. The chiefs directed the crier to call up the men who claimed honors, in the order in which they declared that they had struck an enemy; the man who claimed the first coup first, he who claimed the second coup second, and so on. The man making the oath walked up to the sacred objects and stood over them, and stretching up his hands to heaven said, *Mā i yūn asts'ni ah' tū*, "Spiritual powers, listen to me." Then bending down he placed his hands on the objects and said, *Nā nit'shū*, "I touched him." After he had made his oath he added, "If I tell a lie, I hope that I may be shot far off."

He narrated in detail how he charged on the enemy and how he struck him. Then were called the men who counted the second and third coup on this same enemy and each told his story at length. Next the man who touched the second enemy was called, and he was followed by those who had counted the second and third coup on the same individual. In the same way all claimants told their stories.

If, under such circumstances, a man made a false statement, it was considered certain that before long he or some one of his family would die. The Cheyenne feared this oath, and, if a man was doubtful as to whether he had done what he claimed, he was very likely not to appear when his name was called. On the other hand, each of two men might honestly enough declare—owing to error—that he first touched an enemy. Or, a man might swear falsely. In the year 1862 a man disputing with another declared that he had first touched the enemy. The next year, while the Cheyenne were making the medicine lodge on the Republican River, this man died, and every one believed, and said, that he had lied about the coup of the year before.

When two men were striving to touch an enemy and others were watching them, and the thing was close, the spectators might say to one of the two, "We did not see plainly what you did, but of what he did we are certain." In this way they might bar out from the first honor the man concerning whose achievement they were doubtful.

As already said, the relatives of each claimant were active partisans of their kinsmen.

If enemies were running away and being pursued, and one fell behind or was separated from his party, and was touched three times, if he escaped serious injury and later got among his own people once more, the coup might again be counted on him up to the usual three times.

As an example of the odd things that have happened in connection with the practice of touching the enemy, according to Cheyenne rules, the curious case of Yellow-shirt may be mentioned. In the great battle that took place on Wolf Creek in 1838 between the allied Kiowa, Comanche, and Apache on one hand, and the Cheyenne and Arapaho on the other, coup was counted on Yellow-shirt,[17] a Kiowa, nine times. When the charge was made on the Kiowa camp, Yellow-shirt was fighting on foot and was touched three times, but not seriously injured. Later, he reached his village, mounted a horse, came out to fight and was touched three times on horseback. Almost immediately afterward his horse was killed and his leg broken, and he sat on the ground, still fighting by shooting arrows, and was again touched three times and killed. So in all nine coups were counted on this man, all of which were allowed. In another case coup was counted nine times on a Pawnee, who was not killed and finally got away.

If, through some oversight, the third coup had not been formally counted on an enemy, the act of taking off his moccasins as plunder has been decided to be the third coup, because the man who removed them touched the dead man's person. Coup, of course, might be counted on man, woman, or child. Any one who was captured would first be touched.

There were other achievements which were regarded as sufficiently noteworthy to be related as a portion of a triumph, but which were in no sense comparable with the honor of touching an enemy. Such brave deeds, among the Blackfeet, were the taking of a captive, of a shield, a gun, arrows, a bow, or a medicine pipe, any of which acts might be coupled with touching an enemy.

Among the same people it was highly creditable to ride over an enemy on foot, and in the old-time dances of the different bands of the All-comrades, horses were frequently painted with the prints of a red hand on either side of the neck and certain paintings on the breast intended to represent the contact of the horse's body with the enemy.

Among the Cheyenne the capture of a horse or horses was such a brave deed, and, if the man who had touched an enemy took from him

[17] So called by the Cheyenne from his war shirt. His Kiowa name was Sleeping-bear.

a shield or a gun, the capture of this implement was always mentioned. The drum would be sounded for touching the enemy, sounded again for the capture of the shield, again for the capture of the gun, and—if the man had scalped the dead—for the taking of the scalp.

I believe that the high esteem in which the act of touching the enemy is held is a survival of the old feeling that prevailed before the Indians had missiles and when—if they fought—they were obliged to do so hand to hand with clubs and sharpened sticks. Under such conditions only those who actually came to grips, so to speak, with the enemy— who met him hand to hand—could inflict any injury and gain any glory. After arrows came into use it may still have been thought a finer thing to meet the enemy hand to hand than to kill him with an arrow at a distance.

The general opinion that the act of scalping reflects credit on the warrior has no foundation. The belief perhaps arose from the fact that, when an enemy was killed or wounded, brave Indians rushed toward him. White observers have very likely inferred that those who were rushing upon an enemy were eager to take his scalp. As a matter of fact they cared little or nothing for the scalp but very much for the credit of touching the fallen man. Most people are untrustworthy observers and draw inferences from their preconceived notions, rather than from what actually takes place.

As already said, among the plains tribes a scalp was a mere trophy and was not highly valued. It was regarded as an emblem of victory and was a good thing to carry back to the village to rejoice and dance over. But any part of an enemy's body might serve for this, and it was not at all uncommon among the Blackfeet to take off a leg or an arm, or even a foot or hand, to carry back and rejoice over for weeks and months. Very commonly, a party returning from war would give one or more scalps to a group of old men and old women, who would paint their faces black and carry the scalp about all through the village dancing at intervals, singing the praise of the successful warriors, making speeches in their honor, and generally rejoicing. Scalps were sometimes sacrificed among all these tribes, perhaps burned, as by the Pawnee, or among Cheyenne and Blackfeet tied to a pole and left out on the prairie to be rained on and finally to disappear in the weather. Scalps were used to trim and fringe war clothing—shirts and leggings —and to tie to the horse's bridle in going to war. Usually the scalps taken were small, a little larger than a silver dollar, but like any other piece of fresh skin they stretched greatly.

Æsthetic and Religious Culture

37. DECORATIVE ART OF THE NORTH PACIFIC COAST [1]

BY FRANZ BOAS

IT HAS been shown that the motives of the decorative art of many peoples developed largely from representations of animals. In course of time, forms that were originally realistic became more and more sketchy, and more and more distorted. Details, even large proportions, of the subject so represented were omitted, until finally the design attained a purely geometric character.

The decorative art of the Indians of the North Pacific Coast agrees with this oft-observed phenomenon in that its subjects are almost exclusively animals. It differs from other arts in that the process of conventionalizing has not led to the development of geometric designs, but that the parts of the animal body may still be recognized as such. The body of the animal, however, undergoes very fundamental changes in the arrangement and size of its parts. In the following paper I shall describe the characteristics of these changes, and discuss the mental attitude of the artist which led to their development.

In treating this subject, we must bear in mind that almost all the plastic art of the Indians of the North Pacific Coast is decorative art. While some primitive people—for instance, the Eskimo—produce carvings which serve no practical ends, but are purely works of art, all the works of the Indian artists of the region which we are considering serve at the same time a useful end; that is to say, the form of the object is given, and the subject to be represented is more or less subordinate to the object on which it is shown. Only in the cases of single totemic figures is the artist free to mold his subject without regard to such considerations; but, owing to the large size of such figures, he is

---

[1] Selected from Franz Boas, "The Decorative Art of the Indians of the North Pacific Coast," *Bulletin of the American Museum of Natural History*, Volume 9, pages 123-176, 1897.—The tribes are the Tlingit, Haida, Tsimshian, Bella Coola, Kwakiutl, etc.

Fig. 1

Fig. 2

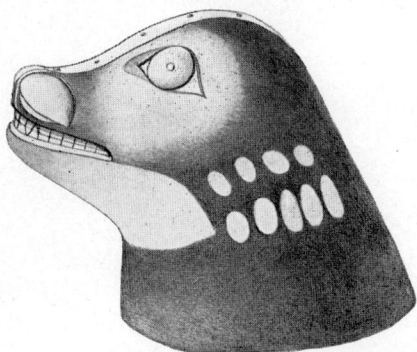

Fig. 3

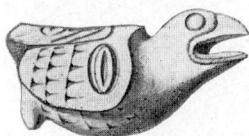

Fig. 4

Fig. 5

Figs. 1-5. Realistic carvings.

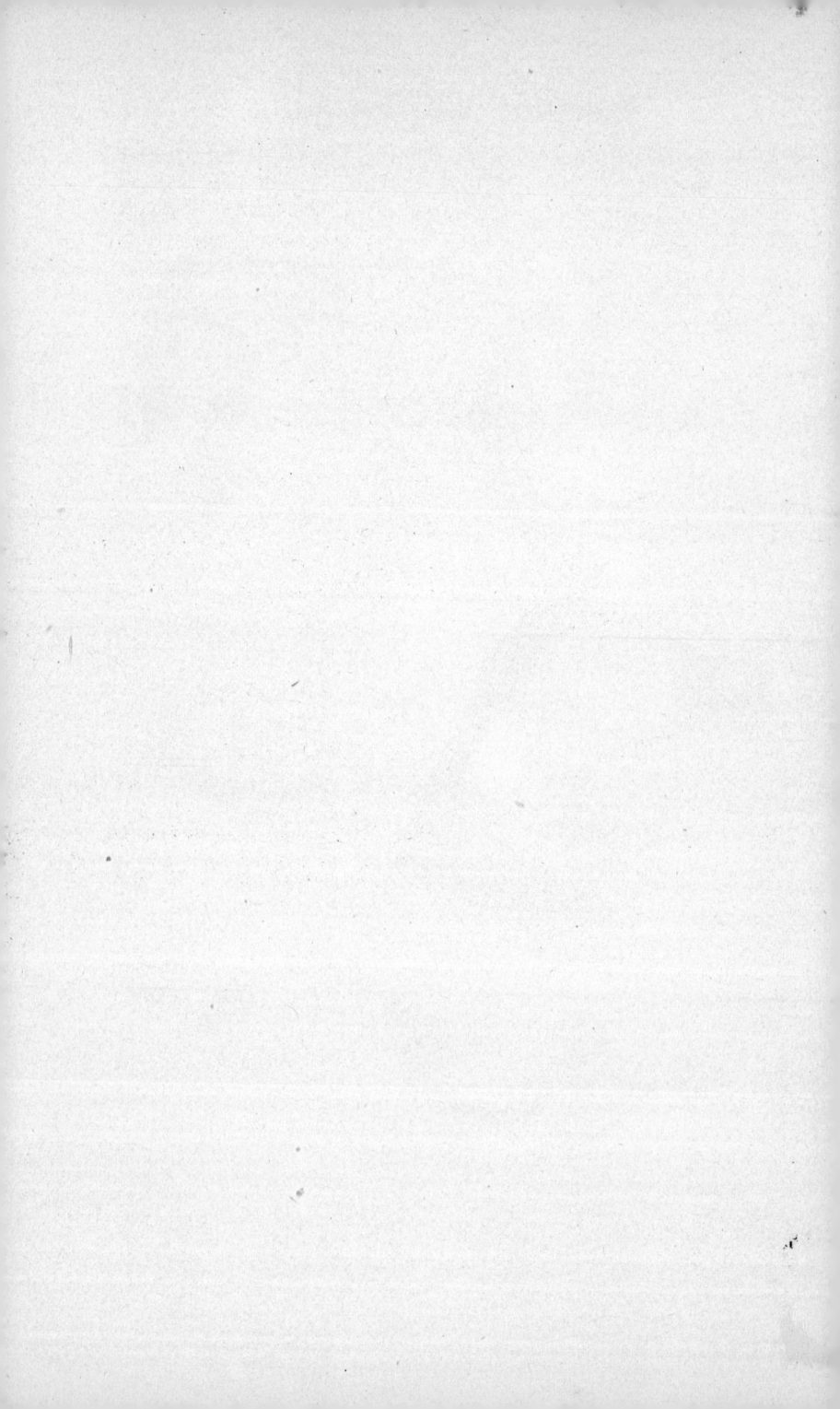

limited by the cylindrical form of the trunk of the tree from which he carves his figures. We may therefore say that the native artist is in almost all his works limited by the shape of the object on which he represents his subject.

The plastic arts of the Indians are carving and painting, in which latter we may include tattooing and weaving. Carving is done mostly in wood, but also in stone and horn. It is either in the round, bas-relief, or, although more rarely, in high relief. There is no art of pottery.

The artists have acquired a high technique, which proves that realistic representations of animals are not beyond their powers. The following are a few exquisite examples of realistic carvings. The helmet (Fig. 1) is decorated with the head of an old man affected with partial paralysis. Undoubtedly this specimen must be considered a portrait head. Nose, eyes, mouth, and the general expression, are highly characteristic. The mask (Fig. 2) represents a dying warrior. The artist has represented faithfully the wide lower jaw, the pentagonal face, and the strong nose of the Indian. The relaxing muscles of the mouth and tongue, the drooping eyelids, the motionless eyeballs, mark the agonies of death. The conception is so realistic that the mask creates a ghastly impression. Figure 3 represents a dancing hat decorated with the design of a seal. Figure 4 is a small float representing a swimming puffin. Figure 5 is a rattle in the form of a swimming goose. The characteristic bend of its neck and the characteristic color of head and neck are very true to nature.

In these cases the artist has rendered the form of his model faithfully. The object on which the representation of his model was placed allowed him the use of the figure without any alteration. This is not often the case. Generally the object to be decorated has a certain given form to which the decoration must be subordinated, and the artist is confronted with the problem of how to adjust his subject to the form of the object to be decorated.

Before attempting an explanation of the method adopted by the artist in the solution of this problem, we must treat another aspect of our subject. We must premise that in consequence of the adaptation of the form to the decorative field, the native artist cannot attempt a realistic representation of his subject, but is often compelled to indicate only its main characteristics. In consequence of the distortion of the animal body, due to its adaptation to various surfaces, it would be all but impossible to recognize what animal is meant, if the artist did not emphasize what he considers the characteristic features of animals. These are so essential to his mind that he considers no representation adequate in which they are missing. In many cases they become the symbols of the animal. We find, therefore, that each animal is characterized by certain symbols, and great latitude is allowed in the treatment of all features other than symbols.

I will illustrate this feature of the art of the Indians of the North Pacific Coast by means of a number of characteristic examples.

Figure 6 is a figure from a totem pole, which represents the beaver. It will be noticed that the face is treated somewhat like a human face,

Fig. 6   Fig. 7   Fig. 8

Figs. 6-8. Carvings representing the beaver.

particularly the region around eyes and nose. The position of the ears, however, indicates that the artist intended to represent an animal head, not a human head. While the human ear is represented, in its characteristic form, on a level with the eye, animal ears are indicated over the forehead; that is to say, approximately in the position in which they appear in a front view of the animal. Their characteristic shape may be seen in figures 6 and 7, and in many others. While the ears characterize the head as that of an animal, the two large incisors serve to identify the rodent *par excellence*—the beaver. The tail of the animal is turned up in front of its body. It is ornamented by cross-hatching, which is intended to represent the scales on the beaver's tail. In its fore paws it holds a stick. The large incisors, the tail with cross-hatching, and the stick, are symbols of the beaver, and each of these is a sufficient characteristic of the animal.

Figure 7 is another representation of a beaver from a totem pole. It resembles figure 6 in all details, except that the stick is missing. The beaver is simply holding its forepaws raised nearly to its chin. There are other carvings in which the beaver is shown with four or five toes, but the symbols described here never vary.

In figure 8, which is the handle of a spoon, we find only the first of the symbols of the beaver represented, namely, its incisors. Only the

Fig. 9. Headdress representing a beaver. The dragon-fly is shown on the chest of the beaver. Tribe, Haida.

head and the forepaws of the animal are shown; and in its mouth are indicated an upper and a lower pair of incisors, all the other teeth being omitted. There is nothing except the teeth to indicate that the artist intended to represent the beaver.

Figure 9 is the front of a dancing head-dress, which is attached to a framework made of whalebone, and set on top with bristles of the sea-lion. To the back is attached a long train of ermine skins. The outer side of the carved front is set with abalone shells. The squatting figure which occupies the center of the front represents the beaver. The same symbols which were mentioned before will be recognized here. The face is human; but the ears, which rise over the eyebrows, indicate that an animal is meant. Two large pairs of incisors occupy the center of the open mouth. The tail is turned up in front of the body, and appears between the two hind legs, indicated by cross-hatching. The fore paws are raised to the height of the mouth, but they do not hold a stick. It will be noticed that on the chest of the beaver another head is represented, over which a number of small rings stretch towards the chin of the beaver. Two feet, which belong to this animal, extend from the corners of its mouth towards the haunches of the beaver. This animal represents the dragon-fly, which is symbolized by a large head and a slender segmented body. In many representations of the dragon-

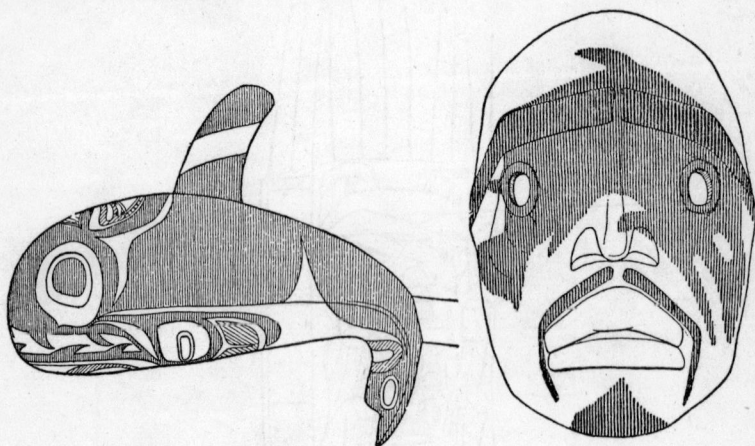

Fig. 18   Fig. 19

Figs. 18-19. Rattle and mask representing the killer-whale.

fly there are two pairs of wings attached to the head. The face of this animal resembles also a human face; but the two ears, which rise over the eyebrows, indicate that an animal is meant. Combinations of two animals of this sort are found very frequently, a smaller figure of one animal being represented on the chest of a large carving. . . .

Figures 18 and 19 are representations of the killer-whale. In the rattle (Fig. 18) the form of the whale will be easily recognized. Its tail is bent downward. The large head, one of the characteristic features of the whale, is much more pronounced in this than in the next figure. The eye appears on the front part of the rattle. Under the eye we see the large mouth, which is set with a number of curved spines. They are intended to represent the teeth. Immediately behind the mouth, on the lower part of the carving, we find the flippers. The painted ornament, which has the form of a small face, in front of the huge dorsal fin, is intended to represent the blow-hole. . . .

The following series (figures 21, 23) are representations of the shark. Whenever the whole body of this animal is represented, it is characterized by a heterocerc tail, a large mouth, the corners of which are drawn downward, a series of curved lines on each cheek which

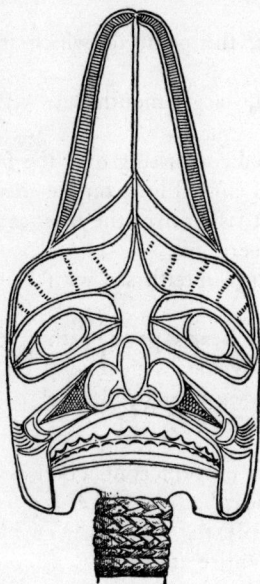

Fig. 21   Fig. 23

Figs. 21, 23. Tlingit dagger handle and Haida tattooing, representing sharks.

represent the gills, and a high tapering forehead, which is often decorated with two circles and a series of curved lines similar to those found on the cheeks. . . .

Figure 21 is the handle of a copper dagger on which the mouth with depressed corners, the curved lines on the cheeks, and the ornament rising over the forehead, characterize the shark. . . .

Figure 23 is a copy of a tattooing on the back of a Haida woman. Here we have only the outline of the head of a shark, again characterized by a peculiarly high forehead, the depressed corners of the mouth, and curved lines on each cheek. . . .

Let us briefly recapitulate what we have thus far tried to show.

Animals are characterized by their symbols, and the following series of symbols have been described in the preceding remarks:

1. Of the *beaver:* large incisors, scaly tail, and a stick held in the forepaws.

2. Of the *sculpin:* two spines rising over the mouth, and a continuous dorsal fin.

3. Of the *hawk:* large curved beak, the point of which is turned backward so that it touches the face.

4. Of the *eagle:* large curved beak, the point of which is turned downward.

5. Of the *killer-whale:* large head, large mouth set with teeth, blow-hole, and large dorsal fin.

6. Of the *shark:* an elongated rounded cone rising over the forehead, mouth with depressed corners, a series of curved lines on the cheeks, two circles and curved lines on the ornament rising over the forehead, round eyes, numerous sharp teeth, and heterocerc tail.

7. Of the *bear:* large paws, and large mouth set with teeth, with protruding tongue.

8. Of the *sea-monster:* bear's head, bear's paws with flippers attached, and gills and body of the killer-whale, with several dorsal fins.

9. Of the *dragon-fly:* large head, segmented, slender body, and wings.

So far I have considered the symbols only in connection with their use in representing various animals. It now becomes necessary to inquire in what manner they are used to identify the animals. We have seen that in a number of the preceding cases entire animals were represented, and that they were identified by means of these symbols. When we investigate this subject more closely, we find that the artist is allowed wide latitude in the selection of the form of the animal. Whatever the form may be, as long as the recognized symbols are present, the identity of the animal is established. We have mentioned before that the symbols are often applied to human faces, while the body of the figure has the characteristics of the animal. . . .

It appears, therefore, that as, first of all, the artist tried to characterize the animals he intended to represent by emphasizing their most prominent characteristics, these gradually became symbols which were recognized even when not attached to the animal form, and which took the place of representations of the entire animal.

Having thus become acquainted with a few of the symbols of animals, we will next investigate in what manner the native artist adapted the animal form to the object he intended to decorate. First of all, we will direct our attention to a series of specimens which show that the native artist endeavors, whenever possible, to represent the whole animal on the object that he desires to decorate.

Figure 31 is a club used for killing seals and halibut before they are landed in the canoe. The carving represents the killer-whale. If the principal symbol of the killer-whale, its dorsal fin, were placed in an upright position on the club, the implement would assume an exceedingly awkward shape. On the other hand, the artist could not omit the dorsal fin, since it is the most important symbol of the animal. Therefore he has bent it downward along the side of the body, so that it covers the flipper. The tail of the whale would have interfered with the handle, and for this reason it has been turned forward over the back of the whale, so as to be in close contact with the body. . . .

We have now to treat a series of peculiar phenomena which result from the endeavor on the part of the artist to adjust the animal that

Fig. 31. Tlingit club representing the killer-whale.

he desires to represent to the decorative field in such a manner as to preserve as far as possible the whole animal, and bring out its symbols most clearly.

Figure 39 is the top view of a wooden hat on which is carved the figure of a sculpin. The animal is shown in top view, as though it were lying with its lower side on the hat. The dancing hats of these Indians have the forms of truncated cones. To the top are attached a series of rings, mostly made of basketry, which indicate the social rank of the owner, each ring symbolizing a step in the social ladder. The top of the hat, therefore, does not belong to the decorative field, which is confined to the surface of the cone. The artist found it necessary, therefore, to open the back of the sculpin far enough to make room for the gap in the decorative field. He has done so by representing the animal as seen from the top, but split and distended in the middle, so that the top of the hat is located in the opening thus secured.

Figure 40 represents a dish in the shape of a seal. The whole dish is carved in the form of the animal; but the bottom, which corresponds to the belly, is flattened, and the back is hollowed out so as to form the bowl of the dish. In order to gain a wider rim the whole back has been distended so that the animal becomes inordinately wide as com-

pared to its length. The flippers are carved in their proper positions
at the sides of the dish. The hind flippers are turned back, and closely
join the tail. A similar method of representation is used in decorating
small boxes. The whole box is considered as representing an animal.
The front of its body is painted or carved on the box front; its sides,

Fig. 39

Fig. 40

Fig. 39. Dancing-hat: sculpin. Fig. 40. Grease-dish: seal.

on the sides of the box; the hind side of its body, on the back of the
box. The bottom of the box is the animal's stomach; the top, or the
open upper side, its back. These boxes, therefore, are decorated only on
the sides, which are bent of a single piece of wood (Fig. 41). When
we unbend the sides we find the decoration extended on a long band,
which we may consider as consisting of two symmetrical halves. The
center is occupied by the front view of the animal, the sides by a side
view, and the ends by one-half of the hind view at each end of the
board. An actual unbending of the sides of the box would not give a

symmetrical form; but, since the ends are necessarily sewed at the corner, the hind view of the body will occupy one end.

In the decoration of silver bracelets a similar principle is followed, but the problem differs somewhat from that offered in the decoration of square boxes. While in the latter case the four edges make a natural division between the four views of the animal—front and right profile, back and left profile—there is no such sharp line of division in the round bracelet, and there would be great difficulty in joining the four

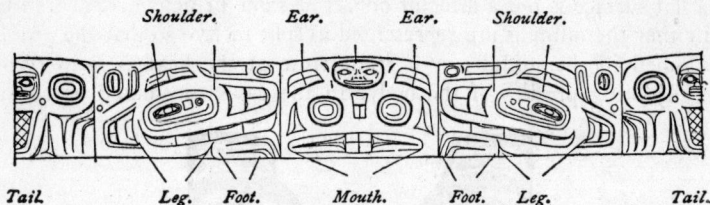

Fig. 41

Fig. 42

Fig. 41. Carving on the sides of a dish, representing a beaver. The sides of the dish are bent of a single piece of wood, and are shown here flattened out.
Fig. 42. Design on a bracelet representing a bear.

aspects artistically, while two profiles offer no such difficulty. When the tail end of each profile is placed where the ends of the bracelet join, then there is only one point of junction; namely, in the median line of the head. This is the method of representation that the native artists have adopted (Fig. 42). The animal is cut in two from head to tail, so that the two halves cohere only at the tip of the nose and at the tip of the tail. The hand is put through this hole, and the animal now surrounds the wrist. In this position it is represented on the bracelet. The method adopted is therefore identical with the one applied in the hat (Fig. 39), except that the central opening is much larger, and that the animal has been represented on a cylindrical surface, not a conical one.

An examination of the head of the bear shown on the bracelet (Fig. 42), makes it clear that this idea has been carried out rigidly. It will be noticed that there is a deep depression between the eyes, extending down to the nose. This shows that the head itself must not be considered a front view, but as consisting of two profiles which adjoin at mouth and nose, while they are not in contact with each other on a level with the eyes and forehead. The peculiar ornament rising over the nose of the bear decorated with three rings, represents a hat with three rings, which designate the rank of the bearer. . . .

The transition from the bracelet to the painting or carving of animals on a flat surface is not a difficult one. The same principle is adhered to; and either the animals are represented as split in two so that the profiles are joined in the middle, or a front view of the head is shown with two adjoining profiles of the body. In the cases considered heretofore

Fig. 43. Painting representing a bear. Tribe, Haida.

the animal was cut through and through from the mouth to the tip of the tail. These points were allowed to cohere, and the animal was stretched over a ring, a cone, or the sides of a prism. If we imagine the bracelet opened, and flattened in the manner in which it is shown in figure 42, we have a section of the animal from mouth to tail, cohering only at the mouth, and the two halves spread over a flat surface. This is the natural development of the method here described when applied to the decoration of flat surfaces.

It is clear that on flat surfaces this method allows of modifications by changing the method of cutting. When the body of a long animal, such as that of a fish or of a standing quadruped, is cut in this manner, a design results which forms a long narrow strip. This mode of cutting is therefore mostly applied in the decoration of long bands. When the field that is to be decorated is more nearly square, this form is not favorable. In such cases a square design is obtained by cutting quadrupeds sitting on their haunches in the same manner as before, and unfolding the animal so that the two halves remain in contact at the nose and mouth, while the median line at the back is to the extreme right and to the extreme left.

Figure 43 (a Haida painting) shows a design which has been obtained in this manner. It represents a bear. The enormous breadth of

Fig. 44   Fig. 46

Fig. 44. Painting from a house-front, representing a bear.
Fig. 46. Hat painted with design of a beaver.

mouth observed in these cases is brought about by the junction of the two profiles of which the head consists.

This cutting of the head is brought out most clearly in the painting (Fig. 44), which also represents the bear. It is the painting on the front of a Tsimshian house, the circular hole in the middle of the design being the door of the house. The animal is cut from back to front, so that only the front part of the head coheres. The two halves of the lower jaw do not touch each other. The back is represented by the black outline on which the hair is indicated by fine lines. . . .

The beaver (Fig. 46) has been treated in the same manner. The head is split down to the mouth, over which rises the hat with four rings. The split has been carried back to the tail, which, however, is left intact, and turned up towards the center of the hat. The importance of the symbols becomes very clear in this specimen. If the two large black teeth which are seen under the four rings, and the tail with the cross-hatchings, were omitted, the figure would represent the frog.

In the following figures we find a new cut applied. Figure 53 . . . represents the shark. I explained, when discussing the symbols of the shark, that in the front view of the animal the symbols are shown to best advantage. For this reason side views of the face of the shark are avoided, and in representing the whole animal a cut is made from the back to the lower side, and the two sides are unfolded, leaving the head in front view.

The painting (Fig. 53) has been made in this manner, the two halves of the body being entirely separated from each other, and folded

Fig. 53. Painting representing a shark. Tribe, Haida.

to the right and to the left. The heterocerc tail is cut in halves, and is shown at each end turned downward. The pectoral fins are shown unduly enlarged, in order to fill the vacant space under the head. . . .

In figure 62, which represents the design on a circular slate dish, we see a good case of the adaptation of a profile to the decorative field. The design represents a killer-whale with two dorsal fins. The animal is bent around the rim of a dish so that the head touches the tail. The two dorsal fins are laid flat along the back, while the large flipper occupies the center of the dish. . . .

I have described a number of sections applied in representing various animals. Heretofore we have had cases only in which the sections were rather simple. In many cases in which the adaptation of the animal form to the decorative field is more difficult, the sections and distortions are much more numerous and far-reaching than those described before. . . .

We can now sum up the results of our considerations. In the first part of this paper I described the symbols of a number of animals, and pointed out that in many cases there is a tendency to substitute the symbol for the whole animal. The works of art which I describe in the second part of my paper may be said to illustrate a principle which is apparently diametrically opposed to the former. While the symbolism developed a tendency to suppress parts of the animal, we find in the

Fig. 62. Slate dish with killer-whale design. Tribe, Haida.

efforts of the artist to adapt the form of the animal to the decorative field a far-reaching desire to preserve, so far as feasible, the whole animal; and, with the exception of a few profiles, we do not find a single instance which can be interpreted as an endeavor to give a perspective and therefore realistic view of an animal. We have found a variety of methods applied which tend to bring the greatest possible part of the animal form into the decorative field. I conclude from this that it is the ideal of the native artist to show the whole animal, and that the idea of perspective representation is entirely foreign to his mind. His representations are combinations of symbols of the various parts of the body of the animal, arranged in such a way that if possible the whole animal is brought into view. The arrangement, however, is so that the natural relation of the parts is preserved, being changed

only by means of sections and distortions, but so that the natural con-
tiguity of the parts is preserved.

The success of the artist depends upon his cleverness in designing
lines of dissection and methods of distortion. When he finds it impossible
to represent the whole animal, he confines himself to rearranging its
most characteristic parts, always of course including its symbols. There
is a tendency to exaggerate the size of the symbols at the expense of
other parts of the subject. I presume this is the line in which the two
principles of the decorative art of the Indians of the North Pacific
Coast of America merge into each other. The gradual emphasizing of
the symbol at the expense of other parts of the body leads in many
cases to their entire suppression, and to designs in which the animal is
indicated only by its symbols.

38. AMERICAN LOT-GAMES AS EVIDENCE OF ASIATIC INTERCOURSE [2]

BY E. B. TYLOR

THE group of games to which our *backgammon* belongs is ancient
and widely spread over the world. In it a number of pieces are moved
on a diagram or board, not at the player's free choice as in draughts or
chess, but comformably to the throws of lots or dice. One can hardly
doubt, from the peculiar combination of chance and skill here involved, that all the games coming under this definition must be sprung
from one original game, though this cannot now be clearly identified,
and may indeed have disappeared many ages since. The closeness of
correspondence between the abacus or reckoning-board with its little
stones or calculi moved on its lines or spaces, and the board and pieces
for ancient backgammon, which were even called by the same names,
strongly suggests the idea that the original backgammon arose out of
the sportive use of the calculating-board. Its descendants, the backgammon family, fall into two groups of games: those played with
numbered dice, and those played with two-faced lots which can only
fall in two ways, as we say "head or tail." These two groups of games

[2] This is a combination of extracts of two articles on the subject by Tylor:
"On the Game of Patolli in Ancient Mexico, and Its Probably Asiatic Origin," in
Journal of the [Royal] Anthropological Institute, Volume 8, pages 116-129,
1879; and "On American Lot-Games as Evidence of Asiatic Intercourse Before
the Time of Columbus," in *Internationales Archiv für Ethnographie*, Volume 9,
pages 55-67, 1896. The account of the Arab and Hindu games is from the
former article; the remainder of the selection from the latter.

may be conveniently called *dice-backgammon* and *lot-backgammon*. Dice-backgammon makes its appearance plainly in classic history. The game of the "twelve lines" (*duodecim scripta*) was played throughout the Roman Empire, and passed on with little change through medieval Europe, carrying its name of *tabulæ*, *tables*; its modern representatives being French *trictrac*, English *backgammon*, etc. Among ancient Greek games, the *kubeia* or "dice-playing" is shown by various classical passages to have been of the nature of backgammon. It appears from Plutarch that in early times it was played in Persia, where it still flourishes under the name of *nard*. There are also in Sanskrit literature mentions of related games in ancient India. For the purpose of the present paper, however, it will not be needful to go at length into the history of dice-backgammon. It is with the less familiar lot-backgammon that we are principally concerned. This, there is fair reason to believe, was the earlier, as it is the ruder form; dice-backgammon being a later improvement. That such is the case is made likely by the following descriptions of lot-backgammon, which show how clumsily the throwing of a whole handful of lots accomplishes what is done easily with one or two numbered dice.

One variety of lot-backgammon is to this day popular in Egypt and Palestine, under the name of *tab* or "game." It is described in Lane's *Modern Egyptians*, and in Hyde's *De Ludis Orientalibus*, part ii, p. 217. The lots thrown are tab-sticks, four slips of palm-branch about a span long, cut smooth on one side so as to be white, while the other side is left green, these sides being called the white and black respectively. The tab-sticks are thrown against a wall or stick, and the throw counts according to how many white sides come uppermost, thus:

Whites up,	none,	one,	two,	three,	four,
Count	6	1	2	3	4
	(go on)	(go on)	(stop)	(stop)	(go on)

Here there is an evident attempt to fix the values of the throws according to the probability of their occurrence, though this is very crudely carried out.[3] Not only do the rarer throws of none-up and four-up score high, but they and one-up (tab) give the player a new throw, whereas the common throws of two-up and three-up lose the lead. This principle runs through all varieties of lot-backgammon. If, as is probable, such lot-scoring represents the earlier form from which dice-scoring is derived, then the privilege of a new turn being given to the extreme throws is the origin of the same privilege being given

[3] The calculated odds are 6, 1½, 1, 1½, 6.—Archiv article, p. 57.

to doubles in our backgammon. Next as to the tab-board. This is divided into four rows of squares, each row having 7, 9, 11, 13, or other odd number of squares or "houses," thus:

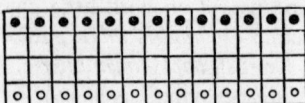

Rows of holes on a flat stone or on the ground will serve, and the pieces or "dogs" are bits of stone for one side and red brick for the other, the players starting by putting a piece in each square on his own side as shown in the figure. Now a "dog" or draught can only be moved from its original square by a throw of tab (one-up). While still inert in its original place the draught is called a Nasara or Christian, but by the throw of tab it is made a Moslem, and can go out to fight. Suppose a player at the beginning throws tab, then four, and then two, he uses the first to bring forward his right-hand draught to the square in front, then moves it on six squares to the left, and then, his last throw having lost the lead, the other player takes his turn. When a throw enables a draught to be moved to a square occupied by one of the enemy's draughts, this is taken, but a square occupied by several draughts is safe. That is to say, our familiar rule of taking a man or hitting a blot belongs to lot-backgammon. The game is ended by one player losing all his men. It remains to be pointed out that the lot-throwing part of the game is sometimes played by itself. The player who throws four is called Sultan, and he who throws six receives the title of Wezir, while the unlucky thrower of two or three gets blows on the soles of his feet.

We now turn to the kind of lot-backgammon played in India, and now generally known under the name of *pachisi*. It is a popular mode of gambling in India, and even Europeans have been known to catch the enthusiasm of the natives, as witness the well-known story of that English official who, having paid his servants' wages, would sit down with him to match at *pachisi* and sometimes win his money back. At the time of reading this paper, the best account of the game accessible to me was that in Herklot's *Qanoon-e-Islam*, but Mr. Arthur Grote has since kindly procured, through Dr. Rajendralala Mitra, of the Calcutta University, a more complete and consistent set of rules, which are here followed. The game may be played by two, three, or four persons severally, or by two pairs, the partners sitting opposite one another. A cloth, with colored patches on it, to form the pattern or diagram, is generally used as a board, zealous players often carrying one rolled round in their turbans. The diagram or board is as shown in the illustration.

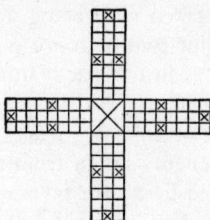

Each of the four arms contains 24 squares, of which the three crossed squares are called forts (*chik*). The pieces played with (*got*) are usually of turned wood or ivory, of a conoidal shape, much like our present rifle-bullets, and in sets of four, each of the four players having a set all of one color, red, green, yellow, black. The moves of the pieces on the board are determined by the throws of cowrie-shells, which count according to how many fall mouth upward. The scoring is as follows when six cowries are used:

Mouths up,	none,	one,	two,	three,	four,	five,	six [4]
Count,	6	10	2	3	4	25	12
	(go on)		(stop)			(go on)	

Suppose now four players to be seated, each at the end of one cross-arm. The object of each player is to move his men from home down the middle row of his own arm, and then along the outside lines of squares from right to left (against the sun) till having made the circuit of the whole board, they come back to the end of their own arm, move up its middle row where they came down, and get back into the central space or home, the winner being he who gets his four men round first. The pieces move onward as many squares as the score of the throw. But a piece can only be started in the game when its owner throws a 10 (*das*) or a 25 (*pachisi*), which throws give a starting 1 (*puá*) in addition to the ordinary score, by which 1 a-piece is put on the first square and so started on its course. The high throws 6, 10, 12, 25, entitle the player to a new throw as doublets do in our backgammon, but at the lower throws the lead passes to the other player. Thus when the game begins, the throws are useless till one player throws 10 or 25; suppose he throws 10, and this giving him a new throw, afterwards 2, he is able

---

[4] A five-cowrie form of the game has the same count, except that scoring 12 for all six cowries is omitted. The count of 6, 10, 2, 3, 4, 25 corresponds to calculated odds of 25, 5, 2½, 2½, 5, 25.—Archiv article, p. 58.

to start a piece on the first square, and then move it 10 and 2 squares onward. A single man on a square is taken by an enemy's man moving on to that square, and the taken man being dead (*mará*) is put back in the home to start afresh, but two or more men of one set on a square hold it safely, all which is as in our backgammon. In *pachisi*, however, taking or cutting (*kátá*) a man gives the player a new throw. Also in *pachisi*, the crossed squares or forts are places where a single man is in safety, and even blocks an enemy's man from moving there. The throws just mentioned, 10 followed by 2, are favorable as entering a man and putting him in safety in a fort; a 25 followed by a 4 is good in the same way. When a piece, after making the circuit of the board, comes back to go up its own middle row, it is called ripe (*pakká*) and is laid on its side to distinguish it from the starting-pieces on their way down. If the ripe piece gets again on the last square before home, it can only be got off the board as it got on, by a throw of *das* or *pachisi*.

The comparison of this Hindu game of *pachisi* shows close connection with the Arab tab; we have even the privileged throws giving a new throw, and a particular throw required to start a man. In India there is also played another game like *pachisi* except that the cowries are superseded by a kind of long dice, numbered on the four long sides but not at the ends; as thus played the game is called *chûpur*. The *pachisi* board has been introduced into England, with four sets of four small draughts as the pieces, and ordinary dice. In this state the game has made its nearest approach to our backgammon, and any one who tries the set of games will be likely to admit that in the *pachisi* played with cowries as lots, he has before him an early and rude stage of the game as lot-backgammon, out of which it passed into dice-backgammon. He may be disposed to think that our own dice-backgammon, though tolerably ancient, came into existence by a similar course of development. It should be added that both as played with cowries and dice, games like *pachisi* are ancient in India. Having looked into the Sanskrit references and consulted Professor Jolly, of Würzburg, I am inclined to think that a game called *panchikâ*, played with five cowries, may represent one of its earliest forms, for the name of *pachisi*, meaning "five-and-twenty," is clearly derived from the scoring of the throw of five cowries. Leaving this for further examination, it will be sufficient to have given an idea of the nature of the Hindu *pachisi*, for it is to this game that a variety of lot-backgammon appearing in Old Mexico will now be seen to present the most striking analogy.

. . . There is a Chinese variety of the game of four sticks, popular under the name of *nyut* in Korea, where Mr. Stewart Culin describes it. Four lots are used, made of bow-wood, plano-convex and with one black and one white side. . . . The scoring is

Whites up	 4	3	2	1	0
Score	.... 4 $+$	3	2	1	5

Four blacks give another throw. The calculated values would be 4, 1, ⅔, 1, 4.

Little sticks or other objects are used as markers or pieces, called horses (*má*) of which each player has from one to four, which move and take along the spots of the diagram. . . .

As early as 1519, the Spanish invaders on their way to the city of Mexico noticed cloths worked in chessboard-pattern from which they judged that the dice-boxes of checkers were also in use in the country. The only known Mexican game for which these cloths were likely to have been intended was *patolli*. Of this game the description by Lopez de Gomara was written between 1540-50, as follows: Sometimes Montezuma looked on as they played at *patoliztli*, which much resembles the game of tables, and which is played with beans marked like one-faced dice which they call *patolli*, which they shake between both hands and throw on a mat or on the ground where there are certain lines like a merell-board, on which they mark with stones the point that came up, by taking off or putting on a little stone. Juan de Torquemada partly follows this account but gives further details: "There was another game they called *patolli*, which somewhat resembles the game of royal tables, and is played with beans having points made in them after the manner of one-faced dice, and they call it the game of *patolli* because these dice are so called; they throw them with both hands on a thin mat which is called *petate*, with certain lines drawn on it in the form of a St. Andrew's cross and others across them, marking the point which fell upwards (as is done with dice) taking off or putting on stones of different color, as in the game of tables." Bernardino de Sahagun has other details to contribute, especially as to the marking of the beans. He mentions *patolli* as a pastime of the lords, describing the lots as "four large beans, each having a hole," and again that "they made on the mat a painted cross full of squares . . . they took three great beans with certain dots made in them, and let them fall on the painted cross." By the time of this writer the game, at which gold and jewels used to be staked, had been given up under suspicion of idolatry.

The already mentioned History of the Indies bearing the name of Diego Duran appears from the critical examination by Ramirez and Chavero to have been more or less an earlier composition written by a native Mexican, probably in his own language. The picture-writing accompanying it, though so late as to be much Europeanized, is an authentic document. The whole may be taken as a record from, or near, the first generation after the conquest in 1521. Chapter C. treats chiefly of *patolli*, at which and other games the Indians not only would gamble themselves into slavery, but even came to be legally put to death as human sacrifices. So covetous were these gamblers that they took as their particular gods the instruments of their game, if it was dice-playing they held the dice as a god and the lines and figures marked on the mat, as seen in the picture, which gods they worshiped with particular ceremonies not only at this game but at all their other games. They played the game of *merells* or draughts imitating the game of chess played by the Spaniards, taking one from the other the black and white stones or pieces. "There was another game, which was that they made on a plaster floor little hollows after the manner of a game-board, and one took ten stones and the other ten others, and the one placed his stones on the one edge and the other on the other on contrary sides, and taking some reeds split down the middle they threw them on the ground so that they sprang up, and as many reeds as fell with the hollow side upward so many places he moved his stones forward, and thus one followed the other, and all such stones as he overtook, he took one after another till he left his adversary without any." There was also the game of the mat, which was the keenest they played, at which many could play jointly and in company, "the game they played on this mat they called *patolly*, which is the same word we now use for cards. On this mat they had painted a large St. Andrew's cross filling the mat from corner to corner, within the hollow of which cross there were some transverse lines serving for squares, which cross and squares were marked and drawn with diluted olin (caoutchouc) . . . for these squares there were twelve small stones, six red and six blue, which stones they divided between the players so many to each; if two played as was usual, each took six, and although many might play, one always played for all, they following his play . . . who had the best throws of the dice, which were some black beans, five or ten according as they wished to lose or gain, which had some little white holes in each bean by which were marked the number of squares which were gained on each hand, where five were marked they were ten, and ten twenty, and if one, one, and if two, two, and if three, three, and if four, four, but marking five they were ten, and if ten, twenty, and thus these little white dots were the lots and counting of the lines which were gained, and for moving the stones from some squares to others." . . .

I pass over descriptions of *patolli* by later writers, who had no direct knowledge of the game and in no way improve on the statements of

Aztec patolli.

the early chroniclers. The foregoing citations from these may have seemed to the reader of tedious length, yet there is hardly a sentence in them which is not evidence in the case. The accounts of the popularity of the game at the time of the conquest, the mention of its special god and the ceremonies of his worship, preclude the idea of the Europeans having brought it into the country with their own cards and dice which have long since superseded it. The descriptions given by the Spaniards indeed show that the game was new to them, for they noticed its re-semblance to the game of tables and in a less degree to draught-games; had they known anything nearer they would have said so. The only difficulty lies in the descriptions of the lots and the scoring, the very con-fusion of which seems to show that the Spaniards were not familiar with the device of lot-scoring, as a Hindu or Arab would be, or they would have expressly distinguished it from the use of numbered dice or tallies. . . .

. . . This description may be compared with the particulars noted by Mr. Robert Frazer of Philadelphia as to the Apache game of *tze-tiehl* or "stone and sticks," which account he kindly sent me with the

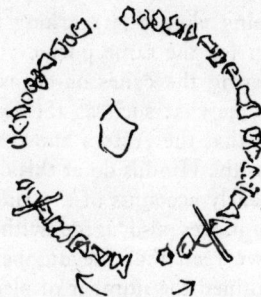

Fig. 13.—Apache scoring circuit for lots.

diagram and a set of the lot-sticks on his return from a visit to the Apache country in 1884. These lot-sticks are thrown against the center stone shown in the diagram and score thus:

Convex up	3	2	1	0
Score	10 +	3	1	5

According to calculation the numbers would be 10, 3⅓, 3⅓, 10. Three-up gives another throw. Fig. 13 shows the position of 40 small stones placed in quadrants round the center, the two players moving their marking-sticks, which are the pieces in the game, in opposite directions, and the player whose stick falls on his opponent's taking it up and sending it back, from which it is evident that the game is won by getting first round. If now this Apache game be compared with the Chinese-Korean game of *nyut* the resemblance will be seen to be so close that the Indians might conceivably have learnt it from the Chinese who for years past have swarmed in this part of America. But in one form or another the game prevails among the native tribes; thus the lot-sticks shown in Fig. 7 [omitted] are those used by the Pueblo Indians of Arizona. It has been seen that the earlier accounts from the district date from times before the Chinese immigration. . . .

Examination has now to be briefly made of the results of the preceding evidence. The existence in Mexico before the Spanish period of a game allied to *tâb* and *pachisi* may be maintained as hardly open to question. How the Aztec players moved and captured the colored pieces along the rows of places on the diagrams according to regulated chance, is known by positive description and even by an authentic picture. The manner of the deciding chances, though sometimes indistinct, is on the whole recognizable. The use of simple two-faced lots, which have lasted on till now among the wilder northern tribes, is unmistakeable; the Aztec split reeds, and the beans with a hole on one side, can have been nothing else. The marking by several lines or dots may very well have been for the same purpose, but it is not impossible that it served for numbering the canes or beans so as to convert them into rudimentary dice somewhat such as the Spanish arenillas. If this were so, it would follow that the Aztecs knew how to play their game either with lots or dice, as the Hindus do at this day; we meet, however, with no trace of dice in early accounts of the Indian tribes to the north. The descriptions of the moves also agree with lots rather than dice. In Duran's first game we read that the number of canes falling with the hollow side up determined the number of places to be moved, which easy method agrees with the play of the Southern Californians. In Duran's second game which was *patolli* proper, we meet with what seems a rule of probability, giving a much higher value to the extreme throws than to the middle or average throws, which as usual show a tendency to follow the mere number of faces turned up, as in the previous more rudimentary game; the reader sufficiently interested in the problem will make the comparison for himself between Duran's numbers and the scoring lists here given.

The idea that the similarity between the American and Asiatic games resulted from independent invention has seemed probable to more than one anthropologist. This suggestion raises the problem, as yet only imperfectly solved, of determining what kind and amount of similarity in the arts or customs or opinions of different districts may justify us in denying the possibility of their independent development and claiming them as results of transmission. Experience has indeed led the educated world to judge positively on this question in extreme cases. If Englishmen landing on a remote island were accosted by natives in their own language, the notion that English had been developed here as well as in England would be treated as a jest. If the natives were seen shooting with guns or playing chess, the suggestion of guns and chess having been twice invented even in approximate forms would hardly fare better. Where, then, is the limit of similarity which proves common derivation? Popular opinion is no doubt led by accumulated experience to consider that highly special or complex phenomena of thought and habit do not so readily recur as the obvious and simple, and probably this judgment is sound. The subject ought, however, to be brought to altogether more accurate definition. I have found it useful at any rate as a means of clearing ideas, to attempt a definite rule by analyzing such phenomena into constituent elements showing so little connection with one another that they may be reasonably treated as independent. The more numerous are such elements, the more improbable the recurrence of their combination. In the case of a language recurrence may be treated as impossible. If the invention of the gun be divided into the blow-tube, the use of metal, the explosive, the lock, the percussion, etc., and classed as an invention say of the 10th order, and the invention of chess with its six kinds of pieces with different moves indicated as of perhaps the 6th order, these figures would correspond to an immense improbability of recurrence. Such a game as *pachisi*, combining the invention of divining by lot, its application to the sportive wager, the combination of several lots with an appreciation of the law of chances, the transfer of the result to a counting-board, the rules of moving and taking, would place it in perhaps the 6th order, the recurrence of which might be less than that of chess, but according to common experience still far outside any probability on which reasonable men could count.

If this argument be admitted, the relation of the *pachisi-patolli* groups of games in the Old and New World must be accounted for by intercourse before the Spanish conquest, other than that of the Northmen, which fails to answer the conditions. If communication across the Atlantic fails, the alternative is communication across the Pacific from Eastern Asia, where the sportive material required could readily be furnished. . . .

39. EGYPTIAN HIEROGLYPHIC WRITING [5]

BY E. A. WALLIS BUDGE

THE ancient Egyptians expressed their ideas in writing by means of a large number of picture signs which are commonly called *Hieroglyphics*. They began to use them for this purpose more than seven thousand years ago, and they were employed uninterruptedly until about B.C. 100, that is to say, until nearly the end of the rule of the Ptolemies over Egypt. It is hardly probable that the hieroglyphic system of writing was invented in Egypt, and the evidence on this point now accumulating indicates that it was brought there by certain invaders who came from northeast or central Asia; they settled down in the valley of the Nile at some place between Memphis on the north and Thebes on the south, and gradually established their civilization and religion in their new home. Little by little the writing spread to the north and to the south, until at length hieroglyphics were employed, for state purposes at least, from the coast of the Mediterranean to the most southern portion of the Island of Meroë, that is to say, over a tract of country more than 2,000 miles long. A remarkable peculiarity of Egyptian hieroglyphics is the slight modification of form which they suffered during a period of thousands of years, a fact due, no doubt, partly to the material upon which the Egyptians inscribed them, and partly to a conservatism begotten of religious convictions. The Babylonian and Chinese picture characters became modified at so early a period that some thousands of years before Christ, their original forms were lost. This reference to the modified forms of hieroglyphics brings us at once to the mention of the various ways in which they were written in Egypt, i.e. to the three different kinds of Egyptian writing.

The oldest form of writing is the *hieroglyphic*, in which the various objects, animate and inanimate, for which the characters stand are depicted as accurately as possible. . . .

Hieroglyphics were cut in stone, wood, and other materials with marvelous accuracy, at depths varying from 1-16 of an inch to 1 inch; the details of the objects represented were given either by cutting or by painting in colors. In the earliest times the mason must have found it easier to cut characters into the stone than to sculpture them in relief; but it is probable that the idea of preserving carefully what had been inscribed also entered his mind, for frequently when the surface outline

[5] From pages 1-39 of E. A. Wallis Budge, *Easy Lessons in Egyptian Hieroglyphics*, Kegan Paul, Trench, Trübner and Co., Ltd., London, 1899. By permission.

of a character has been destroyed sufficient traces remain in the incuse portion of it for purposes of identification. Speaking generally, celestial objects are colored blue, as also are metal vessels and instruments; animals, birds, and reptiles are painted as far as possible to represent their natural colors; the Egyptian man is painted red, and the woman yellow or a pinky-brown color, and so on. . . .

Picture signs or hieroglyphics were employed for religious and state purposes from the earliest to the latest times, and it is astonishing to contemplate the labor which must have been expended by the mason in cutting an inscription of any great length, if every character was well and truly made. Side by side with cutters in stone carvers in wood must have existed, and for a proof of the skill which the latter class of handicraftsmen possessed at a time which must be well nigh predynastic, the reader is referred to the beautiful panels in the Gizeh Museum which have been published by Mariette. . . . But the Egyptians must have had need to employ their hieroglyphics for other purposes than inscriptions which were intended to remain in one place, and the official documents of state, not to mention the correspondence of the people, cannot have been written upon stone or wood. At a very early date the papyrus plant was made into a sort of paper upon which were written drafts of texts which the mason had to cut in stone, official documents, letters, etc. The stalk of this plant, which grew to the height of twelve or fifteen feet, was triangular, and was about six inches in diameter in its thickest part. The outer rind was removed from it, and the stalk was divided into layers with a flat needle; these layers were laid upon a board, side by side, and upon these another series of layers was laid in a horizontal direction, and a thin solution of gum was then run between them, after which both series of layers were pressed and dried. The number of such sheets joined together depended upon the length of the roll required. The papyrus rolls which have come down to us vary greatly in length and width; the finest Theban papyri are about seventeen inches wide, and the longest roll yet discovered is the great Papyrus of Rameses III, which measures one hundred and thirty-five feet in length. On such rolls of papyrus the Egyptians wrote with a reed, about ten inches long and one eighth of an inch in diameter, the end of which was bruised to make the fibers flexible, and not cut; the ink was made of vegetable substances, or of colored earths mixed with gum and water.

Now it is evident that the hieroglyphics traced in outline upon papyrus with a comparatively blunt reed can never have had the clearness and sharp outlines of those cut with metal chisels in a hard substance; it is also evident that the increased speed at which government orders and letters would have to be written would cause the scribe, unconsciously at first, to abbreviate and modify the picture signs, until at length only the most salient characteristics of each remained. And this is exactly what happened. Little by little the hieroglyphics lost much of their pictorial character, and degenerated into a series of signs which went to form the cursive writing called *Hieratic.* It was used extensively by the priests in copying literary works in all periods, and though it occupied originally a subordinate position in respect of hieroglyphics, especially as regards religious texts, it at length became equal in importance to hieroglyphic writing. The following example of hieratic writing is taken from the Prisse Papyrus upon which at a period about B.C. 2600 two texts, containing moral precepts which were composed about one thousand years earlier, were written.

Now if we transcribe these into hieroglyphics we obtain the following:

1. a reed
2. a mouth
3. a hare
4. the wavy surface of water
5. see No. 4
6. a kind of vessel
7. an owl
8. a bolt of a door
9. a seated figure of a man
10. a stroke written to make the word symmetrical
11. see No. 1
12. a knee bone (?)
13. see No. 2.
14. a roll of papyrus tied up
15. an eye
16. see No. 6
17. a goose
18. see No. 9
19. see No. 4
20. a chair back
21. a sickle

On comparing the above hieroglyphics with their hieratic equivalents it will be seen that only long practice would enable the reader to iden-tify quickly the abbreviated characters which he had before him; the above specimen of hieratic is, however, well written and is relatively easy to read. In the later times, i.e. about B.C. 900, the scribes invented a series of purely arbitrary or conventional modifications of the hieratic characters and so a new style of writing, called *Enchorial* or *Demotic*, came into use; it was used chiefly for business or social purposes at first, but at length copies of the "Book of the Dead" and lengthy literary compositions were written in it. In the Ptolemaic period Demotic was considered to be of such importance that whenever the text of a royal decree was inscribed upon a stele which was to be set up in some public place and was intended to be read by the public in general, a version of the said decree, written in the Demotic character, was added. . . .

Hieroglyphic characters may be written in columns or in horizontal lines, which are sometimes to be read from left to right and sometimes from right to left. There was no fixed rule about the direction in which the characters should be written, and as we find that in inscriptions which are cut on the sides of a door they usually face inwards, i.e. to-wards the door, each group thus facing the other, the scribe and sculptor needed only to follow their own ideas in the arrangement and direction of the characters, or the dictates of symmetry. To ascertain the direc-tion in which an inscription is to be read we must observe in which way the men, and birds, and animals face, and then read *towards* them. . . .

Hieratic is usually written in horizontal lines which are to be read from right to left, but in some papyri dating from the XIIth dynasty the texts are arranged in short columns.

Before we pass to the consideration of the Egyptian Alphabet, syllabic signs, etc., it will be necessary to set forth briefly the means by which the power to read these was recovered, and to sketch the history of the decipherment of Egyptian hieroglyphics in connection with the *Rosetta Stone*. . . .

The Rosetta Stone was found by a French artillery officer called Boussard, among the ruins of Fort Saint Julien, near the Rosetta mouth of the Nile, in 1799, but it subsequently came into the possession of the British Government at the capitulation of Alexandria. It now stands at the southern end of the great Egyptian Gallery in the British Museum. The top and right hand bottom corner of this remarkable object have been broken off, and at the present the texts inscribed upon it consist of fourteen lines of hieroglyphics, thirty-two lines of demotic, and fifty-four lines of Greek. It measures about 3 ft. 9 in. x 2 ft. 4½ in. x 11 in. on the inscribed side.

The Rosetta Stone records that Ptolemy V. Epiphanes, king of Egypt from B.C. 205 to B.C. 182, conferred great benefits upon the priesthood, and set aside large revenues for the maintenance of the temples, and remitted the taxes due from the people at a period of distress, and undertook and carried out certain costly engineering works in connection with the irrigation system of Egypt. In gratitude for these acts the priesthood convened a meeting at Memphis, and ordered that a statue of the king should be set up in every temple of Egypt, that a gilded wooden statue of the king placed in a gilded wooden shrine should be established in each temple, etc.; and as a part of the great plan to do honor to the king it was ordered that a copy of the decree, inscribed on a basalt stele in hieroglyphic, demotic, and Greek characters, should be set up in each of the first, second, and third grade temples near the king's statue. The provisions of this decree were carried out in the eighth year of the king's reign, and the Rosetta Stone is one of the stelæ which, presumably, were set up in the great temples throughout the length and breadth of the land. But the importance of the stone historically is very much less than its value philologically, for the decipherment of the Egyptian hieroglyphics is centered in it, and it formed the base of the work done by scholars in the past century which has resulted in the restoration of the ancient Egyptian language and literature.

It will be remembered that long before the close of the Roman rule in Egypt the hieroglyphic system of writing had fallen into disuse, and that its place had been taken by demotic, and by Coptic, that is to say, the Egyptian language written in Greek letters; the widespread use of Greek and Latin among the governing and upper classes of Egypt also caused the disappearance of Egyptian as the language of state. The study of hieroglyphics was prosecuted by the priests in remote districts probably until the end of the fifth century of our era, but very little later the ancient inscriptions had become absolutely a dead letter, and until the beginning of the present century there was neither an Oriental nor a European who could either read or understand a hieroglyphic inscription. Many writers pretended to have found the key to the hieroglyphics, and many more professed, with a shameless impudence which it is hard to understand in these days, to translate the contents of the texts into a modern tongue. Foremost among such pretenders must be mentioned Athanasius Kircher who, in the seventeenth century, declared that he had found the key to the hieroglyphic inscriptions; the translations which he prints in his *Œdipus Ægyptiacus* are utter nonsense, but as they were put forth in a learned tongue many people at the time believed they were correct. More than half a century later the Comte de Pahlin stated that an inscription at Denderah was only a translation of Psalm C., and some later writers believed that the Egyptian inscriptions contained Bible phrases and Hebrew compositions. In the first half of the eighteenth century Warburton appears to have divined the existence of alphabetic characters in Egyptian, and had he possessed the necessary linguistic training it is quite possible that he would have done some useful work in decipherment. Among those who worked on the right lines must be mentioned de Guignes, who proved the existence of groups of characters having determinatives, and Zoëga, who came to the conclusion that the hieroglyphics were letters, and what was very important, that the cartouches, i.e. the ovals which occur in the inscriptions and are so called because they resemble cartridges, contained royal names. In 1802 Akerblad, in a letter to Silvestre de Sacy, discussed the demotic inscription on the Rosetta Stone, and published an alphabet of the characters. But Akerblad never received the credit which was his due for this work, for although it will be found, on comparing Young's "Supposed Enchorial Alphabet" printed in 1818 with that of Akerblad printed in 1802, that *fourteen* of the characters are identical in both alphabets, no credit is given to him by Young. Further, if Champollion's alphabet, published in his *Lettre à M. Dacier*, Paris, 1822, be compared with that of Akerblad, sixteen of the characters will be found to be identical; yet Champollion, like Young, seemed to be oblivious of the fact.

With the work of Young and Champollion we reach firm ground. A great deal has been written about the merits of Young as a decipherer of the Egyptian hieroglyphics, and he has been both over-praised and over-blamed. He was undoubtedly a very clever man and a great linguist, even though he lacked the special training in Coptic which his great rival Champollion possessed. In spite of this, however, he identified correctly the names of six gods, and those of Ptolemy and Berenice; he also made out the true meanings of several ideographs, the true values of six letters of the alphabet, and the correct consonantal values of three more. This he did some years before Champollion published his Egyptian alphabet, and as priority of publication (as the late Sir Henry Rawlinson found it necessary to say with reference to his own work on cuneiform decipherment) must be accepted as indicating priority of discovery, credit should be given to Young for at least this contribution towards the decipherment. No one who has taken the pains to read the literature on the subject will attempt to claim for Young that the value of his work was equal to that of Champollion, for the system of the latter scholar was eminently scientific, and his knowledge of Coptic was wonderful, considering the period when he lived. Besides this the quality of his hieroglyphic work was so good, and the amount of it which he did so great, that in those respects the two rivals ought not to be compared. He certainly knew of Young's results, and the admission by him that they existed would have satisfied Young's friends, and in no way diminished his own merit and glory.

In the year 1815 Mr. J. W. Bankes discovered on the Island of Philæ a red granite obelisk and pedestal which were afterwards removed at his expense by G. Belzoni and set up at Kingston Hall in Dorsetshire. The obelisk is inscribed with one column of hieroglyphics on each side, and the pedestal with twenty-four lines of Greek. In 1822 Champollion published an account of this monument in the *Revue encyclopédique* for March, and discussed the hieroglyphic and Greek inscriptions upon it. The Greek inscription had reference to a petition of the priests of Philæ made to Ptolemy, and his wife Kleopatra, and his sister also called Kleopatra, and these names of course occur in it. Champollion argued that if the hieroglyphic inscription has the same meaning as the Greek, these names must also occur in it. Now the only name found on the Rosetta Stone is that of Ptolemy which is, of course, contained in a cartouche, and when Champollion examined the hieroglyphic inscription on the Philæ obelisk, he not only found the royal names there, enclosed in cartouches, but also that one of them was identical with that which he knew from the Greek of the Rosetta Stone to be that of Ptolemy. He was certain that this name was that of Ptolemy, because in the Demotic inscription on the Rosetta Stone the group of characters which formed the name occurred over and over again, and in the places where, according to the Greek, they ought to occur. But on the Philæ Obelisk the name Kleopatra is mentioned, and in both of the names of Ptolemy and Kleopatra the same letters occur, that is to say L and P; if we can identify the letter P we shall not only have gained a letter, but be able to say at which end of the cartouches the names begin. Now writing down the names of Ptolemy and Kleopatra as they usually occur in hieroglyphics we have:

Ptolemy

Kleopatra

Let us however break the names up a little more and arrange the letters under numbers thus:

Ptolemy.

Kleopatra.

We must remember too that the Greek form of the name Ptolemy is Ptolemaios. Now on looking at the two names thus written we see at a glance that letter no. 5 in one name and no. 1 in the other are identical, and judging by their position only in the names they must represent the letter P; we see too that letter no. 2 in one name and no. 4 in the other are also identical, and arguing as before from their position they must represent the letter L. We may now write down the names thus:

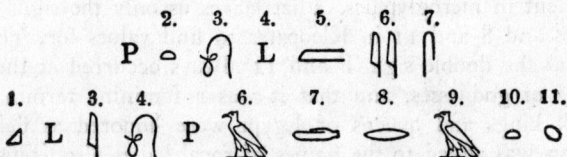

As only one of the names begins with P, that which begins with that letter must be Ptolemy. Now letter no. 4 in one name, and letter no. 3 in the other are identical, and also judging by their position we may assign it in each name the value of some vowel sound like O, and thus get:

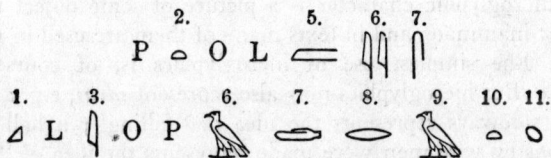

But the letter between P and O in Ptolemy must be T, and as the name ends in Greek with S, the last letter in hieroglyphics must be S, so we may now write down the names thus:

Now if we look, as Champollion did, at the other ways in which the name of Kleopatra is written we shall find that instead of the letter no. 7 we sometimes have the letter no. 2 which we already know to be T, and as in the Greek form of the name this letter has an A before it, we may assume that no. 6 = A; the initial letter must, of course, be K. We may now write the names thus:

$$5. \qquad .6.$$
$$P \quad T \quad O \quad L \quad \rightleftharpoons \quad \text{\textbardbl} \quad S$$

$$3. \qquad\qquad 8. \qquad\qquad 11.$$
$$K \quad L \quad \text{|} \quad O \quad P \quad A \quad T \quad \rightleftharpoons \quad A \quad T \quad \circ$$

The sign no. 3 in the name Kleopatra represents some vowel sound like E, and this sign doubled (no. 6) represents the vowels AI in the name Ptolemaios; but as no. 6 represents EE, or Î, that is to say I pronounced in the Continental fashion, the O of the Greek form has no equivalent in hieroglyphics. That leaves us only the signs no. 5 in Ptolemaios and 8 and 11 in Kleopatra to find values for. Young had proved that the double sign T and 11 always occurred at the ends of the names of goddesses, and that it was a feminine termination; as the Greek kings and queens of Egypt were honored as deities, this termination was added to the names of royal ladies also. This disposes of the sign no. 11, and the letters no. 5 and no. 8 can be nothing else but M and R. So we may now write:

PTOLMIS, i.e. Ptolemy,
KLEOPATRA, i.e. Kleopatra. . . .

Every hieroglyphic character is a picture of some object in nature, animate, or inanimate, and in texts many of them are used in more than one way. The simplest use of hieroglyphics is, of course, as pictures. . . . But hieroglyphics may also represent *ideas*, e.g. a wall falling down sideways represents the idea of "falling"; a hall in which deliberations by wise men were made represents the idea of "counsel"; an ax represents the idea of a divine person or a god; a musical instrument represents the idea of pleasure, happiness, joy, goodness, and the like. Such are called *ideographs*. Now every picture of every object must have had a name, or we may say that each picture was a word-sign; a list of all these arranged in proper order would have made a dictionary in the earliest times. But let us suppose that at the period when these pictures were used as pictures only in Egypt, or wherever they first appeared, the king wished to put on record that an embassy from some such and such a neighboring potentate had visited him with such and such an object, and that the chief of the embassy, who was called by such and such a name, had brought him rich presents from his master. Now the scribes of the period could, no doubt, have reduced to writing an account of the visit, without any very great difficulty, but when they came to record the name of the distinguished visitor, or that of his master, they would not find this to be an easy matter. To have written down the name they would be obliged to make use of a number of hieroglyphics or picture characters which represented most closely the sound of the name of the envoy, without the least regard to their meaning as pictures, and, for the moment, the picture characters would have represented sounds only. The scribes must have done the same had they been ordered to make a list of the presents which the envoy had brought for their royal master. Passing over the evident anachronism let us call the envoy "Ptolemy," which name we may write, as in the preceding chapter, with the signs:

Now no. 1 represents a door, no. 2 a cake, no. 3 a knotted rope, no. 4 a lion, no. 5 (uncertain), no. 6 two reeds, and no. 7 a chairback; but here each of these characters is employed for the sake of its *sound* only.

The need for characters which could be employed to express *sounds only* caused the Egyptians at a very early date to set aside a considerable number of picture signs for this purpose, and to these the name of *phonetics* has been given. Phonetic signs may be either syllabic or alphabetic, e.g. *peh, mut, maāt, χeper,* which are syllabic, and *p, b, m, r, k,* which are alphabetic. Now the five alphabetic signs just quoted represent as pictures a door, a foot and leg, an owl, a mouth, and a vessel respectively, and each of these objects no doubt had a name; but the question naturally arises how they came to represent single letters? It seems that the sound of the *first letter* in the name of an object was given to the picture or character representing it, and henceforward the character bore that phonetic value. Thus the first character P, represents a door made of a number of planks of wood upon which three cross-pieces are nailed. There is no word in Egyptian for door, at all events in common use, which begins with P, but, as in Hebrew, the word for door must be connected with the root "to open"; now the Egyptian word for "to open" is *pt[a]h* and as we know that the first character in that word has the sound of P and of no other letter, we may reasonably assume that the Egyptian word for "door" began with P. The third character M represents the horned owl, the name of which is preserved for us in the Coptic word *mûlotch;* the first letter of this word begins with M, and therefore the phonetic value of the owl sign is M. In the same way the other letters of the Egyptian alphabet were derived, though it is not always possible to say what the word-value of a character was originally. In many cases it is not easy to find the

𓄿	A (א)			
𓇋	Á (ʾ)			
𓂝	Ā (ע)			
or	I (ʾ)		—	S (ם)
or	U (ו)			S (שׁ)
	B (ב)			SH (Ś) (שׁ)
	P (פּ)			K (כ)
	F (פּ)			Q (ק)
or	M (מ)			Ḳ (נ)
or	N (נ)			T (ת)
or	R and L (ר, ל)			Ṭ (ט)
	H (ה)			TH (θ) (ת)
	Ḥ (ח)			TCH (T') (צ)
	KH (χ) (Arab. خ)			

Egyptian Alphabet

word-values of an alphabetic sign, even by reference to Coptic, a fact which seems to indicate that the alphabetic characters were developed from word-values so long ago that the word-values themselves have passed out of the written language. Already in the earliest dynastic inscriptions known to us hieroglyphic characters are used as pictures, ideographs and phonetics side by side, which proves that these distinctions must have been invented in pre-dynastic times.

The Egyptian alphabet has a great deal in common with the Hebrew and other Semitic dialects in respect of the guttural and other letters, peculiar to Oriental peoples, and therefore the Hebrew letters have been added to shew what I believe to be the general values of the alphabetic signs. It is hardly necessary to say that differences of opinion exist among scholars as to the method in which hieroglyphic characters should be transcribed into Roman letters, but this is not to be wondered at considering that the scientific study of Egyptian is only about eighty years old, and that the whole of the literature has not yet been published.

Some ideographs have more than one phonetic value, in which case they are called *polyphones;* and many ideographs representing entirely different objects have similar values, in which case they are called homophones.

As long as the Egyptians used picture writing pure and simple their meaning was easily understood, but when they began to spell their words with alphabetic signs and syllabic values of picture signs, which had no reference whatever to the original meaning of the signs, it was at once found necessary to indicate in some way the meaning and even sounds of many of the words so written; this they did by adding to them signs which are called *determinatives.* It is impossible to say when the Egyptians first began to add determinatives to their words, but all known hieroglyphic inscriptions not pre-dynastic contain them, and it seems as if they must have been the product of pre-historic times. They, however, occur less frequently in the texts of the earlier than of the later dynasties.

Determinatives may be divided into two groups; those which determine a single species, and those which determine a whole class. The following determinatives of classes should be carefully noted:

Character	Determinative of	Character	Determinative of
1.	to call, beckon	6. or	god, divine being or thing
2.	man	7.	goddess
3.	to eat, think, speak, and of whatever is done with the mouth	8.	tree
		9.	plant, flower
4.	inertness, idleness	10. ◇, ⊐	earth, land
		11.	road, to travel
5.	woman	12. ∿	foreign land

A few words have no determinative, and need none, because their meaning was fixed at a very early period, and it was thought unnecessary to add any; examples of such are *henā* "with," *ȧm* "in," *māk* "verily" and the like. On the other hand a large number of words have one determinative, and several have more than one. Of words of one determinative the following are examples:

1. *ȧm* to eat; a picture of a man putting food into his mouth is the determinative.

2. *ānχ* a flower; the picture of a flower is the determinative.

3. *sma* to slay; the picture of a knife is the determinative, and indicates that the word *sma* means "knife", or that it refers to some action that is done with a knife.

4. *ses* bolt; the picture of the branch of a tree is the determinative, and indicates that *ses* is an object made of wood.

Of words of one or more determinatives the following is an example:

1. *renpit* flowers; the pictures of a flower in the bud, and a flower, are the determinatives; the three strokes | | | are the sign of the plural.

Words may be spelt (1) with alphabetic characters wholly, or (2) with a mixture of alphabetic and syllabic characters; examples of the first class are:

	sfenṭ	a knife
	ȧsfet	wickedness
	šāt	a book

And examples of the second class are:

1. ☒ *ḥenkset* hair, in which ☒ has by itself the value of *ḥen*; so the word might be written ☒ or ☒.

2. ☒ *neḥebet* neck, in which ☒ has by itself the value of *neḥ*; so the word might be written ☒ as well as ☒.

We may now take a short extract from the Tale of the Two Brothers, which will illustrate the use of alphabetic and syllabic characters and determinatives; the determinatives are marked by *; and the syllabic characters by †; the remaining signs are alphabetic. (N. B. There is no *e* in Egyptian.)

un	àn	paif	sen	āa	her
		His	brother	elder	

χeperu	mà	àbu	qemātu	àu-f	her
became	like	panthers	southern.	He	

ṭāt	ṭemtu	paif	nui
made	sharp	his	dagger,

àu-f	her	ṭātu-f	em	ṭet-f	un	àn
he		placed it	in	his hand.		

paif   sen   āa   āḥā   en
His   brother   elder   stood

ḥa   pa   sbai   paif
behind   the   door   of his

àhait   er   χaṭbu   paif
stable   to   stab   his

sen   šeràu   em   paif   i   em
brother   younger   at   his   coming   at

ruha   er   ṭāt   āq   naif
eventide   to   make   to enter   his

àaut   er   pa   àhait
cattle   into   the   stables.

40. MELANESIAN RELIGION [6]

BY BISHOP R. H. CODRINGTON

THE religion of the Melanesians is the expression of their conception of the supernatural, and embraces a very wide range of beliefs and practices, the limits of which it would be very difficult to define. It is equally difficult to ascertain with precision what these beliefs are. The ideas of the natives are not clear upon many points, they are not accustomed to

[6] From chapter 7 of R. H. Codrington, *The Melanesians, Their Anthropology and Folk-Lore*, 1891. By permission of the Clarendon Press, Oxford.

present them in any systematic form among themselves. An observer who should set himself the task of making systematic enquiries, must find himself baffled at the outset by the multiplicity of the languages with which he has to deal. Suppose him to have as a medium of communication a language which he and those from whom he seeks information can use freely for the ordinary purposes of life, he finds that to fail when he seeks to know what is the real meaning of those expressions which his informant must needs use in his own tongue, because he knows no equivalent for them in the common language which is employed. Or if he gives what he supposes to be an equivalent, it will often happen that he and the enquirer do not understand that word in the same sense. A missionary has his own difficulty in the fact that very much of his communication is with the young, who do not themselves know and understand very much of what their elders believe and practice. Converts are disposed to blacken generally and indiscriminately their own former state, and with greater zeal the present practices of others. There are some things they are really ashamed to speak of; and there are others which they think they ought to consider wrong, because they are associated in their memory with what they know to be really bad. Many a native Christian will roundly condemn native songs and dances, who, when questions begin to clear his mind, acknowledges that some dances are quite innocent, explains that none that he knows have any religious significance whatever, says that many songs also have nothing whatever bad in them, and writes out one or two as examples. Natives who are still heathen will speak with reserve of what still retains with them a sacred character, and a considerate missionary will respect such reserve; if he should not respect it the native may very likely fail in his respect for him, and amuse himself at his expense. Few missionaries have time to make systematic enquiries; if they do, they are likely to make them too soon, and for the whole of their after-career make whatever they observe fit into their early scheme of the native religion. Often missionaries, it is to be feared, so manage it that neither they nor the first generation of their converts really know what the old religion of the native people was. There is always with missionaries the difficulty of language; a man may speak a native language every day for years and have reason to believe he speaks it well, but it will argue ill for his real acquaintance with it if he does not find out that he makes mistakes. Resident traders, if observant, are free from some of a missionary's difficulties; but they have their own. The "pigeon English," which is sure to come in, carries its own deceits; "plenty devil" serves to convey much information; a chief's grave is "devil stones," the dancing ground of a village is a "devil ground," the drums are idols, a dancing club is a "devil stick." [7] The most intelligent travelers and naval officers pass their short period of observation in this atmosphere of confusion. Besides, every one, missionary and visitor, carries with him some preconceived ideas; he expects to see idols, and he sees them; images are labeled idols in museums whose makers carved them for amusement; a Solomon islander fashions the head of his lime-box stick into a grotesque figure, and it becomes the subject of a woodcut as "a Solomon Island god." It is extremely difficult for any one to begin enquiries without some prepossessions, which, even if he can communicate with the natives in their own language, affect his conceptions of the meaning of the answers he receives. The questions he puts guide the native to the answer he thinks he ought to give. The native, with very vague beliefs and notions floating in cloudy solution in his mind, finds in the questions of the European a thread on which these will precipitate themselves, and, without any intention to deceive, avails himself of the opportunity to clear his own mind while he satisfies the questioner.

Some such statement as this of the difficulties in the way of a certain knowledge of the subject is a necessary introduction to the account which is given here of the religion of the Melanesians; and it is desirable that the writer should disclaim pretensions to accuracy or completeness. The general view which is presented must be taken with the particular examples of Melanesian belief and customs in matters of religion which follow.

(1) The Melanesian mind is entirely possessed by the belief in a supernatural power or influence, called almost universally *mana*.[8] This

[7] It may be asserted with confidence that a belief in a devil, that is of an evil spirit, has no place whatever in the native Melanesian mind. The word has certainly not been introduced in the Solomon or Banks Islands by missionaries, who in those groups have never used the word devil. Yet most unfortunately it has come to pass that the religious beliefs of European traders have been conveyed to the natives in the word "devil," which they use without knowing what it means. It is much to be wished that educated Europeans would not use the word so loosely as they do.

[8] Professor Max Müller, in his Hibbert Lectures of 1878, did me the honor of quoting the following words from a letter. "The religion of the Melanesians consists, as far as belief goes, in the persuasion that there is a supernatural power about belonging to the region of the unseen; and, as far as practice goes, in the use of means of getting this power turned to their own benefit. The notion of a Supreme Being is altogether foreign to them, or indeed of any being occupying a very elevated place in their world. . . . There is a belief in a force altogether distinct from physical power, which acts in all kinds of ways for good and evil, and which it is of the greatest advantage to possess or control. This is Mana. The word is common I believe to the whole Pacific, and people have tried very hard to describe what it is in different regions. I think I know what our people

is what works to effect everything which is beyond the ordinary power of men, outside the common processes of nature; it is present in the atmosphere of life, attaches itself to persons and to things, and is manifested by results which can only be ascribed to its operation. When one has got it he can use it and direct it, but its force may break forth at some new point; the presence of it is ascertained by proof. A man comes by chance upon a stone which takes his fancy; its shape is singular, it is like something, it is certainly not a common stone, there must be *mana* in it. So he argues with himself, and he puts it to the proof; he lays it at the root of a tree to the fruit of which it has a certain resemblance, or he buries it in the ground when he plants his garden; an abundant crop on the tree or in the garden shews that he is right, the stone is *mana*,[9] has that power in it. Having that power it is a vehicle to convey *mana* to other stones. In the same way certain forms of words, generally in the form of a song, have power for certain purposes; a charm of words is called a *mana*. But this power, though itself impersonal, is always connected with some person who directs it; all spirits have it, ghosts generally, some men. If a stone is found to have supernatural power, it is because a spirit has associated itself with it; a dead man's bone has with it *mana*, because the ghost is with the bone; a man may have so close a connection with a spirit or ghost that he has *mana* in himself also, and can so direct it as to effect what he desires; a charm is powerful because the name of a spirit or ghost expressed in the form of words brings into it the power which the ghost or spirit exercises through it. Thus all conspicuous success is a proof that a man has *mana*; his influence depends on the impression made on the people's mind that he has it; he becomes a chief by virtue of it. Hence a man's power, though political or social in its character, is his *mana*; the word is naturally used in accordance with the native conception of the character

meant by it, and that meaning seems to me to cover all that I hear about it elsewhere. It is a power or influence, not physical, and in a way supernatural; but it shews itself in physical force, or in any kind of power or excellence which a man possesses. This Mana is not fixed in anything, and can be conveyed in almost anything; but spirits, whether disembodied souls or supernatural beings, have it and can impart it; and it essentially belongs to personal beings to originate it, though it may act through the medium of water, or a stone, or a bone. All Melanesian religion consists, in fact, in getting this Mana for one's self, or getting it used for one's benefit—all religion, that is, as far as religious practices go, prayers and sacrifices."

[9] The word *mana* is both a noun substantive and a verb; a transitive form of the verb, *manag, manahi, manangi*, means to impart *mana*, or to influence with it. An object in which *mana* resides, and a spirit which naturally has *mana*, is said to be *mana*, with the use of the verb; a man has *mana*, but cannot properly be said to be *mana*.

of all power and influence as supernatural. If a man has been successful in fighting, it has not been his natural strength of arm, quickness of
eye, or readiness of resource that has won success; he has certainly got
the *mana* of a spirit or of some deceased warrior to empower him, conveyed in an amulet of a stone round his neck, or a tuft of leaves in
his belt, in a tooth hung upon a finger of his bow hand, or in the form
of words with which he brings supernatural assistance to his side. If
a man's pigs multiply, and his gardens are productive, it is not because
he is industrious and looks after his property, but because of the stones
full of *mana* for pigs and yams that he possesses. Of course a yam
naturally grows when planted, that is well known, but it will not be
very large unless *mana* comes into play; a canoe will not be swift unless
mana be brought to bear upon it, a net will not catch many fish, nor an
arrow inflict a mortal wound.

(2) The Melanesians believe in the existence of beings personal, intelligent, full of *mana*, with a certain bodily form which is visible
but not fleshly like the bodies of men. These they think to be more or
less actively concerned in the affairs of men, and they invoke and
otherwise approach them. These may be called spirits; but it is most
important to distinguish between spirits who are beings of an order
higher than mankind, and the disembodied spirits of men, which have
become in the vulgar sense of the word ghosts. From the neglect of this
distinction great confusion and misunderstanding arises; and it is
much to be desired that missionaries at any rate would carefully observe the distinction. Any personal object of worship among natives in
all parts of the world is taken by the European observer to be a spirit or
a god, or a devil; but among Melanesians at any rate it is very common
to invoke departed relatives and friends, and to use religious rites addressed to them. A man therefore who is approaching with some rite
his dead father, whose spirit he believes to be existing and pleased with
his pious action, is thought to be worshiping a false god or deceiving
spirit, and very probably is told that the being he worships does not
exist. The perplexed native hears with one ear that there is no such
thing as that departed spirit of a man which he venerates as a ghost but
his instructor takes to be a god, and with the other that the soul never
dies, and that his own spiritual interests are paramount and eternal.
They themselves make a clear distinction between the existing, conscious, powerful, disembodied spirits of the dead, and other spiritual
beings that never have been men at all. It is true that the two orders
of beings get confused in native language and thought, but their confusion begins at one end and the confusion of their visitors at another;
they think so much and constantly of ghosts that they speak of beings

who were never men as ghosts; Europeans take the spirits of the lately
dead for gods; less educated Europeans call them roundly devils. All
Melanesians, as far as my acquaintance with them extends, believe in
the existence both of spirits that never were men, and of ghosts which
are the disembodied souls of men deceased: to preserve as far as possible
this distinction, the supernatural beings that were never in a human
body are here called *spirits*, men's spirits that have left the body are
called *ghosts*.

There is, however, a very remarkable difference between the natives
of the New Hebrides and Banks' Islands to the east, and the natives
of the Solomon Islands to the west; the direction of the religious ideas
and practices of the former is towards spirits rather than ghosts, the
latter pay very little attention to spirits and address themselves almost
wholly to ghosts. This goes with a much greater development of a
sacrificial system in the west than in the east; and goes along also with
a certain advance in the arts of life. Enough is hardly known of the
Santa Cruz people, who lie between, to speak with certainty, but they
appear to range themselves, as they rather do geographically, on the side
of the Solomon Islands. In Fiji it is the established custom to call the
objects of the old worship gods; but Mr. Fison was "inclined to think
all the spiritual beings of Fiji, including the gods, simply the Mota
tamate," i.e. ghosts; and the words of Mr. Hazelwood, quoted by Mr.
Brenchley (*Cruise of the Curaçao*, p. 181), confirm this view. Tuikilakila told one of the first missionaries how he proposed to treat him.
"If you die first," said he, "I shall make you my god." And the same
Tuikilakila would sometimes say of himself, "I am a god." It is added
that he believed it too; and his belief was surely correct. For it should be
observed that the chief never said he was or should be a god, in English,
but that he was or should be a *kalou*, in Fijian, and a *kalou* he no doubt
became; that is to say, on his decease his departed spirit was invoked
and worshiped as he knew it would be. He used no verb "am" or "shall
be"; said only "I a *kalou*." In Fiji also this worship of the dead, rather
than of beings that never were in the flesh, accompanies a more considerable advance in the arts of life than is found in, for example, the
Banks' Islands. It is plain that the natives of the southern islands of
the New Hebrides, though they are said to worship "gods," believe in
the existence and power of spirits other than the disembodied spirits of
the dead, as well as of the ghosts of men. When a missionary visitor
to Anaiteum reported that the people "lived under the most abject bond-
age to their *Natmases*," and called these "gods," he was evidently speaking of the ghosts, the *Natmat* of the Banks' Islands, for the word is no
doubt the same. The belief in other spirits not ghosts of the dead, ap-

pears equally clear in the account given of the sacred stones and places, which correspond to those of the northern islands of the same group, and in the "minor deities" said to be the progeny of Nugerain, and called "gods of the sea, of the land, of mountains and valleys," who represent the *wui* of Lepers' Island and Araga. There does not appear to be anywhere in Melanesia a belief in a spirit which animates any natural object, a tree, waterfall, storm or rock, so as to be to it what the soul is believed to be to the body of a man. Europeans it is true speak of the spirits of the sea or of the storm or of the forest; but the native idea which they represent is that ghosts haunt the sea and the forest, having power to raise storms and to strike a traveler with disease, or that supernatural beings never men do the same. It may be said, then, that Melanesian religion divides the people into two groups; one, where, with an accompanying belief in spirits never men, worship is directed to the ghosts of the dead, as in the Solomon Islands; the other, where both ghosts and spirits have an important place, but the spirits have more worship than the ghosts, as is the case in the New Hebrides and in the Banks' Islands.

(3) In the Banks' Islands a spirit is called a *vui*, and is thus described by a native who was exhorted to give as far as possible the original notion conveyed among the old people by the word, and gave his definition after considerable reflection: "What is a *vui*? It lives, thinks, has more intelligence than a man; knows things which are secret without seeing; is supernaturally powerful with *mana*; has no form to be seen; has no soul, because itself is like a soul." But though the true conception of a *vui* represents it as incorporeal, the stories about the *vui* who have names treat them as if they were men possessed of supernatural power. The *wui* of the Northern New Hebrides are the same. . . .

These spirits, such as they are, have no position in the religion of the Solomon Islands; the ghosts, the disembodied spirits of the dead, are objects of worship; the *tindalo* of Florida, *tidadho* of Ysabel, *tinda'o* of Guadalcanar, *lio'a* of Saa, *'ataro* of San Cristoval. But it must not be supposed that every ghost becomes an object of worship. A man in danger may call upon his father, his grandfather, or his uncle; his nearness of kin is sufficient ground for it. The ghost who is to be worshiped is the spirit of a man who in his lifetime had *mana* in him; the souls of common men are the common herd of ghosts, nobodies alike before and after death. The supernatural power abiding in the powerful living man abides in his ghost after death, with increased vigor and more ease of movement. After his death, therefore, it is expected that he should begin to work, and some one will come forward and claim particular acquaintance with the ghost; if his power should shew itself, his position is assured as one worthy to be invoked, and to receive offerings, till his cultus gives way before the rising importance of one newly dead, and the sacred place where his shrine once stood and his relics were preserved is the only memorial of him that remains; if no proof of his activity appears, he sinks into oblivion at once. An admirable example of the establishment of the worship of a *tindalo* in Florida is given in the story of Ganindo, for which I am indebted to Bishop Selwyn. There was a gathering of men at Honggo to go on a head-hunting expedition under the leading of Kulanikama the chief (himself afterwards a ghost of worship), and Ganindo was their great fighting man. They went to attack Gaeta, and Lumba of Gaeta shot Ganindo near the collar-bone with an arrow. Having failed in their purpose they returned to Honggo, and said they, "our friend is dead." But as he still lived they took him over to Nggaombata in Guadalcanar, brought him back again, and put him on the hill Bonipari, where he died and was buried. Then they took his head, wove a basket for it, and built a house for it, and they said he was a *tindalo*. "Let us go and take heads," said they; so they made an expedition. As they went they ceased paddling in a quiet place and waited till they felt their canoe rock under them; then said they, "Here is a *tindalo*." To find out who he was they called the names of *tindalos*, and when they called the name of Ganindo the canoe shook again. In the same way they learnt what village they were to attack. Returning successful, they threw a spear into the roof of Ganindo's house, blew conches, and danced around it crying, "Our *tindalo* is strong to kill." Then they sacrificed to him, fish and food. Then they built him a new house, and made four images for the four corners, one of Ganindo himself, two of his sisters, and another. Then, when eight men had carried up the ridge covering for the house, eight men translated the relics to the shrine. One carried the bones of Ganindo, another his betel-nuts, another his lime-box, another his shell trumpet. They all went in crouching, as if under a heavy weight, and singing slowly, "*Ma-i-i, ma-i-i, ka saka tua,* hither, hither, let us lift the leg"; the eight legs were lifted together, and again they chanted "*ma-i-i, ma-i-i,*" and at the last *mai* the eight legs went down together. With this solemn procession the relics were set upon a bamboo platform, and sacrifices to the new *keramo* were begun; by Nisi first, then by Satani, then by Begoni, the last, at whose death some four years ago the sacrifices ceased, and the shrine fell to ruin before the advance of Christian teaching. To the natives of Florida this Ganindo was a *tindalo*, a ghost of worship, a *keramo*, a ghost powerful for war; he would be spoken of now by some Europeans as a god, by others as a devil, and the pigeon-English speaking natives now, who think that "devil" is the English for *tindalo*, would use the same word.

41. THE RELIGION OF THE AMAZULU OF SOUTH AFRICA AS TOLD BY THEMSELVES [10]

BY CANON H. CALLAWAY

DIVINERS

THE condition of a man who is about to be an inyanga [11] is this: At first he is apparently robust; but in process of time he begins to be delicate, not having any real disease, but being very delicate. He begins to be particular about food, and abstains from some kinds, and requests his friends not to give him that food, because it makes him ill. He habitually avoids certain kinds of food, choosing what he likes, and he does not eat much of that; and he is continually complaining of pains in different parts of his body. And he tells them that he has dreamt that he was being carried away by a river. He dreams of many things, and his body is muddled and he becomes a house of dreams. And he dreams constantly of many things, and on awaking says to his friends, "My body is muddled today; I dreamt many men were killing me; I escaped I know not how. And on waking one part of my body felt different from other parts; it was no longer alike all over." At last the man is very ill, and they go to the diviners to enquire.

The diviners do not at once see that he is about to have a soft head.[12] It is difficult for them to see the truth; they continually talk nonsense, and make false statements, until all the man's cattle are devoured at their command, they saying that the spirit of his people demands cattle, that it may eat food.

So the people readily assent to the diviners' word, thinking that they know. At length all the man's property is expended, he being still ill; and they no longer know what to do, for he has no more cattle, and his friends help him in such things as he needs.

At length an inyanga comes and says that all the others are wrong. He says, "I know that you come here to me because you have been

---

[10] Selected from pages 259-330 of the Rev. Canon H. Callaway, "The Religious System of the Amazulu," 1870, reissued as *Publications of the Folk-Lore Society, Volume 15, London,* 1884; republished by the Society, 1924. Only the English translation is given here: the original has the Zulu text also.

[11] Diviner, physician, or shaman.

[12] *A soft head*, that is, impressible. Diviners are said to have *soft* heads.

unable to do anything for the man, and have no longer the heart to believe that any inyanga can help you. But, my friends, I see that my friends, the other izinyanga,[13] have gone astray. They have not eaten impepo. They were not initiated in a proper way. Why have they been mistaken, when the disease is evident? For my part, I tell you the izinyanga have troubled you. The disease does not require to be treated with blood. As for the man, I see nothing else but that he is possessed by the Itongo. There is nothing else. He is possessed by an Itongo. Your people [14] move in him. They are divided into two parties; some say, 'No, we do not wish that our child should be injured. We do not wish it.' It is for that reason and no other that he does not get well. If you bar the way against the Itongo, you will be killing him. For he will not be an inyanga; neither will he ever be a man again; he will be what he is now. If he is not ill, he will be delicate, and become a fool, and be unable to understand anything. I tell you you will kill him by using medicines. Just leave him alone, and look to the end to which the disease points. Do you not see that on the day he has not taken medicine, he just takes a mouthful of food? Do not give him any more medicines. He will not die of the sickness, for he will have what is good given to him."

So the man may be ill two years without getting better; perhaps even longer than that. He may leave the house for a few days, and the people begin to think he will get well. But no, he is confined to the house again. This continues until his hair falls off. And his body is dry and scurfy; and he does not like to anoint himself. People wonder at the progress of the disease. But his head begins to give signs of what is about to happen. He shows that he is about to be a diviner by yawning again and again, and by sneezing again and again. And men say, "No! Truly it seems as though this man was about to be possessed by a spirit." This is also apparent from his being very fond of snuff; not allowing any long time to pass without taking some. And people begin to see that he has had what is good given to him.

After that he is ill; he has slight convulsions, and has water poured on him, and they cease for a time. He habitually sheds tears, at first slight, and at last he weeps aloud, and in the middle of the night, when the people are asleep, he is heard making a noise, and wakes the people by singing; he has composed a song, and men and women awake and go to sing in concert with him.

In this state of things they daily expect his death; he is now but skin and bones, and they think that tomorrow's sun will not leave him alive.

[13] Plural of inyanga.

[14] *Your people move in him*, that is, the Amatongo, a class of spirits.

The people wonder when they hear him singing, and they strike their hands in concert. They then begin to take courage, saying, "Yes; now we see that it is the head." [15]

Therefore whilst he is undergoing this initiation the people of the village are troubled by want of sleep; for a man who is beginning to be an inyanga causes great trouble, for he does not sleep, but works constantly with his brain; his sleep is merely by snatches, and he wakes up singing many songs; and people who are near quit their villages by night when they hear him singing aloud, and go to sing in concert. Perhaps he sings till the morning, no one having slept. The people of the village smite their hands in concert until they are sore. And then he leaps about the house like a frog; and the house becomes too small for him, and he goes out, leaping and singing, and shaking like a reed in the water, and dripping with perspiration.

At that time many cattle are eaten. The people encourage his becoming an inyanga; they employ means for making the Itongo white, that it may make his divination very clear. At length another ancient inyanga of celebrity is pointed out to him.[16] At night whilst asleep he is commanded by the Itongo, who says to him, "Go to So-and-so; go to him, and he will churn for you emetic-ubulawo, that you may be an inyanga altogether." Then he is quiet for a few days, having gone to the inyanga to have ubulawo churned for him; and he comes back quite another man, being now cleansed and an inyanga indeed.

And if he is to have familiar spirits, there is continually a voice saying to him, "You will not speak with the people; they will be told by us everything they come to enquire about." And he continually tells the people his dreams, saying, "There are people [17] who tell me at night that they will speak for themselves to those who come to enquire." At last all this turns out to be true; when he has begun to divine, at length his power entirely ceases, and he hears the spirits who speak by whistlings speaking to him, and he answers them as he would answer a man; and he causes them to speak by asking them questions; if he does not understand what they say, they make him understand everything they see. The familiar spirits do not begin by explaining omens which occur among the people; they begin by speaking with him whose familiars they are, and making him acquainted with what is about to happen, and then he divines for the people.

This then is what I know of familiar spirits and diviners.

[15] Lit., We see the head, viz. that it is affected in that way which is followed by the power to divine.

[16] That is, by the Itongo in a dream.

[17] People, viz. the dead, the Amatongo.

If the relatives of the man who has been made ill by the Itongo do not wish him to become a diviner, they call a great doctor to treat him, to lay the spirit, that he may not divine. But although the man no longer divines, he is not well; he continues to be always out of health. This is what I know. But although he no longer divines, as regards wisdom he is like a diviner. For instance, there was Undayeni. His friends did not wish him to become a diviner; they said, "No; we do not wish so fine and powerful a man to become a mere thing which stays at home, and does no work, but only divines." So they laid the spirit. But there still remained in him signs which caused the people to say, "If that man had been a diviner, he would have been a very great man, a first-class diviner."

As to the familiar spirits, it is not one only that speaks; they are very many; and their voices are not alike; one has his voice, and another his; and the voice of the man into whom they enter is different from theirs. He too enquires of them as other people do; and he too seeks divination of them. If they do not speak, he does not know what they will say; he cannot tell those who come for divination what they will be told. No. It is his place to take what those who come to enquire bring and nothing more. And the man and the familiar spirits ask questions of each other and converse.

When those who come to seek divination salute him, he replies, "O, you have come when I am alone. The spirits departed yesterday. I do not know where they are gone." So the people wait. When they come they are heard saluting them, saying, "Good day." They reply, "Good day to you, masters." And the man who lives with them also asks them saying, "Are you coming?" They say, they are. It is therefore difficult to understand that it is a deception, when we hear many voices speaking with the man who has familiar spirits, and him too speaking with them. . . .[18]

POSSESSION BY SPIRITS

When the Amatongo make a man ill, he cries "Hai, hai, hai." They cause him to compose songs, and the people of his home assemble and beat tune to the song the Amatongo have caused him to compose, —the song of initiation,—a song of professional skill.

Some dispute and say, "No. The fellow is merely mad. There is no Itongo [19] in him." Others say, "O, there is an Itongo in him; he is already an inyanga."

[18] Pages 259-267.
[19] Singular of Amatongo, spirits of the dead.

The others say, "No; he is mad. Have you ever hidden things for him to discover by his inner sight, since you say he is an inyanga?"

They say, "No; we have not done that."

They ask, "How then do you know he is an inyanga?"

They say, "We know it because he is told about medicines, which he goes to dig up."

They reply, "O! he is a mere madman. We might allow that he is an inyanga if you had concealed things for him to find, and he had discovered what you had concealed. But you tell us what is of no import, as you have not done this."

As they are talking thus and disputing about concealing things for him to find, at night when he is asleep he dreams that the man of his people who is dead, and who is causing him to begin to be an inyanga, tells him saying, "They were disputing with each other, saying you are not an inyanga."

He who is beginning to be an inyanga asks, "Why do they say I am not an inyanga?"

He replies, "They say you are not an inyanga, but a mere mad man; and ask if they have hidden things for you to discover, since the others say you are an inyanga."

He says, "Tell me who they are who say so."

He replies, "So-and-so and So-and-so were disputing."

The man asks, "Do you say they lie when they say so?"

He replies, "Be quiet. Because they say so, I say you shall be a greater inyanga than all others, and all men in the world shall be satisfied that you are a great inyanga, and they shall know you."

The man who is beginning to be an inyanga says, "For my part I say they speak the truth when they say I am mad. Truly they have never hidden anything for me to find."

Then the man who was an inyanga, he who is initiating him, says, "Just be quiet. I will take you to them in the morning. And do you appear on a hill; do not come upon them suddenly; but appear on a hill which is concealed, and cry 'Hai, hai, hai'; cry thus on the hill which is concealed, that they may hear. When you cry 'Hai, hai, hai,' if they do not hear, then go on to a hill which is open; do not expose yourself much; as soon as you expose yourself, cry 'Hai, hai, hai,' so that they may just hear. When they hear that it is you, go down again from the hill, and return to the one which is concealed. So I say they will see and understand that they have spoken of a man who is beginning to be a doctor; they shall know by that, that when they said you were a mad man and not an inyanga they were mistaken."

So he does so. He cries "Hai, hai, hai," on a hill which is hidden;

they do not hear him distinctly; they hear only a continual sound of Nkene, nkene, nkene, nkene. One of them says, "It sounds as though there was some one singing." Others say, "We do not hear. We hear only an echo."

The Itongo comes to him and tells him that they cannot hear, and bids him go out a little on the open hill, and then return again to the hill which is hidden.

So he departs at the word of the Itongo, and goes out to the open hill, and cries "Hai, hai, hai"; and they all hear that it is he. They are again disputing about him, and as soon as they hear that it is he, they say, "Can it be, sirs, that he comes about the matter we were disputing about, saying, he is mad?"

Others say, "O, why do you ask? He comes on that account, if indeed you said he was not an inyanga, but a madman."

The great man of the village to which the inyanga is approaching, says, "I too say he is mad. Just take things and go and hide them, that we may see if he can find them."

They take things; one takes beads, and goes and hides them; others take picks, and go and hide them; others hide assagais; others bracelets; others hide their sticks, others their kilts, others their ornaments, others their pots; others hide baskets, and say, "Just let us see if he will find all these things or not." Others hide cobs of maize; others the ears of amabele, or sweet cane, or of ujiba, or the heads of upoko.

Some say, "O, if he find all these things, will he not be tired? Why have you hidden so many?"

They say, "We hide so many that we may see that he is really an inyanga."

They reply, "Stop now; you have hidden very many things."

They return home, and wait. Then the Itongo tells him on the concealed hill; for it had already said to him, "Keep quiet; they are now hiding things; do not begin to appear. They wish to say when you find the things that you saw when they hid them. Be quiet, that they may hide all the things; then they will be satisfied that you are an inyanga." Now the Itongo tells him, "They have now hidden the things, and gone home. It is proper for you now to go to the home of the people who say you are mad and not an inyanga."

So he comes out on the open mountain, and runs towards their home, being pursued by his own people who are seeking him, for he went out during the night, and they did not hear when he went out very early in the morning, when it was still dark, when the horns of the cattle were beginning to be just visible. He reaches their home, and his own people who were looking for him, and have now found him, come with him. On his arrival he dances; and as he dances they strike hands in unison; and the people of the place who have hidden things for him to find, also start up and strike hands; he dances, and they smite their hands earnestly.

He says to them, "Have you then hid things for me to find?"

They deny, saying, "No; we have not hidden things for you to find."

He says, "You have."

They deny, saying, "It is not true; we have not."

He says, "Am I not able to find them?"

They say, "No; you cannot. Have we hidden then things for you to find?"

He says, "You have."

They deny, declaring that they have not done so. But he asserts that they have.

When they persist in their denial, he starts up, shaking his head. He goes and finds the beads; he finds the picks, and the kilts, and the bracelets; he finds the cobs of maize, and the ears of the amabele and ujiba and of upoko; he finds all the things they have hidden. They see he is a great inyanga when he has found all the things they have concealed. . . .[20]

THE DIVINER MISTAKEN

Once at Pietermaritzburg a heifer belonging to Mr. G., my white master, was lost. We looked for it, but could not find it. We then asked Mr. G. to give us a shilling, that we might enquire of a diviner, for we were now troubled with looking for it, and did not know where to look for it any further. He gave us a shilling, and we went to a diviner who lives near the Zwartkop. On our arrival we found him sitting in the cattle-pen; and we saluted, saying, "Eh, dear sir," and sat down.

They saluted us, and we replied.

The diviner's people asked us whence we came.

We told them we came from Pietermaritzburg, and had come to enquire of the diviner.

They said, "Why have you come here?"

We told them we had come on our own account, some cattle [21] having been lost. We then asked for snuff, and they gave us some

[20] Pages 273-279.

[21] They say "some cattle," although it was but one that was missing, that they may not give the diviner too much knowledge. They leave him to discover the deception; and if he does not, but proceeds to speak as though many cattle were lost, they know he does not understand divination.

and we took it; and after that the diviner said, "Let us go yonder outside the village."

He went out, and we followed him. He said to us, "Strike the ground, that I may understand, my friends, what is the reason that you have come to me."

We smote our hands together, and said, "Hear."

He said, "You are in trouble."

We said, "Hear."

He said, "Let me just understand what kind of a bullock it is?"

We smote our hands together.

He said, "It is a cow."

We smote our hands.

He said, "No; it is an ox."

We smote our hands.

He said, "No; it is not an ox."

We smote our hands.

He said, "You are in trouble, lads."

We smote our hands.

He said, "But the cow was lost a long time ago."

And there he spoke truly.

We smote our hands.

He said, "Just let me understand if it was stolen by any one."

We smote our hands.

He said, "No, it was not stolen by men; but it is still living."

We smote our hands.

He said, "It is one that is lost."

And there too he spoke the truth.

We smote with our hands.

He said, "Let me just understand of what color it is."

We smote with our hands.

He said, "It is a red and white cow."

But there he made a guess, and did not speak truly.

We smote our hands.

He said, "No; it is a heifer; it has not yet a calf."

We smote our hands.

And there too he spoke truly.

He said, "Let me understand if the heifer is still living or not."

We smote our hands.

He said, "No, the heifer is dead."

We smote our hands.

He said, "No, it is still living."

He said, "Let me just understand where it is."

We smote our hands.

He said, "It is in the mimosa thorn-country."

We smote our hands.

He said, "Just let me understand in what part of the thorn-country it is."

We smote our hands.

He said, "It has gone down the Umsunduze."

We smote our hands.

He said, "Just let me understand if it is still living."

We smote our hands.

He said, "It is still living, and eating umtolo and umunga. Go and look for it there, and you will find it."

We thought we understood that he had now told us the place, for for some time we had not known where to go to look for it.

Then we gave him the shilling, and returned to Pietermaritzburg. When we came to Mr. G. we told him that the diviner said it was in the thorn-country, and that we were to go and look for it down the Umsunduze.

He told us to go and look for it in the place mentioned by the diviner. We went to look for it, going down the Umsunduze. As we went along we looked for it, going towards the thorn-country which he had pointed out. At length we got as far as T.'s, and sought for it in that neighborhood; we could not find it, for the thorns were very thick. As we went we enquired at all the native villages in the thorn-country. The people said they knew nothing about it; and others told us to go to T., the white man who ate up the cattle of the people that were lost. But we were afraid to go to him, for he is a passionate white man who beats any colored men whom he does not know if he see them passing through his land. So we went back to Pietermaritzburg without going to T.; and told Mr. G. that we had not found the heifer at the place pointed out by the diviner. So he told us to give up the search. We did so, and that was the end of it. . . .[22]

ANOTHER INCIDENT

John went to enquire of a diviner when his sister was ill, wishing to know what was the cause of her illness. But when he smote the ground he smote mechanically, assenting to every thing the diviner said, for he said to himself, "For my part I know nothing. It is the diviner that shall point out to me the real facts of the case."

[22] Pages 300-304.

The diviner reproved him, saying, "Surely, my friend, did you ever enquire of a diviner in this way before?"

John replied in the affirmative, saying, "O, it is I indeed who enquire,[23] for I am now the responsible head of our village; there is no other man in it; there is no one but me."

The diviner said, "I see. You do not know how to enquire of a diviner." At length he devised a plan with one of his own people, saying, "This man has not the least notion of divination. Just go and ask him, that he may tell you why he has come, that you may smite the ground for me in a proper manner."

So indeed the man said to John, "The diviner says you do not know how to divine. Tell me the cause of your coming. You will see that we smite the ground for him vehemently when he speaks to the point; and if he does not speak to the point, we do not smite much."

John said in answer, "For my part I do not understand what you say. I have merely come to the diviner for no other purpose than to hear of him the nature of a disease. I did not come to talk with you about it. For my part I shall hear from the diviner what the disease is."

So he refused to tell him; and the man went back to the diviner; he said, "Let him come to me again, that we may hear."

So John again smote the ground vehemently, and thus expressed his assent to every thing the diviner said. Until he became quite foolish, and said, "O, my friend, I see indeed that you do not know how to enquire of a diviner."

He said this because there was no point where John assented very much, nor where he assented slightly, that he might see by his assenting slightly that he had not hit the mark. He expected if he hit the mark John would smite the ground vehemently; but if he missed it he would strike gently. So he left off divining, and said, "No, my friend, I never met with a man who enquired like you." He could do nothing.

John said, "O, then, my friend, as you do not see the nature of the disease, now give me back my shilling, that I may betake myself to another diviner."

So the diviner gave him back the shilling. His name was Um-ngom'-u-ng'-umuntu.[24]

[23] The head of the village alone enquires of the diviner, either in person or by his representatives. Great men send messengers to the diviner, and do not go in person.

[24] Pages 328-330.

42. SHAMANS OF THE EAST GREENLAND ESKIMO [25]

BY W. THALBITZER

IT IS a notorious fact that Eskimo culture and daily life is pervaded throughout by a spirit of religion. Not only is the greater part of the unwritten Eskimo literature of a mythical and ritualistic character, but we find a religious atmosphere haunting even their profane legends and historical or semi-historical tales. . . .

The exponents of the Eskimo's religion are called angakoks (angakut) and are in fact their national priests; they resemble in many respects the shamans of the Siberian tribes. I call them priests, because they are men, who after a long period of training and initiation have acquired a special capacity for entering into communication with the gods of the people and with the whole spiritual world in which this people believes. They are able, in contradistinction to laymen, to see the spirits, obtain answers from them and to bring them to interfere in the life of mankind. Thus in virtue of this natural aptitude and training, they are to be regarded as mediators between common mortals and the supernatural powers of the universe. . . .

The Eskimo religion knows two supreme divinities: the moon, Aningáhk, which is regarded as a man, a hunter, who catches sea-animals, who has his house, his hunting grounds and his implements of the chase in the sky; and the old nameless woman of the sea, whose house lies far away at the bottom of the ocean, and who rules over the marine seals, whales and polar bears. Finally the people of Ammassalik speak of a third power in the sky, an old woman of the name of *Asiak*, who procures rain by shaking a skin drenched in urine down upon the earth so that a shower of drops is sprinkled upon it.

The angakok, and the angakok alone, is able to communicate with these powers by the aid of his spirits; and it is by no means all angakoks, but only those who are fully trained, and only the greatest among these, who can travel to the gods through the air and "see" them. Their bodies are left for lifeless on the earth, while their soul, freed from the body, roams through the universe.

Part of the angakok's functions is to heal the sick. The angakok effects this by enquiring of his spirits whither the sick man's soul has gone, bidding them to seek for it and fetch it home again. For, according to Eskimo notions, all disease is nothing but loss of a soul; in

[25] From W. Thalbitzer, "The Heathen Priests of East Greenland," pages 447-464 of *Verhandlungen des XVI Internationalen Amerikanisten-Kongresses, Wien, 1908* (1910).

every part of the human body (particularly in every joint, as for instance, in each finger joint) there resides a little soul, and if a part of the man's body is sick, it is because the little soul has abandoned that part. In most cases the loss of the soul is regarded as due to one of the following causes: either that evilly disposed persons have driven it out by means of magic, or that higher powers, the moon for instance, have removed it as a punishment for men's sins (some sacrilege, breach of tabu, or other). The sick man's relatives send for the angakok, who passes a night summoning his spirits, finding by their aid the spot on the earth, or in the sky or in the sea, where the lost fragment of the soul is, in order afterwards to have it fetched and returned to its place in the sick man's body, who is thereby healed.

Up to the close of the nineteenth century the religious life of the East-Greenlanders at Ammassalik pulsated with well-nigh unimpaired vigor. As late as 1894, the year in which the Danish state founded its colony over there, there were twelve angakoks belonging to the place, being about the same number as in 1884 when G. Holm wintered there. The proportion was about 1 angakok to 34 persons. Since the last named date the population has increased from 410 to 470, but the number of angakoks has sunk during this time from 12 to 5, being the number of the trained angakoks who lived there during my stay there from 1905 to 1906. . . .

Every angakok has, as a rule, had several paid teachers and has received instruction in different branches. *Mitsuarnianga* mentioned *Imaalikutjuk* as his teacher in the actual angakok craft; but, on his being more closely questioned, it appeared that what he had really learnt during the three days his teaching lasted, was only the first directions as how he should prepare himself "for rubbing the stone," which amounts to the same as initiation in the power of acquiring attendant spirits (genii). At the early age of seven or eight the future angakok begins to receive instruction from an older angakok, who is willing and eager to confide his secret knowledge to him. He teaches him first how he is to go in perfect secrecy and fetch a special kind of sea-weed from the beach when the tide is low, and wash himself with it over his whole body; how then he is to go into the depths of the land among the high mountains to the place where he has selected his grind-stone, a large stone with a flat upper surface, often found lying near a lake, a river, a high declivity or a cave. I have seen one lying at the end of an old Eskimo grave. Proceeding according to fixed rules the novice seeks for a little stone to be used for grinding against the flat surface of the large one. Not seldom a little crustacean from the sea or river is laid between the two stones which are rubbed together.

There sits the disciple hour after hour rubbing the little stone in a circle against the large one, in anxious expectation of what is to appear. According to the tradition quite a definite event is to take place. The bear of the lake will rise up, go towards him and eat him, whereby he "dies" i.e. loses his consciousness. It will spit him out again and then leave him. After the lapse of an hour he returns to consciousness, his skeleton clothes itself in flesh again, and his garments come rushing up to him one by one until at last he emerges fully dressed. Every summer of this and the following years he keeps on rubbing the stone and thereby on different occasions acquires his attendant spirits, who are said to be his very own, and whose names he alone knows, and he alone may use. During the time he is rubbing the stone, he must fast i.e. he may not eat the entrails of animals. Similarly he may not work in metal or engage in any noisy occupation whatsoever.

It should be observed, that it is not the disciple himself who announces himself as a candidate for discipleship; it is the older angakok who exhorts the young one, a boy, whom he thinks well adapted for initiation in the religious mysteries, to receive training, in order that a knowledge of the highest powers in existence may be preserved for the coming generation.

Mitsuarnianga was so young when he underwent his first training that he had nothing to pay his first teacher with. On the other hand he paid all his later teachers, partly with bear and seal skins, partly with implements. One of them received from him a sledge and a dog. When the angakok *Takiwnalikitseq* had taught him iliseetsoq lore (iliseen-ilisaat), i.e. such magic means by the aid of which the attempts of the enemy can be warded off, or even pain or disaster brought upon them as a vengeance, he gave him in payment a large fine bear-skin, a sealing bladder and a skin thong in return for the wisdom imparted to him.

In order to summon a spirit or soul it behooves one merely to know its name and to utter it. Thus it is clear that the angakok novice cannot summon the spirits that are to be his attendant genii, on the first occasion; they come of their own accord, or else he lights upon them unexpectedly when he is out rambling alone. But when he has once spoken with them and learnt their names he will henceforward be able to summon them again.

As for the sacred or mystic language in which the angakok holds converse with his spirits, *Mitsuarnianga* declared that no special teaching was required in order to learn it. As, however, it is identically for all angakoks and even, as it seems, more or less the same for angakoks from all quarters, it must be a really stereotyped language preserved through many centuries. Presumably every angakok learns a great part of it by attending the angakoks' colloquies with their spirits, when they conjure them up in their huts; those that are training to become angakoks impress these words on their memory with particular care. The words are not sheer abracadabra, but obsolete or metaphorically used Eskimo words, a kind of inherited art language, which contributes in a high degree to the solemn and mystical character of the spiritual gathering. The religious forms or expressions themselves are made no secret of: only the way in which the disciple receives his training is wrapped in mystery.

During the whole course of his discipleship the angakok novice carefully conceals the fact, that he is receiving instruction, rubbing the stone and having meetings with his spirits. But when—after a novitiate of from five to ten years—he finally grows into a fullfledged angakok, his house-mates begin to have an inkling about it and to pass their comments on the fact. One fine evening he at last goes and proclaims himself to the world: angakittuppoa, "I am an angakok," and admonishes the others to extinguish the lamps, in order that he may for the first time give them a proof of his prowess.

There is only one circumstance, which can compel a novice to divulge his secret, before his time has come, and that is if he falls mortally ill. For by divulging that he is an angakok he will be able to save his life, though indeed at the sacrifice of his career as angakok. . . .

The secret novitiate lasts in no case more than twelve years, if the disciple ever intends to make use of his powers as an angakok.

There are four main occasions in which the services of an angakok at Ammassalik will be called in request, and when he must summon his spirits to a meeting under the floor of the huts: dearth of sea animals in the sea; snow-masses blocking the ways to the hunting-places (on the land or on the fjord-ice); a man's loss of soul (illness); a married woman's barrenness. Any one of these circumstances is sufficient reason for him to summon a meeting of the spirits, when the inhabitants of the place or even people from a distance so demand. Let us now see how a meeting of this kind proceeds in the hut.

The other men in the house fetch out the angakok's skins (atwtaat) from his seat on the platform, two dry hairless skins, which they hang like a double covering or curtain in front of the inner end of the underground passage-way (kattak, the inner door-opening; doors are unknown).

Here, in the front of the wall itself, stand two massive high stones as door-posts framing in the door-way; the latter appears like a dark hole leading downwards and forwards towards the exit, which lies about half a yard or a yard lower than the floor of the hut. Besides the skins, which hang by straps and thongs in front of this aperture, another skin is spread on the floor just in front of it; this is the angakok's place when he is holding a spiritual meeting (torniwoq). When he sits there on the floor, with his legs stretched out at the same height as his seat, he has his back turned to all of the audience, who, according to their custom, sit in their places on the platform along the back wall of the house. His face is turned towards the covered entrance, i.e. towards the sea. His heels rest on the lowest corner of one of the hanging skins which is turned up in such a way that he can set the skins in motion with his feet and produce a noisy rattling with them. His drum lies on a flat stone on the floor to his right. His arms are tightly bound behind his back, being lashed from the hands to the elbows with a long thong which is tied in knots. It is a part of his art to free his hands in the dark and afterwards, before the lamps are lit, to stick them back again in the still fastened thongs. The angakok is supposed to fly through the air (towards the interior of the country) in his doubled-up posture with the hands bound behind him.

It has not yet been mentioned that the angakok brings with him a little characteristic instrument, the so-called makkortaa; it consists of a round, flat piece of black skin, from five to five and a half centimeters in diameter, which is held tightly in the hollow of the hand, while it is struck or rapped-on with a carved wooden stick with the other hand. By the aid of this little instrument the angakok produces a loud rhythmic knocking as a preliminary to his meeting with the spirits below the ground. When the lamps in the hut have been extinguished, this knocking goes on unintermittingly, while the angakok's voice, keeping time to the knocking, is heard plaintively babbling: aata-aata-aata aahtaah; at the same time the skins rattle and the drum begins to move and to drone faintly. The noise and the movements get gradually wilder and wilder. The drum, they say, rocks or dances standing erect on the floor, and now and then it springs up on the angakok's forehead or the crown of his head, drumming frantically in restless agitation. These are the signs that the angakok's inner vision is "dawning," or, in other words, that his soul is about to pass over into the "other world." When this feeling comes over him, he sinks down into the depths of the earth, crying in mingled despair and ecstasy: aatjiwit-jiwitjiwit ho-hooi-ho-hooi! and at the same moment his drum begins to move in another time.

Teemiartissaq, who furnished me with a great part of this information, had the notion that the angakok at this moment rises and sinks like a man about to drown: "he comes up a third time, before he goes down for good." *Ajukudooq* called my attention to the fact that only the angakok's soul, not his body sinks below the ground. This takes place gradually, and his spirit (taartaa) rises up and enters into him through his anus. It makes its exit afterwards by the same way. His body is thus like a house which changes tenants.

While these mysteries are in progress, the angakok's soul rises several times up from the depths and enters the body turn by turn with his taartaat (this word itself seems to mean "successors"); there can only be one soul at a time in it. But at the moments when the angakok's own consciousness is in it, his spirit monsters, or the manlike animals belonging to the sacred ritual, come—one at a time—stalking into the hut and filling the inmates with religious awe and shuddering. These animals, each of which has his own special name and voice, are called qimarhrat, "they that cause to flee." One of them, *Amooq* ("he that tugs or pulls at something") cries in a sustained and protracted roar "amoo, amoo!" while, invisible in the dark, it tramps along the platform, passing behind those that sit there; at last it disappears through the passage-way. Another monster cries "ongaa, ongaa!" (avaunt, avaunt!"), a third "I will warm my fingers" as it tries to touch those present and warm itself on their naked bodies. There are several similar creatures; most of them seem to be common to all angakoks in contradistinction to their personal attendants, the taartaat, which are identical with the spirits called by other Eskimo tornat (or torngat) and which the angakok has acquired by rubbing the stone during his novitiate.

These attendant spirits have peculiar names and shadows, houses and hunting implements. They are originally nature spirits, often souls of animals that have been formed into men and women. But they all belong to the "other world" (asia), which is only visible to the angakoks. Otherwise they have their being in the same visible world as men—the Eskimo do not see anything self-contradictory in this— and they belong to three kinds of people; each of which have their own special dwelling places and peculiarities: *Timerseet,* who live in the interior of the country, *Eajuätsaat* (=*Taarajuätsaat*) "semi-men" who live under the ground close to men's huts, and *Innertiwin,* "the fire-people," who live on the beach under the rocks of the coast, where the water is shallow. The latter are said to have houses with windows and they can, as distinct from the others, make long journeys in umiaks over to the west coast of Greenland where they buy metal and European clothes. *Timerseet* follow the course of the rivers out to sea when they want to hunt seal. All these beings have the language of men but speak it more or less awry, for instance with distorted mouths, or lispingly, or merely indistinctly on account of obsolete or foreign words.

This last feature applies also to the beings which come from the sea to serve the angakok during the sacred rites. One of these is called Aperqit "the consulted one, the oracle," which sits down by the edge of the sea below the hut and helps the angakok who has been summoned to cure the disease, by answering questions as to the nature of the disease, i.e. as to which souls have deserted the sick man, and as to the place in the sea or on the land where they are now to be found. When the answer has been given, it is for the attendant spirits to search out and fetch back the lost soul.

The other spiritual helper which the angakok has in the sea is Toornartik, the Toornarsuk of the West Greenlanders. As the people of Ammassalik believe, Toornartik is an animal-like creature in the sea, and, it appears, that there are at least two of them. It was described to me as 3 yards long, 1 yard broad across the chest, with the upper part like a man, with arms and legs, but the lower parts looking like a seal.

It is not related to the woman of the sea and has nothing to do with her. Nor is it counted among the angakok's taartaat tornat; it is an independent creature which lives in the sea and can be used by the angakok for different purposes. It serves as his guide, when he flies off to the sea-woman's house with his spiritual retinue, and it hastens the speed of the journey by speeding along in the front.

Last but not least, it is from this being that the angakok receives replies to his questions. Aperqit is only an intermediary, a messenger between Toornartik and the heathen priest. From the hut the angakok addresses his questions to Aperqit, the attendant spirit who listens at the water's edge and thence passes on the questions out to the sea.

I received from the now living angakoks an accurate description of the way the angakok takes to the woman of the sea, and of that which he takes to the moon; and moreover of the obstacles which he and his spirits meet with on their way. These journeys are attended with great toil, hardships and perils, and the angakok will only be instigated to such exertions when it is a question of life or death for a whole settlement or for a single individual whose life is valued so much that his relations are ready to pay the price the angakok demands for the exercise of his double function of doctor and priest.

But, even without such weighty grounds, the angakok frequently summons one or more of his spirits to a meeting in the hut. There are lazy angakoks and diligent angakoks. "A diligent angakok," so the saying goes, "torniwoqs almost every night the whole winter through." "No singing is so lovely as the singing of the spirits; the singing of mortals is nothing to it," said one of the angakoks to me.

43. AZTEC RITUALS

[The following account and pictures are taken from an ancient manuscript or codex which bears on the original sheets the following caption: "Book of the life which was led by the Indians of former days, with an account of the superstitions and evil performances which they believed in and observed." The manuscript consists of seventy-six colored pictures, apparently the work of native Aztec draughtsmen, accompanied by explanatory notes in Spanish, attributed to Cervantes de Salazar. The manuscript in this form was known as the Codex Magliabecchi and was preserved in Florence. A facsimile of it, in color, edited by Zelia Nuttall, but not translated, was published by the University of California Press in 1903, under the title *The Book of the Life of the Ancient Mexicans, part I*. Four of the illustrations in this work are here reproduced minus color, together with the explanatory text on some ten Aztec rituals, as translated by T. T. Waterman. —"Demon" of course means god or idol.]

18

THIS figure represents the festival which the Indians call *Tlacaxipeualiztli* . . ., which means "he skins me and you shall eat me"; because in this festival they kill one whom they call *Totodeci* or *Xipeu*. . . . He is tied to a wheel of stone, which they *tamalacatli*. When tied to this, they give him a club in his hand, very bravely. Then another Indian, covered with the skin of a tiger [ocelot] goes against him, also holding in his hand a club. This second club is set with pointed objects. Then they give it to each other until the one who is tied up is killed. Then he skins him, and later, dressed in the skin of the dead man, he dances before the demon, whom they call *Tlacateu Texcatepocatl*. He who has to fight fasts for four days, and exercises for many days previously to fighting with the tied-up person. He also offers many sacrifices to this demon, so that the demon may give him victory. . . .

20

This festival they call *Gacitocoztli* because they offer before the demon stalks with leaves (consisting entirely of maize) which among them is called *tuctli*. In this festival they offer to the demon a great deal of maize and tamales mixed with beans. In this festival boys at dawn place in their temples such loaves of maize. The demon to whom they celebrate this festival is called *Ocenteutl*, that is to say, deity of the maize. In this festival fathers offer to the demon children at the breast, as in the sacrifice. They invite their elders to feast. This is called *tecoa* which means in their language "sacrifice.". . .

21

This is the festival which the Indians call *Toxcatl.* . . . It was a great festival, because the demon whose rites were celebrated in these ceremonies is *Texcatepocatl,* that is, Smoking Mirror. He was the greatest of the greater gods whom they reverenced. They also give him as another name *Titlacauan,* that is to say, "of whom we are slaves." In his honor they perform dances, and sing songs, and offer roses, and bring labrets and feathers, which are the things they value most. In this festival they cut their tongues and offer the flesh [blood] to the demon. They also make tamales of the seeds of the blite and of maize, which latter they call the body of their god. They eat these tamales with a grand celebration. . . .

26

This figure represents a festival which the Indians call *Huei mical huitl,* which means "great festival." Others call it *Xucutl gueci,* because in it they set up a tree, very tall, on the top of which is seated an Indian. Other Indians knock down from his perch this one who is seated above, going up and clambering on several ropes which are tied to the tree. They take some tamales which they call *teuçoalle,* that is, "bread of god." Trying one of them to outdo the other, they knock him to the ground, where the Indians kill him in order to partake of him as "holy bread." Afterwards they throw into the fire that which they have knocked off of the tree. They put the head in a bath, so that although it be baked, no harm shall happen to the hair or the head until later they eat it baked. The skinned head they set up on another body and dance with it before the demon, called *Hucteutl,* to whom the festival is dedicated. . . .

54

This illustration is an illustration of what occurred when a ruler or principal man dies; namely, they wrapped him in a shroud seated on his haunches, as the Indians are accustomed to sit. And his relatives gather much wood. Then they incinerate him, as the ancient Romans were accustomed to do it, in the time of their heathenism. Before him they sacrificed one or two slaves, so that they could bury them with him, after they had burned them. Also in certain parts of the country where so doing was the custom, there were buried with them their women; for they said that yonder these women were to wait on them. They buried each man's treasure also, in cases where they have any.

q xxj de março dia desant
benito. tlaca xipeualiztli
es gran fiesta

18

55

55

This illustration is an illustration of the same observance. The dead man's children and relatives wailed for him. They also gave him *cavavatl* [cacao, chocolate] for his journey. . . .

58

This is a staff which has on it a drapery, like the Manga de Cruz like those which they make here of feathers. The device was among these Indians used like a banner, which they set up in front of the temple when they sacrifice. It is the first thing in the following picture. The rest of the picture represents the scene when they sacrifice Indians —how they take the victim up to the top and throw him on his shoulders upon a stone and cut out his heart. Another man holds him by the feet so that he shall not struggle. It was the *tlamacaz*, that is the chief of the executioners, who killed him. In order to do this, he tied up his head and his hair with a white mantle, in order to cut out the heart and anoint with it the snout of the demon.

61

In this picture is shown the abominable custom the Indians had, the day they sacrificed men to their idols. Namely, right there before the demon whom they call *Mictlan tecutl* (that is, lord of the place of the dead, as described in another place), they set out many cooking pots of the human flesh [just mentioned] and give it out and serve it to the important personages and officials and to those officials called *tamagatl* [*tlamacaz*, sacrificing priest] who serve at the temple of the demon, and these in turn share that which has been given them with their friends and relatives. They say that it tastes like the pork which they eat today, and for that reason pork is much desired among them.

65

This is a representation of the baths of the Indians, called by them *temezcale*. In the picture they have put at the door an Indian who was an adviser for their sicknesses. When a sick man goes to the bath they make for him offerings of incense (which they call *copale*) to the idol. They hold in veneration the black body of the idol, whom they call *Tezcatepocatl*, one of the greater of their gods. . . .

66

This is a sort of diabolical leechcraft which the Indians practice. When any one was sick they summon the doctor (man or woman) and then [ask] the said doctor to see what the outcome of the illness will be. Then they place in front of the doctor and in front of the sick man an idol, the name of which idol is *Quetzalcoatl*, that is, Feather Snake. The doctor was in the middle, on a mat, and on this mat was placed a mantle of white cotton. He took in his hand twenty grains of maize, (which is the grain from which they make bread). He throws them upon the mantle as when one throws dice. If these grains fall so as to leave in the middle an opening or [word illegible], in such fashion that the grains are all around it, it was a sign that he would be buried there, that is, that he would die of the disease. If one grain fell upon another the doctor announced that his disease had come upon him on account of sodomy. If the grains of maize separated, one half to one side and the other half to the other side, in such a way that it was possible to draw a straight line through the middle without touching a single grain, it was a sign that the sickness would leave the man, and he would get well.

67

This is another picture, where is shown the way which the Indians have of doing penance. Namely, they set up on a high place in a seated position an idol which they call *Mictlantecutli*, that is, "Lord of the Dead." Before this idol they sacrifice [blood] from their ears, and others from their tongues, and others from the calves of their legs. The method was to thrust through their ears and through their tongues thorns, very sharp. This was the way they did penance. . . .

44. MAGIC FORMULAS OF THE HUPA [26]
BY P. E. GODDARD

MORE powerful than any herb were the words recited over it before its use. These words are not prayers but accounts of a former cure. The repeating of the words has power to cure again. It is not necessary for the unclean person to go to the ends of the world that he may

[26] From pages 88, 93, 279, 315-316, 318 of P. E. Goddard, "Life and Culture of the Hupa" and "Hupa Texts," *University of California Publications in American Archæology and Ethnology*, Volume 1, 1903, 1904. The Hupa live in northwestern California.

58

66

become pure. It is sufficient that the priest tell how one went. The spirit of the person follows the words of the priest which he does not even comprehend. Equally powerful are evil wishes. To curse a man was a serious offense, because the words themselves had power to harm. . . .

These formulas may be thought to exert their power in one or all of three ways. The spirit of the reciter may be viewed as undergoing the journey and hardships undergone by the originator of the medicine and in a vicarious manner meriting favor; the good-will of the originator of the medicine may be aroused by the recital of his deeds; or the very words themselves may be thought to have the power of self-fulfillment. . . .

FORMULA OF MEDICINE FOR CHILDBIRTH

He came to the middle of the world where two maidens were living. He smoked himself all day. When the sun went down they came out to look at him. The next day they were pregnant. Their brothers went into the sweathouse after him. They were going to cut the girls open and then kill him. "Wait," said Yīmantūwiñyai, "I will make medicine. Give me a cup." "Make the medicine right here," they said. Right there in the house he made it of ashes. Then he hung up the straps of the carrying baskets. He put some of the medicine in the mouth of one of them and rubbed some of it across her abdomen. When he turned around he heard a baby cry. When he had done the same to the other he turned again and heard another baby cry. "This way it will be with those who know my medicine." . . .

FORMULA OF MEDICINE FOR GOING IN DANGEROUS PLACES WITH A CANOE

Snipe lived across to the south. His canoe was very narrow. It was so shallow it did not come above his ankle. "I am going in it," he thought. "How is it going to be?" he thought. He took the paddles out of the house and went down to the river. He got into his canoe and then he got out again. He turned the canoe around. He placed it with the stern toward the land. "Indians are going to come into existence," he thought. "They will think about me with this." He held it with the stern toward the land, headed this way across the river and down stream. "There must not be many," he thought, "who will say of me, 'That one I hear did this way.'" Then he went into the canoe, beat on the stern with the paddle, and sang. When he started across, his

canoe grew up higher, and floated with him over the world. The boat
did not mind the water. It floated with him over this body of water
which lies around the world. He sang a song as he went along. It
floated back with him across to the south. "It will do that way with
the man who knows my medicine," he thought. "Even if he goes into
a bad place, if he thinks about me, this way the water will not trouble
his boat." . . .

FORMULA OF MEDICINE FOR GOING AMONG RATTLESNAKES

While at Tcexoltcwediñ Yïmantūwiñyai felt dissatisfied with something. "How will the people live?" he thought. He started out and
walked up along the Klamath. When the sun went down, rattlesnakes
which had wings flew about. He looked about as he went along and
thought, "What kind of medicine shall I make?" He saw a bush of
Philadephus standing there. He broke off a shoot, made rings around it,
and used it for a cane. "When I come to Lōknasaûndiñ, that lies ahead
of me," he thought, "I will whip the air with it." When he came out
into the prairie at Lōknasaûndiñ he whipped about himself with the
cane. He found nothing there. He had killed them all immediately.
"This is the way it will happen," he thought, "if any one takes my
cane along. He will go through dangerous places if he carries my cane,
and he will not see rattlesnakes."

45. NAVAHO SONGS AND PRAYERS [27]

Collected and translated by

WASHINGTON MATTHEWS

I. SONG IN THE ROCK

In the house of the Red Rock,
There I enter;
Halfway in, I am come.
The corn-plants shake.

In the house of Blue Water,
There I enter;
Halfway in, I am come.
The plants shake.

[27] Washington Matthews, "The Night Chant," *Memoirs of the American Museum of Natural History*, Volume 6, 1902, pages 77, 78, 81, 85, 143. The Navaho live in northern New Mexico and Arizona.

2. SONG IN THE ROCK

At the Red Rock house it grows,
There the giant corn-plant grows,
With ears on either side it grows,
With its ruddy silk it grows,
Ripening in one day it grows,
Greatly multiplying grows.

At Blue Water house it grows,
There the giant squash-vine grows,
With fruit on either side it grows,
With its yellow blossom grows,
Ripening in one day it grows,
Greatly multiplying grows.

3. MOUNTAIN SONG

In a holy place with a god I walk,
In a holy place with a god I walk,
On Tsisnadzini with a god I walk,
On a chief of mountains with a god I walk,
In old-age wandering with a god I walk,
On a trail of beauty with a god I walk.

4. A SONG TO SWEEP OFF WITH

The corn grows up; the rain descends,
I sweep it off, I sweep it off.

The rain descends; the corn grows up.
I sweep it off, I sweep it off.

5. FREE TRANSLATION OF A PRAYER

In Tse'gihi,
In the house made of dawn,
In the house made of the evening twilight,
In the house made of the dark cloud,
In the house made of the he-rain,
In the house made of the dark mist,
In the house made of the she-rain,

In the house made of pollen,
In the house made of grasshoppers,
Where the dark mist curtains the doorway,
The path to which is on the rainbow,
Where the zigzag lightning stands high on top,
Where the he-rain stands high on top,
Oh, male-divinity!
With your moccasins of dark cloud, come to us. . . .
In beauty I walk.
With beauty before me, I walk.
With beauty behind me, I walk.
With beauty below me, I walk.
With beauty above me, I walk.
With beauty all around me, I walk. . . .
It is finished in beauty.

46. THE CREATION ACCORDING TO THE MAORI [28]

BY SIR GEORGE GREY

MEN had but one pair of primitive ancestors; they sprang from the vast heaven that exists above us, and from the earth which lies beneath us. According to the traditions of our race, Rangi, and Papa, or Heaven and Earth, were the source from which in the beginning, all things originated. Darkness then rested upon the heaven and upon the earth, and they still both clave together, for they had not yet been rent apart; and the children they had begotten were ever thinking amongst themselves what might be the difference between darkness and light; they knew that beings had multiplied and increased, and yet light had never broken upon them, but it ever continued dark. Hence these sayings are found in our ancient religious services: "There was darkness from the first division of time, unto the tenth, to the hundredth, to the thousandth," that is, for a vast space of time; and these divisions of time were as beings, and were each termed a Po; and on their account there was as yet no world with its bright light, but darkness only for the beings which existed.

At last the beings who had been begotten by Heaven and Earth, worn out by the continued darkness, consulted amongst themselves, saying: "Let us now determine what we should do with Rangi and Papa,

[28] Reprinted from Sir George Grey, *Polynesian Mythology*, 1855, pages 1-41. The Maori are the Polynesian natives of New Zealand.

whether it would be better to slay them or to rend them apart." Then spoke Tu-matauenga, the fiercest of the children of Heaven and Earth: "It is well, let us slay them."

Then spake Tane-mahuta, the father of forests and of all things that inhabit them, or that are constructed from trees: "Nay, not so. It is better to rend them apart, and to let the heaven stand far above us, and the earth lie under our feet. Let the sky become as a stranger to us, but the earth remain close to us as our nursing mother."

The brothers all consented to this proposal, with the exception of Tawhiri-ma-tea, the father of winds and storms, and he, fearing that his kingdom was about to be overthrown, grieved greatly at the thought of his parents being torn apart. Five of the brothers willingly consented to the separation of their parents, but one of them would not agree to it.

Hence, also, these sayings of old are found in our prayers: "Darkness, darkness, light, light, the seeking, the searching, in chaos, in chaos"; these signified the way in which the offspring of heaven and earth sought for some mode of dealing with their parents, so that human beings might increase and live.

So, also, these sayings of old time, "The multitude, the length," signified the multitude of the thoughts of the children of Heaven and Earth, and the length of time they considered whether they should slay their parents, that human beings might be called into existence; for it was in this manner that they talked and consulted amongst themselves.

But at length, their plans having been agreed on, lo, Rongo-ma-tane, the god and father of the cultivated food of man, rises up, that he may rend apart the heavens and the earth; he struggles, but he rends them not apart. Lo, next, Tangaroa, the god and father of fish and reptiles, rises up, that he may rend apart the heavens and the earth; he also struggles, but he rends them not apart. Lo, next, Haumia-tikitiki, the god and father of the food of man which springs without cultivation, rises up and struggles, but ineffectually. Lo, then, Tu-matauenga, the god and father of fierce human beings, rises up and struggles, but he, too, fails in his efforts. Then at last, slowly uprises Tane-mahuta, the god and father of forests, of birds, and of insects, and he struggles with his parents; in vain he strives to rend them apart with his hands and arms. Lo, he pauses: his head is now firmly planted on his mother the earth, his feet he raises up and rests against his father the skies, he strains his back and limbs with mighty effort. Now are rent apart Rangi and Papa, and with cries and groans of woe they shriek aloud: "Wherefore slay you thus your parents? Why commit you so dreadful a crime as to slay us, as to rend your parents apart?" But Tane-mahuta pauses not, he regards not their shrieks and cries; far, far beneath him he presses down the earth; far, far above him he thrusts up the sky.

Hence these sayings of olden times: "It was the fierce thrusting of Tane which tore the heaven from the earth, so that they were rent apart, and darkness was made manifest, and so was the light."

No sooner was heaven rent from earth than the multitude of human beings were discovered whom they had begotten, and who had hitherto lain concealed between the bodies of Rangi and Papa.

Then, also, there arose in the breast of Tawhiri-ma-tea, the god and father of winds and storms, a fierce desire to wage war with his brothers, because they had rent apart their common parents. He from the first had refused to consent to his mother being torn from her lord and children; it was his brothers alone that wished for this separation, and desired that Papa-tu-a-nuku, or the Earth alone, should be left as a parent for them.

The god of hurricanes and storms dreads also that the world should become too fair and beautiful, so he rises, follows his father to the realm above, and hurries to the sheltered hollows in the boundless skies; there he hides and clings, and nestling in this place of rest he consults long with his parent, and as the vast Heaven listens to the suggestions of Tawhiri-ma-tea, thoughts and plans are formed in his breast, and Tawhiri-ma-tea also understands what he should do. Then by himself and the vast Heaven were begotten his numerous brood, and they rapidly increased and grew. Tawhiri-ma-tea despatches one of them to the westward, and one to the southward, and one to the eastward, and one to the northward; and he gives corresponding names to himself and to his progeny, the mighty winds.

He next sends forth fierce squalls, whirlwinds, dense clouds, massy clouds, dark clouds, gloomy thick clouds, fiery clouds, clouds which precede hurricanes, clouds of fiery black, clouds reflecting glowing red light, clouds wildly drifting from all quarters and wildly bursting, clouds of thunder storms, and clouds hurriedly flying. In the midst of these Tawhiri-ma-tea himself sweeps wildly on. Alas! Alas! then rages the fierce hurricane; and whilst Tane-mahuta and his gigantic forests still stand, unconscious and unsuspecting, the last of the breath of the mouth of Tawhiri-ma-tea smites them, the gigantic trees are snapt off right in the middle; alas! alas! they are rent to atoms, dashed to the earth, with boughs and branches torn and scattered, and lying on the earth, trees and branches all alike left for the insect, for the grub, and for loathsome rottenness.

From the forests and their inhabitants Tawhiri-ma-tea next swoops down upon the seas, and lashes in his wrath the ocean. Ah! ah! waves steep as cliffs arise, whose summits are so lofty that to look from them would make the beholder giddy; these soon eddy in whirlpools, and Tangaroa, the god of ocean, and father of all that dwell therein, flies affrighted through his seas; but before he fled, his children consulted together how they might secure their safety, for Tangaroa had begotten Punga, and he had begotten two children, Ika-tere, the father of fish, and Tu-te-wehiwehi, or Tu-te-wanawana, the father of reptiles.

When Tangaroa fled for safety to the ocean, then Tu-te-wehiwehi and Ika-tere, and their children, disputed together as to what they should do to escape from the storms, and Tu-te-wehiwehi and his party cried aloud: "Let us fly inland;" but Ika-tree and his party cried aloud: "Let us fly to the sea." Some would not obey one order, some would not obey the other, and they escaped in two parties: the party of Tu-te-wehiwehi, or the reptiles, hid themselves ashore; the party of Punga rushed to the sea. This is what, in our ancient religious services, is called the separation of Tawhiri-ma-tea.

Hence these traditions have been handed down: "Ika-tere, the father of things which inhabit water, cried aloud to Tu-te-wehiwehi: 'Ho, ho, let us all escape to the sea.'"

"But Tu-te-wehiwehi shouted in answer: 'Nay, nay, let us rather fly inland.'"

"Then Ika-tere warned him, saying: 'Fly inland, then; and the fate of you and your race will be, that when they catch you, before you are cooked, they will singe off your scales over a lighted wisp of dry fern.'"

"But Tu-te-wehiwehi answered him, saying: 'Seek safety, then, in the sea; and the future fate of your race will be, that when they serve out little baskets of cooked vegetable food to each person, you will be laid upon the top of the food to give a relish to it.'"

"Then without delay these two races of beings separated. The fish fled in confusion to the sea, the reptiles sought safety in the forests and shrubs."

Tangaroa, enraged at some of his children deserting him, and, being sheltered by the god of the forests on dry land, has ever since waged war on his brother Tane, who, in return, has waged war against him.

Hence Tane supplies the offspring of his brother To-matauenga with canoes, with spears and with fish-hooks made from his trees, and with nets woven from his fibrous plants, that they may destroy the offspring of Tangaroa; whilst Tangaroa, in return, swallows up the offspring of Tane, overwhelming canoes with the surges of his sea, swallowing up the lands, trees, and houses that are swept off by floods, and ever wastes away, with his lapping waves, the shores that confine him, that the giants of the forests may be washed down and swept out into his boundless ocean, that he may then swallow up the insects, the young birds, and the various animals which inhabit them—all which things are recorded in the prayers which were offered to these gods.

Tawhiri-ma-tea next rushed on to attack his brothers Rongo-ma-tane and Haumia-tikitiki, the gods and progenitors of cultivated and uncultivated food; but Papa, to save these for her other children, caught them up, and hid them in a place of safety; and so well were these children of hers concealed by their mother Earth that Tawhiri-ma-tea sought for them in vain.

Tawhiri-ma-tea, having thus vanquished all his other brothers, next rushed against Tu-matauenga, to try his strength against his; he exerted all his force against him, but he could neither shake him or prevail against him. What did Tu-matauenga care for his brother's wrath? He was the only one of the whole party of brothers who had planned the destruction of their parents, and had shown himself brave and fierce in war; his brothers had yielded at once before the tremendous assaults of Tawhiri-ma-tea and his progeny—Tane-mahuta and his offspring had been broken and torn in pieces—Tangaroa and his children had fled to the depths of the ocean or the recesses of the shore—Rongo-ma-tane and Haumia-tikitiki had been hidden from him in the earth—but Tu-matauenga, or man, still stood erect and unshaken upon the breast of his mother Earth; and now at length the hearts of Heaven and of the god of storms became tranquil, and their passions were assuaged.

Tu-matauenga, or fierce man, having thus successfully resisted his brother, the god of hurricanes and storms, next took thought how he could turn upon his brothers and slay them, because they had not assisted him or fought bravely when Tawhiri-ma-tea had attacked them to avenge the separation of their parents, and because they had left him alone to show his prowess in the fight. As yet death had no power over man. It was not until the birth of the children of Taranga and of Makea-tu-tara, of Maui-taha, of Maui-roto, of Maui-pae, of Maui-waho, and of Maui-tikitiki-o-Taranga, the demi-god who tried to drain Hine-nui-te-po, that death had power over men. If that goddess had not been deceived by Maui-tikitiki, men would not have died, but would in that case have lived forever; it was from his deceiving Hine-nui-te-po that death obtained power over mankind, and penetrated to every part of the earth.

Tu-matauenga continued to reflect upon the cowardly manner in which his brothers had acted, in leaving him to show his courage alone, and he first sought some means of injuring Tane-mahuta, because he had not come to aid him in his combat with Tawhiri-ma-tea, and partly because he was aware that Tane had had a numerous progeny, who were rapidly increasing, and might at last prove hostile to him, and injure him, so he began to collect leaves of the whanake tree, and twisted them into nooses, and when his work was ended, he went to the forest to put up his snares, and hung them up—ha! ha! the children of Tane fell before him; none of them could any longer fly or move in safety.

Then he next determined to take revenge on his brother Tangaroa, who had also deserted him in the combat; so he sought for his offspring, and found them leaping or swimming in the water; then he cut many leaves from the flax-plant, and netted nets with the flax, and dragged these, and hauled the children of Tangaroa ashore.

After that, he determined also to be revenged upon his brothers Rongo-ma-tane and Haumia-tikitiki; he soon found them by their peculiar leaves, and he scraped into shape a wooden hoe, and plaited a basket, and dug in the earth and pulled up all kinds of plants with edible roots, and the plants which had been dug up withered in the sun.

Thus Tu-matauenga devoured all his brothers, and consumed the whole of them, in revenge for their having deserted him and left him to fight alone against Tawhiri-ma-tea and Rangi.

When his brothers had all thus been overcome by Tu, he assumed several names, namely, Tu-ka-riri, Tu-ka-nguha, Tu-ka-taua, Tu-whaka-heke-tangata, Tu-mata-wha-iti, and Tu-matauenga; he assumed one name for each of his attributes displayed in the victories over his brothers. Four of his brothers were entirely deposed by him, and became his food; but one of them, Tawhiri-ma-tea, he could not vanquish or make common by eating him for food, so he, the last-born child of Heaven and Earth, was left as an enemy for man, and still, with a rage equal to that of Man, this elder brother ever attacks him in storms and hurricanes, endeavoring to destroy him alike by sea and land.

Now, the meanings of these names of the children of the Heaven and Earth are as follows:

Tangaroa signifies fish of every kind; Rongo-ma-tane signifies the sweet potato, and all vegetables cultivated as food; Haumia-tikitiki signifies fern root, and all kinds of food which grow wild; Tane-mahuta signifies forests, the birds and insects which inhabit them, and all things fashioned from wood; Tawhiri-ma-tea signifies winds and storms; and Tu-matauenga signifies man.

Four of his brothers having, as before stated, been made common, or articles of food by Tu-matauenga, he assigned for each of them fitting incantations, that they might be abundant, and that he might easily obtain them. . . .

The bursting forth of the wrathful fury of Ta-whiri-ma-tea against his brothers was the cause of the disappearance of a great part of the dry land; during that contest a great part of mother Earth was submerged. The names of those beings of ancient days who submerged so large a portion of the earth were Terrible-rain, Long-continued-rain, Fierce-hail-storms; and their progeny were Mist, Heavy-dew, and Light-dew, and these together submerged the greater part of the earth, so that only a small portion of dry land projected above the sea.

From that time clear light increased upon the earth, and all the beings which were hidden between Rangi and Papa before they were separated, now multiplied upon the earth. The first beings begotten by Rangi and Papa were not like human beings; but Tu-matauenga bore the likeness of a man, as did all his brothers, as also did a Po, a Ao, a Kore, to Kimihanga and Runku, and thus it continued until the times of Ngainui and his generation, and of Whiro-te-tupu and his generation, and it has so continued to this day. . . .

THE LEGEND OF MAUI

[I.] The young hero, Maui, had not been long at home with his brothers when he began to think that it was too soon after the rising of the sun that it became night again, and that the sun again sank down below the horizon, every day, every day; in the same manner the days appeared too short to him. So at last, one day he said to his brothers: "Let us now catch the sun in a noose, so that we may compel him to move more slowly, in order that mankind may have long days to labor in to produce subsistence for themselves. . . ."

Then they began to spin and twist ropes to form a noose to catch the sun in, and in doing this they discovered the mode of plaiting flax into stout square-shaped ropes (*tuamaka*), and the manner of plaiting flat ropes (*paharahara*), and of spinning round ropes; at last, they finished making all the ropes which they required. Then Maui took up his enchanted weapon, and he took his brothers with him, and they carried their provisions, ropes, and other things with them, in their hands. They traveled all night, and as soon as day broke, they halted in the desert, and hid themselves that they might not be seen by the sun; and at night they renewed their journey, and before dawn they halted, and hid themselves again; at length they got very far, very far, to the eastward, and came to the very edge of the place out of which the sun rises.

Then they set to work and built on each side of this place a long, high wall of clay, with huts of boughs of trees at each end to hide themselves in; when these were finished, they made the loops of the noose, and the brothers of Maui then lay in wait on one side of the place out of which the sun rises, and Maui himself lay in wait upon the other side.

The young hero held in his hand his enchanted weapon, the jaw-bone of his ancestress—of Muri-ranga-whenua—and said to his brothers: "Mind now, keep yourselves hid, and do not go showing yourselves foolishly to the sun; if you do, you will frighten him; but wait patiently until his head and fore legs have got well into the snare, then I will shout out, haul away as hard as you can on the ropes on both sides, and then I'll rush out and attack him, but do you keep your ropes tight for a good long time (while I attack him), until he is nearly dead, when we will let him go; but mind now, my brothers, do not let him move you to pity with his shrieks and screams."

At last the sun came rising up out of his place, like a fire spreading far and wide over the mountains and forests, he rises up, his head passes through the noose, and it takes in more and more of his body, until his forepaws pass through; then are pulled tight the ropes, and the monster began to struggle and roll himself about, whilst the snare jerked backwards and forwards as he struggled. Ah! was not he held fast in the ropes of his enemies!

Then forth rushed that bold hero, Maui-tikitiki-o-Taranga, with his enchanted weapon. Alas! the sun screams aloud; he roars; Maui strikes him fiercely with many blows; they hold him for a long time. At last they let him go, and then, weak from wounds, the sun crept slowly along its course. Then was learnt by men the second name of the sun, for in its agony the sun screamed out: "Why am I thus smitten by you! O man! do you know what you are doing? Why should you wish to kill Tamanui-te-Ra?" Thus was learnt his second name. At last they let him go. Oh, then, Tama-nui-te-Ra went very slowly and feebly on his course.

[II.] Maui-taha and his brothers after this feat returned again to their own house, and dwelt there, and dwelt there, and dwelt there; and after a long time his brothers went out fishing, whilst Maui-tikitiki-o-Taranga stopped idly at home doing nothing, although indeed he had to listen to the sulky grumblings of his wives and children, at his laziness in not catching fish for them. Then he called out to the women, "Never mind, O mothers, yourselves and your children need not fear. Have not I accomplished all things, and as for this little feat, this trifling work of getting food for you, do you think I cannot do that?

Certainly; if I go and get a fish for you, it will be one so large that when I bring it to land you will not be able to eat it all, and the sun will shine on it and make it putrid before it is consumed." Then Maui snooded his enchanted fish-hook, which was pointed with part of the jaw-bone of Muri-ranga-whenua, and when he had finished this, he twisted a stout fishing-line to his hook. . . .

As soon as it was dark night Maui went down to the shore, got into his brothers' canoe, and hid himself under the bottom boards of it. The next forenoon his brothers came down to the shore to go fishing again, and they had their canoe launched, and paddled out to sea without ever seeing Maui, who lay hid in the hollow of the canoe under the bottom boards. When they got well out to sea Maui crept out of his hiding place; as soon as his brothers saw him, they said: "We had better get back to the shore again as fast as we can, since this fellow is on board"; but Maui, by his enchantments, stretched out the sea so that the shore instantly became very distant from them, and by the time they could turn themselves around to look for it, it was out of view. Maui now said to them: "You had better let me go on with you, I shall at least be useful to bail the water out of our canoe." To this they consented, and they paddled on again and speedily arrived at the fishing ground where they used to fish upon former occasions. As soon as they got there his brothers said: "Let us drop the anchor and fish here"; and he answered: "Oh, no, don't; we had much better paddle a long distance farther out." Upon this they paddle on, and paddle as far as the farthest fishing ground, a long way out to sea, and then his brothers at last say: "Come now, we must drop anchor and fish here." And he replies again, "Oh, the fish here are very fine, I suppose, but we had much better pull right out to sea, and drop anchor there. If we go out to the place where I wish the anchor to be let go, before you can get a hook to the bottom, a fish will come following it back to the top of the water. You won't have to stop there a longer time than you can wink your eye in, and our canoe will come back to shore full of fish." As soon as they hear this they paddle away—they paddle away until they reach a very long distance off, and his brothers then say: "We are now far enough." And he replies: "No, no, let us go out of sight of land, and when we have quite lost sight of it, then let the anchor be dropped, but let it be very far off, quite out in the open sea."

At last they reach the open sea, and his brothers begin to fish. Lo, lo, they had hardly let their hooks down to the bottom, when they each pulled up a fish into the canoe. Twice only they let down their lines, when behold the canoe was filled up with the number of fish they had caught. Then his brothers said: "Oh, brother, let us all return now."

And he answered them: "Stay a little; let me also throw my hook into the sea." And his brothers replied: "Where did you get a hook?" And he answered: "Oh, never mind, I have a hook of my own." And his brothers replied again: "Make haste and throw it, then." And as he pulled it out from under his garments, the light flashed from the beautiful mother-of-pearl shell in the hollow of the hook, and his brothers saw that the hook was carved and ornamented with tufts of hair pulled from the tail of a dog, and it looked exceedingly beautiful. Maui then asked his brothers to give him a little bait to bait his hook with; but they replied: "We will not give you any of our bait." So he doubled his fist and struck his nose violently and the blood gushed out, and he smeared his hook with his own blood for bait, and then he cast it into the sea, and it sank down, and sank down, till it reached to the small carved figure on the roof of a house at the bottom of the sea, then passing by the figure, it descended along the outside carved rafters of the roof, and fell in at the doorway of the house, and the hook of Maui-tikitiki-o-Taranga caught first in the sill of the doorway.

Then, feeling something on his hook, he began to haul in his line. Ah, ah!—there ascended on his hook the house of that old fellow Tonganui. It came up, up; and as it rose high, oh dear! how his hook was strained with its great weight; and then there came gurgling up foam and bubbles from the earth, as of an island emerging from the water, and his brothers opened their mouths and cried aloud.

Maui all this time continued to chant forth incantations amidst the murmurings and wailings of his brothers, who were weeping and lamenting, and saying, "See now, how he has brought us out into the open sea, that we may be upset in it, and devoured by the fish." Then he raised aloud his voice, and repeated the incantation called Hiki which makes heavy weights light, in order that the fish he had caught might come up easily, and he chanted an incantation beginning thus:

> "Wherefore, then, oh! Tonganui,
> Dost thou hold fast so obstinately below there?"

When he had finished his incantation, there floated up, hanging to his line, the fish of Maui, a portion of the earth, of Papa-tu-a-Nuku. Alas! alas! their canoe lay aground.

Maui then left his brothers with their canoe, and returned to the village; but before he went he said to them: "After I am gone, be courageous and patient; do not eat food until I return, and do not let our fish be cut up, but rather leave it until I have carried an offering to the gods from this great haul of fish, and until I have found a priest, that fitting prayers and sacrifices may be offered to the god, and the necessary rites be completed in order. We shall thus all be purified. I will then return, and we can cut up this fish in safety, and it shall be fairly portioned out to this one, and to that one, and to that other; and on my arrival you shall each have your due share of it, and return to your homes joyfully; and what we leave behind us will keep good, and that which we take away with us, returning, will be good too."

Maui had hardly gone, after saying all this to them, than his brothers trampled under their feet the words they had heard him speak. They began at once to eat food, and to cut up the fish. When they did this, Maui had not yet arrived at the sacred place, in the presence of the god; had he previously reached the sacred place the heart of the deity would have been appeased with the offering of a portion of the fish which had been caught by his disciples, and all the male and female deities would have partaken of their portions of the sacrifice. Alas! alas! those foolish, thoughtless brothers of his cut up the fish, and behold the gods turned with wrath upon them, on account of the fish which they had thus cut up without having made a fitting sacrifice. Then indeed, the fish began to toss about his head from side to side, and to lash his tail, and the fins upon his back, and his lower jaw. Ah! ah! well done Tangaroa, it springs about on shore as briskly as if it was in the water.

That is the reason that this island is now so rough and uneven—that here stands a mountain, and there lies a plain; that here descends a vale, that there rises a cliff. If the brothers of Maui had not acted so deceitfully, the huge fish would have lain flat and smooth, and would have remained as a model for the rest of the earth, for the present generation of men. This, which has just been recounted, is the second evil which took place after the separation of Heaven from Earth.

Thus was dry land fished up by Maui after it had been hidden under the ocean by Rangi and Tawhiri-ma-tea. It was with an enchanted fish-hook that he drew it up, which was pointed with a bit of the jaw-bone of his ancestress Muri-ranga-whenua; and in the district of Heretaunga they still show the fish-hook of Maui, which became a cape stretching far out into the sea, and now forms the southern extremity of Hawke's Bay.

[III.] The hero now thought that he would extinguish and destroy the fires of his ancestress Mahu-ika. . . .

Then the aged lady rose right up, and said: "Au-e! who can this mortal be?" and he answered, "It's I." "Where do you come from?" said she, and he answered, "I belong to this country." "You are not from this country," said she; "your appearance is not like that of the inhabitants of this country. Do you come from the northeast?" He replied, "No." "Do you come from the southeast?" He replied, "No." "Are you from the south?" He replied, "No." "Are you from the westward?" He answered, "No." "Come you, then, from the direction of the wind which blows right upon me?" And he said, "I do." "Oh, then," cried she, "you are my grandchild; what do you want here?" He answered, "I am come to beg fire from you." She replied, "Welcome, welcome; here then is fire for you."

Then the aged woman pulled out her nail; and as she pulled it out fire flowed from it, and she gave it to him. And when Maui saw she had drawn out her nail to produce fire for him, he thought it a most wonderful thing! Then he went a short distance off, and when not very far from her, he put the fire out, quite out; and returning to her again, said: "The light you gave me has gone out, give me another." Then she caught hold of another nail, and pulled it out as a light for him; and he left her, and went a little on one side, and put that light out also; then he went back to her again, and said: "O lady, give me, I pray you, another light, for the last one has also gone out." And thus he went on and on, until she had pulled out all the nails of the fingers of one of her hands; and then she began with the other hand, until she had pulled all the fingernails out of that hand, too; and then she commenced upon the nails of her feet, and pulled them also out in the same manner, except the nail of one of her big toes. Then the aged woman said to herself at last: "This fellow is surely playing tricks with me."

Then out she pulled the one toe-nail that she had left, and it, too, became fire, and as she dashed it down on the ground the whole place caught fire. And she cried out to Maui: "There, you have it all now!" And Maui ran off, and made a rush to escape, but the fire followed hard after him, close behind him; so he changed himself into a fleet-winged eagle, and flew with rapid flight, but the fire pursued, and almost caught him as he flew. Then the eagle dashed down into a pool of water; but when he got into the water he found that almost boiling too: the forests just then also caught fire, so that it could not alight anywhere, and the earth and sea both caught fire too, and Maui was very near perishing in the flames.

Then he called on his ancestors Tawhiri-ma-tea and Whatirima-takataka, to send down an abundant supply of water, and he cried aloud: "Oh, let water be given to me to quench this fire which pursues after me"; and lo, then appeared squalls and gales, and Tawhiri-ma-tea sent heavy lasting rain, and the fire was quenched; and before Mahuika could reach her place of shelter, she almost perished in the rain, and her shrieks and screams became as loud as those of Maui had been, when he was scorched by the pursuing fire: thus Maui ended this proceeding. In this manner was extinguished the fire of Mahuika, the goddess of fire; but before it was all lost, she saved a few sparks which she threw, to protect them, into the Kaikomako, and a few other trees, where they are still cherished; hence, men yet use portions of the wood of these trees for fire when they require a light. . . .

[IV.] Maui . . . now returned to his parents, and when he had been with them for some time, his father said to him one day: "O my son, I have heard from your mother and others that you are very valiant, and that you have succeeded in all feats that you have under-taken in your own country, whether they were small or great; but now that you have arrived in your father's country, you will, perhaps, at last be overcome."

Then Maui asked him: "What do you mean? What things are there that I can be vanquished by?" And his father answered him: "By your great ancestress, by Hine-nui-te-po, who if you look, you may see flashing, and as it were, opening and shutting there, where the horizon meets the sky." And Maui replied: "Lay aside such idle thoughts, and let us both fearlessly seek whether men are to die or live forever." And his father said: "My child, there has been an ill omen for us; when I was baptizing you, I omitted a portion of the fitting prayers, and that I know will be the cause of your perishing."

Then Maui asked his father: "What is my ancestress Hine-nui-te-po like?" And he answered: "What you see yonder shining so brightly red are her eyes, and her teeth are as sharp and hard as pieces of volcanic glass; her body is like that of a man, and as for the pupils of her eyes, they are jasper; and her hair is like tangles of long seaweed; and her mouth is like that of a barracouta." Then his son answered him: "Do you think her strength is as great as that of Tama-nui-te-Ra, who consumes Man, and the earth, and the very waters, by the fierceness of his heat? Was not the world formerly saved alive by the speed with which he traveled? If he had then, in the days of his full strength and power, gone as slowly as he does now, not a remnant of mankind would have been left living upon the earth, nor, indeed, would anything else have survived. But I laid hold of Tama-nui-te-Ra, and now he goes slowly, for I smote him again and again, so that he is now feeble, and long in traveling his course, and he now gives but very little heat, having been weakened by the blows of my enchanted weapon; I then, too, split him open in many places, and from the wounds so made, many rays now issue forth, and spread in all directions. So, also, I found the sea much larger than the earth, but by the power of the last-born of your children, part of the earth was drawn up again, and dry land came forth." And his father answered him: "That is all very true, O my last born, and the strength of my old age; well, then, be bold, go and visit your great ancestress who flashes so fiercely there, where the edge of the horizon meets the sky."

Hardly was this conversation concluded with his father, when the young hero went forth to look for companions to accompany him upon this enterprise; and so there came to him for companions, the small robin, and the large robin, and the thrush, and the yellow-hammer, and every kind of little bird, and the water-wagtail, and these all assembled together, and they all started with Maui in the evening, and arrived at the dwelling of Hine-nui-te-po, and found her fast asleep.

Then Maui addressed them all, and said: "My little friends, now if you see me creep into this old chieftainess, do not laugh at what you see. Nay, nay, do not I pray you, but when I have got altogether inside her, and just as I am coming out of her mouth, then you may shout with laughter if you please." And his little friends, who were frightened at what they saw, replied: "Oh, sir, you will certainly be killed." And he answered them: "If you burst out laughing at me as soon as I get inside her, you will wake her up, and she will certainly kill me at once, but if you do not laugh until I am quite inside her, and am on the point of coming out of her mouth, I shall live, and Hine-nui-te-po will die." And his little friends answered: "Go on then, brave sir, but pray take good care of yourself."

Then the young hero started off, and twisted the strings of his weapon tight round his wrist, and went into the house, and stripped off his clothes, and the skin on his hips looked mottled and beautiful as that of a mackerel, from the tattoo marks, cut on it with the chisel of Uetonga; and he entered the old chieftainess.

The little birds now screwed up their tiny cheeks, trying to suppress their laughter; at last, the little Tiwakawaka could no longer keep it in, and laughed out loud, with its merry, cheerful note; this woke the old woman up, she opened her eyes, started up, and killed Maui.

Thus died this Maui we have spoken of, but before he died he had children, and sons were born to him; some of his descendants yet live in Hawaiki, some in Aotearoa (or in these islands); the greater part of his descendants remained in Hawaiki, but a few of them came here to Aotearoa. According to the traditions of the Maori, this was the cause of the introduction of death into the world (Hine-nui-te-po being the goddess of death: if Maui had passed safely through her, then no more human beings would have died, but death itself would have been destroyed), and we express it by saying: "The water-wagtail laughing

at Maui-tikitiki-o-Taranga made Hine-nui-te-po squeeze him to death."
And we have this proverb: "Men make heirs, but death carries them
off." . . .

47. THE CREATION ACCORDING TO THE MAIDU [29]

BY R. B. DIXON

IN THE beginning there was no sun, no moon, no stars. All was dark,
and everywhere there was only water. A raft came floating on the
water. It came from the north, and in it were two persons—Turtle
(A'nōsma) and Father-of-the-Secret-Society (Pehéipĕ). The stream
flowed very rapidly. Then from the sky a rope of feathers, called
Pō'kelma, was let down, and down it came Earth-Initiate. When he
reached the end of the rope, he tied it to the bow of the raft and stepped
in. His face was covered and was never seen, but his body shone like
the sun. He sat down, and for a long time said nothing. At last Turtle
said, "Where do you come from?" and Earth-Initiate answered, "I
come from above." Then Turtle said, "Brother, can you not make for
me some good dry land, so that I may sometimes come up out of the
water?" Then he asked another time, "Are there going to be any
people in the world?" Earth-Initiate thought awhile, then said, "Yes."
Turtle asked, "How long before you are going to make people?"
Earth-Initiate replied, "I don't know. You want to have some dry land:
well, how am I going to get any earth to make it of?" Turtle answered,
"If you will tie a rock about my left arm, I'll dive for some." Earth-
Initiate did as Turtle asked, and then, reaching around, took the end of
a rope from somewhere, and tied it to Turtle. When Earth-Initiate
came to the raft there was no rope there; he just reached out and found
one. Turtle said: "If the rope is not long enough, I'll jerk it once, and
you must haul me up; if it is long enough, I'll give two jerks, and then
you must pull me up quickly, as I shall have all the earth that I can
carry." Just as Turtle went over the side of the boat, Father-of-the-
Secret-Society began to shout loudly.

Turtle was gone a long time. He was gone six years; and when he
came up, he was covered with green slime, he had been down so long.
When he reached the top of the water, the only earth he had was very

[29] From R. B. Dixon, "Maidu Myths," *Bulletin of the American Museum of
Natural History*, Volume 17, pages 39-45, 1902. The Maidu are Indians in
northern California. "Initiate" denotes a member of the secret religious society
of the Maidu.

little under his nails; the rest had all washed away. Earth-Initiate took with his right hand a stone knife from under his left armpit, and carefully scraped the earth out from under Turtle's nails. He put the earth in the palm of his hand, and rolled it about till it was round; it was as large as a small pebble. He laid it on the stern of the raft. By and by he went to look at it; it had not grown at all. The third time that he went to look at it, it had grown so that it could be spanned by the arms. The fourth time he looked, it was as big as the world, the raft was aground, and all around were mountains as far as he could see. The raft came ashore at Ta'doikö, and the place can be seen today.

When the raft had come to land, Turtle said: "I can't stay in the dark all the time. Can't you make a light, so that I can see?" Earth-Initiate replied, "Let us get out of the raft, and then we will see what we can do." So all three got out. Then Earth-Initiate said: "Look that way to the east! I am going to tell my sister to come up." Then it began to grow light, and day began to break; then Father-of-the-Secret-Society began to shout loudly, and the sun came up. Turtle said, "Which way is the sun going to travel?" Earth-Initiate answered, "I'll tell her to go this way, and go down there." After the sun went down, Father-of-the-Secret-Society began to cry and shout again, and it grew very dark. Earth-Initiate said, "I'll tell my brother to come up." Then the moon rose. Then Earth-Initiate asked Turtle and Father-of-the-Secret-Society, "How do you like it?" and they both answered, "It is very good." Then Turtle asked, "Is that all you are going to do for us?" and Earth-Initiate answered, "No, I am going to do more yet." Then he called the stars each by its name, and they came out. When this was done, Turtle asked, "Now what shall we do?" Earth-Initiate replied, "Wait, and I'll show you." Then he made a tree grow at Ta'doikö—the tree called Hu'kīmtsa; and Earth-Initiate and Turtle and Father-of-the-Secret-Society sat in its shade for two days. The tree was very large, and had twelve different kinds of acorns growing on it.

After they had sat two days under the tree, they all went off to see the world that Earth-Initiate had made. They started at sunrise, and were back by sunset. Earth-Initiate traveled so fast that all they could see was a ball of fire flashing about under the ground and the water. While they were gone, Coyote (Olä'li) and his dog Rattlesnake (Ka'udi, *or* So'la) came up out of the ground. It is said that Coyote could see Earth-Initiate's face. When Earth-Initiate and the others came back, they found Coyote at Ta'doikö. All five of them then built huts for themselves, and lived there at Ta'doikö, but no one could go inside of Earth-Initiate's house. Soon after the travelers came back,

Earth-Initiate called the birds from the air, and made the trees and then the animals. He took some mud, and of this made first a deer; after that, he made all the other animals. Sometimes Turtle would say, "That does not look well; can't you make it some other way?"

Some time after this, Earth-Initiate and Coyote were at Marysville Buttes (E'stobüsin yā'mani). Earth-Initiate said, "I am going to make people." In the middle of the afternoon he began, for he had returned to Ta'doikö. He took dark red earth, mixed it with water, and made two figures—one a man, and one a woman. He laid the man on his right side, and the woman on his left, inside his house. Then he lay down himself, flat on his back, with his arms stretched out. He lay thus and sweated all the afternoon and night. Early in the morning the woman began to tickle him in the side. He kept very still, did not laugh. By and by he got up, thrust a piece of pitchwood into the ground, and fire burst out. The two people were very white. No one today is as white as they were. Their eyes were pink, their hair was black, their teeth shone brightly, and they were very handsome. It is said that Earth-Initiate did not finish the hands of the people, as he did not know how it would be best to do it. Coyote saw the people, and suggested that they ought to have hands like his. Earth-Initiate said, "No, their hands shall be like mine." Then he finished them. When Coyote asked why their hands were to be like that, Earth-Initiate answered, "So that, if they are chased by bears, they can climb trees." This first man was called Ku'ksū; and the woman, Morning Star Woman (La'idamlülüm kü'le).

When Coyote had seen the two people, he thought: "That is not difficult. I'll do it myself." He did just as Earth-Initiate had told him, but could not help laughing, when, early in the morning, the woman poked him in the ribs. As a result of his failing to keep still, the people were glass-eyed. Earth-Initiate said, "I told you not to laugh," but Coyote declared he had not. This was the first lie.

By and by there came to be a good many people. Earth-Initiate had wanted to have everything comfortable and easy for people, so that none of them should have to work. All fruits were easy to obtain, no one was ever to get sick and die. As the people grew numerous, Earth-Initiate did not come as often as formerly, he only came to see Ku'ksū in the night. One night he said to him: "Tomorrow morning you must go to the little lake near here. Take all the people with you. I'll make you a very old man before you get to the lake." So in the morning Ku'ksū collected all the people, and went to the lake. By the time he had reached it, he was a very old man. He fell into the lake, and sank down out of sight. Pretty soon the ground began to shake, the waves overflowed the shore, and there was a great roaring under the water, like thunder. By and by Ku'ksū came up out of the water, but young again, just like a young man. Then Earth-Initiate came and spoke to the people, and said: "If you do as I tell you, everything will be well. When any of you grow old, so old that you cannot walk, come to this lake, or get some one to bring you here. You must then go down into the water as you have seen Ku'ksū do, and you will come out young again." When he had said this, he went away. He left in the night, and went up above.

All this time food had been easy to get, as Earth-Initiate had wished. The women set out baskets at night, and in the morning they found them full of food, all ready to eat, and lukewarm. One day Coyote came along. He asked the people how they lived, and they told him that all they had to do was to eat and sleep. Coyote replied, "That is no way to do: I can show you something better." Then he told them how he and Earth-Initiate had had a discussion before men had been made; how Earth-Initiate wanted everything easy, and that there should be no sickness or death, but how he had thought it would be better to have people work, get sick, and die. He said, "We'll have a burning." The people did not know what he meant; but Coyote said, "I'll show you. It is better to have a burning, for then the widows can be free." So he took all the baskets and things that the people had, hung them up on poles, made everything all ready. When all was prepared, Coyote said, "At this time you must always have games." So he fixed the moon during which these games were to be played.

Coyote told them to start the games with a foot-race, and every one got ready to run. Ku'ksū did not come, however. He sat in his hut alone, and was sad, for he knew what was going to occur. Just at this moment Rattlesnake came to Ku'ksū, and said, "What shall we do now? Everything is spoiled!" Ku'ksū did not answer, so Rattlesnake said, "Well, I'll do what I think is best." Then he went out and along the course that the racers were to go over, and hid himself, leaving his head just sticking out of a hole. By this time all the racers had started, and among them Coyote's son. He was Coyote's only child, and was very quick. He soon began to outstrip all the runners, and was in the lead. As he passed the spot where Rattlesnake had hidden himself, however, Rattlesnake raised his head and bit the boy in the ankle. In a minute the boy was dead.

Coyote was dancing about the home-stake. He was very happy, and was shouting at his son and praising him. When Rattlesnake bit the boy, and he fell dead, every one laughed at Coyote, and said, "Your son has fallen down, and is so ashamed that he does not dare to get up." Coyote said, "No, that is not it. He is dead." This was the first death. The people, however, did not understand, and picked the boy up, and brought him to Coyote. Then Coyote began to cry, and every one did the same. These were the first tears. Then Coyote took his son's body and carried it to the lake of which Earth-Initiate had told them, and threw the body in. But there was no noise, and nothing happened, and the body drifted about for four days on the surface, like a log. On the fifth day Coyote took four sacks of beads and brought them to Ku′ksū, begging him to restore his son to life. Ku′ksū did not answer. For five days Coyote begged, then Ku′ksū came out of his house, bringing all his beads and bear-skins, and calling to all the people to come and watch him. He laid the body on a bear-skin, dressed it, and wrapped it up carefully. Then he dug a grave, put the body into it, and covered it up. Then he told the people, "From now on, this is what you must do. This is the way you must do till the world shall be made over."

About a year after this, in the spring, all was changed. Up to this time everybody spoke the same language. The people were having a burning, everything was ready for the next day, when in the night everybody suddenly began to speak a different language. Each man and his wife, however, spoke the same. Earth-Initiate had come in the night to Ku′ksū, and had told him about it all, and given him instructions for the next day. So, when morning came, Ku′ksū called all the people together, for he was able to speak all the languages. He told them each the names of the different animals, etc., in their languages, taught them how to cook and to hunt, gave them all their laws, and set the time for all their dances and festivals. Then he called each tribe by name, and sent them off in different directions, telling them where they were to live. He sent the warriors to the north, the singers to the west, the flute-players to the east and the dancers to the south. So all the people went away, and left Ku′ksū and his wife alone at Ta′doikö. By and by his wife went away, leaving in the night, and going first to Marysville Buttes. Ku′ksū stayed a little while longer, and then he also left. He too went to the Buttes, went into the spirit house (Kukinim Kumi), and sat down on the south side. He found Coyote's son there, sitting on the north side. The door was on the west. Coyote had been trying to find out where Ku′ksū had gone, and where his own son had gone, and at last found the tracks, and followed them to the spirit house. Here he saw Ku′ksū and his son, the latter eating spirit food (Ku′kinim pĕ). Coyote wanted to go in, but Ku′ksū said, "No, wait there. You have just what you wanted, it is your own fault. Every man will now have all kinds of troubles and accidents, will have to work to get his food, and will die and be buried. This must go on till the time is out, and Earth-Initiate comes again, and everything will be made over. You must go home, and tell all the people that you have seen your son, that he is not dead." Coyote said he would go, but that he was hungry, and wanted some of the food. Ku′ksū replied, "You cannot eat that. Only ghosts may eat that food." Then Coyote went away and told all the people, "I saw my son and Ku′ksū, and he told me to kill myself." So he climbed up to the top of a tall tree, jumped off and was killed. Then he went to the spirit house, thinking he could now have some of the food; but there was no one there, nothing at all, and so he went out, and walked away to the west, and was never seen again. Ku′ksū and Coyote's son, however, had gone up above.

Dynamics of Culture

48. ON A METHOD OF INVESTIGATING THE DEVELOPMENT OF INSTITUTIONS [1]

BY E. B. TYLOR

FOR years past it has become evident that the great need of anthropology is that its method should be strengthened and systematized. The world has not been unjust to the growing science, far from it. Wherever anthropologists have been able to show definite evidence and inference, for instance, in the development series of arts in the Pitt-Rivers Museum, at Oxford, not only specialists but the educated world generally are ready to receive the results and assimilate them into public opinion. Strict method has, however, as yet only been introduced over part of the anthropological field. There has still to be overcome a certain not unkindly hesitancy on the part of men engaged in the precise operations of mathematics, physics, chemistry, biology, to admit that the problems of anthropology are amenable to scientific treatment. It is my aim to show that the development of institutions may be investigated on a basis of tabulation and classification. For this end I have taken up a subject of the utmost real as well as theoretical interest, the formation of laws of marriage and descent, as to which during many years I have been collecting the evidence found among between three and four hundred peoples, ranging from insignificant savage hordes to great cultured nations. The particular rules have been scheduled out into tables, so as to ascertain what may be called the "adhesions" of each custom, showing which peoples have the same custom, and what other customs accompany it or lie apart from it. From the recurrence or absence of these customs it will be our business to infer their dependence on causes acting over the whole range of mankind.

Years since, long before my collection of data approached its present bulk and could be classified into the elaborate tables now presented, I

[1] *Journal of the* [*Royal*] *Anthropological Institute* [*of Great Britain and Ireland*], Volume 18, pages 245-269, 1889. The title of the original is as here given, plus the sub-title: "Applied to Laws of Marriage and Descent."

became naturally anxious to know whether the labor had been thrown away, or whether this social arithmetic would do something to disclose the course of social history. The question was how to make the trial. . . . The point I chose was a quaint and somewhat comic custom as to the barbaric etiquette between husbands and their wives' relatives, and vice versa: they may not look at one another, much less speak, and they even avoid mentioning one another's names. Thus, in America, John Tanner, the adopted Ojibwa, described his being taken by a friendly Assineboin into his lodge, and seeing how at his companion's entry the old father- and mother-in-law covered up their heads in their blankets till their son-in-law got into the compartment reserved for him, where his wife brought him his food. So in Australia, Mr. Howitt relates how he inadvertently told a native to call his mother-in-law, who was passing at some little distance; but the black fellow sent the order round by a third party, saying reproachfully to Mr. Howitt, "You know I could not speak to that old woman." Absurd as this custom may appear to Europeans, it is not the outcome of mere local fancy, as appears on reckoning up the peoples practicing it in various regions of the world, who are found to be about sixty-six in number, that is, more than one-sixth of the whole number of peoples catalogued, which is roughly three hundred and fifty. Thus:

AVOIDANCE

Between H. and W.'s Rel.	Mutual	Between W. and H.'s Rel.
45	8	13

Now, on looking out from the schedules the adhesions of this avoidance-custom, a relation appears between it and the customs of the world as to residence after marriage. This is seen in the following computation of the peoples whose habit is for the husband to take up his abode with the wife's family permanently, or to do so temporarily and eventually to remove with her to his own family or home (the reverse of this does not occur), or for the husband at once to take home the wife.

RESIDENCE

H. to W.	Removal	W. to H.
65	76	141

Now, if the customs of residence and the customs of avoidance were independent, or nearly so, we should expect to find their coincidence following the ordinary law of chance distribution. In the tribes where the husband permanently lives with his wife's family (65 out of 350), we should estimate that ceremonial avoidance between him and them might appear in nine cases,[2] whereas it actually appears in 13 cases. On the other hand, peoples where the husband at marriage takes his wife to his home (141 out of 350), would rateably correspond with avoidance between him and her family in eighteen [3] cases, whereas it actually appears in eight cases only. Also, if the thirteen cases of avoidance between the wife and the husband's family were divided rateably among the different modes of residence, two or three cases should come among the peoples where the husband lives with the wife's family, but there are no such cases. On the other hand, five cases should be found among the peoples where the wife lives in the husband's home or family, but actually there are eight. Thus there is a well marked preponderance indicating that ceremonial avoidance by the husband of the wife's family is in some way connected with his living with them; and vice versa as to the wife and the husband's family. Hereupon, it has to be enquired whether the facts suggest a reason for this connection. Such a reason readily presents itself, inasmuch as the ceremony of not speaking to and pretending not to see some well-known person close by, is familiar enough to ourselves in the social rite which we call "cutting." . . . In this first example, it is to be noticed that the argument of a causal connection of some kind between two groups of phenomena brings into view, so far at least as the data proved sound, a scientific fact. But we pass on to less solid ground in assigning for this connection a reason which may be only analogous to the real reason, or only indirectly corresponding with it, or only partly expressing it, as its correlation with other connections may eventually show. This important reservation, once stated, may be taken as understood through the rest of the enquiry.

Let us now turn to another custom, not less quaint-seeming than the last to the European mind. This is the practice of naming the parent from the child. When Moffat, the missionary, was in Africa among the Bechuana, he was spoken to and of, according to native usage, as Ra-Mary—father of Mary. On the other side of the world, among the Kasias of India, Colonel Yule mentions the like rule; for instance, there being a boy named Bobon, his father was known as Pabobon. In fact there are above thirty peoples spread over the earth who thus name the father, and, though less often, the mother. They may be called, coining a name for them, teknonymous peoples. When beginning to notice the wide distribution of this custom of teknonymy, and setting

[2] $45 \times 65 \div 350 = 8 +$.—*Eds.*
[3] $45 \times 141 \div 350 = 18$.—*Eds.*

myself to reckon its adhesions, I confess to have been fairly taken by surprise to find it lying in close connection with the custom of the husband's residence in the wife's family, the two coinciding twenty-two times, where accident might fairly have given eleven. It proved to be still more closely attached to the practice of ceremonial avoidance by the husband of the wife's relatives, occurring fourteen times, where accident might have given four. . . . Were the three customs so distantly connected as to be practically independent, the product of the corresponding fractions $132 \times 53 \times 31 \div 350 \times 350 \times 350$ multiplied into the 350 peoples would show that their concurrence might be expected to happen between once and twice in the list of peoples of the world.[4] In fact it is found eleven times. Thus, we have their common causation vouched for by the heavy odds of six to one. Many of the firmest beliefs of mankind rest, I fear, on a less solid basis. . . .

At this point it will be convenient to examine two institutions of early marriage law, namely, exogamy and classificatory relationship. The principle of exogamy was brought prominently into view fifty years ago, by Sir George Grey, when he described the native Australian rule for a man not to marry a woman of the same family name or bearing the same animal-crest or kobong as himself; and called attention to the coincidence of this with the North American system of clans named from totem animals, a man being bound to marry outside his own totem or clan. Mr. J. F. McLennan gave these customs the name of exogamy or "marrying-out," and showed them to belong to "a most widely prevailing principle of marriage law among primitive races." Much information has since then come in, with the result of showing that exogamy has hardly to do with the capture of wives in war between alien nations, but rather with the regulation of marriages within groups of clans or tribes who have connubium; such clans or tribes may be more or less at strife, but they acknowledge ties of kindred and are usually allied by language. It is now also understood that a people may at once practice endogamy or "marrying-in" within its borders, and exogamy or "marrying-out" of its clans with one another. The situation may be understood among the Hindus, where a man must marry in his caste, but within that caste must not marry in his own gotra or clan. The effect of an exogamic rule is similar whether clanship follows the female or male line of descent. Next, as to the principle of classificatory relationship, an early mention of this is by Father Lafitau, above one hundred and fifty years ago, who states that "among the Iroquois and Hurons all the children of a cabin regard all their mother's sisters as

---

[4] The figure 132 seems to stand for 141 as given above (wife's residence with husband's family) ; and 53 is of course 45 + 8 under "Avoidance."—*Eds.*

their mothers, and all their mother's brothers as their uncles, and for the same reason they give the name of fathers to all their father's brothers, and aunts to all their father's sisters. All the children on the side of the mother and her sisters, and of the father and his brothers, regard each other mutually as brothers and sisters, but as regards the children of their uncles and aunts, that is, of their mother's brothers and father's sisters, they only treat them on the footing of cousins. . . . In the third generation this changes, the great uncles and great aunts become again grandfathers and grandmothers of the children of those whom they called nephews and nieces. This continues always in the descending line according to the same rule." In our own time, Lewis H. Morgan, living among the Iroquois as an adopted Indian, was struck with this system of relationships, so unlike what he had been brought up among, and which he at first thought to be a peculiar invention of his Iroquois. But finding, on inquiry, that it extended to other North American tribes, he eventually by circulating interrogatories succeeded in collecting a great series of systems of relationship, in which he established the wide prevalence of classificatory systems, as he called them from the relatives being grouped in classes. Under the term classificatory systems, Mr. Morgan included not only those approximating to the Iroquois type, but a much simpler and ruder plan prevalent in Polynesia; it is, however, convenient for me to confine my remarks here to the former group only. This system, as found among the American Indians, Mr. Morgan showed to be closely analogous to that of the Dravidian nations of Southern Hindustan. This latter is a well-known source of perplexity to a newly appointed English civilian, who may be told by a witness that his father was sitting in the house, but presently the same witness mentions his father as coming in from the field; the native is sharply reproved by the judge for contradicting himself, whereupon he explains, it was my "little father," by which he means his father's younger brother.

I am placing together the two institutions, exogamy and classificatory relationship, inasmuch as they are really connected, being in fact two sides of one institution. This was made out eight years ago, by the Rev. Lorimer Fison, in the work on the Kamilaroi and Kurnai tribes of Australia by him and Mr. Howitt. This important explanation is still scarcely known to anthropologists, nor indeed, have I much right to reproach others with neglecting it, for I reviewed Fison and Howitt's book without distinctly realizing the bearing of this argument on the theory of exogamy, which only came round to me lately in a way which I had better now describe, as it will enable me to explain shortly and plainly the whole problem. In tabulating the nations of the world, I found a group of twenty-one peoples whose custom as to the marriage of first cousins seemed remarkable; it is that the children of two brothers may not marry, nor the children of two sisters, but the child of the brother may marry the child of the sister. It seemed obvious that this "cross-cousin marriage," as it may be called, must be the direct result of the simplest form of exogamy, where a population is divided into two classes or sections, with the law that a man who belongs to Class A can only take a wife of Class B. Such a division, for instance, is familiar in Melanesia. Dr. R. H. Codrington describes it in the Banks Islands, where the natives have two families, called veve—mother, which implies that descent follows the mother's side, and a man must marry a wife of the other mother from himself, or as they say, not on his own side of the house but on the other. Thus, taking A, A, B, B, as males and females of the class A and B, and bearing in mind that the mother's children are of her class, but the father's children of the opposite class to his, we have:

Two sisters, A, A, their Children, A, A, are of same class = tribal brother and sister = unmarriageable	Two brothers, A, A, their Children, B, B, are of same class = tribal brother and sister = unmarriageable	Brother and sister, A, A, their Children, B, A, are of different class = tribal cousins = marriageable

Fig. 7

. . . Though not proposing to enter fully into the deduction of classificatory relationships in all their varieties from the rule of exogamy, it is necessary to point out that the form of exogamy here contemplated is the simplest or dual form, in which a people is divided into two inter-marrying classes. Systems of exogamy which are dual in their nature, that is, consisting of two classes or groups of classes, stand in direct connection with cross-cousin marriage and classificatory relationship. But if the number of exogamic divisions is not dual, if there are for instance three clans, and a man of one clan may take a wife of either of the other two clans, it is readily seen that the argument of Fig. 7 breaks down. Although at present only prepared to deal with exogamy and classificatory relationship in their dual form, I may notice that the treatment of the problem by the method of adhesions strengthens the view, not wanting in other evidence, that the dual form of exogamy may be considered the original form. In reckoning from the present schedules the number of peoples who use relationship names more or less corresponding to the classificatory systems here considered, they are found to be 53, and the estimated number of these which might coincide accidentally with exogamy were there no close connection between them, would be about 12. But in fact the number of peoples who have both exogamy and classification is 33, this strong coincidence being the measure of the close causal connection subsisting between the two institutions. The adherence is even stronger as to cross-cousin marriage, of which 21 cases appear in the schedules, no less than 15 of the peoples practicing it being also known as exogamous. Here, indeed, the relation is not one of derivation, but of identity, the cross-cousin rule being actually a partial form or imperfect statement of the law of exogamy itself. Such adhesions between two or more customs have been already recognized as proving the existence of causal connection, but it has now to be pointed out that they serve another purpose. The connection, when proved, reacts on the evidence by which it was proved. When once it has been shown that cross-cousin marriage is part and parcel of exogamy, it may be argued that all the 21 peoples practicing cross-cousin marriage are to be set down as exogamous. Now as only 15 of them are expressly recorded to be so, the list of exogamous nations of the world has to be increased by six. So, classificatory relationship being evidence that the peoples practicing it are or have been exogamous, this will add some twenty more to the list of nations among whom further investigation will probably disclose record that exogamic society once prevailed or still prevails. Even if no direct record is forthcoming, the indirect proof may with due caution be sufficient for placing them in the exogamous group, which may thus number above one hundred peoples out of the 350 of the world. . . .

Exogamy lies far back in the history of man, and perhaps no observer has ever seen it come into existence, nor have the precise conditions of its origin yet been clearly inferred. Even the historical relation between exogamy and the system of classes known as totemism is not fully cleared up; whether as Prof. Robertson Smith takes it, totemism supplied the necessary machinery for working a law of exogamy, or whether exogamy itself led to totemism. But as to the law of exogamy itself, the evidence shows it in operation over a great part of the human race as a factor of political prosperity. It cannot be claimed as absolutely preventing strife and bloodshed, indeed, it has been remarked of some peoples, such as the Khonds and the Banks Islanders, that the intermarrying clans do nevertheless quarrel and fight. Still by binding together a whole community with ties of kinship and affinity, and especially by the peacemaking of the women who hold to one clan as sisters and to another as wives, it tends to keep down feuds and to heal them when they arise, so as at critical moments to hold together a tribe which under endogamous conditions would have split up. Exogamy thus shows itself as an institution which resists the tendency of uncultured populations to disintegrate, cementing them into nations capable of living together in peace and holding together in war till they reach the period of higher military and political organization. . . .

The results here brought forward make no approach to exhausting the possible inferences to be drawn from the tables. These need not even be confined to working out the development of customs found in existence somewhere on the globe, but may in some measure restore knowledge of forms of society now extinct. Interesting, however, as these problems are, I am more anxious to bring under discussion the method by which they are here treated, how imperfectly I am well aware. The interpretations offered will have to be corrected, the tabulated material improved in quantity and quality and the principles it involves brought out more justly, yet at any rate it will remain clear that the rules of human conduct are amenable to classification in compact masses, so as to show by strict numerical treatment their relations to one another. It is only at this point that speculative explanation must begin, at once guided in its course and strictly limited in its range by well-marked lines of fact to which it must conform. The key of the position is, as that veteran anthropologist, Prof. Bastian, of the Berlin Museum, is never weary of repeating, that in statistical investigation the future of anthropology lies. As soon as this is systematically applied, principles of social development become visible. . . .

The treatment of social phenomena by numerical classification will, it must be added, react on the statistical material to which the method is applied. It is in classifying the records of tribes and nations that one becomes fully aware of their imperfect and even fragmentary state. The descriptions happily tend to correct one another's errors but the great difficulty is blank want of information. As for extinct tribes, and those whose native culture has been re-modeled, there is nothing to be done. But there are still a hundred or more peoples in the world, among whom a prompt and minute investigation would save some fast vanishing memory of their social laws and customs. The quest might be followed up internationally, each civilized nation taking in hand the barbaric tribes within its purview. The future will, doubtless, be able to take care of itself as to most branches of knowledge, but there is certain work which if it is to be done at all, must be done by the present

49. SUB-HUMAN CULTURE BEGINNINGS [5]

BY A. L. KROEBER

THE last fifteen years have seen a burst of interest in those of the mammals most nearly related to ourselves, the Primates, and among the Primates in the anthropoid or man-like apes. This interest has been partly popular, but has also been reflected in the endeavors of biologists and psychologists to secure reliable evidence and a sound understanding of the behavior of these apes. The work of Koehler, Kohts, Boutan, Yerkes, Furness, has been as critical as is possible in the present development of science. Controlled experiments have been added to systematic observations. Strangely enough, not one of the studies of the great apes has been made by an anthropologist. But there is in this at least the advantage that an anthropological interpretation cannot be challenged on the ground of bias or preconception.

All of the four types of man-like apes have been studied, but the chimpanzee has provoked most interest. The gibbon is very different from ourselves in proportions and behavior; he is thoroughly arboreal. The orang approaches him in this respect; he possesses a sluggish and melancholy temperament. The gorilla, perhaps anatomically closest to man, has been difficult to capture and keep in confinement. His study has yielded some results, but his attitude toward human beings is aloof. The chimpanzee is about equally similar to man, shows definite responsiveness to human association, and is relatively hardy and docile.

THE CHIMPANZEE

The chimpanzee's life is primarily terrestrial, although he is a splendid climber. The body is not carried fully erect, and the knuckles frequently touch the ground in walking; but locomotion is on two feet. The differentiation of the limbs into a locomotory and a manipulative pair is not marked as in man, but approaches it. There are few if any human manual abilities which the chimpanzee does not possess. He is endowed with much greater strength. The available data suggest that his muscular power may be estimated at three times our own.

The infant chimpanzee begins to teethe within two months, walks at the end of six, has all its milk teeth within twelve months, and possesses at that age sufficient muscular coördination to secure for itself part of its food, although it may continue to nurse. A period of play-

[5] From *The Quarterly Review of Biology*, Volume 3, pages 325-342, 1928.

fulness and activity follows. Growth is at first slower than in man, but rapid toward adolescence. Sexual maturity comes at about eight to ten years in females and ten to twelve in males. Accompanying sexual maturity there is a change of temperament. Playfulness diminishes, indolence and irritability increase, the individual becomes less exuberant in his manifestations of sociability, and, on account of his great strength, somewhat dangerous. This appears to be part of a wider process involving a slowing down or at least change in direction of what we call intelligence. In experiments, young chimpanzees have made the best performances. The one adult female of Koehler, for instance, was rated by him near the bottom of his list of seven immature chimpanzees. A human parallel is obvious. The duration of chimpanzee life is not known, but is estimated at not very much less than that of man.

CHIMPANZEE PSYCHOLOGY

The senses of the chimpanzee are similar to our own. Sight, which is the easiest to test in both species, is much alike in perception of color, form, and distance. Hearing appears to be about as acute as in man. Taste and smell are utilized very much as by ourselves, primarily with reference to food. All in all, the sensory equipment is definitely analogous to that of man, and different from that of subprimate mammals.

This is expectable. A body like ours with senses like those of a dog is a combination hardly to be anticipated in nature. The chimpanzee's use of his senses is also human. If he sees something out of his reach but with a string attached to it, he pulls the string with as little hesitation as a human being. If there are several strings, he draws the one lying in most direct line toward himself; or if only one is actually in visual contact with the desired object, he pulls that one. After all, he possesses a string-pulling mechanism—arms and hands and fingers; and this would serve him in little stead if he saw blurred instead of clearly, or if his ability to interpret spatially were deficient.

If food is put on the ground outside a barred window, a string attached to it and led indoors, and an ape allowed to survey the situation, he quickly hauls the food up on the cord. A dog fails to grasp the situation. He may starve before he takes the cord in his mouth and backs across the room to haul the food in. He does not see the relation of food, string, and himself; he cannot connect or synthesize them. . . .

As regards imitativeness, observations are at variance. Koehler interprets the chimpanzee as much less imitative than does Yerkes. But the latter found a gorilla non-imitative almost to the point of being negatively suggestible. This, however, was with reference to use of appliances or solution of problems such as the animal would not en⁃ counter in nature. When it came to eating new foods, the gorilla was willing to follow example—provided no persuasion was applied and it could withdraw to make the test in seclusion. Emotional factors are evidently of the greatest influence as regards imitativeness; and these are conditioned by the social relations in which the ape finds itself. Yerkes' orang and chimpanzees were almost members of his household. Koehler's apes lived primarily in a colony of their own. It is clear that they learned little from one another in the solution of posed problems. Imitativeness is evidently called out largely by association with human culture.

LACK OF SPEECH AMONG APES

On the side of speech it is agreed that the ape is completely deficient in imitativeness. Observations and experiments are uniformly negative. At this point the close human associations and manual adaptations of Yerkes' animals are of high significance. They did learn to brush their teeth, to spit, to eat with a spoon, to go to bed, and a hundred other things which the family was doing. They could not be taught to speak at all.

Furness, by long and repeated practice, taught his young orang to say "Papa," and apparently to realize that this sound-complex in some way related to her master. Whether the animal recognized that "Papa" was Furness' name, as Furness believes, is another question. . . .

Parallel are the results of Boutan, who worked with a gibbon, a particularly vocal species. The gibbon, he finds, is capable of no more than pseudo-language. Its sounds are like those of the other mammals in expressing emotions; they do not convey anything objective. Utter⁃ ances relieve the utterer: there is no semblance of their being purposive as regards conveying information. The chimpanzee, in fact, does not confine himself to vocal utterances: when frightened he rattles a tin pan or thumps the wall of his cage. It is clear that we are beyond the realm of what can profitably be construed as language when we are driven to include the rattling of pans.

All in all, the data at hand are unanimous to the effect that the speech faculty of the apes is substantially on a par with that of a normal six-months-old human infant: namely, nil. When we enquire why this is, it seems likely that however we may paraphrase it in more technical terms, the old reason literally holds: animals do not talk because they have nothing to say.

This fact is particularly striking because the structure of the mouth parts of the apes is so similar to that of man that there is no doubt that they could render reasonably close approximations to the sounds of human speech. They might talk with a brogue, but we could understand them. What a parrot does when with his horny beak he produces effective imitation of a soft lip sound like "p," a primate could obviously do at least as well, so far as his anatomical apparatus is concerned. Yet he never tries to speak, nor apparently can he be induced to try, no matter how close his associations with humans.

HAVE APES A CULTURE?

There are three historic definitions of man designed to set him off functionally from the other animals: man is the speaking animal; man is a political animal; and man is the tool-using animal. Other phrasings, such as the fire-using or clothes-wearing animal, are evidently included under the more general category of tool-using. We have considered the first of these criteria, that of speech, and found it to hold. The second definition goes back to Aristotle. It has been said that, the connotations of words having changed, Aristotle, if he were living now and speaking in English, would make his definition run that man is a social animal.

We still know very little as to the kind of society the apes maintain in a state of nature. Their behavior in captivity, with dependence primarily on human beings instead of fellow apes, evidently is little indication. With a few exceptions, those observed in captivity have been immature. Natural history observations will obviously be extremely difficult. That the apes are sociable is evident but not to the point. Dogs, birds, some other species, are highly sociable toward human beings. Of course if man were not endowed with a gregarious impulse he could not have developed culture; but something more than gregariousness is needed to produce culture; otherwise cattle would possess it. Now it is conceivable that the chimpanzee and gorilla possess something more than sociability or personal attachments; that they pass down from individual to individual and from family to family certain forms or patterns of relation to one another—traditional group habits, which may have begun to take on something of the color of institutions. But that this actually has happened without the presence of speech is difficult to conceive; and there are no positive indications whatever as to the existence of such incipient institutions. It would not be difficult to project backward from the simpler human social institutions to something that seems still simpler and expectable among apes. But experience has shown that such reconstructions are always in part misleading, and quite likely to be unfounded. As regards the question, then, whether the apes are in any rudimentary degree social animals in the sense that man is institutional, we can at present answer with nothing more than a question mark.

It may be thought that there are some evidences warranting a less skeptical attitude. Koehler reports that when a pair of his young chimpanzees in playing began to stamp and circle about a post, others frequently ranged themselves in line until they formed a ring, and presented much the appearance of a savage tribe in a dance. But, while the stamping of each ape was definitely heavier with one foot, there was no unison—only a tendency to keep time together. And there was nothing to show that the dancing followed any pattern—that there was imitation in the cultural sense, with social acceptance of a form. The dancing of one individual stimulated other individuals into analogous behavior; but the performance of each apparently remained a purely physiological response. When the gamboling of one lamb sets others to gamboling, or when one startled sheep runs and the flock follows, the sheep do not possess culture because they follow one another's example. If one ape devised or learnt a new dance step, or a particular posture, or an attitude toward the object about which the dance revolved; and if these new acts were taken up by other chimpanzees, and became more or less standardized; especially if they survived beyond the influence of the inventor, were taken up by other communities, or passed on to generations after him,—in that case we could legitimately feel that we were on solid ground of an ape culture. But of this there is as yet no indication.

It is the same with chimpanzee fashions in smearing white paint, or teasing chickens, which Koehler describes. These are comparable to the vogue which a game or social manner or dress fashion has among ourselves; to the fact that the first boy who brings out his kite or his marbles in spring is almost certain to set other boys of his school to bring out their kites and marbles. What is cultural in such phenomena is not the fact that one individual leads and others follow, but the game or fashion as such. The kite, the manner of manipulating the marbles, the cut of a garment, the tipping of the hat, remain as cultural facts after every physiological and psychological consideration of the individuals involved has been exhausted. Of any such institutional residuum of unmitigatedly cultural material, there is as yet no demonstration among the apes.

When it comes to our third criterion, that of tools, the case is different. The anthropoids use tools; and they make them. Chimpanzees take up sticks to draw to themselves food which is beyond reach of their arms. They beat with sticks for the same purpose, or cast ropes or rope-like objects. If the desired food is out of reach overhead, jumping to reach it has led to failure, and there is no other individual about that can be climbed onto and used as a take-off for a higher leap, many of them finally have recourse to moving a box or other convenient object under the prize. If, after they have learned to use a box, the food is hung still higher, they learn to pile a second box on the first; and the more versatile ones will pile three or four. Gorillas will also do this. As Koehler justly points out, the piling of the second box on the first is psychologically a quite different thing from moving the first box; there is in it the element of combination, or construction. The difference is something like that between rolling a stone and building with stones.

If the convenient reaching tool happened to be a bundle of straws, one chimpanzee, finding the straw too soft to move a banana, without hesitation stiffened the bundle by doubling it. Even then the tool was ineffective, so she redoubled it. That it was now too short to reach the banana rendered the result ineffectual, but does not detract from her credit as an inventor: she got the problem and knew what to do about it.

Especially interesting is the observation that two canes were joined one into the other to draw in food which lay beyond the reach of a single cane. This is indubitable tool making; especially when a stick is chewed down to fit into the hollow of a cane.

How far chimpanzees under proper stimuli might progress in devising tools for themselves is difficult to say; just as the observations leave it somewhat obscure how far slower-witted individuals tend to profit by the discoveries of a more inventive one. There are, however, some interesting observations as to the circumstances of the process of invention.

First, the chimpanzee strongly dislikes the strain of situations which call upon his inventive faculties. The process of invention is visibly and disagreeably arduous for him. His first impulse is to give up, or to become angry, if he cannot arrive at a solution by purely physiological means such as leaping or biting. Characteristic is the fact that if a reaching implement is in line of vision with the desired object, it is usually promptly utilized. If on the other hand, the stick lies behind the ape's back as he faces the food, it will not be "thought of" or noticed and taken up for a long time, when the experiment is a novelty to the animal being observed; in fact, usually not until after repeated renunciations and recurrences of desire. Emotions clearly are important, constituting a strong resistive factor. The individuals that meet difficult problems most readily, and carry invention farthest, are evidently those best able to control or inhibit the emotions which the prospective goal arouses in them.

COMPETITION AS A STIMULUS TO INVENTION

But emotions of another kind can be an impelling influence toward invention. These are the social emotions. His desire for affection, and for approbation from human beings, certainly helps a champanzee to invent tools. In the state of nature it is probable that competitive emotion—jealousy—is even more stimulating. Significant is Koehler's observation of the behavior of his adult female chimpanzee when a loaded box or heavy obstacle was placed to prevent her from reaching her food beyond the bars. She was perfectly capable of moving the obstacle; but the problem weighed on her for two hours. When, however, one of the young animals began to stray in the direction of the food, from which it was not separated by bars, she suddenly seized the heavy box, shoved it out of the way without hesitation, and grasped the prize out of reach of the competitor. Next day she found the solution in one minute.

The same chimpanzee objected to using sticks for reaching unless they were, so to speak, thrust into her hands by their placement. For half an hour she neglected a stick which was close behind her and which, as a retinal image, she saw whenever in aimless irritation she turned around. After a while she stood on the stick. She must have felt it with her sole; but again, as a personality, she refused to receive the sense impression. After half an hour a free chimpanzee came near the food. The jealousy which his approach excited was utilized to repress the sulking emotion that had hitherto baffled her; and suddenly the ignored stick was perceived, seized, and used to draw in the food.

The one gorilla tested reacted less emotionally, but showed less inventive faculty than the cleverest of the chimpanzees.

These observations may not throw much light on the question of how far apes possess culture. They do however suggest much as to the psychology which underlies human culture, and what we are accustomed to term its progress. They indicate that the elimination of the competitive factor among men would deprive civilization of one of its principal and perhaps indispensable impulses. They suggest further why the institutions, codes, and ethics of all peoples have so strongly emphasized inhibition; why, for instance, courage—the repression of fear —has always been esteemed a high if not the highest virtue; and why, similarly, all social groups condemn incest. Not that the anthropoid apes set up moral standards. But all human groups do; they have evidently learned, on the basis of individual life experiences, the social importance of restraints. The inference would be that from soon after the time when men began to possess institutions, and were able to formulate these in speech, they have never seriously swerved from an insistence on a social limitation of the natural sex impulse.

PLAY AS AN ELEMENT IN INVENTION

Play is evidently an important element in chimpanzee invention. Situations are often first met, or devices prepared, not from a desire to achieve a useful end, but as a matter of sport or amusement, as a means of satisfying pure manipulative interest; the utilization is later. Here again we have parallels with human culture. The lodestone or magnet was long a toy, or an object of pre-scientific marveling, before it was used in the compass and still later in machinery. The Chinese placed a compass on "south pointing chariots," where it could have served no purpose other than as a refinement of luxury, nearly a thousand years before they employed it in the serious business of navigation. They knew gunpowder in fireworks centuries before they put it into firearms. In fact, in both cases the Chinese play invention seems to have passed to other peoples, the Arabs and Mongols, to have been turned by them to more practical purposes, and then to have been re-introduced into China.

The domestication of animals, although its whole history is far from clear, appears to derive at least in part from the keeping of pets. To be sure, the keeping of a pet, which may be played with so long as it is amusing, and allowed to starve or escape when it becomes troublesome to maintain, is a different thing from the tiring business of continuously caring for flocks on which living depends. Also, of the numerous species of animals which are interesting enough as pets, many are of no economic utility, and others are incapable of being domesticated to the point where they can be regularly handled and fed and reared with economic profit. Still, it is clear that many primitive peoples who never rear either domesticated animals or plants do keep pets frequently. It can hardly be doubted, therefore, that a stage of play domestication preceded economic domestication of animals in the course of human history.

Among us occidental moderns the process of invention is difficult to understand; perhaps because we cannot yet sufficiently extricate ourselves from our own civilization to look upon its processes with the same objectivity with which we view those of foreign or ancient cultures. Nevertheless, one thinks of the pneumatic tire, first employed on the bicycle in the period when this was a novelty and instrument of sport, but gradually helping the motor car to develop into the important element which it now forms in our economic structure.

Modern invention is of course completely interwoven with modern science. Now, time and again scientists have pointed out, sometimes when they were asking for money and sometimes when they meant what they said, that the progress of applied science or invention depends on the progress of pure science or discovery. Researches which, at the time they were made, could not have been conceived of as leading to practical results, have nevertheless again and again led before long to the invention of useful contrivances. The whole history of electrical discovery is a case in point. Now the significance of this, in the present connection, is that pure science is, after all, play. We are accustomed to think of it as hard work because it requires intense specialization and long application. But in these qualities it agrees with modern sport. Like modern sport, it is, economically and physiologically, immediately useless. It is even more than useless: it is unnatural—a fact often charged against organized sport, but just as true of science. There is in us an element making us strive for mastery or excellence or perfection of achievement for its own sake, apart from the satisfaction of any definable physiological need. It is the driving of this impulse to the point of physiological discomfort, even of bodily strain or damage, that gives sport and science their quality of unnaturalness. At their fullest, they are perversions of the play impulse.

No chimpanzee seems capable of being so perverse: he is too unin‧telligent, from our point of view; but also too sensible, too concordant physiologically. For better or for worse, however, we men are prone to this exaggeration of the play impulse; and, again for better or for worse, the exaggeration has perceptibly aided the gradual accretion of the stock of modern culture, as well as the betterment of athletic records.

The chimpanzee, in his youth, is as playful, restless, curious, and explorative as any human being. He does not go very far in tool invention, because his central nervous system seems to become quickly and healthily fatigued by play which puts on the nervous system any strain that cannot be promptly discharged into striped muscle activity. He is physiologically a clear extravert. The gorilla, on the other hand, is described as an introvert, with more self-respect and sense of value of his personality. It remains to be seen whether in the field of pure intellect the gorilla will prove the equal or superior of the chimpanzee, once we have learned to establish relations with him satisfactory to his temperament.

A demonstrated psycho-physiological trait of the ape is lack of patience in the solution of a problem. As soon as difficulties are encountered which cannot be solved by direct use of hands, feet, or mouth, the chimpanzee tends to take refuge in irritation or sulks; the gorilla becomes dignifiedly indifferent. An added stimulus, such as doubling the reward, or approach of a competitor, may launch him again at the task, and perhaps with success. But the effort is new, not continuous.

The fact is of interest because it finds a parallel in the history of culture. There was required actually less skill to fashion many of the ground or polished stone implements of the New Stone Age than some of the specialized chipped ones of the Old Stone Age, tens of thousands of years earlier. The average modern person who has never worked stone would, if the reward were sufficient, almost certainly turn out on the first attempt a better ground mortar or ground stone ax than a chipped knife or spear point, if indeed he would not fail utterly in the latter. The reason is that while chipping requires definite manual control, it is a very rapid process. A dozen failures occupy little time; each may suggest the possibility of an improvement; and the thirteenth attempt may be reasonably satisfactory. Grinding, however, although one of the simplest of operations, is of necessity slow. Early man was apparently readier to mobilize a fair degree of manipulative skill than a great amount of patience.

INVENTION BY ACCIDENT

That the chimpanzee possesses a beginning of ability to reverse his primary impulse is shown by a series of experiments by Koehler. After the animals had learned to use a stick to gather in food from beyond their reach, the fruit was placed behind a barrier, in a low open box with only the farther side broken out. To get his banana the ape had therefore either to lift it with his stick out over the front or side edge of the box, which was difficult; or he had to reverse his first impulse of scraping the fruit toward himself, and instead push it farther away until it was clear of the box; after which of course the familiar raking-in process could successfully commence. Without exception the apes found this problem difficult. Some never solved it except when the box was partly turned to help them; others only by the aid of accident, such as the banana rolling favorably; and even those who had learned the necessary reversal, tended to relapse into their earlier, direct, impossible efforts. Still, some of them did learn, and with practice came to perform quickly and efficiently. These results are a genuine credit to the more gifted individuals of the chimpanzee species. More observations as simple and significant as this are a desideratum.

This experiment developed a type of success which probably has its parallel in culture: invention partly by accident. The banana, prodded by the stick, rolls or bounces near an open corner of the box, or entirely clear of it, and the animal immediately sees a solution that had been beyond its grasp while the problem remained unmitigated. After this partial aid by chance, the whole problem is soon mastered.

Whether invention wholly by accident occurs in human culture, may be doubted. But that accident sometimes assists, is likely. At any rate, there are devices like the bow and arrow, and the fire-drilling apparatus, which seem to be by-products of other devices subsequently improved or converted when a chance variation suggested a new utilization. A bow which fails to attain a certain efficiency is of no use as a weapon. Yet an efficient bow is a fairly complex implement of delicate adjustment with which a first inventor would be almost foredoomed to fail. Its origin is best conceivable as a secondary stage of a bow used as a toy or musical instrument, which, being later produced with the requisite strength and balance, would be serviceable for propulsion. We do know from archæology that the bow came into culture relatively late—not until the terminal phase of the Palæolithic. The fire-drill is a simple apparatus but needs to be adjusted and operated in a particular way before a spark is obtainable. Drills used for boring, however, would sooner or later be likely to produce smoke or even a spark, and a new application be suggested. It would be rash to contend that any invention was ever due wholly to lucky chance. If there were no insight into problem nor recognition of need, the accident would pass unobserved and unutilized. But it does seem that previous accomplishment, plus insight, plus accident, have at times led to the creation of new cultural material. And the same three factors occur in chimpanzee invention.

The chimpanzee depends much more than we on muscular strength and gymnastic skill. Even the most intelligent anthropoids manifest little sense of statics. They pile three or four boxes randomly and then balance their own bodies to counteract the imbalance of the mechanical pile. Boxes are set on an edge or corner and the animal tries to mount them—in some cases succeeds because of its natural acrobatic capacity. The one gorilla tested proceeded more like a human being in adjusting and trying out the boxes; but this was a proportionally heavy animal, and without jumping impulses. Of course a solution which depends for its effectiveness on muscular skill is in that degree farther from an invention in the cultural sense. An imperfect tool suffices; the congenital body makes up the deficiency. If men had the strength of arm and jaw of the great apes, their enormous canine teeth, they would no doubt have continued for a long time to meet many situations with muscle rather than with tools.

The impulse to perform with his body is strong in the cleverest chimpanzee; performance with a tool is usually clumsy and always an arduous act at first. Given a suspended banana and an available pole, the first impulse is to climb the pole before it can fall and grasp at the fruit—a sort of pole-vaulting. Sticks are brandished threateningly in play combat. But let a chimpanzee lose his temper, and he drops his stick and plunges into attack with hands and teeth.

Nevertheless some use of tools is spontaneous. Stones are hurled. Sticks are used to dig in play or for roots, to tease fowls or other animals, to touch fire, lizards, live wires, or other things that provoke both curiosity and fear. In removing filth from his body, the chimpanzee prefers a stick, chip, leaf, or rag, to his fingers. He will lick up ants, or hold out a straw for the ants to crawl on and then lick them off. He has not been observed, outside of posed problems, to manufacture tools or to lay them aside for the future; he does certainly, without human stimulation, use simple tools that come to hand, and use them in a way that in a human being we should call intelligent.

INVENTION AS A SYNTHESIS OR AS A COMPOSITE

Sometimes an ape sits down in front of a problem that has baffled him, detaches himself from his previous efforts, and looks the situation over, seemingly thinking. How far he may actually study the situation is difficult to say; but he certainly appears reflective. Suddenly then, sometimes, the solution comes and is applied without hesitation or awkwardness. Again, it may come overnight and without warning. When a human being acts in this manner we say that he has thought the problem out. At any rate the ape's solution tends to come as a whole, as an abrupt synthesis.

Now as we think of the course of human culture, it may seem as if the layman conceived of invention happening by syntheses like those of the chimpanzee, whereas the social scientist tended increasingly to view its history as one of gradual accretion. Both are correct. What we call an invention is normally a composite of many inventions gradually assembled. Each unit invention, however, probably depends on one insight made as a synthesis—a simple one, mostly, but a synthesis. Popular imagination, with its love of the dramatic and abhorrence of the analytic, transfers the process operative in the unit to the ensemble. It makes the printing press, the steam engine, the telegraph, the radio, spring like Pallas Athena in full panoply from the head of some human Zeus. As an explanation of what happened, this is pure myth. The steam engine, the telegraph, the automobile, are obvious composites. They function as cultural units, but the process of development of each totality has been a complex and slow one. An automobile represents literally thousands of inventions. Its hundreds of parts, like the screw and the cogs, have each its history of successive stages, each of which was in its time an invention. As Gilfillan has recently shown, the reputed inventor of every machine is regularly that individual among a number of contemporaries who first made a given assemblage of existing inventions pay. In the eyes of the world successful invention is successful economic exploitation. And however we may rebel ethically or esthetically, this verdict has primary culture historical validity. It is when a machine makes money that it comes into cultural use and consciousness. At the same time, a scientific interpretation of culture must penetrate deeper and recognize the antecedent stages and gradualness of development; much as for reckoning our ages we count from the day of birth, but the biologist in studying life history goes back of that act of emergence, into pre-natal life, to conception, and beyond that to the ancestral germplasm.

It is the innumerable minimal unit elements of human invention that find their rudimentary prototypes among the anthropoids in their qualities of discreteness and synthesis. Beyond that, the parellel does not go; for the interrelation and accumulation of these elements is a cultural process, and culture the apes as yet give no indication of possessing.

THE DESTRUCTIVE IMPULSE

Left to themselves, chimpanzees are destructive. They love to demolish. Like small children who have grown up uncontrolled, they derive immediate satisfaction from prying, ripping, biting, and deliberately smashing. Once they begin, they rarely desist until an object has been reduced to its components. They never learn to lace shoes; they find spontaneous pleasure in unlacing them. The impulse to construct is infinitely weaker; it is called into activity only by special problems, and the solution of these is trying.

One of the few exceptions is nest building. This the chimpanzee does from an early age, and apparently without being taught. Here we seem to have a genuine case of what in the older terminology was called "specific instinct." Nest building is of interest because directed toward an objective outside the body. But, according to both Koehler and Yerkes, the building is partly a drawing and tucking of branches under the body. Some of the twigs snap off and tend to hold in place the branches which remain attached to the tree. In this way a tolerable mat or platform is built up. This however remains, during the act of building, in contact with the ape's body; it is built against his skin, he feels it during the process of construction, and the sensations aroused may be an important element in the carrying out of the process. Some chimpanzees, if trees were not available or loose material did not suffice, laid down a ring that outlined the body and merely suggested the nest —a nest gesture, as it were.

The powerful impulses of chimpanzees toward destructiveness may help to explain one phenomenon in the history of human culture already touched upon: the long precedence in time of the chipping over the grinding technique in stone. After all, the earlier and grosser process of production by fracture is one of breaking apart. Grinding, being so slow as to be almost imperceptible in its results, must be quite unsatisfactory as a means of satisfying the demolition impulse. As an object is slowly rubbed into form, there is probably rather a sense of shaping and constructing. Of course, the Chellean picks and other early Palæolithic artifacts are not mere by-products of an interest in cracking bowlders; they are too definitely adaptive, too patternized, too utilizable as tools. But preceding the Palæolithic there are the "eoliths" which have been championed by some and denied by others as the earliest tools. They date back to the Pliocene, if not the Miocene, much beyond the earliest fossils of organisms in the line of human descent. It is generally admitted that the eoliths were not fashioned as tools but produced by natural agencies and then utilized as tools. Their finer fractures, usually confined to one edge, are interpreted as the results of wear during such use, and not as deliberate attempts to produce an edge.

In the light of ape behavior we can venture one tentative step farther. Our ancestors, like chimpanzees and children and human adults, probably took pleasure in demolishing. Learning among other things to smash bowlders, and especially nodules of flint which long resisted and then shattered cleanly, they may have found themselves provided with attractively sharp and shining flakes, affording a new toy. Manipulation of these may have led to the discovery that the flakes furnished the possibility of a new satisfaction in hacking or scraping other objects. From such play in turn might have grown increasing habits of tool use; leading finally, when the mechanism of culture fixation and transmission became sufficiently developed, to the manufacture of tools as tools.

THE ORIGIN OF CLOTHING

We have a few observations that bear on esthetics and religion. The apes are indifferent about being clothed or dislike it, although they appreciate a blanket in which to wrap themselves at night. On the other hand, they voluntarily drape themselves with strings and rags, wearing these for hours or days. The satisfaction is clearly in the wearing as distinct from the act of putting on. As Koehler aptly says, the heightening of bodily consciousness appears to be what gives the pleasure. Chains or strings which swish and sway with the motion of the body are favored; a girdle would probably be meaningless, or its presence be resented. The suggestion is that human dress for protection and human adornment spring from separate sources. This has long been good anthropological doctrine. However, in the history of man, protective clothing and adornment intergrade so extensively that a large class of phenomena can only be described as ornamental dress. Even basically utilitarian clothing is invariably affected by the fashion impulse in man. One may conjecture that there have been two developments little related in origin which secondarily came to overlap; and that dress and adornment, as we know them in the history of human culture, are largely hybrid.

RUDIMENTS OF ÆSTHETICS

Koehler's chimpanzees, in digging, discovered some white earth. Tasting it and finding it inedible, they spat it out. Wiping their lips, they saw the wall whitened. This soon became a game. First with their lips and then with their hands they painted with white earth whatever walls and surfaces were available; but rarely their own bodies. There was no attempt at design or figure. The stuff was smeared on, and the more the appearance of a surface changed, the greater the satisfaction. The pleasure apparently lay in using the muscles to produce a visibly effective external accomplishment. The act of creation gave satisfaction.

These observations accord with the behavior of small children, whose first attempts at what we are wont to call drawing or painting, even when an attempt is made to guide them, normally result in nothing more than smearing. It is rather evident that the small child, left to himself, does not attempt to draw a house or a dog or a man. He converts a white paper into a red or black one, a monotonous into a variegated surface. He defaces as much as he makes. It is again demolition pleasure; or, more generically, the satisfaction of producing an effect; and this, at an early stage of development, is more readily accomplished by destruction than by construction. We tend unjustly to read the child as an adult. It is doubtful whether small children ever try to represent except as the result of cultural influence. In fact, we do not know that a human being become adult without impingement of cultural influences would try to represent anything. So too, when a child makes something like a decorative pattern, his principal satisfaction perhaps lies at first in the rhythmic motion. We, thinking primarily of the effect, are likely to construe into the child an impulse to decorative rhythm and regularity, which it probably does not appreciate until later in life. To understand art, it seems necessary to recognize that there is always a motor impulse involved; that in incipient stages the motor element probably predominates; and that recognition of æsthetic qualities as such is, historically, likely to be an overlay.

ANTICIPATIONS OF RELIGION

Religion is difficult to conceive without formulated ideas and thus without speech. Even its rudiments could therefore hardly be looked for among the apes. Yet there may be some sub-cultural anticipations. Koehler made a rude rag animal with shoe-button eyes which vaguely suggested a miniature donkey. It was altogether too crude to be mistaken for a live animal, yet had sufficient resemblance to one to set it off from ordinary inanimate natural objects, or from artifacts such as boxes or chairs. The apes responded instantly with manifestations of fear. It was not terror as great as an ox or a camel inspired, but can perhaps best be characterized as similar in its expression to what human beings would call awe. There was not a trace of either the indifference or the curiosity which a lifeless object provoked; interest there was, but also respectful staying at a distance for a long time. Even food placed in proximity to the image was shunned, and only at last cautiously snatched with a precipitate retreat ensuing. Koehler observed a dog manifest the same degree of interest in the figure, except that, being a carnivorous and therefore aggressive organism, his interest took the form of hostility. He convinced himself however, as soon as he dared, of the inanimateness of the image; and from then on was completely indifferent to it. The chimpanzee, like ourselves, is less practical, evidently as the result of possessing more imagination. Occasionally however, one of the lower animals will react more like a man or an ape. I have seen a young dog for weeks manifest panic whenever an imitation animal toy was brought into his presence.

The relation to religion of the chimpanzee's reaction lies in his manifesting something like the awe which is regarded as an important or essential ingredient of what we call the religious feeling: the religious

thrill. It is generally recognized that religion could not well originate
without the presence of emotions of which awe may be taken as the
type; and that these emotions tend to persist or to be re-awakened in
religion, no matter how culturally crystallized this becomes. Also, the
kind of object that arouses the awe-like feeling in chimpanzees has a
certain quality of resemblance to the basic concepts of religion. Souls,
ghosts, spirits, like stuffed rag donkeys, do not occur in ordinary experience; like them, also, they are thought to be at once similar to living
bodies and different from them. A dummy donkey with button eyes
evidently is literally supernatural to a chimpanzee. We can then say
pretty positively that the ape does not have a religion; we can also say
pretty positively that he acts at times as if he were religious. . . .

There is a residuum of new understanding which knowledge of the
apes contributes to knowledge of human culture. We see above all the
tremendous influence of the play impulse. We see the unit elements of
invention sometimes made with the aid of favorable accident; more
often occurring as a product of reflection, of a kind of synthesis which
in ourselves we call ideation. We see, perhaps a little more clearly than
before, the relation of these unit elements of invention to the course
of invention; and how culture, in its operations, fixes and settles upon
certain patternized combinations of these elements. It is these combinations, as combinations, which it allows to enter into its consciousness and deals with. We see also that the impulse of destructiveness has
probably played at times an ultimately constructive part in culture development. We are able to recognize more clearly the rôle of the emotions with reference to culture, and of it toward them. Inhibition of
direct and primary emotional impulses is a necessity for culture to acquire material with which it can build; and the existence of inhibitions
has been felt by all cultures as indispensable to the preservation of
themselves and of societies. On the other hand, emotion is also a positive factor. Competitive feelings in particular seem culturally stimula-
tive; and we gather at least an inkling of the part played in religion
by awe.

Many or all of these conclusions have at one time or another been
reached tentatively or positively by anthropologists from the examination of human culture itself. The study of the anthropoids, however,
yields grateful and valuable corroboration. Cultureless these higher
primates are; but with reactions and faculties closely akin to our own,
and manifesting at least some measure of the basal psychic ingredients

which enter into culture. There is infinitely more to be learned from them by wise experiment, and no less by critical observation. We have only begun. In fact, with the wide interest in these animals, it is surprising how scant the significant scientific data on them as yet are. Further study of them is important in itself; it will be invaluable in the illumination of the basic problems of anthropology and all the social sciences; and will in turn be furthered by what it can derive from these sciences.

50. THE AMERICAN INDIAN AS AN INVENTOR [6]
BY ERLAND NORDENSKIÖLD

IN THE following pages an attempt will be made to elucidate, by means of examples from America, one of the more—not to say one of the most—important problems of ethnographical science, viz. that of independent inventions and culture loans. As we all know, this is a much discussed problem, and the attitude taken towards it has mostly proved a matter of faith. To some researchers it is evidently placed beyond any doubt whatever that man exceedingly rarely, if ever, has made the same invention twice. When, for example, we meet with the signaling gong both in America and in the Old World, according to their view the Indians must have learnt its use from the latter, whilst to other investigators it appears quite natural that in different parts of the world the same invention has been made many times over.

Many students opine that a certain invention cannot have been made more than once because of its complicated and difficult nature, whilst regarding another as being so easy and simple that it might quite well have been accomplished at different times and places. This subjective view is, of course, capable of being varied in all possible ways. As a matter of fact, no doubt every open-minded investigator has his own particular opinion as regards primitive man's capacity as an inventor.

So as to get a real grasp of the above-mentioned controversy, I have in the following tried to review what we actually know in regard to independent inventions in America.

[6] From "The American Indian as an Inventor," *The Huxley Memorial Lecture for 1929*, in *Journal of the Royal Anthropological Institute*, Volume 59, pages 273-309, 1929. By permission. Baron Nordenskiöld's purpose of course is not to extol the Indian as specially original, but to study the processes of invention among a group of peoples whose isolation and circumstances render it practically sure that certain elements of their culture have not been borrowed but have been devised by themselves.—*Eds.*

To that end I shall endeavor, so far as it is possible, by way of concrete instances to show how inventions have been made—or apparently have been made—by the Indians. My aim will be to avoid showing that personally I hold one view or the other, even in cases where I possess a subjective opinion—which I naturally cannot escape having. My object is to express nothing that is not purely objective. In my view it is better to be satisfied with small results that are sure than to propound wider ones that are uncertain. I do not wish to draw conclusions from facts before I know their true value. Thus I have purposely avoided expressing any definite opinion as regards questions concerning Melanesian, Polynesian, or Asiatic influence in America. I have only attempted to adduce facts calculated to throw light upon the value of certain more or less theoretical speculations.

Generally speaking, it is on the question whether identical culture elements occurring in the New and the Old Worlds are explainable as independent inventions in two or more different places, or as culture loans, that the opinions of Americanists are so divergent. This is quite a mistaken limitation of the problem. Graebner is certainly right when he remarks that those who believe the same invention to have been made at different times, are inconsistent when they hold that this can only have happened when the invention occurs in two areas separated from each other, whilst they consider that the invention has only been made once when it is a case of a connected area. For of course an invention may just as well have been made twice, although its area of distribution at the present time is a connected whole.

The same invention may, for instance, in one part of America be a culture loan from the Old World, whilst in some other part it is an independent invention, or an earlier loan from the Old World, but nevertheless the area of distribution may by now have become a connected whole. A cultural element of this kind is, for example, the skin-membrane drum which in large tracts of America is of pre-Columbian origin, whilst in other parts it has been introduced by whites and negroes.

Before proceeding any further, I wish to emphasize that a study like the one I am here placing before the reader ought to be valuable, inasmuch as it focuses our attention upon the collating of material from view-points that so far have not been sufficiently taken into account. For the study of culture loans and minor inventions, the influence of the whites, for example, on primitive tribes is of great importance. Objects originating from a primitive people, who no longer exist in their pristine condition, but have changed owing to influence from the whites, are, however, more or less at a discount with many collectors.

For my own part I am prepared to confess that, for example, I have not always given due appreciation to such objects as the Indians have manufactured from old scrap-iron and such like, objects which nevertheless offer much that is interesting, seeing that they show how primitive man utilizes a raw material which is new to him. These products also tend to convey to us an idea as to his more or less marked conservatism.

I shall now proceed to discuss Indian inventions in some detail. It should be of interest, I think, to begin by pointing out what must have been invented and discovered by the Indians themselves, for the simple reason that it was unknown in the Old World prior to the discovery of America. By this we shall obtain a very fair picture of the Indians' capacity as discoverers and inventors. After that, we may well ask ourselves whether it is not possible that the Indians, who have discovered and invented so many things that were unknown among the variegated cultures of the Old World, might have been capable of hitting upon something or other that also was known there. It is a question that to me, at any rate, appears in a high degree pertinent.

In the first place, then, we may consider the cultivation of all the purely American cultivated plants. These the Indians must have found in their wild state, and by degrees brought under cultivation. These plants, as we know, are very numerous, and I shall confine myself to mentioning only the most important ones. They are, generally speaking, quite well known, but in this connection it is necessary that I should mention them, however briefly.

Of outstanding importance is maize. At the time when America was discovered this plant was being cultivated in a number of varieties all the way from Central Chile to 55° of northern latitude. A good many of the implements that were used in connection with the cultivation of maize, such as grinding-stones on three or four feet, graters, husking-pins, etc., must necessarily be Indian inventions. The different dishes prepared from maize must also be of Indian origin, as well as different methods of storing maize.

As I have already indicated, the cultivation of maize is of exceedingly wide range in America, and the Indians have found out how to adapt the method of cultivating this American plant according to the varying climatic conditions. Among other things, in Peru and in southwestern North America, for example, there were in pre-Columbian times very large-scale irrigation constructions with an important canal system. As to whether the idea of these is native to America is a question that I for the present prefer to leave unanswered.

Next to maize, manioc is the most important of the cultivated plants of the New World. The Indians cultivate both a non-poisonous and a poisonous variety of manioc. In this case the Indians have made a very remarkable invention, in that they have discovered how to eliminate the deadly prussic acid from the manioc roots, and then use them for food. It thus follows that the Indians must have invented that most peculiar straining-bag of basketwork by means of which the poison is squeezed out, and also the various kinds of graters that are used for reducing the manioc to a pulp. Of the former there are two varieties, and of the latter many different types. To these I shall recur.

Another very remarkable thing is also the Indian invention of utilizing the juice squeezed out of the manioc, for preserving meat against putrefaction in a tropical climate.

A plant very important to the Indians of the Andes in pre-Columbian time was—and still is—the potato. The Aymara Indians of Bolivia distinguish between no fewer than 240 different varieties of potato. The method of preserving potatoes by freezing and drying in the sun, for preparing so-called "chuño," must be an Indian invention.

Other important food plants that we have received from the Indians are our common beans, pea-nuts, Jerusalem artichoke, sunflower, as also cacao, quinua, tomatoes, etc. These and many others have been discovered by the Indians.

The tobacco plant is one of the most well-known Indian discoveries, as well as smoking, snuff-taking, and chewing. Thus we see that snuff, cigarettes, cigars, pronged cigar-holders, and tobacco-pipes are Indian inventions. If we study all the different kinds of Indian pipes in America we shall find that they vary most considerably as to shape, and that in this department the Indians have achieved quite a number of more or less ingenious inventions, as, for example, the use of a filter for draining off the tobacco juice. It is possible in America to note down the evolution of a number of pipe types from the simple tubular pipe.

The coca bush, from which we obtain cocaine, also hails from America. All of the very complicated cultivation of the coca bush must have been tried out by the Indians, just as they have discovered the remarkable qualities of the coca leaves. Coca is chewed together with ashes or lime, and in this we meet with a noteworthy parallel in betel-chewing. Therefore we are unable to declare, off-hand, that the idea of chewing coca together with lime was invented in America independently of influences from Oceania, among other things because the receptacles for the lime in America and Melanesia are so strikingly similar, and, in addition, they are even made from gourds (*Lagenaria*), i.e. one of the few cultivated plants that were common to the Old and the New Worlds in pre-Columbian times.

Cacao, too, is another of the important cultivated plants that we have originally obtained from the Indians. In pre-Columbian times the Indians drank cacao unsweetened, or sweetened with honey.

Among textile plants cultivated in America, cotton is the most important, and it was known to the Indians in pre-Columbian times. At that time the species of cotton that were cultivated in America were different from those that were cultivated in the Old World before the discovery. Hence we cannot, of course, know whether the spinning of yarn or the art of weaving cloth was independently invented by the Indians.

The Indians of America cultivate a spice plant, Spanish pepper (Cayenne pepper), which is of the greatest importance to them. They have discovered that by the burning of this pepper there is developed a sort of "poison gas" that proves effective in laying siege to villages fortified by palisades.

The great majority of Indian cultivated plants are tropical or subtropical, and must in the first instance have been discovered in Central America or in the tropical section of South America. In this department the achievement contributed by the North American Indians north of Mexico is inconsiderable. Of the above-mentioned really important plants tobacco is the only one that possibly may have originated there. Among the less important ones the sunflower and the Jerusalem artichoke derive their origin from North America.

If we knew the history of the American cultivated plants, then we should know the history of the Indians from very far back in time. Of course, the Indians did not discover all the cultivated plants at the same time or in the same place. As has been shown by Guernsey and Kidder, the Basket-makers of southwestern North America were acquainted with maize, but not with beans, and it is probable that also in South America beans were disseminated much later than maize, as is evident from so many Indian tribes possessing their own words for maize, whilst having borrowed the names for beans from Quichua and Guarani. Cotton appears to have been originally propagated in South America by means of the migrations of the Caribs and the Guarani tribes.

The following important plants were probably cultivated everywhere in America where there were agriculturists, and where their cultivation was possible from climatic conditions: maize, pumpkins, and tobacco. The following have not attained their widest possible distribution: beans, sweet potatoes, cotton, potatoes, *Lagenaria* (bottle-gourd), manioc, cacao, and coca.

There are many wild-growing plants that the Indians have put to use for different purposes, and in this direction they have made a number of important inventions. It is to Indians that credit is due for the discovery of rubber and its utilization in the form of rubber balls, enema syringes, waterproof fabric, elastic rings, etc. It is a matter of fact that in pre-Columbian times the Indians were acquainted with all the qualities that make rubber so valuable in modern industry. No corresponding discovery had ever been made in the Old World prior to the discovery of America, in spite of the fact that both in Asia and Africa there are found rubber trees of various kinds.

The Indians have discovered a number of poisons, among others the terrible curare poison which they produce from certain *strychnos* varieties, including *Strychnos toxifera,* and principally used for their blowgun darts. A horrible cardiac poison is obtained by the Chocó Indians from a tree called pakurú-neará. These Indians also produce a very virulent arrow-poison from the secretions of a certain frog.

In addition to cultivated narcotic plants, the Indians know several wild-growing ones, as for instance, parica (*Piptadenia*). They have invented curious tubes, which they use in snuffing up powdered parica seeds, whereby a strongly intoxicating effect is produced. They are also known to have used parica for intoxicating enema injections. Guaraná, peyote (a kind of cactus), and Paraguay tea (maté) have also been discovered by Indians.

The Indians possessed a considerable knowledge of medicinal plants. Among the most important discovered by them are quinine, balsam of copaiba, and ipecacuanha. It is probable that the Indians, before it was known in the Old World, understood the application of aseptics, seeing that certain tribes dress their wounds with boiled water, without having learned this from the whites.

The Indians have discovered how to make use of a number of wild-growing American plants for making cord, etc. Among these, caraguata (*Bromelia serra*) may be noted. A certain proportion of the tools they used in working up the fibre are undoubtedly also Indian inventions.

From the bark of certain trees the Indians manufacture bast cloth, but as a similar manufacture is also known from Oceania, it cannot definitely be asserted that in this case the Indians have made an entirely independent discovery. Similarity between the implements used both within and outside America in the preparation of bark-cloth even speaks against such a supposition.

From the above it will be seen that the Indians in a wonderful way have known how to utilize the plant world by which they were surrounded, and in this province the peoples of the Old World have learnt a very great deal indeed from the Indians. In fact, during the period exceeding 400 years that Europeans have been in America, they have achieved not one single important discovery in this department. Evidently the Indians have carried out tests and experiments with everything they found available.

Here I may add that the very idea of cultivation must, in America, be an Indian invention, for if it had been introduced from abroad it must have been imported in association with some alien cultivable plant. For we have no reason whatever for supposing that the plants first cultivated by the Indians were the sweet potato and the bottle-gourd (*Lagenaria*)—plants that in pre-Columbian time probably they had in common with Oceania—cultivation having instead been inaugurated with some purely American utility plant. It is in fact evident that the sweet potato is in America a plant whose cultivation began at a later date than, for example, maize. This is apparent from linguistic comparisons, upon which I cannot here enter into details, as that would carry me into too lengthy a discussion.

If we now pass on to domestic animals we shall find that not many are of purely American origin. For this we cannot blame the Indians, but the American fauna. They have domesticated the llama, alpaca, guinea-pig, musk-duck and the turkey. The dog's companionship with man is of such remote antiquity that it was possibly brought along when man first immigrated into the New World. It is, however, probable that the Indians have domesticated also one or more indigenous species of the Canis family. A couple of American bee species have also been adopted for cultivation by the Indians. That this was a perfectly independent development is quite obvious. The cultivation of the cochineal bug, for the production of red pigment, is also an Indian invention. The employment of the llama as a beast of burden must necessarily be an Indian invention, as also the pack-saddle pertaining to it.

Plants and domestic animals of the New and the Old Worlds respectively with one or two exceptions differ from each other, hence we are able to ascertain that their discovery and utilization must have been independently made in the New World. This does not, however, apply in the case of metals, as the same metals are found both in the New World and the Old. It is nevertheless probable that it was the Indians who first discovered, at any rate, one metal which is found in the Old World as well as in the New, namely, platinum. In regard to the working of metals, the Inca Indians achieved an invention that we of the Old World only in recent times have succeeded in accomplishing—and then by a method quite different to that of the Indians—namely, the art of welding copper. Thus we have in the Gothenburg

Museum a copper rattle from Peru, in which the different parts are not soldered together, but welded, as has been shown by one of Sweden's leading metallurgists, Mr. Hultgren.

If we turn to the subject of dwellings, clothing, ornaments, tools, weapons, and so on, we shall find that the Indians do not possess much that is not also found in the Old World and which may, off-hand, be stated as having been invented by them, but nevertheless it appears improbable that man would find it easier to subject a new plant to cultivation than to invent some new implement or process in order to benefit by it.

We shall see that the Indians have invented more than one thing that was not known to any of the innumerable peoples of widely variegated culture in the Old World—that is to say, that they have made certain inventions that cannot be explained by the fact that they alone possessed the raw material. I have already referred to those objects which they manufacture from rubber.

In the realm of ceramics the application of sponge spicules in the clay, for cohesion and durability, is an invention made in Amazonas, and, so far as I am aware, not known from any other part of the world. The spicules, which act as do iron rods in reënforced concrete, impart great strength to the clay vessels. Of ceramic forms many exist in the New World that are not met with in the Old. Thus, for example, vessels with a hollow rim probably represent a type that is of a purely American origin.

The hammock is an invention that we have received from the Indians. Its autochthonous occurrence in New Guinea may well be considered highly doubtful. It is, moreover, unquestionably established that this comfortable form of bed was unknown outside America prior to the discovery of that continent. The hammock is an essentially Amazonian cultural element.

The reduction of head-trophies, by removing the skull and shrinking the head to the size of a fist, whilst still retaining the shape of the facial features, as the Jivaro Indians do, is a strange custom which is not known outside America.

Among musical instruments in America there are many that do not occur in the Old World, such as a quaint wind-instrument from Guiana, a strange-looking flute in the shape of an ax, described by Bolinder, from the Motilones. Many forms of signaling gongs, too, are of purely Indian origin, as is also the "teponatzli," the well-known "Zungen-trommel" of the Mexicans. To this subject I shall recur later.

Of weapons there is none of especially Indian type, but, on the other hand, the Indians have made certain minor inventions as to weapons that are not found in the Old World, such as several methods of affixing feathers to arrows: for example, Peruvian cemented feathering, sewed feathering, and others. Neither can it with certainty be maintained that any Indian method in hunting is entirely original. Nor—as regards fishing—can there be any method pointed to that only the Indians know. This latter is quite interesting to note in view of all we know of their important contribution as agriculturists to the progress of human culture . . .

A really thorough-going knowledge of the culture in certain parts of the Old World, as of the New, would probably result in showing that considerably more than what I have here adduced had been invented by the Indians and was not known outside America prior to its discovery. Also in regard to social structure and the spiritual world, notions may no doubt be found that have a purely Indian origin. This is, however, not possible to prove conclusively unless one possesses a thorough knowledge of the geographical distribution all over the globe of the different conceptions on these subjects. A custom like, for instance, cremation in association with endocannibalism is probably purely Indian. This to give one example only. In great part the Incan state organization may well be supposed to be original.

If we study the distribution of those discoveries and inventions which the Indians must have independently made, on account of their non-occurrence in the Old World, we shall find that a surprisingly great proportion of them fall within the Amazon region. The impression is also forced upon one that the independently made inventions belong more to the agricultural tribes than to those living by hunting and fishing. It is also evident that the Inca region was at least as important a culture center as Central America and Mexico. As the present paper principally deals with South America it is probable that I have overlooked some discoveries and inventions made by the Indians of North America.

It is mostly where the Indians have been prosperous that one meets with a large proportion of inventions and discoveries. I am afraid it is not always true that necessity is the mother of invention. If it were true, then inventions ought to have been made in places where the struggle for existence was very hard. But instead they are made where conditions of life are easy.

We should bear in mind that migratory movements are productive of inventions, or of loans of new cultural elements and modifications of old ones. In the history of the earliest inventions we may therefore be certain that substitutes have played an important part, and these are worth a thorough study. A people may, for example, have emigrated from a district in which was found an excellent material for carrying-baskets, and entered another where such material was absent. Thus they have had to find some substitute which probably led to the invention of new basket types that were better suited to the new conditions. Where the new district was inhabited by people that possessed carrying-baskets or satchels made from some indigenous materials, then it is probable that the existing forms made from that material were simply copied. But in case nothing similar was met with, the immigrants were obliged either to invent something new, or else to leave off carrying in the way they were used to. This sort of adaptation to natural conditions of the locality of abode must have played an exceedingly important part in the history of inventions.

I shall here confine myself to mentioning one particular kind of substitute that in America has been fruitful of a number of inventions, namely, substitutes for stone. America contains many large regions more or less devoid of stone. Among such regions I have myself visited El Gran Chaco and Mojos in South America, and the Sacramento River delta area in California.

The Chaco is in certain parts so bare of stones that one may live in them for many months without finding a stone as big as one's hand. In my books I have pointed out that these conditions have caused the inhabitants to cast about for various substitutes for stone. There the Indians manufacture knives of hard wood or bone, similar to those found in archæological excavations in districts richer in stone, nearer the Andes. In the same way they also have saws, or scrapers, shaped like those of stone that are in use farther west. In the Chaco I have seen the Indians use their spades, which are of lignum-vitæ, as whetstones. In those parts they also use bolas stones made of hard wood. . . .

An interesting point is the use of hearth-stones made from burnt clay. These are even found in localities where stones occur, as will be seen from a map which I have published. This is an instance of substitutional invention having spread into regions where the substitute was not needed. The form has also been modified and made barrel-shaped instead of pyramidal, its supposed original shape. Among substitutes for stones I also think we should count the shell axes of the West Indies. But this provides no reason for supposing any connection between the shell axes of Oceania and those of the West Indies. . . .

I have now given some account of such inventions and discoveries as must have been made in America, for the reason that they were unknown in the rest of the world prior to the discovery of America, as well as of such as obviously constitute adaptations to extreme physiographical conditions. My next aim will be to discuss some further inventions which, although possessed in common by the Old World and the New at the time of the discovery, appear to have been independently made in America.

If the Indians of western South America had possessed bronze in which the tin and the copper were mixed in the same proportion as in the Old World, and if it could be proved that their bronze age followed immediately upon their stone age, then it would be quite clear that bronze was an importation from the Old World. Now we know that such was not the case, but that the bronze age was preceded by a copper age, and that the Indians of Bolivia only in a later stage of the bronze age succeeded in discovering an effective proportion between tin and copper. This discovery, which appears to have been made not far from Lake Titicaca, subsequently spread to the Peruvian coast and Mexico. It is therefore evident that bronze is an invention independently made in America. In the same way we ought in every case to examine whether in any given district an invention occurs in its completed stage or whether we there find preliminary stages of it, in which latter case it is very probable that it is indigenous, or that at any rate the improvements have been achieved in America.

To choose a few examples. In a special paper I have made a study of the distribution of palisades in South America, and then found that there occur both very complex types with loopholes, pitfalls, and so on, and with double rows of poles, and also palisades consisting of nothing beyond fences of thorny trees, more or less elaborately constructed. It is quite obvious that the earliest palisades in South America simply consisted of fences, and that subsequently these protections round the huts developed into palisades of more or less complicated nature. This circumstance speaks in favor of palisades having been independently invented in America.

The socketed ax-head—that is, axes in which the handle is inserted into the head—in America occur only within the culture region in Peru. After Ambrosetti I have, in vol. 4 of my series, "Comparative Ethnographical Studies," clearly shown that in that region the Indians, to begin with, possessed T-shaped axes of copper, which they fastened to a handle with a piece of rawhide taken round the handle and sewn together at the back. On other axes this binding was at a later stage imitated in metal, and a shaft-hole ax resulted. Even the stitches by which the rawhide used to be secured were reproduced in the metal, so that they remained as an ornament. As a matter of fact, it can here be clearly seen how the process developed by which the socketed axe was invented in America, where otherwise it was unknown, and the socketed ax represents a very important invention whose distribution in the Old World is, and even formerly was, very extensive. That it did not become so widely spread in America is probably ascribable to the circumstance that it was invented at a relatively late period—that is to say, not very long before the discovery. Socketed stone celts are not known from America. . . .

The liana bridge is also counted among the culture elements that certain investigators consider as having in America a Melanesian origin. Nevertheless, many more important bridge constructions of this kind are known from America than from Melanesia, as is evident, for example, from Cobo's excellent description of the bridges of the Incan kingdom. There had also existed a type of bridge, "uruya," which is probably unknown in Melanesia. In America, too, Botocudos and Sirionós have exceedingly simple bridges consisting of one or two lianas stretched across the river.

Those who believe that the liana bridge is a culture element imported from Melanesia into America, is it their opinion that the primitive Sirionó and Botocudo Indians have independently produced these inventions, or that their bridges are a simplified form of other tribes' more elaborate bridge constructions? According to them, it would appear that it is neither the poorest nor the superior suspension bridges that the Indians have learnt from Melanesia to construct, but only such as are somewhere in between. It is, moreover, to be noted that the Indians possess several other types of bridges: floating bridges (Aymara), footbridges of poles laid across (Huari), and cantilever constructions (Quichua). Consequently it appears probable that the art of bridge-building was independently invented in America.

To the Oceanian culture elements also belong maces with heads in the form of stone rings, either smooth or more or less star-shaped. Correspondence between certain Melanesian maces and others recovered in Peru is indeed striking, and appears to furnish proof of a common origin.

It should, however, be noted that the stone-ring mace was preceded by the digging-stick of the type used by the Bushmen, and that these implements at the time of the discovery existed both in California and southern Chile. The digging-stick would thus have been an exceedingly ancient culture element in America—unless it was independently invented both in the extreme south of South America and in California. Strictly speaking, a mace with a smooth stone head is nothing but a digging-stick used for whacking people over the head. Thus we must either believe that in remote antiquity the Indians received the digging-stick with the stone ring from Oceania, or that from that quarter they have only learnt how to give more of a star-shape to their mace-heads, or else that in this department they have not learnt anything from anywhere. The idea of making mace-heads of metal, such as the Indians of Peru possessed at the time of the discovery, must, of course, be their own. In this they have partly imitated the stone forms, but have, in addition, invented one or two things originally of their own. . . .

The manioc-grater must, as I have already said, be an American invention. It is also interesting to note how this invention has been improved upon all the way from simple spiny roots up to well-made boards artistically encrusted with quartz splinters.

In the same way the manioc press is, as I have said, an Indian invention. Its distribution has been studied in detail by Métraux, who points out that its origin appears to lie in Guiana. This invention is not known by the tribes inhabiting the upper Xingú, who squeeze out the poisonous juice through a basketwork sieve. The Uitoto, Yamamadi, and Kayapó employ a very primitive form of press, which Métraux no doubt rightly supposes to be more original than the well-known basket bag. These tribes who, as far as we know, have not for a very long time had any intercourse with each other, inhabit the extreme edge of the distribution area of the manioc press. The migrations of the Guarani Indians have evidently contributed to the dissemination of the manioc press. To Central America it has only penetrated in post-Columbian times, along with the black Caribs transferred to that territory from the West Indies. Seeing that the manioc-grater is found on the upper Xingú, it appears there to be older than the basketwork bag. Even of this implement the highest forms are found in Guiana, whilst its simpler forms occur peripherally in its area of distribution.

A culture element of which I have made special study is the enema syringe. In this we have before us an invention that we are able to prove to be purely Indian in part, seeing that we know the rubber syringe to be an Indian invention. At the same time it is an invention of which in America there are two forms, namely, the enema tube and the enema syringe, of which the latter is supposedly an improvement upon the former. In favor of the enema tube also being an American invention speaks the circumstance of its not being known either in Oceania or northern Asia. As regards the rubber syringe, it is an invention which was preceded by the hollow rubber ball.

In the foregoing I have shown the development of variation in form of several inventions that must have been made in America because they are not found elsewhere, such as the manioc press, the manioc-grater, and the enema syringe made of rubber. I have also shown that the socketed copper ax was invented in America. Moreover, I have pointed out culture elements common to America and the Old World which in America present similar developments of variation as to form, from the most primitive types up to the most elaborate.

In respect of several other culture elements much the same thing can be shown to be the case. I would therefore like to put the question: Just *where* did the foreign influence come into play; was it when the first attempts were made, or when improvements were being achieved—or must we suppose that these inventions have always been controlled from the Old World? For my own part I cannot but find it logical to suppose that such cultural elements as the liana bridge, the signaling gong, etc., have in the same way as the manioc press and the manioc-grater been invented in America, and there successively improved. This way of thinking does not in any way contradict that pre-Columbian intercommunication existed between the New and the Old Worlds, but only maintains that all common cultural elements are not necessarily derivable from a common origin.

Before passing on to inventions that appear to be American because of their having an isolated distribution in America, I wish to give a few words to inventions that appear to be in some way connected because of being founded on the same principle. I intend to show how certain inventions may have been made.

When the same principle is capable of being applied to two fairly divergent inventions, that circumstance may have been of importance, as thereby one invention may have supplied the idea for another. Inventions that to us appear enormous leaps in human progress may in this way prove to be much less isolated than is *prima facie* apparent. Of this I shall adduce one or two examples.

It is well known that the beam scale as well as the Roman steelyard were known in western South America at the time of the discovery. This is evident from the literature of that period. The question then arises as to whether the beam scale is found in America as a fully completed invention or whether it was suggested by some previous device. This, to me, seems to have been the balanced double-load pole.

It is evident that the carrying pole was in use in America at the time of the discovery, and it was then still employed by the Seri Indians of Mexico. Of these Indians McGee thus writes: "Ordinarily women are the water-bearers, each carrying an olla balanced on the head with the aid of a slightly elastic annular cushion, usually fashioned of yucca fiber, though in some cases two ollas are slung in nets at the ends of a yoke after the Chinese coolie fashion (this device being apparently accultural)."

From this it appears that he considers the "coolie yoke" to be a post-Columbian culture element in America. This is certainly an erroneous opinion, seeing that this contrivance is mentioned by Oviedo, and other writers from Mexico and Darien even as early as the very beginning of the era of the discovery. Oviedo, in fact, has depicted a man carrying by means of such a pole. . . .

It is a very noteworthy circumstance that this mode of carrying loads, of such common occurrence in eastern Asia, was practiced in America at the time of the discovery. That the Indians of northern Mexico did not merely by chance happen to employ this method of carrying burdens, is evident from the fact that they suffered terribly when the Spaniards compelled them to carry loads on their backs, a thing they were entirely unused to. . . .

Another interesting example of isolated distribution connected with a specific purpose is the following. We know that in the extreme north of North America, the Eskimo, and certain neighboring Indian tribes, possess sledges with runners. In all the rest of America the sledge fitted with runners is unknown. One of the Fuegian tribes, the Alakalouf, possess, however, this vehicle in an embryonic stage, as their plank-boats are provided with runners in order to facilitate their being dragged overland from one water to another. A plank-boat fitted with runners is a sort of sledge. As the runner-fitted sledge among the Eskimo no doubt is a comparatively late invention, it must be taken as probable that the Alakalouf in this respect present an independent invention made for a special purpose. The origin of the Eskimo sledge is, on the other hand, presumably to seek in the Old World. Many other examples similar to the above might be adduced.

As has already been pointed out by Max Schmidt, it is of great interest to study the form variations in such implements as have a two-fold purpose. An implement may at the outset have been used for a certain purpose and later for another, a procedure likely to entail modifications. Wegner mentions an implement partly used as a digging-stick and partly as a pestle. Should for some reason or another it be used exclusively for one purpose, its form would probably be affected. The Indians on Lake Titicaca used triple-pointed poles that are used both as fish-spears and to punt their raft along. It is not at all unlikely that it is the multi-pointed pole which has suggested the fish-spear. These poles are multi-pointed in order that they may be used in swamps, to punt their canoes along. It was natural that the Indians should try with these poles to have a thrust at any fish they might see. Then, if they migrated to a district where many-pointed poles were no longer needed, these poles lived on as fish-spears.

Lastly, in this connection, I wish to bring forward, as examples of the Indians' ability as regards inventions, a few minor achievements in that line made by them in post-Columbian times, on the basis of newly introduced culture elements or new raw material obtained from the whites.

In Patagonia, the Indians have invented a baby-carrier for use on horseback, which is a modification of the ladder-like baby-carrier they previously used on foot. This is an invention they could not have borrowed from the whites. The horse being post-Columbian, this invention, too, must be post-Columbian. The Patagonian spur cannot but be an independent type, like the wooden spurs that formerly were used by the Mocovi, and in our days by, for example, the Ashluslay Indians of El Gran Chaco, as well as by the Pima Indians of North America. In this case Indians of different parts of America have, independently of one another, arrived at the same result. In California the Indians have invented a pump-drill with a movable disk, which supposedly is a modification of the type of pump-drill the Indians have seen the whites using. The Tehuelche have modified the Spanish pack of playing cards according to their own particular taste. The Tepiete and the Toba manufacture cleverly contrived boxes of armadillo tails, which they use as containers for tinder when they strike fire with flint and steel, an art which they have learned from the whites. These tinder-boxes must have been invented in post-Columbian times.

As is well known, snow-goggles and eye-shades are common among the Eskimo. In South America eye-shades are only known from the Karajá, who use them for protecting their eyes when staying on the sun-flooded banks of Rio Araguaya. These shades are plaited from palm leaves. In the mountain regions of Bolivia and Peru, where snow is very prevalent, the Indians do not know of any way of protecting their eyes, so that sun-blindness is consequently very common among them. . . .

In conclusion, to summarize what I have said in the foregoing, I think we must admit that the Indians' contribution—as discoverers and inventors—to the cultural progress of man is considerable. It is a proven fact that the Indians have achieved many discoveries and inventions that in pre-Columbian times were unknown in the Old World. They have invented many things that are adaptations to exceptional geophysical conditions. They have, further, made a number of inventions in connection with culture elements that in post-Columbian times have been introduced to them by whites and negroes. Many inventions have in America such an isolated area of distribution that they may properly be supposed to have been made there. Seeing that the Indians

have discovered and invented a great deal that was unknown in the
Old World at the time of the discovery of America, it does not seem
unreasonable to wonder whether they may not also have invented something or other that also was known there. The actual fact of their
having done so is proved by its being possible to trace several inventions
of that class from their simplest to their most elaborate forms. In the
case of certain very important inventions it can be shown that in America they were in all probability preceded by simpler devices founded on
the same principles.

Lastly I wish to say that we must from our experience collect all
that we actually know as regards inventions and culture loans, so that
we may possess a sure foundation on which to build further, if we
propose to study cultural intercourse between the New and the Old
Worlds, or even within the continent of America, as well as between
other parts of the globe. We have to bear in mind that the question of
independent inventions and culture loans is a much more complicated
one than certain ethnographers would appear to think, to whom the
mere occurrence of a number of similar culture elements in two separated areas suffices as evidence of cultural community. We must not
simplify the problems too much, for then we run the risk of having
to do it all over again.

51. THE INFLUENCE OF THE HORSE IN THE DEVELOPMENT OF PLAINS CULTURE [7]

BY CLARK WISSLER

ONE of the important problems pertaining to the Indians of the Plains
is the relation of the European horse to their culture. The initial difficulty lies in our inability to determine the precise dates at which the
successive tribes came into its possession. . . .

The great Spanish expeditions to explore the southern parts of the
United States were well equipped with horses and even cattle and hogs.
The adventurers were cavaliers; hence, horses were a necessity. De Soto
carried some of his horses across the Mississippi in 1541. At about the
same time Coronado reached the present bounds of Oklahoma from
Santa Fe. Oñate is believed to have visited the Pawnee and Kansas,
1599-1601, and Peñalosa conducted an expedition to the Mississippi
in 1662. From Coronado's time on there was a growing trade with

[7] Extracted from the article of the same title, *American Anthropologist*,
new series, Volume 16, pages 1-25, 1914.

the Indians of the Gulf coast, and trade to the interior from Santa Fe as a base began about 1600. The pueblo village of Taos soon became the trade center for the Plains Indians. This trade seems to have reached its maximum about 1630. . . . In 1719 du Tisné, a Frenchman, visited two Pawnee villages in Oklahoma where he counted three hundred horses. As early as 1682 Henri de Tonty found horse-using Indians on the lower Missouri. La Salle also states (1682) that the Gattacka (Kiowa-Apache) and Manrhoat (Kiowa?) had many horses. . . . It seems, therefore, safe to conclude that some time during the interval 1600-1682, at least, the Caddoan tribes, the Tonkawa, and the Comanche, as well as the Kiowa, became fully equipped with horses. . . .

It is thus clear that the Indians below the Platte and lower Missouri were quite well supplied with horses by 1682, and there is no reason why many of them should not have had horses as early as 1600. Presumably those to get them first would be the Ute, Comanche, Apache, Kiowa, and the Caddo. As we move northward our historical data become a little more definite.

The sons of La Verendrye made a journey to the Rocky Mountains from the Mandan in 1742-43. They encountered horse Indians, also mules and asses, and on their return to Canada mention the horses of their Assiniboine companions. . . . On one point they are definite: that horses were in use all along their route after they left the Mandan country.

Next we turn to the journal of La Verendrye's Mandan discoveries, 1738-39. He set out from a camp of Cree on the Assiniboine river and made the journey overland with a body of the Assiniboine. It is clear that the whole party were afoot, for "the women and dogs carry all the baggage, the men are burdened only with their arms; they make the dogs even carry wood to make the fires, being often obliged to encamp in the open prairie, from which the clumps of wood may be at a great distance." No mention of seeing horses among the Mandan and the adjoining villages is made. . . .

A little later (1751) Saint Pierre states that he saw horses and saddles which the Indians obtained by trade from the west, and notes a report from Fort Lajonquière in the Blackfoot country that the natives there traded for horses and saddles to the westward. This is the earliest suggestions of horses among the Blackfoot peoples. . . .

For the Dakota and other tribes above the mouth of the Missouri we seem to have negative evidence. . . . Le Sieur penetrated the country of the typical Plains Dakota in 1700, and, though he goes into much detail, we find no hint of horses being in the vicinity. Before his day neither Hennepin nor Du Luth mentions them for the Sioux country.

Then we come to the journal of Peter Pond, 1740-45, where we are told that the Yankton division of the Dakota had horses in abundance. . . .

The result of our survey is then quite definite. Horses were numerous among the Blackfoot as early as 1751, and they were used by the Assiniboine about the same date. They had not been acquired by the Mandan in 1738, but were among their immediate neighbors to the south. They are first definitely mentioned for the Teton Dakota in 1742, and for the Yankton at about the same date. The Iowa seem to have had some horses in 1724. . . .

If these dates for first mention of the horse are tabulated or plotted on a map, we have a progressive series northward, beginning with 1682 and culminating on the Saskatchewan in 1751. In every case, however, we must assume an earlier date for its introduction. There is no good reason why the Pawnee should not have had horses in 1650 or even in 1630, since they were available in the Spanish and Pueblo settlements of New Mexico. . . .

In this connection we may give brief consideration to the use of horses east of the Mississippi. From the very first, the Spaniards were great importers of horses and other domestic animals. In this respect they stand in contrast to the French of Canada where the first horse (just one) was imported in 1647, the first cargo in 1665. The English colonists imported horses moderately, except in Virginia, where the cavalier element, as among the Spaniards, brought in the horse, and where in 1669 wild horses became a pest. The first horses imported by the New England colonies came in 1629. Horses spread among the Indians of the Atlantic slope, but it was only in the south that they were numerous. According to Adair the Cherokee and other southern tribes were good horsemen. While these Indians could have secured their stock from Virginia, it is much more probable that they first came from Spanish settlements on the Gulf and even from the tribes west of the Mississippi. According to Swanton, Du Pratz and others speak of horses as numerous in the south and note that they seem a different variety from the European horse, which suggests the Indian horse of the west.

Adair gives us a good description of the riding gear of the Choctaw and other southern Indians. They had the rope for a bridle, made saddles with wood and green buffalo hide, and mounted from the "off-side," in all of which he recognizes the Spanish type and which reminds us of the Plains. Even the saddles made by the Iroquois of

New York are of this same western Indian type. All this strongly suggests that the dominant traits of horse culture among all the south Atlantic Indians came from across the Mississippi, or at least indirectly from the same source as the western culture. The ultimate source was most likely the Spaniards. The French are a negligible factor because they settled at the mouth of the Mississippi after the horse had reached the Missouri. Even the English settlements in Virginia scarcely reached a point where they could supply horses to the Indians of the east before horses are reported in the west. It seems therefore clear that the Spaniards must be credited with the introduction of the horse to the Indians of the Plains and the lower Mississippi both east and west; the greater number of horses must have come from their more numerous settlements in the Southwest and Mexico. . . .

The phenomenon we have is now plain: Indian horse culture spread rapidly from the Spanish settlements of the Southwest and Mexico upward between the Rocky mountains and the Mississippi river, and thence northward between the Missouri and the mountains, to the west of the Black hills and thence to the Saskatchewan country. On the south it spread out over the Gulf states, but did not become prominent north of Virginia, or between the Ohio and the Great Lakes, and reached the Upper Mississippi relatively late. It reached the lower Colorado on the west, but did not reach far into California or any part of the Pacific coast to the north. Likewise it reached up into the Plateau area, and even to the Déné area.

The subject we have chosen for discussion is the relation of horse culture to other Plains traits and not the historical investigation of the introduction of the animal by Europeans. The preceding data are presented solely to define the problem and make no claim to completeness. However, we cannot well discuss the influence of horse culture without fixing its relative time of origin, for, if it greatly preceded other strong European influences, its value as a cultural characteristic is high. While the fixing of such a date is quite speculative, we have its limits clearly defined, for we find the horse in the far north in 1751 and know that it could not have reached the Indians before 1500. . . .

Thus we may ask—

1. Is the Plains culture as a whole older than the introduction of the horse?
2. What changes in culture traits can be attributed to the influence of horse culture?
3. What had the environment to do with the distribution of horse culture?

If we take up the first and look for traits older than the introduction of the horse, we can lay hands upon at least one such. The use of dogs for transporting baggage is mentioned by Coronado's men, a date before the era of the horse. Furthermore, we have linguistic evidence in the names for horse, such as "mysterious dog" and "elk-dog," certainly implying a resemblance in the uses of the two animals. We should expect no one to doubt the assumption that dog traction, one of the most distinctive traits of Plains culture, was fully diffused over the area before the horse was known.

As to the tipi in the form familiar in the nineteenth century, we are far less certain. Obviously dogs could not have transported the tipi of horse days with its long heavy poles and bulky cover. Descriptions of the tipi have not been found by us at a period when the horse was unknown. The tents mentioned by Castañeda appear to be tipis, but we cannot be sure of their detailed structure. They were, however, transported by dogs. The distribution of the tipi among a few of the Central Algonkin and its analogous forms to the eastward among the Cree, may warrant a guess that it was diffused over the Plains in some form along with dog traction; but a mere guess will not help us here. However, in another place we have called attention to the apparent relation between the travois and dragging tipi poles. The horse travois is made of tipi poles and the few dog travois we have seen had their poles pointed at the butts precisely like the tipi poles. Yet the true travois was found in the northern part of the Plains; the tribes of the south placed the load upon the horse and dragged the tipi poles at the sides. In Castañeda's time this was the way for dogs. In short, there are several reasons for assuming that the northern travois was developed from the tipi poles dragged by dogs. If we accept this explanation, it is clear that a tipi of some form and the travois are historically associated and that the former is the older.

Turning to less material things we may cite the coup and methods of warfare. It would seem that since almost everywhere in the Plains a war party set out on foot, even though they went after horses, it is safe to assume that the entire procedure had become a fixed custom before the advent of the horse. The coup is so fundamental a matter in the warring system of the Plains that it also must have been there for a long time. . . .

If we turn to some of the intermediate tribes, like the Mandan, we can prove by archeology the existence of the earth-lodge before the horse. Maize also was among the Mandan. It seems most certain that Mandan culture was essentially developed long before 1738.

The net result of this survey is, then, that we have positive evidence of the dog travois development before the horse, but that on other traits of culture we have only presumptions for the area at large. . . .

We may recapitulate then by stating that while there is a presumption that the horse stimulated periodic ranging on the Plains, there were other factors capable of exerting similar influences; but that actual migration was due to the horse is quite unlikely. The existence of former periodic ranging is proven by historical evidence in some cases and made inferential in others by the previous development of dog traction. In short, we may say that only those traits directly associated with the horse can be taken as later; the most characteristic traits, for want of evidence to the contrary, must be given priority, and that while the horse along with other European influences may have intensified and more completely diffused the various traits, there is no good evidence at hand to support the view that the horse led to the development of the important traits. In other words, from a qualitative point of view the culture of the Plains would have been much the same without the horse. It does not follow though, that these Plains traits were diffused over the same area as found in 1850. For example, the characterization of the southern Plains Indians in the Icazbalceta manuscript can scarcely be improved upon as defining the Plains type of culture, but we have no way of determining its extent.

We may be reminded that in the Plains area are several subtypes of culture. There are first of all the nomadic tribes of which the Blackfoot, Crow, Teton, Kiowa, Arapaho, Cheyenne, and Comanche may be taken as types. These are the great horse and buffalo Indians as we know them. They ranged north and south in the true plains while on either border were tribes of less intense culture and varied by additional traits. Our problem, therefore, is as to whether the development of this typical group in which the horse seems so important a factor did not occur after the acquisition of the horse. If so, then the true Plains culture may properly be said to have developed with the introduction of the horse, even though every trait may have been in existence somewhere in the area long before. A rather extended argument could be presented on this point, but a few suggestions must suffice.

1. Though true migration since horse days is rare, there is a very strong presumption that several of these typical tribes had scarcely reached their historic ranges by 1600; and in that event could scarcely have developed their present culture before the horse came.

2. The high tide in typical Plains culture seems to have come in the eighteenth and nineteenth centuries. While this was the era of trade, yet the horse increased the economic prosperity and created individual

wealth with certain degrees of luxury and leisure; also it traveled ever ahead of white trade and the white trader.

3. The horse was a great inciter of predatory warfare which must have increased the range and intensity of operations, thus intensifying tribal contact and increasing intertribal knowledge, all of which would favor diffusion.

4. The culture of these tribes takes its individuality from apparent adjustments of traits to a more nomadic and intense form of life, the practical inhibition of such traits as pottery, basketry, agriculture, and fixed houses; rather than from the introduction of any new traits except those directly associated with the horse.

Hence, we may formulate for further consideration the proposition that while no important Plains traits except those directly associated with the horse seem to have come into existence, the horse is largely responsible for such modifications and realignments as give us the typical Plains culture of the nineteenth century, or which differentiate it from the subtypes in the same area. Thus we can see how practically all the essential elements of Plains culture would have gone on, if the horse had been denied them; but it is difficult to see how the vigor and accentuated association of traits forming the typical group and their intense occupancy of the true plains could have been what it was in 1800 without the horse. A type of culture, we should note, is the conception of an associated group of traits, and it is the manner of the association rather than the identity of the traits that determines it.

We may now turn to a more specific examination of the point as to what distinct modifications of culture were produced.

In the first place, the horse brought with it all its own associated elements of culture. Our collections show that saddles and other riding gear are quite uniform in type for the Plains and are on the whole after Spanish patterns. Even the use of the reata seems to be of Spanish-American origin. Riding itself was, of course, intrusive. Knowledge of how to care for horses would also come in from the Spanish. So we must surely have had a whole group of associated culture traits carried along with the horse.

Thus we have a fine example of diffusion, like the sun dance, men's societies, etc. Could we show that the diffusion of horse culture preceded the diffusion of these other traits, we should have a strong case for the horse as a modifier of culture. As we have seen, what little evidence there is points in the other direction. . . .

While the problem we have discussed is far too complex to permit a paper of this kind to be more than a suggestion of new lines of research, the following conclusions seem permissible: The horse reached most, if not all, of the typical Plains tribes from three hundred to two hundred years before they lost their cultural independence. In its diffusion over the area a large number of associated traits were carried along as a whole, or as a cultural complex. At least some of the tribes had developed dog traction to meet their nomadic wants before the horse came, and needed, therefore, but to substitute the horse for the dog in their own dog-culture complex and to take over the necessary parts of the Spanish horse-culture complex. Thus among the less sedentary tribes the whole basic structure of the later horse Indian culture was in existence when the horse came. We have found no reason to believe that the introduction of the horse did anything more than intensify and perhaps more completely diffuse the cultural whole previously formed. As such, however, it seems responsible for reversing cultural values in that the earlier dominant sedentary cultures of the Siouan and Caddoan tribes were predominated by the Shoshone and other formerly struggling nomads of their old frontier. As the leading horse carriers, the Shoshone played a large part in this development, but they lacked many of the strong cultural traits which the Crow, Teton, etc., received from the original Plains culture, in consequence of which they now fail to qualify as typical tribes. Finally, it appears probable that the accidental presence on the New Mexican frontier of a well-developed dog-traction culture was the chief determining factor in the direction of horse-culture diffusion though there were other ethnic factors as well as environmental conditions that could have contributed to the result.

52. THE ARCHITECTURE OF THE AMERICAN INDIANS [8]

BY T. T. WATERMAN

LOOKING over the distribution of different kinds of buildings erected by Indian tribes, it is possible, with the aid of inference and some imagination, to surmise what has happened in the past, and to reconstruct the story of the Indian's building arts, from the earliest times to now. The problem of how the Indian ever came to build his more remarkable works seems to be worth assailing. Many beautiful photographs have been taken by investigators, of very sensational pieces of native architecture, which would help to make certain points clear, and would serve to make any presentation of the facts more digestible for a reader,

[8] From *American Anthropologist*, new series, Volume 29, pages 210-230, 1927. Slightly revised from the original.

but only a few of them can be included within the limits of this article. I wish to propose a sort of archæological jaunt through the centuries, to find out what the Indian did, and to view his progress, stage by stage, from his first simple beginnings in building.

THE FIRST HOUSES

When the original ancestor of the Indians came wandering over the region about Behring Strait, he evidently brought with him some very definite' notion of how to build houses. This statement is easily made: but we can believe it without straining ourselves, for otherwise the original Indian could never have made the journey across the arctic wastes, nor have populated a hemisphere with his descendants after he got here. We may well ask ourselves what kind of a house he brought with him. The apparent answer is, he brought in a circular type of dwelling. The fact that the original type of house in the Behring Strait region was circular suggests this inference. Houses were built in a circular style when the first European explorers arrived, and nobody as far as I know has ever suggested the existence of any type that preceded the circular ones in that region, though the evidence of course remains scanty in the extreme. Taking the evidence as it exists, we seem to see the introduction into America across Behring Strait, of a circular form of house, back when human history began in this area.[9]

My feeling is that the habit of building circular houses, introduced in this way, spread over the whole of the New World. When we glance over the two Americas, we find that circular houses are widely used even yet. We seem to see at first glance, to be sure, a sort of olla podrida of house types, round houses and square houses more or less mixed up and alternating, of a thousand varieties of form and materials. Circular houses, however, are still encountered here and there from the Hudson Bay region right away to Cape Horn. When the different forms of houses are plotted on a map, an arrangement emerges which is not exactly helter-skelter. On the contrary, the distribution of types of houses follows a sort of dim logical plan. Circular houses, namely, are without exception found among the more primitive and backward

[9] Lest some critic object that the Eskimo in this region build square houses of planks, citing Nelson and Murdoch, and not circular houses, I may remark that these square plank houses of the Alaskan Eskimo are modern. The first white man who came into the region, the explorer Captain Cook, reported circular dwellings. His artist sketched them, both on the Aleutian Islands and on the mainland north of the Strait. The square houses of today seem to be due to contact with the Russians, for they have been in use for several generations.

tribes, while rectangular houses are built invariably by the more progressive groups. Square houses are found in a central region, circular houses in the peripheral regions towards the Poles. This hints at a conclusion. Perhaps the circular habitation is the original or primitive type, the square houses being an afterthought or modification or improvement which came with advance in knowledge and culture.

Let us give some examples (assuming for a moment that what I have just said is true) of some of the adaptations of the "primitive" or "original" round house. The Eskimo snow house is, from this point of view, an adaptation of a primeval round dwelling. The earth lodge or semi-subterranean house of our Northwestern plateaus is another form of the same thing. So is the earth lodge of the Plains tribes, such as the houses of the Mandan and the Pawnee. So is the "tipi" of the Dakota and the Blackfoot. So is the "grass lodge" of the Osage, the "hogan" of the Navaho, and the earth-plastered "kee" of the Pima. For that matter, so is the ramshackle "wickiup" of the Paiute of Nevada. The "wigwam" of the Ojibwa is another form of the round dwelling, and so, to my way of thinking, are all other circular structures wherever they may be found, including the lodges of the Tehuelche of Patagonia, and the lunatic windbreaks of the Yahgans of Tierra del Fuego. Imagination tells us that this round form of habitation was brought into the New World by the ancestors of the Indians, became diffused subsequently to the uttermost limits of things, and persists today wherever tribes have remained backward in their way of living.

SQUARE HOUSES

Dropping now into narrative, we may recount what happened next. As the Indian became more civilized (and this occurred in some regions at a very early date) he abandoned the round house, and took to building a square one. This was a first step forward in experimentation with the building arts.

From this point of view, the tribes of Iroquois in New York state were one evolutionary stage ahead of the Ojibwa mentioned above, since the Iroquois built rectangular structures, and the Ojibwa, round ones. The Iroquois "long house" was long ago described by Morgan. All the accounts picture the owners of these long houses as somewhat more advanced in the arts of life than their Ojibwa neighbors were. They had for example a more perfect political organization, and made better pottery, to mention only two things. All the tribes living in the southeastern and southern regions, Powhatan, Creek, Cherokee, Seminole, and the rest, also built houses which were I think without exception rectangular, and in general these tribes were somewhat ahead of the hunting tribes of our West in the arts of life. The association of complicated and advanced ways of living with rectangular houses, the association of primitive ways with round houses, seems to my mind to be a real correlation, and by no means blind accident. All the sedentary tribes and nations in our Southwest, in Mexico, in Central and many in South America, built rectangular habitations. In South America as in our own northern region, as we pass away from the highly advanced tribes into the region where tribes lived by hunting, we notice always a shift to circular dwellings. Speaking as briefly as possible, the area where square dwellings are found is much smaller than the area where dwellings are round, and is included within it. Square houses seem therefore to be historically later.

If any one should insist on knowing where in my opinion the square house was invented and brought first into use, I should answer, on the Atlantic side of northern central America. Here architecture reached its most elaborate form, and seems to have had a longer history behind it. A conviction that houses ought to be rectangular seems to have spread from this focus until it reached the tribes far to the south in Chile, and, in another direction, reached the Iroquois on Lake Erie. The distribution of square houses is continuous over this middle area, though the houses become more primitive as we pass from the focus toward the periphery. Two historical processes are therefore visible, one a diffusion southward over both continents of a round type of architecture, and the other a diffusion of a later and rectangular habit of building from a focus in Central America. The second movement passed in both directions and caused the old round houses to be replaced, among those tribes which lay in the path of diffusion, by square ones.

The map which accompanies this article illustrates this point. The outlines of areas on this map are of need somewhat conventionalized. All shaded areas, whatever their complexion, are intended to represent regions where houses are square. The unshaded parts of the map indicate the regions where houses are round.[10] I feel positive that the square structures scattered from Utah to Chile are all modifications of one type of building. I feel a lively persuasion also that the unshaded area in the north represents the distribution of round houses that have

[10] In "1B" of the map, namely the unshaded area in South America, rectangular houses of poles occur in several tracts, but not in eastern Brazil, nor south of the tropic of Capricorn. In other words, the horizontal shading could be extended to areas adjacent to those already shaded, but not to the parts of South America most remote from these. The addition therefore improves the symmetrical arrangement north and south of the focus of the building arts in Central America, and correspondingly strengthens the main argument.

their close relatives and counterparts in the unshaded parts of South America. A formerly continuous distribution of circular houses has seemingly been interrupted by the evolution of square forms of archi-

tecture in the middle region. What has been said therefore accounts in a general way for the appearance of square houses in America, and the matter so far is rather easily understood.

A second focus for square houses appears on the northwest coast of North America. The shading on the map extends vastly too far to the right. If the shading had been limited to the actual fringe of coast where rectangular houses are found, it would not have been visible at all. Here the houses are all rectangular, built in many cases of enormous planks, and put together in a most elaborate style of carpentry. The habitations in this region used at one time to be round. I have elsewhere gone into the evidence which indicates a shift here from circular to square styles. The change rose perhaps in part out of the singular ease of splitting planks out of the enormous conifers of this region, and may have been connected also with the high cultural level of these tribes in other respects; in art, for example, social institutions, and economic life. . . .

A well-known and interesting area where square houses are known to have followed round houses in point of time, is our Southwest, where the well-known Pueblos and Cliff-dwellers were preceded by Basket-makers. The Pueblos built square habitations, while the more ancient Basket-makers built themselves round huts. There are several known cases also where tribes built rectangular rooms to live in, but round structures for *religious* uses. Thus the Pueblos lived in rectangular rooms, while their ceremonial chambers or *kivas* were circular. This always suggests that religious chambers are a survival of an older style of building. In many of the existing Pueblos, ceremonial chambers are still circular. The Natchez tribe who lived at the mouth of the Mississippi built rectangular wooden houses, but had a circular "temple." The latter was a wooden structure on a mound with an image of the sun in it. . . .

HOUSES OF STONE

If the shift from round to square was the first improvement in the Indian's house, what was the second? The obvious answer is, the use of stone. The occurrence of buildings made of stone is represented by the darker shading on the map. Difficulties arise in plotting this matter. The Eskimo, for example, in the eastern part of their area, build stone walls for their huts. This seems to be anomalous, for they are usually regarded as a primitive people. I do not know what to say about it, except that the Eskimo are anomalous anyhow, and in a sense they had to employ stone, for in the eastern part of their habitat (from Hudson Bay to Greenland) there is no timber. I hasten over this point, merely remarking that all the Eskimo built circular dwellings, of a very primitive sort, and I think the Eskimo themselves played no real part in the evolution of architecture above its primitive stages.

The data, aside from that on the Eskimo, suggest certain conclusions relative to the steps in the development of building methods. For instance, as we pass from the northern region of frame dwellings into the region of masonry, we encounter walls built of stones without mortar. As we pass *out* of the region of masonry into the regions of frame houses in South America, we find the same sort of mortarless walls. The Cliff-dwellings of Arizona are beautiful and very familiar examples of this preliminary stage of masonry without mortar. The ancient cliff-dwellers raised walls of stone, well laid, but used mud, or nothing at all, to bind the wall together. Mud came before mortar.

THE BEGINNING OF ÆSTHETIC EFFECTS IN STONE BUILDING

As we pass into the region of fine stone buildings, we can watch, stage by stage, the beginnings of æsthetic development in architecture. The Indian built in stone through long ages before he developed any architectural sense to speak of. The Pueblo dwellings, again, are examples of an early stage of building in stone, showing little or no effort at architectural "effect"; at least, no conscious effort on the part of the builder. The "effect" which they have is largely due to their quaintness, and their state of ruin. The lack of architectural sense may be illustrated by the fact that there are no windows, properly speaking, and doorways are mere holes to crawl in at. The Pueblo never thought of arranging his doorways to improve the appearance of his buildings. The buildings for the most part are mere haphazard accumulations of rooms. Each structure is largely formless, except where its situation, in a cave, for example, may give it a form.

The Indian's earliest essay toward architectural effect in his structures was expended on stairways. As we deal with the edifices of outlying areas, often there is nothing to suggest any care for how the thing looked, except the long labor and thought expended on the approaches to buildings. Judging from the fairly wide distribution of examples, the Indian came rather early to the conviction that stairways can be constructed so as to appear fine and imposing. The Pueblo never advanced to that stage, even. He made buildings of stone, with square chambers, but he usually provided mere ladders for climbing to his building, and for climbing about its various levels. He occasionally built stairways of masonry, but they are hardly more than ladders of stone, and in effect are leaned against the building. They give the effect of being incidental, utilitarian, and without design, except the design of enabling people to mount to their rooms. Stairways built for looks belong to a more advanced stage of the building art than the Pueblo. To find examples we must proceed to Mexico. Here some splendid effects in stairways are to be seen, as at Teotihuacan and Papantla.

Stairways are what the Indian architect did first, and what, to the end of his history, he did best.

During the time when stairways were being elaborated, lime mortar seems to come into use. At least, the two things appear together. The area where mortar was used is continuous, and this invention was never achieved but once, all the tribes which use it having apparently borrowed it directly or indirectly from one source. I do not know how the Indian came in the first place to think of making mortar, but at certain sites he made mortar of admirable quality by burning limestone, and before the end of his building operations, he learned to depend on it utterly. The ancient buildings in Middle America are more like our concrete constructions than like our masonry. There is a hearting of stone or rubble, set in liberal quantities of mortar, which makes up more than half of the bulk of the building. The wall is then evened up and covered with a thin veneer of very finely dressed stone. Such a building is practically monolithic. Even buildings of this stage of architecture, in spite of the use of elaborate foundations and complicated embellishment, remain excessively homely and squat, once the stairways and approaches are omitted from view.

When the Indian builder finally came slowly to the idea of beautifying his building proper, instead of beautifying the approaches merely, he hit upon one very good idea. He realized that doorways are architecturally interesting, that they strike the eye, and he began to use them for "effect." Buildings remain square and squat, but the native builder multiplied doorways, far beyond the limits of actual need or convenience, because he liked the looks of a series of portals. Such a series of entrances gives character at once to the façade of the building. He multiplied openings therefore, and carefully spaced them. At the summit of his success, he loaded on to such a building the most complicated ornament he could devise. He did not develop any sense for form in his buildings until late in his history, and even then his efforts were by no means crowned with perfect success.

In a stage of advancement where the Indian built elaborate pyramidal foundations (enormous some of them were), fine sweeping stairways with balustrades, and house fronts with fine successions of doorways, he still made his roofs and ceilings of poles or logs. An example of architecture at this stage of progress, fortunately well preserved, is to be seen at Mitla, in the Mexican state of Oaxaca. The ornamentation is elaborate to an extreme, and very striking and successful, and the workmanship shown in the cutting of the stone is a thing to marvel at. Even with all this, the native builder never thought of giving the structures any artistic shape. One of these buildings, once the embellishment is discounted, is no more pleasing to the eye than a packing case is.

Nobody, however, has ever carried embellishment to a higher pitch than the Indian builder did. On the House of the Governor at Uxmal in Yucatan the embellishment is worked out to represent five layers of ornamental design, conceived separately, but combined in one magnificent incrustation. Many of the finest buildings of this region are in ruins, utterly, for the labor and love were expended on the external veneer, which suffered first of all the parts of the building from time, the climate, and the plant life. In form these buildings are quite primitive and undeveloped, except for a few buildings erected during a rather brief period. The best the Indian could achieve in form was the making of square corners and vertical walls: but in embellishment he worked genuine marvels.

Some very good sculpture, for example, was worked into such façades as architectural ornament. Faces or heads were often carved on the ends of blocks, and the whole set into a wall by means of tenons. Some of this sculpture is really remarkable, with amazing spirit and fire. One might remark that the Indian not only failed to be an architect such as the classical Greek was, but did not even try, caring little for form and proportion, staking everything on external richness of pattern. He loaded on decoration as a pastry-cook spreads icing on a cake, with lavish hand, and loving care, and with a certain amount of taste. It is curious, considering the magnitude and the boldness of his enterprises, that he had no better sense for form.

THE GENESIS OF COLUMNS

His love of doorways arranged in series led him step by step to a rather surprising result, the invention of round columns. In Egypt, too, columns seem to have evolved out of sections of wall. Narrow sections of masonry left between doorways certainly seem to have been gradually sensed by the builders in Egypt as square piers. Later on these square piers were rounded off, and turned themselves by a sort of metamorphosis into round columns. Square pillars in any case are early in Egypt, appearing in temples of the pyramid age, 2800 B.C., at a time when round columns may be searched for without success. In a later period, the Age of Nobles, 2000 B.C., square columns are replaced by round columns, fluted, and exhibiting capitals. Still later, enormous round columns with capitals representing parts of plants were built into the temples of the Empire, around, say, 1500 B.C.; the most imposing pillars, though not the best proportioned, in history.

When we turn to America with this in mind, we find similarly that the oldest cities in actual date have no columns. In Tikal, which is very ancient, we find no pillars, but we see façades with numerous doorways. In Palenque, a city somewhat later in point of time, the doorways in the typical buildings are so numerous, and the intervening sections of wall so skimp, that square piers seem gradually to have emerged. When we look at a Palenque building, it is impossible to discern whether the builder intended his structure to be a room with numerous doorways, or an open veranda, fronted with a row of pillars.[11] In late towns such as those in Yucatan (later by a number of centuries, as the inscriptions and other data show clearly) square piers are sometimes employed, but round columns are very numerous. In some of the structures, such as one at Chacmultun, the columns are quite well proportioned, and have a finished look, quite in the Old World Style. Some of the towns, such as Chichen Itzá, supply examples of enormous round columns, most elaborate and fanciful.

VAULTS

The Indian toward the close of a long period of architectural experimentation discovered a way to ceil over rooms, and to span portals, with masonry, without the help of timbers. Through the earlier stages of his building enterprises, he depended always on a wooden beam to span every opening. Wooden lintels are an element of weakness in a stone building, for the wood sooner or later decays. Some of the best and finest of Indian structures have fallen into collapse and wild ruin, because the timbers in them have rotted out. It is noteworthy, then, that in late times (but earlier by a thousand years than the coming of Columbus and the Spaniards) the American Indian succeeded in building a kind of arch or vault. This achievement was the handiwork of the Maya Indians of Guatemala and Honduras. Later the idea migrated into Yucatan, but it never passed out of the tropical area.

The Maya, when they wanted to close over a room, caused the successive courses of masonry in the side walls to project toward the center, so that one wall leans forward to meet the other. The result is by no means a true arch. It therefore goes by the name of the "false" arch, the "corbelled" arch, the "cantilever" arch, the "offset" arch, or, among Americanists, the "Maya" arch. The contrivance is of course

[11] See Figs. 2, 3, Selection 19.

identical in principle with the "arches" of Greece in the Homeric age, as seen for example in the Tomb of Atreus and other "bee-hive" tombs, in the Lion Gate at Mycenæ, and the famous galleries at Tiryns.

The earlier "arches" in Central America, compared to the later ones in the same region, are cautious and tentative. The engineer seems to have felt that the thing was going to collapse on him. The walls lean toward each other very gingerly, and the vaults are accordingly narrow and high. In later buildings the architect became relatively bold, and his vaults are lower and broader. . . .

The story of the building arts in America therefore has a number of chapters; round houses, square houses of wood, square houses of stone without mortar, square houses of stone laid in mortar (but minus all attempts at form or proportion); fine stairways and approaches, buildings of stone with amazing embellishment, and finally, vaulted ceilings, columns, and an attempt at form.

DISTRIBUTION OF TYPES OF HOUSES ON THE MAP

A few words about the map on which I have plotted the styles of architecture may not be amiss. Apparently the data do not lead to perfectly clear and satisfactory conclusions. For example there is a region in northern South America where houses are made of poles, a region wedged in between two areas where houses are built of stone. There seems no very obvious reason for this. The region of square plank houses on the northwest coast of North America interferes with what would otherwise be a simple and logical distribution. The two areas of masonry-minus-mortar are wedged apart by the area where mortar was employed. The device of building in stone without mortar apparently went out of style in this intervening area, and out of use. Very ancient buildings here, if they could be found or dug out of the ground, ought to exhibit the archaic building methods, without the use of mortar. The area where vaults are found, if time enough had been granted, would presumably have wedged apart the mortar area, and would have made two separate areas of it. The map suggests that the building arts developed most rapidly in the small area in Middle America which is colored solid black. In every period of history, the knowledge of how to build better houses became diffused from this area to the northward and southward. As we pass from this focus toward the periphery, we find increasingly archaic types surviving in use, until we encounter the areas of primitive round lodges in the regions about Hudson Bay and Cape Horn. Conversely, as we pass from the periphery toward the center, we are following step by step the actual evolution

of the art of building. . . . Critics who look at the map will very
likely be pained when they observe that the architecture of Peru is
represented as equivalent to the Pueblo and Cliff-dweller architecture
in our own Southwest. Though I know little enough about Peru, I am
familiar at least by hearsay with the gigantic character of the masonry
in some of the structures there. I admit that at first glance, Sacsahua-
man is quite different from Pueblo Bonito. None the less, this mortarless
Peruvian architecture seems to me to find its counterpart not in the
architecture of Yucatan, nor even central Mexico, but in the mortarless
buildings of our Southwestern states. On the southern fringe of the
Peruvian-Chilean area, stone buildings are reported which have a
rather startling resemblance to the pueblos of our own Southwest.

THE SOURCE OF THE INDIAN'S ARCHITECTURAL IDEAS

Certain authorities profess that architectural missionaries came from
somewhere and taught our Indians how to build. Some on looking at
American Indian buildings cry "Egypt," others, "China." In the
meantime, the one architecture in all the world which to me looks like
that of Middle America is not the Chinese anyway, nor yet the Egyptian, but the architecture of extreme southeastern Asia, particularly
Siam, Cambodia, and Java, with analogues in India. This raises a point
which I would rather enjoy discussing, but meanwhile it ought to be
remarked that a solitary voyager, a pilgrim, a castaway, or a missionary,
could hardly have induced a barbarous people to plan cities, or adopt
new building and engineering methods. One traveler, or a ship load of
them, can have little effect on an alien culture, in any case. It is a true
saying, and worthy of being noted, that two nations begin to affect
each other's way of living, when there is an interchange of com-
modities. Missionaries accomplish little in changing externals. Trade
and business relations quickly shift all the scenery on the stage.

We know that Lief Erickson, the Norseman, landed among the
Indians somewhere on our Atlantic seaboard, but these chance Norse
voyagers did not at all change the Indian's way of living, nor his way of
doing. The sojourn of the Norsemen left apparently not one single
relic behind, and we would not know that they had been here if they
themselves had not told us. If any Asiatic people had really been in
position to introduce a new way of building among the Indians, they
would probably have introduced along with it rice, tea, and porcelain,
not to mention pigs, chickens, and metals. They would have taken back
maize, potatoes, and tobacco. Within eighty years after the landfall
of Christopher Columbus, American plants like maize and tobacco

spread over the Old World, from one end to the other and into all the corners, not merely into Spain and Italy, but into Africa and Tibet. In brief, an architecture cannot be introduced overnight by a chance arrival, while if there had been any communication, and business relations, other things than architecture would have made the jump, and the flux and the currents of ideas and artifacts would have passed in both directions. The fact that the ideas and inventions, the domestic animals and cultivated plants just mentioned, did not pass in either direction until Columbus came, is rather clear evidence that previous to his voyage there had been no sufficient contact for the spread of ideas of any sort. That nobody had ever crossed the sea is a proposition that is not worth disputing. No business relations were established which took New World products into the Old, and it seems unlikely that Old World ideas could have come into the New. Such a plant as maize is of a thousand times more moment than a style of architecture, and a thousand times more likely to migrate.

It seems to my mind, in brief, that in the hasty dash we have just finished among America's ancient monuments, we have seen how one step in architecture follows another and grows out of it. Borrowing from abroad, if it occurred, must have been continuous over thousands of years. What the Indian actually did in his building operations was what he would have done if he had been feeling his way along. We witness among the aboriginal structures what seem to be experiments, and these timid essays marched only very gradually toward the finer masterpieces. The Indian built houses and other structures of fifty materials, and five hundred shapes, but when we look for evolution in the shapes and materials, stages in progress seem to be visible, and the advance from one stage to the one just next beyond it, seems to be in each case a simple matter. The one place where architecture seems to have gone ahead most rapidly seems to be on the Atlantic side of Central America. Here is perhaps the place where the Indian began first to build in stone, and where he later did his best work. I do not know why.

53. THE DISAPPEARANCE OF USEFUL ARTS [12]

BY W. H. R. RIVERS

THE civilized person, imbued with utilitarian ideas, finds it difficult to understand the disappearance of useful arts. To him it seems almost

[12] Pages 109-130 of *Festskrift Tillägnad Edvard Westermarck*, Helsingfors, 1912.

incredible that arts which not merely add to the comfort and happiness of a people but such as seem almost essential to his very existence should be lost. He assumes that the loss is only to be accounted for by such factors as the total lack of raw material or the occurrence of some catastrophe which has wiped out of existence every person capable of practicing the art. The object of this tribute to Professor Westermarck is to show that arts of the highest utility have disappeared in Oceania and to suggest that the causes of the disappearance are not of a simple character but that there must be taken into account social and magico-religious, as well as material and utilitarian, factors. I shall deal with three objects: the canoe, pottery, and the bow and arrow.

THE CANOE

It might be thought that, if there was one art of life which would have been retained by people living in small groups of islands, it would be the art of navigation. Even putting aside the need for intercourse between the inhabitants of different islands of a group and with the inhabitants of other groups, one would have thought that its usefulness in obtaining food would have been sufficient to make people strain every resource to the utmost to preserve so necessary an object as the canoe. Nevertheless we have clear evidence that in two places in Oceania the canoe has once been present and has disappeared.

In the Torres Islands (not to be confused with the islands of Torres Straits) the people have at present no canoes and in order to pass over the narrow channels, which separate the islands of their group from one another, they use rude catamarans of bamboo. These craft are so un-seaworthy that they are of little use for fishing; how little is shown by the fact that in order to catch the much prized *un* (the *palolo* of Polynesia) the people stand on the reefs and catch the worms with a net at the end of a long pole.

It is quite certain that we have not to do in this case with people who have never possessed the canoe. The Torres Islands form only an outlying group of the Banks Islands which in their turn form a continuous chain with the New Hebrides, and the general culture of the Torres islanders is so closely allied to that of neighboring peoples and there is such definite tradition of intercourse with them that even if there were no more direct evidence we could be confident that the people must once have shared the prevailing outrigger canoe of this region with their neighbors. Direct evidence, however, is not wanting. Dr. Codrington records that the canoe-makers had died out and that the people had in consequence resigned themselves to doing without an art which must once have taken an important place in their daily avocations.

While the canoe has thus disappeared in the Torres group there is evidence that it has degenerated in the adjacent Banks Islands. The canoe of these islands is now a far less seaworthy and useful craft than it must once have been. There are clear traditions of former communications with the Torres and New Hebrides, if not with more distant islands, but now the canoes only suffice for journeys within the Banks group and are not even good enough to fulfill this purpose completely. The canoe of Mota cannot be trusted to take its people to the island of Merlav which forms the southern limit of the group. Further, Dr. Codrington records that at Lakon, a district of Santa Maria, one of the largest of the Banks Islands, the people for a time went without their canoes though, unlike the Torres islanders, they had relearnt the art.

It is clear that this disappearance or degeneration of the canoe is not due to modern European influence. The canoe had already disappeared in the Torres Islands when Dr. Codrington was in Melanesia and this was not long enough after the settlement of Europeans to allow the loss to be ascribed in this cause.

The other place in Oceania where we have evidence of the disappearance of the canoe is Mangareva (Gambier Islands). When this island was first visited by Beechey he found the people using large rafts capable of carrying twenty men, together with smaller craft of the same kind; and yet, as Friederici has pointed out, there is one fact which shows that these islanders had formerly possessed the canoe. The Mangareva people call their raft *kiatu*, which is a widely distributed word in the Pacific for the outrigger of the canoe. We can be confident that this word indicates a direct relation between the Mangareva raft and the ordinary Polynesian canoe. Even if it would be rash to conclude that the raft is the direct descendant of the outrigger of an ancient canoe, we can be confident that the natives of Mangareva were once acquainted with the canoe but had it no longer when their island first became known early in the last century. When Beechey visited Mangareva the people sailed their rafts and could do so much with them that it would not be correct to say that they had lost the art of navigation, as may be said about the Torres Islanders. Nevertheless the art must have been very inferior to that which was given to them by the possession of the canoe.

POTTERY

Pottery is less essential to the life of an islander than a canoe but yet its convenience must be so great that its manufacture would seem to be an art most unlikely to disappear.

The distribution of pottery is one of the most remarkable features of the material culture of Oceania. In southern Melanesia it is now found only in two places, New Caledonia and Espiritu Santo (usually called Santo), and then, passing northwards, we do not meet with it again till we come to the Shortland Islands, Bougainville and Buka, and then it goes again to reappear in New Guinea. Eastwards it is found in Fiji but is totally absent from Polynesia.

Its distribution, however, was once more extensive. Fragments of pottery are found scattered about in Malikolo and Pentecost, in neither of which islands is pottery now used and in Malikolo the people have a myth to explain the presence of the fragments. Further, pottery has been found buried at considerable depths in two places, and promises through its indestructibility to become in these distant islands as important a guide to past history as in the older world. In Lepers' Island (Omba) Glaumont has found coarse potsherds lying nine feet below the surface and in Ambrym pottery has been found accompanying an ancient burial. We have here clear evidence of the use of pottery over an extensive region in only one corner of which it is still made.

Similar discoveries of ancient pottery have been made in New Guinea. Here pots are still made in the districts where this ancient pottery has been found, but in southeastern New Guinea the ancient pottery is far superior to that now made, though similar to it in several respects. The modern pottery which most nearly approaches the old in character is that used in Murua (Woodlark Island) as a receptacle for the bones of the dead. If, as is probable, this modern pottery is the direct descendant of the old, we may note that it has survived in its completest form, not for a utilitarian purpose, but as part of the ritual of death.

There is thus clear evidence that pottery has disappeared from some islands where it was once in regular use, and that in others where pottery is still used, the art has fallen far below its former level of excellence.

THE BOW AND ARROW

There is definite evidence that the bow and arrow was once a far more widespread and important weapon in Oceania than it is at present. In Polynesia it is only definitely known to have been used as a weapon in Tonga and Samoa. In Tahiti the use of the bow in war is doubtful but it was used to shoot at a mark in sport and it is difficult to understand the existence of archery as a sport if the bow had not once had a more serious use. In other parts of Polynesia the bow is used in sport especially to kill rats, and also to shoot birds and fish for food. Here again there can be little doubt that these uses are only survivals of a time when it was employed as a weapon. What little doubt remains is dissipated when we find that the word for the bow of Polynesia is often *pana*, *fana*, or *ana*, forms of a widespread word for the bow in Oceania and used in places where the bow is the chief weapon.

In Melanesia the conditions are much as in Polynesia, the bow and arrow being used as a toy or to shoot birds and fish in places where there is evidence of its former use in war.

In New Britain the bow is only used in war by the Kilenge people of the north coast and since they obtain it from the people of New Guinea it might be thought that it has only recently been introduced. The bow is used in war in the middle of New Ireland but the people at the southern end use it only to shoot pigeons. In New Hanover the bow and arrow is said to be now unknown and in the Admiralty Islands it has hitherto only been known as a toy, though the Hamburg Expedition has recently discovered a bow once used in war.

There is clear evidence, however, that in some of these islands the use of the bow in war was once more general. The ancient voyagers record that the natives of these islands shot at them with arrows and there is some evidence in favor of a progressive diminution in the importance of this weapon. Again, though the bow was till recently used in war in the British Solomons, it was certainly a less important weapon than when the islands were visited by the Spaniards two centuries earlier.

In many parts of New Guinea, and especially among the people who speak languages of the Melanesian family, the bow and arrow is now absent, or used only as a toy or to shoot birds. In this case there is more justification for the view that the bow has been introduced recently, for in parts of German New Guinea the bows and arrows used by the coastal people to shoot birds are obtained from the natives of the interior, while on the south coast of British New Guinea they are obtained from the people of the Papuan Gulf.

In German New Guinea, however, a fact has been recorded which points clearly to the bow and arrow being a survival rather than a recently introduced element of culture. Pöch found that the Monumbo living on the coast opposite Vulcan Island in German New Guinea do not use the bow and arrow. They have, however, a word for the bow in their language, and in their marriage ceremony the bride holds in her hand a symbolic bow and arrow, this ceremonial use pointing unmistakably to the ancient importance of the weapon thus symbolized.

Again, in British New Guinea the storing of the bow and arrow in the *marea* or clubhouse among the Roro suggests that this weapon is an ancient possession of the people, and this is supported by the fact that even the Papuan tribes from whom the bow is obtained apply to it terms which are almost certainly Melanesian. In New Guinea, as in Melanesia, there is thus reason to believe that the bow and arrow was once a more important element of the culture than it is at present.

Having now established the fact that in certain parts of Oceania there have been lost three arts the utility of which would seem to make their disappearance most unlikely, I proceed to consider to what causes this disappearance is to be ascribed. I will consider these causes under three heads, material, social and magico-religious.

MATERIAL CAUSES

The most obvious cause of the disappearance of an art, however useful it may be, is the absence of the raw material out of which it is made and I have first to consider whether the disuse of the canoe and of the bow in many parts of Oceania may have been due to lack of suitable wood and that of pottery to the want of clay.

There are certain features of the art of canoe-making in the Pacific which suggest the lack of raw material as a possible cause. There are islands of the Pacific where there are no trees from which a dug-out canoe could be made and the people have to depend on the arrival of driftwood. Further, this dependence on driftwood may be necessary even in islands where there are suitable trees owing to the implements of the people being incapable either of cutting down a tree of sufficient size or of hollowing it after it has been felled. It is not difficult to see how a people may allow their implements to degenerate till they are incapable of felling or hollowing trees so that after a time they become dependent upon driftwood, and that then some change of current or other cause may allow so long a time to elapse without arrival of suitable wood as to explain the loss of the art.

There is no reason, however, for supposing that this has been the cause of the disappearance of the canoe in either the Torres Islands or Mangareva. The Torres Islands are well wooded and their implements are not notably, if at all, inferior to those of neighboring groups of islands where the canoe is still made. Again, the picture of the Mangareva raft in Beechey's book shows that the natives were able to use large planks of wood, and absence of suitable material may be put on one side here also.

There is no reason whatever for supposing that absence of suitable material has played any part in the disappearance of the bow but with pottery the case is different. The geological character of many of the islands of the Pacific shows that they must be quite devoid of any material from which pots could be made and the absence of raw material is probably a most important, if not the essential, factor accounting for the absence of pottery from Polynesian culture. Absence of clay, however, will not explain the disappearance of pottery in Melanesia and the ancient pottery of Lepers' Island was covered by many feet of clay-like earth which would probably have been suitable for the manufacture of pots if the art had not disappeared through some other cause. Though absence of raw material may have caused the loss of the potter's art in Polynesia, it cannot explain its disappearance in Melanesia, nor can it explain the loss of the canoe and of the bow and arrow. . . .

A more probable motive for the disuse of the bow in Polynesia has been suggested by Friederici who points out the unsuitability to the physical conditions of Polynesian warfare. He believes, almost certainly with right, that the bow was a prominent, if not the chief, weapon of the ancestors of the Polynesians. The warfare of the Polynesians is conducted in canoes or on shores affording little cover from the wind and Friederici has himself seen how the strong winds of the Pacific make the arrow a fluttering and harmless missile. He suggests that the bow was the weapon of a people accustomed to fight in the bush who found it ill adapted to the more open character of the islands of Polynesia.

This factor, however, will not explain the disuse of the bow as a weapon over large regions of Melanesia where there is present the condition of bush-warfare to which Friederici supposes the bow and arrow to be especially adapted. Nevertheless, it is possible that the disappearance of the bow has been due here also to the special nature of the warfare. The leading principle of the strategy of many parts of Melanesia is the use of surprise. The object of an invading party is to come to close quarters and destroy the enemy in the early morning, while he is still asleep. The importance of this mode of warfare cannot, however, fully account for the disappearance of the bow and arrow, for this weapon is still used by some of the people who practice this war by stealth. It is probable that the causes of the disappearance of the bow and arrow in so many parts of Melanesia have not been purely material but that other motives have been in action.

SOCIAL CAUSES

A second group of factors which may bring about the loss of useful arts are of a social nature. Many of the objects used in the every day life of Oceania are not made by any member of the community but their manufacture is confined to special groups of craftsmen. Thus, in Tonga and Tikopia canoes are only made by certain men called *tufunga* who are succeeded in this occupation by their sons. Though in Tikopia a man can become a *tufunga* through his own efforts, the obstacles in the way of his success are very great and the craftsmen thus form a body limited in number, definitely distinguished from the rest of the community. It is only necessary for such a limited body of men to disappear either as the result of disease or war or through some natural catastrophe, to account for the disappearance of an art. As we have seen, there is evidence that this dying out of skilled craftsmen has been the cause of the disappearance of the canoe in the Torres Islands, and Seligmann and Strong have recorded the dying out of skilled craftsmen as the cause of the disappearance of the art of making stone adzes in the Suloga district of Murua (Woodlark Island). The dying out of skilled craftsmen within a community is thus established as a cause of the loss of useful arts.

This factor, however, will only explain a localized loss here and there. It will explain the loss of the canoe on isolated groups of islands but it will not account for the absence of the bow and arrow or of pottery over large areas of Oceania. The skilled craftsmen would not be likely to die out simultaneously among all the peoples of an extensive area.

In certain parts of Oceania there are, however, conditions which make the extensive loss of useful arts more intelligible. Useful objects are often made only in certain places whence they spread over a large area by means of trade. Thus, the people of the Papuan Gulf obtain their pots from the Motu and Koita round about Port Moresby and trade in pottery is also found among the Massim. Again, in New Caledonia pots are said to be made only in three places. The extermination of the people who made pottery by warfare or by some natural catastrophe might thus be limited to a small region and yet it might lead to the disappearance of the use of pottery over large and even remote regions. There is some reason to suppose that a catastrophe of a volcanic character may have led to the loss of pottery in the northern New Hebrides. The fragments of pottery found in Lepers' Island lay under two layers of soil, the deeper of which consisted of scoriæ. In this region where volcanoes are even now active, it is possible that the use of pottery throughout an extensive region was wiped out by the destruction of some special people from whom the pottery was obtained. It is even possible that the pottery of Santo may have been introduced later into a region from which pottery had many ages before been eliminated by a volcanic catastrophe. We should have in such a case a combination of material and social factors. If pottery were once made in every island and district of the northern New Hebrides, it is very unlikely that any volcanic catastrophe would have wiped it out completely; but the limitation of the art to one district is a social factor which makes intelligible such an effect of the material agency. The material factor acting alone would not have abolished the art but in combination with the limitation of the manufacture to special tribes it would enable a localized catastrophe to destroy an art over a wide region. Even this combination of causes, however, would not destroy an art over such extensive regions of Oceania as some of those in which useful arts have disappeared.

It is possible that social causes may have assisted the utilitarian motives suggested by Friederici as the cause of the disuse of the bow and arrow as a weapon. In many parts of Polynesia, if not generally, fighting had largely a ceremonial character, the killing of a man on either side or even the drawing of blood being sufficient to put an end to a fight. In such a condition strictly utilitarian motives would count for very little and thus would be made easy a process by which one weapon was changed for another of a less deadly character.

Again, among a people so advanced as the Polynesians it is a question whether the mere play of fashion may not have had a great influence. If war were the deadly process it is with us, it is most unlikely that a weapon capable of killing at a distance should give way to one which can only be used at close quarters, but if war is largely ceremonial it is possible that the bow and arrow may have been supplanted by the club. The great development of the club in Polynesia, its manifold development in form and ornament, show how great a part it has played in the interests and affections of the people. It does not seem unlikely that the club may have so become the fashion at one stage of Polynesian history and so excited the æsthetic, and perhaps the religious, emotions and sentiments of the people that the bow and arrow ceased not merely to be an object of interest; it ceased to be used at all for the serious business of warfare and persisted only for the relatively unimportant purposes of shooting birds, rats and fish or for the pure sport of archery.

Useful arts may also disappear through the influence of an immigrant people. The contact of two peoples has social consequences of a complicated character in which elements of the material culture may be involved. It is unlikely that immigrant influence would ever lead people to discard such useful objects as pottery and the canoe, but it is probable that it has played a part in the disuse of the bow and arrow in Melanesia. It is even possible that the change of fashion I have supposed to have occurred in Polynesia may have been connected with the presence of a new ethnic element in the population.

RELIGIOUS AND MAGICAL FACTORS

In the last section I have suggested that religious factors may have assisted the development of the club in Polynesia and thus helped to bring about the disappearance of the bow and arrow as a weapon. There is another religious factor which may have worked in the same direction. People whose highest hope it is to die in battle, to whom this end opens the way to a future life in a special paradise, are not likely to be swayed by utilitarian motives in their choice of weapons. If the bow and arrow had a great superiority as a weapon, and if war were waged in earnest, we could have trusted to natural selection to ensure its survival, but in the absence of such superiority, the Polynesian contempt for death may have had a share in its disappearance.

It is also possible that religious or magical motives may have assisted the loss of useful arts dependent upon the dying out of special craftsmen. To our utilitarian minds there may seem to be a serious objection to the view that useful arts have disappeared through the dying out of craftsmen. We can readily understand how such a factor would produce a great falling off in workmanship and ornamentation, but from our point of view it would seem most unlikely that people would stand idly by and allow the disappearance of arts so useful as those of making pottery and canoes. Nevertheless we have found that arts have disappeared for this reason and it remains to discover why. In many parts of Oceania an art practiced by a special group of craftsmen is not a mere technical performance but has a definitely religious character and may be regarded as a long series of religious rites. It is not enough to be able to make a canoe but you must also know the appropriate rites which will make it safe to use it for profane purposes without danger from ghostly or other supernatural agencies. To go in a canoe which has not been the subject of such rites would be to put oneself into the midst of all kinds of hidden and mysterious dangers. In Polynesia this religious character of crafts is shown even in the terms applied to those who practice them. The *tufunga* of Tonga and Tikopia is only one form of the *tohunga* of the Maori, the *tuhuna* of Tahiti, the *taunga* of Mangaia, the *tahunga* of the Low Archipelago and the *kahuna* of the

Hawaian Islands. Most of these words are used both for priests and craftsmen, thus pointing clearly to the religious character of the occupations they follow. In combination with rites which so often accompany the process of manufacture this common nomenclature suggests that the disappearance of useful arts through the dying of craftsmen may not have been due solely, or even chiefly, to the loss of their manual skill but that the quenching of their spiritual power, the *mana* of Oceania, may have been another and most potent factor. . . .

I can now consider briefly some problems of general interest towards the solution of which the conclusions of this paper may contribute. . . .

I hope that I have made it clear that in studying the history of culture we must be prepared for changes not to be accounted for by the likes and dislikes of the civilized and almost incredible from the utilitarian point of view. We must be very cautious in assuming that elements of culture are so useful or so important that they would never be allowed to disappear. If islanders can lose the canoe, of what features of culture can we safely say that they can never be lost?

A second most important aspect of my subject is one in which the loss of the canoe is especially concerned. In many regions of Oceania and in other parts of the world, islands are now to be found inhabited by people whose present means of transportation are wholly insufficient to have brought them from the nearest land. In dealing with such problems it has sometimes been assumed that under no circumstances is it credible that people could ever lose the art of navigation and it has therefore been concluded that the islands must have been peopled when they were connected with some continent by a connecting bridge of land. On similar grounds it has even been supposed that scattered islands are the mountain peaks of submerged continents, of whose people the natives of the islands are the survivors. Thus Giglioli, starting from the assumption that the frail canoes of the Tasmanians could never have brought them from Australia, has argued that the Tasmanians must have reached their island when it was connected with the mainland and, accepting Giglioli's statement that no case is known in which people have lost the art of navigation, Howitt has adopted the supposed passage of the ancestors of the Tasmanians by dry land. Again, the culture of Easter Island has led some to suppose that it is one of the mountain-peaks of a Pacific continent. The grounds for such hypotheses and conjectures are swept away if it be established that even an art so useful as that of navigation can disappear.

Another way in which use has been made of the supposed impossibility of the loss of the art of navigation is in the ascription of an indigenous character to the culture of certain regions. Thus, Mr. Joyce has lately argued against any influence of people from the Pacific Ocean upon South America on the grounds that along the whole of the coast of South America nothing but the most primitive raft was found. The facts I have brought forward deprive this argument of its cogency, though it may be noted that the absence of the canoe is only one of several features which Mr. Joyce believes to point to the indigenous nature of the Andean culture.

Lastly, I cannot forbear from pointing out an allied aspect of human culture which points in the same direction as the special subject of this article. Quite as striking as the loss of useful arts is the extraordinary persistence of elements of culture which seem to us wholly useless, and perhaps are so even to those who seem to carefully preserve them. This persistence of the useless combines with the disappearance of the useful to make us beware of judging human culture by purely utilitarian standards. I have perhaps in this paper gone beyond the limit warranted by my evidence in assigning the loss of useful arts to religious motives. I have done so without misgiving, however, because I am sure that I cannot be far wrong in bringing forward views, hypothetical though they be, which will put us on our guard in estimating the motives which guide the conduct of peoples with cultures widely different from our own. I hope that the facts brought forward in this paper have been sufficient to show that utilitarian motives are less important in determining the course of the ruder stages of man's history than we suppose them to be among ourselves.

54. SOME FUNDAMENTAL IDEAS OF CHINESE CULTURE [13]

BY BERTHOLD LAUFER

OF ALL the numerous problems with which the scientific research of China is concerned, the problem of the early origin and development of Chinese civilization is the most important, and at the same time the most fascinating. In former times, when the exploration of China was still in its infancy, two main theories, in strong contrast with each other, were advanced in regard to the origin of the Chinese. In the eighteenth century, when both China and Egypt were imperfectly known, it was almost inevitable that the two should be linked together by a common source of origin; and in more recent times the romantic

[13] From *The Journal of Race Development*, Volume 5, Number 2, October, 1914. By permission.

school of sinologues, headed by T. de Lacouperie, stamped the Chinese as emigrants from Babylonia, bringing from there all the essential elements of West-Asiatic civilization. The French Count Gobineau is responsible for the not very serious hypothesis that the culture of China in its total range may have been derived from India. Other scholars endowed with a lesser degree of imaginative power insisted on the independence and originality of Chinese culture, and vigorously stood on the platform of a Monroe doctrine, "China for the Chinese." But this theory of perfect seclusion and isolation of ancient Chinese culture can no longer be upheld; for we begin to recognize more and more its historic and prehistoric connection with other culture-groups of Asia, and to understand that also the Chinese were a people among peoples.

Indeed, no culture on this globe was ever exclusive or singled out, or had a purely internal development prompted by factors wholly within itself. The growth and diffusion of culture are due to historical agencies, and must be comprehended in connection with the universal history of mankind. No historical problem can be understood and solved with any hope of success by limiting our attention to one particular culture-sphere to the exclusion of all others, and even in the minutest specialization of our work we must never be forgetful of the universalistic standpoint. Aside from the lack of critical methods, the principal error of those who simply reduced Chinese culture to a loan received from the west, was that the antiquity of the fundamental elements of civilization was far undervalued, and that a purely imaginary drama of migration of tribes was staged which has no basis in fact. Beyond any doubt, the foundations of civilization are far older than the period to which the oldest extant documents of the Egyptians, Sumerians, and Chinese, carry us back. The impression even prevails at present that they are still older than we are now inclined to assume on the ground of archæological facts and internal evidence. The acquisition of cultivated plants, their wide distribution over immense geographical areas in Asia and Europe, the introduction of agriculture, the domestication of animals, the mining and working of metals, the conception of the important technical inventions, in order to come into being, must have taken, even within the boundary of reasonable calculation, not centuries but millenniums of human labor and exertion, and are removed far beyond the bounds of all historical remembrance. As to the question of migrations, it is not tribes but the very ideas of culture which have constantly been on the path of migration, which were transmitted from people to people and fertilized and advanced the life of nations. In the earliest records of the Chinese we meet no tradition pointing to an immigration from abroad. All that the conservative historian may safely assert is, that they inaugurated their career in the fertile valley of the middle and lower course of the Yellow River and its affluents, and gradually expanded from this center of their early habitat eastward toward Chili and Shantung, and in a southerly direction toward the Yangtse. In their onward march they encountered a large stock of an aboriginal population of most varied tribes, partly related to them in language, with whom they struggled many centuries for the supremacy in China. The comparative study of Indo-Chinese languages has brought out the fact that the Chinese are a member of an extensive family of peoples, the best-known representatives of which are the Siamese, the Burmese, and the Tibetans. In early historical times all these peoples lived in close proximity to and relation with the Chinese, in the western and southwestern part of China. We are able to trace from their records and tradition the history of their migrations into the countries which they now occupy. The Tibetans designate themselves Bod (Sanskrit Bhota), and Ptolemy knows them by the name Bautai inhabiting the river Bautisos, identified with the Upper Yellow River. The present territory of Western Kansu and Szechuan was the cradle of the Tibetan branch which moved from there westward into the present territory of Tibet, probably during the first centuries of our era. The province of Yünnan is the home of the forefathers of the modern Siamese formerly known as Shan or Ai-lao (the modern Laos), who formed the highly organized kingdom of Nan-chao. Their state was destroyed by the Mongols in 1252, and the Mongol invasion gave the incentive to an emigration of the Shan from Yünnan down into the peninsula, where they founded the Kingdom of Siam in about 1350.

In the extreme southeast of Asia, scattered over the mountains and littorals of Indo-China, we meet another large group of peoples whose languages show no affinities with Chinese, and who form a distinct family. The most prominent members of this stock are the Annamese, the Khmer of Cambodja, the Mon of Pegu in the delta of the Irra-waddy, the Khasi, and the Colarians, whose remnants are dispersed over the hill tracts of Central India. In prehistoric times this group extended also into southern China; it is probably due to the expansion of the Chinese that they were subsequently driven back farther southward.

These ethnical movements render it clear that the present Chinese territory is in the main composed of two distinct culture-areas,—a northern one, decidedly Chinese; and a southern one, originally non-Chinese, but later colonized, absorbed by and assimilated to Chinese rule. Present-day China is a political not a national or ethnical unit. The antagonism that still prevails between the people of northern and southern China, and which nearly resulted in a partition of the country during the recent revolution, has come to the notice of everybody. It amounts not only to a question of racial differences, but to a far-reaching divergence of culture and economy as well. The farmer of the north grows wheat, barley, and various species of millet, and tills the ground with the ox as the draught-animal of his plow. The south is engaged in the cultivation of rice, and the peasant avails himself of the water-buffalo, an animal domesticated in southeastern Asia. His method of farming, corresponding to the subtropical flora characterized by palms, evergreen shrubs, fragrant woods, and tropical fruits, consists essentially in gardening, where that primitive system of hoe-culture still partially survives in which not the plow, but solely the hoe, is employed. The north is traversed by highways, and the two-wheeled cart drawn by mules is the usual means of conveyance; besides, the horse, the donkey, the camel, are in evidence as pack-animals and for riding. The south is densely intersected by rivers and a net of skillfully laid out canals connecting rivers and lakes, so that boats are the favorite method of journeying and transporting goods; on land, the sedan-chair carried on the shoulders of bearers is the means of transportation, whereas horses and mules are almost absent or scarce. The northerners are typical children of the soil, conservative, and somewhat heavy; the southerners, more alert and quick tempered, are sons of the watery element, river boatmen, bold seafarers, enterprising merchants, emigrants and colonists. The Chinese, of course, are by origin a purely continental race; and one of the most attractive chapters of their history is the one telling how they gradually extended from their inland seats toward the seacoast, how their naïve astonishment at the grandeur of the ocean produced a marine mythology and legends of distant lands and blessed isles, and how they learned and acquired the art of navigating from the seafaring nations along the shore of Indo-China. The north, in close contact with central and northern Asia, was constantly engaged in perpetual defensive wars against the restless hordes of Turkish and Tungusian nomads, and subject to influences coming from that direction. The horse, the donkey, the camel, the tactics of mounted archers and cavalry, felt and rug weaving, are due to this contact. The south was always deeply influenced by currents of thought pouring in from Malayan and Indian regions, and still visible in the laying-out of settlements, in domestic architecture, in every-day implements, and in certain industries and products.

The knowledge of the geographical distribution of such culture-elements as are here pointed out is naturally the basis for the understanding of their origin and historical development. For this reason let us now turn our attention to that northern culture-province which represents the original culture of the Chinese, and which was subsequently welded with the south into that unit which is now included under the name "China." The main question to be raised is, What relation did that culture hold to the other cultures of Asia? When we attempt to reconstruct by comparative and intense methods the oldest accessible primeval forms of the ancient civilizations of Asia, we are ultimately led to the result that in an undefinable pre-historic age a great universal and uniform culture-type must have existed in the northern or central hemisphere of the Old World, in strong contrast with the cultures of all primitive tribes which we encounter in the rest of Asia, in Africa, and in America. In the earliest stages of Sumero-Babylonian, Indo-Iranian, and Chinese cultures (leaving aside the manifold subsequent differentiations due to indigenous development) we are confronted with a number of traits which most strikingly coincide, and which cannot be attributed to a chance accident. Conspicuous among these is the economic system of the three peoples, which was founded in like manner on agriculture and cattle-breeding; that is to say, it was then already on the same basis as our modern system of economy. Their agricultural implements were highly developed, they tilled their fields by means of the plow drawn by an ox that was regarded as a sacred animal, and cultivated several cereals, chiefly wheat and barley. Methods of artificial irrigation were perfectly known, and elaborate agrarian laws were in force. Cattle were exclusively employed as draught-animals, particularly in connection with the plow, and were originally raised, not for their milk, but for their meat only. Carts and chariots built on the principle of the wheel are found alike in the three groups; while it is a notable fact that transportation by means of wheels is obviously absent among all primitive tribes of Asia, Africa (except ancient Egypt), in the South Sea, Australia, and America. It is remarkable also that the cart appears everywhere hand in hand with the plow, and consequently must be an invention made in the agricultural stage of civilization. The peoples of Babylonia, India, and China, in the same manner, employed chariots for making war, to which horses were harnessed. As the ox was domesticated in the interest of agriculture, the camel in the interest of commerce, so the horse was essentially an animal of war, and in its military capacity was employed as the draught-animal of war-chariots. Horseback-riding is a much later art conceived by the nomadic tribes of Scythia and inner Asia. Of other domestic animals, dog and swine were reared. As to the importance of swine, ancient China offers a striking analogy to the prehistoric cultures of central Europe, with which it has also millet and the water-chestnut in common. The offensive arm of that period

was the composite bow—a very complex affair, consisting principally
of flexible wood combined with horn, to which are bound layer upon
layer of pliable sinew—while most of the primitive tribes of Asia know
only the simple wooden bow. Of metals, only copper and bronze were
employed. In the manufacture of ceramics, the potter's wheel has been
utilized since early times in the East as well as in the West. Homer,
in a verse of the Iliad (XVIII, 600), compares the movements in the
round of a dance to the whirling motion of the disk turned by the potter's hand. The ancient Chinese philosophers likened the action of
Heaven in evolving the universe and its beings to a potter fashioning
the objects of clay by the revolution of his wheel; and Heaven, for his
creative power, is directly styled a molder or a potter's wheel. Again,
this contrivance is unknown wherever pottery is worked in the primitive
stages of culture. Furthermore, we find in ancient Babylonia and China
a highly-developed stage of knowledge of astronomy combined with an
intelligent chronological sense, time-reckoning, and a calendar system.

The time and locality in which this reconstructed primeval culture
common to Western Asia, India, and China, was developed, certainly
escape our knowledge, and I must forbear on this occasion discussing
this side of the problem. The point which should be emphasized is, that
the characteristic features, particularly the system of economy, are
fundamental principles and factors of civilization, and exactly those
which still form the fundament of our own modern life. We still depend
for our subsistence, in the same manner as the prehistoric culture-groups
of Asia did ages ago, upon the products of the soil, the cultivation of
cereals, the breeding of cattle; and in principle, our methods of
farming, despite all technical improvements, are still the same. We
may reform almost everything in our life; we may change our language,
our manners and customs, our political institutions, or our philosophy;
but we cannot change that one most stable and persistent factor of
our culture which we may briefly sum up in the words "cereals,"
"cattle," "plow," and "wheel." Whatever our modern progress in the
perfection of land transportation may be, whether we consider our
steam-engines or motor-cars, they all depend upon the basic principle
of the wheel—that wonderful invention of prehistoric days, of the
time, place, and author of which we are ignorant.

The main contribution, however, to the problem under consideration, is that ancient Chinese culture in its earliest stage cannot be the
product of an isolated seclusion, but has its due share and its root in the
same fundamental ideas as go to build up the general type of Asiatic-
European civilization. This opinion certainly does not imply that the
basis of primeval Chinese culture is merely derived from the West,

but only that it has a substratum of ideas to be met alike in the other great culture-groups of Asia from which we may reconstruct the common ancestral form of culture that must have once prevailed in most ancient times.

While, thus, the place of China is determined in the general history of civilization, there are, on the other hand, visible symptoms in existence which warrant the belief that as early as prehistoric times the Chinese must have undergone a development during several thousands of years entirely independent of any Western influence. And here we touch on one of the most interesting problems in the oldest history of Asia. Ancient Asia with its European annex is split into two large, sharply-defined economic camps, as regards the production and consumption of milk and other dairy products. The entire East-Asiatic world, inclusive of China, Korea, Japan, Indo-China, and all Malayans, does not take animal milk for food, and evinces a deep-rooted aversion toward it; and this was the state of affairs even in remotest times. On the other hand, all Indo-European peoples, the Semites, the ancient Scythians, and all nomadic tribes of northern and central Asia, as Turks, Mongols, and Tibetans, are all milk-drinkers, and were so in early historical times. The remarkable feature about this case certainly is not the bare fact that the East-Asiatics abstain from milk,—for the aboriginal tribes of America and Australia and others, simply for the lack of milk-producing animals, do exactly the same,—but the essential point is that the Chinese and their followers adhere to this practice, despite an abundance of milk-furnishing domestic animals in their possession, and despite long-enduring intercourse with neighboring milk-consuming peoples, whose habits and mode of life were very familiar to them. They rear cows, buffalo, mares, camels, sheep, goats, all animals from which milk could be derived, but they do not even understand how to milk them. They were at all times surrounded by Turkish and Mongol peoples, whose daily sustenance depends upon milk and kumiss, butter and cheese. This fact has been perfectly known to the Chinese, but, notwithstanding, they never acquired the habit. In India and Indo-China we face the same striking fact, in that the aboriginal inhabitants, though willing to submit to the higher civilization of the Aryan Hindu, never adopted from them the custom of milk-drinking. It follows, therefore, that our consumption of animal milk cannot be looked upon as a self-evident and spontaneous phenomenon, for which it has long been taken, but that it is a mere matter of educated force of habit. As natural as it appears to us, owing to time-honored practice and tradition, so just as unnatural, tedious, and barbarous does it strike the Chinese and other peoples of eastern Asia, who uphold that it is cruel to deprive the calf of its mother's milk. This ethical opinion, surely, does not give the true reason for their abstinence from milk, but is no more than a speculative after-thought. No less remarkable is it that no religious taboo is placed on milk in any of the Eastern religions, and that the aversion is not prompted by motives of any religious character; it is purely a matter of social and economic life. Thus we are led to distinguish in the history of the domestication of cattle two main and fundamental stages. In the primary stage, the milking faculty of the cow was unknown to man, and the ox was exclusively the sacred animal of agriculture, drawing the plow; and the invention of the plow and the cultivation of cereals are events closely affiliated with the taming of the ox. This is the very point which Chinese society has in common with the rest of Asia and Europe. At the close of this initial period, the western portion of the Old World subsequently advanced to a further stage of development, from which the Chinese were debarred,—the acquisition of dairy economy. This was an exceedingly complex, slow, and long process, moving along two lines—one in the producer, the animal, in which the productive power was gradually trained; the other in the consumer, man, who just as slowly acquired the habit of taking to milk. It should be understood that the obvious advantages which we derive from domesticated animals are not the reasons which prompted their domestication. These material advantages are but the effect and result of prolonged activity in matters of domestication, and could not have been anticipated by primitive man when he first conceived the idea of rearing and training animals. Wild fowl, e.g. when they are first being taken care of by man, do not propagate to a large extent, nor do they lay eggs in great numbers. The egg-laying habit of our chickens, to such an extent that it was of some advantage to man, was only attained in the course of the gradual process of domestication. Consequently other reasons than material considerations must have led to the first step in this direction. Likewise the productive power of our milk-animals is only the consequence and the ultimate result of long-continued domestication. This development, which must have been in operation for millenniums, ages before any recorded history, remained confined solely to the western part of Asia, while the East was never affected by this movement. This effect is still obvious in the division of labor brought about between cow and ox in the West, the ox performing duty as working-beast, the cow being the milk-animal. The same is reflected in language: all Semitic, Indo-European, and Ural-Altaic languages have separate words for "bull" and "cow," while the Chinese express the same notions with one word only.

There are other such negative criteria of peculiar character which conspire to prove a lengthy prehistoric period of Chinese independence. The ancient Chinese raised sheep and goats, but never utilized the wool of these animals for the making of material for clothing, as was done in the West. The employment of wool for felt and rugs is an idea of nomadic peoples of inner Asia, and was taught by them to the Chinese in historical times. The latter always used for their garments vegetable fibers obtained from various kinds of hemp, and silk, which most clearly stands out as a preëminently brilliant example of their power of nature-observation and of their technical genius. The art of baking leavened bread, which was first applied by the Egyptians and adopted by the Greeks and Romans, has always remained unknown in China, where no leavening or fermenting agent is employed for bread-making.

Speaking of mental achievements, we observe that the Chinese, like all other peoples of eastern Asia, have never produced any epic poetry. Epic poems are met with among all Indo-European nations, among the Finno-Ugrians, the Turkish, Tibetan, Mongol, and Tungusian tribes; and it is a peculiar coincidence that all these peoples of epic songs are also milk-consumers, while those abstaining from milk are deficient in epic poems. I do not mean to say that there is an interrelation between milk and epics, but merely wish to point out the fact of this curious coincidence.

Thus the conviction is gaining ground, on the one hand, that Chinese culture, in its material and economic foundation, has a common root with our own; and, on the other hand, that it independently marched along its own way and evolved its own ideas for numberless ages, until at the time when the nation emerged from prehistoric life it had grown to full maturity. The keynote of its rapid progress in historical times is chiefly signaled by the sound development of all social and civic virtues, finally culminating in the political and ethical system expounded by the sage Confucius. The sane family organization based on the religious institution of ancestral worship, the high conception of the sacredness and purity of family life, filial devotion, and the subjection of the individual to the ideal of the family and the state, must be regarded as the principal manifestations accounting for the racial and national continuity of the Chinese, that indestructible vital power and tenacity of their culture and institutions. No nation has ever presented a more sensible and effectual solution of the problem of the sexes than China by her commonsense marriage-laws, which enjoin marriage on every one as a moral obligation due to the ancestors. Despite its religious function, it has always been strictly a matter of civil law, and was never usurped by a Church or bound to ecclesiastic sanctions, as has so long been the case among ourselves. Early marriages were always made possible in consequence of a just economic system, with an almost equal distribution of landed property among single owners, in which a large, probably the largest, portion of the population, enjoys a share; while great real-estate owners are few, resulting in a leveling process of economic and social equality. Husbandry was at all times upheld as the bone and sinew of society, and encouraged and promoted by Government. In the social division the farmer ranks next to the scholar or official, and precedes the laborer and merchant. Wholesome principles in matters of nutrition, frugality, and temperance—in general, a good share in the knowledge of that greatest of all arts, the art of living—have contributed to the stability and persistency of Chinese society. An extraordinary capability for passive resistance, and an unlimited power of absorption, are prominent characteristics of this civilization, whose vitality has been tested many times. Military defeats and even widespread conquests have never been able to make a deep impression on this people. By dint of intellectual force and superior diplomatic tactics they have usually overcome the most serious conditions. The Huns could overrun Europe; but the very same Huns, knocking at the gates of China for many centuries, were unable to bring about her downfall. The Mongols trampled the Occident under the feet of their horses; but under their sway in China they became converted into Chinese, and made art, literature, and commerce flourish. In the same manner they absorbed the Khitan, the Manchu, and others of their foreign rulers.

We are all familiar with the fact that we are indebted to the inventive genius of the Chinese for the mariner's compass, gunpowder, fireworks, rag-paper, wall-paper, paper money, silk, porcelain, the goldfish, tea and many other valuable cultivated plants. All these things, being exceedingly useful and practical, come within the daily reach and experience of every one. They have also enriched the field of our popular games and entertainments by the addition of kite-flying, shuttlecock, playing-cards, dominoes, checkers, and that jolly theatrical performance the shadow-play. But all these advantages sink into insignificance when we come to consider the intellectual gain which has accrued to us from the wonderful development of the mental and moral forces alive in the Chinese nation. They follow suit with us in their eminently chronological and historical sense, one of their most striking and admirable intellectual traits. Next to the Greeks, they are that nation which has furnished the most solid and extensive contributions to our scientific knowledge. While ancient India revels in mythology but gives us no clew to her history, the Chinese have recorded for us with minute accuracy and painstaking conscientiousness, and above all with objective impartiality, every event in their internal history and in their relations with foreign peoples. The continuity of their traditions laid down in their twenty-four national Annals may be styled, more justly than many other things, one of the great wonders of the world, and this stupendous work is the most permanent monument that they have built to themselves. They are born philologists and students, and there is no domain of human thought which their fertile literature has not efficiently cultivated. . . .

55. THE RÔLE OF THE INDIVIDUAL IN SAMOAN CULTURE [14]

BY MARGARET MEAD

IN THE evaluation of the rôle of the individual in culture, it is fair to assume that the importance of the individual as innovator and stylist will be in great measure a function of the particular culture into which he is born. And it is of interest to investigate in what types of culture individual talent is given the freest play. The following study is based upon field-work in the Manu'a Archipelago of the Samoan Islands. The Manu'an culture presents such a striking picture of flexibility, rapid slight changes, easy acceptance of innovation and deviation, that it would seem to give each gifted individual a particularly open field for the exercise of his peculiar talents. This flexibility is probably the exception rather than the rule in primitive cultures, and therefore presents a good test case of the relation between flexibility of culture and individual initiative.

I shall first discuss the attitudes in Samoan society (Samoan being understood to refer to Manu'a specifically) which are relevant to the problem of individual initiative: the logical limitation implicit in the culture, attitudes favorable to individuality, and attitudes unfavorable to it. After which I shall examine briefly the personal life of the Samoans and the opportunities open to the individual in the fields of industry, art, religion and social organization. It must, however, be borne in mind throughout this discussion that social organization is the principal preoccupation in Samoa; industry, art and religion all are dwarfed beside it.

[14] From an article of the same title in *Journal of the Royal Anthropological Institute*, Volume 58, pages 481-495, 1928. Reprinted entire, with minor revisions by the author.

The Samoans regard the social structure, a hierarchy of titles carrying with them specific privileges, as of paramount importance. The individual has neither rank nor sanctity in his own right, nor by virtue of the blood which flows in his veins. It is only as the holder of a title the accession to which has been validated by large distributions of property, that he is honored and obeyed. Coincident with this attitude is a disregard of the rules of primogeniture and of direct descent—not to the extent of ignoring them entirely, but sufficiently to set them aside in favor of special ability in heirs-aspirant with a weaker blood claim upon a family title. Each large family can hold several titles of varying importance. As a result there is no chiefly class as opposed to a class of commoners. In a family of four brothers one may hold a high chief's title, the second an ordinary chief's title, the third a talking chief's title, and the fourth be a *taule'ale'a*, without the right to sit in the council of the titled, but condemned to associate with the "young men." Yet, in the next generation, the son of the *taule'ale'a* may perhaps hold the high chiefly title if he has shown the greatest promise among the children of the four brothers. Selection for a title is based on two major considerations—personal qualifications of strength, charm, leadership, integrity; and the possession of special abilities: skill as a carpenter, orator, or fisherman.

The possession of special gifts exacts recognition from the society in two ways; a gifted man is more likely to receive a good title early in life; and, also, a man of skill accumulates wealth through which he can advance his prestige by large distributions of property. The social structure further recognizes the master craftsman by according him all the prerogatives of chiefly rank, special terms of address, precedence in the *kava* ceremony, and position in the house, on the occasions when his craftsmanship is concerned. So the chief carpenter is the guest of honor at a house-warming ceremony or the launching of a canoe.

Where there is no system of usury, the initial possession of wealth does not give any one a disproportionate start. The *Gross-familie* system makes it easy for a young man to borrow a fishing canoe or collect a bride price. The land is only partly under cultivation and it is always possible to clear new land. Wealth consists of houses, canoes, food, bark cloth, and mats. Because the mats and cloth are made only by women, and the canoes and houses only by men, a household is more likely to be crippled by the lack of one *kind* of property, owing to a disproportion of the sexes, than by actual poverty. Cleared land goes back to a natural state in a very few years. The best houses, constantly repaired and reënforced, last only nine or ten years. The supply of pigs and chickens can be greatly increased in the course of three or four years. Breadfruit trees and coco-nut palms are slower to reach maturity, and are therefore the most valuable property; but here again the system of obligatory mutual aid within a large relationship group makes it possible to translate industry in fishing into breadfruit beams for a new house with very little delay.

The crafts are neither exclusive organizations nor controlled by heredity. The boy who desires to learn a trade attaches himself to a master craftsman until he has acquired sufficient proficiency to complete a piece of work himself.

So that neither birth, nor wealth, nor inherited craft privilege are sufficiently determining factors to seriously weight the scales as against the possession of natural ability.

Age is a serious handicap to the politically ambitious, for the political affairs of the village are in the hands of the titled men—the *matais*, to which body a man is seldom admitted until he is twenty-nine or thirty years old. But the very postponement of a genuine political majority increases the zest of the struggle to master the intricacies of the social organization, and some special wealth-producing prestige-meriting skill.

The fact of being a woman presents more serious obstacles to the free play of individuality. The property owning system is such that, with a few outstanding exceptions, property can only be held by heads of families—*matais*. At the present time there is only one woman *matai* in the Samoan Islands. They seem to have been as rare as European queens and must be regarded as non-typical in every respect. The girls belonging to families of high rank who are given the title of *taupo* receive a great amount of social adulation and ceremonious recognition, but in return more services are demanded from them, and they can neither own property nor openly participate in political affairs. The public rôle of a woman is entirely confined to the private manipulation of the men-folk within her sphere of influence. That sphere is often very wide, as a woman is able to use her manual skill as well as her knowledge of intrigue in obtaining recognition within the household. The man owes his position in the village organization to the possession of a title, originally conferred upon him by his family; but the duties incident upon holding the title are so onerous that an old man is usually forced to resign it in favor of a younger one. His prestige within the household diminishes enormously, while that of the woman, subject to no such spectacular rise and fall of social position, suffers no such eclipse; and it is as an old woman, relieved of child-bearing and child-tending, famous for her skill as mat-maker or midwife, that a woman finds the freest vent for her individuality.

Physical defect has few far-reaching consequences. Blindness or deafness disqualify an individual for occupations in which the particular lost sense is specifically needed. The society is more likely to give absolution to the disabled in perfectly irrelevant matters than to penalize them unfairly.

There is no rigid series of tests or ordeals which may serve unfairly to eliminate those who, while possessing special abilities, nevertheless lack particular character or mental traits necessary to carry them through preliminary encounters with set tasks. There is scant premium set upon fortitude and endurance. Neither fasting, self-torture, or significant self-denials are enjoined upon young or old. Entrance into the *Aumaga,* the organization of young men, is the social stamp of young manhood; the entrance requirement is a gift from the father or *matai* of the initiate to the group; the initiation ceremony is a feast. Within the *Aumaga,* a tattooed and an untattooed group are distinguished, so that tattooing may be postponed several years beyond puberty. The tattooing itself may be prolonged over several months, and any number of groans are permitted.

No other sharp trials confront the youth. He is left to work out his own salvation slowly, without undue pressure. His choice of a profession is in his own hands, and professionally he is subjected to no atmosphere of harsh and unfriendly criticism. When he has studied carpentry long enough so that he feels capable of building a house himself, some relative will give him his first commission. If he completes the house satisfactorily, he receives the final payments in the stately ceremony of the *Umu Sa* (the Sacred Oven); the chief carpenters of the village all partake of the feast, at which the successful novice is given highest honor. He is then recognized as a *tufuga fau falé* (a master house builder). If, on the other hand, the novice has overestimated his skill and bungled his job, the others will go to his assistance, but neither in triumph nor rebuke, and help him to finish his too ambitious task. His defeat will be glossed over, revamped into a step in his education, and not viewed as a signal and crushing defeat.

Bravery in warfare was never a very important matter in Manu'a. War was a matter of village spite, or small revenge, in which only one or two individuals would be killed. The most dangerous posts were allotted not to those who had watched their arms or seen a vision, but to the young men living in a special division of the village. Where the war-making and war-leading powers were vested in men holding special titles and the service as scouts was residentially determined, any selection on the basis of prowess was of little importance.

No religious experience was demanded of any individual, neither skill in communicating with spirits, nor, in fact, any important communication with them whatsoever. A careful observance of the taboos surrounding special places; the village god—where there was one—and one's family god; a libation poured to the family god at the evening *kava* ceremony, completed one's religious duties.

In only one respect does the society impose an ironclad choice—the acceptance of a title. A man who through self-distrust, laziness, or fear of responsibility refuses a *matai* title is for ever marked as a social backslider; he can never be awarded any other title, and remains a titular "young man" until his death. But only here, where the very base of the social order is rejected, can an act, one moment's failure, damn an individual for life. In all other respects most of a man's life is regarded as a painless, casual sort of novitiate, offering repeated small occasions for making a mark. The reward is a very brief period in which the fruits of these not too strenuous efforts are enjoyed, before old age and decreptitude relegate him again to a cup of *kava* by courtesy and a seat in the back of the house.

In contrast to this flexible scheme there are other attitudes definitely hostile to the development of individuality or the exercise of peculiar talents. Complementary to the *laissez-faire* attitude toward slow development, toward the awkward gangling boy who gradually finds his tongue and at thirty-five learns to speak in council, is a feeling of rigid intolerance toward precocity, youthful innovators, or short cuts to prestige. All of these crimes were summed up in the expression *"tautala lai titi"* (talking above one's age, or, less importantly, one's status). No stigma, not even the reputation of tale-bearer or thief, can so thoroughly wreck a boy's whole career as receiving this brand. Such an attitude, never relaxed except on the dance floor, serves to discredit the gifted and discourage the prematurely ambitious, and so becomes an even greater leveling force than the social tolerance of tardiness. Where the precocious are execrated and the slow plodders treated gently and rewarded according to their ultimate achievements, titles and positions of equal importance may be held by middle-aged men of very different natural gifts.

This attitude toward youth is aggravated rather than relieved in the case of children of men holding high rank. There is rigid chaperonage of the girls, severe and exacting tutelage of the boys. Because there is so little permanent wealth, and a chief's expenditures are heavier than those of men of lesser rank, the young people of a chief's household work harder and have less freedom and less chance for self-expression than the children of households of fewer pretensions.

Furthermore, the very democratic nature of the competition for titles has a deterrent effect upon the attempt to attain virtuosity. A man's accession to a title means endless responsibility for ten or fifteen individuals in the household under his charge—responsibility to the village council for their care, guidance, and peaceful behavior; responsibilities in the affairs of the village. Holding a title also carries with it a status fenced about with prohibitions. A *matai* may not associate with the young men, play games with them, or take light-hearted part in any youthful frolic. Whatever his age, status, not age, determines his behavior, with the result that many gifted boys, unwilling to accept these responsibilities, hide their lights under bushels; and lights so hidden for years are likely to go out for ever.

But offsetting these deterrent social attitudes are others—most importantly the eager acceptance of the new, and a premium upon the incomprehensible, the esoteric and the elusive. On the dance floor and in the minor industrial arts even very young people are permitted to initiate, and in adult life individual variations of the pattern are accepted with hospitable acclamation. Because all social ceremonials are combinations of a number of relatively independent elements, each one of which is regarded as a unit subject to manipulation and variation, the innovator can give immediate and free play to his desire to make himself felt by introducing some slight change. The native delight in a proverb which no one understands, a change of phrasing, a hint of some knowledge of esoteric lore, results in an atmosphere more favorable to individual variations than the sort of society in which everything is conceived of as having been done in one particular way from time immemorial, and the knowledge of the tradition-sanctified procedure is shared by the entire group.

PERSONAL LIFE

The young child is allowed many startling privileges. The developing individual is conceived of as gradually growing in a quality designated as *māfaufau*—a word best rendered as "an ability to exercise good judgment in personal and social matters." Character deficiencies are explained by a lack of this quality; any particular breach of group standards carries with it the accusation *"Lē ai se māfaufau"*—"lack of judgment." Although regarded rather as a unit quality, there is also the suggestion that judgment on particular points may develop at different ages. The natives look upon the development of this quality as a pure matter of growth; they meddle with it neither by magic nor profane formulas.

The enforcement of the most severe and important sex taboo in the society—the brother and sister taboo—is left in the hands of the younger of the siblings. When the younger child has sufficient *judgment* to feel ashamed at any contact—then the taboo comes into play. The older child is expected to make no move, but to wait upon the younger's maturing judgment.

The selection of a residence is also very much in the children's hands. Any child over five or six is an economic asset; little truants are welcomed by any relative, and a ten-year-old may change his or her residence two or three times before settling down. This freedom of choice actually serves as a powerful deterrent of specific adult tyrannies, and the child is often content to remain in one household, serene in the reflection that he can always run away if he wishes.

The selection of tutors is also left to the young people themselves, with the exception of children of high chiefs. These latter must be taught by the talking chiefs and their wives, the education of the chief's children being one carefully defined item in the complicated reciprocal relationship existing between a high chief and his talking chiefs. Social pressure is exerted in indefinite terms—"It is time Tuli learned to weave blinds"; "It is time Lele began a fine mat"; "It is time Palo should be able to go bonito fishing"—and the choice of a teacher who will teach Tuli to weave blinds, Lele to begin her fine mat and Palo to fish, is left to Tuli, Lele and Palo individually. Very often a child's own father and mother are the teachers, especially in the simpler tasks, but as often the *matai* and his wife, as persons of more prestige and skill, are chosen; and the boy in search of a special technique, like carving, netting or lashing, will range far afield to the very edges of his wide relationship-group, and occasionally even beyond it.

Boys are circumcised at puberty; and here again they make their own choice of physician and occasion, two boys usually repairing together to an older man skilled in the operation.

The same freedom is permitted in the matter of personal names. As a name is regarded as a tangible entity, it cannot be both retained and given away. So constant name-changes occur through an older girl or boy "giving away a name" to a younger child and assuming a new one; the younger child in turn "throws away" the old name. In this way there is among the youth of the community a non-significant aping of the important adult mechanism of changing from one title to another. The choice is left almost entirely in the children's hands.

Also, for all the young people, except the daughters of houses of rank, there is comparative freedom of choice of partners in sex-experience. This does not apply to marriage, but it does result in a gradual development of the emotional life free from any warping compulsory factor. The idea of forceful rape or of any sexual act to which both participants do not give themselves freely is completely foreign to the Samoan mind. This applies also to freedom of divorce; marriage is a socio-economic matter, but divorce is not. Either party to a marriage may leave it at any time and return to his or her home. Such freedom is possible because women always retain a claim on their parents' property, which needs only to be validated by actual participation in the labor of the household and on the plantation.

Members of chiefly families are deprived of a great deal of this freedom. The chief's child is named more formally, is educated and circumcised by the talking chiefs, and, in the case of a girl, denied premarital sex-experience. Similarly, adultery with the chief's wife is a crime punishable with death. The marriage of women of rank is a source of profit to the talking chiefs; so is the remarriage of chiefs, on whom pressure is often exerted to divorce one wife that his councilors may fatten upon the dowry of a new one. Less definite, but very important in the development of individuality, are the thousand minute rules of etiquette which hedge about those of high rank, from the plight of the *taupo* who is strictly forbidden to scratch mosquito bites in public, to the chief who may not climb his own coco-nut tree if any one of lesser rank is present to climb it instead.

Fatal to the prosecution of private plans is the lack of power over one's own time. Only the *matais*, subject to the demands of the village council, can make their own times and occasions; every one else must suffer continual interruptions without irritation. The young child is subject to every single older relative in the village. This ascendancy of age continues throughout life, cut across by accession to a title for a fortunate man, while the young and unfortunate must accede to the demands of the titled as well as those of their elders. Village matters take precedence over household, household over individual, the affairs of the older over the affairs of the younger—and all this constitutes a network of exactions through which the young can seldom count upon escaping for more than an hour at a time.

With the exception of the *matai*, no individual has any privacy or control of personal property. Ten to twelve persons eat and sleep in a one-room house. The *matai* alone can exclude others from his house, and even require some one to wake and keep intruders away while he sleeps. Every word, every act, is the property of an interested inquisitive public. Similarly, a ring, a dance skirt, a fishing-rod might be the handwork or the nominal property of an individual, but it is liable to seizure by the *matai*, or, as an obligatory loan to a relative, or simple confiscation by an elder at any time.

In the selection of his rôle in the social structure the individual is allowed very little positive choice. Marriage is an economic matter ratified by an exchange of property between the two contracting families. The wealthier and more important the family, the less chance the young people have of selecting their mates. No act of theirs, not an elopement resulting in children, could legalize a union from which the customary exchange of property had been omitted. Similarly, a man may refuse a title, but he can never select one and take it for himself. He may aspire to a title, labor zealously to attain the necessary skill, knowledge, and wealth; the choice still lies with some one else. The individual is still a pawn on the social chess-board.

ARTS AND INDUSTRIES

There is a virtual absence of formal industrial procedure as far as the artist himself is concerned. He does not need to prepare for his task by a long series of ritual acts, treat his materials with religious deference, nor consecrate the finished object. Work is primarily secular in character. Only when it involves several individuals, a contracting chief and a craftsman of standing, is social ceremonial between the participants introduced. Education in industrial matters is definitely a question of imparting actual techniques. The relationship between pupil and teacher is secular, casual and uninstitutionalized. There are no charms, no secret formulas, to be imparted, except in the case of medical formulæ. Material is regarded unreverentially and as subject to repeated experimentation and manipulation.

There is no symbolic art. Certain kinds of tapa patterns are most esteemed and put on the best tapa, which is worn by those of highest rank. But this implies merely a demand for the best for the highest; rank only plays an indirect rôle. There is no absolute number of tattooing stripes, or house beams or platform terraces permitted to men of different rank. But if several boys are tattooed together, and the chief's son has five bands of tattooing, the sons of the talking chiefs may not have more than four. If the highest chief in the village has only three terraces around his house no other chief may have more than two, but if he has seven the next ranking chiefs may have as many as six. But rank sets no premium upon special designs or special styles of decoration, and so provides no stimulus to development along particular lines. A premium set upon size, breadth, length and thickness, while developing routine craftsmanship of a high order, has much less influence upon individual initiative than would have come from setting a price upon new and original forms of decoration or actual variations in style.

While a Maori chief was distinguished by the possession of a carved house, a Samoan chief boasts principally of the possession of the house with the greatest number of cross-beams (this makes it automatically the highest) and the greatest number of pebbled terraces in the village.

In the details of a craft innovations were welcomed. There is no set style from which it is inadmissible to deviate, no stringent taboo against change. On the contrary, there is a strong feeling against making any two things alike, which extends even to a prejudice against making two sides of the same house or both ends of the same piece of tapa cloth exactly alike. The deadening effect of the use of pattern-boards in stamping tapa is continuously and consciously evaded by the introduction of asymmetrical variations in the subsequent free-hand emphasis given to parts of the design. There is a genuine feeling for individual choices in decoration and a vivid distaste for slavish imitation. The innovation tends to become completely identified with the originator, and so the more striking the departure from established usage the more conspicuous becomes any attempt to copy it, and the more likelihood is there of the new pattern's perishing with its author. I once particularly admired a fan in which the usual form was varied with conspicuous success. I tried to persuade some of the women on Taū to make fans like it, but without success: "A woman on Olosega makes that kind."—"But why don't you make them too?"—"Because a woman on Olosega makes them. I make my own kind of fan." Surrounded by the easy social expectancy of at least some slight rearrangement of the old designs, deprived of the flattery of imitators and any social or economic premium upon stylistic variation, the artisans take but little significant advantage of the unusual freedom allowed them. Their audiences are easily satisfied—a new combination of dance-steps; the transfer of a weaving pattern used on baskets to a food platter; a leaf design reversed —these are sufficient innovations.

In the larger industrial undertakings, such as house and canoe building, the question of departures becomes a socio-economic matter. An additional house post means an additional feast and consequently additional expenditure. Where variations have such far-reaching consequences, the whole craft-group retains a firm control, and unlicensed changes are punished by the village council; the deviating carpenter is deprived of the right to practice his trade.

The practice of medicine presents a somewhat striking contrast to the other arts. Although there are no charms or incantations, the formulas are secret and handed down from an old woman to her daughter or niece. Each formula is regarded as a personal possession: "Lale has a good medicine for the stomach"; "Tofi has a good medicine for the toothache." Sometimes six practitioners have six different medicines for the same ailment; they are regarded as probable equivalents, just as today native remedies and white men's remedies are often resorted to indiscriminately. This secrecy, this easy acceptance of the possibilities inherent in half a dozen remedies, militate against the accumulation of any general store of medicinal knowledge. The individual practitioner has the formula she learned from her elders, a knowledge of a few general medicinal herbs with cathartic qualities, and a free field for unchecked, dangerous and profitless experimentation.

In striking contrast is the practice of surgery, which is a public affair—a matter of skill, a technique to be learned; and so efficient have the natives become that mis-set bones come under the care of the American doctors with surprising infrequency.

RELIGION

Institutionalized religion and personal psychic experience were both exceedingly undeveloped in aboriginal Manu'a. Through the existence of the taboo system much of the social ceremonial took on a quasi-religious character, but innovations here really belong in the field of social organization. When the solemn *kava* ceremonies, in which the *kava* is poured to the gods in a prayer to avert misfortune, and other social functions of the same sort are subtracted from the sum total of religious activity very little remains.

In his relationship to the family god and the spirits of the dead a very free rein was given the individual. The origin of village gods or local gods worshiped by a number of families seems to have been in an extension of the worship of the god of some gifted individual who combined psychic powers with a general worldly success which testified to his possessing much *mana*. Sometimes he assumed the position of a priest or oracle and was richly rewarded by offerings. This prestige he might perhaps transmit to a son, but there it seemed to lapse, resulting in a shifting pantheon and no genuine priestly institution. There were no priestly families.

Aside from this enhancement of his own inherited god's prestige, an individual who possessed special psychic gifts might gain considerable prestige and wealth from their exercise. His services would seem to have consisted in exorcism of evil spirits and ascertaining the cause of disasters. These special gifts range the whole gamut—from the ability to go into a trance, to the medicine-makers who talked to the ghosts as they gathered their herbs, and when the herbs could not be found knew that the patient would never get well. But there was no point in the social life at which the services of such people were absolutely necessary—a priestless *kava*-drinking ceremony would always do just as well. The unstable were rare; they were regarded as gifted, not skilled, and there was no tradition of apprenticeship.

SOCIAL ORGANIZATION

But art and religion and the basic economic operations themselves are all mere background and by-play compared with the social organization. A man holds his title first; his skill, his character and his god are less important. And this very overpowering importance of the social structure, coupled with the fact that the individual and the title never became completely molded into one unit, makes for flexibility and change.

The titles are arranged in an ideal structure, based on the seating positions to which they entitle their holders in a great ideal council (*fono*) of all the Samoan Islands. This ideal structure is repeated on a smaller scale for each island, island division and village. In each local replica of the great plan, fewer of the great titles appear and titles of smaller and smaller rank are inserted. On the island of Taū there are three village *fonos*—one for Fitiuta, one for Faleasao and one for Taū; a second scheme includes Taū and Faleasao, necessitating the omission of some of the lesser *matais* from the seating arrangement; and a third includes all three villages, in the *Fale Ula*, the great council of the Tui Manu'a.

These titles belong to two main classes—chiefs (*alii*) and talking chiefs (*tulafale*). Within these two groups there are endless shades of rank and precedence, but the two main classes remain distinct; their relationship to each other is an elaborate system of reciprocal services. It is the duty of the talking chiefs to maintain the honor, prestige and public high estate of the chiefs; to act as their ambassadors, spokesmen, grand viziers, bankers and campaign managers. In their hands lie all the traditions, the regulation of etiquette and inter-village social intercourse, the ordering of all important social events such as the marriage or death of a chief of high rank, his princess (*taupo*) or his heir-apparent (*manaia*). For the talking chief of highest rank, called in Manu'a "*to'oto'o*" and "*suāfanu'u*," these functions are conceived more as services to the whole village, organized as it is around one or more high chiefs, than as personal services. Talking chiefs of lower rank perform definite services, such as preparing the chief's food, or representing him for several months before his marriage in the family of his betrothed. The talking chief must also provide the chief with food upon all important occasions.

In return for these services, they receive fine mats and tapa, payments ranging from the great distribution of the bride's dowry among the talking chiefs of the high-chief bridegroom to the gift of a length of tapa to each talking chief who has danced beside the *taupo*. And, more importantly, they possess great power. Theoretically the chief is a noble figure-head, of too high rank to make his own speeches in council or propose for his own wife. And the talking chief who obsequiously sings his praises also makes most of his decisions for him.

A *matai* title is conferred upon a man by his family group, and carries with it a place in the social structure. Theoretically this place is fixed and invariable; actually, if the holder of the title is poor and unpopular, the position of the title may be radically altered by the powerful and disaffected talking chiefs who wish to exalt some other and wealthier individual instead. Such changes necessitate the manipulation of old myths, or the outright invention of new ones, to validate the claim of the *nouveau riche*; changes in the *Fa'alupega* (the courtesy salutation formally recited by visitors); changes in the geography of the village and even in the dating system. It is customary to refer to events of the past hundred years as happening during the time that such and such a high chief held his title. When a high chief is quietly, insidiously relegated to an inferior position, the conversational habits of the village historians must be revised so that their references are not to his forebears but to the undistinguished forebears of his successful rival. I have one case where this happened in the course of twenty-five years. It is possible to check these local changes by the talking chiefs of distant villages, who visited the now metamorphosed village some twenty years ago and had studied the then existing social organization carefully for the occasion.

Such conditions were made possible by several different factors. The social organization was known in detail to only some twelve or fifteen old men in a village; the more incomprehensible they make it to the rest of the population the greater their prestige. The relationship-group controls the title, and the talking chiefs have, with one exception (the Tui manu'a), nothing to say about the choice of an incumbent. Not being able to choose the individual, they, instead, manipulate his formal status, greatly increasing the strange disassociation between the individual and the position which he holds.

Furthermore, there are other premiums set upon innovation and originality of social form, quite aside from the desire of the talking chiefs to exercise their power or increase their wealth and the way in which the ambitious *nouveau riche* exploits these desires. Every village seeks to have a different social structure from the neighboring village, and there is no standard of better or worse. The stress is all laid upon difference. If one village derives its prestige from having seventeen chiefs of such high rank that each one has to be mentioned in the introduction to every formal speech, the next village retaliates by exalting one chief so high that no one else's name can be mentioned with his. If one village has four *to'oto'os* the next village is unique; it has only one *to'oto'o*. If Fitiuta has the most systematic *fono,* in which each pillar seat is named not only after one *matai* but after others who are entitled to sit in his place during his absence, Ofu can boast of having three entirely different ways in which the *fono* can be arranged. Similarly with the courtesy language, a common word on one island may become the highest chief's word upon another; and the courtesy language also gives wonderful opportunities for the invention of new esoteric phrases known only to the locality and designed to puzzle visiting orators. A talking chief's prestige depends upon his knowledge of the minute details of the social organization not only of his own districts, but of other districts, for upon this knowledge, more even than upon rhetorical skill, depends the choice of orator for great occasions. And a village is proud of the reputation of being *faigata* (difficult) for the visiting orator.

Because of the extreme variety of social ceremonials, composed as they are of the same elements in endless recombinations, the Samoans really see them as combinations, not as fixed sequences. An intelligent talking chief never has to begin at the beginning and go through a ceremony in order to arrive at some detail. It is possible to ask directly, "How many *kava* bowls are used at the marriage of Tui Manu'a?" "What kind of girdles do the *Suafanū's* wear in the funeral ceremony?" and get an immediate answer. (Needless to say, the actual procedure varies enormously from occasion to occasion.) This is also due to the fact that the highest pitch of etiquette is reached not by observing the fixed procedure, but by pointedly reversing or rearranging it. One of the principal reasons for knowing who *should* receive the *kava* cup first is so that one may honor another by giving it to him instead. In this dexterous, graceful play with social forms the Samoans find their chief artistic expression. In the more serious manipulation of the social structure, for purposes of economic gain or political ambition, lies the most powerful dynamic force in Samoan society.

CONCLUSIONS

Only by placing Samoa against the Polynesian background is it possible to arrive at a basis of comparison and say, for instance, that the art of Samoa is relatively undeveloped or that the religion plays a minor rôle. Thus, in religious development, Hawaii, Tahiti, New Zealand, and the Marquesas all out-distance Samoa in richness and variety of religious forms and beliefs and in the relative importance of religion in the lives of the people. Samoan tattooing is of negligible artistic intent beside that of New Zealand and the Marquesas, as is Samoan wood-work. In tapa-making the Samoans never approach the beauty of Hawaiian tapas. It is for its intricacy and complexity of social organization that Samoan culture is particularly conspicuous.

When the comparison is made, not with other cultures of Polynesia but within the Samoan archipelago, the same result is reached—social organization occupies most of the thought and interest of the community; all other activities are at least partly subordinated to it and made to minister to its ends.

With this preponderance of the social interest in mind, it is possible to ask: How important is the influence of the individual upon the different parts of this flexible culture which is hospitable to innovation, omnivorous of variation?

In the field of personal relationships the freedom of choice allowed the individual is prevented from having more important results by the low level of appreciation of personality differences. Choice is possible among homes, among teachers, among lovers; but the consciousness of personality, the attitudes necessary to make such choices significant, are lacking. So that the freedom in personal choices operates mainly in reducing the poignancy of personal relations, the elements of conflict, the need for making painful choices. The emotional tone of the society is consequently more moderate, and less charged with strain and violence. It never exerts sufficient repression to call forth a significant rebellion from the individual. The suicides of humiliation so common in parts of Polynesia do not exist in Samoa. The individual need commit no murder, need not even muster up a fine rage to escape from a disagreeable situation—he simply slips out of it into the house next door. Such a setting does not produce violent, strikingly marked personalities; it is kind to all and does not make sufficient demands upon any.

In the decorative arts, the freedom given to the individual is rendered nugatory by the absence of cultural recognition of the innovator and by the strong prejudice against active imitation; so the gifted individual receives but passing praise for his work. The variations are taken for granted; they do not become distinguishing marks of high rank, nor do they enhance greatly the economic value of the object. And his ingeniousness is seldom directly perpetuated in the work of those who come after him. Tattooing and tapa designs retain the same fluid, slightly differentiated style, containing endless, non-significant variations, imitation of no one of which permits a real trend in a new direction to develop.

In religion the premium set by society was also very low, giving slight economic gains and only small increase in social prestige; and the man who had been a medium or local priest in his day was still remembered more for the place which he had held in the social structure. The most famous "priest" in Samoan history is probably O le Tamafaiga of Manono, who usurped the great secular title of the family of Muagututi'a. So in religion the same nondescript variation occurs—one village with two gods, another with none, a pile of stones where the god of some family had once been worshiped by the whole neighborhood. The society contained no mechanism by which an individual religious genius could permanently institutionalize his inspiration. In a generation they were back again to the casual service of their family gods, and the occasional formal recognition of the high gods in the course of social ceremonial.

In the social organization the individual is given the freest hand and meets with the greatest rewards. So flexible is the social structure, so minutely adapted to manipulation, that it is possible to change the appearance of the *fono* in twenty years. But this very sensitivity to slight change proves in the end to be a conservative factor. The social innovator runs against no hard-and-fast wall of caste, no religiously sanctioned ritual, no jealously guarded body of tradition. Would he make a change—a few fine mats, a little judicial diplomacy—the social landscape is completely altered. His ambition, his itch toward manipulation, and his desire for revenge meet with too slender opposition. The social structure offers too slight a challenge; it is too complacent to the innovating hand. And so the recent history of Samoa contains few records of important changes introduced by individuals. The daring coups of the Hawaiian kings and the lonely, dangerous rôles of Maori outlaws are absent from Samoan chronicles. And the ever-yielding, ever-accommodating social structure has remained much the same, generation after generation, while the talking chiefs with original minds and social ambitions slid, sated with too easy victories, into undistinguished grooves.

Without seeking to generalize beyond the limits of the material, it is possible to summarize: In Manu'a the individual plays the most significant rôle in the most complex and important aspect of his culture, the social organization. The whole flexibility of Samoan culture, which at first blush looks so favorable to the display of individuality, so pliant to the molding hand, is also a powerful conservative force. It possesses all the strength of the tough willows, which bend and swing to every passing breeze but never break.

Index

$3\,^{00}/_{00}$